Fellows in Foolscap

Memoirs of a Publisher

DESMOND FLOWER

One hates an author that's *all author*, fellows
In foolscap uniforms turned up with ink.
Byron, *Beppo*

ROBERT HALE · LONDON

ISBN 0 7090 4473 9

Robert Hale Limited
Clerkenwell House
Clerkenwell Green
London EC1R 0HT

Photoset in North Wales by
Derek Doyle & Associates, Mold, Clwyd.
Printed in Great Britain by
St Edmundsbury Press, Bury St Edmunds, Suffolk.
WBC Print Ltd,
Bound by WBC Bookbinders Ltd, Bridgend, Glamorgan.

Contents

Illustrations

DF, Coronation Day, 1910
Winning the 440 yards against Eton, 1925
Helping Guy Butler train, 1926
Graduation Day, 1929
Donald Beves, Lay Dean of King's College, Cambridge
Frank Adcock, Professor of Ancient History, Cambridge
Newman Flower, 1915
DF, 1931
DF by Feliks Topolski, 1942
Winston Churchill laying the foundation stone, Red Lion Square
Model of the Cassell building, Red Lion Square
La Belle Sauvage, David McFall RA
Cartoon, *Punch*, 14 November 1959

Life without memory is no life at all.

Luis Buñuel

It has long been an axiom of mine
that the little things are infinitely
the most important.

Sherlock Holmes

The steady stream of small facts from which the
overall meaning will emerge.

Guy de Maupassant

Foreword

Some years ago I was telephoned by a retired naval officer who had been captain of the first corvette on which Nicholas Monsarrat served early in the Second World War. He had written his memoirs and wanted some advice about publication. He said that he had been in touch with Monsarrat who advised him to cut out all chapters dealing with his childhood because 'everyone's childhood is the same and it is a bore'.

I find it difficult to believe Nicholas said that, because it is not a rule which he observed when he wrote the story of his own life. Perhaps the officer, whom I never met, misunderstood him; or perhaps Nicholas thought that this man's early years had been so uneventful that any account of them might be tedious. Anyway, at the risk of there being, as Tallulah Bankhead said, 'rather less than meets the eye', I have started at the beginning.

Writing any memoirs at all is egocentric. It has been alleged that the publication of Lord Mottistone's book, *Fear and be Slain*, was delayed because the printer had run out of capital 'I's; it would be a matter for some distress if the printer of these pages were to find himself in the same predicament. Yet if I am to describe in these chapters my experiences of people in various realms, I feel that anyone who cares to read them may want, perhaps need, to know what kind of animal I am and what kind of life I have led, so that against such a background, including as honest a picture as I can give of my often extreme opinions, an assessment may be made of the validity or otherwise of my descriptions. Despite their egocentricity, perhaps any memoirs can contribute a few threads to the tapestry of the age with which they are concerned. The eight decades through which I have lived have been among the most dramatic for centuries and have witnessed many changes, socially as well as in technology. As in many other fields, my own profession – that of book-publishing – has been virtually turned upside down; in addition I have been privy to certain facts which, so far as I am aware, are not widely known. In consequence here and there I have dwelt on these changes – sometimes things now passed, sometimes fresh aspects. I hope that I have not been too garrulous, for I feel with Luis Buñuel who wrote: 'These details are excruciatingly boring, I know, but if you want to follow the sinuous route of a simple life, if you want to see where it came from and where it went, it's impossible to tell what's superfluous and what's indispensable.'

Apart from my childhood – when, through my father, I was already privileged to meet interesting people – my life has fallen into two categories: publishing and soldiering. Ben Huebsch, one of the great American publishers of this century, has written: 'Is there any business so paradoxical, so self-contradictory, so baffling as that of the book-publisher? It calls for scholarship, artistic taste, psychological insight, business acumen, critical ability, poker sense and a few more endowments. There never was a publisher who had what it takes!'

However few of Ben Huebsch's possible attributes I may have possessed, to whatever extent I may have enjoyed these other virtues, I cannot escape the heartache I have caused which remains like the albatross round the ancient mariner's neck, however deep the remorse that I may feel, and however I may realize the mistakes I have made and appreciate their consequences. Yet, as Hemingway has summed up: 'There are some things which cannot be learned quickly, and time, which is all we have, must be paid heavily for their acquiring. They are the very simplest things, and because it takes a man's life to know them the little new that each man gets from life is very costly and the only heritage he has to leave.'

Whatever little I have got worth leaving, I have tried to put into this book.

Desmond Flower
London 1990

1 Early Days

I was born on 25 August 1907 in north London in a street made up of tidy houses joined together, which must have been quite new then, in the heart of Muswell Hill. They remain unchanged today, for they were sturdily built; it must have been a quiet street then, and indeed is quiet now – the sole visible change being the endless rows of cars parked on either side.

My father came from the West Country, of an old family which seems originally to have been in Devonshire, but by the nineteenth century had gravitated east into Dorset, where for generations they were brewers.

Father was born in the brewery house in Fontmell Magna, near Blandford, and remained deeply devoted to the county. When he was old it was a joy to hear him read aloud the poems of William Barnes, in which he reverted to a rich Dorset accent as redolent of the soil as John Arlott's is of Hampshire. His father was the master brewer who later transformed himself into an engineer, a designer and manufacturer of machinery for the brewing trade, and moved his works to Wimborne.

My mother came from Wells-Next-The-Sea, in Norfolk, where her father, the village organist, lived in one of the charming old houses on the Buttlands. She had an interesting ancestry. In 1588 one of the ships of the Armada, attempting to get home by the northern route, sank off the Norfolk coast with all hands except one, who swam ashore; he was well treated by the locals, settled down, and married a local girl. There is remarkable evidence of this strange story. I knew all my aunts and uncles, her relations, and without exception they all had pink and white complexions, blond hair and blue eyes; whereas my mother was very small, with a swarthy skin, jet-black eyes and very black hair in which there was never a touch of grey. Put her down in a Seville street and you would have lost her in two minutes. The genes skipped me but returned in one of my daughters, who in fond memory has as her third name Cayetana. But I was caught in the morphogenic field, propounded by Dr Rupert Sheldrake; a strange feeling went through me when I first crossed the border into Spain, and it recurs every time I go back to the country which I have grown to love so much. It is an uncanny feeling that I am coming home.

Both father and mother were interested in sport. Mother was a crack rifle shot, a good golfer, sound at tennis and badminton. Father was a wonderful game shot and a fine fisherman, and had remarkable green fingers. But he was never good at ball games; when I was ten I used to walk round with him when he played golf; a fierce blow with his cleek – now No 1 iron – which sent a large divot rather farther than the ball would produce a volley of oaths which substantially widened my knowledge of the English language.

Some people smile when they hear 'Flower' and say 'that's a nice name', but few realize that it has nothing to do with gardens. In Anglo-Saxon *Flow* was an arrow and *er* a maker, with *y* put in for ease of pronunciation, as 'Lawyer' was a law-maker. In time the *y* was dropped, although there are still Flowyers in Devonshire. When the Normans brought their French as a parallel language, an arrow-maker was called a *Fléchier*, which became Fletcher.

Having no interest in engineering but a distinct bent towards writing, father came to London after he left school and found employment in journalism, and there flourished. At the time when I was born he was editing periodicals for Lord Northcliffe, of whom he told me many stories. There is one I remember because it has in it the same testiness as father himself could occasionally display. When Carmelite House was built Northcliffe used to inspect it with a feeling of some pride. As he was going down a back staircase one day a boy bumped straight into him crying 'Out of my way, I'm in a hurry!' Northcliffe said, 'I like that; go to the secretary and tell him to double your wages.' The youth, who was not employed by the company, found the secretary and said, 'Some fat geezer says I'm to be taken on,' and the secretary, recognizing the description and not daring to offend the boss, made 15/– (75p) into 30/– (£1.50). Not long after the same thing happened on the same staircase; Northcliffe, looking down, recognized the boy and thundered, 'Once is enthusiasm, twice is rank carelessness; you're fired!'

In 1909 father was offered the editorship of all the magazines published by Cassell & Co. The company was doing badly and all his friends advised him not to take the job as, they said, he would be digging his own grave. But he decided that he would take the risk, and lived never to regret it. With confidence in himself, he insisted that in addition to his salary he be paid royalties on the sales of the magazines which he was certain he could lift to success. This renaissance he achieved, but he had no means of knowing that in five years events would open a market which could never have been foreseen: the Great War began. In those days there were no paperbacks, no radio, and the only entertainment that the War Office could find to relieve the boredom of the trenches in some way was magazines. There was no profiteering, the prices remained the same, but the demand was almost insatiable, and from his contract negotiated five years before father became a rich man.

Shortly before my first birthday we left Muswell Hill and went to Sevenoaks, in Kent, and from then on father had gardens of increasing size in which to exercise his skill.

Soon came my first memory in life, when I was three years old. It was the day of celebration for the coronation of George V in 1910. Mother and I were staying with my grandfather in Wells. I had been got up in the uniform of the Royal Horse Artillery, and from the photographs of me holding my pony afterwards I seem to have been a big boy for my age. There was a procession in which I rode and wept bitterly throughout – for in front of me was what seemed to be a huge horse ridden by a man representing a Red Indian, bare to the waist, his body stained brown with walnut juice, and a feather in his long black hair; it was a fearsome sight, never to be forgotten. I was only comforted at the end by one of my aunts, a discreetly veiled Lady Godiva on what seemed an equally enormous white horse.

My next memory came a year later and should have been genuinely frightening, but it remains vividly in my mind not so much from fear as from fascination. As servants we had a married couple living in; the short-tempered husband suffered from exophthalmic goitre – the red bulging eyes which made the comedian Marty Feldman so conspicuous. One morning, not long after father had left for London, the man made up his mind to kill his wife with an axe, but she managed to lock herself in the cellar. At the other end of the passage mother shut herself and me into the study where the telephone was, and called the police. Her appeal to them to come quickly was punctuated by the thud of heavy blows as the demented man hacked at the cellar door; it sounded like the final curtain of *The Cherry Orchard*. When the police arrived, the man retreated to the top of the stairs, brandishing the axe and shouting, 'Come and get me.' 'All right, I will,' said a young constable who, slowly mounting the stairs, tackled the man round the legs so that the two of them rolled from top to bottom. We did not see the couple again, but I still remember the wild eyes and hear the sound of those heavy blows.

1912 was a landmark year. Father was asked if he would take on the book list of Cassells as well as the magazines, and when he accepted found that there were just two titles with which to build an autumn list. And he bought his first car: an open four-seater De Dion Bouton, chocolate with all the metal-work in brass, including huge acetylene headlamps. Again we moved, this time to a house called 'Idehurst' which was to be our last family home. At first it was rented, and next door lived our landlord, a Colonel Fulton, who was a wireless buff. After tea one evening mother and I were invited round to hear this new marvel; with headphones on, we listened in awe to the steady crackle of morse, and at one point the colonel told us that a signal which we could hear repeated again and again was a ship's S.O.S. This must have been before 1914, because I cannot believe that radio hams were allowed to continue once we were at war with Germany.

The red brick house was not exactly beautiful, nor was it ugly, but it was comfortable, and large enough to be turned years later into a boys' prep school, which it remains to this day – the large grounds father loved so much sadly neglected and the tennis court asphalted over as a playground.

My parents had their two rooms at one end of the house while at the other, over the back stairs and through a glass door, were my day and night nurseries. At each end narrow stairs led up to the servants' bedrooms and large attics in one of which were shelves crammed with books which I was strictly forbidden to read. This was an obvious attraction, and there I made my first acquaintance with Zola's *La Terre*.

But very soon father bought 'Idehurst', and with it extra land for rockeries, lily pond and rose garden – then, further, an orchard with another pond and a strange assortment of wildfowl, including Chinese geese, golden pheasants and a pair of peacocks. All this was the inspiration for a volume of verse which he had privately printed, called *Through My Garden Gate*.

I was an only child with a romantic imagination, living in a world of books, music and sport. Father was a workaholic, very temperamental, with a very slight sadistic streak which does sometimes seem to appear in the sentimental. It may also have been fostered by the merciless bullying to which he had been subjected as a boy at Weymouth College. Throughout his life there were bony protuberances on his wrists, a malformation caused by a master who made him grip the edge of his desk so that the forearms could be hammered with a heavy wooden ruler like a rolling pin, which I remember still in common use for its proper purpose. Fortunately my grandparents moved up for a while to Croydon, so that father finished his formal education with a year at the Whitgift, a civilized school which he always remembered with affection, and he became a member of the old boys' committee. He was quick tempered and often intolerant, but he was also extremely generous both in thought and deed. Those friends he kept – he quarrelled with many – loved him, for he was both kind and witty.

Mother was quiet and withdrawn, a great reader of history and historical novels. There was a great deal of knitting, and jigsaw puzzles of enormous dimensions. She needed these quiet forms of concentration because as soon as dinner was over father sat down at his desk. He worked all hours of the night, long after mother and I had gone to bed. Frequently he got hungry and we knew that he used to boil an egg because the stock in the larder decreased, but no one could discover how he did it. One morning cook came to mother in triumph: 'I've found the answer.' she said, 'he broke one last night – in the kettle.' He was usually either writing or reading manuscripts, occupations punctuated by trips down the hall to the wine cupboard, for he consumed a considerable amount of whisky. Mother was quite unmoved by his potations, and by his peccadilloes which I think were many. She was a very good hostess to the many business and personal friends who came at weekends, although it was a side of life which gave her little pleasure. They lived largely separate lives with different interests. Mother did not seem much interested in sex, and father sought his pleasure elsewhere – their attitude was one of affectionate indifference.

In the years before the Great War, and for two years after it, my parents took their summer holidays abroad, and I was left with my grandparents. But mother was such a bad sailor – so bad that she could quite easily be sick before the ship left Dover harbour – that soon after the war she opted out and did not go abroad again until air travel, which she enjoyed and which agreed with her, became general.

My grandparents lived at Parkstone, outside Bournemouth, whence grandfather had an easy journey by train to his works in Wimborne. Both of them were very kind to their only grandchild, and in addition there was my Aunt Blanche, who was also my godmother, whom I adored. Neither she nor her brother or sister ever married or had children, so that I was the last of our line. My memories of that time are vivid, if episodic. Clear to me are the serried ranks of bathing-machines drawn up by the water's edge and the bored old horse waiting to pull them further back when the tide came in. And my grandfather in a long bathing-dress of light blue and white horizontal stripes, inviting me to sit on his back while he swam; but he had burst a blood vessel in one eye and this, with his flowing moustache, made him look like an enraged walrus, so I, terrified, refused. I asked what the fur on his face was and, when told, could not pronounce it, so I called it 'starche' and to everyone he remained Starche until his death.

There is one tiny vignette which I cannot resist. I used to sleep in a cot by the side of my grandparents' bed. One night the sound of voices and the gaslight turned up caused me to wake and I opened my eyes to see grandmother sitting up in bed stark naked with a piece of soap in her hand chasing a flea. I tactfully went back to sleep. What has happened to all the fleas now? At that time these little beasts were quite common in clean and respectable houses; but anyone would be horrified if they were found in comparable quarters today, and I have not encountered any for certainly fifty years.

It was from the garden of that house that I first saw an aeroplane loop the loop. The pilot was a Frenchman, Pégoud, who was the father of aerobatics. He had to perform at several thousand feet because the trick was considered dangerous; and after he had done it several times I was still amazed that an aeroplane could make a circle in the air.

By then a family habit had been formed which lasted a long time. My grandmother had a collie called Scott, presumably named after the Antarctic explorer who had died so tragically in January 1912. If I came into the room and the topic of conversation was unfit for young ears, one of the grown-ups would say 'Scott enjoyed himself' and the talk was turned or froze into silence. This went on for many years until, no longer needed for its original purpose, it came a family joke.

At five I started going to dame school. It was only about half a mile away, but to get there involved crossing the main London road, so for several years I was taken and fetched.

Whether it was by good fortune or temperament or a combination of both I do not know, but I was happy throughout my education. I was happy at this dame school, called 'Newry', happy at my preparatory school, and supremely happy at my public school. My first year at

University was marred by ill health, but apart from that I was happy
there too. With certain exceptions I loved the work; I never found
discipline irksome and I was never bullied or even mildly oppressed at
any time.

I have mentioned that mother loved the cinema, and she took me to a
matinée every Saturday – for even before 1914 there were two cinemas
in Sevenoaks. We saw *The Birth of a Nation* and *Intolerance* when they first
appeared, as well, of course, as the dangerous but never catastrophic
adventures of Pearl White. Mother also drove me over to Tonbridge to
see Buffalo Bill's Wild West Show; it was the great man's last
appearance before the war broke out. There were plenty of Indians, of
whom I had lost my earlier fear, and covered waggons; and at the end
Colonel Cody himself rode into the ring, an erect figure in fringed white
buckskin, a white ten-gallon hat, white gauntlets, with a long silver
beard and riding a snow-white horse. He looked magnificent. With
enormous dignity he raised his hat to acknowledge the applause, and
then slowly rode backwards out of the ring.

Early in 1914 my grandparents moved to a house in Bournemouth,
which was exciting for me because at the top end of the garden – oh joy!
– was the mass of railway lines running into Bournemouth West Station,
and leaning over the fence I could practically touch the huge
locomotives steaming in from London. At one side of the house was my
Aunt Blanche's apiary. I was always allowed to watch and, in time, help
her when she opened the hives for the cells of rogue queens before they
hatched or fed the swarm its glucose drip in winter. Years later when
she had moved from her parents' home to a place of her own with a
large apiary, she won the only world championship that a Flower has
acquired. The world congress of apiarists was held in London and she
won the award for the finest honey from any country. The trophy was a
magnificent bronze bee, nearly six inches long, which stood on her
mantelpiece until she died at the age of ninety. Bees were her business,
but she had many other activities and whatever she took up she did
well.

Christmas was for many years spent at this house. Dinner, following
the eighteenth-century tradition, was at four, and at the end, from the
age of seven, I was made to get up and propose the health of the family.
I found this early practice gave me confidence later in life. After crackers
we all moved into the sitting-room and made music, for that was about
the only form of entertainment there was then – apart from drinking and
playing cards. Grandmother played the piano, Aunt Blanche and Uncle
Arthur (if he was there) played the violin, father sang in a good baritone,
and I contributed two songs of which one was a very sentimental ditty
called 'Alone on the raft'.

Christmas Eve was always nerve-racking: father worked a full day in
London and then began the long drive to Bournemouth in the De Dion.
Not only did he bring all the goodies for the morrow – the *marrons
glacées*, the crystallized fruits, various kinds of coloured rock with nuts in
it, and fruit – but on the long drive he had to pass through the New

Forest, a vast area devoid of garages, service stations and telephones. As we waited, long past my bedtime, it was always 'hope he gets through the New Forest', which made that beautiful stretch of the country seem to my mind like some prehistoric vastness inhabited by dragons. He always made it, however deep the snow, and the glare of his enormous acetylene headlamps and the toot of his bulb horn brought us running to the door to greet the frozen figure in his big leather coat, tweed cap and goggles.

It is an interesting thought that although, particularly towards the end of the first war, we nearly starved, there was never a shortage of sweetmeats (perhaps they were imported from France which had its big sugar-beet industry); whereas in the second war food, although it might be dull, was never short, while all sweets were rationed and extremely scarce.

On 4 August 1914 the world blew up. To a small boy France and Belgium seemed a long way away, but they were soon brought very near both to Sevenoaks and to our home. There was no question of father getting into the armed forces because he was desperately short-sighted and without his glasses could see virtually nothing. But he had always been fascinated by military matters – his first job had been on the small staff of a periodical called *The Regiment* – and he became a good war correspondent, going many times to France. Once he nearly did not come back; he and his great friend Sir Philip Gibbs injudiciously showed themselves on the skyline of Vimy Ridge and received a personal saluta- tion from the German artillery. But he never forgot his garden and found time to gather seeds and at the bottom of the orchard there soon grew a mass of Flanders poppies.

Once the B.E.F. was settled across the Channel, the retreat from Mons was over and the long war of attrition began, a large map was put up on my nursery wall and the first task after breakfast was to move the innumerable little flags pinned into it in accordance with the morning's news; alas, too often they moved very little. As time went on, mother would take me to the look-out in Knole Park, at the top of Pole Hill with its superb view over the Weald of Kent towards the sea, where we could plainly hear the never-ending roar of the barrages on the Somme.

My seventh birthday was something to remember. With the war just three weeks old, father's present was two hundred tin soldiers represen- ting the armies of all the belligerents; they were drawn up in lines on the table in my nursery. There were things called Chinese crackers then, about an inch long, as thick as a pencil with a fuse at one end. By chance at one side of the tennis court there was a small vein of yellow clay; father used to wrap the crackers in this clay and bake them – then battle commenced. My grandfather was staying with us at the time, so he took one end, father took the other, the fuses were lit and the missiles were thrown. They exploded with a loud bang and the hard clay fragmented. The carnage was terrible, the noise deafening and the smoke like a thick fog; I crouched under the table with fingers in my ears, shivering with fear, while overhead my elders had a high old time with my birthday present.

But one day before that, in the blazing hot first weeks of war, mother was giving a tennis party and I was ball-boy, when I turned round and saw an officer, immaculate in service dress and riding-boots, walking up the drive. He was the billeting officer and said that we were to have soldiers in the house and had a choice: we could have two officers or ten other ranks. Mother said that she would consult her husband when he came home and ring in the morning. When father got back he said that no way would he have officers; it would mean giving them wine and dressing for dinner every night, and while they would be welcome to all the wine they could drink, nothing on earth was going to make him put on a black tie. So we had ten men. I suppose they slept in the attics, but by day they had the use of a garden-room which was warm and quite comfortable. Various drafts came, and then left for France, and all of them were charming. The last I can remember, in the spring of 1915, was from the Liverpool Rifles, and they stayed quite a long time. Since their training was finished and they had nothing to do, one of them, a private with black hair, used to walk me to school and fetch me in the afternoon; we got to know them well and they became friends of the family. Very soon after they had departed to France it was reported that the battalion had been annihilated the first time it went over the top; one of our ten was said to have been cited for the Victoria Cross, but that did not matter – he and the young man who used to walk me to school were dead. There was silence in the house; we were thinking of them and had nothing to say to one another.

At the beginning of the war mother drove an ambulance, with a soldier in attendance in case of difficulty – such as a puncture, for the wheel was too heavy for her to change. She had to pick up the wounded at Chatham Docks and drive them to Sevenoaks Hospital. After some time she resigned because she said she could not bear the screams of the stretcher cases as they bumped from pot-hole to pot-hole over the abominable road. Then she ran a canteen in the woods opposite our house; when I was at home from school I used to try to help, emptying ashtrays and doing any job that was useful and harmless.

Sevenoaks Hospital was big, and one day Queen Mary came in the course of her visits to the ever-increasing wounded up and down the country. Going round the wards, she stopped beside one man and quietly asked where he had been wounded.

'Wipers, lady,' was the reply from the bed.

'Ypres,' murmured the Queen.

"Orrible place, Wipers.'

'Ypres.'

'Shelling was something terrible round Wipers.'

'Ypres.'

Etc.

After the visit was over, the nurses crowded round the man's bed and said, 'Aren't you lucky to have had such a long talk with the Queen!'

'What Queen?' said the wounded man. 'Do you mean that lady with hiccups?'

Then there was the matter of the air raids. At first the zeppelins came across the North Sea from Cuxhaven, so that their targets were nowhere near us; although from mother's bedroom window one night I did see the fearsome blaze of the one which was shot down over Potters Bar in North London. Later the Germans developed the gigantic ten-engined Gotha and, as in the second war, the run-in to London from airfields in Northern France was over Sevenoaks. The air-raid warning was by changing the gas pressure: when the lights went up and down twice all window curtains had to be drawn. Sevenoaks was a vast nest of anti-aircraft guns which barked continually at the giants lumbering overhead; shell fragments pattered down like rain, but that would never prevent father from parading around outside to see what was going on, however much we implored him to come in. One night I stayed awake for a long time listening to a bomber groaning round and round trying to find a way out of the box barrage in which it was caught; it did not succeed – when it was shot down the droning stopped and I went back to sleep.

Nearing eight, I and another boy were the only ones to have started Latin, which I must admit I have found more of a necessity than a pleasure in life, apart from Horace and Catullus. Since I read a great deal and seemed to have some aptitude for English, I was directed to go downstairs to the girls, who were mostly somewhat older, for play-reading; in my last year tackling the male parts of *Julius Caesar* was as difficult as it was exhilarating. But my days were numbered; my prep school was chosen, at Oxted about ten miles from Sevenoaks, so we went over to look around and be looked at. All was arranged, but I rather enjoyed a letter which came from the headmaster a few days later saying 'by the way, in our discussion nothing was said about religion,' to which father replied 'As I am a Quaker and his mother an atheist, he had better be C. of E.' Mother was furious; she said that she was an agnostic, not an atheist; anyway the die was cast: I was to go to the Oxted Preparatory School in the autumn term as a weekly border.

My years at my prep school were just like any other boy's; work went as well as could be expected, and in sport I discovered that I had some gift for running which was counterbalanced by the unpleasant fact that in cricket I could not catch – a disability which haunted me as long as I played the game.

In the last years of the war food was very scarce; we were not actually starving, but were always hungry. Nothing was allowed to remain on our plates; if one put something aside because one hated it (in my case, parsnips) a tearful stalemate ensued until it was forced down.

But at last the end of the war came. The news cannot have reached us children until late in the afternoon of 11 November 1918, because I remember that we paraded round the garden in our night clothes blowing anything that would blow and banging anything bangable, such as a tea-tray. 'Now,' as Robert Graves wrote, 'the country was in the full sunshine of peace ... People no longer spoke to one another in trains as a matter of course without introduction.' It was to take another war for people once again to chat with strangers; and now in the golden reign of peace the mugging is such that one is once again chary of that.

In my last term at Oxted there was an unexpected crisis. Years before I had been put down for Charterhouse and promised a place. But out of the blue came a letter from Fletcher, the famous but rather dictatorial head, saying that after all he had no vacancy, but I could try for a scholarship if I liked. Without any preparation I went up to London and sat the exam at the Old Charterhouse in the City, which I was very glad of having a chance of seeing; but there was little hope and my failure was no surprise. In the ensuing panic father's stockbroker came up with an idea; he said that Lancing, at which one of his partners had a boy, had just opened a new house and therefore probably had more vacancies than usual – for all public schools at that time had enormous waiting lists. Father wrote off at once to the headmaster, Henry Bowlby, who replied that all vacancies were already taken, but he had one place in his personal gift; I would have to take the scholarship exams and if I showed distinction in any subject, he would consider me. This time I was allowed to take the exams in a small room at Oxted, with the second master invigilating; the results were awaited with bated breath. At last a letter came; of course I had not won a scholarship, but of all those who had sat, including the successful scholars, I had come out top in English, and would therefore be accepted. There was not only a sigh of relief, but it was the best thing that could ever have happened to me; because great and famous as the other establishment is, I found at Lancing a congenial atmosphere which made me successful and happy.

So I left Oxted, grateful for all the goodness and kindness which had been shown to me, and full of great expectations.

2   Intermezzo

Although school takes up the major part of life for so many years, there is a great deal which goes on at home during the same time and contributes so much to the process of growing up.

One of father's wisest dicta, uttered to me when I was in my early teens, was 'Travel, keep on travelling; it is essential to the development of the mind.' He certainly travelled whenever he could. However bad a son I was, that saying of his struck a chord in my mind which has never been forgotten.

When I was small my imagination sometimes got the better of me. Once I ransacked the cupboard where various fancy dresses were kept, and got myself up as Lord Nelson. The admiral, of course, had to have a shave, so I took one of the cut-throat razors which father used throughout his life; I stropped it, as I had seen him do so often, and tested the edge. The great hero did not look very heroic crying his eyes out at the head of the stairs with the top of his thumb cut off.

The thought of heroes reminds me that in the early years of the war I met for the first time in my life a celebrity: Field Marshal Sir Evelyn Wood, V.C. Father published his memoirs and they were good friends. When a film was made from one of father's novels (he wrote three) called *Resurrection*, mother and I went to the trade show, and the Field Marshal was invited. I was enormously impressed when he arrived: a tall man in his eighties, erect and as stiff as a ramrod, and I was in awe of him because he had commanded the British Army in the Zulu War of 1879, and also because of an interesting story – a good example of E.S.P. After the war the Empress Eugénie asked Sir Evelyn to take her to see the grave of her son, the Prince Imperial, who had been killed under his command at the age of twenty-three. Riding across the veldt, the Empress suddenly got off her horse crying, 'Violets, I smell violets; they were his favourite flowers,' and ran by herself two hundred yards unerringly to the barely marked grave.

While I was still at Oxted the summer holiday of 1919 was very important. The treaty of peace had been signed at Versailles in June, and in August my parents took me to France. At the impressionable age of twelve I was to see the Somme. The bodies and the artillery were gone but nothing else had been touched, and the engineers were still gathering up the unspent ammunition. We stayed in Arras and father

21

hired a car with a driver. We drove first to Albert, a town reduced to a heap of red brick rubble with only the church tower standing: the Madonna on its summit had been reduced to the horizontal and it was a tradition that if she fell off completely, the allies would be defeated. Then north to the vast mine crater of Thiepval: I believe it was the biggest of all – so vast that six storeys of dug-outs had been hewn into the chalk sides with paths zigzagging down to the bottom a hundred and fifty feet below, like a nightmarish megalithic settlement. Then north to Delville Wood, where a battalion of the West Kents – so dear to me – had been wiped out, Trônes Wood, and everywhere trenches running in all directions like the lunatic labours of some army of demented burrowing animals. Then south past the Butte of Warlincourt, a pimple in the plain soaked with the blood of thousands of soldiers from both sides because it gave the only observation over the surrounding desert, to Bapaume; and Villers-Bretonneaux, famous in Australian history, in the main street of which was gathered a pile of small arms ammunition twenty feet high. Every day there were sudden explosions and mushrooms of smoke climbing slowly into the blue sky as ammunition dumps were detonated. I have spoken of 'woods' but there were no trees, only stubby tormented trunks a few feet high, plastered with clay, so that they were the same dirty grey as everything else. Not one leaf was to be seen, not one blade of grass. By the roadside would be a board giving the name of a village no longer there. The chalk and clay was baked hard by the summer sun. It was described, I believe, by those who were in it as a lunar landscape, and today when we are familiar with the black and white photographs taken by the astronauts, that is just what it was. Except that it was more pitted than the moon; the shell craters were edge to edge. The land was a rumpled overturned grey to the far horizon, and silence: no people, no birds, no life.

When at the end of hostilities Sevenoaks Hospital went back to its normal civilian life after coping with thousands upon thousands of wounded, a lot of reorganization had to be done and this required money. Father decided that he would arrange a series of lectures by some of his authors, and these were a great success. They took place on Saturday evenings and the author always stayed for the weekend with us. I remember only two of them: William Le Queux and Rosita Forbes. Le Queux, a prolific writer of spy stories now long forgotten but at one time allegedly Queen Alexandra's favourite reading, had been connected with the Secret Service, and I was very impressed when he said that the plans of every German warship were on the Admiralty's table before the keel had even been laid – a claim also made by the notorious Sidney Reilly, but not proven.

Rosita Forbes was a very tall, beautiful woman, whom later in life I was to know well. Then, as a schoolboy, I idolized – as did a great many adults – a lady who at such a tender age had led an expedition to the little known oasis of Kufra. When she arrived she apologized to mother for the appearance of one of her eyes: in the desert some sort of beastie had laid eggs in it and the eye was taking a long time to heal. It was a lantern lecture and mother and I sat in the front row. After it was over she asked us if we had noticed any untoward movement during the lecture; we said that we had seen something but could not make out what was happening.

'Thank God,' she said, 'you see, I lost so much weight in the desert that I have no hips to keep my pants up. They fell down round my ankles and I was trying to kick them behind the screen before the lights came on.'

Immediately after the war American publishers began coming to London and some were asked down to 'Idehurst' for the weekend. The first was William Morrow who had founded a firm under his own name. He was a big, jolly man, and I played set after set of tennis with him in the hot summer weather. I never saw him again, he died in 1931, but his name remains so clear because the man who later took over the firm – Thayer Hobson – was to become a great friend and influence in my life.

The next were the Knopfs – Alfred and Blanche. Father was very fond of Alfred but did not care for Blanche, feelings which were not unusual. Many years in the future I was to find that I liked them both very much, for different reasons, and had respect and love for them.

The weekend was chiefly memorable for the fact that Blanche made the first of several attempts to take her own life. While our doctor ministered to the patient with a stomach pump, mother stamped up and down the corridor fuming. 'I don't care a damn whether she commits suicide or not, but I won't have her doing it in my house!'

At that time, too, there was a very small incident which I mention only because it had an effect on my life. A barn-storming pilot arrived in a field beside the main road through Brasted, next door to Sevenoaks. Mother and I learned that he was taking people up at ten shillings a time, so we drove over. We climbed into his string-bag and for the first time saw our beloved land from above. It was thrilling. Of course, people today who are accustomed to going by jet to every corner of the world will say, 'So what? Big deal.' But seventy years ago it *was* a big deal: one's first entry into an element hitherto reserved for the birds. Clive James has put it so well, as he always does. 'In just my lifetime, long-distance flying has stopped being an event and started being a cliché. But a miracle is no less miraculous for having become commonplace.'

We told father that evening that we had been up and he was furious. But that first adventure gave me a love of flying which I have never lost – I really *enjoy* travelling all over the world in aeroplanes and no 'incidents', of which there have been several, have diminished my pleasure.

Music was becoming more and more important in the family, and father was already collecting manuscripts, first editions and *libretti* of Handel to whom he was deeply devoted. In all, the collection comprised seven hundred manuscripts, bound in three hundred volumes, including fifty-one full scores and a nearly complete set of instrumental and vocal parts for all the operas and oratorios, instrumental parts for the whole of *The Water Music*, a large number of *libretti* and two autographs.

Not long after the war father began his *Life of Handel*, which appeared in 1923. It was dedicated to me, and he sent me the first copy to come from the binders. It was a large book, still a treasure on my shelves where it stands next to the autograph manuscript, but I used to read it during meals in Hall, propped up against a jam pot. Sixty years later it was still in print, and has only recently been succeeded by a newer biography.

While he was engaged in writing *Handel*, he thought that it would be a good idea to learn German; so a lady from Cologne came to live with us. Her name was Hedwig Evers and she was a gentlewoman temporarily in distress because of the economic situation in Germany; fortunately all her property was in land, so that when things stabilized she was able to live in comfort for the rest of her days. But when she came to us she had no money and her wardrobe represented the height of fashion in 1914, which caused a certain amount of ribald comment; also she was the first German to be seen in Sevenoaks since the war, which raised a few eyebrows. But she was a tall woman of such dignity and grace that any ill-feeling was short-lived; father, mother and I all loved her deeply, for she was so genuine, good and kind that no one could do otherwise. The lessons, however, were not a success, father had a huge job to cope with at Cassell's from which he came home tired and, whereas in the evening he could write or read manuscripts, he was in no state to learn a language for which, unfortunately, in any case he had little gift. There was every justification for calling off the operation, but Hedwig had become so dear to us that she stayed for two years.

In the summer of 1923 father decided that he and I should go to Munich. Shortly before we were due to depart he took me to lunch at the Garrick Club; Arnold Bennett, who was a friend as well as a Cassell author, was there alone and we sat with him. It was the first time that I had met that charming man whom I was to know well later. In the course of conversation he asked if we were going away and father said that we were just off to Munich. Arnold said that was nice because he was, too. Father asked him where he was staying and, making the best use of his stammer which he could do when he wished, he replied, 'I can't remember. Find the most expensive hotel. I-I-I'll be there.' And he was. This was a memorable journey for me for two reasons. First, I heard an opera for the first time; it was *Lohengrin* which I found rather boring but not sufficiently so to put me off opera, to which in time I became devoted. Mother loved ballet and was off to London like a shot, particularly when Pavlova was dancing, but this was one taste of hers which I never shared; I have always disliked ballet as much as I love opera. I have on occasions been unpopular for saying that if one has to go to the ballet, the only way to survive is to shut one's eyes and listen to the music.

In the following year, together with Hedwig we went to Vienna, and I discovered to my delight one of the loveliest cities in Europe: a world of peace and enchantment. It must be difficult not to be carried away by the beauty of the two Belvederes, St Stefan's, Schönbrunn and the innumerable other treasures of that lovely place. Since father was working on his life of Schubert, we ate at a charming restaurant with shutters and pale grey walls called *Zum Grünen Anker*, where the composer took his meals every day. Whenever I visited Vienna I ate there, until after the conflict – of which it was perhaps a casualty – it had disappeared.

The country's finances had by then been stabilized, but father had been there before during the collapse and told me of his endeavours to cash a £5 note. In a bank the cashier, visibly shaken, said that he could not oblige that day, but he would do so on the following morning, furthermore advising father to come with a taxi. It was as well that father took the advice because £5-worth of paper schillings and himself completely filled the cab.

But the high point of this visit was to wipe away the slightly sour taste of *Lohengrin* with just one glorious performance which imbued me with a love of opera for the rest of my life: *Rosenkavalier*. Father did not like Strauss, so Hedwig and I went together. To mount the great staircase of that wonderful opera house for the first time is a beautiful adventure in itself. We sat in what had been the imperial box, which meant that its position and the acoustics were perfect, and there we were carried to heaven by the two stars then at the height of their youthful powers: Lotte Lehmann and Elizabeth Schumann. Could any small boy, attending only his second opera, ask for more? I do not think so; and to have heard Vienna's own opera sung by those two divas at that time left *Rosenkavalier* with a very special place in my heart.

Another essential visit was to the Albertina where naturally I wanted to see the two most wonderful Dürer drawings – the praying hands and the Hare – and, of course, had a portfolio of very fine reproductions placed before me. Examining them closely, I complained to Hedwig that they were reproductions; she made a terrible fuss in the nicest possible way and after a long wait the sacred originals were produced. I can only say thank you to the kindly custodians of the Albertina by recording that more than half a century later the sight of those two drawings remains a golden moment in my life. I understand from a recent article by Bernard Levin that they can no longer be seen by anyone. I was a very lucky and a very happy young man.

In 1921 the Government made a rather rash experiment, which did not last long: it reduced the age for driving licences. Cars went down from eighteen to sixteen and motor-cycles from sixteen to fourteen. Of course I wanted a motor-cycle on my fourteenth birthday, but my parents were against it. They made me an offer: I could be taught to drive a car at fifteen, and they would pay any fines if I was caught without a licence, provided I gave up the idea of riding a motor-cycle. Agreed; so a year later I was taught to drive by Bone, our chauffeur-gardener. There were no driving tests in those days, and on my sixteenth birthday I received a licence, and thereafter drove back to school feeling very proud.

My sixteenth birthday was something special. Father had become greatly attracted to Scandinavia and had joined the Swedish Club in the City of London. There he met a number of prominent Icelanders, and as a result it was decided that we would go to their country in August 1923. We embarked at Leith on a small tub called *Botnia* which was nearing the end of her long life; she was much smaller than the average Channel steamer. The voyage took four and a half days, and from start to finish we struggled through a North Atlantic gale. I never left my bunk and lived on dry biscuits which enabled me, a very poor sailor, to survive. A hardy man, father attended meals, but on the third day even he was sick, for the first and last time in his life. The porthole of our cabin was usually under water, but when it was not I watched with awe the huge waves coming at us which broke right over the superstructure of the ship. The only peace was when at stops on the way, in comparatively calm water, I could peer out at the forbidding grey cliffs of the Faroes and the Westmann Islands.

There was only one hotel in Reykjavik then. It was homey and comfortable. Once a month a cargo ship arrived with fresh vegetables from Europe; the day she docked was always a *fiesta*, and in August she came on the morning of my birthday. Father had invited three members of the Cabinet and two other Icelanders to dinner that evening. But we were not the only visitors. At that time the American Air Force was flying three seaplanes round the world, with two destroyers as support and supply vessels. Also a lone Italian called Locatelli was trying to fly round the world by himself, without even a navigator. The dining-room was full that evening and there were three main tables: my birthday party, at which to my embarrassment I had to take the chair, the American airmen, and, sitting alone, Locatelli. The management had decorated each tablecloth with its national flag in coloured granulated sugar; ours, of course, was the Red Ensign – for those who normally see only merchant ships have long assumed this, rather than the Union Jack, to be our national flag. Now that our merchant navy is virtually non-existent, the Red Ensign is less familiar.

To celebrate the arrival of the vegetable ship there was a small orchestra that night, and in honour of the guests it played only three tunes throughout the evening: *God Save the King*, *The Star Spangled Banner* and *Giovanezza*; as a result people were popping up to attention in three corners of the room with monotonous regularity. Finally the Americans shouted over to me, 'For God's sake, can't you get them to play something else?' but my efforts met with no success. Friendships made that night were valuable: the Americans, worried about Locatelli, fixed a wireless link with him and as a result, when he crash-landed in Greenland, they were able to rescue him.

Iceland's great sculptor, Einar Johansson, was alive then, and in his honour the Government built a gallery to house his enormous sculptures – very Nordic and impressive – and appointed him custodian of it for life. We called and rang the bell which was answered by the sculptor himself, a rather dour figure like a character out of *Rheingold*. He was not very communicative, which is understandable, and retired to his cubbyhole, leaving us the place to ourselves. What we saw we both thought wonderful, and father had a wild idea of arranging an exhibition of Johansson's works in London; but it would have taken an entire ship's hold to carry these huge works, even if they were allowed out of the country – and where could they have been shown? Burlington House would be ideal today, but was not interested in such matters then; and the Hayward Gallery did not exist.

Since there are so many rivers rich in salmon throughout the country, father asked if there was anywhere he could fish within reach of the capital. The answer was that there was a very good river about ten miles down the only road in the country; being so near to town, it was over-fished but he could have a rod for the day if he wished. He did wish. We took a picnic and were driven out by a taxi which was to pick us up in the late afternoon. I sat on a rock painting, while father continued with the seemingly endless amusement of casting a fly, only stopping at intervals to change to a fly of another feather. Against all the odds, he had a big one on in the early afternoon. He played it for hours, and insisted that I take the rod for a while – but I soon gave it back to him because I found coping with the struggles of the victim was as boring as it was unpleasant. Eventually the fish was landed, all twenty pounds of it, and we were driven back to Reykjavik in triumph. After dinner we set out to dispose of the spoil. In those days Icelanders lived off their native products, mutton and fish, so salmon was more common than vegetables. Since the hotel was not interested, we carried it round town, an awkward job because one had to hold it up to stop its tail dragging in the street. We called on all father's friends, who politely shut the door in our faces. At midnight we were still on the move, and passed a man who had just come out to start painting his house – for in August the sun sets at four and rises again at six. Our last desperate call was on the mother of one of father's Government friends. She opened the door and said, 'Ah! I see you have caught a fish and can't get rid of it. I don't want it, but I will take it so that you can go home to bed.'

Two very weary but relieved travellers crept back to the hotel.

It was time to go inland. The only road ran forty miles from the capital to the livery stables. With a guide we were taken there by a six-seater open car which, serving as a bus, went at a rate of knots in a cloud of dust. The stables were huge: they contained not only ponies for hire – such lovely sturdy little animals, not unlike those to be seen wild in the New Forest – but they also put up all the mounts of those who rode in with business in the capital, finishing their journey in the same hair-raising bus. We set off with four ponies: one each and a pack-horse.

Iceland is superbly beautiful. The air is crystal clear, there are no trees, and the soil is powdered lava. As a result one sees as far as the eye can carry. The ground at one's feet is royal purple and each line of hills in the distance is a lighter hue until, a hundred and twenty miles away, the ultimate range is the palest lavender. It is a land with a strange beauty unlike anything I have seen anywhere else in the world. It was extremely hot day after day without a cloud in the sky, and in a silk shirt

I was always soaked with sweat. Wherever one looked there were the waves of mauve and violet, seldom a habitation, no life except occasional sheep, almost the only animals that can get sufficient nourishment from the coarse grass which sprouts here and there from the lava soil.

We rode for two hundred miles. At intervals there were isolated farms, all of which put up travellers for the night, with dinner and breakfast, at a tariff laid down by the Government. Sometimes we stayed in a low stone farmhouse with a turf roof, lulled to sleep by the restless movement of the horses stabled in the next room, and the natural fatigue of a long day in the saddle. Once we were put up by a pastor with a tiny church in the middle of nowhere. His small house was very comfortable, with a wonderful library, and he spoke flawless English. The Icelanders are remarkable linguists; they read enormously during the long winter months when there are only two hours of daylight. Now, of course, there is television and radio; but then there was nothing to do but read and learn languages. Our pastor, who seldom went to the capital – let alone abroad – said that he had taught himself English from reading *The National Geographical Magazine* to which he was a regular subscriber. His cook-housekeeper produced for us a memorable meal in the evening. It consisted of ten platters – I will not call them 'courses' – of which the first four were of salmon prepared in various ways and the last six were mutton in every conceivable form from curry to meat balls.

We rode up the volcano Hekla, and visited the geysers into which we threw bars of kitchen soap which act as a catalyst that makes them shoot their huge spouts of boiling water into the air. Next we rode on to the Gulfoss, the huge and superb river falls in the middle of which protrudes the sheep-saddle rock on which Rider Haggard's hero, Eric Brighteyes, is said to have sat, although I do not believe this to be possible. The current is so strong that not even the most powerful Viking could ever have swum his way back up against it. The spray from the tumultuous cauldron two hundred feet below forms, when the sun is right, a remarkable rainbow. We paid our respects to the ruins of Thingvellir, the oldest democratic parliament in the world. At last we arrived back at the stables, bronzed and fit, and committed ourselves once more to the hazardous car ride to the capital. There, before our departure, I learnt to swim. I am physically allergic to cold water and at home had never been able to stay in the sea or a bath long enough to learn before turning blue. But at Reykjavik the baths are filled by warm water out of the earth, so that I could stay in long enough to master the art; after that all was well and I became a not unreasonable swimmer.

The voyage south on a new ship, the *Gulfoss*, was not quite so fierce as that on the way up, but it was bad enough. Waves broke constantly right over us, and two Americans who were playing cards in the lounge one evening had to spend the night there because the decks were awash and they could not get back to their cabin. I was to see the *Gulfoss* once again, when I was stationed at Kiel in 1945; she was in the harbour, small, decrepit and rather sad.

Of all the countries I have visited and the things that I have seen over so many years, the beauty of Iceland remains very high. I have only been there once since: a flight stop at Keflavik, on the way to New York. From the airport, built by the Americans during the Second World War, I saw again the vistas of purple, lavender and mauve; a wave of nostalgia came over me and I wanted to go back. But it would be unwise. The Icelanders, I am sure, would be as kind and friendly as ever; but, of course, Reykjavik is a different city now, and I am told there are metalled roads spreading from it in all directions across the wilderness through which I rode and which I loved so much. Some memories are best left untouched.

In 1925 Hedwig Evers wrote, inviting me to go to Cologne to see the big trade fair which opened in September. It is an indication of how much more quickly the young grow up today that at seventeen I had never been away by myself, whereas now some can be much travelled and even married by that age. I told mother that I wanted to travel by air, and she said that I could, provided that I flew on a British airline. As green as a gooseberry, I went up to London and entered the first office I saw; it was SABENA which opened in Lower Regent Street in 1923. Only after I had bought my ticket did I discover that it was Belgian, instead of Imperial Airways on which I should have booked. I really did not care, I was so pleased to be off on my own, so I kept quiet and in due course departed from Croydon. The plane, which was a converted Vickers Vimy bomber, came down at Brussels, where the airport was little more than a field; there was no restaurant or café and, since it was midday and I was starving, the sole sustenance I could get was a packet of chocolate from a small kiosk. On the second leg to Cologne the only other passenger was a general who told me that he was a director of Imperial Airways. I offered him some chocolate which he accepted. In those days one flew at 1500 feet; the windows, which were of talc, slid back and one could stick one's head out into the cooling wind, for it was an extremely hot day. I dozed in the sunlight until I was prodded by the general who shouted, 'Your damn chocolate has made me sick!' Apart from that it was an extremely nice flight.

Hedwig and I looked at as much of the fair, on both banks of the Rhine, as we felt like. One important attraction was the stand of the Soviet Union, which contained a small cinema in which they were showing their newest masterpiece, *Battleship Potemkin*. In England it was banned by the censor for years, so I was lucky to see it – numbed into horrified attention at scenes which are now familiar to every film buff: the perambulator, the hysterical mother, and the Guards in their white blouse uniforms advancing slowly and steadily down the Odessa steps.

Equally important was a concert in the Messehalle, built for the occasion with wonderful acoustics and a splendid orchestra, conducted by a man nicknamed 'the butcher' because his fierce up-and-down beat resembled the wielding of a meat axe. Nevertheless, he certainly got results, and I shot up in my seat as if a bolt of electricity had gone through me as he produced a series of shattering ascending chords: I was hearing Brahms' First Symphony for the first time. Although the very first symphony I ever heard was Dvořák's the 'New World', which I loved, I do not think that I had ever before been so stunned by a piece of music; after the final notes I was a different person – I do not know if I was any better, but I was different, as though I had just gone through an ordeal by fire. It remains my favourite of all symphonies, and even now an atavistic shudder goes through me when I hear those opening chords.

About this time spiritualism played an important part in our lives. Father was a firm believer in the hereafter, convinced of the possibility of communication between the two worlds and of reincarnation or 'recycling'. He used to sit regularly with the most famous voice medium of her day: Mrs Leonard. By the time I was fifteen he usually took me with him. A voice medium goes into a trance and her vocal chords are taken over by a 'control' who says what people wish to say to those on the other side, and repeats what they have to say – very occasionally the vocal chords themselves may be used by one of them. The voice of the control – Mrs Leonard's was named 'Feda' – is quite different from the normal tones of the medium, but this in itself means nothing because it could simply be play-acting. The 'art' of testing the veracity of the sitting is to have a conversation with someone on the other side about a subject of which the medium could know nothing and which is not originated by the receiver, so that there can be no auto-suggestion or thought transference. Always in attendance to communicate were my Aunt Gertrude and Sir Evelyn Wood; Handel sometimes turned up, drawn by father's absorption in his life and work. A completely unsolicited incident I can remember was when Feda said that Aunt Gertrude was screaming with laughter and indicating that she had something round in her hand, and that a white substance from it had come up into her face and that of father who was, she said, with her at the time. Father was temporarily nonplussed, and then he remembered that he and his sister had, in 1913, cut open a golf ball to see what was inside and found that it was filled with a milky chemical substance which squirted all over them – the 'gutty', a short-lived type of ball which preceded the modern core of wound rubber; he had never thought of it since then. On one occasion only the voice of Handel was heard for a few moments; at that time this was the earliest voice transference known. I think that it would have been very difficult indeed for Mrs Leonard herself to produce a deep bass voice with a thick German accent, but who knows? Two volumes of recorded sittings with Mrs Leonard were published, the first called *The Bridge* by father, published in 1927; the second, *Through a Stranger's Hands, New Evidence for Survival*, appeared from Hutchinson in 1935, both with a foreword by Sir Oliver Lodge, with whom father was in constant communication on this fascinating and controversial subject. I doubt if these things will ever be proved or disproved, but from the many sittings which I attended with Mrs Leonard up to the time I finally left home, I was convinced that what I heard hour after hour, month after month, was genuine. And I remain convinced.

These are some of the things which happened at home in my school years. During those days if one is an only child, one lives two lives: at school one is never alone; one is part of a constant *va et vient* of friends, acquaintances, even enemies; whereas at home one is constantly in the company of one's parents – if one is lucky and they are around. Even though my father and mother were to a certain extent indifferent to one another, they had still a great deal in common, and my great good fortune was that both seemed to take pleasure in gathering me into whatever each was doing. This continued throughout their lives, to the very end.

3   The School Beneath the Chapel

The situation of Lancing is remarkable. Everyone who drives along the south coast between Brighton and Worthing sees the college standing on top of the downs, its superb chapel dominating the whole valley of the River Adur and towering above the knapped-flint buildings which lie gathered round its base like pigmy children of a noble giant.

I know of some who have been to Lancing and hated it, which must surely be the case with every school. But there have been many more who have been awed by their first view, by their first arrival, and come to love the place deeply, I am among the latter: I succumbed on the first afternoon when my parents drove me up the college hill.

I was put in Field's, one of the two houses opened in 1912. To me it is the nicest house, not only because it is comfortable but because it forms a wing jutting out southwards from the main buildings with superb views of the rolling fields, the woods, Shoreham's airfield and the sea. It is exposed to all the winds that blow, which are considerable, but the view is worth it.

All schools have their ups and downs, such variations depending upon the personalities running the place at any given time. During my years there, Lancing was very much up; it had, perhaps, just passed a particularly high peak. There were troubles to come later, from which it has now long recovered. My first four years were the last four of Henry Bowlby, one of the great headmasters who was by then getting old and tired, but he had ruled the school so well that the diminution of his powers had no deleterious effect. Agatha, his wife, was still the very kind twittering sparrow she had always been – judging from the long-told story of the garden party they gave in 1912, during which she was called to the telephone. She came back somewhat upset and said, 'Oh Henry, there's been a boating accident,'; her caller had told her the news of the sinking of the *Titanic*. In his last years Bowlby himself produced some verbal aberrations, even *non sequiturs*. His main interest was the building of the war memorial cloister: indeed a fascinating business. All the stone was cut and the carving done on site; it was absorbing to watch the craftsmen and the aged but dictatorial foreman Dick Gale, who might have come straight from his last job building Salisbury Cathedral ten centuries ago. One summer Sunday, Douglas Goodhart, a prefect and captain of athletics, had spent a profitable afternoon in a haystack with the daughter of one of the masters, enjoying himself so much that he missed Evensong. His absence was noted and reported to Bowlby who sent for him and admonished him in these stern words: 'Last week two boys accidentally damaged one of the stones of the cloister and came at once to me to confess; you cut chapel and you say nothing.' But he was a fine figure and admirably portrayed in the painting by the once fashionable Philip de Lazlo, whose sons were there with me.

The figure who most commanded my envy in my first term was Evelyn Waugh, about to go up to Oxford, because he was head librarian – and that was something which I deeply wanted to be before my time was done. Whenever I saw him, he was always running, as if he were perpetually late like the White Rabbit. He has written that he did not like the school because he did not learn much. I must have sat under some of the same masters as he did, and I learnt a great deal. I did not know him because he was older and in another house, but it occurs to me that he may already have been a difficult young man and perhaps the masters did not like him: nothing will come unless there is *rapport* and good will between master and pupil.

Another character who was also in his last term was Tom Driberg (eventually Lord Bradwell). At the time I remember him chiefly for the solemn, sanctimonious expression on his face when he carried the cross at the head of the choir which processed round the chapel on major saints' days. But I got to know him later in life, when the four years between us were of no account, and liked him a great deal. There was a quietness about him springing, I think, from certainty of his own mental superiority which he felt no desire or necessity to parade.

Homosexuality at public schools has always been a subject of acrimony, because it has frequently been considered as encouraged by the monastic setting in which boys approaching manhood with all its budding desires are confined. It does not seem to me that the monasticism has got anything to do with it; the 'gay' – as they are now called, so debauching a fine old English word – are now recognized as a distinct psychological type, and I very much doubt if their incidence is in any way decreased by the existence today of a sixth form for girls in a hideous new building which has destroyed the pleasant open space between the Masters' Tower (suites for bachelor masters) and the Rugby fives courts. An article in *The Times* in 1984 specifically mentions Lancing and says that it has had an effect. Adolescence and adulthood have swung back so far in the past half-century, nearer, but not quite, to the first Elizabethan age in which Sir Philip Sidney graduated from Oxford at the age of fifteen; hence I presume that human desires are engendered correspondingly early. But I still do not see why this should affect in any way one's sexual appetites: one likes one's own sex or the opposite, or sometimes none at all. One is born that way, not made – although admittedly a proselytizing homosexual can cause considerable trouble.

How much homosexuality existed at Lancing in my time I have no idea. Certainly this was the reason Tom Driberg was asked to leave. As he had already won a scholarship to Christ Church, this unfortunate incident did not stop him from going up to Oxford, from which he was sent down for something entirely different. His was the only case of which I heard in my five years. I am not aware that there was any practised in Field's House. Since one was not allowed into other houses, I have no idea what the life of their occupants was like – if one wanted to speak to a friend in another house, one had to go to the entrance, send in a message and wait. It would be too much to suggest that there was no covert activity; I can only say that I was not aware of it.

Another question which is constantly being debated today is that of corporal punishment, no longer practised at Lancing. The policy at the school in the twenties was very enlightened for its time. There were two types of offence which merited chastisement: breach of a school rule and breach of a house rule. If a school rule (such as being out of bounds or smoking) had been broken, the head of the school had to apply to the headmaster for permission to punish the accused, who was publicly summoned to the prefects' common-room. The statutory sentence of 'common rooming' was six strokes. When I was head of my house I was once called upon by the head of the school to carry out the sentence, but he compassionately stopped it after four which he thought was enough. I think the psychological effect of the ceremonial was a greater deterrent than the actual cane.

House offences were more frequent, the trespass minor – such as being out of bounds in the building (the dormitories were taboo all day and the changing rooms before lunch) or making an affray. The head of the house had to explain to the housemaster what had happened and, if punishment was approved, the maximum penalty was three strokes – although very occasionally a fourth was allowed if it seemed justified. Another prefect or house captain had to be present to ensure that there was no irregularity. A book was kept in the housemaster's study in which had to be entered the date, the name of the victim, the nature of the offence, the punishment administered; and this had to be signed by the Head of the House.

Masters never administered corporal punishment.

The only other punishment was lines, given for such offences as talking in evening prep. I always hated these because they were such a waste of time, an unprofitable use of leisure better spent painting or reading. Much better a beating which was quickly over and soon forgotten.

After trials I was accepted by the music master, Alexander Brent Smith, as a treble in the choir, which was very important to me, for the choir was excellent and we sang a great deal of very good music. I learnt the old notation of plainsong, and the anthems on Sunday at Evensong were a joy. There was a good one by Beethoven which we seldom sang; but my favourite – everyone's favourite, I suppose – could never come round often enough: Bach's *Jesu, Joy of Man's Desiring*. It occupies a special corner of my mind and I find myself singing it at the oddest moments – driving a car or playing golf.

If Easter fell in term the choir sang the grail music from *Parsifal*. This happened twice, in my second year and in my last. On the first occasions as an angel I was singing way up in the triforium; since I have no head for heights, I kept my eyes away from the audience a hundred and twenty feet below. The second time I was one of the knights on *terra firma* beneath the organ loft.

After the summer concert we were invited by the Dowager Duchess of Norfolk to sing to her at Arundel Castle. She asked a number of friends to tea at one end of the great hall while we were at the other. She was a gracious but formidable lady. After we had sung all the numbers from the concert, she got up and walked slowly across to Brent Smith to whom she said, 'Now I would like you to sing something that you know.'

Brent Smith was taken aback and looked slightly miffed.

'No, no,' she said in explanation, 'I mean something that you just know by heart.'

After we finished we were regaled with tea and then she led us through the castle, throwing the doors open and marching ahead with throw-away descriptions of each room.

For some reason she had a very soft spot for Lancing and wanted her son Bernard to come to the College. When Bowlby gently pointed out to her that Lancing was a markedly C. of E. school, she is said to have replied, 'Oh, that is no matter. He will have his own chaplain.'

Alas, Bowlby could not do anything and we did not have the pleasure of the Duke's company.

In my second term there arrived in Field's the boy who became my greatest friend: Michael Fletcher. He was the son of a Protestant Irish clergyman who in winter had charge of the English church in San Remo. His mother bore a remarkable physical resemblance to Virginia Woolf, but healthier. He was the only son, but he had three sisters: Diana, Pamela and Romola (known as Rummy). They were a wonderful family and were so kind to me that for the first time in my life I felt as if I had a brother and sisters. He used sometimes to come to stay with me at Sevenoaks. It is remarkable how sensitive one can become to the well-being of a person to whom one is very close. All of four years later when Michael went to Oxford to sit his entrance exams for Worcester College (which he passed), he arrived back when we were all going to bed in the senior dormitory. I took one look at him and said 'My God, what's the matter?' Nothing, he replied, he felt fine, and everyone else agreed with him. But before breakfast the next morning an ambulance rushed him to Brighton to have his appendix out.

In the autumn term soccer was played by everyone; but after Christmas there was some soccer, some hockey, but mainly running and athletics – the school's speciality. Apart from the sports at the end of term, *the* event was the five mile. Lancing has one of the two best cross-country courses among public schools – the other is at Bradfield. It starts at the boiler – literally an old boiler on wooden legs which is a safety look-out when the shooting-range is in use – on the downs at the back of the school. Along the ridge of the downs, through Lancing Ring, down into the valley, a long pull up to Cow Top, a quick gallop downhill to a little Saxon church, and then a long slog home through the fields which contain some two dozen water obstacles, including the showpiece, the twenty-foot valley dyke. Each house entered a team of eight, so there were fifty-six starters. The first twenty home were awarded their house colours, and I was immensely proud to be given mine at the first attempt.

I also began to win a number of under-sixteen events, and was good enough to attract the attention of Douglas Goodhart, captain of athletics (he of the adventures in a haystack). He advised me to give up cross-country running and concentrate on track, and not to run at all in the spring following my sixteenth birthday; so many immature athletes, he said, were ruined by trying too hard in their first year as a senior. Any temptation to disregard his advice was removed by an accident which ruled me out until the following season.

After my second year I left the Lower School, skipped Remove, and went into the Lower Fifth. This was the form in which the scholars were put when they arrived, and I then made three new friends. They were Peter Burra, who played the violin – he was killed in an air crash not long after coming down from Oxford, but not before he had written a good short life of Wordsworth; Peter Pears, the famous singer and monarch of Aldeburgh, who played the piano; and Edward Croft-Murray, who was to spend his life in the Department of Prints and Drawings at the British Museum, also a violinist. Teddy was my science partner; I was an incompetent scientist, but he was worse. He suggested an equable arrangement: if I would carry out as best I could whatever we had to do with test tubes and retorts, he would do his best to relieve the tedium. This worked very well: I muddled through, while at each class he produced from his pocket some object of beauty – an exquisite piece of carved jade or a Japanese netsuke; he seemed to have an inexhaustible collection.

There were other friends whom I liked very much but with whom I cannot claim to have been so close. John Ramsay Willis (a beautiful medium-pace bowler in Gibbs House) who, when we compared notes, said 'I wondered who it was who pipped me at the top of the English scholarship paper,' (later Sir John Willis, obit 1988); John Godfray, also in Gibbs, who produced the first Oxford bags seen at the College and was to be my golf partner for many years playing for the school; a slim, dark boy in Second's, also destined for fame as the Right Hon. Sir Robert Megarry, Judge of the High Court; Gino Watkins and his friend Quentin Riley who later accompanied him on his three Arctic expeditions (on the last of which he was drowned at the age of twenty-four). There was a peaceful assurance about Gino, so different from Quentin who was always ebullient. He spoke so quietly that one could hardly hear him, and was always extremely neat. Also he had a habit, which I have observed in only one other man, of standing and walking with his left arm behind his back clutching his right arm at the elbow. The other man was T.E. Lawrence. Of course they are not the only people to have had this habit, but I wonder if there was not some psychological similarity between them: both intrepid men of action, yet personally withdrawn as though containing within themselves something not of this world.

English was taught by F.A. Woodard – 'Baggers' – a great-nephew of the founder of the school, who was in Holy Orders. He was a teacher who achieved results by sheer love. When we came to take the School Certificate – the equivalent of the modern 'O' Level – the special subject was Keats. So well did he convey his feeling for the poet that the national examiners gave four of us over 90 per cent: Holland a brilliant boy who died soon afterwards, got 98 per cent. 'Baggers' gave me as a memento an inscribed copy of Colvin's *Life of Keats*, which still sits on my shelves next to the annotated text which I used at the time.

How marked was the contrast a year later. We found ourselves 'learning' English from a useless individual called James whose idea of instruction was to make his pupils read aloud so that he could sit and do nothing. The book he chose was *Treasure Island* which the two Peters and I had read several times years before, so we sat in the back row and talked in whispers. I am sure that it was supremely irritating for him, but to us conversation was more interesting than listening to others reading a good book rather badly. The indolent tyrant tried to get his revenge on me later. There was one unique institution at Lancing: at the end of the summer term the entire school from top to bottom, except the Sixth, took the same all-embracing English paper. In my term report under *English* James wrote 'Has neither aptitude nor interest.' The gloss from Bowlby – I never realized that headmasters actually *read* reports before they signed them – was: 'This is difficult to credit as he has come out top of the School.'

Having broken, my voice now had settled down as a baritone, so I asked Brent Smith if I could come back into the choir. He said that he was full up with basses, but could I manage tenor? I knew quite well that I could not really, but I was desperate, so I said yes, and was accepted. I could in fact manage all but the highest notes. Back in the choir, I was next to Peter Pears (he had Peter Burra on his other side). I explained my predicament and he agreed that if I saw a note coming which I could not manage I should nudge him, shut up, and he would sing a little louder for us both. It worked perfectly.

At the end of the school year in summer 1925 when Bowlby retired, he wrote to father saying that I should learn another language: it could be Greek or German, and he recommended the former. Father did not mention the matter to me and wrote back agreeing, which was surprising in view of his own interest in all things German. Thus without choice I was condemned to a language at which I proved to be remarkably inept – the only good I ever got out of it was to be able to read the street signs in Athens – and denied an alternative which later I was badly to need.

During this year there was the Great University Row which raged for months. It was agreed that I should go to a university, but which? Father had made up his mind that I should go to Geneva. I protested; mother

took my side, saying that she did not see why I should be sent to a
university abroad if I did not want to. Father was adamant. I was adamant
– I would not go to Geneva. In the end father relented and said I could go
wherever I liked as long as it was not Oxford, which at that time enjoyed a
reputation for being effete. I doubt if there was ever any foundation for
such a reputation; perhaps a few flamboyant individuals may have
caused remark, rather in the way that Cambridge in the thirties is now
regarded quite erroneously as having been a hot-bed of Reds. Anyway, I
said that I wanted to go to Cambridge, and finally this was agreed –
father's Parthian shot being that I would have to make my own arrangements since he would have nothing to do with it. After this decision I was
victorious but clueless. Matters were eventually settled during a visit to
Lancing by C.L. Chamberlain, 'Monkey', who had been head of Field's
the year before. I explained my trouble and he said why did I not come
where he was, King's? He said that I would have to read for honours and
must pass the college exams. I jumped at it and he sent me the forms. In
the following spring I went up to King's, sat the exams in history and was
accepted. I must say that father, when he did give in, did so with good
grace: in due time he gave me a most generous allowance.

My last year began with the arrival of a new headmaster, Cuthbert
Blakiston. He was a bull of a man, with a club-foot; a bachelor of great
charm and positive views. He was much more of an intellectual than
Bowlby. He had been a housemaster at Eton where I am told that he
was brilliant. He was to be head of Lancing for only nine years. I think
that he was a forward-looking man, perhaps too outspoken for his own
good, and it is possible that he was better with a house than with the
distractions of a whole school. He was interested in individuals and did
not suffer fools gladly. At any rate, his reign marked the end of a golden
age: after him Lancing went down. Happily that is long passed and
today the school is right at the top again. He was good to me in many
ways, and I owe him a great debt of gratitude.

There was a lot of writing going on in the school, and for this there
was no outlet, since the school magazine was confined to news and
reviews of activities. So I went to Blakiston and asked if there was any
possibility of starting a literary periodical. He said it was a good idea; the
material was gathered and edited by a friend of mine in Gibb's called
Davis and myself, and it was printed by W.H. Smith. So the *Lancing
Miscellany* was born. Among the first contributors, Peter Pears wrote an
'Ode to Music'.

In the spring after I had passed my exams for King's, Blakiston said
that I need no longer attend any classes unless I wanted to. I chose to go
to Lucas on history, and Blakiston's own class on the Greek Testament –
the latter not because I particularly enjoyed it but because I felt that it
was good for me. The rest of the time I spent in my pitt (Lancing study)
reading history and writing a weekly essay for the head. Many of them
were strange legends built round some town in Northern Italy, for I was
deep in the Renaissance at the time. It meant an hour of intelligent adult
conversation when he went over each effusion, and very occasionally he

invited me to dinner and talked wisely over roast pheasant and a glass of claret. He was a great raconteur and I was fascinated by the tales he told me. One in particular was like a detective story. I cannot now remember all the details, but it concerned the loss in mysterious circumstances of a magnificent painting – I think that it was a large Delacroix – which eventually turned up equally mysteriously in a dim corridor of a country rectory. It was a very good story and I told it at a dinner party many years later. Everyone around the table was riveted as I drew towards the climax; with a rather unfortunately phrased flourish I delivered the punch line: 'And where do you think the picture was found? In the rector's back passage.'

To return, for a moment: a new master to arrive in 1925 was Guy Butler. He became assistant housemaster of Head's House. He was a huge man who ran the quarter mile in the 1923 Cambridge team – the greatest team ever produced by a university, most members of which ran for Britain in the 1924 Paris Olympics; he won a bronze in the 400 metres. He was in charge of athletics and in this respect had a considerable influence on me.

I emerged from my sabbatical in the spring of 1925 and started to train seriously. I suppose I interested Guy as the best prospect at his own distance, and he went to the trouble of taking photographs – very little used in training at that time – of me in action, and from the prints pointing out flaws in my style which I had to work to eradicate. He also had his own shoemaker come to the school and measure some of us for really fine spiked shoes, and silk shorts were ordered. He spared nothing to make us as dedicated as we could be. The most important match of the season was always against Eton; we usually beat them because we specialized more than they. That year they came to us. I was first string for the quarter, which I won; Eton took second and third, the latter being Luke Lillingstone, whom I mention because he was to cross my path again. I also won the quarter in the school sports.

In the following year I felt honoured to be asked by Guy to help him in his training for an assault which he intended to make alone on the world 400-metre record. It was speed work; given a start, I had to try to force the best out of him by acting as a target. He made his attempt at a meeting in Glasgow and failed by the narrowest margin to achieve his ambition.

So the last year wore on. I had achieved my ambition of becoming head librarian. I was head of Field's, and captain of athletics. I painted a lot, and wandered up to the music school to hear others doing what I could not do myself; one afternoon Peter Pears asked me what I would like him to play. When I asked for Liszt's *Liebestraum*, he said, 'Can't you think of anything better than that?' But to my delight he played it all the same.

Athletics came round again, and for the annual match we went to Eton. Arriving by coach, we were given lunch by our opponents. I sat with the Eton captain, a very good athlete, particularly in hurdling, who won the Victor Ludorum twice and was a debonair, distinguished individual, named Ian Fleming. We won the match, and I won the quarter, beating Lillingstone again.

Unexpected things can happen. As we took the coach back to Lancing I did not suppose that I would ever see Ian Fleming again, but I was wrong. Chiefly because we both became book collectors a friendship began that day which lasted until Ian's death. It was patchy – there were long periods when we did not see one another at all, then there were casual meetings when we both happened to be in the same place at the same time; but the warmth remained, for, as a close friend has said, 'He had such magnetism and generosity of heart that to know him well was to be filled with affection for him.' The last time I was to see him was far in the future, not long before his death, when we were lunching together at the *Etoile*; he introduced me to Raymond Chandler, and I sat between two masters neither of whom I published. It was a flourish which Ian would have enjoyed if he had realized that it was an *envoi*.

My last school sports came round, in which the quarter was a very close thing. I was just first – the only boy to win two years running since 1888 – and I broke the school record. Mother had come down to watch and I was all the more happy that I had made it.

There only remained the Public School sports at Stamford Bridge during the Easter holidays. I won my heat of the quarter, and knew that there was one outstanding runner whom I had to beat in the final. My plan was the classic one: I would stay behind his right shoulder, pushing him as hard as possible, until we came out of the last bend when I would take him. With the tape in sight I was accelerating when I heard a pop in my chest, and, to my horror, started practically to mark time. I dropped back to fourth place and was bitterly disappointed. I concluded that I was not sufficiently robust to run two fast quarters in one afternoon; but in the autumn I was to discover that something far more serious was wrong.

Every summer term there was a stock-taking of the library. As head librarian I had to see that this was done and report the state of the shelves to Gordon, the master responsible. This led to a most disreputable incident. In the course of checking the books with the other librarians, I discovered that a number of Browning's works available for borrowing were first editions, including *Sordello* which was already a rare book. I told 'Gordo' this and suggested that they should be withdrawn into reserve and modern editions substituted for everyday use; to my horror he simply was not interested. This was a situation which, as a rabid book-collector, I just could not tolerate; so I removed the first editions and took them home: I stole them. However by the autumn my conscience was pricking me severely so I sent them back to 'Gordo' with a rather feeble letter saying that when I left the school they had got into my luggage by mistake; I heard no more.

So my last term drew to an end.

I packed up everything and stood at the top of the hill waiting for the car to take me away. On a hot July morning I looked up at the chapel and felt very grateful for five years of happiness.

4   The Game of King's

I went up to Cambridge in September, 1926, agog with excitement. At first I was disappointed to find that I had been given lodgings a mile from College, out on the Ely Road. The Cambridge system was, and I presume still is, for undergraduates to live out for the first year and then spend the next two in College – the opposite of that which pertains at Oxford. This was to prove in one way a disadvantage, yet one which was more than offset by the personality of the only other lodger in my distant house.

Charles Hasse, of Alsatian origin and a few years older than I, was a descendant of the composer Johann Adolph Hasse, who had married Handel's great soprano Faustina Bordoni. Under the same roof we became very close friends and remain so to this day – though I do not see him as often as I would wish since, like his illustrious forebears, he has long chosen to live in Italy.

The first thing I did was to call on the lay dean, the economics historian Sir John Clapham, and ask if I could switch from history to English literature. An austere but kindly man, he looked down his long nose at me and, pointing out that I had been accepted by the college as an historian, asked what made me think I could read for an honours degree in a different subject. I told him that my father was a publisher and, brought up in literary surroundings, I thought that I had leanings in that direction. After considering the matter at some length he granted my request and told me that my supervisor would be F.L. Lucas. This was an important decision for me and had I not made it or had my request not been granted, a great many things in my life would have been different.

I reported to 'Peter' Lucas and as I got to know him, which was not easy, I developed an enormous admiration for him, ripening into a friendship which, though I had little inkling of it at the time, was to last until the end of his life.

My next call was on the captain of athletics to whom I gave a brief résumé of my running at Lancing, and I was soon up at Fenner's to start training. The changing-rooms piled with clothes, spiked shoes everywhere, snatches of conversation on distances and times: it was a part of my life and I loved it. I was sufficiently experienced to train myself, and I would retreat into a far corner of the track with my little trowel to dig the holes in the cinders, the way it was done before starting blocks were invented. But I was not happy; I had no speed out of the holes and my acceleration was not there. The first event of the season was the inter-college relays. I was picked for second leg in the 4 × 220 yards; I not only ran abominably, but I felt rotten afterwards. 440 yards is the killer and after the sprint I should not have felt more than a little puffed; something was wrong.

I made an appointment to see Salisbury Woods, the doctor who for so many years ministered to the ailments of every athlete in the university. I had heard the pop inside my chest when I had suddenly lost ground in the spring, but my utter disappointment at my performance distracted me from my physical condition; this latest manifestation was too much. X-rays were taken, and I came back a few days later to hear the news: it was catastrophic – I had blown the side out of my heart. No more running, no sport of any kind, no bicycle, walk no further than essential, go up stairs slowly – for a year. I left his consulting-room in a nightmare of misery. I had to tell the captain of athletics in College and I can see now the scorn on his face; just another schoolboy wonder turning out to be a damp squib. Ironically, the Blue for the 440 which I had once had hopes of gaining in my third year was awarded to Luke Lillingstone (also in King's) whom I had beaten on both the occasions on which I ran against Eton.

I did not hate that first year; I just lived through it like a zombie remembering little. Charles Hasse's comforting friendship was the sheet anchor that saved me from being blown away. To avoid the long walk from and to my lodgings more than once a day I did my work in the College library or the Junior Common Room. During the great amount of time which I spent in the latter I used to notice with some surprise the frequent visits of Professor Arthur Pigou, the economist and mountaineer, whose tall, spare figure with fluffy hair round his bald pate seemed to have little to do with the undergraduates. But in this I was wrong, for at the time neither I nor, so far as I am aware, anyone else realized that for many years he was the most secret and in many ways the most effective Soviet agent in Britain, his financial advice as much appreciated by the Kremlin as his success in recruiting fellow-travellers, an activity which apparently he called 'picking out the Marxist plums'. He must, I think, have been a friend of Leonid Krasin, Commissar for Foreign Trade and twice Soviet ambassador to the Court of St James, who was largely responsible for building up his country's economy.

I was paroled half-way through the May term. Taking a fresh set of X-rays, Salisbury Woods said that my heart was now healed, indeed that the scar tissue was tougher than the muscles which it had replaced; now, he said, I could do what I liked. In spite of his reassurance I did not feel sufficiently confident to submit myself again to the rigours of the quarter mile, and was at an unexpected loose end. It must have been through Charles that I met Walter Churchill, who was to be a dominant figure in my life, and the three of us were soon inseparable. Walter was an epéeist and he suggested to me that I should take up fencing, which I did.

At that time the *salle d'armes* was in a yard off Petty Cury and was shared with the boxing club. The *maître* was a famous and successful teacher, Nicholas Dapp – a tall, handsome French ex-sergeant-major who had been badly gassed at Verdun. His star pupil was a Kingsman senior to me and possibly the finest foilist this country has ever produced: Emrys Lloyd – a name beyond Dapp, who always called him 'Leeodd'. Equally distinguished was the best *sabreur*, Robin Brook, also a Kingsman, who was to become a lifelong friend. Both were selected for two Olympic Games, though Robin was only able to attend the second for which he was chosen – Berlin, 1936.

I was in the *salle* pretty well every afternoon, and after a lesson and five hits with everyone present I would stay on for hours talking philosophy with Dapp – who, incidentally, never wore a mask when giving a lesson, even after some clumsy pupil had got him in the eye with a foil. These long conversations helped to nourish my penchant for France and everything French. The first seeds were sown, I am sure, by father's complete distaste: he never had a good word to say for the French, I don't know why; certainly he was not alone. There have always been people in these islands who share this dislike – and in consequence generally find it reciprocated. Human beings are animals and have all the same instincts as, for instance, dogs and cats. I love the French and now after so many years can put my hand on my heart and say that I have never at any time had a cross word with a French man or woman in my life, or received from them anything but courtesy.

That spring there was an event of considerable importance. For a number of years Cassell's had belonged to the Berry brothers who became Lords Camrose and Kemsley. They made up their minds that their interest lay in newspapers and periodicals, not books, so they decided to dispose of that side of the business – with the imprint – and move all the magazines to the Amalgamated Press which they owned. Since father had been running both the books and the periodicals for a long time, he had become very friendly with them; and in consequence they gave him first refusal. The price for the book list and the imprint was £100,000, a considerable sum in those days. Father accepted and set about raising the money. Everything he owned was hocked, but he was still short of the target; the final balance, how much I never knew, was produced by my grandfather.

The next move was that the lawyers engaged in the matter found the company structure so complicated that they declared the wishes of a willing buyer and the willing sellers impossible, which was ridiculous. The Berrys turned to an eminent company lawyer, Ernest Jacobson, who found a way round the impasse. After a frightening period of hanging on the brink, on 6 May 1927 I got a letter from father saying that the deed was done; and on the same morning it was announced in the press that 'Mr Flower bought all the ordinary shares in Cassell and Company, Ltd, from Sir William Berry and Mr J. Gomer Berry, and as the

Preference share capital about to be redeemed, Mr Flower becomes the owner of all the shares in the company.' Later the company was dissolved and Cassell & Company (Holdings) Ltd was created – which would in the distant future lead to unimagined trouble. I sent him a telegram which expressed surprise and relief after so long: 'My God. Congratulations.' This, however, was too much for the Post Office and he received instead the rather sissy message, 'My good congratulations.'

In the following autumn, when I had moved into College, there was a postscript. Father telephoned me to say that he had been offered a handsome profit on his investment (I always forgot to ask him from whom it came, but my guess was always Walter Hutchinson). He said that if I wanted to follow him as a publisher he would turn down the offer; but if I did not so wish, he would accept, and then give me the capital to set up as an antiquarian bookseller. My reply had to be immediate; there was no time for reflection. I said that I wanted to be a publisher, and such I became, thanks to his confidence and generosity.

One of the greatest events of that year was the opening of the Arts Theatre, under the management of Terence Gray – predecessor of the theatre which under Maynard Keynes was established near the market square. Being on the outskirts of town, it was very near to Charles and me; we never missed anything in the repertoire. The plays, their production and actors were of dazzling quality. Michael Redgrave, who came up at the same time as us, described Tyrone Guthrie's production as 'witty, inventive, very theatrical'; three of the company – Maurice Evans, Torin Thatcher and Jessica Tandy – went on to make their reputations in the United States. The last was described on Broadway as having 'the fascination of that rare combination of star power and acting virtuosity'; and also in 1990 won an Oscar. But the most beautiful actress was Leonora Corbett, tall, statuesque and golden haired. The plays I remember best were O'Neill's *The Emperor Jones*, Strindberg's *Miss Julie*, Čapek's *Insect Play* and *The Man Of Mode* which gave me my love for Etherege.

For many years father, as editor of the *Dorset Annual*, had known the greatest living Dorset man – Thomas Hardy – and was a frequent visitor at Max Gate. As soon as I was old enough he would take me with him. Florence Hardy was very particular about allowing visitors because of her husband's great age and the fact that people from all over the world wanted to see him. It was a pilgrimage which she had actively to discourage. Father always respected this and never took anyone without Florence's permission. My grandfather wanted very much to meet Hardy and in the spring of 1927 father rang Max Gate to ask if he might bring his father with him; Florence said 'Of course, don't be silly.' So all four of us, which included mother, drove over from Salisbury, whither my grandparents had moved.

Inside the front door of Max Gate is a sitting-room with a little alcove, to the left of which is the dining-room. Starche and Hardy, being of much the same generation, hit it off at once, sitting together in the alcove – Hardy as usual like a meditative Buddha. When it was time for tea he said to Florence, 'All of you (for there were some relations present) go and have your tea in the dining-room; Mr Flower and I will have ours here.'

So we left them deep in converse, and all chattered away. There is that old wives' tale, so often true, that silence falls at twenty past and twenty to the hour. Suddenly there was one of those inexplicable pauses and in the stillness I heard one of them (which I do not know, for their voices were not unalike) say:

'Do you remember that highwayman who used to lurk behind the gibbet?'

Hardy's eighty-seventh birthday, which was to be his last, was on 2 June 1927. The weather was glorious and father asked him if he would like to go for a drive and a picnic. Yes, he said that he would like to be driven for the last time round those places in the county which were nearest to his heart. It took most of the day and he talked without ceasing of his memories of each field, each village and each wood as we drove by. My clearest memory is of the picnic on High Stoy, overlooking father's birthplace, and Hardy sitting on a rug in the sunshine, waving a lobster claw and still talking.

Seven months later father and I were in Westminster Abbey, among the small number invited by Florence, silently watching his urn lowered into the floor of the Poets' Corner. Little did we know, as we stood there silently, of the back-biting and confusion which had preceded the service. As soon as Hardy was dead Sydney Cockerell rang up James Barrie at the Adelphi in London asking him to fix an Abbey funeral, and got an immediate reply that all was arranged. As was said of him at another funeral, 'Cockerell took charge and ordered everyone around.' In this case Florence was particularly unhappy because she knew that Hardy in his Will had stated flatly that he wanted to be buried at Stinsford beside his parents, his sister and his first wife, Emma; she consulted the local vicar who suggested the solution ultimately adopted: the heart was buried at Stinsford and the ashes were sent to the Abbey.

Florence, who hated Sydney Cockerell, always accused that unfortunate man of causing her husband's death. She said that not long before it he had talked at Hardy without stopping for seven hours, after which the dear old man, exhausted, took to his bed and never got up again. This is not entirely true, although there is considerable substance in it. Hardy took to his bed finally on 11 December 1927, and Cockerell did not arrive at Max Gate until New Year; on the other hand, his reputation in Cambridge was that 'when he appeared at a distinguished bedside, no doctor's skill could save the patient'. Hardy died in January.

Everything changed in my second year. One's last task at the end of the previous academic year was to go to the college office to see what accommodation would be available in the autumn and choose rooms according to one's taste and means.

Walter Churchill and I seemed to be aiming at a similar price-range, so we decided to live on the same staircase in Bodley's down by the river. We chose E staircase, which has since been changed to W; I was to live on the first floor, opposite Professor Adcock, who held the chair of Ancient History, and Walter had those above me facing Frank Birch, an historian who became a theatrical producer. Birch and Frank Adcock, later knighted, were old friends having been in Intelligence during the war. In 1939 they both went back to it, Birch as head of the naval section and Adcock as the main recruiter for Bletchley Park, to which he took no less than ten fellows of King's, including Peter Lucas.

Charles chose rooms in another part of the college. But that made no difference; we remained inseparable and thought of ourselves in a rather juvenile way as the three musketeers: our epigraph is the last photograph taken together in front of the Senate House on graduation day.

The college fell markedly into two parts: heterosexual and homosexual. There was nothing personal and the two parties were perfectly civil to one another; but they did not mix. There could be a light-hearted side to these variations. One spring afternoon I had been to see Lowes Dickinson and was standing on the steps of Gibbs', the lovely eighteenth-century building which divides the college in the middle, talking to Lytton Strachey and Maynard Keynes. In front of the Hall and Senior Common Room not far away stood the best-looking man of my year whom I knew only by his name, which I have forgotten. Strachey was focusing a small camera. Keynes said, 'Lytton, what on earth do you want to take a photograph of that for? It's the worst building in College.'

'Ah,' was the reply, 'but look at the foreground.'

My view then, and I do not think that it has changed very much since, was that everyone is entitled to his own code of conduct; but that he should also respect the codes of others. Lack of such respect can be dangerous, and may lead to easily avoided trouble. Regrettably today, in some quarters, it is regarded as queer to be heterosexual; the pendulum must swing too far before it can come to a reasonable rest.

Father's serious suggestion that he would, if I wished, put up the money for me to become an antiquarian bookseller shows that I was already immersed in old books, and I was sunk further by friendship with two Kingsmen whom I was to know for the rest of their lives: John Carter and John Hayward, the former, tall, handsome, brilliant and fastidious, the latter equally brilliant, an acid wit, a Caliban who had a streak of great kindness when he chose to let it peep out; at that time he could still walk, although it was painful to watch and he was soon to be confined permanently to a wheelchair. They were both a year senior to me, and a year at that time makes a lot of difference. In their presence, therefore, I felt a tyro, as indeed I was. John Carter had already formed his large collection of early editions of the classics and was beginning on Sir Thomas Browne. John Hayward's collection of Saint Evremond was at an advanced stage and already top of its class, while I was swivelling indeterminately between Edith Sitwell, Eric Gill, Tennyson and Browning, like a yacht tacking in light weather before the start of a race. They treated me with condescension, which was quite proper, but being gentlemen they tempered it with sympathy and kindness. As a result I learned from them to such an extent that when I found my collecting *métier* I was able to get on with it without any more backing and filling.

One of the pleasures, in those days, if one was a book collector, was the weekly gallop to David's stall near the main square at nine o'clock on Saturday mornings. Dear old David, with his long Jewish nose pitted with blackheads hanging over the yellowed stub of a long dead home-rolled cigarette, an ensemble topped by an Anthony Eden hat of such old age that it shone; he was a genius. He loved books as a lioness loves her cubs, and could round on the unwary with the same ferocity. He bought in the sale-rooms during the week and the fruits of his labours were first offered on Saturdays. One had to be there absolutely on the dot when business began; and since his stalls (he had two) were only five minutes walk from King's, I usually went in my pyjamas and dressing-gown. Ferocious as he could be, if you were in, you were in. For some reason he accepted me; as I scrabbled about, looking into the distance like an umpire rejecting an appeal for LBW, he would murmur, 'Nothing there, look down the other end.'

About this time I had an unhappy musical experience; mother took me to hear *The Yeoman of the Guard*. It was well done, but I found it trivial and boring. I have throughout my life heard many of the songs of the Savoy operas – one cannot avoid them – but as to the complete works, that first performance was enough and I have never sat through one since. This was a taste which I shared with father, who couldn't stand them: which may seem surprising since he this year wrote and published the first major life of Sullivan – ostensibly with the collaboration of the composer's nephew, though Herbert Sullivan's sole but vital contribution was to produce the diaries. Arthur Sullivan kept his diary in annual volumes bound in green leather, each closed with a heavy brass lock, the key to which had long been lost. At regular intervals father sat at his desk with a hacksaw, and when he got a volume open, his hair used to stand on end at the horrifying details; he would regale mother and me with tasty titbits and then say 'I can't publish that!' Although he hated the Savoy operas, he loved Sullivan as a musician, a great conductor and a serious composer *manqué*; and he had great sympathy for an obviously unhappy man.

The diaries went back to Herbert Sullivan who had no children and presumably they passed to a relative who also inherited from him all the autograph manuscripts. So far as I know, they remain in private hands; but Arthur Jacobs has had access to them in writing his life of Sullivan, published in 1984. Mr Jacobs takes father to task for whitewashing his subject in his first use of the diaries. There is considerable justification for these strictures of a book which has been described as 'hagiographical'; father, in what he wrote and in what he would publish, was, by modern standards, a prude. On the other hand, in his defence it must be remembered that he was collaborating with Sullivan's nephew and had to tread delicately; furthermore, fifty years ago the 'warts and all' school of biography was in its infancy – one might hint but one did not state – and a book which descended to the level of prurience common today would then not have been published, or, if it had, would have been utterly damned.

The manuscripts did once very nearly find a more public home. Father was staying with Bertie Sullivan when Sydney Cockerell, the peppery but highly successful director of the Fitzwilliam Museum, came to call, asking about the manuscripts. Bertie said that he could not make up his mind what to do with the autographs, so father said, 'My son's at Cambridge. Why don't you leave them to the Fitzwilliam?'

'That's not at all a bad idea,' said Bertie, and there the matter rested for the moment.

At eight o'clock the following morning there was a loud knock at the front door. Bertie, probably with a hangover which was not altogether unusual, saw Cockerell and two men standing below.

'What the hell do you want?' he asked.

Cockerell replied, 'I have here a form of Will and two witnesses.'

'Bugger off,' said Bertie, slamming the window. So that was one of Cockerell's few failures.

Eric Gill had now become one of my main interests. Almost as soon as I got into College I began to receive catalogues from a young bookseller in Bristol, Douglas Cleverdon, who later became a dear friend and has remained one. From him I bought the Golden Cockerell *Canterbury Tales* and *The Four Gospels* (plus a number of Nonesuch Books). It was only recently when visiting Chichester Cathedral after many years that I noticed and studied the two superb panels of Saxon carving which Gill must have known so well when he lived at Ditchling, and which in my view surely influenced his style in the treatment of drapery.

In good time father asked me what I would like to have as a twenty-first birthday present, and I asked for a piece of sculpture by Gill. I knew that there was a link with him because Cassell's were to publish his first large volume of essays, *Art Nonsense*, in the following year. Before 25 August it arrived from Capel-y-ffyn: a lovely half-length of a woman with a comb in her hair. She belongs now to my daughter Susan, but not long after she was carved she was to lead me to her creator.

Apart from collecting books, I drew quite a lot and did a number of caricatures, two of which, of Donald Beves and Frank Adcock, appeared in *Basileon*, the College magazine. Another, the best, of the new provost, Sir John Sheppard – about whose character the college was very much divided into pros and cons (I was a con) – was so satirical that the editors would not publish it.

Then, too, my interest in the black races, and then in jazz, was born. Started by Romer Wilson's *Latterday Symphony* which the Nonesuch Press published in 1927, it quickly spread with the rage of a prairie fire. I wanted to see the coloured peoples treated everywhere as equals both in public and in private; obviously I was only a very small one of many, but it became an obsession. With wild idealism I predicted that by the year 2000 the population of Europe and America would be khaki – an ignorant assumption which left out of consideration the basic fact that coloured people do not wish to marry or cohabit with whites any more than whites do with coloureds, except for love – a commodity which is too often in short supply in the world today.

Mother and I never missed an opportunity to hear Paul Robeson sing spirituals gloriously. He was much criticized at the time for dressing up in a morning coat and singing to sell-out audiences in the Albert Hall, an Uncle Tom attitude of which Louis Armstrong was also accused in the United States. It struck me as a load of hypocritical prejudice; we went to hear him sing, not admire his sartorial appearance. It used to make me mad, just as today I get angry when people whinge about the vastly inflated sums paid to men and women in sport. Of course the amount of money such professionals earn is absurd, but like everyone else they take what they can get; if people disapprove of it, largely from jealousy, the answer is simple: stay away. If the interest were not there, neither would the money be. It was Henry Cotton who first insisted that if he was a good enough golfer for people to come from far and wide to see him play, he was a good enough man to have the run of the clubhouse. Similarly it is immoral and obscene to be entertained by and applaud a black musician who has to enter and leave the establishment by the back door and who is fed, if he is fed at all, in a corner behind the scenes like some badly house-trained dog.

There have always been wonderful concerts at Cambridge and I went to a great many, often with Eddie Allum, who was an organ scholar. Sometimes he used to invite me up into the organ loft at King's when he was practising, and one day said, 'Now I am going to play the *Chromatic Fantasia and Fugue* entirely on eighteenth-century stops,' and I can remember now the peculiarly golden sound which rolled from one end to the other of that glorious building.

He was on the committee of the Cambridge University Musical Society. We sat together one evening when Beecham was conducting. At that time Sir Thomas was flogging with all his might his idea of an Imperial Opera League. After the interval he made a stirring appeal beginning, 'When I came here this evening I did not expect to have to make a speech; nevertheless …'

'Bloody liar,' Eddie whispered to me, 'he said he wouldn't come unless he could speak.'

No matter; it is a tragedy that Beecham did not succeed in turning his dream into substance.

One eccentric figure who came to play was Vladimir de Pachmann, then eighty years old and under restraint. He was accompanied on to the platform by his keeper who sat silent and unmoved at one side. The concert was a sell-out, so there were several rows of people round the back of the stage behind the piano. Pachmann was notorious for talking while he was playing. On this occasion his attention was caught by a remarkably unattractive middle-aged woman only a few feet away on his left, and all his remarks were addressed to her. Far from being a distraction, his ramblings were most illuminating, such as: 'Now you will see that I introduce the second subject in the left hand … now I go back to the first subject in another key with my right.' While he was talking he played quite beautifully.

His homey performance was far removed from that of Paderewski, whose playing was, of course, superb; but even more so was his presence. He struck the piano as if it were privileged to receive the attention of his wonderful hands, and acknowledged the plaudits of a full house with the aloof dignity of the statesman that he was in Poland.

But I was totally captivated by Cortot. He came first with Thibault and Casals, who must have played as well as three men have ever played together. Generally, much as I admire it, I must confess that chamber music is beyond me; while appreciating the beauty, I am not clever enough to enjoy the subtleties which make it such an important part of music. But those three I could listen to for ever.

The next time he came it was to give a recital of which the whole programme was devoted to Chopin. I am inclined to think of Chopin as the greatest of all composers, I suppose because of the shattering effect which he has on me, wafting me to heights of beauty so that I could wish to die with the sound of it upon my ears or tearing me with a despair which makes me weep. Chopin is the god and Cortot was the high priest who led me, the neophyte, to the shrine. I do not miss a recital devoted entirely to his music if I can help it, but I do not think that I have ever heard anyone – even Malcuzynski at his remarkable best – who expressed to such perfection the far away gentleness, the touching purity, the yearning for something which perhaps there never was, the fierce pride, the sometimes uncontrolled power which are all part of Chopin.

There were many other visitors – the best, perhaps, Kreisler, a tall, military figure with iron grey hair *en brosse*, coaxing a slightly wistful yet rich, golden tone from his Strad.

There was one occasion when I came near to striking Eddie. I had been to Vienna where I had had another unforgettable operatic experience: I had heard Maria Jeritza singing Marietta in Korngold's *Die Tote Stadt*, a role which she had created in 1920. A glorious golden voice: I could never forget it. I came back with a record of her singing the two finest arias in the opera, and when I played it triumphantly to Eddie, he pulled his forelock – a habit he had – and said in a far-away tone, 'I didn't know it was so old fashioned.'

For more than a year I had been sedulously courting Michael Fletcher's sister, Pamela. Apart from other meetings, I used to drive over every Sunday to her family home which was at Mousehill, on the road to Hindhead. Her parents were always very kind to me and did not seem to mind how often I turned up.

With the deepest respect to those dear to me, I think that Pam in her youth was the most lovely woman I have ever seen. She was not unlike a beautiful version of Yvonne Printemps, Sacha Guitry's wife. She had enormous blue eyes, a perfect complexion, a mass of hair which can only be described by the corny phrase, spun gold, and a stunning figure: the only flaw – there had to be one, otherwise it would have been too much – was her legs which were rather solid, mainly, I suppose, because she played so much tennis. In addition she was extremely witty and gay; with an extremely good mind, though it was then still growing.

I asked her up for May Week and she accepted. Mother was to be her chaperone; I was too dazzled to remember how Pam arrived, but mother came by coach, sitting next to Walter's father about whom she had heard so much but whom she had never met. A happy chance.

We went to watch the last day of the May races in the 1½-litre supercharged Lee Francis which I had recently acquired which, apart from its speed, turned out to be an unsatisfactory car. It was a hot day and she did not like it a bit, boiling in the traffic jam before we had even got out of the field in which we had parked. Jesus went head of the river, and in celebration they rowed up the Backs on Sunday afternoon with Jackie Brown, who had not long before coxed the University boat to victory for the fourth successive year, ringing a crier's bell and bellowing, 'Make way! Make way!' There wasn't much room, and several young gentlemen punting their girl friends downstream fell overboard in trying to oblige. Incidentally there was then some query as to whether it was in order for Brown to be in the boat at all, as not being in *statu pupilari*. Half a century later it seems permissible for an oarsman to row for as many years as he is invited and so chooses; any year now the first greybeard will be seen on the tideway and bald pates will be commonplace.

The King's Ball is always on a Monday. Mother said good night and bade us enjoy ourselves. Pam in a long dress of ivory watered satin looked ravishing. She was a very good dancer, and she taught me the Charleston and the Black Bottom. I never danced the former nearly as well as she: it had arrived from the States nearly four years before and has been called 'as indigenous to the twenties as the *pavane* was to the Escorial'. The latter had just arrived from *George White's Scandals* in New York and was the sensation of the year; I became fairly efficient at it – or at least I presume so. It was a very sensual dance in which the limbs of the participants were closely intertwined; and at one point of the evening she suddenly said, 'Stop it!' from which I gather that I must have been doing quite well.

By the time we had consumed a great deal of champagne at supper it was after midnight, when all the balls are thrown open, so we thought that we would go and see how Ambrose was playing at Trinity.

It was a good idea as his band was playing extremely well. We stayed for about an hour, then took a punt up the Granta, moored by the bank, and went to sleep.

Les étoiles en feu brillant dans le ruisseau
Et le ciel n'a pas un nuage ...

I woke first. It was a wonderful morning, warm and the birds were singing. She stirred and in a moment I was looking down at her glorious blue eyes. When young one is wide awake in a second, and in any case I was startled by this constellation of beauty, soft with sleep and a gentle smile. Time to punt back, get out the car and drive to Newmarket for breakfast. There was quite a gathering at the hotel, all white ties, tails and lovely dresses, tucking into bacon and eggs.

We left that day. I had asked her to marry me and she had said no, we were too young. She was eighteen and I was nearly twenty-one. Today couples, married or unmarried, have had children by that age, but in our generation all those years ago I suppose that she was right. Of course I was upset. And if fate had not had another card to play, would I have pursued my love, bided my time and tried again? Only the stars can tell. May Week was over.

After two years I had taken Part I of the English tripos, and at home I opened *The Times* with shaking fingers every morning, until the results came out; I had got a 2 (1). What should I read in my third year? I was thinking of switching to history because I had no intention of wasting my time learning Anglo-Saxon which had hitherto been *de rigueur* in the second part of English. Early literature had few attractions for me, and I have never been able to read even Chaucer with any pleasure. There was one exception: Langland's *Piers Plowman*. But my decision was made for me by two things. First, I did not wish to depart from Peter as my supervisor; and secondly the authorities, thank goodness abandoning the useless Anglo-Saxon, created a completely new examination with as set books *La Vita Nuova* and those tales of Boccaccio which had provided plots for Shakespeare. It meant learning Italian, but that was something beautiful and useful.

In August came my twenty-first birthday. Whether to get up his strength for the ordeal or not, I do not know, but father went off for a holiday in the South of France with a friend, Hugh Edwards, a Welsh Member of Parliament. They were in Menton when they saw a most impressive cortège on its way to the cemetery, which turned out to be the funeral of Blasco Ibañez. 'Who's he?' asked Hugh Edwards, and father explained that he was a famous Spanish novelist who had written *Blood and Sand*. They decided to follow, and after the coffin had been lowered into the grave, listened to the orations: first Spanish, followed by French, German and Italian. 'Isn't anyone going to speak in English?' said an outraged Hugh Edwards, and with all the Welsh command of oratory gave an impassioned address lasting nearly half an hour on a man of whom he had never heard.

My parents were extremely generous over the celebration of my twenty-first birthday, which was in two parts on the same evening. The first half was a dinner party at which father and mother left me discreetly alone to take the chair with my best friends. The only absentee was Walter, who had taken a tutoring job in the United States for the summer. After that, with my parents presiding, there was dancing at the Mayfair which was then quite new.

Walter and I arrived up on the same day for the autumn term, and we stood in his rooms talking about our summers. He had come back tourist on the *Olympic*, and he was telling me about an American girl he had met on the boat. From his deck he had looked up at first class and seen her looking down through lorgnettes; they were unusual and he thought they looked snooty, so he put his hand up to his eyes, imitating her. But she was also very attractive, so he and a friend travelling with him put on their dinner jackets that evening and made their way up to first class to find her.

As we were talking, looking out of the window, we saw a neat figure come over King's Bridge. She wore a cloche hat, so I could not see very much of her face, and a very smart suit, the skirt tight until it flared out below the knees, the whole in beige; it was a vision of simple elegance.

'Look,' said Walter, 'that's the girl I was talking about who was on the boat.'

I was already looking.

'I'm going to marry her,' I said.

It did not take long to meet her. Her name was Margaret Cameron Coss and she had come to Cambridge for a year after taking her degree in English at Bryn Mawr. She was extremely beautiful. She was short-sighted and, with pardonable vanity, she did not like to use glasses – hence the lorgnettes until they were for a time superseded by contact lenses. She was the belle of the year and quickly made an enormous number of friends. Through her some of them became friends and acquaintances of mine; they were an interesting collection: Michael Redgrave, Robin Fedden, Bill Empson and John Marks in Magdalene: Michael wrote that Margaret, 'though attractive, was a rather over-earnest intellectual'. (Nonsense – intellectual, yes, but over-earnest, never.) Robin Fedden, a charming man who used his stammer as effectively as Arnold Bennett, I saw at irregular intervals until, after rising to responsibility in the National Trust, he died comparatively young. Bill Empson, I.A. Richards' most promising pupil, was after his death described as 'the most famously over-sophisticated man of his time'. I remember a small man with pebble glasses over which hung an uncontrollable mop of black hair, too clever for me by half and already at work on his *Seven Types of Ambiguity*. John Marks, later literary editor of the brilliant but short-lived *Night and Day*, became the equal if not the master of Hemingway as an authority on bull-fighting. In Trinity the charm and kindness of Anthony Blunt is forgotten in the clouds which surround his end. Alistair Cooke in Jesus I never saw after he went down, though decades later I called him in New York and he had not forgotten. Corpus Christi produced Basil Bartlett, a handsome baronet who went on the stage, and André Mazower, a Russian who remained a friend for a long time until he disappeared abroad; I do not know whether it was by chance or design that they both took part in the Dunkirk evacuation. In Trinity Hall were Denis Blundell and Brooke Crutchley (future University Printer). Denis Blundell, a New Zealander, was a cricket blue who represented his country in the late thirties, admittedly before they became the giants they are today; he was New Zealand High Commissioner in London and eventually Governor General.

Spring came and then early summer. I was unremitting in my attendance on Margaret, who has said that I introduced her to the

Pre-Raphaelites to whom I was devoted at that time. I lost a lot of that devotion later, except for the formal designs of Burne-Jones, the poetry of Morris, and the richness of Rossetti's best paintings.

The time for exams arrived; I had done very little work, and I nearly met total disaster when I walked nonchalantly into the Senate House one morning to find myself faced by a paper I had completely forgotten existed and for which I had in consequence done no preparation. The wind was tempered again: by good fortune this 'special period' which I had forgotten about was the Romantic Movement which had been my own speciality ever since I had been made to love Keats at school, so that I could put up a reasonable show *ad lib*. In the circumstances I was lucky to sink no further than from 2(1) to 2(2).

May Week was coming up, and I had asked Margaret to go with me to the King's Ball on Monday and St John's on Wednesday. Her sister Mary arrived, met everyone, and a close rapport developed between her and Michael Redgrave. She was as beautiful as Margaret but quite different. Tall, willowy, very dark, with grey-green eyes (not brown, as Michael Redgrave, who fell in love with her, said in his memoirs). At the balls they looked stunning in dresses identical except for colour: Margaret's was coral pink and Mary's pearl grey. They were gluttons for punishment; they went to balls on all three nights and slept by day.

The Charleston and the Black Bottom were out: the tango was in. It was a dance I loved and convinced myself that I did quite well. I remember little of the King's Ball, although I think that we had Roy Fox's band. Tuesday I went to an early bed; but John's on Wednesday remains very clearly in my mind for two reasons.

The first was the band. A wealthy Mexican named Fred Elizalde had, when up at John's, formed a band called the Quinquagintas, and, although he had gone down, the college had persuaded him to get it together again for the ball that year. They were superb and played the best traditional jazz I had heard up to that time. I can see and hear now the piano of Elizalde and the soaring clarinet of Skinny Donaldson (small world: nearly half a century later at Walton Heath Golf Club I got to know very well Leonard Joseph, who had been Elizalde's relief pianist!). They were so good that they stayed together and moved into the Savoy Hotel, the first place to offer dance music with dinner, for three years, until they broke up.

My other memory is of a young Argentinian millionaire whose name I never knew; he was, I recall, rather good-looking. Around midnight one of my friends asked me if I felt all right; I said that I did. Then another and another asked me the same question. When I was asked yet again, I rounded on my questioner and said, 'Of course I feel all right. What is this all about?'

'Well, you see,' was the reply, 'that Argentinian has been putting cigar ash in your champagne all evening; it is supposed to be a drug, and he wants your girl.'

I have no idea how many Havanas I consumed in powdered form, but fortunately they had no effect.

Degree Day came; the Three Musketeers were photographed together in cap, gown and hood, looking neither more nor less foolish than any other group. I asked Margaret to marry me and she said she would think about it. She was soon going to Belaggio on Lake Como, and I to Germany. Cambridge was over. My furniture was sold back to Nightingale for the next generation and a removal firm took all my personal possessions to Sevenoaks. In doing so they damaged the top of my sculpture. I wrote to Eric Gill who told me to bring it to him at High Wycombe and he would reshape it; so began my friendship with that great artist.

5 Weimar Twilight

When I came down from Cambridge father decided that I should go to Germany. Had he not made me learn Greek at Lancing, I could from the first have got around all right; as it was, I did not know a single word. It was typical of him – his kindness, a spurt of energy after which he was so busy that his attention was distracted by something else – that he arranged for Hedwig Evers to find me a room, continued my allowance, and washed his hands of the whole thing. At the time I was irritated, but on reflection I suppose that there is a lot to be said for being thrown in at the deep end.

There were some days at home before I departed, and Margaret was in Paris with her parents before going to Italy. Lying on my back in the rose garden at home sunbathing, I watched an aeroplane go over and thought of her on the other side of the Channel. Asking mother's permission, for it was her territory, I cut a huge bunch of roses, got in the car and rushed over to the airport.

Everything today is such a huge organized shambles; half a century ago there was still time to stand and stare. I arrived at Croydon (then London's airport) at about a quarter to twelve and discovered that there was a noon flight to Paris. Asking if there was any chance of getting the flowers on it, I was answered by a man standing beside the desk who said, 'Yes. I am the pilot and I shall be very happy to deliver them to the lady's hotel for you myself' – and he kindly did.

Then I went over for a quick visit also. Apart from the Louvre, with my first sight of the Mona Lisa and the Winged Victory of Samothrace, my only memory is of the last evening and my departure. We spent the night at Zelli's, which was then fashionable. There was an excellent band and a famous pianist between sets (to whom I shall refer later under 'jazz'). It was also the first establishment to have a telephone on every table, and I got furious because two Americans a few tables away rang Margaret and engaged her in endless conversation; I succeeded in making sure that was as near as they got. Jöe Zelli, who later opened the Royal Box in Montmartre and took it to New York where he died in 1971, made a short speech before each set and always finished, 'And now you will dance to the music of ten thousand musicians.'

I was taking the first plane home. There was no time to change, no time for breakfast, and in those days there was no question of checking in an hour before flight time. I took a taxi to Le Bourget, arriving twenty minutes late, and was properly admonished: 'Oh, do hurry up; we're all waiting for you!' And they were; I walked out to the little de Havilland in top hat, white tie and tails to face the disapproving stares of the other nine impatient passengers.

And then off to Germany.

In Cologne I had a large room in the house of a Frau Schröder at 101 Löthringerstrasse, a quarter of an hour or so by tram from the centre of the city. There were four others besides myself: two Dutch, an American and a German from Berlin. The Schröders had a married son who lived somewhere in town and a teenage daughter named Hella, a remarkably beautiful girl.

I spent the first day or two exploring the city and racking my brains as to how I was going to learn German. Some of my explorations were with Hedwig Evers and we walked a lot around the outside of town. Cologne was one of the first cities to be completely surrounded by a magnificent green belt. This had been constructed by the mayor who had by 1929 retired from office, covered with praise, his work accomplished. He was to become even better known to the whole world very much later as Chancellor of West Germany, Conrad Adenhauer.

Faute de mieux I went first to the Berlitz school. This did me little good: hardly the fault of the system, which has benefited many millions, but of myself. I have never been able to learn anything if I cannot understand the object of the exercise – such as algebra at school; similarly pointing to a door and saying *Tür* or a window *Fenster* did nothing for me. But I soldiered on for lack of an alternative.

My day soon developed a pattern. A daily Berlitz lesson, then to a gymnasium which I had found. Like that at Cambridge, it was for both fencing and boxing. It was run by a large agreeable man who spoke some English. I would have a good work-out with him pretty well every day. The rest of the time he spent sparring with a tall good-looking black man. To me one day he said, 'Why don't you put the gloves on and get in the ring with him?'

I said I was no boxer, but he replied, 'Go on, have a go; he won't hurt you.'

I did as I was told and found myself in the ring with Larry Gains. I warily circled about him for a few rounds and came to no harm, but it was an extraordinarily interesting experience in speed and timing. Gains was a charming Canadian; he had been one of Jack Dempsey's sparring partners before coming to Europe; four years before this he had knocked out Max Schmeling in the second round in Cologne. He was at the moment training for a fight in Vienna, and it is said that only racial prejudice kept him from a crack at the European title; but he was Commonwealth Champion from 1931 to 1934, a title which he lost to the incomparable Len Harvey. He made his home in Cologne and lived on to his eighties, dying there in 1983.

Then I went on for tea at a café on the Rhine called *Zum Bastei*, a roofed-over concrete searchlight tower from the war, and after that to the station where *The Times* arrived at five o'clock. Unlike the Germans in the south who are prepared to live and let live, the Prussians of the Rhineland can be very insular and pleased with themselves. I was to find this again and again, sometimes to my fury. The first instance occurred quite soon after my arrival on one of my trips to the station to pick up the paper. Sometimes I would be wearing informal clothes not altogether unusual for a Britisher of my age who happened to play golf: big grey flannel plus-fours (equivalent in size to 'Oxford bags') with black and white check stockings; and if it was raining I armed myself with a black and white golf umbrella. I must have looked unusual; I may have looked uncouth; but, whereas almost anywhere else I would have been ignored as a (presumably harmless) lunatic, numerous Prussians audibly expressed their disapproval, tut-tutting loudly like a lot of old hens. These unfortunate characteristics are widely recognized, and after both world wars plans were discussed at great length (though never brought to fruition) for separating the Slavic Prussians from the rest of Germany. I was to meet further examples.

By frantic and urgent enquiry I found the name of the crammer who taught most English diplomatic and consular candidates. I quickly enrolled and it is entirely due to him that I attained the level of proficiency in German that I did. He lived in Jünkersdorf, about half an hour by tram from the centre of the city. I went out pretty well every day at the same hour, and there was always the same tram conductor.

Now, since even an idiot knows that in German J is like Y, it is impossible to mispronounce the name of this village so badly as to be incomprehensible. But this little bully saw a sucker and decided to enjoy himself. When I asked for a ticket, he said: '*Jünkersdorf? Wo ist dass? Dass weiss' ich nicht.*' I could only mumble 'Jünkersdorf', turning scarlet, to the vast amusement of all the other passengers. This went on every day for four months and I never said a word. I waited until my German was fluent and then exploded.

To the usual '*Jünkersdorf? Dass weiss' ich nicht,*" I shouted at him, a printable version of my words being 'You bloody little bastard, I've been coming on this rat-ridden tram of yours for months. You know perfectly well where I'm going. Now give me a ticket and shut up.'

The result, of course, was a revoltingly servile '*Ja, mein Herr; jawohl, mein Herr*', and thereafter when I got on he had a ticket all ready before I could even get out the money.

Outside the Wallraf-Richartz the street turned through a right-angle and the tram had to come to an almost complete stop to negotiate it. I used to step on it there, going home. One hot day, when all the windows were lowered, the conductor shouted at me: 'This is not a stop, you can't get on here,' and all the passengers leaned out and shouted 'This is not a stop, you can't get on here'; I shouted back in German, 'Shut up, the lot of you' and all their heads disappeared like puppets on a string. I was, of course, in the wrong: but there is, I regret, sometimes something to be said for shouting at the Prussians – they certainly do it enough to one another.

But, by contrast, there could be so much kindness and desire to help. I remember with affection a man in a camera shop just after I had arrived. In those days one mounted photographs in small albums of stiff grey paper and wrote the captions under them with a white pencil. I went into the shop and asked in English for the latter.

A furrow came upon the young man's brow as he struggled to summon up some English from his schooldays – and anyone who knows a little German will appreciate the verb which was to be his downfall. A beatific smile came over his face when he had worked it out and he said with great solemnity:

'Today I have no white pencil. But on Monday I *become* a white pencil.'

Largely I got on well with my fellow boarders. The oldest, in his thirties, was a New Yorker named Irving Cranford. He had no gift of tongues and nothing anyone could do would stop him pronouncing the first person singular *Ich* as *Ik;*. and since the Cologne accent is very soft, somewhat similar to Andalusian in Spanish, his frequent use of this ugly word sent a shudder through everyone at the table. The next oldest was Barth Landheer, a Dutchman who went on to a distinguished academic career. We remained friends for years to come, and in the hot September weather went walking through the Eifel Mountains, blue and green, the pine needles crackling under our feet, down to Alf an der Mosel, and then back to Cologne by steamer. He was expelled summarily for making some sort of pass at Hella. When I came back that evening I found Frau Schröder's son in the hall; I did not like the look of him a bit, and I would take a bet that he was bound before long to become a stormtrooper. Also he had with him the biggest and nastiest Alsatian I have ever seen, which was about to be unleashed when Frau Schröder shrieked, 'No, not him! He's all right.' Unscathed, I went up to my room without a word.

Next was a Jew named Krauskopf. He was an amusing wastrel whose father had sent him to Cologne to get him away from the decadent bright lights of the capital. He told me that he had been married to a rich wife, but when he had spent all her money and she was penniless, he left her – for of what further use was she to him? He considered it a joke, but the funny side of it escaped me.

The youngest was a very nice Dutchman who had an Amilcar, then a well-known *marque* of French sportscar.

When I had thoroughly 'done' all the many churches in town, I found that my favourite of all was St Alban's, a superb Romanesque building down by the river in one of the seedier parts of the city. It was next door to Cologne's equivalent of Hamburg's Reeperbahn – a straight street of horse-boxes, the upper half of the door open and the whore, bored to tears, leaning over the lower part of each one, a cigarette perpetually in her over-ripe scarlet mouth; there were policemen on duty day and night at each end. All that quarter was razed to the ground during the war; the street was no loss, but of that wonderful church not a stone remains.

But the greatest attraction of Cologne was the music. The most beautiful concert *salle* was the Gurzenich, a fifteenth-century guildhall, now also completely gone. I went to various concerts with Hedwig, of which the one I remember clearly was a recital by Horowitz, then twenty-five, a fiery, elegant, slim giant.

The opera at that time was said to be the best in Germany outside Berlin. Whether this was true or just an expression of local pride I cannot tell; but I do know that it was very, very good. I went three times a week until I left the city, and the repertory was large. The season opened on 1 September with *Schwanda* by Weinberger, the Czech opera which was then just two years old. It continued chronologically with *Fledermaus, Hänsel und Gretel, Freischütz, Cavalleria Rusticana* and *Pagliacci, Meistersinger, Traviata, Carmen, Flying Dutchman, Tales of Hoffmann, Sly, Trovatore, Marriage of Figaro, Rosenkavalier, Tiefland, Louise, Götterdämmer-ung, Madame Butterfly, La Bohème, Tosca, Salome, Tannhäuser,* Gluck's *Don Juan, Aïda, Rheingold, Walküre* and *Siegfried.* Such a catholic selection – and I missed none of it – was ideal for me, experiencing a full diet of opera for the first time; most of my tastes, good and bad, were formed then and have not changed much since. The Puccini productions were not particularly outstanding, but they were sufficiently good for me to discover that here was my operatic hero; I still regard *Tosca* (the only opera of which I claim to know every note of the score) as one of the two works – the second I heard later – which for me conform most nearly to the definition of *opera in musica,* a drama to be sung. Of course devotees of *The Ring* would no doubt place its four parts on a higher plane.

Cologne was wealthy enough to retain in the company a gypsy who sang nothing but *Carmen* and a tenor who appeared only as *Hoffmann;* they were devoted specialists, so that their interpretation of these two roles was more exciting, more rounded and deeper than performances I have heard from many more famous singers. I was particularly fond of *Hoffmann* to which I went every time it was played, and subsequent hearings have not altered my opinion – the lovely melodies combined with overwhelming sadness make it something special. Perhaps they did it so well with pride because Cologne was the city of Offenbach's birth.

My first encounter with *The Marriage of Figaro* brings me to a painful subject: my inability to get along with much of the music of Mozart. With the exception of *Bastien und Bastienne,* a charming cameo, it must be of some significance that the four great works which I find overwhelming are all products of the closing years of his restless and often unhappy life: *Figaro, Don Giovanni,* the *Jupiter* symphony and the deeply moving *Requiem.* My 'repertoire' increases slowly, including such glories as the *Haffner* and the Clarinet Concerto, and then my depression is summoned up once more by a composition which seems to me facile and fiddling. I know that this is abysmal heresy to such experts as Bernard Levin, to whom every note Mozart committed to paper is magical and sacred. I know that it is my loss, my ignorance, my shortcoming, but it is a heresy which no amount of trying on my part can dissolve. The heresy may have begun in my formative years when Mozart was not thought of very highly – Wagner was fashionable – and little played compared with the abundance of today. So when I meet others who share my view – yes, they do exist – I feel a little less as if I suffered from some form of leprosy.

Cologne produced some unusual operas which I have had little chance to hear since. Wolf-Ferrari's *Sly* was only eighteen months old then and I loved it; many years were to pass before I heard the later, better known and more successful *Jewels of the Madonna*, but perhaps because it was new and I was young, I liked this earlier work just as much.

I do not think that I have ever had another chance of hearing d'Albert's *Tiefland*, and Charpentier's *Louise* is not all that frequently performed. But both remain in my mind visually as much as musically because their *décor* was by Hans Strobach, the great designer then at Cologne. Strobach was an imaginative genius. Soon after this time an Oxford undergraduate who had been studying under him tempted him to England to design three productions for the Oxford University Opera Club, and he also did some work for Covent Garden before the political atmosphere brought about his loss to Europe. But he had free rein in Cologne; and, without closing my eyes, I can see now the most moving moment which I have ever experienced in a theatre, his Act III of *Walküre*. It was largely an imaginative use of projection. The night sky was an electric blue cyclorama across which the Valkyries rode higher and higher. Upon a black rock stood Wotan (a glorious voice) wearing a huge dark blue cloak which, with the aid of a wind machine, streamed horizontally from his armoured shoulders. As he invoked the fire it began as a modest circle round the sleeping Brünnhilde. With the music rising more and more in its glory, the fire too spread, creeping up the rocks, filling the stage, then over the proscenium arch and the boxes, so that finally the theatre was a blaze of flame through which could still be seen the giant Wotan, his cloak still streaming in the silent wind. Words cannot describe the beauty, the miracle of that scene; I sat silent, small and trembling. It does not happen very often.

I remember coming out of the opera house one night to a smell of burning, and milling crowds. I asked a German what was going on and he replied, 'We've just been beating up the Nazis; we do it every Saturday night. This evening we thought we would make a job of it and burn down their headquarters.' The headquarters was a small office in one of the streets leading off the Opernplatz. Although I am sure that in Bavaria, where at Munich and Nuremburg they were strongest, the Nazis were much in evidence, I never saw one in uniform in Cologne. How many there were walking around in mufti, of course, I cannot tell. But the fact remains that within only four years of the day when big business engineered the evil corporal into the office of Chancellor, the party was so weak in the Rhineland that the people of Cologne could still treat it as a bad joke.

In the early winter the weather was beautiful – crisp sunshine for days on end – and I decided to see as much of Germany as I could. Setting off on my travels, my first stop was Bremen.

Bremen is – or was – a lovely city. After dinner I went to the *Ratskeller*, beneath the town hall, where for centuries they have laid down a barrel of *Rheinwein* every year. When one is finished, the next is tapped; then they were drinking the 1726 and a small glass cost DM4. I took a sip of what looked and tasted like almost colourless water; I held it on my tongue for a long, long time until it warmed in my mouth and slowly, so slowly my taste buds were rewarded by the glorious fragrance of two centuries before.

Hamburg was memorable for Hagenbeck's Zoo, then I think the only open zoo in the world. Used as I was to wild animals in cages often pathetically small, and famous as the place was, I still found it a shock to come face to face with twenty lions, for the water obstacle round their large home was cunningly hidden. Of course today there are many similar, including our own. Then for a few minutes I watched with horror the deposition of the head of a large tribe of monkeys. The flea-bitten old monarch, too tired and worn to protest, sat motionless on a ledge of the monkey hill while the young braves darted up to him, bit him and ran away again chattering with laughter. I suppose they killed him in the end, but it was an unpleasant sight and I hurried away to the art gallery.

None of the pupils at the crammer's in Jünkersdorf had become a close friend since we only met briefly, day by day, but the man I knew best was Denys Lowson, later the youngest ever Lord Mayor of London. We found that we were going to be in Berlin at the same time, both staying at the Adlon, so we agreed to spend an evening together in this centre of the world's decadence.

Together we went to see possibly the greatest actress in Europe at the time – Elisabeth Bergner – in *Seltsames Zwischenspiel*, the tongue-twisting German title of Eugene O'Neill's *Strange Interlude*. It must have been considerably cut in translation because the performance was not much over the duration of a normal play.

After watching her spellbound, we were hungry. There were then two houses of entertainment which catered for every taste: *Casanova* and *Haus Vaterland*; we decided to go to the former. On entering one was met by a wordly *maître d'hôtel* who decided to what floor one should be taken. He said 'top floor' to the lift man and we were whisked away. Half-way up we heard some rather good jazz and said that we would like to stop there, but the lift man said, 'Certainly not; that is for middle-aged couples'; so we were borne upwards to the top. We emerged into a pretty, gay, more or less circular room. At one side was a long bar at which were sitting a large number of extremely beautiful whores. We immediately realized that the *maître d'hôtel* had thought he discerned a lustful gleam in the eyes of two young men in dinner jackets.

We explained to the head waiter that we had merely come for supper; but he said 'never mind' and put us at a table plumb in the centre of the room. It was too early for real business and we were the only visitors; we ordered dry martinis and buried our noses in the menu.

The 'sport' soon started. The girls first tried seductive coo-ees to attract our attention, without success. These were followed by less seductive whistles. Finally they began to throw paper streamers at us. This they thought was rather fun and it became a free for all. As the multitude of streamers landed over our heads they built up into a tent; we must have looked ridiculous sitting under it solemnly stuffing ourselves. After working through several courses and a couple of bottles of wine, we clawed our way out of the paper tent and left amid the derisive hoots of the ladies.

The next day I spent at Potsdam which was important to me because I went over Sans Souci and saw the room of Voltaire who within a few years was to become my god. And that evening I had the good sense to see Pabst's latest film *Die Büchse von Pandora* – good sense because a generation was to pass before the censors allowed it to be shown in England. Now, of course, it is a legend.

I arrived in Dresden full of hope, first because of the wonderful art gallery and second for the famous opera. I settled into the large handsome hotel on the banks of the Elbe in which Goethe had always stayed – now no more. I stood rapt before the 'sleeping Venus' of Giorgione, the only Venetian painter I like, and admired Rosalba's pastel of Faustina Bordoni, so familiar to me since early years for the very good copy of it which father had commissioned. I had one night in the city and I hoped to hear one masterpiece at the opera. To my horror I found that they were performing for the second or third time (for the first night had been on 2 November) an expressionist work called *Maschinist Hopkins*, words and music by Max Brandt. Disappointed, I nevertheless went and sat through it. By the length of a very long street it is the worst opera I have ever heard. I can remember like a nightmare a chorus of workmen in grey overalls advancing down stage, step by step, rasping chord by rasping chord, fist uplifted in proletarian menace, throughout a repeated chant of 'hard work, hard work'. No work of reference admits its existence, but the critics got quite excited when the BBC performed it on Radio 3 during February 1986, describing it as 'one of the Weimar Republic's most successful operas'. *The Sunday Times* even produced a photograph of Brandt, looking remarkably like Scott Fitzgerald; and in its columns, describing it as 'an excellent example of exuberant, innovative creativity', said rightly that the characters are all anti-heroes, all more or less morally corrupt. This was typical of the Weimar Republic in general and Berlin in particular – the sun was beginning to go down.

At least I was consoled by the Zwinger, Pöppelmann's early eighteenth-century confection, surely the most beautiful sugar icing in the world.

I had to go to Halle because of Handel. And the great church with its two organs, one of which was played upon by Mr H. and the other by Bach. I stayed the night at the Elephant Hotel, and while eating my solitary dinner I did not know whether to be amused or disgusted by the antics at the next table. It was occupied by one of the few generals allowed to the *Wehrmacht* by the treaty of Versailles and his ADC, both in uniform. He said to the young man, 'You choose the wine', and the popinjay with great sniffing and gargling made the wine waiter open *twelve* bottles before he would accept one as drinkable. I would take a large bet that the one he finally passed was no better than the first, or any of those in between; he was just showing off and the waiter had to bear it with an expressionless face of stone.

Leipzig, Eisenach for Bach's restful and impressive home, Nuremburg, Ulm where the cathedral organist was practising the *Chromatic Fantasia and Fugue* when I looked in, Trier, Baden Baden for several days with Walter who was learning German there, the Wartburg where in Luther's study the dent made by his ink-pot which he threw at the devil was by then the size of a football from centuries of people picking out bits of plaster as souvenirs: I zigzagged across the country before and after my Mecca – Weimar. I loved Cologne because I lived there; but next of all the cities, towns, villages and hamlets I have visited at one time or another in Germany that is the one for which I have a particular veneration. For one thing, with Sacher's in Vienna and a tiny place in Paris which no longer exists, I think the Erbprinz is (or was) my favourite hotel in the world. In a lovely late eighteenth-century building, filled with Biedermeier furniture, each bedroom is named after a distinguished visitor. I had the Schiller room; I do not think that there was any evidence that the great dramatist actually slept in it, but one somehow felt his presence. In the drawing-room over the front door, just down the passage, Napoleon received the Queen of Prussia when on her knees she begged forbearance for her country the day after Jena.

I was there for two nights and went twice to the theatre. On the first evening I sat through Goethe's magnificent but almost interminable *Faust, Part I*, and on the second enjoyed Schiller's *Maria Stuart* with its extremely exciting imaginary confrontation between Mary and Elizabeth, and its study of the difference between worldly and psychological justice.

In my short stay two things happened which I cannot forget. First, I went to the Art Gallery. The only person in the place was the director looking out of the window at the early morning mist. I said good day, and we started talking and then, hearing a Rheinland accent, he said, 'Ah, so you're from Cologne'; I said I was from England and he did not believe it. What greater and more flattering proof could I have had that I had not wasted my time all those months than to be taken for a native.

Then I set off across the park to visit Goethe's garden house. On the way I found two men planting young trees in the unseasonably mild November weather. I asked if I might plant one and they replied that I would have to ask the ranger. 'Ah,' one of them added, 'here he comes.'

I introduced myself to him and said that I could think of no greater honour than to plant a tree in Goethe's park.

'By all means do,' he said cheerfully.

I chose a rowan tree and tamped the earth round its tender roots with loving care. Then over the sapling we shook hands; I said, 'May there never again be war between our two countries,' and we bowed to one another. I wonder if it still stands there, a big strong beautiful tree, or whether bombs blew it into scattered twigs.

On my way back to Cologne I spent a night at Kassel, and here I was as lucky with the opera as I had been unfortunate in Dresden. It was a beautiful city, on which the Elector of Hesse-Kassel had lavished so much care and love. The opera house was enchanting; the attendants still wore scarlet tailcoats edged with gold braid, and powdered wigs. The opera that night was *Dreigroschenoper*, the masterpiece of Kurt Weill and Bert Brecht which had had its first production in Berlin the previous year.

At the first interval I walked out past one of the attendants standing stiffly to attention and looking just like the frog in *Alice*. He bent slightly forward and in deep conspiratorial tone said, *'Ganz Quatsch, nicht wahr?'* ('Absolute rubbish, isn't it?') I did not agree with him but I could not be bothered to argue. I thought it was superb; even then, thirty years before Louis Armstrong got around to it, I came away humming 'Mack the Knife'.

And so back to Cologne to await the arrival of my parents (how father persuaded mother to cross the Channel in midwinter I shall never know). They came, and father gave a dinner party for the Schröder family, Hedwig Evers and a few of my friends. Then goodbye to the city for which I felt such affection. Christmas at the Bristol in Vienna. Walter was there for a day or two to see the annual ice-hockey match between Cambridge University and Vienna in which Cambridge, captained by his younger brother Peter, beat the powerful city team for the first time ever. Then back to England. Learning was over; it was time to work.

6   Life with Father

We got back from Vienna after Christmas and I went into Cassell's on 1 January 1930. I had only one more year living at Sevenoaks.

Father marked my appearance by giving a dinner for the whole staff, which was rather overwhelming. His particular friends Warwick and Phyllis Deeping were there, and Olive Wadsley – a popular novelist now long forgotten.

I was given a nice office next to father, with a bow window overlooking La Belle Sauvage yard – premises in which the company had been since almost its beginning, retaining the crooked shape of the coaching inn which it had been for centuries.

We went up to town together and walked to the Belle Sauvage, which was on Ludgate Hill, from Cannon Street. There were three trains in the morning – at 8.50, 9.01 and 9.10 – and the passengers on them were known as the Strivers, the Thrivers and the Thriven; we were part of the middle group. I was generally late, having to run most of the way, and, as father left the house in reasonable time, his last words while I was still eating my egg were always 'You'll never make it.'

The first months I spent training; first in production where I learned how to compute the length of a book, lay it out and estimate its cost; then to the Company Secretary to see how the wheels went round.

My editorial experience was supposed to be learned at the feet of father, whose assistant I was intended to be, but in this last and very important part of the work I really learned most from the editors, of whom there were three senior ones. The oldest was Arthur Fish, a slight case of Parkinson's disease, deaf and about to retire. He had been Oscar Wilde's assistant when Wilde was editing *The Woman's World* at Cassell's. Although old he was still very competent; a gentle soul who must have been very handsome when he was young. Willy Steer was a precise little man almost all of whose time was spent on the publications of the Automobile Association which we produced at that time. Arthur Hayward, who had been a young gunner officer in the war, was a man of wide erudition who became chief editor later, and was a pillar of the establishment on whom I leaned heavily until his eventual retirement in the fifties. The dictionaries, which were to become of particular interest to me, were in the hands of a brilliant cripple named Heron Lepper; there being no lift at La Belle Sauvage, it was painful to see him manoeuvring his misshapen body up and down the twisting stairs.

Invited to take over the books in 1912, father had built up a formidable list which on the fiction side included Arnold Bennett, Robert Hitchens, H.G. Wells, Compton MacKenzie, H.M. Tomlinson, Sheila Kaye-Smith, Warwick Deeping (the biggest seller in the country after the tremendous success of *Sorrel and Son*), Ernest Raymond and Alec Waugh.

Warwick Deeping had been with Cassell's for years, writing historical novels of which the sale of about 9,000 yielded enough for a quiet life until, originally trained as a doctor, he was called up in 1914 and spent the next five years operating in a cellar in the Ypres salient, up to his ankles in blood. He kept his sanity – just – but the subject of the war was taboo, until one surprising day years later. Hedwig Evers' brother, who spoke English, was over from Cologne and came to 'Idehurst' one Sunday for lunch when the Deepings were also with us from Weybridge for the day. Warwick and Evers discovered that they had faced one another on either side of the much disputed Butte of Warlincourt; they went off to another room and spent the rest of the afternoon swapping reminiscences. This was the key which opened Warwick's mind, so that he finally was able to write a novel about an army surgeon. When he did, I had a design done for the jacket of a surgeon as one normally thinks of one; sterilized overalls, rubber gloves and a mask. When I showed it to Warwick, he laughed. 'No mask, no gloves,' he said, 'just an apron and one's shirt-sleeves rolled up'; back to the drawing-board. He was a gentle, quiet, scrupulously honest man, yet possessing a violent temper if roused. There was always a fight whenever he delivered a new novel. Father was very straight-laced; even what is today the most common of words – 'bloody' – offended him, and he used to say that Warwick put it in just to be difficult. However, they always reached a friendly agreement.

Ernest Raymond hit the jackpot with his first novel, *Tell England*, in 1922. A padre in the army, he was so sickened by Gallipoli and later campaigns that he lost his vocation. He worked some of the bile out of his system in this book, and I remember father, after dinner, muttering over the typescript which he had brought home, 'My god, I've got something here.' He had indeed, a best-seller, a consistently successful author far into the future, and a very good friend. It sold and sold, for it was perfectly attuned to the mental atmosphere of the time. Still punch-drunk from the horrors of the war, readers fell eagerly upon anything romantic, religious, class-conscious, with an idealized homosexual ethos, an ethos still Edwardian. There were immediately many serious memoirs by leaders on all sides which were largely ignored; father himself published Jellicoe's *The Grand Fleet* (1919), the rival Scheer's German *High Seas Fleet* and Hindenburg's memoirs (1920), but was disappointed by all of them. The floodgates were not opened until the runaway success of *All Quiet on the Western Front* in 1928 followed in the next year by Robert Graves' *Goodbye to All That* and R.C. Sherriff's tragic *Journey's End* which broke box-office records all over the world. 'The country was psychologically better prepared for the Second

World War,' Graves himself wrote, and, far from mentally exhausted, was within three years more ready avidly to welcome Liddell Hart's conversations with the German generals (*The Other Side of the Hill*) and novels such as Alexander Barron's *From the City, From the Plough* and Nigel Balchin's *The Small Back Room*.

Sheila Kaye-Smith was also a friend as well as a client. She naturally lived in Sussex, about which she wrote so many of her books. It cannot have been long into 1930 that father gave a lunch party for her in the private room on the left as one went into the old Berkeley Hotel, at which I was present – nearly to my undoing. With coffee, cigars came round, and I chose a full corona – of what brand I cannot remember. When one smokes one's first cigar, one is supposed to turn green and leave the room in a hurry; I was determined that this should not happen to me. As I puffed my way through this large unfamiliar object I felt worse and worse, but I stuck it out and remained seated, though I think I rather dropped out of the conversation.

I am reminded at this time of another female author from whom father had parted: Radclyffe Hall, Cassell's had had considerable success with *The Unlit Lamp*, of which father thought very highly, but when she delivered *The Well of Loneliness* he refused to publish it. First, he did not approve of its lesbianism, and secondly he said that it was certain to be prosecuted – although today the book's morals seem very ordinary, at that time he was right.

Published eventually by Jonathan Cape, the book was taken to court by the Public Prosecutor as an indecent libel, and he won. Olive Wadsley, who I still think (without proof) was more to father than just an author and friend, and who could be hilariously funny, described a lunch with Radclyffe and her lover Una Troubridge. 'It was time to leave,' she told me, 'and I had just got to the door when Radclyffe Hall barked "You've heard about the case of course?" Like a damn fool I said no, and was forced to go back and listen to the whole thing; it took the rest of the day.'

Authors wandered in without appointments, and if father was not there it was my duty to receive them. Michael Arlen, whose stories father used to publish in his magazines, passing from the south of France to New York; Hilaire Belloc, like a becaped and fat sergeant-major, not particularly pleased to see Flower junior; Admiral Jellicoe, who had had a room and a safe for secret papers when he was writing the three books we published, on his way to a wedding in St Paul's. H.M. Tomlinson, very deaf, rather sad, and much neglected today. The most interesting in one particular way was Seton Gordon, who occasionally descended on London from his home in Skye. I knew that he was one of the finest judges of the pipes at Highland gatherings, and yet was reputed to be stone deaf. I just did not believe this and decided to put it to the test. One day when he was standing in my office looking out of the window I addressed him in a loud voice from behind so that he could not read my lips. There was no response. It was true; he could not hear a thing except the pipes which registered perfectly on his otherwise unresponsive eardrums.

One quite unexpected but delightful visitor who said that he had just looked in for old times' sake was a nattily dressed, very old Frenchman, very precise and rather diffident. We talked for a long time, and I do not think that he ever came to the Yard again. It was Paul Martin who had designed the Cassell colophon in 1883, when we had a branch in New York, and is now so highly regarded as a *genre* photographer of the London at the end of the last century.

I did not appreciate at the time how close the relations had been between father and the Asquiths – the ex-Prime Minister, first Earl of Oxford and Asquith, and his famous wife Margot – throughout the twenties. The extent of them is plain from her letters, sold after father's death without my knowledge, but now, I am happy to say, in the Bodleian. I was startled when father burst into my office saying, 'Margot's here, we must go down.' We descended, and there in the Yard was a big high Daimler such as the Royal Family used at the time, and perched in the back a bird-like, determined figure with distinguished, if raddled, features. She could not be expected to climb up to the first floor, and we stood bare-headed chatting affably. Suitably impressed, I bowed as though to Royalty as she drove out.

American authors passing through London would often pay us a visit. One whom we acquired with Alfred Knopf's London list in 1931, a deal to which I will return later, is now completely forgotten but was once a figure of considerable prominence: Joseph Hergesheimer. *Java Head* was, I think, his best known novel, and he also wrote travel books. Anita Loos, who in addition to writing about her dizzy blonde was a woman of great perspicacity, liked him and considered him a man of real talent, but she wrote that he was 'a born figure of fun, a self-made patsy who practically begged for the humiliations that dogged his footsteps. He was crowding sixty, fat, semi-bald and married, but nothing interfered with his ambitions as a Casanova'. One of his which we did was *Berlin*, an interesting forerunner of Isherwood, and his concern over detail was instanced by a little he told me of his research for this. He said that when studying a city the best source of information is the prostitutes, who know everything that is going on. Accordingly, arriving in Berlin, he picked up an intelligent-looking woman and took her to dinner at the Jockey, then one of the most fashionable restaurants in town. Over drinks, talking around things to get to know her, he asked who were her most lucrative customers.

'Oh,' she said, without hesitation, 'the Japanese.'

They looked at the menu, ordered, and started with caviar. Russian caviar came in flat round kilo tins, and for all I know still does, but this is one of my greeds in which I can no longer afford to indulge. The waiter came with a full one, spooned out two generous portions and left the tin on the table. Hergesheimer called him back.

'I ordered two portions of caviar, not a whole bloody sturgeon. Take it away.'

The girl shook her head sadly, and said, 'No Japanese gentleman would have done that.'

Cassell's this year published a translation of Maeterlinck's *Life of the Ant*, which so attracted father's interest that he acquired a formicarium, kept normally in a cupboard, which was of perpetual interest. The nest comprised two sheets of glass about a foot square and an eighth of an inch apart, the space between filled with sand, and the whole framed; in one corner from time to time some honey was put in, and in another a few drops of water. The ants were never still; they burrowed shafts through the sand like some highly complicated trench system, then changed their minds and did it all again. Getting the nest out of the dark cupboard, we could watch them at work, and from time to time see the queen lay her eggs which a praetorian guard watched over until they hatched.

Although when I was younger I remember going to London theatres with both my parents, by now we very seldom went *en famille* and I had the best of two worlds – being taken out by both. Partly this was a difference of interest: father, for instance, liked going to boxing matches which mother detested. At Olympia in June that year he and I saw the world middleweight title fight between the holder, Micky Walker, and Tommy Milligan. The American won in the tenth and I distinctly remember the Scot's face being badly cut. A great champion, Micky Walker, when he retired, became a very successful painter – surely a fact worthy of *The Guinness Book of Records*. Father also took me to the Ring, Blackfriars, opposite Waterloo Station, which was completely destroyed in the Second World War and never rebuilt. Here the good, the bad and the indifferent would fight for £5.00 a time, and many a champion's career began in that rather seedy establishment. Later in the thirties Robert Atkins, who started the open-air theatre in Regent's Park, realized that the Ring was the nearest resemblance in London to Shakespeare's Globe, and put on a fine production of *The Merry Wives of Windsor* in which the famous Vanburgh sisters appeared.

The idol of the period was Josephine Baker, whom Hemingway described as 'the most sensational woman anybody ever saw'. And it was said that 'Her body stunned all who saw it.' I saw her three times, in London, Paris and Stockholm, and I certainly was so stunned at the Palladium and the Casino de Paris that I can remember nothing about her performance, nor with whom I went. It is only clear to me that on all three occasions she wore no more than the famous string of bananas, was totally fascinating, was quite different each time, and that the most lascivious performance – if that is the right word – was in Stockholm where I was on holiday with father. She came down into the stalls and sat on the laps of wealthy tycoons, twisting their grey hairs into spikes like unicorns as she whispered in their ears; they loved it.

Both my parents took me to a number of concerts. I do not think that mother shared my father's passion for Handel, since I cannot remember her coming to any of the many performances of *Messiah* to which I was taken from early childhood. But she did take me to my first symphony (which was the 'New World') and to a recital by Rachmaninov both at the Queen's Hall, then London's chief concert hall, destroyed in the blitz, in

Langham Place, where the St George's Hotel now stands. I can see now that enormously tall figure hunched over the piano, which he dwarfed, with a gloomy expression which was never enlivened by any sign of emotion except when he was forced to play his famous *Prelude*, of which he was so sick and tired that a look of extreme distaste came over his lined visage. But, great as his reputation has always been, I did not enjoy his playing as much as that of my all-time favourites: Paderewski, Cortot, Arrau, Malcuzynski and Richter.

One weekend that year each of them took me to a concert on following days. Saturday night father and I went to the Queen's Hall to a concert conducted by Sir Thomas Beecham; one of the items was *The Emperor* with Cortot as the soloist. Half-way through Cortot forgot where he was and stopped; Beecham, conducting as always without a score, was shaken out of his beaten track and flummoxed; the whole performance came to a halt. Silence reigned – it seemed a long time, but it can only have been seconds until Cortot shouted '*Violons! violons!*' and started off again four bars further on. At the conclusion conductor and pianist shook hands with some relief.

On the following afternoon mother and I went to the Cambridge Theatre to hear a recital by Cortot, and when he was playing one of Debussy's *Voiles*, studies in endless ascending scales each differing by no more than a note from the one before, he suddenly stopped, looked at the audience and said, 'I think I had better go and fetch the music.' He went into the wings, and came back trailing the sheets behind him like a sheepish schoolboy. His bad memory was notorious, but surely to lose it twice in one weekend must have been unusual.

Although mother and I spent so much time at the cinema, which A.J.P. Taylor described as 'the essential social habit of the age', we did not miss Paul Robeson's Othello in 1930. He was, I have always understood, the first coloured man to play the part; and it has now been made known how much hostile racist mail was received by Peggy Ashcroft, his Desdemona. He was frighteningly superb; he threw himself into the part and the frustration and jealousy got him to such an extent that saliva was running down his chin when, in Act IV Scene i, he stormed off the stage with the desperate cry of 'Goats and monkeys!'

The Film Society was started in 1925 for performance of unlicensed films to members only on Sunday afternoons at the New Gallery Cinema in Regent Street. We must have joined early because I remember that we saw Pudovkin's *Mother*, which was made in 1926; other great films of the twenties we saw were Eisenstein's *October* and Pabst's *The Love of Jeanne Ney*, and all the German masterpieces including *The Cabinet of Doctor Caligari*, *Waxworks*, *Dr Mabuse* and *Metropolis*. There was one contribution from France: Carl Dreyer's *La Passion de Jeanne d'Arc*. The one great film directed by Pabst which did finally meet with the censor's approval (because it showed the German army being beaten) was his *Westfront 1918*.

The other memorable occasion was the showing of Pudovkin's latest film, *Storm over Asia*, at the New Gallery, for which the great director had come to London. Afterwards we all crossed the road to a café and he gave us a lecture on how he saw the future use of sound, which had recently arrived. I cannot, of course, remember much of what he said, but the one ingenious point which I do recall I think never came into use. He was most emphatic that the director of a sound film had complete liberty and was not confined to using the human voice; for instance, the sound issuing from the mouth of a man in a rage could be the roaring of a lion.

I began to think seriously about printing types. The Golden Cockerel and Nonesuch Books which I was buying were so beautiful that I wanted to know more about the printing of them; thence there burgeoned an interest in typography, which led me to want my own press, and finally I asked father if there was any possibility. With his usual generosity he bought an Albion which was assembled in the attic at 'Idehurst'. With it came a fount of type; it was not very good type – a sort of bastard Jenson – but first I could not look a gift horse in the mouth, and secondly I had to find out just how much printing I was going to do before I started getting fussy over typefaces.

But working in the office all day, often reading manuscripts in the evening, on Saturdays shooting in the winter and playing cricket in the summer, I realized that I would never have the time – nor, I admit, the application – to produce anything worth while, nor might I have room for the press in any future home. So I wrote to Eric Gill and asked if he could use an Albion, and, since he and René Hague were just beginning to print their handsome books, he said yes. I dismantled the press and sent it to Piggotts, where I was to see it on later visits and where it was put to much better use than in my amateur hands.

The most memorable event in 1930 was the Passion Play at Oberammergau. Walter was still living in Germany and it was his idea that we should go together. I joined him in Baden Baden and we set off in his car through the Black Forest, to Freiburg and along Lake Constance into Bavaria.

When we arrived in Oberammergau we found that we had been given rooms in the house of the High Priest; he was extremely jovial and very pleased to have on his hands two young foreigners who spoke German. In the hot twilight after supper he took us for a stroll·through the little town, regaling us with all the gossip about the people whom we passed; once he pointed – 'See that chap over there. He's Judas Iscariot, and what he's up to with the Virgin Mary is just nobody's business!'

Millions of people have seen the play and millions more know all about what it is like. Of course it is deeply impressive; but we both agreed that, while the drama is spell-binding, we could have done without the interminable choruses. But then it would not be the same thing; I suppose one should think of each monologue as a lengthy sermon. The chorus that year was for the first time the famous Anton Lang, it having been reluctantly decided that at last he was too old to play the part of a man who died on the cross at thirty-two; he had a glorious voice and his lengthy rhetoric rolled round the vast theatre. The new Christ was his nephew, whose vitality and almost brutal force, when, for instance, driving the money-changers out of the Temple, made his end seem even more tragic. And I can hear now the stirring command of his irresistible apostrophe: '*Wahrlich, wahrlich, sag' ich euch ...*'

Back home, literary agency was beginning to explode and proliferate as a profession. I suppose that everyone interested knows that as a way of making a living literary agency started quite by chance – although it would have begun somewhere anyway. The story is that, with his rise to fame, Rudyard Kipling wrote to his friend A.P. Watt in England saying that the offering of his stories and the resulting correspondence had become an intolerable burden for him in India, so that he would be grateful if Watt could deal with it all for him and, in return, keep 10 per cent of the proceeds.

We have seen exactly the same thing happen in recent times when Arnold Palmer, then the most successful and popular golfer in the world, complained that constant badgering to endorse this or support that left him no time for practice, and in a pro-am tournament asked Mark McCormack, an Ohio lawyer and a very good golfer, if he would take the whole thing over on a percentage basis. From that has grown Mark's colossal International Management Group, and, with his imitators and rivals, another profession has been created.

A.P. Watt enjoyed his profitable association with Kipling and turned it into a business. Then came J.B. Pinker, who had two sons: one, Ralph, ran the London office while his elder brother, Eric, was stationed in New York; both came to unhappy ends, but that lay in the future. The third literary agent was an American who started in his own country and then came to England: Curtis Brown. I remember him when he was getting on in years, a burly man who looked remarkably like Colonel Saunders of Kentucky Fried Chicken fame. His firm grew and prospered, a breeding ground for a number of influential figures in publishing affairs. Next followed John Farquharson, which today is amalgamated with Curtis Brown. Comparative newcomers were A.D. Peters, a singularly upright man (with his charming partner Nick Roughead who, of all unlikely things, had captained Scotland at rugby); Hughes Massie; and D.C. Benson.

I might here refer to some important developments which were to take place in the next few years. In 1933 there was an exodus from Curtis Brown. Laurence Pollinger and Nancy Pearn left, and founded the agency of Pearn Pollinger; they were joined later by David Higham, who, after resigning his regular commission in the army, had joined Curtis Brown in 1925. Michael Joseph departed and founded his own publishing firm. Albert Curtis Brown in due course was no longer there and left the business to his son, Spencer, of whom more anon.

The Watts were always austere, although over the years considerably more warmth crept into their blood. They remained completely upright and commanded great respect; they were, in cricketing terms, Gentlemen as opposed to Players – before that distinction ceased to exist.

I used to have, and still have, a passion for Fragonard's *Le Chiffre*, that tiny painting in the Wallace Collection which I covet madly. One Saturday morning in the early thirties my passion was uncontrollable, and at breakfast I said that I must go to feast my eyes upon it. Unshaven, in pyjamas, I put on wellingtons, an old macintosh, and drove to the Wallace. Standing rapt in front of my target, I glanced to my left and saw Alec Watt, immaculate as ever in a pin-stripe suit, bowler hat and rolled umbrella. Since we knew one another very well, I was about to hail him when I realized that I was somewhat improperly dressed. I refrained. He brushed past me without a glance, for he obviously could not number among his acquaintances such an obvious bum.

Nancy Pearn, who dealt with the periodical side of the P.P. & H. business, died in 1950, and this left Pollinger and Higham head to head. They were temperamentally very different, and it was unlikely to last; they parted and set up under their own names – but that was far into the future.

It is hardly surprising that I knew both of them well. Socially I saw much more of David Higham for musical reasons. Laurence Pollinger's private life was more private, and his greatest pleasure was to disappear to his home in Devon. Using that old cliché, David Higham was an extrovert, L.P. was an introvert. But I am not sure that so easy a definition fits either of them properly. David was friendly, occasionally looked faintly naïve but wasn't, and could be irritatingly pompous – which is why we, because of the large moustache which he had retained from his army days, nicknamed him 'flue-brush'.

Pollinger was a portly man, like Higham seldom seen without his pipe, who spoke slowly in a slightly high-pitched voice. He was a remarkable business man; he could drive a hard bargain but also be extremely understanding. I think mostly of his kindness, and also that nothing happened in the world of writing and publishing without his hearing about it first. As I have said earlier, I am wary of absolutes – the greatest soldier, the greatest picture, etc. – so that I do not think that one can speak of a greatest literary agent; a number of them had virtues and special abilities in certain cases. But I will risk an absolute and say that the greatest personality in the profession in my time has been Laurence Pollinger.

When I started work I suppose that at least half the books we published were contracted direct with the author; by the time I retired agents of all sorts and sizes had proliferated and it was unusual to find a writer who was not represented by one of them.

In the early thirties so many unsolicited manuscripts were submitted to the house that we had a man named Packe (who had been in the juvenile department, by then unhappily defunct) whose sole task was to look at what had come in and divide it into two piles. One pile was completely hopeless; the other made up of manuscripts with varying degrees of possibility which were not to be sent back until some muggins in authority had said so. I became the muggins. Every Friday Packe and I went through the piles. I listened to his experienced views and sampled those with any hope, the best of which would be sent to outside readers (unless something unusual caught my eye and I decided to read it myself). We averaged about eighty manuscripts a week.

As the literary agents increased in number and strengthened their hold on the market, this heavy inflow of junk dwindled, because more would-be authors sent their work to agents who made no bones about telling them if they were beyond hope. Of course the position never arose in which everything offered by a literary agent was accepted because there is always the exercise of personal taste – which is one of the joys of publishing. By the end of the second war, so well organized and sagacious had the profession become, that I believe it was virtually unknown for us to receive from an agent a manuscript which did not merit serious attention.

From the first father generously encouraged me, as the next generation, to bring in new authors. To begin with I never accepted anything on my own, but recommended it to him; a few fine fish slipped through the net, but generally speaking this worked well. As I grew in confidence and experience, he acquiesced in my building my own list which was parallel and supplementary to his own galaxy of successful authors.

It is not surprising that our tastes differed in emphasis, if not in general. It seems to me that, as a writer of fiction (particularly short stories) himself, his greatest strength – and I might add his soundest judgement – was in the novel; next, he had a deep interest in memoirs concerning warfare, an interest – macabre as some may find it – which I share; and travel and exploration because he loved travel himself. For me, I think that history and biography came first, with fiction second despite which I managed to acquire for the list some good writers, and my interest deepened with the passage of time. There are few things which I did as well as my father, but one is perhaps that I took a more personal interest in the progress of our language dictionaries; reference books of all kinds deeply interested me. One thing for which father had had no time and less inclination was typography, a subject which assumed a re-born importance in my generation and in which I had something to contribute.

There was one thing upon which I always insisted when the time came for me to be entrusted with the buying of books: I would offer precisely the same terms to an author whether he sent in his manuscript himself or through a literary agent. This was not directed in any way against the agents, who as I 'grew up' in the course of time nearly all became friends. I never wanted it to be said that any author would be at a disadvantage by dealing direct because he either did not want to employ an agent or did not know one he felt he could trust – I am not being funny; there were a few in the latter class. Byron coined the phrase 'Barabbas was a publisher' – why I cannot think, since he was treated lavishly by Murray – but I never wanted it to be said of me. Every book has its fair price in every age, and we paid a lot of money sometimes, but I can clearly remember that our standard offer for a first novel was £50 advance on account of a royalty of 10 per cent, rising to 12½ per cent and eventually 15 per cent. Today this sum may seem derisory, but in terms of present money it must be multiplied by fifteen; furthermore there were very few subsidiary rights, and paperbacks did not exist.

At that time there was a Holy Trinity made up of three publishers who were personal friends: Walter Hutchinson, father and Charlie Evans, head of Heinemann. At one point in the twenties Charlie was fed up, father was browned off, and they were thinking of both resigning and going in together; what a firm that would have been! Anyway, they didn't, and when Dwye, Charlie's son, and I became good friends years later, the opportunity had passed.

The 'Trinity' never poached one another's authors. There was and always will be a good deal of changing horses, sometimes for financial reasons, sometimes a matter of temperament (I was to experience examples of both). If, for instance, father was offered a Heinemann author – either direct or by an agent – he would ring up Charlie. If the answer was 'Yes, we've had a disagreement', then O.K.; if the reply was 'I don't know anything about it', then no dice. This remained sacrosanct so long as all three were at the head of their affairs. The only Heinemann author that I can think of who came to us was Margaret Kennedy, and father never told me the reason for her changing stables.

There was one other chore that I was, from the first, required to do, which in the end had important consequences. One of the rules of the house was that the page proofs of every book had to be signed by a director before they could be sent to press. Although I was not yet on the Board, I was, as it were, of the hierarchy, so my initials were acceptable. There was no such animal at that time as a publisher's designer. Manuscripts were just sent off to the printer, who laid them out himself to the best of his ability. The great work of Stanley Morison had not yet breathed its remarkable inspiration into British commercial printing, and there were only three people who could always be relied upon to produce a handsome book: Oliver Simon at Curwen, Walter Lewis at Cambridge and William Maxwell at R. & R. Clark in Edinburgh. Only just below them was John Johnson at Oxford. I put him slightly lower because his abiding interest was typographical history and, while he could produce good books, I do not think that his overall achievement was as great. The rest of the trade was so far behind, it was out of sight.

In consequence the proofs presented to me were so abysmal that I soon refused to sign them. As the books had to be got to press somehow, I started by re-designing the title pages so that the opening looked – to my eye at least – presentable. But this was a waste of time and money, and the logical solution was to lay out the book before sending it to the printer in the first place. Thus the craft of publisher's designer took one more step forward. I started this practice at about the same time as Wren Howard at Faber & Faber, but there was a great deal of difference between us. I soon had so much to do that I could only design those books which I thought mattered – or, if you like, which mattered to me – so I was not much more than an amateur. But Wren Howard was a complete professional and a perfectionist, and laid down a house style which was clear, handsome and simple, a jewel in the crown of British typography which has shone ever since.

I also took on responsibility for jackets and cloth for bindings.

There is no mechanical device which can work quite so fast as that natural phenomenon, the grape-vine, so that within days of its becoming known that someone at Cassell's was interested in typography I received my first visitor from the trade: Oliver Simon. Although there are, I believe, some who find his work too dry, for me Oliver is one of the greatest typographical designers of this century. One critic, Marcus Brumwell, has written: 'Oliver's sensitivity about printing, typography and applied art was outstanding, but if I were to single out one facet of his wisdom, I would choose common sense, in which he was unshakable and sound. This solidity, strangely enough, went with an emotional sensitivity which was almost feminine.' (Herbert Simon, *Song and Words*, 1978). And I myself years later wrote: 'Oliver was never satisfied: certainly not in the early thirties. Every book was a new experiment. Although one could pick up a book and say "That must be Curwen", there was always enough vitality and originality for one to say to oneself "Well, it could be someone else, but I wonder who else could possibly do it". The answer was that it was always a Curwen Press book.'

Oliver, his brother Bobby, Francis Meynell and I had one common interest outside business – cricket; there were some tales to tell which I have put in an appendix on the great game.

Historic links existed between Curwen and Cassell. Three quarters of a century before, John Cassell had invited the Reverend John Curwen, promoter of the tonic so-fah system and pastor of a chapel in Plaistow where the Curwen Press had always been, to contribute music lessons to *Cassell's Popular Educator*, which were highly successful. In 1929 they had produced for us *The Legion Book*. Reprinted many times, it was an anthology of leading writers, sold, as its title implies, in aid of the British Legion.

More *recherché* was the first of two books done at the suggestion of Arnold Bennett: a story of his, *Elsie and the Child*, illustrated by McKnight Kauffer. The illustrations were stencilled, a process long used in France, but in this country unique to Curwen where it was destined to last for only six years after its introduction by Harold Curwen in 1925. Since it is no longer in use, I should perhaps give a short description of the process. Originally a black image was printed on the page by lithography. The colours were applied, in accordance with the artist's design, by hand through plastic stencils by skilled women operatives. It was an expensive business, but at its best could produce results virtually unequalled by any mechanical process.

Elsie was 'stencilled with opaque gouache. The result has a depth of colour and a brilliance which could hardly have been achieved by any other printing method'. Bennett lived then in Chelsea where he knew Kauffer and persuaded father, if any persuasion were needed, to do this lovely book. In it Ted Kauffer 'disposed – for the first time in book illustration – of the key altogether; in other words, the girl who had to do the stencilling started with a blank sheet of paper and had to key all her stencils to one corner. In addition he made great use of broken stippled tones such as are found in Toulouse Lautrec's posters.' (H. Simon, op. cit.) For this Lautrec used a toothbrush; I never asked Ted if he used the same instrument.

Ted Kauffer lived with Marian Dorn, a designer of carpets, and they were such good people. Ted – who designed for Frank Pick at London Transport the finest posters seen in this country at that time, perhaps ever – had a tremendous reputation, and was unofficial Art Director of Lund Humphries who specialized in colour printing. In 1939, turning down a chance to become a war artist, he returned to the United States and was never the same again 'because of lack of understanding on the part of the American people' as Bobby Simon put it.

The firm published one other handsome volume in 1929: *Art Nonsense*, a collection of essays by Eric Gill which was printed by Walter Lewis at Cambridge. It was the first book to be set in Gill's Perpetua, which was so new that the italic was not ready and every word that the author wanted to emphasize had to be underlined. Eric cut on wood two special Belle Sauvages for the title page; black on white for the 'trade' edition and the reverse for the *edition de luxe*. Beatrice Warde, the brilliant and beautiful American typographical authority, whom I later came to know well, sat – or in this case stood – as the model. The book had been brought to Cassell's by Donald Attwater, author of our *Catholic Encyclopaedic Dictionary*, who was acting as secretary to Gill and through whom my sculpture had been commissioned.

Shortly afterwards Attwater produced a version of William Langland's *Vision of William concerning Piers the Plowman*. As this happens to be the only fourteenth-century poem which I admire, I leapt at it and a very handsome limited edition was produced illustrated with woodcuts by Denis Tegetmeier, who was also in the Gill entourage which had just moved from Wales to Piggotts, near High Wycombe. It was, of course, printed by Oliver Simon.

Oliver was one of the extraordinary group which in little over a quarter of a century poured out of Bradford – such men as Delius, Sir William Rothenstein and his brother Albert Rutherston, J.B. Priestley, Humbert Wolfe, and his own brother Herbert (Bobby) who went first to the Kynoch Press in Birmingham and swiftly turned them into one more fine commercial printing house. With the exception of Priestley, they were all descendants of the Jewish immigration, mostly from Germany, to the textile industry in the last century. Oliver was Rothenstein's nephew.

On his first visit my life took another step along the road; we became friends immediately, our lives were intertwined in work and play, and he was responsible for my meeting the man who had an even greater influence on the way I was to go. Towards the end of our first conversation I said that I knew *The Bibliophile's Almanac*, a pretty little annual which he had produced in the previous year, and asked him what he proposed to do with it. It must obviously have lost money, for he said that his colleagues were against continuance, and, if I liked, I was welcome to the idea. He added that if I did decide to take it over, I should solicit an article from A.J.A. Symons, of whom at that time I had never heard.

By an extraordinary chance Arthur Symons, a gaunt relic of the nineties, came to see me a few days later in the hope of selling me a volume of essays which he had scraped up from the bottom of the barrel. I should have felt sorry for this sad old man, whose first book, *An Introduction to the Study of Browning*, was published by Cassell in 1886. But I didn't; I felt emanating from him an aura of evil which shook me and which I could not explain. I thought that he was the most odious old man I had ever met, and I was overwhelmed by a dislike of which I have never been able to rid myself. However, here was the only Symons that I had ever heard of, and, thinking mistakenly of Oliver's advice, I asked him if he would care to write an article for me. The thought of doing any work was too much for him, and he shuffled hastily out of the room muttering that he would think about it.

Something was obviously wrong, so I rang Oliver who quickly put me on the right track. I made an appointment with A.J.A. Symons and called at the First Edition Club, which was then in its heyday, occupying one of the handsome houses on the north side of Bedford Square. I found myself in the presence of the most remarkable man in the world of letters in this country of the period between the wars. Now he is a legend. To me he became a very close friend whom I dearly loved and whose early death I mourn to this day.

Having described his literary works, his brother Julian has said of him: 'He was also a dandy, a wit, a gourmet, an elegant calligrapher and a skilful amateur forger. He collected many things from books and musical boxes to Victorian card cases, glass obelisks and transformation scenes: and he managed to do all these things without, in any serious sense, having any money.'

Physically he was very tall and dark, handsome rather than good looking. A brilliant conversationalist – and conversation was very important to him – he was the only person I have ever known who in the middle of an esoteric discussion could suddenly change sides and argue just as convincingly the other way, to the delight of all present, not least himself. He was extremely generous – not with money of which he had little, but with his time and friendship. He was probably one of the few from whom the world would have benefited if he had enjoyed a really solid income; so much of his time was taken up wheeling and dealing (such as ferreting out cheap good wines and selling them to his friends at a profit) to keep going, which was greatly detrimental to the quantity of his writing. He might, for example, have had time to complete his life of Wilde, which we can see from the extant fragments would have been a masterpiece. On the other hand it is possible that, had he been a man of means, he would have written no more than he did because his ingenious mind enjoyed the wheeling and dealing; it was part of his convoluted nature that he enjoyed complication for complication's sake.

He could be quite remarkably tortuous, and I remember that he – fastidious in his conversation and a master of English prose – on one occasion uttered one of the finest mixed metaphors it has ever been my pleasure to hear. He made a publishing proposition to me of which I thought little at the time and told him so. But after reflection I rang him up a few days later saying that I had changed my mind. I sensed at once that he was a little embarrassed; after a pause he said slowly, 'When you turned down my proposal I had to try elsewhere; as a result I started several hares – and one of them has come home to roost.'

He had a heart of gold, but he could be an unscrupulous enemy. I once asked a bookseller in the Midlands to send me a book on approval. He replied that he would be glad to do so if I could give him an assurance that I was not in business with A.J.A. Symons. After the matter was settled satisfactorily, I asked A.J. what he had done to this wretched dealer to engender such bitterness. A far-away look came into his eye and after a moment he said, 'Ah, yes, I remember him. A foolish fellow.'

When I went to see him on the first occasion to ask him for an article for my little Annual, I was ushered into his lovely green and silver room at the top of the First Edition Club. It was in this same room in this same year that he was to say to me, 'Today is my thirtieth birthday. I depart from the age of promise and enter the age of achievement.'

On the first occasion he stood warming himself in front of the fire, with a glass of very dry sherry in his hand, listening sympathetically to what I had to say. Then, holding a glass of very dry cold sherry in my hand, I listened with equal sympathy to the ideas which he expounded mellifluously and with such persuasive grace. I left eventually with another friend for life, and a periodical on my hands – subject to the agreement of the Board. They agreed. And so *The Book Collector's Quarterly* was born. He gave me a copy of his *Emin* inscribed 'to mark the beginning of a collaboration' – and what a collaboration it was; long, rewarding, with total mutual confidence.

The agreement stipulated that we supplied the *B.C.Q.* free to members of the First Edition Club and had the rest of the world to ourselves. It was a perfectly fair and reasonable arrangement, but in the end it led to the Quarterly's demise – but not the demise of the close relations between A.J. and myself. Owing to the Depression it turned out that there were not enough collectors around who were not members of the club to make the periodical viable.

I was *ipso facto* an honorary member of the club and spent a great deal of time there meeting some of A.J.'s friends. One of the first was Thomas Harrison, the book binder, for whom I developed a great reverence and deep affection. Technically he must rank as the greatest binder in the country at that time, a superb craftsman from Kirkby Lonsdale, who was to live to a great age and leave behind him a reputation which almost canonized him. He was the last surviving apprentice of the great Bedford, and had been binder to the Empress Eugénie when she lived at

Chislehurst. Books for repair used to be brought in by her nephew, the Prince Napoleon, who always said, 'Please do them quickly; the Empress does not like holes in the *bibliothèque*.'

When I met him, he was running the firm of Henry T. Wood, in Rathbone Place off Oxford Street. Kenneth Hobson, who decorated books as well as binding them, was with him. This firm too was a casualty of the Depression and was eventually sold to Sangorski and Sutcliffe. Indeed, the whole craft eventually got into such a bad way that those who cared about it (of whom I, under Tommy Harrison's aegis, was one) feared that there might be a total collapse. But that didn't quite happen, and now I don't think it ever will. But Tommy's great knowledge died with him. Many years later I asked another binder, de Coverly, if Tommy had any apprentices to whom he could pass on his skill; the answer was 'No. None would work under him. Because he was such a perfectionist they could not stand the strain.'

A.J. used to have twenty-five copies of a book he liked bound by Tommy for Members of the Club, and I also got into the habit of designing bindings, which Tommy carried out as gifts for friends on special occasions.

Another friend in the printing world was Tony Barrett. The managing director of the Edinburgh Press had decided that he needed a personal representative to call upon publishers, and sent to London his son, J.A. Hamilton Barrett. There are some people one meets, perhaps initially through business, who one feels instinctively are going to become something in one's life quite out of context; that instinctive feeling is like driving the first spike of a new railway which will in time stretch far away into the distance. Tony Barrett was one of those. The fact that we did a good deal of business with the Edinburgh Press was sufficient reason for Tony to ask me to lunch in the rooms at Gray's Inn which he shared with Dwye Evans of Heinemann, whom at that time I did not know. It was at that lunch that the first spike was driven in. I knew that I would like him as a friend, and he must have felt the same of me because it takes two to make a bargain. He was frank and open, with an almost child-like straightforwardness – if he occasionally tried to be devious, you could see it a mile off. He had an enormous sense of humour, and delighted in asking impertinent questions so that he could enjoy the often embarrassed replies. But he was charming in a Scottish way, extremely kind and a man of honour.

We saw one another regularly, played some squash, at which he was much better than I, but he was a bachelor and moved in his own circles. He was in the H.A.C. and of course disappeared on the outbreak of war. Gone out of my life, the railway progressed unseen from the day of the first spike, until a decade later it was to be opened in running order.

In the spring father decided to go to the United States. He said to me, 'You don't know much about the business, but you'd better come along; you can carry my bags.' I said that suited me anyway as I had some unfinished business to attend to.

We sailed on the *Majestic*. Before we began work in New York we went up to Toronto – by train, of course. We were represented in Canada by McClelland & Stewart, an agency which carried the lists of a number of American publishers. John McClelland was a tall, kindly Scot; but I must confess that, young as I was, I found myself less than impressed by his business acumen or that of his partner, George Stewart. I felt that in those days the Canadians – with certain marked exceptions – were rather sleepy people. Toronto was a dull city; nothing ever happened there except that a troop or squadron of their mounted guards, in the same gleaming uniform as our Household Cavalry, would clatter through the streets from time to time. There were no bars; but there was good golf. Father, for some prophetic reason, was deeply interested in diabetes – indeed, every aspect of medicine and surgery fascinated him – so our one extra-curricular activity was to take tea with Dr Banting, one of the two discoverers of insulin (the other was dead). I can see him now with his long jowl and bald head, but I cannot remember the conversation in which, I am sure, I took no part.

Back in New York we started the customary round of calls on publishers looking for books. By far the most important part of the expedition from my point of view was my unfinished business in Philadelphia. After some telephoning, we were invited for the weekend by Margaret's parents. After calling on Lippincotts, the biggest publishers in Philadelphia, on Friday, we went out to their house. Mr and Mrs Coss had one guest-room, so father stayed there, and I was put in the dormy house of the Merion Cricket and Golf Club, which started as a cricket club and had its famous golf course added.

On Saturday Margaret and Mary took me to the theatre in Philadelphia to see Chekhov's *Three Sisters* played by the three Gish sisters. Everyone remembers Dorothy and Lilian, but it is now forgotten that there was a third, and they were all superb.

After lunch on Sunday Margaret and I went for a walk through the woods. There, sitting on a fallen tree trunk in what seemed to me like Arcady. I once more asked her to marry me, and she accepted. We arrived back for tea feeling and probably looking rather pleased with ourselves. I was in such a state of euphoria that I cannot remember formally asking John D., as he was always called, for Margaret's hand, but I presume I did.

My unfinished business was most happily concluded, and we went back to New York. A few days later Margaret came up to the Big Apple and we all had dinner at one of the few good restaurants in the city; the fourth member of the party was Margaret's friend, Edna Klein, a tall, stunningly beautiful blonde Jewess (blonde Jewesses are a rarity; the few I have come across have all been beautiful. I have never seen a plain one. Why should this be so?). Father called for a bottle of champagne, which was produced without demur – the manager only asking if we would please put it under the table when not actually pouring; I don't think that we were subjected to the indignity of drinking out of tea cups.

One of the reasons why there were so few good restaurants in New York at that time was Prohibition. There were thousands of speak-easies; it was a cut-throat business, and the only advantage that one could claim over its neighbours was in the quality of the food it served. As a result practically all the good chefs in town were earning a fortune cooking in one joint or another. We were introduced to the one we used by Charles Scribner. There was the traditional mumbo-jumbo – the knock three times and when the little grille in the door opens, say 'Joe sent me' sort of thing – but once inside it was extremely comfortable and the food was excellent.

Apart from Alfred Knopf whom I had already met at home, I remember few of the publishers upon whom we called except George Doran, then head of Doubleday, Doran & Co.; Charles Scribner who introduced us to our speak-easy; the Viking Press, started in 1925 by Ben Huebsch and Harold Guinzburg after Ben had been on his own for a number of years – it has been written that 'what Harold and Ben accomplished together was even greater than the sum of the parts'; and Bennett Cerf, forming with Donald Klopfer another redoubtable pair at the newly founded Random House.

When told that we had been invited to a party at Bennett's apartment, I said that we must go because he was married to that lovely film star Sylvia Sidney; but when we got there, I discovered to my chagrin that she had walked out on him just the week before.

There were many parties, and one is very clear in my mind. It was at the apartment of Katharine Brush, an enormously successful author now, unhappily, forgotten. We had published her *Young Man from Manhattan* and *Red Headed Woman* (which she was herself); the latter had made her a fortune, and the MGM film, which had a script by Anita Loos, catapulted Jean Harlow to stardom and was the first appearance in Hollywood of Charles Boyer. She was also at that time married to a banker, and they were installed in a luxurious duplex apartment. He had had built for her a circular study which went up through both floors, so that she could have complete silence and seclusion for her work. It destroyed her, for she never again wrote anything as good as her previous books; she said that when she shut the door on herself in her large circular cell, in silent solitude, she froze and could not write a word.

She was a beautiful woman, a magnetic extrovert with an endless stream of glittering conversation. When in later years I came to know her better, I found her one of the most exhilarating people I have known and also one of the kindest. On this occasion I silenced her without meaning to.

It was a pretty high-powered party and I felt very shy. I had not made much of a go of it with the people to whom I had been introduced, and I was sitting silent at one end of a big sofa. Kay came across and, gazing down at me, said, 'You don't really like American girls, do you?'

Looking up, I replied, 'I don't know. I'm just going to marry one. I'll find out.'

Alec Waugh, who was standing beside her, afterwards said that it was the only time he had ever known Kay left speechless.

For many years father had written short stories for *The Saturday Evening Post*; they valued him highly, and paid him extremely well. One sunny day the editor, Cuddahy, drove us for lunch to a charming inn at Montauk Point, the northern tip of Long Island, the proprietor of which had a reputation for making the finest Old Fashioneds in New York State. We were early and no one else was there; drinks were ordered. Then a policeman in uniform came in and sat at the other end. Eventually the proprietor appeared with our drinks, saying, 'I'm so sorry to keep you waiting. That's the local cop and he's very crotchety if he doesn't get his dry Martini at once.' A good advertisement for Prohibition, which still had three years to run!

We made social calls on three Cassell authors, one of whom was Russian and another Polish, both living in New York. One was the Grand Duchess Marie whose *Things I Remember* we were about to publish. She was *chef de vendeuses* in a *maison de haute couture*, very much the Grand Duchess. I neither liked nor disliked her; I merely found her *hauteur* slightly offensive.

The other, Princess Catharine Radziwill, was quite different. She was Polish and minute, a busy creature like something out of Beatrix Potter. We published three books by her: *Nicholas II, the last of the Tsars, The Taint of the Romanovs* and *The Empress Frederick*. She once had the temerity to sue the Tsar over some land, and, since she obviously lost the case, had to leave Russia. She had been the mistress of Cecil Rhodes, and could not come to England because his family was longing to serve a writ on her for some alleged misappropriation of property. Not very long after, she rang up father in London and we took her to lunch at the Savoy. To father's remark that he thought it unsafe for her to be in England, she airily replied that she would be out of the country long before the law could catch up with her.

In both apartments every available space was crammed with photographs in silver frames of everyone who had been anyone before 1917. Both had made new lives, but the past was still there like an overcoat which hangs behind the door, seldom used but never forgotten.

A much larger apartment was that of the third author on whom we called, the famous and very successful crime writer Mary Roberts Rinehart. She lived in great state on Park Avenue. She was charming in a slightly daunting way – or perhaps I was only daunted because I was already cowed by the ineffable superiority of the butler in morning coat and white gloves who opened the door to us. But charm she had, and she passed it on to her son, Stanley, the publisher with whom in the future I became very friendly.

I played hookey one morning to go to the Morgan Library, where I was ushered into the presence of the great Belle Green, whose fame had spread throughout the world of books. She was a stately lady, with greying hair and a daunting presence. When, in answer to her question, I said that I would like to look at the English literary manuscripts, she bade me follow her. Through the main library, she unlocked the door of a small room and said, 'There you are, young man. Come to my office when you have finished.' Dazzled and a little bewildered, I was left alone to browse through the shelves of this treasure house.

Years later in the library I asked my good friend, Fred Adams, if I might see a certain manuscript.

He said, 'Just a minute, I will send for it.'

I remarked that there had been no such formality in Belle Green's day.

'Ah,' he said, 'in her time it was the private library of a gentleman; now I am responsible to a board of trustees.'

The film of *All Quiet on the Western Front* had just come on and we saw it at Roxy's. They gave one a lot for one's money in those days, and in addition we heard Paul Whiteman's band (see Appendix 3). But the film, one of the classics of the new sound era which I have seen several times since, had a profound affect on me. The French attack, in which the infantry is caught on the wire which their barrage has failed to destroy, was etched for ever on my memory. I made a vow then and there that if I ever had to be a soldier I wanted to be a machine-gunner and to fight in France; it was not a vow which at that time I ever thought I would have to honour.

I cannot recall how many books father bought, but I know that he acquired Louis Bromfield, who began on the Cassell list with *Twenty-four Hours* and never left it. In fact, as well as being a most successful author, he became very much a personal friend. It was most marked that nearly all father's authors were also friends. I can think of four – Margaret Kennedy, Neville Shute, Belloc and Storm Jameson – with whom his relations were never more than 'correct', to use a useful gallicism. But otherwise, provided it was geographically possible, he liked to be on the closest terms with them all. If one loves the job – and it is almost impossible to carry out successfully a job which one does not love – this is one of the joys of publishing. I certainly tried to feel and behave towards my own authors in the same way, I hope reasonably well, although I did successfully publish the books of one author whom I personally disliked. And with the increasing prominence of the literary agent, there were some authors whom one never met at all unless one went out of the way to do so.

As a reward for helping to read through the pile of manuscripts which accumulated in our hotel room, and also, no doubt, as a sort of test, father said that I could choose one book myself and he would buy it without comment. Because of my concern with the problem of the coloured people in the United States, in addition to its merits as a novel, I selected *Death in the Deep South* by Warde Green, the story of a lynching. It came out in the autumn; three months was enough time in which to produce a book then, two months if one were in a hurry. I was naturally on tenterhooks – my first personal choice, my ewe lamb – and correspondingly down-hearted when it showed little signs of life. Then the miracle happened; Arnold Bennett noticed it. There has never since Bennett's death been a book critic with the extraordinary drawing-power which he possessed through his weekly article in *The Evening*

Standard. He was supremely honest; if he had known of my personal
interest or been in any way concerned by the fact that the publisher was
his own, he would have just ignored it. Imagine my feelings, therefore,
when I opened *The Standard* one Thursday and read Bennett's article
beginning, 'Wondering what to write about today, I looked along my
shelves and came upon an excellent first novel entitled *Death in the Deep
South ...*' The book was sold out completely within a week.

The one sad thing about that trip had nothing to do with publishing.
Father and I were walking to our first appointment one morning when I
noticed that he was weaving along the pavement. I was worried, because
there was no question of any drinking, and he was worried too. On our
return to London he went at once to his doctor, to be told that he was
seriously diabetic. He had to inject himself with insulin twice a day for the
rest of his long life. I often wondered, but never asked him, if he had any
premonition of this when he had insisted on meeting Dr Banting in
Toronto.

We came home on the *Olympic*, a nice ship. It had been a memorable
trip, happy and successful. My wedding was fixed for the following
March.

The end of the *edition de luxe* was near in 1931 so far as Cassell's was
concerned. We did the second of the Arnold Bennett stories which
McKnight Kauffer illustrated, *Venus Rising from the Sea*. It was the last
book Ted illustrated, apart from a brief St Martin's summer more than ten
years later. He took immense pains over the book and actually produced
three sets of illustrations, the first of which went no further than the
drawings, the second got right up to passed stencil proofs, and the third
was used. Oliver also laid out the text three times before he and Ted were
satisfied that words and illustrations married happily. But it is significant
that 750 copies of *Elsie* were printed, but the edition of the second one was
reduced to 350: 'Sad evidence of the economic difficulties which were
paralysing so many good things in our daily life ... This time the artist
chose transparent water colour and the illustrations are beautiful in their
delicacy and almost ethereal.'*

It was early in 1932 that Oliver staggered me with his quite unexpected
suggestion. When Bobby Simon was writing his *Songs and Words, A
History of the Curwen Press* he asked me for my thoughts about Oliver and
from the considerable contribution which he quotes I may perhaps
extract the surprise: 'He asked me to go and see him at his office, which
was then in Great Russell Street. When I arrived he proposed to me that
we should produce one of the most lovely illustrated books in the
history of British typography; it was to be *Urne Buriall*.' I sat on the edge
of my chair. To be invited, at the age of twenty-four, to take a hand in
the production of a book which, it was intended, should stand for all
time, was quite something. I rushed back to the office, saw father and
his senior colleague (Aubrey Gentry) and, somewhat to my surprise,
both gave me the go-ahead. Paul Nash was to be the illustrator, I asked

* H. Simon, op. cit.

John Carter to edit the text, while Oliver and I were to see that the book was born. It appeared in 1932, and I think it is accepted as one of the great illustrated books; its fame is due enormously to Oliver who, with his tact, expertise and firmness, produced results which satisfied even the hypercritical Nash.

There are no absolutes. Jenson's *Hypnerotomachia* was by many ages considered the most beautiful book ever printed; though some may still think it is so, it is a dangerous claim to make. Tastes change. I count Audubon's *Birds*, Redouté's *Roses*, Moreau's *Monumens du Costume* and Lautrec's *Bestiaire* as books of illustrations, not illustrated books. But there are, after all, Delacroix's *Faust*, the Kelmscott *Chaucer*, Gill's *Four Gospels*, and Rex Whistler's enchanting *Gulliver* which Dennis Cohen produced so lovingly at his Cresset Press. And there are some individual achievements of the highest merit, such as the frontispiece of the Nonesuch *Don Quixote* which Francis Meynell described as 'the finest of any book I know' – a portrait of the author by Ted Kauffer which moves me almost to tears when I see it and often haunts me when I am away from it. It is enough that *Urne Buriall* is a wonderful, beautiful book, and I am very proud to have been part of its creation.

The whole production went extremely smoothly. Knowing that Sir Thomas Browne was one of John Carter's specialities, I asked him to edit the text, which he did admirably. There were thirty drawings, and Paul Nash wrote to Curwen, 'I would like to tell you how very good the stencil work is.'

But it was the last book ever produced by the stencil department of the Curwen. The Depression had bitten hard and the 270 copies sold very slowly. Some time later Aubrey Gentry raised with me the possibility of remaindering the balance, but I flew at him. 'Pulp them if you wish, but remainder – never.' They all sold in the end, though it took a long time. And today, with Oliver, Bobby Simon and Harold Curwen all long dead, even the Press itself has closed.

Paul Nash and I got on extremely well, though I was never as close to him as I was to Ted Kauffer. In a way there was a similarity between them. Shortly after his death in 1954 I wrote of Ted: 'He was an aloof person not because he meant to be, but because so much of his time was spent in his private world. He took everything seriously, most of all himself.' In a lecture in 1938 I said: 'With the world as it is, and social values as they are, there is an almost inevitable tendency for thoughtful and creative people to seek sanctuary in a private world ... The artist, therefore, is inclined to look for symbols and meanings that will express for him a reality different from the one in which he is compelled to live. By those who are unable to follow him, his mode of expression is termed abstract and his conduct is commonly described as escapist.' My description could apply equally to Paul, and these words could equally have been said by him.

Ted was almost certainly the greatest artist to have applied himself to the poster in this country and who, at the same time, illustrated eight books, each a different problem solved in a different manner, and each containing work – such as the portrait of Cervantes and the frontispiece of *Benito Cereno* – of wonderful quality. Paul was a painter, a designer of designs, who distilled the essence of his talent into one book, so that in the short stencil age it stands on the highest peak in a noble and inspiring mountain range.

One of the casualties of our withdrawal from the field of illustrated books was an edition of one of the novels of Aphra Behn which I had planned. Since Charles Hasse and I had been devoted to Restoration literature at Cambridge, I asked him to edit it, which he did very well, having time while he was working at his entry into the film profession – which eventually and successfully became his life's work. We also prepared together a treatment for a film about the affair between Byron and Mary Chaworth-Musters, probably the only woman the poet deeply and sincerely loved, and by whom he is believed to have had a child. We called it *Morning Star*, the name which he had given to her. This was another victim of the slump; the British film industry was in the doldrums until the dramatic appearance of Alexander Korda, and Laurence Pollinger could not find anyone who would look at it – but there was an interesting sequel.

When I came to London I kept on fencing and got to know an excellent epéeist named Terence Beddard. Once he asked me to join a team which he took annually to fight against his old school, Eton. In between bouts, I wandered from the *salle* into the gymnasium next door where the school boxing competitions were taking place. As I did so the P.T. sergeant was announcing the next bout: '... and on my left,' he said, 'in the blue corner, Master Chaworth-Musters.' I looked up sharply, and there to the life, pink-cheeked with curly hair, was the perfect image of Lord Byron.

7   Sailing in a Chill Wind

At the end of the year the first number of *The Book Collector's Quarterly* appeared. Everything had gone smoothly from the start and Oliver, of course, printed it at Curwen. A.J. and I would toss around ideas for the next number over lunch, his acquaintanceships seemed endless, and even though I was a new boy, I was already beginning to make useful friends. A.J. wrote all the editorial notes.

The survey of new and forthcoming well printed books was compiled by Molly Fordham, who also canvassed for advertisements. She was the enchanting wife of the eminent child psychiatrist, Michael Fordham, who used to play cricket with the Simons and me. Years after the *B.C.Q.* was over, her life came to a sad end; in 1940 she evacuated her little son to Jamaica, and as she was returning to Michael her ship was torpedoed.

The hundred best produced books, which used to be selected and displayed annually at the First Edition Club, were reviewed by Hamish Miles. He was a slight, rather vague Scot, but a very good translator from French whom I would put in the top *échelon* with Bonamy Dobrée, Vyvyan Holland, Gerard Hopkins and Scott Moncrieff (who got most of the limelight because of his Herculean labours with Proust).

Early in the discussions I suggested that there should be a limited edition in hard covers, but A.J. was not interested and said that if I wanted it, I should do it myself; so thinking up special additions for these numbers became my province.

For the first number I asked Eric Gill to print four pages of his new type, in which all the books produced by him and his son-in-law, René Hague, were in future to be printed; it was named *Joanna* after the daughter whom René had married.

In the second number there was an article on fashion plates by Vyvyan Holland, Oscar Wilde's son whom I got to know very well. At that time we were close to the Sun Engraving Company; the senior director, Hunter, was a great friend of father's and I believe helped him in some way over the acquisition of Cassell's – though I never discovered how. The other, David Greenhill, was a particular expert on colour printing, and designed the whirlygigs on the back of our pound notes, which were supposed to be unforgeable (at least any attempt to do so was quickly apparent to an expert), for which he was paid a small royalty on every note issued. I knew them both; Hunter I found a bit daunting, but Greenhill was a quiet spoken, firm but almost shy man. I went to see him and said that I was tired of being told that the only good colour printing in the world was produced by the Germans or the Swiss, and added that I thought we in Britain could do just as well if we tried. He agreed with me, so I asked him if he would like to reproduce a fashion plate of 1850 to show what he could do, and he said that he would. While the plate was going through, the Sun representative ('Happy' Pearson, an old Cassellite) came into our production department; he asked the manager, Horace Tickell, if he had gone out of his mind – 'because,' he said, 'this plate we're doing for you is nine printings. What's going on?'

The answer was, 'Well, chum, you're paying for it, not us.'

'Happy' as he went out uttered one word: 'Christ!'

But the result was quite lovely, could not have been bettered anywhere in the world, and vindicated my point that we could do it if we tried. This is still true. Britain is old, tired and run down, as Greece, Rome and Spain once became, and the outward sign is all too often we are content with second best. But when we try – if we try – there is almost no field in which we cannot equal, or surpass, the best that the world can offer.

There were only eight numbers of the *de luxe B.C.Q.*, and the two most beautiful inserts both came from the Gregynog Press. The first was a wood-engraving by Blair Hughes-Stanton for their *Comus*, a lovely delicate design. The other was a broad and powerful coloured woodcut by William MacCanse, *The Dreamer of Dreams*, for a volume of poems then in preparation, *The Singing Caravan* by Sir Robert Vansittart, who within the decade was to become the light of hope for all of us whose hearts were broken by Munich.

At the end of the second year the Depression was beginning to bite. At first it had had little effect on publishing, and I was lucky that the red light did not shine until *Urne Buriall* was well on its way. But I was told that the limited edition would have to go, and I was not altogether sorry because finding special features for inclusion in each number was becoming increasingly difficult.

1931 began with my being appointed to the board of directors, which, with only one year's experience behind me, I think was too soon – although Ian Parsons, who had been at Cambridge with me, was made a partner in Chatto & Windus at the same time. On the other hand, our board was so small that an addition was needed for practical reasons. There were only three directors: besides father, there was the chairman, Thomas Young, a canny Scot who was in the Berry-owned Amalgamated Press and only appeared at the Yard to preside over formal board meetings. The third was the business manager, Aubrey Gentry, who had not long been in Cassell's but to whom father had offered the position when the Holding Company was formed.

Aubrey Gentry was very important to the company and in my life. Of his great ability in management there can be no question, but he was at the same time schizophrenic. One side of him was kind, friendly, helpful and charming. On the other hand he had an ungovernable temper which he did not lose very often, but he went quite berserk when he did (he told me that his father had had it, and it was inherited by his son, Bryen, who was to join us later). He could be obtuse, and his reaction to any proposal was either 'No' or he would think about it; he also had in him a streak of fear: he liked everything to proceed normally and something extra large or unusual was unwelcome. Yet this element of fear must not be over-stressed, because he reacted with surprising grace to some odd things which I came up with over the years. But the difficult side of his nature is evidenced by the fact that he was disliked by the whole staff, with the exception of his faithful secretary.

It was quite soon after my appointment that, lunching with A.J. at the Café Royal, discussing the next number of the *B.C.Q.*, I suddenly saw that it was three o'clock. 'My God!' I said, 'There's a board meeting *now*,' and fled. Of course there was nothing like the traffic then that there is now, but even so it was obvious that I was going to be very late indeed; I sat in a taxi, sweating and wondering what on earth I could say, other than that I had just forgotten. At Temple Bar there was an unexpected jam and my taxi ran into the one in front with a sickening bump. Both drivers got out, examined their vehicles and decided that no serious damage had been done. As he climbed back in, my driver apologized; sitting back, smiling like a Cheshire cat, I said, 'That's all right, my good man, take your time.'

At La Belle Sauvage Yard I ran up the stairs and burst in, panting: 'Sorry – I'm – late – been in – a – taxi – accident.' Instant solicitude; did I want a doctor? Would I like a drink? Waving a martyred hand, I declined both. Of course it was outrageous, but it taught me a lesson; I was never late for a board meeting again.

I think that it was a lesson which aroused in me something of father's insistence on punctuality. After that I do not think I was ever wittingly late for anything – it might happen through circumstances beyond my control – until recently when the total unpredictability of traffic and the passing of years have made me sometimes less prompt. But I still loathe being late for anything; it is so ill-mannered. With father punctuality was a fetish – in fact he overdid it, as I had found in our travels together. If he were having a guest for lunch – usually at the Garrick or the Devonshire – and whoever it was had not arrived by ten minutes past one, he departed, leaving with the hall porter a note which said simply, 'I thought that we had a lunch engagement at one o'clock. Please get in touch with me some time at your convenience.'

The next thing was my marriage in March at St Nicholas, Sevenoaks. The verger filling out the register in the vestry, in answer to his question, entered John D.'s occupation as 'retired gentleman'; it sounds like a short joke in *The Reader's Digest*, but that is what he wrote. After lunch at 'Idehurst' we went up to the Savoy for a reception, at which Margot Oxford proposed our health and I must have replied, but of what I said I have no memory. What I do remember turned out to be tragic. I was going round offering wedding cake and came to Arnold Bennett.

He said, 'No, I won't, if you don't mind, Desmond; I don't feel very

well.' These were his last words to me, as he left early. He took to his bed
that night with typhoid, and we got a cable on our honeymoon to say
that he had died on the 17th. Dear Arnold; he was the last person for
whom straw was laid in the street. He lived, and died, in Chilton Court,
the block of flats over Baker Street station, and Baker Street itself was
covered to deaden the sound of traffic; it has never been done again
since. Although they had known one another for years, H.G. Wells, who
lived in the same building, did not even put his head round the door to
see him; and afterwards, let off one of his friendly aphorisms: 'Poor
Arnold. He knew all about women, but made a mess of his marriage. He
knew all about money, but could never keep any. He knew all about
Paris, but died from drinking the water.'

Before our marriage we had had time to take a lease on a house, have
it redecorated and move in the furniture. It was a charming corner
house: 2 Gordon Place, off Church Street in North Kensington.

We went to Taormina, and on the way south we broke the journey in
Rome where we had a wonderful cicerone in a friend, Maurice Rena.
Maurice was the son of father's friend who ran a restaurant in London;
he thought that he would like to be a publisher and had come to train in
Cassell's. At the moment he was taking time off to do his stint as a Page
of the Cloak and Sword in the Vatican. Although Maurice decided
eventually that publishing was not for him and switched to law,
becoming a successful barrister, he and his French wife became friends
of whom we used to see a great deal. My favourite story concerns his
attending a shoot in Belgium, a country where, like certain others in
Europe, anything that moves is fair game.

His full name was Ercole Maurizio Conti Rena, and he was an Italian
count, a title he never used in this country. He was also a very good
shot, and about the only able one on this very fancy occasion. At the end
of the day the bag, for most of which Maurice had been responsible, was
laid out by the head keeper for the host to present his share to each of
the guns. It was all, of course, done strictly by protocol: first the dukes,
in order of seniority, followed by the marquises and viscounts. Finally
the host turned to Maurice. 'And here, my dear Count, is your share,' he
said, proffering with suitable ceremony a starling.

And so home. My salary was £850 a year, supplemented by dividends
from the shares in Cassell's which father had generously given me, if
and when they were paid. On this we could afford to live in Gordon
Place with two servants.

Life quickly settled into something like a pattern. Across the road in
Gordon Place there was the sight of James Joyce at work at a desk in the
window, and our first caller was a little old lady, Violet Hunt, who
wanted to know who had the house now because she used to visit it
often as a child when it was occupied by Dante Gabriel Rossetti. Within
days we were invited to the Sunday afternoon 'at home' of Sir William
Rothenstein. He and his wife were the monarchs of Campden Hill and
most people coming into the district were summoned. We were
honoured to receive the summons.

Sir William was a very small man, whom his elder son closely resembles, though he is not so dark. John was there and we began a friendship which was to last for many years. The younger son, Michael, the painter, took more after his mother. She had been one of Will's models and was a tall, statuesque figure with a mass of tawny hair, and must have been remarkably attractive in her earlier years; she was also forthright in a bubbling and sometimes surprising way.

At this first meeting she sweetly performed her part as a hostess, asking me who I was and what I did and chatting about people we knew. It appeared that we shared a dislike of H.G. Wells. I must admit that my views were founded largely on descriptions from my parents of which I did not like the sound, and my own meetings with Wells had done nothing to improve matters. Lady Rothenstein's views were more explicit. She went off at once in a rapid staccato:

'Dreadful little man. Couldn't stand him. First time he came here he tore open his shirt and said, "See my lovely white chest. Wouldn't you like to go to bed with me?" "Ach", I said, 'no good to me. I like 'em with hair on it." '

As soon as we were settled in London, I joined the R.A.C., to go on with my fencing. It had a fine old *maître d'armes* with a big moustache, and I begged him to teach me sabre which became my favourite weapon. There were several squash courts at the club but all of them were slightly sub-standard in size so that they could not be used for any championships. I had not been there long before the committee decided to build a standard match court, and in consequence the fencing *salle* and the miniature rifle range had to go. By great good fortune the Lansdowne Club was being built at the time, incorporating the eighteenth-century ballroom and some other parts of the old Lansdowne House and, through the good offices of, I understand, the great sportsman Lord Aberdare, room was found for a fencing *salle* and we all moved over in a body. Soon we got a quite young *maître d'armes* from France who stayed with us until 1939, when he was recalled for military duty and was taken prisoner in the Maginot Line. His assistant was a Territorial named Richards who came back after the war and took charge; but all that was far in the future. It was a fairly small but happy *salle*; our most eminent member was Ian Campbell-Gray who reached the final pool of the *epée* in the Berlin Olympics.

The most important event to take place at the Lansdowne, a few years later, was a match between London and Paris, for which a *piste* was laid down the centre of the beautiful ballroom, and there was a large audience. The restaurant was cleared and after the match supper was served for a hundred. For some reason I got saddled with arranging this, and it is not a night which I shall easily forget. As I started to put out the place cards the lights on the upper floors fused, and there was I rambling round with a candle in one hand and the table plan in the other, sweating that I would never get the job done before the fencing finished downstairs; I succeeded with minutes to spare.

One member of the Paris team was a charming young man, junior *epée* champion of France, who was killed a week later when his opponent's blade broke and the splintered end went through his heart. When in 1984 a similar accident caused the death of an R.A.F. man there was a hullabaloo and a court of enquiry into whether the bib of masks should be bigger or tougher (in this case the blade penetrated the throat). Blades break frequently in fencing, but it is unusual for an *epée* to splinter. If it does, and it is not noticed instantly, nothing will keep it out – for it is like a needle. However small, there is always some element of risk in fencing, and I still have two scars from *epées* which went through my protective clothing half a century ago.

I imagine everyone knows that life was much more formal in the thirties. I used to dress for dinner every night. This was not to uphold the dignity of the Raj, but for comfort; I felt dirty coming home from Ludgate Hill, and as I was going to change my clothes anyway it seemed natural to put on a dinner jacket. Of course, as another version of the same habit many men wore smoking jackets: usually Burgundy velvet with silk facings, though they could be seen in splendid brocade. They were very handsome and their going out of fashion is a sad loss. The same may be said of fancy waistcoats which came in for a time, but have now disappeared (partly due, no doubt, to the appalling cost of clothes) – though I still have one friend in the literary field who has a superb collection of these beautiful garments; I do not recall ever seeing him in the same one twice. It is his personal foible and an agreeable hobby.

Usually the hostesses who invited us to dinner stipulated black tie, and sometimes we did so ourselves. For the theatre or opera one dressed, and any occasion out of the ordinary demanded tails. The worst solecism was to wear a made-up tie or a wrist watch. One tied a bow tie so often that one became very good at it, although there were some who never mastered the art and had to have it tied for them by their wives. A few years ago when Edward Fox played the Duke of Windsor on television his bow tie, white or black, looked so immaculate that a letter appeared in *The Standard* from an outraged reader pointing out that under no circumstances would the Duke have worn a made-up tie. To this there was an equally outraged reply from a gentleman who said of course not; he was Mr Fox's dresser and he had himself tied his master's tie for every scene.

Even on our small means we gave a dinner party every week, and once a week we went to the opera, a theatre or a cinema. Margaret also played a good deal of bridge. She enjoyed it, and the fact that she is so very good was the reason why I never learnt to play. She and her father had been champions of the east coast of the United States, and it was quite obvious that if I, with no gift and little taste for cards, were to start to learn I would at first be an irritation to her and at best would never reach anywhere near her high standard. We agreed that she should play as much as she wished and I never; I had plenty to do collecting books and writing.

It was the cocktail age; Marcel Boulestin, who founded the legendary restaurant, wrote: 'Cocktails are the most romantic expression of modern life ... but the cocktail habit as practised in England now is a vice.' Everyone gave parties and at them one made more acquaintances who in turn issued more invitations. We drove from one to another, often meeting the same people over and over again; for instance I seemed always to run into Moura Budberg, who must once have been beautiful but was now fat and blowsy; she seemed to have a good opinion of herself, and had I known then that she had been an agent of the Soviet authorities, who had planted her first on Gorky and then on H.G. Wells, I would have found her less of a bore.

I clearly remember the record, when we appeared at six parties in one evening, which sounds ridiculously frivolous, but I mention it because in spite of driving from one end of London to the other, evening after evening, it did not seem to affect the amount of work one got through in a day. By the end of the decade it was nearly over and the war finished the cocktail age. After 1939 parties there were, of course, but they tended to be in one place and last longer, since dashing hither and thither in the black-out was not on. The old tempo never seemed to return for us. Slowly but surely, of course, a new frenetic tempo became fashionable, and life is faster now than we ever knew it. There is an altogether later tempo for, however many parties we went to, the whirlwind was always over in time for supper at home. I understand that parties start later now and go on forever.

We never saved any money; we just got by on what we earned, and from time to time I parted with treasures to plug a gap. This life was the tinsel on 'the black years, the devil's decade', which has for so long been looked upon with a distaste which has been described by A.J.P. Taylor as expressed in the phrase, 'mass unemployment and appeasement'. At that time the country and its government were equally unprepared for the rapidity with which the Depression overtook them; it could not all be blamed upon the Wall Street crash. The disparity between the employed and the unemployed became daily more ominous, yet there were two sides to the problem.

For the latter the situation was terrible. A skilled man out of work, and there were so many, 'is ashamed of his lapse from higher standards, but the shame only depresses him more ... a ghost among living men, inhabiting a no-man's-land, without hope, without purpose, without human contact'. (A.M. Cameron, *Civilization and the Unemployed*, 1943).

And, 'What is astonishing is not that there are some unemployed men and women who are nervous wrecks and psychopathic cases ... but that there are not more.' (A.M. Cohen, *I was one of the Unemployed*, 1945). Years later in the second war I knew a Sergeant Hickman who came from Jarrow and I asked him what things had really been like; he summed it up in one sentence: 'In my school there was not one boy whose father had a job.'

For those in employment times were hard but steadily improving. While in 1933 the British Medical Association stated that 'a significant proportion of the people are suffering from an inadequate diet', those fortunate enough to have a job found that their wages rose by a third during the thirties, while the cost of living fell slightly and the consumption of food rose by 33 per cent. So while in 1934 in some areas the entire population was out of work, other parts of the country were experiencing almost boom conditions, and the rift between north and south was already widening. One symbol is the number of private cars on the road: in 1920 it was 500,000, 1,500,000 by 1929 and 3,000,000 in 1939. British annual car production rose from 95,000 in 1923 to 500,000 by 1937. While nothing but sorrow was felt over such moving events as the Jarrow march – fine men in despair who presented their pathetic case with order and dignity – the middle classes became better off by just attending to their jobs, by simply treading water in a country where the population was relatively static. It has been said that 'the legacy of bitterness and suffering caused by mass unemployment helped to spur the creation of the Welfare State'; what have we done with it?

Despite the serious state of the nation there were still enough lucky people around to fill the Lyceum when Sir Thomas Beecham brought Chaliapin's Russian Opera Company from Paris, and we were among them. It was wonderful; they did five operas: Mussorgsky's *Boris Godunov*, Rimsky-Korsakov's *Sadko*, Glinka's *Russlan and Ludmilla*, Borodin's *Prince Igor*, and *A Life for the Tzar*, also by Glinka. We went to all of them.

Clearly in my mind remain the glorious voice of Oda Slobodskaya, already in her forties but singing in London for the first time, and Act II of *Rousalka*. In this the tenor, alone on the stage, was singing a long aria when the scenery began to fall down. As he jumped bravely from side to side to avoid the huge fifty-foot flats collapsing around him he never missed a note, and Beecham, who was conducting, continued unperturbed, although I am sure he had a few words to say back stage afterwards.

But the zenith was *Boris Godunov*, an opera which is bracketed with *Tosca* at the top of my list of favourites. At that time the controversy was beginning over which version should be used, and the music critic of *The Times* wrote, 'There are those who declare that Rimsky-Korsakov's instrumentation and editorship of the whole score detracts from the crude grandeur of Mussorgsky's conception.' Those who made such a declaration have over the years become larger in number and louder in their vociferation, so that today I think one would be a little shocked to hear any version other than the composer's own. And the same critic then continued: 'Chaliapin's performance has lost nothing of its dramatic power and very little if any of its vocal beauty.' At fifty-eight his voice was perhaps ever so slightly showing its age, but his utter mastery and superb presence were spell-binding. Furthermore, the other bass part, the monk Pimen, was sung by Gitovsky, a young Russian with a glorious voice, and I noticed some dirty looks from Chaliapin when they were on stage together: no one should sing that well in the presence of the master. After they went back to Paris a report was published that during a performance of *Boris* Chaliapin could bear it no longer and delivered a fierce right hook to the button of the presumptuous monk. He was thinking, I suppose of the golden tones which had once come so easily to him; but he could have restrained himself – in spite of his age he was still *stupor mundi*.

A memorable event that summer was the last Schneider Trophy flown at Southampton. My King's friend, Ian Mackenzie, asked us to stay for the weekend in the Isle of Wight and we had a grandstand view from his garden. The excitement was not so much the speed (Squadron Leader Boothman flew the course at 547.30 k.p.h., the Italians failed to get airborne, and on the following day Stainforth raised the world speed record to 610.02 k.p.h.) as the planes. The trophy, given by Jacques Schneider in 1912 and now forgotten since Britain won it outright in 1931, was for seaplanes. The winning Supermarine, resplendent in royal blue, had a slim fuselage unlike any aeroplane one had ever seen before, as those who have looked at it today in the Science Museum will agree. But little did we know then as we watched R.J. Mitchell's design flashing past in the clear blue sky that we were looking at the immediate forerunner of the Spitfire.

We went to Skye to call on our author Seton Gordon, joint monarch of Skye with the Macdonald of Dunvegan, and back to the mainland to stay with Compton Mackenzie. If there is a more beautiful drive than that from Kyle of Lochalsh to Inverness, through Glen Affric, I have not seen it.

'Monty' Mackenzie was well known for his love of islands. He had lived on Barra in the Outer Hebrides, and had taken a sixty-seven year lease of Jethou in the Channel Islands; and now the Lovats had offered him an island in the middle of the river at Beauly, by Inverness. It was small, with room for a comfortable house, built in the eighteenth century by the Sobieski Stuarts, and with peaceful woods. The river divided round it: on one side shallow and easily forded by the deer coming for the silence of the trees; on the other beneath rocky cliffs a torrent racing through a narrow gorge. It was a happy if strange stay. Immediately after dinner Monty retired to begin his day's work; he wrote through the night and next appeared at lunchtime. After breakfast alone there was plenty for us to do: walk around the island, and play music – for as editor of *The Gramophone* Monty had all the newest records.

He was a wonderful host and a fascinating talker. Since among many languages he spoke fluent Greek, he had during the war been in the Secret Service in Athens, and it is said that the revelations in his *Athenian Memories*, which was suppressed, caused the Foreign Office to have to move every British spy in Europe. As a rich source of information he ran a brothel in Athens, and when the Greek government requested him to leave, I was told that his departure was dramatic, to say the least: packing his girls into a large, open car, he drove out of town discharging a pistol into the air.

Some time not long after I joined the firm father decided it would be a good thing if authors could see how their books were made. So he invited a fairly large party – I think we were about twenty in all – to go over Graycaines at Watford. They were not the world's best printers, but

they had some interesting machinery, and a bindery. After the tour we
sat down to lunch in a private room at a large hotel in Bushey. Monty, a
complete extrovert, got into an amicable argument with someone
opposite – I think Warwick Deeping. He became so excited that,
plunging in knife and fork, he devoured indiscriminately not only his
own salad but that on his right as well; the owner was Ernest Raymond,
a shy man, who recoiled in disbelief rather like a tall rabbit in
unwelcome proximity to a rattlesnake.

Throughout his life Monty appears always to have been short of
money, but his moves from island to island placed him in real straits. He
asked for higher and higher advances until father finally said he could
go no further. With mutual expressions of regret Monty moved to
Chatto's, who, being good publishers, I am sure looked after him very
well.

Not long after I started at the office Monty wrote *April Fools*, for which
I asked Edward Bawden to do the jacket; it was a memorable book
because the jacket was the best that Bawden did for me and Monty gave
me the autograph manuscript as a wedding present. I was sorry when
he left us, but we parted with good will and remained friends for the
rest of his life.

8   The State of Play

Oliver Simon did me the honour of proposing me for the Double Crown Club, and in November 1932 I was elected. There was what James Moran, the club's historian, had described as 'the customary confusion' over who had been nominated, so that I had no inkling and was all the more delighted by the flattering news.

The Double Crown Club is a unique institution, enjoying a prestige and standing far beyond its own pretensions which have been admirably described by Francis Meynell: 'Born in 1924, [it] is a fraternity of experts in the several crafts of printing. It was Oliver Simon's brainchild and the *accoucheurs* were Hubert Foss* and my cousin, Gerald Meynell. We meet at dinner four times a year. We are professionals meeting as amateurs' (*My Lives*, 1971). The first president, Holbrook Jackson, said a few years later that 'it had not been the business of the Double Crown Club to make history, being content that history should be made by its members, who have been responsible for most of the events of typographical importance in this country since 1924'.

I do not know if it is because I felt so honoured that it seems to me to have been harder to become a member then than it is now. The answer is perhaps yes and no. The illustrious founders had remarkably high standards in an age of great progress, while today the work produced by the new methods is, with some honourable exceptions, at its best dull but worthy, frequently bad, and in the case of one university press which should know better frankly appalling. Printers seem like children with Meccano or Lego, too occupied by the mechanics of putting the bits together to build a crane. Nor do there seem to be publishers who are interested any more, and we are waiting for the new technology to produce its Stanley Morison, its Oliver Simon, its Wren Howard.

My election to the club brought me in touch with a number of my elders and betters, some of whom became personal friends from whom I learned a great deal.

Holbrook Jackson was president and also dinner secretary, arranging excellent menus, always at the Café Royal. One dinner there remains

---

* Of the O.U.P. Music Department, father of Christopher, who today has a bookshop in Baker Street.

embarrassingly in my mind. It was in 1935. Calligraphy had always been an interest of the club: Edward Johnston, Graily Hewitt, Percy Smith and Alfred Fairbank were all members at various times. On this occasion Percy Smith was to read a paper on Lettering, and I was responsible for the design of the menu. It was a lantern lecture; the tables formed a U with the fourth side of the square taken up by the screen. Percy Smith was a very nice, gentle person who, of course, knew his subject from A to Z, but he had a soporific manner, and was intolerably and interminably dull. This last proved to be a delusion, for he stopped with unexpected suddenness and the lights were switched on – to reveal a member from the far sprig, who could bear no more, crawling on all fours to avoid the lantern's beam, towards the door and liberty.

But my greatest friend whom I first met at a club dinner was Francis Meynell. The Nonesuch Press was at the height of its fame, so great that apparently it had not yet been eroded by the Depression. Francis had already enjoyed a life of distinction (although there was still so much to come) and I was only in the second year of my profession. Some friendships ripen slowly over many years, others are born suddenly into full bloom. That between Francis and myself was of the latter variety and the roots went very deep. We shared so much; in addition to so many other interests there was cricket – the game itself and our respective teams. Francis ran his at Great Yeldham and I started the Savages at Cassell's, and we used to play for one another's sides. For convenience I have put my memories of this beloved game together in an appendix, but I must pay tribute here to Margaret. She has many attributes, not the least remarkable of which is that she, an American, not only has a deep love and encyclopaedic knowledge of the game, but also is an adept who kept score at nearly all the Savages' matches until the team became a casualty of the Second World War.

Although I had joined the Bibliographical Society as soon as I came to London, I do not know how such skills as I have in that fascinating science became known, but they did, and Francis asked me to compile the bibliography for *The Nonesuch Century*, the volume with comments by Francis himself and an introduction by A.J., which records the first hundred books of the press and which was published in 1934. I did it in my spare time – by which I mean that, snatching a quick sandwich, I could manage two hours in the middle of the day, and the secretary of the company, Edwin Harper, had the next lot of books ready for me every time I went there.

A year later, Francis, finding that the Depression had now struck and the Nonesuch could no longer give him a decent income, and that the Harmsworths, who had been putting money in, had reached the end of the line, reluctantly decided that he must sell. One day he asked me if I would like to buy, and after some calculations I decided that if I hocked everything I could just raise the price that he was asking. This figure was a reasonable one because it was entirely for the name and goodwill; the limited editions were sold out and the press was just what one made of it. I was very excited; to have my own list with such a famous name! It would not be difficult for me because it did not have to give me a living, I had my job; Margaret and I could publish as few books as we liked until the economic storm, which no one believed could last for ever, had come to an end. But my hopes were soon dashed; Thomas Young, as Chairman of Cassell's, gently but firmly pointed out that Cassell's articles of association clearly stated that no director might be on the board of or have any concern with any other business. Crestfallen, I told Francis this. He sold it to George Macey of the Limited Editions Club in New York (although with George's good will it was to be returned to him years later).

Some time after that Francis told me that Edwin Harper, who had lost his job at Nonesuch, was at the *Daily Express* and desperately unhappy; could I perhaps find room for him? I was able to get him the position of second-in-command of our Publicity Department, which he accepted. That was a good deed done which earned a rich reward. Apart from five years in the navy during the war, he was to spend the rest of his life at Cassell's and eventually took his seat on the board. He was a soft-spoken, very private man, extremely able and with great charm. He was also scrupulously honest and upright; many years later I came to look upon him as a friend on whose confidence I could always rely.

It was during 1932 that I had some short-lived relations with Richard Aldington and H.D. I do not know how it began, but I presume that it was about a book; at any rate it was arranged that I should go to call upon them at the Cavendish Hotel. I appeared and was shown up to their room where we had a long, friendly but fruitless chat; I then said goodbye and went downstairs.

As I was walking out an imperious voice said, 'Young man, come here.'

I stopped, turned and went into the first door on the right of the entrance.

'Sit down and have a glass of champagne.'

I did both.

It was Rosa Lewis, sitting in an extremely comfortable chintz-covered armchair facing the door, so that she could see everyone who came in or went out, the champagne bottle in a bucket by her side.

She was a noble, rather large figure with a mass of beautiful hair pinned up in the manner fashionable in the twenties, the way my mother's used to be. Her face had splendid bones and when younger must have been lovely. When she was not shouting imperiously at passers by, her voice was low-pitched, but it had about it an air of authority as though she were monarch of all she surveyed – as indeed she was.

She wanted to know who I was, everything about me; the conversation rambled on happily until with a gracious nod and a kindly smile she dismissed me. It was a small thing, but I deeply appreciated talking even for so much as an hour to one of the goddesses of a past age.

1932 was a good year for new authors, of whom the most important, to me, was Stefan Zweig. We began with *Fouché*, considered by some to be one of his best books – not my favourite, but still extremely good. He was then offered to us on a more permanent basis by Ben Huebsch of The Viking Press, a remarkable man who was a personal friend of Zweig and acted as his representative in all matters concerning the English language versions of his work. Stefan was to remain with us for the rest of his life.

I bought from Viking at this time an enchanting small book by a German Jewess called Helene Eliat, *Sheba Visits Solomon*. Margaret and I were going to Germany for our holiday that summer, and as it turned out that we and Huebsch would all be in Berlin at the same time, we agreed to meet so that we could go to see Helene Eliat together.

We drove via Cologne; it was an extremely uncomfortable journey because the roads were bad and the chassis of the little MG so short that we bumped from pothole to pothole like a trawler in a choppy sea. There was as yet no Führer to build autobahns to sop up the unemployment and facilitate his vast troop movements, as Napoleon had done with the *routes nationales*, and earn the grateful admiration of an innocent public.

We met up with Ben and saw our author who turned out to be beautiful and as charming as her delightful book. Ben was eager to see the homosexuals and transvestites for whom Berlin was notorious: we knew the types well from the drawings of George Grosz, but actually to see them enjoying themselves would be as good as a three-ring circus. Ben said that he had the address of the bar which was the fashionable meeting place, so after dinner we set off. A taxi dropped us at a bar of which we were the only occupants. After sitting in sepulchral solitude over a glass of wine for a while, Ben told the bartender that we understood this to be a gay headquarters.

'Used to be. They all moved on about six months ago.'

Where did they go? The barman gave us another address; another taxi; another silent vigil; another question – again they had moved on; another address; another taxi. We covered most of Berlin, getting back wearily to the Adlon Hotel in the small hours. The three-ring circus had eluded us, and Ben sadly went about his business.

We had to visit the Planetarium, since these fascinating constructions were still a novelty – the first one having been built by Carl Zeiss at Jena only in 1913; we had the place to ourselves. The lecturer was rather like the schoolmaster in the film of *All Quiet on the Western Front*, with the same pompous voice; the appearance of the evening star was greeted in deep foreboding tones with: 'Jetzt kommt Frau Venus.' One evening we went to Haus Vaterland, the other mass entertainment emporium like Casanova at which Denys Lowson and I had looked so stupid three years before. Going up in the lift from floor to floor in the same way, we heard some good jazz and said 'Stop – that's for us.' We spent the evening in the Wild West Bar listening to Sidney Bechet; I thought it wonderful, but Margaret confessed many years later that she did not enjoy it all that much (I have touched upon it in the appendix on jazz).

On the way home we stopped in Verdun to visit Fort Douomont. In those days visitors were allowed down to the bottom floor where, when each side possessed half of the corridor, the French surrendered; forty years later, when I went once more the foetid bowels were no longer on view. It is a wonderful position overlooking the long flat plain across which the Germans had to advance; their losses were appalling – in fact it is not generally realized that their total casualties in front of and in the forts were higher than those of the French. But in the hedgerow of the lane which led from the main road to Douomont was, plain to see, a skeleton; fourteen years after the end of the war and no one had troubled to lay this poor soul to his eternal rest.

Willa Cather and R.C. Hutchinson joined us with, respectively, *Shadows on the Rock* and *The Answering Glory*. Ray Hutchinson had published one novel elsewhere when he was brought to us by Curtis Brown. Father considered him to be one of the finest English novelists of the century and idolized him. Though I do not think that I felt quite so fanatical – except for *Shining Scabbard* which I loved because it was about France – Ray and I got on very well. I liked him, we were in constant touch, he came frequently to the office and was a voluminous correspondent.

But I blundered over the jacket of both novels through not familiarizing myself sufficiently with the text before making up my mind. Both should have had type jackets, and I gave them pictures – dignified pictures, but still pictures. Both authors complained in writing and the offence was not repeated; but many years later Ray was to return to the subject.

My team of favourite jacket designers was now forming and in a few years would be complete. Finally it comprised Edward Bawden, Eric Ravilious, Eric Fraser, Edward Ardizzone, Barnett Freedman and Feliks Topolski. Type jackets I designed myself, and novels of a more popular nature were commissioned by the Art Department. What gave me the idea I do not know, but I had a shot at having one or two novels illustrated. Edward Bawden, who on his eightieth birthday said 'I died fifty years ago', produced some enchanting drawings for Compton Mackenzie's *Buttercups and Daisies* in 1931, but his work was by no means to everyone's taste then, certainly not to that of my elders, and when his designs for a later novel by Gide were delivered while I was on holiday, they were set aside and the book sent to press without them. My rage on my return was quite impotent, for it was too late.

I discovered quite by chance in the Production Department swatches of patterns which could be impressed upon cloth if one took the trouble to order in advance. No one seemed to be particularly interested, and I cannot imagine now why I did not use them far more often. The first effort was on a complete edition of Chekhov's plays, and ten years later I used a handsome one on Stefan's posthumous *Balzac* – which an antiquarian bookseller recently described as 'a remarkably attractive and unusual cover'. Attractive it certainly was, but unusual only because book producers, myself included, took too little notice of what was there under their noses. There was another instance about which I felt very aggrieved. Barcham Green, the producers of hand-made papers, developed a chemical process which would make its product extremely strong. The paper could be printed on, coated with the chemical and then used for binding. It was very tough; the representative selling it carried with him a machine which demonstrated that it was, in fact, stronger than cloth – and it was washable. I used it on a volume of Gauguin's letters; on the front cover was printed his self-portrait, and it looked rather handsome. But the booksellers would have none of it; the binding was paper and a paper binding they did not want. The fact that it was more durable and also washable, which cloth is not, meant nothing and I could never use it again – nor, I believe, did anyone else make the attempt.

So an attractive step forward was stillborn through ill-founded prejudice – until in 1986, more than half a century later, I saw someone remarking in print that the same product was a rather good idea.

The most showy trade bindings I produced were for the three volumes of *The Story of My Life* by Queen Marie of Rumania, 1934–5, on which I was given *carte blanche*. Cased in red cloth, they were emblazoned with the royal arms, which were almost as colourful as she was, for she left behind her a dubious reputation somewhat characteristic of the Rumanian royal house.

Another production problem which persisted for years and is still not dead is which way the lettering should read on the jacket and, when relevant, the binding: upwards or downwards. In this I was the blinkered conservative. Historically (for instance on a narrow book before jackets came into use) it has always read upwards, because the human head tends to lean to the left and the eyes read upwards. The opposite crept in during the late twenties and early thirties for a purely commercial reason. Booksellers set out their wares in piles which lie uniformly with the top copy displaying the front cover; when that is done lettering reading upwards on the spine is facing the wrong way. I understood this point of commercial neatness, but never considered it sufficient reason for a change from the natural and aesthetic; various other publishers felt the same way as I did, and still do. But after sticking to my guns for about twenty years I came to the conclusion that the battle was lost; it was crazy to have books on the shelves side by side reading differently, and, since we supporters of the 'correct' were in the minority, I gave way, following the old pusillanimous adage 'If you can't beat 'em, join 'em.'

Publishing on both sides of the Atlantic at that time was always a different ball game and there were three difficulties. In the first place, only a certain proportion of a publisher's books successfully survived the ocean crossing – either way – and those that did could not produce enough revenue to maintain an overseas establishment. Secondly, the rights of most successful authors across the water were already sold separately. Thirdly, in his forays to the other side in search of new authors, a publisher had to have some *quid pro quo* to recommend in return; if all his ripening plums grew on a branch of his own tree, he could hardly expect young plums to fall into his hands from his opposite numbers' trees.

I have put this in the past tense because taste and circumstances have now entirely changed. The herring-pond has become much smaller; the Americans and British seem to appreciate one another's literature more; the walls now have fallen like those of Jericho. The Oxford University Press were the first to find a successful formula; an interesting group set up an organization which handled O.U.P. books but was autonomous and had a different name – the St Martin's Press. The changes have accelerated enormously and I shall return to the subject later.

But earlier all attempts to change the facts of life had failed. In the 1880s Cassell's had opened a branch in New York and failed. Conversely, Alfred Knopf opened a branch in London and failed; he started in 1928 and it took him just three years to learn the lesson – in 1931 he went into voluntary liquidation. Father had first choice from the list; we bought the stock of some beautiful books illustrated by Anthea and Vera Willoughby, and took into our list Carl Van Vechten, André Gide, Sigrid Undset and Dashiel Hammett. The rest went to Allen & Unwin.

In the same month Hamish Hamilton was founded, and it was announced that certain of Jamie Hamilton's books would be issued in the United States by Harper Brothers. Such was the atmosphere of distrust at the time, so deep the cleavage, that the new firm in London was widely rumoured to be merely a branch of Harper's under another name, and that therefore there was no point in offering one's wares to that much respected New York house because one would never get anything in return. The rumour was entirely without foundation and after some time died away.

Also this year I thought that I, too, would have a go at changing the facts of life. It was always said that the *novella* bore the kiss of death and I refused to believe it; I considered that the short novel, if it was good enough, would sell sufficient to earn its keep, if nothing more. So I started with Paul Morand's *Orient Air Express*, and followed it with a Maurois, a Schnitzler, a Gide and another Morand. All of them were good, yet I was wrong – all had the kiss of death all right. The facts of life remained unchanged for another thirty years until the fetish was triumphantly destroyed by Hemingway's *Old Man and the Sea*.

In parenthesis, *Orient Air Express* was my first translation from French. I admired Morand's writing, particularly at that time *Open All Night* – one story which inspired us to go to the six-day bicycle race at Olympia in the small hours when the competitors pedal round and round half asleep until the tannoy announces 'Mr Smith of Hackney offers £50 for a three-lap sprint' and everything springs into feverish activity.

It is interesting that such a rebel as Céline admired the writing of Paul Morand, who, he said, had 'jazzed up' French prose and put new life into it.

I followed it in the following year with *Indian Air*, a travel book which

Margaret remembered so well that it inspired her to suggest forty years later that we go to Peru for a holiday. Morand came to London and in my copy wrote 'Each translation is a journey – and this one came out beautifully.' That was kind of him, but I did mis-translate one word which his Rumanian wife noticed and this led to his asking to see the proofs of the third and last book of his which I did: *A Frenchman's London*. His wife, I was told, very much fancied herself as an English scholar and when the proofs came back they were scrawled all over with pencil emendations in a hand unfamiliar to me – presumably hers. In his covering note Morand said 'You must excuse the handwriting; I was doing it in a boat.' About a third of the scribbles were different ways of saying the same thing, the other two-thirds were gibberish, and I threw them in the waste paper basket. Not in any sense of tit for tat, I did point out an historical error of eight hundred years and his insouciant reply was 'If one is going to make a mistake, make a big one.'

Another debt which I owe to A.J., and another example of the breadth of his acquaintance, is Wyndham Lewis as an author. I would not have thought that they had much in common, nor do I know how or why they met. I am not alone in my surprise; Julian Symons has written 'The friendship between my brother ... and Wyndham Lewis was upon both sides a curious one ... The two had apparently nothing in common ... They were both individualists, dedicated to personal survival in a generally hostile or uncaring world; and it is true also that A.J. was like many others fascinated by Lewis' personality and, more surprisingly, admired his work. On Lewis' side it may be said that young admirers are almost always agreeable; and when they are vivid and intelligent personalities in their own right, that makes them even more attractive.' (*A.J.A. Symons to Wyndham Lewis*, ed. Julian Symons, 1982).

A.J. suggested that I see Wyndham Lewis, and as a result I 'launched, to not much effect, on an Audenary, unsuspecting world in 1932 *Snooty Baronet*'. These words are those of Alan Jenkins, reviewing the Black Sparrow edition fifty years later, who sums it up as 'an anarchic, inhuman panache which makes it one of the most accessible and funny of his novels'.

Lewis and I became very friendly, and he asked father and Margaret to sit for inclusion in his portfolio, *Thirty Portraits*, in which A.J. was also included. Those of father and A.J. were extremely good. In some of the drawings Lewis at the last moment added a pale brown wash, presumably to make the head stand out more strongly from the paper; this displeased father who remarked that it made him look like the Aga Khan – which, if you choose to look at it that way, it did – and Lewis was deeply miffed. Liking it very much, I bought it and hung it in my office, where with everything else it was destroyed during the war.

That of Margaret, which she has, I never cared for. Although fundamentally it is a good enough likeness, it lacks the charm which, even to an eye less biased than mine, was a characteristic of the sitter. It is not that Lewis was better at portraying men than women, because the drawing of Rebecca West in the same series is brilliant. I think that its comparative failure was caused by the hat. So long as a hat was part of the *tenue* of a well-dressed woman, Margaret always had a limited but fascinating collection. When she went to Lewis' studio she wore a small black straw turned up at one side, rather like an Australian soldier's hat, and the flap was covered by a tight mass of minute white artificial flowers. It was a tricky hat; Lewis chose to draw her in profile wearing it, and I feel that he became so interested in the technical problem of rendering the flowers that the features beneath them faded into secondary importance.

The portrait of A.J., on the other hand, came off extremely well. In October A.J. wrote to me 'I hear you have bought my portrait. I envy you, but I am glad you have it'; he was soon to discover that I had bought it as a present for him, and it now belongs to his brother Julian.

Lewis came to dinner at Gordon Place with John Rothenstein and A.J. What they talked about after dinner I no longer remember, but the sight of them sitting together on the sofa remains like a photograph in my mind because the conversation was spell-binding. We asked him again later, but he cried off with an abrupt postcard: 'Regret can't come to dinner. Severe dose of clap.' This was in March, 1933, when A.J. wrote to him 'Where and how are you? When last heard from, you were suffering from a roaming wild oat come to roost.'

In 1935 we published another novel by Lewis: *The Revenge for Love;* it did not have an easy birth. While writing it Lewis was hard up and A.J. was trying to help with the aid of Ian Black, a slim, dark, laconic financier to whom A.J. turned on many occasions. When in proof it was shown, as was the custom in the trade, to Boots' library reader, who took exception to some passages which Lewis was not prepared to alter. Lewis appealed to A.J. who replied, 'As you say, it is a serious matter. I have myself attacked the lending libraries (in my speech at the *Sunday Times* exhibition) but this purity nonsense is a fresh offence ... Don't think that because I am friendly with D.F. and Cassell's that I am on their side in this difference. I see their dilemma, but it is merely the dilemma of all publishers.' (Ibid, ed. Julian Symons). After the difficulties were resolved, on publication A.J. wrote congratulating Lewis and said, 'It is even better than I remember it; better than *Snooty* ... I look forward to the next masterpiece.' Alas, there was not to be another – at least not from us; it was no more successful than its predecessor and the red light was shining. The Depression which had ruled out illustrated books was now biting hard into the general list, and I had the uncomfortable task of telling Lewis that we could not go on; I dreaded his coming in, but in the event he was calm and dignified.

He arrived, of course, in his usual wide-brimmed black sombrero, and snorted several times through his nose – a habit, as though there were some obstruction; perhaps there was. He never disputed or criticized what was to me an unhappy decision; quietly he said 'All right' and walked out of my office and my life. Mentally, if not physically, I went into mourning.

The mention of the deference paid to Boots' librarian needs explanation today, and a little history.

To begin with, the nineteenth century had been the age which had displayed such a general thirst for knowledge. Gentlefolk who were not sufficiently wealthy to buy every book they required were catered for by that invaluable institution, the London Library in St James's Square, the need for which had been clearly seen by Thomas Carlyle who founded it in 1856. But literacy was now general and with it came a thirst for knowledge, on which were made the fortunes of men like John Cassell with his *Popular Educator* in penny weekly parts and other publications of a similar nature. Books had become so essential a part of community life that the Public Libraries Act was passed in 1850, and the setting up of libraries by local authorities was given an enormous boost fifty years later by the staggering philanthropy of Andrew Carnegie, a Scot who crossed the Atlantic, made an immense fortune and returned to his homeland. But the purpose of public libraries was fact, not fiction – and whereas now the amount of shelf space in libraries allotted to novels far outstrips anything else, it was not the original intention.

Since the eighteenth century, if not before, there had been private lending libraries; the multi-volume novel was expensive, so circles of friends bought them and handed them around amongst themselves. It was the vast expansion of the empire, and consequently families living abroad with little to do but embroider, gossip and read – even their children were cared for by nurses and sent home to Britain to school – which created the need for subscription libraries; and crates of books were despatched to every corner of the world and, one hopes, eventually returned. Mudie's was the first and became a household name; I was too young to know why it declined, but I can just remember it before it finally shut down. But the age of the lending library was not over; Harrod's, purveyors of everything to everybody, had a library service for its customers, distant as well as near at hand; and the shelves of The Times Book Club in Wigmore Street were at the service of the 'better' class readers at home. Into this field in the twenties stepped Boots; there was to be a library at the back of every major branch, leaning preponderantly but not exclusively to fiction, and they were so successful that if one recommended a novel to anybody the reply was invariably, 'I'll make a note of that and get it out of Boots.' Notice that they were always at the back of the shop; they were intended to be a loss leader – the idea being that a customer on the way out from changing his book would remember that he was short of soap, or loo paper or what have you. When they died for a variety of reasons after the Second World War, I am told that they were losing £30,000 a year, but how many millions poured into their tills which might have gone into those of other chemists one will never know. In their heyday they were of primary importance in the sale of fiction, and if they gave the thumbs down to a novel it was a disaster.

There was also for a time a commercial enterprise – the 'Tuppenny Libraries' – which hired out popular fiction at a fraction over a penny in present money per title for two weeks; the margin must have been too small and they disappeared.

Business in general did not alter very much over the years before the war, nor, indeed, for some time after it. In 1952 the eminent American publisher, Ben Huebsch, writing about publishing on the sixtieth birthday of his illustrious rival, Alfred Knopf, said, 'Looking back over the intervening years one notes that public taste has changed less than the clangour of today's methods might imply.' But the clangour had started and during the last twenty years changes have come about at a hurricane pace; I have already referred to the merging of imprints across the Atlantic – and there has been much else.

We used to have seven travellers on the road and added an eighth when it came to light that the territory of the country representative did not quite meet that of the two in London. There was a kind of *cordon sanitaire* around the capital which no one was covering; this was given to a member of my cricket team who longed to get out on the road, and a splendid job he made of it. While at the office we saw the West End representative every day – he had almost senatorial rank, and there were only three during the whole of my time: Bob Hazelton, Ken Smith and John Knight. The men in the country were a law unto themselves. Our rep in the West Country had the reputation of being one of the best in the business, and only after his sudden death did we discover that he was an alcoholic; as one bookseller said, 'Many's the time I've let him sleep it off at the back of the shop while I filled out his order forms for him' – perhaps that is why his figures were so good. Scotland was virtually hereditary; when Alec Hutton was ill his wife travelled for him and got a square deal all round, and on his death if anybody but his son Jim had been given the job, the trade would have turned its back.

An old custom which still survived, but is now, I think, obsolete, was the '13 as 12' (the baker's dozen): any bookseller ordering twelve copies of a title was given one for free; how or when this simple incentive ever started I cannot imagine. A constant problem was the production of editions, subsequent to the original one, at a low enough price to get at a wider market which everyone felt existed but did not know how to reach. Every novel (with extra lengthy exceptions) was published at 7s. 6d. (*c.*38p) and more were printed than the estimated requirement; if the book went better than expected, well and good – if not, the surplus was later given a cheaper binding and issued at 3s. 6d. (*c.*18p). But this ploy only reached the already known market, it did not reach the Outback which we were sure existed. Various 'pocket editions' appeared, of which the most handsome were Martin Secker's Adelphi Library, those of Chatto & Windus and Jonathan Cape. Benn's made a big effort in 1930–1 with their Sixpenny Library (2½p), a series of short books covering art, history, economics and philosophy; they published some two hundred titles. At the same time we had a go with a large number of popular novels in simple hard covers at 1s. 0d. (5p), of which we sold just under two million, and we came within a hair's breadth of a big breakthrough. Our chairman, Tommy Young, knew one of the directors of Players and discussed at Norwich a plan to give our novels as a bonus for so many cigarette packet wrappers; but it was long before the age when everything, almost the kitchen stove, was given free as a sales inducement, and in the end nothing came of it. Another five years were to pass until the real break was made by Allen Lane, to which we shall come later.

Taste has not changed much over the half-century of my experience, but there naturally has been evolution.

Before the First World War, apart from Sherlock Holmes and the Australian *Mystery of a Hansom Cab* of which the earliest surviving copy is the 100,000th, there was little crime fiction except stories, now forgotten, about an investigator named 'Cleek'; published by Cassell's, the author, who lived in Bromley, was a friend of my parents and I have a vague memory, refreshed by photographs, of being a page in a white satin suit at the wedding of one of his daughters. But after the war the crime story burgeoned into full flower and has never faded – and, interestingly, all the successes were women, except for men of distinction such as G.K. Chesterton and Father Ronald Knox. During the thirties the balance between the sexes was restored, starting in our own list with S.S. Van Dine, and it now appears the odds are slightly in favour of the male.

The thriller was already with us. But the inscrutable Orient – represented, for instance, by Fu Manchu with whom Sax Rohmer and Cassell's had such a roaring success – has been replaced by spies who came in from the cold. The Iron Curtain created a no-man's-land which supplied unlimited possibilities for villainy attractive to adventure writers such as Ian Fleming – even Dick Francis has had a go – and a galaxy of which the stars are Deighton and Le Carré. Between the wars there was also on both sides of the Atlantic the widely read tough school of varying literary merit, from *No Orchids for Miss Blandish* to *They Shoot Horses, Don't They?* and *The Postman Always Rings Twice*.

Romantic fiction remains unchanged: there is little difference between Elinor Glyn, Ruby M. Ayres and Barbara Cartland; but loosened morals now permit lubricious novels such as the notorious *Lace* which no one would have published in the thirties.

The completely new element in fiction is the 'blockbuster', a phenomenon made possible partly by the expansion of the market far beyond the confines of years ago, partly by the taste of a vast public for drama, usually but not always liberally laced with sex. 'Cometh the hour, cometh the man', and the top figures – among them Irving Wallace, Irving Stone, Harold Robbins, Arthur Hailey and Frederick Forsyth – a generation ago simply did not have the demand to write what they write so successfully now. There is a tendency among the higher brows to look down on such authors because of their success, which is unfair because they are able craftsmen – the fact that he earns a lot of money does not make MacEnroe's tennis any less beautiful. Whatever one may think of Harold Robbins as a whole, the early chapters of *The Carpetbaggers* are extremely moving; and there cannot be a more exciting way of learning about a subject of considerable importance than *Strong Medicine* by Arthur Hailey, an Englishman by birth. Fifty years ago we did have one unique 'blockbuster' who was similarly looked down upon, yet with a grudging respect: Edgar Wallace. His fecundity was prodigious; father, in a tight corner with one of his magazines, rang him up and asked if he could possibly write a full-length serial and deliver the first instalment in a fortnight, to which the reply was 'No, I can't do that, but I will deliver the whole thing in ten days' time.' A glance with unprejudiced eyes at his clean, straightforward prose might be a salutary experience for some writers with more elevated pretensions.

The subject which showed the most dramatic increase between the thirties and the fifties was history. The only reason for this which I can think of was that after the first war the British Empire was still in one piece while the troubles at home centred our interest upon ourselves; but after the second war empires fell to pieces, the world was in disarray and people looked outwards and backwards, suddenly interested in where all this turmoil had come from. In the thirties also Lytton Strachey planted the first seeds of the 'warts and all' school of biography, which by now has grown to such an extent that those writing lives of anyone well known have become learned chiropodists gleefully slashing at feet of clay.

One literary historian has written of the last half-century that 'there is little evidence that Book Clubs seriously influence writers' choice of what they shall write, or publishers' of what they shall publish (as they do to some extent in America).' This is a true comment, and the reason is not difficult to find: it is a question of size. Somebody who likes to have books around him may in Britain complain that he is miles from a decent bookshop, but his opposite number in the United States may be hundreds of miles from anything similar. For an intelligent middle-of-the-road family deep in the heart of Texas or Nebraska it has therefore been a godsend to have a book more often to their taste than not arrive through the post regularly, so the Book of the Month Club and the Literary Guild both reached an enormous size which could optimistically and understandably affect a writer's or a publisher's mind when contemplating a project; a Choice made a great difference. In Britain no such circumstances existed and book clubs did not proliferate or particularly flourish. The Left Book Club and The Folio Society were special cases; the former was political and people like Margaret and I joined on principle (though I cannot swear that we read every one of the books which arrived in their distinctive red covers every month), and the latter we shall come to later. The Book Society, admirably run by its founder, Alan Bott, was never large enough to affect the views or judgement of anyone in any branch of the business; and The Reprint Society, also started by Bott, was merely a special edition of acknowledged successes.

Lastly there is the bookseller, this willing beast of burden who always claims to be on the verge of bankruptcy but seldom seems to slip over the edge. There is money to be made, but, even more than in publishing, success depends upon the personality of the individual. Between the wars the London scene was dominated to an extraordinary degree by J.G. Wilson of Bumpus in Oxford Street – so much so that with his departure the shop withered and died. There has never been anyone like 'J.G.', though since the second war his kingdom has been admirably divided between Cadness Page and Tommy Joy. These are names graven in the history of the trade, with Hubert Wilson in the City, Basil Blackwell in Oxford, Heffer in Cambridge, Hudson in Birmingham and Thin in Edinburgh. In the Charing Cross Road, Willie Foyle, who rose from a barrow to a vast assemblage which might not unkindly be described as an inspired shambles, and Zwemmer to whom anyone wanting an art book flew like a homing pigeon – and one's own favourite round the corner. Now there are new names; may they be graven with honour in the roll of their ancient and honourable calling.

DF ready for the procession at Wells, Norfolk, on Coronation Day, 1910

Winning the 440 yards against Eton for the first time, 1925

Helping Guy Butler train for his attack on the world 400 metre record, 1926

Graduation Day, Cambridge, 1929
Left to right: DF, Walter Churchill, Charles Hasse

DF's cartoons, *Basileon*, King's College magazine
Left Donald Beves, Lay Dean; *right* Frank Adcock (later Sir Frank),
Professor of Ancient History

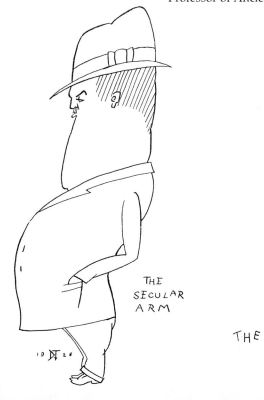

THE
SECULAR
ARM

THE
PWOFESSOR

My father, 1915

Right: DF by Feliks Topol
1942 (later misdated by
ar[

DF, 1931.

Winston Churchill laying the foundation stone of the Cassell building,
Red Lion Square

Model of the Cassell
building, Red Lion
Square

La Belle Sauvage by David McFall RA. Maquette of the figure placed in
front of the Cassell building

THESE LOOKS SPEAK VOLUMES

A Panorama of Publishers

SHERRIFFS.

4. Dr. DESMOND FLOWER

THE middle of three generations of Flowers now at Cassells (father Sir Newman is President, son Nicholas is Up and Coming), Desmond Flower became Literary Director in 1938 and retired in 1940 to devote himself to soldiering (M.C., dispatches). In 1946 he resumed, became Chairman in 1958. An enthusiastic Francophile, he is a Chevalier of the Legion of Honour and a D.Litt. (*honoris causa*) of Caen University. The foundation-stone of the firm's building in Red Lion Square (laid by Sir Winston Churchill in 1956) is part of the fabric of the Chateau de Versailles. His list of books of which he is proudest is eclectic, includes an illustrated (Paul Nash) edition of *Urne Buriall*, Nicholas Monsarrat's first novel, Churchill's *Second World War*, *Cassell's Encyclopædia of Literature*, Sir William Slim's *Defeat into Victory*, *The Collected Letters of Edward Gibbon* and *Cassell's Spanish Dictionary*.

314

Cartoon, *Punch*, 14 October 1959

9   Literature and Gastronomy

Father was a great admirer of the poetry of Ernest Dowson, not only for its own merit but because he could never forget that when he first came to London he had seen the poet – probably at the Café Royal. A.J. had fabulous treasures from the nineties, but he would never reveal the sources from which he had obtained them, and among these was Dowson's manuscript notebook which contained a considerable amount of unpublished work. In 1931 he had come to know of father's interest and mentioned the notebook to me; in the end father bought it and put it in my hands so that I might produce the complete poetical works of Dowson. This took me two years and the book appeared in 1934 as a handsome large octavo, the first time Oliver Simon had used Walbaum, a beautiful type.

It was through Dowson that I came upon the most important figure in my book-collecting life. Dowson made a translation of a large part of Voltaire's *Pucelle*, and, as I proposed to include some of it in my edition of the poems, I thought that I ought to compare his version with the original; he was in fact a remarkably able translator.

Although I was told that the stalls in Farringdon Street were nothing compared with what they had been – nothing ever is – there was still one man who had a row of four stalls piled with books on which one might find anything. I used to go there several times a week unless it was pouring with rain. No sooner had I made up my mind to look at *La Pucelle* than I found on the stalls a mid-eighteenth-century edition bound up with other works by Voltaire. Of course I had to go to the London Library to look for a bibliography which would tell me what I had got, and I found the four volumes of Bengesco, published in 1888. Like everyone else interested in Voltaire, I genuflect before this Rumanian diplomat's astonishing feat. Superseded it must be, for like all sciences bibliography has progressed enormously since the last century, and we now know Bengesco to be incomplete and often inaccurate, but we are nonetheless deeply in his debt. I found that my volume was an interesting one; *La Pucelle* was very early and the pamphlets bound with it were first editions.

Constantly collecting, constantly disposing, I parted with books for two reasons: to raise money to help keep our heads above water, and because I had not yet found a subject which absorbed me. I already admired *Candide* and knew a good deal about the author and his other works, and that day as I looked at Bengesco the penny dropped. Like Hillary at base camp with the unconquered height towering above him, I would tackle one of the giants of world literature; I would collect Voltaire.

I had tried very hard over Dowson; nevertheless, when I sent a copy to Peter Lucas he produced a list of errata to the notes – most of them to the Greek which I had never mastered. In the L.C.C. library I delved into piles of documents concerning Bridge Dock which had belonged to the Dowson family, and pursued as many of the poet's friends as I could find. Knowing Sir William Rothenstein, I went first to him. He said that he had seven letters from the poet but could not find them, and indeed they never have been found. He told me how it was that he came to draw his portrait of Dowson – the finest ever done, the present whereabouts of which is a mystery; I had a photograph of it once, and twice reproduced it. Dowson used to come up from Bridge Dock, which he did not enjoy, to see his many friends at the Café Royal or one of a group of pubs such as the Fitzroy in Charlotte Street, or the one which lay between the Empire and the Alhambra music halls, or to see his beloved Missie at her parents' restaurant in Sherwood Street. Sometimes if he lingered too long he missed the last train back to Limehouse, and would knock up a friend to beg a few hours' rest on a sofa. Once it was Rothenstein, who said the next morning, 'The charge for bed and breakfast here is that you sit still while I draw you.' With the skill of all Rothenstein drawings, the result has caught the shy and sad good looks to perfection and is the only portrait of Dowson in his prime, before his health gave way and led to the heartbreaking sketch of him by Charles Conder which is in the National Portrait Gallery.

I went to Edinburgh to see Father Gray who was kind and gave me a strong feeling of what a nice person Dowson must have been – although after so long as a priest he dwelt more clearly than most on the poet's faults; indeed, he was not particularly concerned any more with the nineties or the fact that his own book of verses, *Silverpoints*, was the most beautiful book of its time.

Arthur Moore, who collaborated with Dowson in three novels, two of which – *A Comedy of Masks* and *Adrian Rome* – were published, was still a solicitor in Gray's Inn. He told me that the two of them were seldom together; having agreed upon a plot, they wrote alternate chapters in a notebook which they posted backwards and forwards.

Although I had met neither of them before, both Gray and Moore trusted me with all the letters from Dowson which they had kept – a considerable number. I exchanged letters with Conal O'Riordan, and the son of Greene, who had been secretary of the Rhymers' Club, came into my office one day with the letters to his father. In reading and copying all these I discovered what an extremely good letter writer Dowson was, and considered gathering together and publishing all his correspondence. But I was distracted by other things, and perhaps I lacked the true detective instinct (as A.J had) to pursue the matter through thick and

thin. Anyway, the project lay dormant for over a decade until in 1947 I
was called upon by a boy at Eton named Henry Maas. He was tall and
charming, with about him an air of shy determination. He loved
Dowson and knew from my introduction to the poems that I had copies
of certain letters. We talked for a long time and it was in reverse very
similar to my first meeting with A.J. when we had finished up as
co-editors of the *B.C.Q.* Henry and I decided upon a collaboration. His
was the touchstone which revived my interest; he was the bloodhound
who smelt out letters from unimagined corners; even so, it still took
twenty years. As the task was nearing completion, we found that we
had amassed so much information about Dowson that we knew in
considerable detail what had happened to him, so we decided that the
letters should be supplemented by a narrative which would in fact
altogether amount to a biography. In close consultation I wrote the
narrative, and finally in 1967 *The Letters of Ernest Dowson* appeared.

Time and taste never stand still and later criticism may place a
different interpretation upon Dowson, but nevertheless I feel that
Henry, Mark Longaker of Philadelphia and I presented pretty well all
the facts that are likely to be gathered about him. Imagine then my
surprise and, indeed, annoyance to see recently an anthology of nineties
verse in which the editor in his introduction has progressed no further
than the unfounded drink-sodden image fabricated by Arthur Symons
in the early years of this century.

In 1931 at an agreeable lunch of a few friends the subject of George
Saintsbury, now old, nearly blind and alone in Bath, came up, and as a
result it was decided to found the Saintsbury Club in his honour. A.J.,
quite rightly, had a low opinion of the sage as a man of letters, but all
present admired him for the remarkable Cellar Book which he had kept
in his palmier days. Members were to be limited to fifty, all wine lovers,
and the club flourishes today. It holds two dinners a year in the Vintners
Hall, at which the quality and quantity of the wines are naturally the
main feature. There is a chairman who is elected annually; the first
Secretary was A.J. and the Yeoman of the Cellar was André Simon – an
office which he continued to hold until 1960. André, father of the well
known wine merchant today, was one of the nicest and most kind men I
have ever met, and a complete encyclopaedia of food and wine. The one
remarkable thing about him was that, although he spent his life in this
country and had a flawless command of the language both spoken and
written, he never bettered his accent – it was appalling. Perhaps he did
not want to; perhaps the stream of fractured, sometimes unintelligible
sounds were an essential part of his bubbling character. He did
enormous good for the standing of both wine and food in this country,
which badly needed it.

Through them both I was elected a member in the mid-thirties. The
entry fee was a case of wine for the club's cellar. One could present what
one liked, and, being smart-Alecky and knowing that in every bad year
there are one or two exceptions as much as vice versa, I went to my wine
merchant and asked him to find me a really beautiful '23 Bordeaux.

When he made his suggestion I wrote to André, who telephoned me – he was not happy, would I allow him to advise me? Politely I said no, that was what I was giving, period; afterwards my heart sank – what a fool I would look if the wine turned out to be sour plonk! Several years later my heart sank again when I looked at the menu and saw that my wine was on it. But I need not have worried – it drank beautifully, and at the end of the table Vyvyan Holland, the son of Oscar Wilde (knowing all about what had happened) raised his glass and winked.

Vyvyan, who like so many others I first met through A.J., became someone whom I admired and respected. He was a small man, with the right side of his mouth very slightly drawn up and a staccato laugh. I thought that these two characteristics came from what he had been through and, indeed, in his autobiography in 1954 he wrote, 'As a result of the secrecy with which I was surrounded in my childhood, I have suffered all my life from embarrassing shyness ... In these pages I have tried to show what it is like to be the son of Oscar Wilde. On the whole my life has been one of concealment and repression.' Nevertheless, 'in his time' it has been said of him, 'He was probably one of the dozen best judges of wine in the world ... He was never happier than when dispensing hospitality to a few chosen friends in his house in Carlyle Square.' I remember one such evening when Margaret and I were among those invited after a Wine and Food Society dinner. The others were drinking pink champagne while I was looking at his superb collection of books with pornographic illustrations by Kenneth Hobson, the bookbinder. Whatever the subject of conversation was, I profoundly disagreed but was prevented from expressing my views by a prolonged bout of hiccups – most frustrating. During the second war he married Thelma, an enchanting Australian 'beautician', and I am sure that this was the best thing that ever happened to him. He died in 1967.

The most memorable dinner of the society in my mind was one at which we finished with Madeira. On the island, poking about in one estate's cellars, André found a pipe covered in dust marked in chalk *'pour l'Empéreur'*, and bought it. The ship bearing Napoleon to St Helena put in at Madeira, the Emperor went ashore and ordered a pipe to be sent on to him, but when he arrived at his last home, Dr Barry O'Meara ran the rule over him and said, 'Your liver is horrible, you will not eat or drink the following,' – a list which included Madeira. So the wine was never sent and more than a century later it arrived at the Vintners Hall. Apart from the feeling of awe at its pedigree, it was the most sublime nectar.

On 2 June 1932 A.J. wrote to me, 'I shall probably be helping to start yet another society next week.' This was the Wine and Food Society which he and André Simon finally founded together in the following year. To A.J. it was both a good and a bad thing. There is no doubt that the amount of work which the society entailed ate into his time for writing. As his brother Julian has put it, 'His love of entertaining and of being entertained grew by what it fed on and as the Wine and Food Society flourished it filled his life pleasantly but in a way that had nothing to do with literature,' and A.J. himself wrote to Julian, 'Alas. What dozens of distractions I have invented to persuade me from my own purpose.'

Margaret and I quickly joined. Regional dinners were held regularly, most of them very good; and two I remember specially. A Russian dinner in the beautiful dining-room of the Ritz; it was customary at the end for the chef to appear to receive congratulations – the chef that evening was a quite young, dark, good-looking Frenchman. He acknowledged the applause with aplomb and, before retiring to his kitchen, added, 'May I say that I think the standard of female beauty here this evening is remarkably high.'

The other, the eleventh meeting in October 1934, marked the centenary of the death of Antoine Carême. It was held in the banqueting hall of the Brighton Pavilion where Carême had been chef to George IV. There were eleven courses and twelve wines reproducing, it was made clear, not a banquet but an everyday dinner put before the King. A.J. decorated the tables with his collection of silver snuff boxes. Obviously we ate and drank a great deal, and at the end of the meal I put one of the snuff boxes in my pocket as a joke. Shortly afterwards I handed it with a flourish to A.J., who said, 'Oh good, now only five are missing.'

Another important event for those who cared was the appearance of Barry Neame at the Hind's Head in Bray. Previously head of the Savoy laundry, an unlikely provenance, he rapidly became one of the most remarkable hoteliers in the country. The food, the wine, and the comfort of the whole establishment made it an oasis of supreme pleasure. To drive out to dine there was like a pilgrimage, which could happily be repeated as frequently as one's inclination and one's pocket allowed. Of course, A.J. was closely involved. He first told us of it, and was frequently there.

Barry Neame was a large man whose *bonhomie* was genuine and endearing. Physically he bore some resemblance to a pleasant version of Strindberg. A bonus for us was that he considered word of mouth to be the best form of advertising, and to this end he gave occasional dinner parties to which he invited representatives from different walks of life; Margaret and I represented publishing. Of course it worked. The Hind's Head was never far from one's mind and recommended to anyone considered worthwhile who had the means of getting there. When we were invited we were shamelessly pampered; oysters and champagne on arrival before going up to dress, a superb dinner, a comfortable night, and back to the grind the next morning.

My last memory of Barry came from a telephone call. 'We're getting a bit low on whites; could you come down for a tasting?' Of course I could. It was a beautiful day in early summer. There were ten of us, including Barry and A.J., and we sat down to a simple meal at a long table under an oak tree in the garden. We tasted eleven wines. At the end a photograph was taken of us looking rather pleased with life round a table loaded with one hundred and ten glasses; I raise the one hundred and eleventh in his memory.

By 1932 A.J. had been forced to give up the lovely house in Bedford Square. The First Edition Club went into liquidation, and was refounded in the church hall of St George's, Hawksmoor's handsome church unique in having a statue of George II on top of the steeple. There was a lot of sadness and muttering that things would never be the same again, but really, once one got used to the change, the new quarters were very pleasant.

Soon after the move I looked in and found A.J. talking to a smallish man with a fresh complexion and boyish mien. I was introduced to Lord Alfred Douglas, who was naturally not in the least interested in me since he had things to talk about with A.J., whom he knew well, but I was of course interested in him. Two years passed and by chance the same thing happened – except that Lord Alfred was alone, awaiting A.J.'s return, and we talked about nothing in particular. But I was shocked; the face was grey, not pink, and it had fallen. In twenty-four months the boyish figure had become stooped – and I thought silently of *The Portrait of Dorian Gray*.

I gathered that the liquidation in Bedford Square had cost the original backers quite a lot of money, because I was subjected one day to a tirade from one of them, the chairman, a pompous old man called Dr G.C. Williamson. I understood that he was not pleased, but otherwise had no idea what he was talking about. Whatever their loss, most of the backers accepted it philosophically, especially Lord Esher and Albert Ehrman.

Ehrman, with his secretary, occupied a small office in Holborn at the north end of the Old Bailey; since La Belle Sauvage was near the south end, we were only three minutes apart. He was a small, dark man with beautiful deep brown eyes and a pointed nose which gave him a slightly foxy look (I mean literally, not unkindly, since I had great admiration and affection for him). Apart from his business he had one abiding passion: book collecting. He lived in Hertfordshire and his splendid treasures – bindings, type specimens, the first printed books from towns all over the world – were called after the village where they were housed: the Broxbourne Library.

He developed the endearing habit of ringing me up and saying 'I've just got something I think might interest you,' and I would reply that I would come round as soon as possible. Since he was a diamond merchant, getting into his office was rather like gaining admittance to Fort Knox, but once I was in and sat down he would carefully unwrap his latest acquisition. It might be a Lyons binding or the first book printed in Beirut; he would handle it with all the love of a parent for a new-born child and I would be the first to admire it before he took it home to Broxbourne.

Many years later he proposed me for the Roxburghe Club, that remarkable assemblage of bibliophiles who have either inherited great libraries or formed noteworthy collections themselves, or both. Since the membership is limited to forty, a candidate cannot be elected until another member dies; hence entry can take a considerable time. I felt sad that when after the usual lapse I was received into what I find the most interesting body of like-minded people I have ever come across, Albert Ehrman was dead.

Another event in that remarkable year was the marriage of Alec Waugh to a wealthy Australian girl, Joan Churnside, at the Old Church in Chelsea. We took a pew behind two women whom we knew and who were great friends, Theodora Benson and Margaret Lane (now Countess of Huntingdon), both writers. The former was striking, the latter a great beauty. Joan was on time but Alec was twenty minutes late. As time ticked away and the guests sat in mute expectancy, one of these two said to the other in a conversational tone which echoed through the heavy silence, 'There, I told you he wouldn't turn up.' But he did eventually, and after their honeymoon they went to live in Joseph Conrad's house at Bishopsbourne, in Kent, where they were extremely hospitable.

There can seldom have been two brothers so unalike as Alec and Evelyn. Of the younger one's greatness as a writer there is no question, but remarkably few people have anything good to say of him as a man. Alec was the opposite, a generous friend, yet as a writer, although he was able, he was not in the same class as his younger brother; and with perhaps two exceptions, he was a better travel writer than he was a novelist. They were both small, while their father, Arthur, was a tall and dignified figure, a publisher – head of Chapman & Hall, in which both Alec and Evelyn served for short stints. I did not know the father well enough to ask him what he thought of his younger son, but Alec told me of one occasion when he was as angry as he was bewildered. Evelyn lived in the country, and if he was in town would descend without warning on his father's Hampstead house for the night. In due course Waugh senior went to bed while Evelyn wanted to stay up longer to read. Later he fell asleep and a cigarette dropped from his fingers on to the carpet. He woke up to find the library in flames. The fire brigade came and put out the fire, but the damage done to the splendid collection of books can be imagined. Some time was spent clearing up, the firemen were given beer, but where was the culprit who had caused the disaster? Amidst the confusion Evelyn had packed his bag and left.

Through Alec we met Peggy Wood, the enchanting star who in 1929 had been the hit of Noel Coward's *Bitter Sweet*. Her first husband was John V.A. Weaver, a small, dark man whom I liked and two of whose books I published – a straight novel and a novel in verse called *Trial Balance*. He was also a very good golfer – a combination with poetry not found since until Patric Dickinson. Alas, *TB* finished him not long after. In November 1932 Peggy starred with Basil Rathbone in *Tonight or Never* (a musical which I don't think lasted very long), and after the first performance we went to her dressing-room to congratulate her. More people came in, and then a photographer for whose benefit Peggy formed a trio with Gladys Calthrop, who had designed the *décor*, and Noël Coward. Having done his work, the photographer got out his notebook and pencil, saying, 'Mrs Calthrop, yes; Miss Wood of course; and who is the gentleman?' There was a stunned silence, and then Coward in a high falsetto screamed, 'He doesn't know me! He doesn't know me!'

Musically we enjoyed a very full life of opera, concerts and recitals throughout the thirties. I cannot remember many events and a list of them would be very boring if I could, but some memories are bad, and it is perhaps for that reason that they have stuck in my mind. For instance, the disappointment of hearing Schnabel who was so widely heralded as the greatest living interpreter of Beethoven; that, indeed, he may have been, but his playing seemed so dry that it was like a lecture from a schoolmaster. And a prom at the Queen's Hall when we sat behind the orchestra and were facing Sir Henry Wood, of blessed memory, who was conducting. He is always said to have referred to those two great composers 'Ravl and Diboosy', and that evening he was having a go at *Bolero*. Unfortunately in the constant repetition one half of the orchestra got two bars behind the other, and throughout the resulting cacophony the thunderclouds on Sir Henry's face grew so black that we feared for his health.

A much happier and superbly successful event was Gigli's first London *Tosca* in 1934. Phyllis Deeping took us, and she looked very impressive in her usual green and wearing a tiara. It was a Friday night, and when we went down to Sevenoaks the next morning, we were still bewitched by the beauty of Gigli's voice. Describing its effect on us, I said to father how lucky he was to have heard Caruso so often. With a far-away look and a nostalgic tone, he said 'Ah, but you should have heard Jean de Reszke.'* I nearly struck him.

A few years later there was a concert which was memorable for an unusual reason in addition to the wonderful music. It was announced that Sir Thomas Beecham would give a performance of Berlioz's *Te Deum* and we decided to go with our friends the Renas. Composed in 1849, this great work in honour of the victims of the revolution the previous year was originally intended to be performed in the open air in the Place de la Concorde. Berlioz made sure that it could be heard by everyone and, given the full Beecham treatment, the vast noise which generated within the confines of the Queen's Hall can be imagined. It was marvellous, it was electrifying, and when the interval came we turned to one another chattering excitedly; not one syllable could be heard – we were all stone deaf.

Another author whose work came out from Cassell's at this time was J.S. Collis, whose elder brother, Maurice, had recently done very well with a book on Burma. Throughout his life Jack was only once to enjoy anything like the same commercial success, but I had an enormous admiration for his prose and I tried very hard. Although the company accounts were no concern of mine, I do not suppose that we made any money out of the three books which he brought to me in the years before the war; I persisted, and this was Act I of a two-act drama.

Very early in my career I came to believe strongly that since one gains – or perhaps I should say *can* gain – a livelihood from publishing as profitably as possible the works of authors of varying literary merit

* Distinguished Polish tenor, 1850–1925.

(some of no merit at all, but good sellers), it should be a matter of conscience to put something back by publishing works of value but little profit. It is only possible to carry this out with safety if there is a sheet anchor to help in weathering storms. There have been a number of good publishers, Grant Richards and Martin Secker among them, who have tried to publish to their own taste without a sheet anchor, and they eventually foundered. Our sheet anchor was provided by our dictionaries and our educational and medical books; if these took care of the overheads there was more room for personal idiosyncrasy in the general list and it was possible, without looking at the figures on the bottom line, to do things which seemed of value. Allegiance to Jack Collis was an example of my contention. I was happy in my certainty that he would never write a bad book, and I feel that it may have been of some help to him during this period to know that whatever he was writing, there was an enthusiastic publisher waiting for it. He was a man whose company I always enjoyed, but he could be peculiarly secretive about his life. For instance, although I went to his cottage at Otford, near Sevenoaks, and played golf with him on the goats' course nearby, it was some time before we came to know that all the while he had a wife and two children in London.

The search for new authors was constant, and I published a number who were not always entirely unsuccessful but are now forgotten. One first novel was by an author who has later achieved considerable renown: Lawrence Durrell's *The Pied Piper of Lovers* appeared in 1935. It did not do very well – despite a lovely jacket which I can still recall – and I was understandably not offered anything further by the author who prefers not to remember this book in his *Who's Who* entry.

We remained in touch with both Charles Hasse and Walter Churchill. The former, having made his mark in the film business, moved into one of the delightful eighteenth-century houses in Hammersmith Terrace, just above Hammersmith Bridge; the neighbour on his right was A.P. Herbert, and both of them always gave parties on Boat Race day. As long as he lived there, Charles always asked Margaret and me to watch the race, because we are among the millions who have never had anything to do with rowing but are glued to the Boat Race, the reason for which I have never been able to understand.

As soon as the boats had shot Hammersmith Bridge and disappeared up river we all crowded round the wireless to listen to John Snagge's commentary. Charles had six rockets set up in his garden and as soon as Cambridge had won – they were in the middle of a successful streak even longer than that recently enjoyed by Oxford – he set light to the blue paper and a hiss of triumph leapt into the sky. Next door Herbert, then M.P. for Cambridge which was one of the independent university constituencies the abolition of which was regretted by many, always had a grandstand of tubular scaffolding erected for his guests. One year five of Charles's rockets ascended to heaven rejoicing, but the sixth had other ideas and after devious gyrations landed, still burning, at the feet of Clement Attlee in the stand next door. Herbert could be very funny, but Charles said that he was neither amused nor amusing on this occasion.

Until Walter married and set up his own establishment in Leamington, his parents invited us every year to Malvern during the festival, in which the plays, produced by Barry Jackson, were usually extremely good. Our visit was to us one of the high points of the year. His father, a large very quiet man, was in his study much of the time, while his mother, who was a formidable enchantress, talked for hours in the summer house – for they always seemed to be halcyon days. Walter and I played golf, or we walked on the Malvern Hills, and Peter, the middle brother who was like a fish in the water, taught me to dive – something which I had previously been unable to master.

Their house in Malvern was large and comfortable. Nevertheless, there was a time when they thought of moving and went *en famille* to look at various properties in the neighbourhood. They had a German *au pair* girl at the time who came along for the ride. In the gloomy Victorian servants' quarters of one property Mrs Churchill exclaimed, 'My God, it's like the bowels of a ship!' and Walter heard a German voice from the rear, 'Wass ist powells?'

Walter had joined the Auxiliary Air Force in 1932 and was in 605 (County of Warwick) Squadron commanded by Lord Willoughby de Broke, who died recently at a great age. The following year he asked us if we would like to go to the Hendon Air Display, as they were going to do a bombing demonstration flying Wapiti biplanes. The day was wet and windy and we huddled in our car. Eventually Walter found us. He was giggling. They had already been airborne when it was decided that the weather was too bad for the operation to be carried out and they were ordered to return to base; no – repeat no – bombs were to be dropped. Walter had little confidence in his observer-bomb aimer, so he was more angry than surprised when, immediately after receipt of the message, he felt the plane shudder. The wretched man behind him had pulled the plug. As soon as they had landed a group of them had set off by car, in some trepidation, to find out where the bomb had finished up, and eventually they found a small crater in the middle of Hendon High Street. As they were regarding it ruefully, Walter was attacked by an irate old lady who brandished her umbrella under his nose and barked, 'Young man, can't you find *anywhere* else to drop your bombs?'

I have remarked before that at this time we did not and could not save any money, which led to our missing one heaven-sent opportunity. We had met and become friendly with two figures in film production, Jack and Winifred Holmes. Jack, tall and dark, died many years ago, but Winifred remains the small energetic figure that she has always been. They knew in Paris Catharine Hessling, who at one time had been the housekeeper-companion of Renoir. The aged painter was by then so crippled with arthritis that he could no longer grip a brush and she used to strap it to his hand. The time came when he could no longer move, and she painted under his instruction, putting each stroke of colour on to the canvas as he wished. When he died in 1919 she was left with a considerable number of paintings. Later she became a star of the silent screen, and was Nana in the first film made of Zola's great novel in 1926.

But then she became involved in a scandal in the same way as Fatty Arbuckle in Hollywood; there was a party at her flat in which someone died or was killed, and as a result no studio would offer her a part again. Unable to get further employment, she wished to dispose of the canvasses which she had, and the price was £50 for a Renoir and £25 for one which she had painted under the master's instruction. There was one condition: that a buyer should promise not to sell his picture during his lifetime; we would willingly have taken the oath, but we had not got the money.

There were various changes in the editorial department, as a result of which John Marks arrived. I had not known him particularly well at Cambridge, but he quickly became a close friend and occupied a special place in my existence until his death. He eventually left for a better job at Chatto's, and became features editor of *Night and Day*, the brilliant but ill-fated periodical modelled on *The New Yorker*. It had a constellation of superb contributors, as may be seen by the selections from it recently published, but it did not catch the public taste as it deserved and finally foundered, fatally holed by a libel action. While it was still alive, it seemed a natural early call for an artist who had just arrived from Poland, Feliks Topolski. John suggested that he should come to see me, and I believe that I was the first publisher to commission jackets from him, before he was the famous and much admired painter which he became; many will have seen the rooms beneath the arches by Waterloo Station decorated with frescoes depicting the world as he saw it. Feliks, with his great flair and free flowing style, used quickly to produce four or five roughs, all so good that it was difficult to decide which to choose.

One of 1933's events on our list was the appearance of the first volume of Ernest Newman's monumental life of Wagner. I put this in the hands of the Kynoch Press which, under Bobby Simon with Harry Carter as designer, had come right up as a printing house. They made a fine job of it, a beautiful small quarto. Newman was a crotchety old thing, a severe though fair critic, who could be a charming man. When I first went down to Tadworth, near Epsom, to tea with him and his wife, I found him doubled up with laughter at a record of Donald Duck and other similar voices singing the male quartet from *Rigoletto*. He was always kind to me and appreciative of the production of his book. Unfortunately the story had a sad ending which I had better record now. Volume II appeared in good order, but volume III was delivered during the Second World War and the last volume not long after. Under the stringency of paper rationing the office decided that they would have to cut down the size of the third volume, which appeared as an immaculate but smaller brother to its predecessors. By 1947 it might have been possible to have returned the final volume to the original size, but this would merely have compounded the disaster. *Wagner* was Newman's life work and the disparate size of the volumes infuriated him and he would never speak to any of us again; I cannot say that I blame him.

At the end of 1933 the first *Sunday Times* Book Exhibition took place at

Sunderland House in Curzon Street, for one week in November. Publishers took stands on which they exhibited their wares. It was a good idea, and the introduction to the catalogue said, 'This exhibition is an impressive demonstration of the success with which through difficult times, they [the publishers] are keeping up the best traditions of English book publishing'. The literary editor at the time was Cyril Lakin, whom, with his wife Vera, we knew well; he was very able as well as charming. Later he left the literary scene, went into politics, and was tragically killed in a motor accident in France. He knew about my book-collecting and asked me if I would mount an exhibition of rarities as a sort of icing on the cake. It was a fascinating task and I really went to town. The display was in four parts: the first showed masterpieces of our literature from a couple of Caxtons to Oscar Wilde; the second was autograph manuscripts of modern authors from Auden to Henry Williamson; the third was bookbinding from the seventeenth century to the present; and finally a Century of Best Sellers, from Scott to *The Good Companions*.

Through this, my first exhibition, I made a number of friends and met many interesting people. The trade were wonderful to me, and indeed they have been ever since. The two great collectors whom I had not known before were Sir John Murray and Sir Leicester Harmsworth. The firm of Murray had not only kept the manuscripts of their authors, such as Byron, but were themselves for generations great collectors. Somewhat deaf, Sir John Murray received me with a patrician dignity softened by an enormous kindness. He listened to what I had to say, gently gave his consent, and the details were worked out with his nephew, Jock, who runs the firm so ably today. Sir Leicester was a near neighbour of ours on Campden Hill and the treasures of his library were legendary. I went to call upon him with trepidation; first, I needed the loan of some of his treasures very badly, and secondly I was in awe of a man who had used his wealth to assemble such wonderful books, the material objects about which I cared most in life, and I could not disguise my feelings. A big man, old, four square, crippled with, I think, arthritis, he sat motionless with his eyes fixed upon me as I said my piece. Then he said firmly, 'Young man, flattery will get you nowhere.' But it was not flattery, it was admiration; and at any rate, he lent me everything I wanted, which was a lot.

Ted Dring of Quaritch I never forget, and forty years later we found ourselves members of the same golf club. But I made one particular friend for life, P.H. Muir of Elkin Mathews and (then) Marrot. Percy was a great and dear man whom I had already met through the *B.C.Q.* but had never known so well as I came to then, and he remained in my deepest affections until he died.

A Century of Best-Sellers interested Maurice Marston, the founder of the National Book Council, and he asked me if I would write an introduction on what constitutes a best-seller and on author-publisher relations during the past hundred years, and he issued the whole as a pamphlet. Few people remember Maurice Marston now. It was his idea that there should be an organization representing every aspect of the

British book, as distinct from sectional bodies such as P.E.N. – also, of course, a British foundation. He founded the National Book Council in 1925 and ran it pretty much as a one-man show in Henrietta Street in the face of the 'unqualified resentment' of the Publishers' Association. In 1945 it was considered a good thing, John Hadfield was appointed as the first director, funds were raised, a lease taken on the then bomb-damaged Albemarle Street property (a lovely house which used to be Grillon's Hotel where Louis Philippe stayed), and the name was changed to the National Book League. (Recently changed again to the Book Trust). Marston remained secretary. He was a gentle soul, a woolly bear – but it was like a Corinthian Casual being made to play as striker in a First League side; the increased pace, the wider scope seemed too much for him, and he quietly faded out. But when we think of the great days and the considerable influence of the N.B.L., let us remember that it was Maurice Marston's idea in the first place.

From the Sunderland House beginnings I found that I had what might be called a mania – with, I hope, a little flair – for organizing exhibitions, of which there were to be a considerable number in the years to come. With an office job to keep going, it was hard work but sheer joy. I always learnt an enormous amount, however well I thought I knew the subject – someone said 'If you want to learn something, write a book about it' – and I also got immense satisfaction from gathering together and setting out for public delectation artefacts of such beauty and interest.

The *Sunday Times* show continued the following year and was held in the ballroom of Grosvenor House. The main theme of my exhibition was music. Here Stefan Zweig, whose wonderful collection of autographs has now been presented to the British Library, gave me enormous help and was most enthusiastic. He put me in touch with a number of collectors of music and himself lent several including his own favourite, Mozart's *Das Veilchen*. Musical manuscripts and first editions were not fashionable then, and I think that the exhibits surprised a lot of people because they had not really thought about them before. Percy Muir lent an uncut copy of the first edition of Beethoven's Ninth Symphony, and he wryly remarked to me, 'My price at the moment for that is £25, yet artistically it is on a level with any of Shakespeare's plays – and imagine what you would have to pay for a first Quarto of that if you could find one.' In the catalogue I dropped one quite unnecessary clanger. A dealer in music – not Harold Reeves from whom father had bought so much Handel – generously lent Chopin's passport. In the haste of getting everything ready, I failed to do my homework and in the catalogue gratuitously added a note: 'What a pity he never came.' The irate owner rang me up the next morning and I grovelled, because of course Chopin came to London and spent the last year of his life there, consulting doctors about his lungs and giving recitals, the piano on which he played being treasured in the Polish Embassy today. It taught me a sharp lesson; check every fact, and never write a word more than necessary.

The third and last *Sunday Times* exhibition in 1935 was held at Dorland

Hall in Lower Regent Street, and my display was in two parts. One was
devoted to calligraphy – thirty-seven specimens of the handwriting of
living authors who mostly had no interest in how they wrote, and
twenty-nine examples of people who were conscious of and careful
about the style of their hands, such as Eric Gill and Francis Meynell. The
other part was a show of the best books in print on every imaginable
subject chosen by an expert. The books on architecture were chosen by
Sir Edwin Lutyens, food Marcel Boulestin, the countryside Glough
Williams Ellis, and so on; how I persuaded them all to do it I do not
know.

I have mentioned Stefan Zweig's enthusiasm over the music section
of the second exhibition, and I should explain how it came about that he
willingly gave me so much help.

When we published his *Fouché* and the very successful *Marie
Antoinette* he was still living with his wife Fredericke in his beautiful
house, Kapuzinerberg, in Salzburg; he and Max Reinhardt were the two
local celebrities. An exchange of letters and cards began, in which he
invited Margaret and me to visit him and repeated the invitation several
times. The opportunity passed, and he soon came closer than being just
an agreeable correspondent.

More and more harassed by the situation around him he had, he said,
lost the joy of developing his home and his collection; he could not
concentrate, he needed to make his life simpler and more mobile; he had
to leave. 'It is Rome or London that attracts me most,' he wrote to a
friend. The latter won and on 20 October 1933 he arrived at Brown's
Hotel. Within a week he had taken a flat at 11 Portland Place and,
although he returned unhappily to Austria for a while, early in the New
Year this had become his home.

As father in his memoirs put it, 'He and I and my son Desmond
became close friends. We lunched together, Stefan and Desmond talked
art, which was the only thing Stefan cared for outside his work.' While
up to a point this is true, I think that father is unfair to himself; his own
interest in art was extremely strong, though it would be right to say that
he kept it very much within self-imposed guidelines. Yet without in any
way minimizing father's admiration of and affection for Stefan, there
was building up away from the office a quite different relationship
between him and me which I cannot claim was unique but which was
certainly unusual. I was the master in the sense that I was the publisher,
but I was the pupil as a younger man sitting at the feet of one whose
philosophy I respected and whose work I admired. I was later to find
myself in something like the same position with Winston Churchill.

I cannot now recall the Portland Place flat, but early in 1936 Stefan
moved into a newly built block round the corner at 49 Hallam Street, and
this I remember as clearly as my own home. Before the *Anschluss* there
was no restriction on his having whatever he wished sent from Austria,
though in fact he had but few of his treasures; Salzburg was *vorbei*. There
was his large Blake drawing, and his desk – what a desk! A noble piece
of furniture which had belonged to Beethoven.

At both flats it became a habit for me several times a week to drop in on my way home and sit for as long as possible, talking and talking. Sometimes his secretary, Lotte, whom he eventually married, was there, often not; sometimes an old friend, Victor Fleischer, came in, and once his then wife, Fredericke. There always seemed to be a sadness about him as though, having left his beloved Salzburg, he was a voyager who might one day have to resume his reluctant travels. I told him once that my ambition – quite impossible, but I had a good go – was to own a first edition of every work that Voltaire published.

'Whatever for?' he asked, 'Selection is the secret. Look, I have reduced my autograph collection to the size of one suitcase, so that if I have to go I can carry it with me.'

The flat was so familiar to me that when years later I produced Stefan's works in a smaller format I named them the Hallam edition.

Of course, we also met outside. He was fond of Parmigiano's, a comfortable Italian restaurant not far from Hallam Street which was destroyed in the Blitz. And in 1937 he asked me if I would like to go to a Toscanini rehearsal at Queen's Hall in Langham Place, also a casualty of the war. Toscanini would not allow anyone at his rehearsals except his closest friends (of whom Stefan was one) and their closest friends. The maestro was rehearsing Brahms' *Requiem* with the B.B.C. orchestra. On the previous day they had played so badly that he had stormed out, and no one knew whether he would turn up this morning or not. Paul Beard, the well known and distinguished leader, addressed them and said that if the maestro appeared they were to behave as though nothing had happened.

Shortly after that, sitting alone with Stefan at the back of the circle, I saw through the side window a car draw up; Signora Toscanini had told her husband that he had a duty and brought him to the hall herself. After a brief delay he marched on to the podium amidst a ripple of applause from the players discreetly beating bows on instruments. They started on the superb theme *The grass withereth, the flower fadeth*; they were nervous and played abominably. After a few minutes Toscanini laid down his baton and cursed them; he cursed them in English, in Italian, in French and in German. Then, verbally exhausted, he went back to work. The effect was miraculous; from then on they played like angels.

As we spent so much time together, I felt particularly close to Stefan. It may be sentimental, it may be hindsight, but I used to think that when I left he seemed a little more at peace.

10   The Beloved Country

We were bound to go one day to Spain, that great country which is a complex enigma of similarities and dissimilarities: 'Varied but one the land, varied but one the people,' as Salvador de Madariaga has wisely said. But it was the publication of *Death in the Afternoon* in 1932 which made up our minds for us. As members of the generation which had seen English prose miraculously changed before our eyes, like so many we read it at once.

During the spring we learned Spanish. A Catalan, Francesc Vinyals, came to Gordon Place to give us lessons; Margaret, a brilliant linguist, found Castilian simple and later in the year he taught her Catalan. From a very good teacher he became a very good friend and was to be later drawn into Cassell's. We decided that we would begin by driving to Bilbao for the *fiesta*, which is in the early days of May, because Hemingway said that there they prefer bulls to men, so that the former are always of the best. Disposing of the little MG because we had found the previous year that her short chassis was unsuitable for long distance touring, we bought a second-hand Lancia Lambda, the famous 'flying bedstead', considered one of the great designs in the history of the motor car. It was ideal for driving in mountains because its perpendicular spring gave it a look like a taxi and, as one writer has put it, 'took the corkscrew turns with the rhythm of a fast pendulum'. Ours had several faults which were to plague us, but it admirably stayed the course.

The printed notes sent to us by the AA with the triptyque (required in those days) would be a surprise to motorists visiting Spain today. The two pieces of advice which I remember most clearly were (1) take Keatings powder to sanitize dirty hotel beds, and (2) never drive at night because of bandits.

We had to leave very early in the morning to catch the car ferry at Dover; it was a bitterly cold morning and I left the car running while I fetched out the bags. Now I must admit that the Lambda was not the quietest of cars, so I was not altogether surprised when the bedroom window opposite shot up and there emerged the head of Clifford-Smith, an irascible gentleman who was something in the V. & A.

'Must you make such a bloody awful noise at this hour of the morning?' he roared.

Mildly I replied, 'I am so sorry to have disturbed you; we are leaving in a minute for the Continent.'

'Continent? What Continent?' he shouted and slammed his window down again in umbrage.

We were to drive many times to and from Spain, and we tried never to go by the same road so as to see as much as possible of France. On this occasion we went by the most direct route, and stopped at the Michelin depot in Bordeaux because we had discovered an ugly blister in one of the front tyres. Putting a sleeve in it so that there was no danger of a burst, they said that if we could call at the factory in Clermont Ferrand we were sure to get complete satisfaction. Since we came back by the Mediterranean border, Port Bou, it was simple for us to do as they had suggested. As we drove up to the factory gates a foreman appeared, I showed him the tyre, and saying 'Sit there' he drove the car away; less than ten minutes later he drove back with a brand-new tyre fitted with the compliments of the company. I was impressed. We stayed the night in town, and I was even more impressed – and still am, when I think of it – by the little basilica of Notre Dame du Port, a superb small Romanesque church. It must have been a major saint's day, for in the evening Mass was being sung and the tiny church was packed. Several hundred candles made the rugged dignity of the architectural style which I admire above all glow as if it had a patina of gold.

Someone said that Europe ends at the Pyrenees, but I cannot find out who; but the reverse – that 'Africa begins at the Pyrenees' – is attributed to Alexandre Dumas – is true, for south of them lies the sometimes parched, sometimes cold mountains and plains of El Cid, a land held in fief for eight centuries by the Moors – so much so that the Duke of Alba, when ambassador in London, said to me that there is not a family in the country without Moorish blood in it, including his own. Apart from the attributions about which I get so sentimental, I cannot believe that any sensitive person can cross the international bridge at Irun, with the threatening hills leaning over him higher and higher on his left, without some feeling of expectancy, of meeting for the first time something special, something which one will reject or be rejected by, or love deeply for ever.

We had booked rooms at the Torrontegui, a comfortable hotel opposite the church of St Nicholas de Bari on the Paseo del Arenal. Now long demolished, it was a fine piece of early twentieth-century architecture, featuring miradors – those balconies which are completely glazed in addition to the windows of the room itself. The place was like an oven so I set to, opening all the outside windows. They were the type of which one pushes the bottom half up until the pawls each side click into their retainers. It had been such a hot day that the frames were swollen and, hard as I slammed them up, I could not get the pawls to engage; they were immovable, firmly stuck, so I left them. Hurriedly, as instructed, dusting Keatings into the beds which were as immaculately clean as beds in Spain always are, we went down for dinner at about ten o'clock; the first person we saw on entering the dining-room, dining alone, was Papa Hemingway. The room was on the first floor and when, after our first and very good meal in Spain, we left, we were met by the manageress who hissed, 'Don't go downstairs; the police are looking for you!' What had happened was that in the cool of the midnight air the wooden frames had shrunk and the windows had crashed down, showering the crowded street below with broken glass. It was only the second year of the Republic; the police were still jumpy and they had entered the hotel, suspecting sabotage.

The Bilbao *fiesta* always begins on 2 May. We became completely enamoured of the *fiesta brava* and were to see many *corridas* in the future. In the fifty years following this first experience I have attended over sixty *corridas* in Spain, Mexico and South America, and have seen every *torero* of note from Marcial Lalanda (the best in 1933) to Antonio Ordoñez, the greatest of the next generation – including Manolete and El Cordobés, names which publicity may have made known to those who generally are not interested.

To many people, the majority of whom have never seen it, bull-fighting is simple cruelty, an abstract which can be absolute or relative. If I like bull-fighting and boxing, I cannot be absolutely opposed to cruelty; and relativity at once brings in the question of personal taste. There are people who will abuse a child, maltreat a dog, but feel slightly sick at the thought of a bull being killed; but then, man is not only the most cruel animal in the world, he is the most hypocritical. I deplore the use of horses in the ring, I regret that their fate is dictated by technical necessity – which does not in any way detract from the cruelty; and the fact that most horses are shipped over from the U.S.A. for the purpose contains an element of hypocrisy.

Perhaps we all split hairs; my own objection is to the peaceful country occupation of fishing. To catch a hook in the mouth of a fish and, if it is a big one, 'play' it for hours seems to me to be the height of cruelty. Don't anyone try to tell me that a fish, being cold blooded, has no feeling – someone might as well pretend that a horse positively enjoys being hit in the flank by two and a half tons of bull travelling at the speed of an express train. At least a matador takes on something his own size – in fact something several times as large as himself – and is in considerable personal danger, which can hardly be said of a fisherman sitting in comfort on a leafy bank.

Since views on this subject will forever differ and I have no desire to give offence, I will write no more about tauromachy – except in one short instance in which politics are concerned. It was prophesied, I remember, that the eventual rise of Spain's professional footballers to eminence would spell death to the *fiesta brava*, but this proved to be untrue. Both today enjoy favour, and at the bull-ring only one thing has changed: the way of the world. Half a century ago, with no television and little football, the bulls were almost the only attraction and the *corrida* was a wonderful spectacle. For many years the ring was a blaze of colour; the vast crowds wore their best clothes, the ladies large hats or, if they were near the front, combs, mantillas and bright shawls which they spread in front of them on the *barreras*. Today that has all passed, partly due to the development of tourism. Not only are hats seldom worn, but all sense of formality, of occasion, has departed. Shorts and T-shirts are commonplace; only the fighters were the same beautiful traditional hand-embroidered garments – and still pass their parade capes up to their girlfriends sitting in the front row.

During the day we drove, of course, to the caves of Altamira, now closed to visitors. The first view of prehistoric art is overwhelming. Those who have been there know that, the caves being low, there are trenches dug so that visitors may see the paintings in comfort. I presumed that the men who made these lovely designs must have been tiny; but I was wrong, for Marvin Harris, in his remarkable *Cannibals and Kings*, points out that the average height of a man 30,000 years ago was five feet eleven inches. Did man, as he painted by the light of flickering flames, move about on all fours, or has the detritus of ages raised the level of the floors?

If there is a paradise in Spain, it must be just down the road from the caves: Santillana del Mar, in which nothing has been built since 1750. Chickens scampered in the marble halls of the small palaces which were then occupied by farmers, and I had hopes of acquiring one of them some time. But now the whole little town is, most properly, a national monument, and one has to be very rich indeed to live in one of the lovely houses and fill it, as it should be, with contemporary Spanish furniture.

As we were in a hurry to get to Madrid, we decided to ignore the AA's second piece of advice and set off from Bilbao in the dark and get as far as we could. The Lancia roared up the mountain's hairpin bends most satisfactorily, over the crest, and the descent to Vitoria began. There was a level-crossing ahead and as we approached it we could see a lantern being swung from side to side. Ah, we thought, perhaps the AA was right after all: bandits. We had to stop as two figures were blocking the road; it turned out that they were plate-layers who were hungry and asked if we could spare them any food.

On the road south to Madrid the place which always fascinated me was Templeque. The main street, as narrow as a country lane, is a hubbub of varicoloured life; carts, mules, donkeys and children indiscriminately jostled, dark-skinned women carrying bundles on their heads, and the air loud with the hooting of cars threading their way through at walking-pace. Today there is a by-pass; and, dashing down it, I think nostalgically of the women, children old men and animals who now have to themselves that hot, dusty street, threading through the small Moorish town that slumbers in the sun.

Madrid was Madrid: a city which I like rather than love as one might a distant cousin, though one's first sight of *Las Meniñas* is something which is ever memorable. My initial encounter with a Spanish policeman was a heart-warming experience. Having worked out the route to our hotel, I was dismayed to find, crossing the wide, extremely busy Puerta del Sol where the traffic has been described as '*un poco maniaco'*, that the street I wanted was No Entry. I stopped dead and all the traffic built up around me, hooting. A policeman appeared, blowing his whistle and shouting, 'Get back! This gentleman does us the honour of visiting our country and all you do is hoot at him; get the hell out of it!' Thanking him profusely, I shot up the very street I was trying to avoid. There was no going back; I had to endure the deserved derision of all the cars coming up the right way. Half a century later the traffic is worse and I don't think the reception would be quite the same.

A night spent in Zaragoza produced a baffling experience: we saw there was a Clark Gable film on and decided to go. It started at eleven o'clock and we missed the first few minutes. It was, of course, dubbed into Spanish, but, although we could understand it, neither of us could gather what they were on about. In the middle there was an interval and everyone went out to have a drink; when we got back to our seats the film started again with the credit titles – no wonder we could not make it out: the projectionist had shown the second half first.

While I was there I fell in love with the Pilar, which vies with Santiago de Compostela as being my favourite church in Spain. It is dark, mysterious and very lovely; one tiptoes lest the peace might be disturbed and no sound may echo about the black wood with its occasional gleam of gold in the choir; much more beautiful than the cathedral, despite the latter's Goya frescos.

A quick look at Lérida and on to Barcelona which, unlike the capital, I think is a lovely city. Today there are still flower stalls down the middle of the Ramblas, but half a century ago there were infinitely more; it was a riot of colour from side to side and one end to the other. And off the Ramblas the Barrio Chino enticing with its web of narrow lanes where one is happy to get lost. One night we wandered into a club full of sailors where an attractive young thing was singing a remarkably dirty song and making the most obscene gestures with a large doll; I suppose we should have been shocked, but it was in fact extremely funny.

On a higher level we were lucky enough at a large music hall to see the great Pastora Imperio dance. Once the mistress of Alfonso XIII, she had become a legend in her lifetime. She was a little past it by then and was not going to attempt anything dramatic; but her deportment was so gracefully arrogant and every movement of her hands so beautiful that everyone sat in mute admiration. Accompanying her, sitting at the back of the stage dressed in black with his Cordobese over his eyes, was the equally great Carlos Montoya. To see the most famous dancer and hear the most famous *flamenco* guitarist: fortune could not have favoured us more richly.

We had been so occupied with the bulls in Bilbao that we did not have a chance to see in its native territory *pelota* (simply 'ball'), in the Americas *Jai Alai*, the fastest and, for me, the most exciting court game in the world. But this was remedied in Barcelona.

Although Spain has become a holiday playground for so many million foreigners. I do not suppose that the game is any better known now that it was when we first saw it half a century ago. First, it is only played in the north, and secondly, in the holiday season few people other than enthusiasts want to sit indoors. What do they know of 'the most emotional country in the world'? What do they know of the historical remains in Castille, of the beautiful evocation of Salamanca, of Avila, of the hanging houses of Cunca, of the Roman arch at Medinaceli?' wrote Norna Middleton. So perhaps I may indulge myself a little about a game which I have enjoyed so much.

As in all sports, there are amateurs and professionals. In every Basque village will be found a tall white wall standing at one end of an open space: that is the *frontes*, or front wall. Like lacrosse which can extend for ever, the playing area is as big as the space available. All the village boys and young men play in any numbers that will make up two sides of manageable proportions. Professionals, however, play indoors in a court, called a *fronton*, by which name the game is familiarly known. The *fronton* can be built as high as you like, but the playing area is officially eleven metres; it has three walls – the *frontes* or front wall, the back wall (*rebote*) and the side wall (*pared izquierda*) – the fourth side, behind wire mesh, is made up of tier upon tier of spectators.

The two teams are always the Red and the Blue; singles and doubles are played (there are other more complicated and less interesting variations). The professionals are all from Basque families so that there are wonderful names on the advertisements of the day's play, such as 'Uributu I vs Uributu IV'. The ball is smaller than a cricket ball and is made of wood covered with buckskin. The player wears a *cesta*, a curious curved wicker talon some two feet long which comes to a point at one end and at the other forms a cup, having on the back a glove into which the hand fits. Pelota players are said to offer any odds against a stranger, putting on a *cesta* for the first time, despatching the ball to the end wall because of the unpredictable direction and speed imparted by the curve.

Standing behind a line, the server bounces the ball and then slings it hard against the end wall; it must be caught by his opponent either on the volley or first bounce in his *cesta* and returned: play is on. A game is thirty points and an agreed number of games make a match. I prefer doubles to singles (as, for that matter, I do in lawn tennis); the strategy is more complicated and more interesting. One of the most exciting moments is when one player hits a high ball soaring miles away to the back wall. A member of the opposition awaits it half-way down the court and, if he has judged the long bounce right, catches it, swivels and slings it back to the front wall like a rocket; the ball hits the concrete with a pistol crack.

But the sound of the ball and the cries of the players are almost drowned by the hubbub on the other side of the wire netting. *Fronton* is a tremendous gambling game, bets are placed as fortunes fluctuate right up to the last point; the system is unique. The bookies (*corredores*), say a dozen or so, stand facing the spectators with their backs to the game. They do not lay the odds; they are agents for placing bets (*apuestas*) between onlookers. Someone at one end will offer a bet and his odds may be accepted by someone else some distance away; a bargain struck, the *corredor* scribbles it down, inserts the betting slip in the slit in a tennis ball which he throws with uncanny accuracy to each party. He gets 18% commission on the deal, but I have never stayed after a game to see how the accounts are settled. Even if one's Spanish is very good, it is virtually impossible to understand and quite impossible to participate, since the transactions are conducted at the speed of an American cotton auction and tennis balls are flying in every direction. It is bedlam, but the atmosphere is extraordinary, and I defy anyone who appreciates the skill of cricket and the excitement of football not to be carried away by it.

After a few days we felt like sea and sun, so we set out northwards on the coast road. After twenty-five miles we rounded a corner and saw on the left a small hotel, the Estrach, in Caldetas, a rambling village of which the Catalan name is Caldas d'Estrach. We had found a home from home. It was very simple – only cold water in the rooms, a hot bath by arrangement – but with wonderful food and run by a wonderful family. Alvaro Constanceau was the boss, with his wife and sister-in-law, and there were four children: one son, Alvarito, who was to succeed him, and three girls, the eldest soon to marry. Across the road, down some steps, over the railway track, was twenty miles of golden sand with no one on it except ourselves.

There was soon a strong bond with the family. Whenever we went to Spain, we always spent the last part of our time at the Estrach; there the welcome was always warm, and the evenings spent chatting with the family on the patio. When Margaret had learnt Catalan, sometimes deputations would arrive. Because she had been taught properly and with her gift for languages she had a thorough command of grammar, while the locals, brought up at their mothers' knees when under the monarchy the language was illegal, talked fluently but could not parse. Arguments echoed in the local over the conditional or subjunctive of a verb and, when no agreement could be reached, someone would say, 'Let's go up to the hotel and ask Señora Flower.'

In 1934 when Stefan Zweig had moved to London, since we were going through Paris, he gave us a letter of introduction to Salvador Dali who had just settled there; foolishly, we were in a hurry and did not use it. At Caldetas Alvaro asked if we would care to drive up to Cadaqués so that he could see his cousin, the local carpenter. The three of us set off north, past the Bay of Rosas, that huge expanse of water used by every navy on manoeuvre for centuries, surrounded by flat, wild but, alas, no longer deserted country.

Our host's house was on the harbour's edge and, as we stood chatting in the sun, we saw a long black ship, black sail hoisted, the eye in bright colours painted on the bow, steered by a large oar at the stern, slipping out to sea: the ship in which Odysseus embarked for Cythera. Its darkness stood out strikingly against the blue of the sea and the brilliant white of the harbour wall. I asked, 'What ship is that?'

'That is the Greek ship,' replied the carpenter. 'It has been coming here for coral each spring for the last two thousand years.'

Alvaro had said that his cousin would cook us a good lunch: it was not merely good, it was memorable. The two main courses were lobster in a hot chocolate sauce (unexpectedly sublime) and chicken roasted in laurel leaves which gave the flesh a pungency which I have not tasted before or since.

After lunch we walked down to the Ateneo, the social club, watched the fishermen playing billiards and got talking. 'Ah,' they said excitedly, 'so you came through Paris. Then you must have seen Salvador. How is he?'

I was touched by the thought that we would run into a Spaniard as easily in the *ville lumière* as one might on a street corner in Cadaqués, and touched that these tough, bronzed men, whose lights at night seen from the corniche road to the frontier look like a network of stars on the dark sea, should care so lovingly for the fate of a young painter who had left them. I felt more sorry than ever that we had not used the introduction.

1934 was the year in which the exodus of Jews from Germany developed from a stream into a river. Stefan Zweig, as I said, had left his beloved Kapuzinerberg in Salzburg for a flat in Portland Place. Robert Neumann arrived with a considerable reputation as a novelist; his agent was Ralph Pinker, and whether it was by Neumann's recommendation or for some other reason I do not know, Ralph had a long string of well known German and Austrian *émigré* authors. We did not do very well with Neumann and he soon moved elsewhere; and from Bruno Frank we only had one novel, *A Man Called Cervantes*. Highly regarded in their own countries, a number of these authors were quite unknown to the English public and, not receiving the attention they expected, were understandably restless and tended to flit from publisher to publisher until eventually they settled down.

After Stefan the most important to us personally was Paul Frischauer, a Viennese, who, like Stefan, was content to stay at Cassell's until the war once again set us all adrift.

Paul was a man of fantastic vitality who had a knack of getting to know everybody. He and his Yugoslav wife, Maritza, took a flat about ten minutes' walk from us and we quickly became on very close terms. His elder brother Willie was a well known Fleet Street journalist, but I gathered that they were not particularly friendly, so I never met him.

Paul was just old enough to have been in the first war and, surprisingly, could be very funny on the subject. In 1914 when the two brothers were in their early teens their father was a regular soldier commanding a battalion of motor-cycles with sidecars. The day approached when the unit was to be inspected by the Emperor on the gravel parterre outside the palace of Schönbrunn, and the boys badgered their father to get them on to the parade so that they could see the aged Franz Josef. Able to withstand the nagging no longer, their father had uniforms run up for them, saying that they could occupy the last motor-cycle and sidecar on the extreme left of the rear rank and, whatever happened, were not to move a muscle. But he had completely forgotten that the old Emperor had a set drill for inspecting a body of troops. He always bowed to the right marker in the front rank and said '*Guten Tag*'; then walked very slowly down the ranks until he came to the last file of the rear rank to which he also addressed himself. Very old, very upright, the Emperor progressed slowly until he came to the last motor-cycle where, too blind to notice that the occupants were hardly soldiers, he bowed to the petrified boys and uttered his customary parting words: '*Es hat mir sehr gefreut.*'

By 1918 Paul was commanding a battery of field guns on the Italian front. His men were all Czechs; with the war clearly lost and the Empire about to collapse they degenerated into respectful insubordination. Told to engage a target at a certain range on a bearing of 180°, their shells winged their way in quite the wrong direction; to his remonstrances the battery sergeant-major would reply, 'Oh, 180°, I'm so sorry, sir, I thought you said 80°,' and there was nothing that Paul could do.

At the beginning of the year Margaret's edition of Shakespeare's sonnets appeared, printed by Hague and Gill at Piggots; it is a lovely little book, but not everyone liked the wood engraving which Eric used as a frontispiece – A.J. was scathing! We asked Eric to lunch at home and he said that he would be delighted if I would pick him up at Broadcasting House where he was carving the sculptures. When I arrived he was on the scaffolding and called for me to come up. I ascended gingerly, having no head whatsoever for heights, but it was worth it to stand there and watch him at work.

Also in 1934 A.J.'s *Quest for Corvo* was published. He had previously begun a Life of Wilde (in March 1931 he had written to me 'I am now committed to Wilde') but this unfortunately had only got as far as a few chapters when he became completely involved with Baron Corvo and – with the participation of the peculiar Maundy Gregory, 'not the first but by all odds the most successful honours broker in recent times' – he gained control of much new material from which I published two novels, *The Desire and Pursuit of the Whole* and *Hubert's Arthur*. He decided to set down the whole extraordinary story, and the result is one of the most remarkable and fascinating books of this century. He sent me chapters to read as he progressed, as he did to other friends, and I had little or no criticism but much admiration to offer, for the whole is a solid and complete achievement on which A.J.'s reputation will last long after many other activities of his may be forgotten. I was delighted that we published it; Oliver Simon printed it splendidly, it was extremely well received and enjoyed good sales.

It is known that A.J. was a remarkable searcher after and finder of rare books and manuscripts, and there was one volume which he was seeking at this time which I do not think he ever found. It was a Portuguese–English phrase book produced in Portugal for sale to the officers of Wellington's army. He had once seen the book and was delighted by it and was fond of quoting one phrase from it: 'Never was I seen a so much bad horse; it can neither to go forwards nor to go back.'

Stefan Zweig now delivered his *Erasmus*, which I regarded then as his most important work, and despite the many which were to come I still feel the same. Stefan wrote, 'From the earliest days of my youth I strove only to stress the "European man", the "European mind" ' – he was a man to whom every sort of jingoism, every variety of oppression was abhorrent, a mind with all its doors and windows open so that through it might blow every wind of human thought. When I first met him and talked with him he had reminded me of Erasmus, so it was in a way no surprise to me that he should write so moving a book about the man whom he regarded as his spiritual forebear, and of whom I could think of him as a reincarnation.

I took special pains over the design of the book, which I admit was pastiche; I wanted to give an impression of the great Swiss printer, Froben. When I had had my press at 'Idehurst' I had bought from Tregaskis (an excellent antiquarian bookseller opposite the British Museum, now long gone) a set of sixteenth-century woodcut initials and I used these for chapter openings. The result pleased me, but I do not know if it did anyone else.

Stefan suggested to me that he thought there was a need for selections from the letters of monarchs of this country. I liked the idea and started *The Royal Letters* series, beginning with Charles II because he was my favourite king. Of course I asked Arthur Bryant, whose life of Charles had recently had such a resounding and richly deserved success, and when I called upon him at his flat in Chelsea his answer was cryptic and prophetic: 'I will do it, but you will lose money on it.' There were three more which all came out in 1935, but Bryant was right: they did not do well. They were too early; the interest in letters as illuminating character had not yet become so great to the public at large as it is today (although, of course, there were collected correspondences such as that of Keats). No more were commissioned, but I still found letters fascinating. Margaret and I began an enormous collection entitled *Elizabethan Letters*, to illustrate the whole reign, which remained still a heap of typescript when war came in 1939. And I took time off from that to compile a collection of poets' letters which appeared in 1939 as *The Pursuit of Poetry*, which had a good press but hardly got off the ground because the entire stock was destroyed in one of the first air raids of the following year.

One of our most interesting publications of this year, and one of the scarcest if anyone wants to get hold of it second hand today, was *Unit One*. Paul Nash, who was the editor and moving spirit of the group, asked me if I would like to do it and I was delighted. The group's idea was to offer a customer a complete service by artists with principles in common; they would design, build and decorate a house. They did not hold together long, but I understand the idea is being tried again today, with what results I do not know. There was an introduction by Herbert Read and a uniform entry on each artist: a photograph of his head and hands (the latter very interesting), an essay by him on his beliefs and practices, and reproductions of his work. The artists were Barbara Hepworth, Henry Moore, John Armstrong, John Biffe, Edward Burra,

Tristram Hillier, Paul Nash, Ben Nicholson, Edward Wadsworth, Wells Coates and Colin Lucas. The last two were the architects. Unfortunately I did not meet them all – some lived far from London – but I met several, and Margaret and I were asked to Wells Coates' house. He was a good host; but I could never quite get over my uneasiness talking to a fully clothed Mrs Coates when out of the corner of my eye I could see, over the living-room mantelpiece, a life-size nude of her like the front view of a twentieth-century Rokeby Venus – though I suppose it was less embarrassing than *vice versa* would have been.

As an artistic body Unit One did not last long, but it is not forgotten. In the early eighties there was a detailed historical exhibition at the Portsmouth Art Gallery, and in 1985 another at the Mayor Gallery of which one art critic wrote: 'Unit One is best seen now as a rallying point for many of the more significant British artists of the period, each highly individualistic, but each also trying to find a "modern" art, contemporary in spirit and expression of the age.' I did not think of it in such high-sounding terms at the time.

After Thomas Hardy's death father and I remained in touch with his widow, Florence. She could be abrupt and had strong prejudices, both for and against people. I think that she liked us because father always respected her and treated her with kindness, which is by no means so of all her husband's friends, and in return she looked kindly on me. I do not feel that she was quite as miserable in her last years as Robert Gittings (in *The Older Hardy*) has made out. Florence sold Max Gate and moved to London, first to a flat in the Adelphi, over which Barrie, who lived there, helped her, and upon its barbarous demolition she moved to Artillery Mansions. At both she used to give a lot of luncheon parties, and once in this year she invited me, and on the telephone mentioned that Gwen ffrancon-Davies was going to be there. I would have gone anyway, but to meet my favourite actress I accepted with more than usual alacrity.

When I arrived I listened perfunctorily to the introductions, my attention being fixed calf-like on the object of my admiration. Through lunch I hung on her words – and there were a lot of them – until I felt an increasing unease; there was a distractive magnetism drawing me away from her. The cord, if one can so describe an absorption in someone else's conversation, was broken and I looked to my left to find fixed upon me a pair of periwinkle blue eyes. Suddenly I recollected the name Shaw to which I had hardly listened on my arrival; it was T.E. Lawrence. At the end of lunch the two of us left together and walked and walked for hours. It is a pity that I made no notes of what we talked about, argued and discussed during all that time, but of the supernatural strength which made me turn towards him I have the most vivid memory – and of his holding his right elbow with his left hand, which I had noticed Gino Watkins do at Lancing. It was the last year of Lawrence's life.

Florence Hardy's deep dislike of Sydney Cockerell had increased since the bitter row which had broken out in Barrie's flat in the Adelphi after the funeral in 1928, and later when he had attacked her in *The Times Literary Supplement* their relationship became impossible. He was Hardy's co-executor and trustee, but with the help of Irene Cooper Willis, whom I remember at Max Gate, she obtained the sole trusteeship. It is true that Cockerell could be pompous, peremptory and overbearing. Father was furious one day at Max Gate when Cockerell, about to show him a manuscript, barked 'Have you washed your hands?' At which father who was most scrupulous in such matters, muttered, 'What does he think – that I've got raspberry jam on them?'

Florence would have nothing more to do with Cockerell, and when, in 1934, she wanted to have produced *An Indiscretion in the Life of an Heiress*, an adaptation by Hardy of his first story, *The Poor Man and the Lady*, written in 1878, which had never appeared in book form, she turned to me. I went naturally to Oliver Simon; Florence accepted his estimate and a hundred copies were produced in a numbered edition which she gave to her friends. Cockerell was furious, but I cannot imagine what he could expect after the way that he had behaved.

Her health had never been good and she had for years been in and out of a nursing-home in Fitzroy Square. In 1937 she went there for good, riddled with cancer. By then she was a very sad figure; there is nothing more pathetic than a person who has been forceful, even belligerent, when her defences are gone. Father and I took it in turns visiting her – one of us went every day until the end which came on 17 October.

While I was at Cambridge Peter Lucas had been at work on his great edition of John Webster's plays for which he was contracted to Chatto & Windus, and the lectures on Tragedy which I had heard him deliver in the hall of King's were published as a small book by Leonard Woolf. He had never come into my mind as a potential author, and therefore I was surprised and delighted when he offered me his new volume of essays, *Authors Dead and Living*, during this year, and I accepted with alacrity. Thereafter I published almost all his books except his translations of Greek poetry and drama which he most properly gave to Dent. In addition to the pleasures of publishing, it gave me regular opportunities to see again someone whom I venerated. For a pupil to become his master's publisher may not be unique, but it is surely unusual.

He was an extremely withdrawn person with a nervous manner, almost as though he could not express his feelings and would not if he could. So it was something of a surprise to learn after his death in 1967 that in addition to his wives, whom I knew, there were quite a number of other women in his life. In a way I think that, frightened of him because he towered so far above me intellectually, I was pathetically pleased to do anything which earned his approval, and it would have comforted me to think of him as any ordinary man. Whenever he came to the office before and after the war I was reminded once again of his remarkable physical resemblance to Keats. Of the fifteen books of his which I published, my own favourite was *Style* which did not come out until 1955 and then ran through a number of editions; apart from his great Webster, it also seems to me the most important – but it is a matter of taste and they were all good. I used to ask him to inscribe my copies of his books, which he was not particularly keen on doing because he said that he never knew what to put. But in the first one he wrote '*Discipulus delectissimus*' – flattering, perhaps, but to me he was most certainly *auctor delictissimus*.

A.J. at this time was having fifty copies of selected works bound in full leather by Henry T. Wood for sale to members of the First Edition Club, and decided to do Dowson, for which I produced the design; it led to the nearest A.J. and I ever came to a quarrel. On the upper and lower covers a small flower ornament is enclosed within diagonal lines which I intended should meet as apexes on the spine, linking the whole into one symmetrical pattern. While I was on holiday A.J., on the grounds of cost, altered it so that the back is crossed by horizontal lines, thus losing the point. When I came back I was furious; if I had been available I would either have altered the design or paid the extra cost of the brasses to retain my purpose. But the deed was done and I simmered down; but it was a pity.

The Depression was deepening in publishing, although in other professions the worst was over, so I was told that the ordinary edition of the *B.C.Q.* would have to share the fate of the *édition de luxe* and come to an end. The sixteenth and last number that we published appeared in October 1934. A.J. asked if I would mind his carrying on, and I agreed – reluctantly because I did not think that he had the resources to do it alone; he did produce one number and that was all.

For our last number I was offered an article on *Anstey's 'Election Bill' and the 'Epistle to Bamfylde'* by A.N.L. Munby. It was a good article, and I was particularly interested because the author was an undergraduate in King's. When he came down he went into Quaritch, the eminent antiquarian booksellers with whom I had a good relationship, and there I met him in person and our friendship ripened very quickly. He was very gentle and by nature took a kindly view of the human race; I am sure that if he considered you to be the vilest specimen alive and for some reason had to tell you so, he would have done it with the greatest courtesy. It is well known that his chief interest was the collection and preservation of books and manuscripts, in which he became most erudite, and he was held in the highest regard by librarians and collectors all over the world.

I suggested to him that we should together prepare a volume of facsimiles of poetry, and *English Poetical Autographs* appeared in 1937. Curwen produced it, and it was the only book to come from that august establishment which disappointed me; the collotype plates were not sharp enough. But collotype could do that; it was capable of giving finer results than any other form of reproduction, but if anything went wrong, it went very wrong.

Tim was a Territorial officer in the K.R.R.C., the headquarters of which was in Davies Street, just five minutes walk from his office, for he had moved to Sotheby's. He used to ask me to lunch in the very pleasant mess which was not much used – sometimes we had the place to ourselves. Of course he disappeared on 3 September 1939, and was put in the bag the following year, at Calais, where the stubborn defence put up by his battalion caused the Germans much trouble – even if to little avail in the end. While in Offlag VII he entertained his fellow prisoners with his bibliophilic ghost stories in the manner of M.R. James which were published in 1949 as *The Alabaster Hand* Six years later he was the librarian of King's and our friendship was renewed.

I like to remember him from the last time I ever saw him. It was at a King's dinner held at Armoury House, the headquarters of the Honourable Artillery Company. He said, 'As I am in the chair, I consider that I have the right to choose who should sit next to me; I want you on my right, please.' That was so typical of his gentle courtesy.

We published one book, *Now a Stranger*, by Humbert Wolfe, then highly thought of as a poet and now completely forgotten. We used to meet frequently in what are pretentiously called 'literary circles' and I think that it was through him that I met Viola Garvin, literary editor of *The Observer*. She was deeply in love with him at the time, a forlorn affair since, although he loved her too, he had a wife. She was the eldest daughter of J.L. Garvin and was unusually close to her father.

She was a tall, beautiful woman with lovely grey eyes, and she limped. She had had an accident as a small child; indeed, while she was still a child her leg was only saved from amputation by a remarkable surgeon in Germany. Perhaps she resented this flaw and, never quite coming to terms with life, extravagance was her compensation, for 'in money matters she was incorrigible' and her father several times had to settle her debts. She always seemed a generous but sad person, which made her giggle all the more touching when it suddenly effervesced. We became friends and she added me to her list of reviewers, of which I was glad because, although I knew Cyril Lakin so well at *The Sunday Times*, he did not make use of me in this way. I reviewed regularly for her, and in 1935 she gave me a real plum: Hemingway's *The Green Hills of Africa*. I thought that it was a wonderful book and said so. I was surprised that my enthusiasm was not shared by other reviewers; at best they were luke-warm, some even critical. I read it again recently and cannot understand the lack of enthusiasm; I still think it is a wonderful book.

Success in publishing is as exciting as the failures are disappointing. When I bought the British rights in *The Memoirs of Caulincourt*, I thought that I had got a certain winner, but they turned out to be a comparative failure. Caulincourt, Duke of Vicenza, had commanded a division as early as 1805, and two years later was sent as French Ambassador to St Petersburg, where he had considerable influence with the Tsar Alexander. Asking to be recalled in 1811, he warned the Emperor against the invasion of Russia in 1812, but when Napoleon insisted in going ahead, he went with him. Napoleon trusted Caulincourt implicitly, with every justification, and when he decided to abandon the *Grande Armée* and return to Paris before there was trouble, it was this staunch supporter whom he chose as his companion on the long sleigh and coach ride home – all the way reminiscing about his past campaigns and expressing his views about the world in general. The first volume, which I asked Hamish Miles to translate, covered this period, 1812–13, and seemed to me to be the most important memoirs of the Empire, so in 1935 I was bitterly disappointed that they did not have the success which they merited. Caulincourt was then appointed Foreign Secretary and was the Emperor's personal representative at the congress of Châtillon which met to decide what to do, which resulted in the exile to Elba. The second volume, covering these historic matters, appeared three years later with no greater success, which I found surprising and saddening.

A.J. put authors my way when he could, but I do not remember whether it was to him that I owed the arrival on our list of Philip Gosse, though it is possible since they knew one another well. My parents were acquainted with Sir Edmund Gosse, his father, who I gathered was austere and somewhat pompous, though a great critic, while the son was quite different – rather roly-poly, with an outrageous sense of humour, whose company I found a constant joy. The first book he gave us was *Go to the Country* in 1935, but the most important appeared three years later – *St Helena*, a book which is highly thought of by those who know that remote and historic island. He was a doctor of medicine, and, with so many called into the forces, he resumed practice in Cambridge when the war began. Afterwards he told me that, with surgery over and patients visited, he wanted to broaden his mind, and the presence among them of a man in his fifties slightly surprised the undergraduates of Trinity Hall. He was a beautiful writer and all his books were good.

The success which we had had with S.S. Van Dine was followed that year by the publication of *The Case of the Howling Dog* by Erle Stanley Gardner, and the immortal Perry Mason made his first appearance on our list. Gardner's books sold well for many years, but not nearly as well as they did in other countries – particularly his own. I never met him, but I gathered that he was arrogant and cantankerous – although he did much good with his Court of Last Appeal. We published nearly all his books, but his American publisher (a close friend of mine) years later had to say, 'Can't you try and do a bit better so that I can keep the old so-and-so quiet?' But in that kind of situation there is very little that one can do. An author who churns out at regular and frequent intervals books which hardly vary in quality, displaying always the same degree of slick competence, establishes a level in the market; he is not likely to drop below it (unless the public suddenly tires of the cult), nor is there any reason why he should suddenly rise above it. A novelist, not a writer of detective fiction with a stock character, can change his subject and his approach; Alec Waugh, for example, doubled his sales in the mid-thirties by writing *The Balliols*, a family novel of a type people rather liked at the time, after which his sales dropped back again until many years afterwards he wrote his most successful book, *Island in the Sun*, about which there is a curious tale to tell later.

A quite different type of novel, appeared in France that year, of which I bought the English rights and which I translated: *Les Traqués* by Michel

Matveev. I chose *Bitter Draught* as the English title, from Sterne: 'Disguise thyself as thou wilt, still, Slavery ... thou art a bitter draught.' It describes the sufferings of a Jewish family in their wanderings from Russia via Rumania to Paris; it begins with a pogrom. Although it is beautifully written, why did I choose to acquire the rights in and myself translate a book of such unrelieved gloom, without hope?

Looking back half a century later I think I know. Mine was the generation which grew up in the belief that those before us had fought and died in the war to end wars. With outraged feelings we realized that we had been conned; the world was not only in depression, it was in turmoil. Hitler had walked out of the League of Nations, Mussolini had marched into Abyssinia. The Japanese seized Manchuria; as Fisher said, 'The new Republic of Spain treads uneasily on burning lava'; Greece was torn asunder. In the blurb I wrote, 'We encounter in this book a callousness which should be inconceivable.' Of course it should; yet today, long after, when crime and savagery are without limit or restriction, one can only look on and realize how ingenuous it was to find any cruelty inconceivable. Mine was the generation of Burgess, Maclean, Philby and Blunt who thought the grass was greener on the other side. I am not a political animal; drowned in an indifference which ill becomes anyone reasonably intelligent, I have never felt satisfied with the policy of any party in the country during my lifetime, and my individual views have unusually been at odds with the majority. At every general election between the wars Margaret (who then had dual nationality) and I voted Labour not from any conviction, but because the Royal Borough of Kensington was so conservative that we felt we should try to help the underdog save his deposit. So in this deepening gloom I published a novel about man's inhumanity to man; it was a minor thing, maybe, but it was my two cents' worth. The fact that when I offered the American rights to Alfred Knopf, he took them like a shot, encourages me to think that I was not just whistling down the wind.

In the whole ethics of publishing, too, I found myself in a head-on collision with conservative views. Allen Lane, having failed to gain the agreement of his fellow directors in the family firm, went off on his own and founded Penguin Books. In July 1935 the first ten titles were published at sixpence each, which made them available for Woolworth's in which that small coin (now less than 3p) was the maximum price of any object.

There had, of course, for a hundred years been the library of paperbacks produced for travellers abroad by Bernard Tauschnitz in Leipzig, the importation of which into Britain was forbidden. But Penguin, apart from a small venture by Benn Brothers of which little was heard, was the first firm to produce a paperback edition (after an agreed period of time) in the country of a book's origin.

We all know that this was an epoch-making event which changed the face of society, the half-century of which was in 1985 celebrated with much pomp and circumstance. Its followers and imitators have become legion, but not many of them have taken the same trouble over the typography – for Allen Lane first used Jan Tschichold, the eminent Swiss designer, and then on Oliver Simon's recommendation Hans Schmoller, who was head of Penguin's production for twenty-five years.

Allen Lane had written to every publisher, asking for the lease of titles for the new venture. Many agreed, including Jonathan Cape, who remarked later, 'You were bound to go bust and I thought I'd take four hundred quid off you before you did.' Father was one of a group, including Stanley Unwin and Victor Gollancz, who flatly refused, holding that the introduction of paperbacks would result in the collapse of serious publishing which was in enough trouble already. I equally flatly disagreed with this decision; I argued and I pleaded. Father and I did not have a row because he was adamant and I was powerless; I just shut up – but I vowed that if I was ever in a position to do so I would reverse the decision.

11   The Edge of the Precipice

King George V died on 20 January 1936. There cannot have been many people in this country who did not admire him from afar. I certainly did. I can see now in my mind's eye the occasional photograph of his enchanting smile when he bent down to speak to a child, showing a gentleness which seems to have deserted him with his own family; the fate of the eldest we know full well, and of him his father once said, 'After I am dead he will ruin himself in twelve months.' Apart from this misfortune he seemed such an admirable, caring man. We remember him as the first monarch to speak to his subjects on the air, and the last to speak with a German accent; he had a good voice, even if he was speaking to us more from a sense of duty than of pleasure. Now he was gone.

I got up early to hear Edward VIII proclaimed at St James's Palace, and climbed on to a ledge of the chapel opposite Friary Court. Apart from the dignity of the proclamation itself by Garter King at Arms, there was quite a lot of entertainment. Drawn up in Cleveland Row facing the Palace was a troop of the Household Cavalry. They were there a long time and the horse at the far end got very bored, so he leaned against his neighbour, who in turn leaned against the horse next to him. The pressure increased as it passed down the line so that the last horse at my end crossed his legs, fell over and his armoured rider hit Pall Mall with a clatter like a pile of saucepans. The trooper was not hurt and tried to get up, but, being above the crowd, I could hear the police sergeant hiss to him, 'Lie down, you fool' while two constables produced a stretcher on which he was removed amid general sympathy.

In front of me on both sides of the road was a platoon of Grenadiers deployed at five-pace intervals. At the conclusion a sergeant-major at the Pall Mall end gave the order, 'Ranks, right and left turn,' whereupon half the guardsmen facing me turned to their left and the other half to their right. Following the command, 'Quick March' they set off smartly. I saw the last of the party heading towards the Mall growing more and more uneasy as the gap grew wider and he could hear no sound of boots behind him. In Pall Mall the sergeant-major was screaming his head off, his face the colour of a ripe mulberry. Discipline demanded that the rear guardsman of the errant party should look to his front, but I saw his head begin to twitch, and finally he could bear the strain no more; he looked round, saw nobody and gave a wild cry of 'Oi!'. One, two, three, four, they stamped an about turn and headed back to the fold. It was extremely funny to watch, but I am sure that the orderly room at Wellington Barracks was busy later that morning.

On the 28th I got up early again to watch the funeral and found a good place in the front row at Marble Arch. At the lightning speed with which such rumours always spread, it was hinted that following a heavy night Carol of Rumania was so poorly that a masseur had to be sent for to get him on his feet, and furthermore, as there was some element of doubt as to whether the King would stay the course, the masseur was put into uniform and made to march beside his patient. Obviously I know nothing about the truth of such rumours, only with my own eyes I saw that next to King Carol, whose features were unmistakable, strode a figure from beneath whose greatcoat protruded six inches of white apron. After the crowned heads came the representative of the Spanish Republic, a figure soon to become rather more familiar to us: General Franco.

I was a fervent supporter of the new King, partly for himself and partly because of my growing antipathy towards Baldwin whose negative attitude to Nazism filled me with trepidation. At the 1935 General Election he had said, 'I give you my word that there will be no great armaments,' – small wonder that he was described by Churchill as 'the greatest non-statesman'. Paul Frischauer, who knew a mole in cabinet circles whom I was never able to identify but whose veracity was startling, told me of the Prime Minister's reaction to a report from the British air attaché in Berlin that the Luftwaffe now mustered, trainers and all, 30,000 aircraft: 'Thirty thousand! The House will never stand for it; I shall say three thousand.' Difficult as the position in which the King was to place himself may have been, so mendacious a minister seemed hardly the man to find a solution, if one existed.

It was an interesting year in publishing, and our list contained the first of two long novels by an American highly thought of at the time, but now apparently forgotten: Ayn Rand's *We the Living*. I was excited by another American of whom I thought very highly, Richard Sale. Hitherto a crime writer, his first straight novel, *Not Too Narrow ... Not Too Deep*, has been described as a 'tour de force'. Beautifully written and very moving, it is a story which haunts me to this day. I liked Sale enormously and made no secret of my admiration for the few novels which he wrote; but, alas, he was also a very good script writer and so sank without trace in Hollywood – not quite without trace, since he got credit titles on a number of classic films, to the great benefit of his bank balance, I am sure, but to the detriment of the world of fiction.

A.J. introduced to me Richard Wyndham who was as good a writer as he was a painter. Wyndham had recently spent a considerable time among the Dinkas, a little-known primitive tribe in southern Sudan, and as a result wrote *The Gentle Savage*. When the Dinka warriors prepared for war they plastered their faces with ashes and dyed their hair blond with urine, and the jacket was from a superb painting by Dick of a man ready for battle. It was an extremely good book, and I came to like the author very much. During the summer he asked me down for the weekend. He lived in Tickeridge Mill at Blackboys, near Tunbridge Wells, which was to be the last home of Vivien Leigh. There were three other guests: A.J., Constant Lambert and Tom Driberg. It was a busy weekend, and I do not think that any of us got much sleep because a complicated war game was set up and each side spent a vast amount of time contemplating and making its next troop movement, like a potted Karpov-Kasparov contest. During daylight hours there was croquet, and here A.J. was in his element. To have played croquet on a lawn as smooth and level as a billiards table would have been dreary, but Dick's lawn sloped at a steep angle, and the resulting problems brought a gleam of cunning to A.J.'s eye and skill to his hand.

During his time in the Sudan, Dick had stayed with the District Commissioner, Captain J.R. Poole, and when 'Aginejok', as he was called, completed his service and came back to England Dick decided to give a welcoming dinner for him. A private room at the Savoy was done up entirely to look like the surroundings from which the guest of honour had recently returned, even down to candles stuck in the tops of wine bottles and huge black men standing impassively on guard in the background. Poor Dick. A kind and talented man, he came to a tragic end; having survived the war, he was sent to troubled Palestine as the *Daily Telegraph* correspondent and stood up at the wrong moment somewhere near Jerusalem.

The fiction market in 1936 was dominated by the extraordinary success of *Gone With The Wind*, which was published on both sides of the Atlantic by Macmillan and reminds me of a story which perhaps is worth retelling. The chief editor of Macmillan's, New York, named Latham, regularly roamed the country looking for talent and when in Atlanta, Georgia, he was told that Mary Mitchell – one of the top reporters on *The Atlanta Journal and Constitution* with Erskine Caldwell and the famous sports writer Grantland Rice – had for some time been engaged on a novel, the characters of which were drawn from her own life, as a form of therapy after an accident. Latham called, persuaded her to let him read the vast pile of typescript, and made publishing history. Latham himself was a 'vast pile', a huge eunuch who lived with his mother. I remember him when he was in London doing the rounds, in the course of which, of course, he called upon Harraps. English publishers did not have much to do with one another in those days, unless they happened to be personal friends; American publishers have always been much more gregarious. So although I knew Walter Harrap quite well, I never met the other leading light, George, who I was told might be described as a 'bit of a rough diamond'. When mother's boy walked into the office, he was greeted warmly by George Harrap. 'Well, Mr Latham, this is indeed a pleasure after corresponding with you for so many years. I tell you what,' – looking at his watch – 'why not come back here at six o'clock, we'll go down to Piccadilly and pick up a couple of skirts.' His enormous visitor in shocked tones replied, 'MR HARRAP, you have mistaken your man.'

Without any success I had a go at Italian literature this year with Alberto Albertini's *Two Years to Live* and a little later Alberto Moravia's *Wheel of Fortune*. Neither took off, and I could hardly have chosen a worse time to try my hand in this field. Mussolini had savagely attacked Ethiopia and everything Italian was out of favour, in marked contrast to the post-war years when anything became fashionable because of the spate of films like *Open City*.

Then came an event which was to be very important to Cassell's. The New York publisher Charles Scribner, 'a silver-haired, gentle-featured man of charm and good humour', conceived the idea of asking Winston Churchill if he would write a history of the English-speaking peoples. He naturally went to Harraps with whom he was in collaboration over the publication of *Marlborough*, which appeared in volumes from 1933 until 1938. The answer of the board of Harrap directors was that they were already losing enough money on their present commitment without taking on anything further from the same pen – no. Charlie then came to La Belle Sauvage and father said that he would be happy to join in the venture. The next move was a cable from New York saying that the board of Scribners had come to the same conclusion as their opposite numbers at Harraps in London, and in consequence father was welcome to the idea if he wanted to do anything about it on his own. Father did indeed want to and, as I remember and as recorded by Martin Gilbert in his biography of Churchill, signed a contract for the complete copyright for £20,000. This was a considerable gamble if one considers the state of trade at the time, the need to multiply the sum by at least twenty in today's money, and also that at the time Churchill was not only politically a lone voice but he was also involved in the production of a vast biography which, great as it might be, was not paying its way. Father lightened the load somewhat by selling the American book rights to Houghton Mifflin of Boston. The author set to work.

I should mention here that there was a dramatic development during the war. Churchill rang up father saying that Alexander Korda had offered him £70,000 for the film rights, which he saw from the contract belonged to Cassell's. (I very much doubt if Korda had any intention of making a film about the history of the English-speaking peoples, although it was possible as a piece of expensive propaganda; it seems to me more likely to have been a nice way for Korda to express his great admiration for the Prime Minister, who had done some literary work for him in days gone by.) Churchill said that if father ceded him these rights, he would undertake that Cassell's should have the first offer of anything which he might write about the present conflict. It was not difficult for father to agree.

It was now six years since a director of the company had visited the United States. Father was not keen and I had family interests, so Margaret and I went, making the round trip on the *Ile de France* surely, with every respect to the many great liners this country has built, the Queen of the Atlantic.

Our journey began with all the British passengers going down the

Solent in a tender to await her arrival. She arrived all right, storming past at a rate of knots, a vast black ghost towering over us in the dark; a magnificent sight, a black ghost lit from stem to stern like a thousand Christmas trees. She turned and came back so that our tender could nuzzle against her and we climbed up the companion way into a warm, welcoming world of France with all the excitement of boarding a great ship for which, alas, there is no substitute.

It was a happy voyage. For meals – what meals! – we were put at a table with Charles Maduro, a composer from Curaçao, his wife and two daughters. On the last night the composer was kind enough to say that he and his family had enjoyed our company so much that he would like to take us out for an evening and asked us to choose the *venue*. We looked through the bible, the front pages of *The New Yorker*, and the following week I phoned him to say that we would like to be taken to the Lincoln. He said, 'Can't you think of anything better than that?' I was polite, but firm. The Lincoln was, and probably still is, a large, unattractive workaday hotel on the West Side, which had a large ballroom. We had done our homework; the band was that of 'The King of Swing' himself – Benny Goodman, at the first great height of his career (there is more about this in the Appendix on jazz). I came very near to meeting my end; I had asked one of the Maduro girls to dance when he went to town on a very good number, *Organ-grinder's Swing*, and jammed it, chorus after chorus, for twenty minutes. After twenty minutes of vigorous dancing to a wonderful band playing a wonderful tune, we crawled off the floor ecstatic but almost terminally exhausted.

Louis Bromfield was at that time working on his best-known novel, *The Rains Came*, and since a very close relationship had grown up between him and father – and at second-hand with me – we were asked to his apartment. Present there was George Hawkins, his right-hand man, who was having a passionate affair with Libby Holman, whose husky contralto voice made her one of the most popular singing stars of the period. We were to leave New York before we learned whether the affair was consummated or degenerated into *passé* gossip, but when on the following night we went to the Cotton Club (South) to listen to Cab Calloway, our attention to the flamboyant band leader (known later in London as a wonderful Sportin' Life in *Porgy and Bess*) was distracted by, three tables to our right, George Hawkins and Libby Holman. Why should the affair of a man barely met with a woman famous but never encountered prove such an attraction that I remember it? Human nature – or the nature of some humans – is such that the sight was riveting and we wished lasciviously that we could lip-read. If we could have, we would probably have found that they were talking about Bromfield's growing interest in agriculture, or her next engagement in a town she didn't like. But even triumphant proof that two people about whom we had heard so much gossip actually did know one another could not distract us from the dancing of Bill 'Bojangles' Robinson. With a bowler hat cocked over one eye like a miniature agile version of Fats Waller, he was a black Michael Fokine of tap dancing, as far above his fellows as the

Matterhorn is above its neighbouring peaks. There is a satisfaction, a form of restful excitement, about seeing something done better than anyone else can do it. And 'Bojangles' ' dancing, from the faintest whisper to the loudest cross-rhythm, stays in my mind like the *Water Music* or the *Three-cornered Hat*. He was supremely fit, and remained so until years later practically the whole of New York turned out to applaud him when he danced his way around the boundaries of Harlem on his eightieth birthday.

It was a good trip which paid off, and I laid the basis of many friendships which were to grow when I went to the United States regularly in later years.

But everything in 1936 was overshadowed by Spain. We decided to go to the Córdoba *féria*, which is spread over three days in late May. As soon as we drove across the border we could sense something was wrong; there was a threatening, brooding atmosphere which we had never felt in the country before, and in Barcelona there was the sound of shots occasionally during the night. On the road south from Madrid we toiled slowly in our little car up the Sierra Madrona, to find at the top the entire population of Los Correderes, all the men armed with shotguns and rifles, blocking the road. My first thought was that if I stopped we would be robbed, so I changed gear and charged them. They gave way and as I drove on I told Margaret to keep her head down. I must say that the back of my neck felt very vulnerable; but, whatever or whoever they wanted, it wasn't us.

Hot and dusty, we rattled into Córdoba without much time to spare before the first *corrida*. Faced by the brilliant white walls of that lovely town I was uncertain which road to take until a mischievous imp of about twelve asked us where we wanted to go. I told him the Hotel Simón, and, hopping on to the bonnet, he said that he would guide us, which he did very well. But at one point I stuck my head out and said to him, 'You know we're going the wrong way up a one-way street?' 'That doesn't matter,' he happily replied, 'my father's the Mayor.'

In those days I never checked a bill or locked anything up because I found the Spanish to be a people of impeccable honesty, apart possibly from those in the extreme south about whom I always had slight reservations. The Simón was in that tradition which, like itself, belongs to the past. It appears in a 1912 Baedeker which I have, but it is gone now; there are various modern structures of which I have no knowledge. Then it was the height of old-world elegance. There were no keys to the rooms because there were no doors; air-conditioning was that of nature, little breezes which whispered in from the balconied courtyard. If one wished for privacy, there was a curtain to be drawn, but that one should be disturbed was quite out of the question.

Everything else was unforgettable. The mosque, despite the interpolation by Charles V, is still a building which leaves one nearly in tears. The maze of streets of the Barrio de Judio round it, dazzling white with countless tiny courtyards ablaze with flowers which seem so silently private. The young blades riding in *traje corto*, reins in the left hand, right hand on thigh, their *queridas* on the crupper, cascading flounced skirts, high comb, like a come-hither poster for Spain, yet when you see it putting such mundane thoughts joyfully out of mind. The stalls, noisy with laughter, selling everything literally under the sun. The gentleman on a street corner showing off the dressage of his favourite horse for public admiration and amusement. The herds of wild horses driven in for sale across the Guadalquivir bridge in a cloud of dust. The gypsies lined along the river beneath the trees, every tent and caravan with its fire beside it like a dwindling lane of dull red lamps in the dark of night. A town to remember.

Back in Madrid, and then we went out to Toledo on the 29th, saw the Alcazar for the last time it would be intact, lunched overlooking the Tajo, and bumped over a horrible unmade road to Aranjuez, where there was an incident at the *corrida*. The arena of the ring there is the biggest in Spain but the tiers of seats are low and handsome, unlike Madrid or Barcelona where a place in the back row can produce vertigo. Punctually, to the trumpet call, the two *alguaciles* (stewards) galloped in to collect the key of the bull-pen from the President, both with their fists raised in the Communist salute. There was instant pandemonium; while the crowd's roar of disapproval would have drowned the noise at a Wembley Cup Final, everything movable was thrown into the ring. The two horsemen sat in the middle defiant for a while, but the hail of bottles forced them to withdraw. It took half an hour to clear up before they could ride in again and do their job without political gestures.

We left Spain in mid-June and a month later the tragedy began. Like everyone who loved Spain, we were appalled, and wrote to Alvaro in Caldetas saying that we would be happy to have the two younger girls for the duration, put them in a Spanish school and see that they were brought up as good Catholics; but he replied that the family must stay together, come what might.

There have been few events in history which have engendered such divided and bitter feelings, and left behind questions which half a century later are still debated, no nearer positive resolution. For the poet Cecil Day-Lewis the Republican cause was 'a battle of light against darkness', but not everyone was so certain, for it was said that 'those who have lines as straight as steel rails, inserting Spain into a Fascist, anti-Fascist plot, are mistaken. Spain is mysterious, elusive and nearly always unexpected'.

I have often wondered if Sanjurjo (who never got to take up command as he was killed on the way) and Franco would have started the war, insurrection, intervention, call it what you will, if either had known that it was to plunge their beloved country into misery and bloodshed for three long years. I feel very doubtful. But there was plenty of evidence that within the country it was realized that a clash was coming. A few years ago a Spaniard who had been a brigadier in the Republican army wrote in a letter to *The Times*, 'I belong to a well known Republican family and during the months preceding the outbreak of the Civil War I heard ministers of undoubted loyalty to the regime express in private at my parents' home their despair at the course events were taking, their deep concern at the government having lost control of the situation, and their horror at being unable to restore order in what could be fairly described as mob-rule conditions.' And an important aspect of the tragedy which is often overlooked has been expressed by Salvador de Madariaga, himself a member of the Republican cabinet, in all his wisdom: 'The Civil War was a strictly Spanish event and its two initiators were men of the truest Spanish character at the head of two institutions which in the truest Spanish tradition revolted against the state through sheer inability to resist the temptations of the power which they happened to possess. Neither Communism, Russian or otherwise, nor Nazi-Fascism, German or otherwise, had the slightest possibility of provoking a Spanish Civil War in 1936, even if they had tried, which they did not.'

But the waters were muddied by the foreign help given to both sides, which was in total less than has often been thought; as Hugh Thomas has pointed out, it was the timing rather than quantity which tipped the balance either way from event to event. The best-known supports of the 'light' were the International Brigades which came from many countries. The British brigade totalled only two thousand and suffered very heavy casualties. 'There was in the rich innocence of their muster, a naïve innocence only equalled, perhaps, by the Children's Crusade', for when they landed 'it was discovered nothing tallied, neither love, death, God nor government, with what those terms meant – even in the broadest sense – outside Spain ... The initial shock as they journeyed into this huge strange land was to see its churches burning, hearing its priests being executed and watch ordinary people apparently thankfully piling their personal religious aids, statues, holy pictures and rosaries on to bonfires.' John Marks when he got back to London told me that he had witnessed a very good night's hunting. Caught in Spain, he was kept with many others on a train in a siding at Barcelona Station awaiting the arrival of a British destroyer to take them off. White-faced and terrified, a priest ran past, doubling back between the carriages as in some macabre Waterloo Cup, with the hounds in full tongue, gradually catching up until they could overtake him and tear him to pieces. 'By far the worst of the old Spanish customs the International Brigade volunteers and idealists had to endure, and this whether their internationalism was for or against Franco, were the judicial murders carried out daily by both sides. At the close of the war it was estimated that more than 800,000 people had been executed, which was exactly double the number of those slain in actual battle.'

Of course there were other forms of foreign intervention: German aeroplanes, the Condor Legion, Russian artillery and technicians cynically withdrawn by Stalin later (there was a suggestion that Stalin was afraid of the consequences of a Republican victory), and Mussolini's contribution – the Littorio Division which got itself cut to pieces by the Italian Garibaldi volunteers in a fratricidal affair at Guadalajara.

Furthermore, the chances of the democratically elected government were not improved by its internal divisions. Andrés Nin, one of the founders of the Spanish Communist party who had changed his stance and become leader of P.O.U.M., was arrested and murdered at the behest of the Soviet secret police; George Orwell on his emergence from hospital was arrested in Barcelona and thrown into jail because his political views were not 'correct'. As Leon Trotsky said in his essay on Spain in 1937, 'The "Republican" military commanders occupied themselves more with crushing the social revolution than with winning military victories.'

Some lily-livered racists regarded the use of African troops in Europe as barbarous, but no one has yet disproved the truth of Sherman's contention that war is hell, and it seems to matter little what colour the devils stoking the conflagration may be. A Moorish corpse is just a pathetic bundle of rags like any other; there is little dignity in sudden death.

Because we had discussed Spain so often and at such length, Viola Garvin gave me a daunting task; I was to review for *The Observer* all the books coming from both sides during the war. The daunting side of the task was to perform it with enough dexterity to avoid falling foul of Garvin, who was way out to the right and quite early stated firmly that 'the true government of Spain is already the government of Bourgos' – a view hardly acceptable to the predominately pro-Republican British people; but long afterwards the historical verdict was that 'Garvin's attitude may have lost readers, but it made sense.'

Since Viola and her father were particularly close, I am sure that they must have discussed the literary pages and Garvin obviously saw what I had written. I tried very hard to be fair because I was myself torn two ways. But despite Garvin's political views my copy was never cut or altered by a word. As an exception from my task Viola gave one book to Archie MacDonnell who belittled the heroic defenders of the Alcazar in Toledo; this brought a rebuke even from the Duke of Alba, and the author of *England, Their England* was not called upon again. I found that both sides produced some good straightforward stuff, but equally some absolute stinkers, and it was like a man finding water in the desert when in 1938 I set about reviewing the only book to come out of the three years' tragedy that anyone can now remember: George Orwell's *Homage to Catalonia*.

September of that year was a day marked white by the birth of our son, Nicholas, in a Blackheath maternity home. At the time I was playing cricket, and I think that I should explain how I came to be engaged in such a frivolous pursuit at such a time. Always on the look-out for new fixtures for the Savages, I had rung up Sir Stenson Cook and asked if we could have a match with the AA, to which he kindly replied that all their sporting arrangements were made by their company, the Motor Union, to whom he would give the necessary instructions. A few days later I was rung up by the cricket secretary who said, with bad grace, 'We have been told to give you a game'; we fixed a date and then he said, with rather worse grace, 'I take it you're medium to strong.' You bastard, I thought, while replying, 'Yes, indeed.' I got the team together, told them of the conversation, and invited the two weakest members to stand down so that I could bring in two friends who were good cricketers, and to this the pair cheerfully agreed. When the day came, with Margaret in the nursing-home, I found myself in the embarrassing position of having asked two friends who did not know the team to play and not turning up myself. I phoned Blackheath; there were no signs of labour, so I risked it and went. The match was hilarious and the story of it is in the cricket appendix, but while I was absent things had been happening and the baby was born. All was well, and he was enchanting.

It was not done then for fathers to be present at births, but what was fashionable at that time was never to say 'No' in bringing up a child. The idea of, short of the risk of serious physical injury, letting a child do what it liked, was to encourage innate common sense, and ignore overt naughtiness. So often a child's actions are intended solely to get an angry rise out of the parents, and if the actions are totally ignored there is no fun in repeating the mischief. My mother was horrified; but, difficult as it often was, we stuck to it. I have no idea how much influence this upbringing had upon Nicholas; I can only offer a slightly prejudiced opinion that he is one of the nicest and sanest people I know.

12   Downhill All the Way

In spite of the fact that business was still difficult, I was tempted back into the limited editions field by Stefan Zweig who had found a good Austrian wood-engraver named Margaretta Hammerslag, and he suggested that she should illustrate an English edition of *The Buried Candelabrum* which had appeared in German at the beginning of 1937. This story meant much to him and brought some solace to many Jews. We did an edition of 1,000 copies, which Oliver Simon printed beautifully as ever; 990 were numbered and ten, bound in full leather, were signed by Stefan. Things must have been looking up because we sold them quite quickly.

Another indication that things were getting better was the opening of the *Ecu de France* in Jermyn Street, the first new good restaurant since the beginning of the slump.* The cellar was chosen by André Simon, who warmly recommended the place to me, and I became a regular, well known to the *Maître d'Hôtel*, Lherian, who always looked after me well, as we shall shortly see. But I did not desert Boulestin, and it was at this time that we published a most original book which the great man had compiled, *The Finer Cookery*. Apart from the magnificent recipes, the originality of the book lay in the fact that it was in two volumes: one in washable cloth for the cook, and the other, on good paper and handsomely bound, from which the mistress could choose the meals. I knew Boulestin well: a rubicund, jolly man who had originally been an interior decorator. During the war he was liaison officer with a British unit, in the mess of which he found the food so bad that he insisted on taking over the cooking himself. Afterwards there was little architectural work to be had, and a friend suggested that he should go to London and open a restaurant. The other side of him came out in the ornamentation, the crowning glories of which were paintings by Laboureur and Marie Laurencin. It is an infinite pity that the best of them has now been prised from the wall and sold.

On publication day he invited me to lunch. He was the first restaurateur to have specialities flown in from France, and on that day the *pièce de résistance* had arrived from his beloved Marseilles – which of course we had to have. It was stuffed calf's hoof, and I am sorry to say

---

* The *Ecu* has now unfortunately gone.

that I thought it perfectly filthy. There was no question of going to Spain in 1937, so we went as near as we could, to St Jean de Luz, and gazed wistfully at the beloved country across the Bidassoa, the river in which so many Republican refugees had died when General Mola took Irun on 3 September 1936.

On the way home we stopped in Paris to visit the International Exhibition, of which I have three memories: in the Cambodian exhibit the half-scale model of the Angkor Wat; the stalls of the French colonies, each serving free its own delicious coffee; and the Spanish pavilion, which was completely empty, except at the far end where, doubly impressive through its very isolation, was Picasso's latest canvas, painted in fury: *Guernica*.

A year later the situation in Spain had changed considerably. The Marqués del Moral, with whom I used to fence at the Lansdowne Club, asked me why I did not go as I loved the country so much, adding that if I asked the Duke of Alba for a visa I would get one. So I did. Margaret took our son Nicholas to Frinton, and I arranged to meet John Marks at Irun. It was a surprising and informative visit.

We spent the first two days at Zarauz, which was then no more than a sleepy fishing-village. There the heavy hand of the law showed itself: a civil guard, plodding through the hot sand in ammunition boots, ensured that no one lay down on the beach; for some ridiculous reason to do so was considered morally lax, but it was in order to sit up.

I was anxious to see the *Cinturón*, the famous 'Ring of Iron' round Bilbao against which General Mola, and after his death General Davila, had flung his infantry to so little purpose, because, certain by now that we ourselves would soon be in a war, I wanted to see what a modern impregnable position looked like. It was a perfect defensive line and a frontal attack made as much sense as the Union's advance at Fredericksburg which I had gone over eight years previously. It was never pierced: it was outflanked by the first use of a tactic soon to become painfully familiar to us – *Blitzkrieg*. Lining up every tank he had on the main road from San Sebastian, the army commander gave the order to go, with no stopping for anything or anybody. Any vehicle broken down or knocked out was to be pushed off the road. Such radical action was as successful as it was to prove in 1939 and 1940.

In Bilbao we stayed in the comfortable Torrontegue, a new version of the hotel Margaret and I had known; now even that has gone. In a café near by the law appeared for the second time. We were having drinks before dinner when the musicians played *Ouriamendi*, the Nationalist anthem. Everyone got up, arms stiffly raised; we stood to attention. Immediately afterwards I went to the gents and I was followed by a plain clothes policeman who, curious to know why I had not given the salute, demanded to see my passport; leafing through it, he was satisfied. We had no further trouble.

We visited Durango and Eibar, both small arms manufacturing towns (the latter centred round a pistol factory) which had both been seriously damaged; and so to Guernica.

To this day aspects of the Guernica tragedy remain enigmatic. Philip Knightley, reviewing the five hundred pages that the American historian Herbert R. Southworth devoted to the subject in 1977, wrote, 'The dispute remains as alive today as when it started,' and Southworth himself says, 'I do not know why Guernica was destroyed as it was,' and on the fiftieth anniversary of the outbreak of the war Brian Crozier, in a letter to *The Times*, referred to 'the apparently invincible myth of Guernica'. I cannot help wondering how many of the vast army of those who have written about this little town, which produced at the time such horror stories, such propaganda from both sides, Picasso's great painting, and even in 1984 a paean of sentimental horror on television, have ever been there.

We found the destruction much less than we had been led to expect, though the fact that the town was bombed by German aircraft is not in question.

That this act of war took place on market day can be dismissed as valueless sentiment. I do not think that the RAF took much notice of whether it was market day or any other day when they needlessly bombed Caen, a few miles from where I was watching, in 1944; but on the other hand they knew that the city was packed with refugee women and children when they ruthlessly destroyed Dresden with such appalling slaughter in the following year.

The squadron of the Condor Legion which made the attack had written off the railway station which was a legitimate military target since it is an important junction. Next door two streets of workers' dwellings had been destroyed by fire, and the prevailing wind spread the flames through one section of the town. Both high-explosive bombs and incendiaries had been used, but from my observation the two areas of destruction were so distinct that there cannot have been any question of a bomb mix which became so common in the Second World War; but there is a possibility that they might have been dropped separately by succeeding waves of aircraft through negligible ack-ack.

It has been suggested that the bombing might have been a strategic exercise designed to break the Basque morale; this I cannot accept, because the one act which would most effectively have achieved this would have been the destruction of the sacred tree which makes Guernica of such importance to all Basques.

Apart from the station and its environs, up the road the main town of largely late nineteenth-century architecture, the big church on the hill with, flourishing beside it, the sacred tree, all smiled happily in the sunshine with not a mark, not a scratch upon them. Wondering if my eyes and memory had deceived me so long ago, I took Margaret to the town again in the late seventies; I had made no mistake. Although the place has sprawled to the west, the original town which I first saw in 1938 remains intact in its old-fashioned and sedate dignity.

What of the two burnt streets and their environment? They must have made a spectacular blaze at night, which would easily have provided all the cinema footage shown in the 1984 television documentary. It must be remembered that all the photographers present were on the Republican side, as was G.L. Steer who wrote such a moving and dramatic account for *The Times,* and would avidly shoot a good fire – that is their job. In one of the books I read for *The Observer* the Nationalists claimed that before the town was evacuated the Republicans set fire to the streets for propaganda purposes; the justification for this story, if there were any truth in it, would be the surprising survival of the sacred tree which the Basques would have been careful to spare, and the extraordinary proximity but sharp division of fire and high explosive. I do not know any more than the historian, Herbert Southworth, who destroyed what or why; I do not know the truth, but 'What is truth? said jesting Pilate.' I have only the evidence of my own eyes as to what was not destroyed.

Like so many others, I was already becoming more and more unhappy about the international situation. I decided to publish an anthology about the horrors of the First World War as a cautionary tale, a warning, and I asked Guy Chapman, the husband of Storm Jameson, whom I knew and admired, to undertake it. He made a fine job of this huge volume which we called *Vain Glory.* I wonder how many people who have seen a copy recognize that the title on the spine is printed in imitation of the metal strips with name and number which were punched out and nailed on the wooden crosses of the dead before their final resting place was marked by the traditional headstone of the War Graves Commission. It was published in 1937 and the whole thing backfired. Far from a cautionary tale, far from a warning against similar folly, it was received with ecstatic nostalgia and sold in large quantities.

During the preparation of the book Guy Chapman lunched with me at my club. At the next table was David Higham, his host a notorious member of the Pitt-Rivers family who was to be sent very smartly to the Isle of Man on the outbreak of war in 1939. On the latter's lapel were the three metal emblems of Mussolini, Hitler and Franco. Guy looked at them and said to me, 'The Fasces I know, the Swastika I have heard of; but what is that bunch of arrows tied by with a girth – the local toxophilite society?' His voice carried – it was meant to, and Pitt-Rivers roared, 'Are you talking to me, sir?'

I wrote to the secretary that I objected to having my guest shouted at in the club, and received a grateful reply saying that the committee had been trying to get rid of this member for some time but until now had not been able to pin anything on him.

A less successful publishing venture, but in one way a pleasant experience, was Errol Flynn's *Beam Ends.* As he was the new big film star, I thought that a book by him about his early life was bound to sell, but I was wrong. Passing through London, he had a day to spare which we spent together. I remember him as tall, lithe and handsome, so unlike the bloated figure of his last years. He had been a beachcomber in Australia, and he vividly – too vividly – portrayed all his old companions of that vagrant life. One of them got hold of the book, considered himself libelled, consulted a lawyer and won his case. He passed the word along the East Coast of Australia and in all we had to settle twenty-nine cases out of court; this must constitute some kind of record – and the book did not sell.

A great disappointment to me also was Hughes Panassié's *Hot Jazz*: when it was translated into English I jumped at it because there was nothing in this country to help me in my pursuit of traditional jazz except occasional articles in *The Melody Maker*. Unfortunately my own interest did not seem to be shared by many other people. It is fashionable now to deride Panassié; the *cognoscenti* say that he was inaccurate and that in the States they had already done it all; perhaps they had, but they succeeded in keeping their findings remarkably dark and we on this side of the Atlantic who were thirsting for knowledge got no drops from their overflowing pitchers of wisdom.

I got more than I expected when I took a rather good first novel called *You Play the Black and the Red Comes Up* by Eric M. Knight. Knight was to write only three more books before his death early in the war in the Far East: two novels, of which *This Above All* was very good, but he left behind to be published posthumously a book which was quickly received into the canon of children's literature, *Lassie Come Home*.

Since there must always be progress and new ideas if there is to be life, it seemed perfectly natural for the AA in the late thirties, when the career of Sir Stenson Cook as its founder and first secretary came to an end, to wish to have control of its own publications – at that time in the singular: there was only the handbook for members. Someone in the organization realized that they had a captive public, the handbook was removed from us perfectly amicably, and the list was slowly developed into a major publishing house, producing superb books of history and towns and villages and atlases, of which I, like many members, have a shelfful, and then more recently into a motorist's emporium offering everything from tool-kits to sheepskin coats.

On 7 January 1938, I met Robert Graves for the first time. Martin Seymour-Smith quotes from Graves' diary: 'Good impression ... decent and intelligent,' Robert wrote, which was very kind of him; for myself, I think I was frightened stiff.

Robert had a problem. He had finished a new historical novel, *Count Belisarius*; he also had Laura Riding. They had met in 1927, only six months after she had come to Europe from the United States. An extraordinary situation developed in which Laura and Robert lived together with the consent of his wife, Nancy, who had her own establishment with their children. Laura's importance at that time was that she could relieve him of his 'vivid, nerve-shattering recollections' of the First World War, which he finally exorcized with the publication of *Goodbye to All That*, in 1929. On the proceeds of this success he bore Laura off to Deyá in Mallorca. In the following year Laura wrote, 'Bodies have had their day', and the two ceased to be lovers but remained together, Robert seeming to feel himself under some sort of obligation. Evacuated like many others by a British destroyer in the early months of the Civil War, they returned to England.

By now Seymour-Smith says that 'Graves' (alleged) "debt" to Riding was probably paid,' but Robert still insisted on offering a package deal: his novel and her work. Again 'the ease with which he could sell his own work and the difficulties he had in selling Laura's proved greatly embarrassing to him.' Heinemann said No; father and I were offered the package and took it. In our view this was not doing anyone any great favour: I thought then (and still do) that she was a fine writer but a difficult property.

Book production could be fast then and we had *Belisarius* out by April, printing 20,000 and selling it well. But Laura's poems were longer in the press and did not appear until the autumn. She was a powerful figure and was always fussing about the publicity. Julian Symons has said, 'She was ... beautiful in a ferocious way: sharp nose, thin lips, eyes dark and snapping.' There was a lot of snapping, and finally, lunching at their flat one day, I too snapped. She kept up her demands all through the meal and finally I said, 'Oh, Laura, don't be so dictatorial!' Forty-eight hours later I got a letter from her saying that, as a publisher, I presumably knew the meaning of words in the English language, and to call her 'dictatorial' was to put her in a class with Hitler and Mussolini; was that my meaning? From time to time I have found myself shooting off letters which are short and to the point and my reply to this was one of them:

> 'Dear Laura,
> 'Yes, that is my meaning.
> 'Yours.'

The upshot was a meeting with a rather subdued and gentle Robert who said that Laura had made him promise never again to offer a book to Cassell's; but that nevertheless he would return at the first opportunity. The break with Laura became 'official' early in 1940. Robert had had enough, he had paid his dues; but true to his promise to her he asked his agent, Alec Watt, to offer his next two novels concerning Sergeant Lamb to Methuen (who had acquired Arthur Barker's firm when it folded in 1939 and therefore had the Claudius books); they published the first in 1940 and the second in 1941. A year later, however, Robert honoured his word to me and returned to Cassell's with *Wife to Mr Milton*, but by then I had gone for a soldier and father, who, as we shall see, had returned to the office, received him with open arms. Father particularly liked *King Jesus* which followed *The Golden Fleece* (1944) and wrote to Robert, 'A grand piece of work ... easily the finest book you have given Cassell's.'

No one had been deeply concerned by the murder of Dollfuss in 1934; after all, he was a dictator and we had had enough of Mussolini and now Hitler was Chancellor of Germany. Although the crime was organized by the Nazis, it seemed like neighbours squabbling in their back garden; but we should have known better, for in March of 1938 came the *Anschluss*. It was, of course, a terrible shock, but it should not have been unexpected.

As the German troops were crossing the border Paul Frischauer had a frantic telephone call from the cellarer of the Hofburg, whom he knew, asking if he would like some wine at a nominal price. He was, he said, trying to get rid of as much as possible from the Imperial cellar before Hitler started guzzling it. Paul rang me, and we decided that we could afford two cases each. When they came, my share was a case of Johannisburg 1915, sent to the Emperor by Prince Metternich as rent for the vineyard, and a case of Tokay Essenz. The essenz is not like the wine of the same name, but a wonderful and most potent liqueur which has a reputation as a life-restorer (in the following year when my grandfather was dying of bronchitis father phoned me and asked if I still had any; I had, I took it to Salisbury, and within twenty-four hours the dear old man was back on his feet, completely restored).

The Austrian ambassador, Baron Frankenstein, who had contracted to write his memoirs, *Facts and Features of my Life*, which we published in the following spring, was extremely well liked in London. Three days after the *Anschluss* Margaret and I had been invited to one of the baron's famous musical evenings, a Schubert concert at the embassy in Belgrave Square. Before the music began we saw Paul Frischauer and asked how our host stood with the Nazis. Paul said that Hitler had invited Frankenstein to continue as ambassador under the changed conditions, and he had refused. Hitler had then stripped him of his nationality and title, and given him forty-eight hours to get out of the embassy. It was now the third day and I said, 'So, actually, he is trespassing?' 'Exactly,' said Paul. No one would have believed it as the erstwhile baron welcomed his guests and presided benignly over the wonderful music. The end of the story was a happy one: King George VI granted him immediate British nationality, knighted him and set him up in a grace and favour apartment at Hampton Court. This is said to have caused one of the Führer's carpet-biting exercises, although that is probably no more than wishful thinking.

Apropos, we published one more rather sad book in 1938, fortunately already in our hands in view of what was about to happen: *Farewell Austria* by Kurt von Schuschnigg, appointed Chancellor on the death of Dollfuss; totally opposed to the Germans' intrusion, he was promptly put in prison from which he did not emerge until their defeat seven years later.

Another interesting book that same year was *The Story of S.T.25* by Sir Paul Dukes. It was an account, which he felt able to tell after twenty years, of his adventures during the Russian Revolution. 'S.T.25' was his number when he and Sidney Reilly were the two most important British agents in Russia, and he enjoyed a reputation as being a master of disguise. When things became too hot and he was recalled to this country, he had been received in audience by King George V, who listened avidly to all that he had to tell, and said that if it were not confined to the armed services he would give him the Victoria Cross – there being no George Medal at that time. His reputation was not unknown, and at this time he was asked privately to go to Czechoslovakia to trace a missing businessman; he succeeded in outwitting the Germans, already a majority in the Sudetenland, and he described his successful mission two years later in *An Epic of the Gestapo*. He was a tall, ascetic man whom, although friendly, one never felt one knew at all; it was not surprising that years later he wrote a book on Yoga which we published.

It has always been a mystery to me why occasionally authors, out of the blue, offer a book to another house instead of to their regular publisher. John Cowper Powys, who had a considerable reputation at the time, now brought to us *The Pleasures of Literature*, which was an interesting book and I enjoyed meeting him; but there had been no relations between us before nor were there to be any after. It was similar to John Buchan offering us his life of Sir Walter Scott a few years earlier; again, I enjoyed the unexpected pleasure of his company, but I really did not think that we could have done any better with a good, solid biography than the highly reputable house which had published him for years. Another example was Eddie Sackville-West who brought to me *Flame in Sunlight*, his life of Thomas de Quincey; I had never met him before, and I never saw him again after the book's publication. Some authors, I know, are footloose and enjoy change for its own sake; sometimes a misunderstanding can send an author away in a huff; occasionally a fresh face is pleasurable – there can be many reasons; nevertheless, I have never felt that the 'one off' is particularly good for either side.

The happiest event of 1938 was father's knighthood. He had told me in the strictest confidence (any honour is automatically cancelled if the would-be recipient opens his mouth) that he had received a letter from the Prime Minister. Remembering the many occasions at home when he had ranted against all honours, I said, 'I take it that you have declined?' He looked a little sheepish and said, 'No, I have accepted.' I was surprised but delighted.

It came out in the Birthday Honours list, and then there was the usual wait until the investiture. That wait used to be an embarrassment because the knowledge was public but the title did not apply, an anomaly which has now been rectified. When the day arrived, father came straight from the Palace to give mother, Margaret and me lunch at the *Ecu de France*. Dear Lherian welcomed us, and at the first opportunity I slipped a note into his hand: 'My father has just been knighted; will you please produce a bottle of champagne and I will pay for it.' He quickly slipped a note back to me: 'I will serve it at once – but it is on the house.' Father was understandably in a state of nervous excitement and when the bottle appeared he exploded, 'I didn't order champagne. Take it away!' When the situation was explained to him, he was distressingly contrite – but it was a very good wine, consumed with relish.

Stefan Zweig expressed his pleasure, and asked me if he should now address father as 'Sir Flower'; curiously, although his knowledge of the English language was so wide, he still had some blind spots – for instance, I could never cure him of referring to *The Ballad of Reading Goal*.

The agent Christine Campbell-Thomson offered me a novel which was not a first, because its author had previously written three comparatively trivial books which he – in common with the rest of the world – preferred to forget; this was his first 'serious' novel. I read it immediately myself because I was struck by its opening line which I think is one of the most memorable in English fiction: 'I was unusually drunk the night my father died.' It was called *This is the Schoolroom* and the author was Nicholas Monsarrat. I bought it at once and my confidence caused me to print (and sell), 7,500 copies – a figure which in later years the author regarded as 'derisory' but was just two and a half times as many as one normally printed of a new author at that time. It appeared in the autumn, and led, *inter alia*, to my writing another of my short letters. One Clarence Paget wrote to me saying that he was doing so because Monsarrat, a fellow Wykehamist, did not like to write himself, yet felt that his novel was not getting enough publicity and he (Paget) hoped he was not being impertinent in drawing attention to the matter. I replied: 'Dear Mr Paget, You may hope that you are not being impertinent. You are. Yours sincerely.' A decade later Clarence, an extremely nice man, came to work with me, reminded me of the letter, and we chuckled.

Overshadowing everything that autumn was the Munich Pact, which affected the whole nation and created rifts within families; the Flowers were no exception. In common with so many others, Margaret and I had been growing more and more unhappy at the increasing policy of appeasement, and regarded the attitude of Neville Chamberlain as treachery. Nor was the Prime Minister alone; Geoffrey Dawson of *The Times* was as bad, and even the film censor's reader in recommending a ban on the March of Time film, '*Inside Nazi Germany*', gave as his reason: 'In my opinion the public showing of this picture in England would give grave offence to a nation with whom we are on terms of friendship.'

Another example of the current pusillanimity was the attitude taken by the authorities towards *Idiot's Delight*. A brilliant and grimly prophetic play, it was written by Robert Sherwood in 1936 and played with enormous success on Broadway by the Lunts. Two years later this great pair were coming to London to play (magnificently) Giraudoux's *Amphritrion 38*, so Raymond Massey had the chance which he had always wanted of taking the lead himself here. But the Foreign Office requested the Lord Chamberlain to ban the play because it might cause offence to the Fascist powers. Lord Cromer, the then censor of plays, was most distressed and happy to reach a compromise with Massey which set the play in an unnamed Middle European country. Massey played to capacity houses for six months, was then replaced, and the curtain was finally rung down by the Munich agreement. The night we went was an experience which I shall never forget. Most people were convinced that war was imminent and it was accepted that as soon as it started London would be razed to the ground. The play is concerned with a dance company on tour in Europe at a time of acute international tension. At the end of the last act the players listen to and the audience hear a sound soon to be all too familiar – the sound something between a whistle and tearing calico – as the first sticks of bombs rain down. Despite the wonderful acting of this great play, there was not one note of applause; at the end the audience got up and slunk out in complete silence.

When the pact was signed in September the scenes in London were lamentable. The weather was glorious; Margaret and I walked in Kensington Gardens watching the rise and fall of pick-axes as slit trenches were frantically dug and the solid mass of traffic stood for hours in Kensington Road, slowly heading out of town. I particularly remember a stationary pearl-grey Rolls-Royce with, strapped on its roof, a large perambulator; it seemed sadly incongruous.

We debated as we walked as to what country we should emigrate to, and decided on New Zealand. It may seem illogical to regard with contempt the stationary traffic while planning permanently to leave the country, but there was a difference. The occupants of the cars were impatient to reach their funk-holes: we in our young arrogance, mindful of the axiom that every country gets the government it deserves, had no wish to remain in an island the honour of which had been besmirched, which made us feel ashamed; we could be just as useful somewhere else within the Empire. After so many years it is difficult to believe that we felt so strongly, but it was very real at the time.

Father, with his pro-German and anti-French sentiments, and Aubrey Gentry, both with sons who would be involved if there was a war, regarded the Prime Minister with a warmth little short of idolatry. At the office the rows between us became constant, waxing more and more abusive. Any communication during working-hours was confined strictly to business; attempts at conversation were avoided because they inevitably ended up in a slanging match on the same old subject.

However, there was no time to organize anything before Christmas, and by then it was apparent that Chamberlain was tied round Hitler's little finger by a granny knot which would soon give way and there could be only one outcome. That was a different moral issue: we were for it, and we were part of it.

Another unhappy aspect of that year was the serious decline in father's health. His years of hard work and the need for alcohol to keep him going were catching up with him and he was not doing a very good job. I was to go the same way at the same age: was this an inherited weakness or merely coincidence? Aubrey Gentry tried to persuade me to join with him in forcing father to resign, but there was no way that I was going to gang up on someone whom I loved and to whom I owed so much. I refused. A period of uneasy stalemate followed, brought to an end in a way which took me by surprise: he announced his own decision to retire.

When I took over his office, my first task was to try to negotiate a treaty of peace in a *casus belli* which had already led to harsh words between us. Storm Jameson, one of the real stars on our fiction list, had recently delivered to us her new novel, *Cousin Honoré*. It was bitterly and brutally critical of Neville Chamberlain and the Munich pact, and father set about it with his blue pencil. He showed me his handiwork and I pointed out that not only did I agree with all the passages which he wished to see deleted, but no serious author would ever accept such cuts. There was, of course, a row, but he sent off the list of deletions which he wished made before he would publish the book and met with the expected refusal.

In the changed circumstances I asked Storm Jameson if she would be so kind as to come and see me. She arrived with her husband, Guy Chapman. I explained that I did not see eye to eye with my father on political matters and had objected to the cuts being suggested in the first place, asking her to forget about them except for one small remark about Chamberlain which was clearly libellous. But she had arrived firmly in the saddle of her high horse: no, she said, she would not alter a single word. One line: that was all I wanted out, and to object to this was clearly not very reasonable. I turned to her husband and said, 'Guy, what do you think?'

'Nothing to do with me.'

Exasperated, I nearly asked him why the hell he had bothered to come, but I didn't, and that was the end of the matter. A good start to my time in office – to lose an eminent author! But she was a generous woman and had the last word; several years after the war we met at a P.E.N. party, and with a gentle smile she said, 'I should never have left you; silliest thing I ever did.'

After that I turned to something more agreeable which I had vowed to do as soon as I was in a position to: I wrote to Allen Lane reversing the previous decision and saying that he could have any Cassell titles he wanted for Penguin; he was pleased, took me up on it, and we became friends for the rest of his life.

My next move was to call upon our most eminent author, whom I had never met: Winston Churchill. I went to his flat in Morpeth Mansions to enquire how he was getting on with his *History of the English-speaking Peoples*. He was dressed in a gorgeous blue brocade dressing-gown and there was a very large cigar in his mouth – my first sight of an image which is part of history. He had, he said, finished the Wars of the Roses with which he was very pleased because he thought that he was the first historian to make any sense out of that conflict, and he hoped to finish the whole work in the following year, which turned out to be a pious dream. Then we talked about the international situation. 'The lights are going out all over Europe,' he said and, walking up and down, repeated the phrase which I ignorantly did not recognize as the famous words of Sir Edward Grey in 1914. In years to come I found that he would often repeat a phrase that pleased him which he intended to use, probably in the House, as though he were trying it out on the dog. I was to see him countless times in years to come and because a situation developed similar to that between Stefan Zweig and myself – in a way as his publisher I was the master, but in every other way very much the servant – I was never in awe of him, but, like so many others, felt a deep affection, a love such as one might feel for a revered and favourite uncle. He was always kind, considerate (except when he would ring me up at one o'clock in the morning) and courteous; he never lost his temper with me – one has heard of monumental explosions – and indeed once it was I who was rude to him, when under considerable strain, which happily he chose to ignore.

The first event of the New Year was Pamela's wedding on 5 January. She had become engaged in the previous year to Patrick Hoare-Ruthven, son of the Governor-general of Australia, and invited us to her party. I spent the entire time talking to her fiancé whom I found delightful. Neither of us seemed to want to talk to anyone else; there was, I suppose, a bond, if nothing else, between us; he was the man in possession and I long retired but still admiring. The wedding was in Henry VII's chapel at Westminster Abbey, and we were kindly asked again. It was the last time that I was to see her for many, many years. She looked ravishing in ivory satin, and I do not think that any more beautiful bride can ever have walked to the altar steps of that superb building. She bore Patrick two sons, of whom the elder is the present Earl of Gowrie, before he gave his life in the Long Range Desert Group.

During the spring I received a visit which remains vivid because of its sadness. The brother of Hedwig Evers – he who had talked of the Butte of Warlincourt with Warwick Deeping so many years ago – came into the office to tell me that she was dead. He was a good man. We stood by the door as he got up to leave and I said:

'Do you think it is going to be war?'

'Yes, I am afraid so.'

'Then I am glad that she has gone because she would have hated to see it all again.'

We shook hands and he departed.

The first of the two most important events of the year came in May: the end of the Spanish Civil War. We made immediate plans to go there. It was a joyful reunion with the Constanceau family at Caldetas. They were all well and for, alas, the last time we sat on the patio in the warm evenings, chatting. The war had produced much suffering and little good except for the great advances made in blood transfusion. As an example of the muddle the whole thing had been, I asked the son-in-law what he had been doing for the last three years. He replied that he had been in the Ministry of War and had never worked so hard in his life; after a full day's activity it took him most of the night to encode the orders and radio them to the insurgents. In a war between nations that is blatant treachery; but how can one describe it when people fight their own brothers, and so many find themselves geographically on what from choice they might consider the 'wrong' side? It is a heartbreaking element of any civil war. So goodbye Caldetas; the Estrach is no longer there, but various monstrosities have sprung up – as they have all along that lovely coast.

We went into Barcelona and, after the hair-raising accounts of the destruction, we were surprised to find it virtually intact, except that the Hotel Colón had gone and one block of flats was seriously damaged.

Denyse Clairouin had invited us to call at her country house at Villers, near Honfleur, on our way home, and said that two members of the cabinet whom she would like us to meet would be there. But by the time we arrived the international situation was extremely grave, the French army had mobilized, and we were hardly surprised when Denyse, in greeting us warmly, regretted that the two ministers were otherwise engaged in Paris. She took us to the church in Honfleur in which William prayed before setting sail for Hastings, and remarked that as the direct descendant of one of the Conqueror's knights she had the right to ride into the church on a white horse – a right which I was disappointed to learn she had never exercised.

Fortunately we had our car already booked on a definite date from Dieppe, or we would have been in real trouble getting home. The quay was a shambles. For one thing it was crowded with car-owners who had cut their holidays short (in the end most of them got home somehow while their cars were driven by the AA and RAC to Belgium where the ferries were less overloaded); for another it was littered with wrecks. Holidaymakers returning from the south had to cross the path of the mobilizing troops moving west to east, and the results were disastrous. In those days if an insurance claim was to be made the car had to be produced in England, whatever its condition, so it was necessary for wrecks to be towed to the docks. I remember one in particular which was in a shocking state: its left-hand door had gone and the front seats were drenched in blood.

Not long after we got home we were invited to lunch at Chartwell; on a gorgeous day, it was our first visit to a place I was later to know well. There was only one other guest outside the family: Professor Lindeman. At the end of lunch the ladies left us three men to our port. Winston and the 'Prof' started a conversation between themselves in riddles, to which I realized that I knew the answer. If it was secret, they should not have been discussing it in front of me anyway, and I thought it slightly rude of them to ramble on, completely ignoring the only other person in the room. After a while I could bear it no longer and said bluntly, 'If you are talking about the compressed air bombs which the Luftwaffe is supposed to have dropped on Barcelona, I can tell you they're no bloody good.' The two great men looked startled and then there was a general conversation on the subject.

Over the last few years we had become very friendly with a good-looking American with an attractive white streak in his black hair, Bob Low, who was one of the heads of Twentieth Century-Fox in London, and he used to ask us to previews of films at their headquarters in Soho Square. One day he rang me and asked if Margaret and I could do him a favour. In 1938 the beautiful young film actress, Corinne Luchaire, had had such a success in *Prison Without Bars* that Twentieth Century-Fox had bought the rights and were bringing her to London for tests before the English-language version was made. She was to be chaperoned by her mother who spoke no English. Since we spoke French, would we take them both out? Of course. Eventually Margaret took Mama to Harrods to shop, but first we went for the evening to the Café de Paris. Corinne and I had a dance or two. She was remarkably attractive, but there was a steely, acquisitive undertone which is difficult to describe but to which I felt a deep aversion.

The next morning Bob rang me up at the office and asked me what I had thought of her. I said, 'She's the biggest two-timing bitch I've ever met.' After a pause he said, 'I'm so sorry; I was thinking of marrying her.'

I had no idea that he had any personal interest and I could have bitten my tongue off, but in the end perhaps I did him a good turn, since she turned out to be not a very good character, although it must be said that had they married she would not have had the opportunity to disgrace herself as she did. History relates that, if she did not herself share the bed of Otto Abetz, she was certainly the closest friend of his 'steady' and spent most of her time in the headquarters of the German governor of Paris. At the end of the war her father was hanged for his collaboration, while she was one of the wretched women forced to march with her head shorn through a hostile crowd down the Champs Elysées. Fortunately she died of T.B. soon afterwards, for she would never have been allowed to work again.

We were not back from Spain in peace for long. My last memory of the halcyon days was tea with Oliver and Ruth Simon in their garden in Hampstead. W.H. Auden, whom I knew slightly and whom the Simons knew rather better, looked in and sat on the back doorstep, chatting in the hot sunshine. I said to Nicholas, 'Go and hold that gentleman's finger; he is a great poet – it will bring you luck.' Auden extended his forefinger and Nicholas shyly took it, looking up at him. I wonder what legacy that symbolic gesture bestowed upon the child – if any.

Then in a matter of days the Germans had marched into Poland and we were listening gloomily to the news of their inevitable victories. Bad as the German tanks were at that time, they were still less vulnerable than horses, and heroism is not enough. Down at Sevenoaks for the weekend, I was lying on the sofa in the Handel Room, basking in the hot sun, waiting for the eleven o'clock news; and when it came, it was the dry voice of Neville Chamberlain announcing that Britain had declared war. When the inevitable finally occurs it is like the lancing of a boil, the drawing of a thorn; our spirits rose, but it was not long before they sank again; what were we going to do to help Poland, with whom the Prime Minister had allied us with promises which he could not keep? Nothing.

This was the last shooting-season. For a number of years father had had a shoot in Kent and kindly asked me every Saturday, and we stayed the weekend. My shooting was a pale shadow of father's; he was very good. There were four guns on the final day at Cranbrook: we two, the stationmaster at Tubbs Hill, Sevenoaks, who was a beautiful shot, and a tall, athletic Italian named Bertucelli who had a business making buttons out of Brazil nuts. After a long stand at midday we began the best part of a mile's walk back to the forester's cottage for lunch, I with the Italian, the other two behind. As we went along a ride through light, open woods, a magnificent cock-bird hastened ahead of us nervously. This aroused all the Italian's predatory instincts and he started to stalk it, his gun thrust forward at the ready. The bird showed no inclination to take off, but turned right into the sparse undergrowth and quickened its pace. Bertucelli followed and went faster until he was brought to a sudden halt by a roar from father: 'Bertucelli, what the bloody hell do you think you're doing?'

He slunk back with his head down like a truant schoolboy.

At twilight the duck flighted in to the small silent reed-lined lake; I bagged one, and I have shot only once since.

13   Change of Life

At first things were much as usual, and I was surprised when the list of reserved occupations came out to find that directors of publishing houses over the age of thirty were on it; I could not think why, but presumed that there must be some reason and decided to conform. In the upheaval caused by the nation finding itself once more engaged in 'The executive and brutal business of war', books did not at that time flourish. Later, when the air raids started and people had time on their hands, business was to be very good.

But now there were new circumstances to be met. Against considerable opposition in the House, I got out an A.R.P. book which sold 13,000 in two weeks. And I remembered that a friend of father, Captain Robinson, who had won the King's Prize at Bisley, had written a small book on rifle-shooting which we had done. Digging it out, I found it good and reprinted it for the Home Guard; the first edition of 10,000 went immediately and it had to be put back on the machine.

Our most active friend was Paul Frischauer, who moved to a house near Crawley in Sussex which became a centre for the dissemination of culture; he believed, rightly, that it was a time when everyone should be proud of his country and its achievements. He made a series of records of English folk songs, sung by David Carver, who had a lovely voice and whom I came to know well years later when he was secretary of P.E.N. Paul also thought up a series of colour-plate books each presenting some aspect of the British genius. He brought the idea to me and I liked it, but when I discussed it with Aubrey Gentry the answer was an uncompromising 'No'. Since he controlled the finances, I was stymied. Paul took the idea to Collins who produced the series *Britain in Pictures* which was a runaway success.

Looking back, I think that a lot more went on at that Sussex house than I ever knew about, probably to do with Intelligence, because in the following spring Paul told me with high glee that the French wished to bestow an honour upon him. He had asked for the *Légion d'Honneur*, only to be told that in time of war that became an entirely military Order, so he said that if he could not have the best, he would have the worst. This, in his opinion, was the Order of Neftim Tafari, holders of which wore a broad cordon of all the colours in the spectrum, bestowed by the Bey of Tunis on the breeders of prize donkeys.

Late in the following February I was summoned to the Admiralty by Winston Churchill, who said, 'I have to tell you that I can no longer work upon *The History of the English-speaking Peoples* now that I am in office.' I replied that I clearly understood that and we went on to other matters. Going to the wall, he pulled down a huge map of the world, saying, 'I had this installed when I was here on a previous occasion so that the whereabouts of every warship at sea could be marked upon it,' reproachfully adding, 'since when it has not been touched.'

He invited me to stay for lunch and we went through to the beautiful eighteenth-century rooms which are the abode of the First Lord. We sat at a long table with him at one end and his wife at the other. I sat on her right, and next to me was Brendan Bracken; opposite were the three daughters whom I had met at Chartwell.

It was the first time I had met Brendan, and we took a liking to one another. Everyone is familiar with his appearance, the odd shape of his head and the masses of wiry hair, but I do not know if anybody really understood him. I certainly didn't, but I was drawn by his sense of loyalty and, to me, his great generosity which continued until the end of his life.

Winston spoke of his appearance on the previous day at the Guildhall to which the victorious seamen of the battle of the River Plate had marched. In his speech, he said, he was the third person to confuse the names of Captain Woodhouse of *Ajax* and Captain Bell of *Exeter*, and 'I don't think they liked it very much.'

Then the girls started to play a guessing game, posing questions about the appearance of an unknown figure; Brendan and I looked at one another in bewilderment, but all was soon made clear. When they got to, 'Who wears collars too big for him? ... Who has a neck like an old turkey?' the immortal voice interrupted, 'I will not have the Prime Minister mocked at my own table.'

After lunch the First Lord said that Chamberlain was making a speech in his own constituency in Birmingham and I had better stay and listen to it. In the drawing-room round the wireless the speech droned on while the First Lord, sunk deep in an armchair with his hands over his eyes, as so often when listening, kept up a running commentary, 'an inexactitude ... a *non sequitur* ... a split infinitive ... a solecism ... another *non sequitur* ...' throughout.

The first Christmas of the war and nothing, apart from the River Plate, was happening. Margaret's mother, imagining or having read in the American papers that we were already short of the niceties of life, sent her a tin of Earl Grey tea; Margaret, with equal solicitude, sent her mother a tin of Earl Grey tea. On Christmas Day I listened to General Von Brauschitz, the Commander-in-Chief, addressing his troops in the Siegfried Line. He spoke extremely well with a quiet dignity, and I realized again what an extraordinary language German is. From its basest mishandling to the rantings of Hitler (to which I often listened before the war with amazement) it can be the ugliest language in the world; yet from a good speaker and in the words of Goethe or Heine it has a resonant and haunting beauty.

In the spring I suggested to Churchill that it would be a good idea if we were to publish a volume of his important war speeches. He agreed and left the task of preparing it to me. I managed to finish my selection, write the necessary commentary and deliver the manuscript to Number 10 before I went off to other things, but the Prime Minister and Brendan Bracken were both too busy for either to run his eye over it and release it to Cassell's for publication, so Randolph Churchill was asked by his father to go over it, which he did, putting his name on the title page as editor. (Randolph himself also later went into the Forces and subsequent volumes were prepared by Charles Ede.) When the first volume, *Into Battle*, finally appeared with great success, I was frankly upset to see that there was no reference to the work which I had done. I protested, Randolph apologized and added a line of acknowledgement in subsequent editions. Actually I never met Randolph; a great many hurtful things have been said about him, and if they are true perhaps it is not surprising that he should have had to be jogged into a reference to someone who had handed him a completed manuscript on a plate. I do know that after the war when he had occasion to telephone me over various matters, if I was not in my office he used to be extremely rude to my secretary, and that I find hard to forgive.

At this time Doris Langley Moore invited us to stay for a weekend with her in Harrogate. Doris, a South African by origin, had long enjoyed renown in many fields; her studies of Byron, her great knowledge of costume and the foundation of the museum in Bath, her concern with Victorian jewellery – an interest which she shared with Margaret – her appreciation of all that is good in food and wine. She was, I think, the most fastidious woman I have ever met; although her circumstances were quite different, she was in some ways the female counterpart of A.J. While perhaps not beautiful, she was in her prime extremely striking, and with her wonderful clothes she had a remarkable presence. The rooms of her Victorian house in the famous spa were a succession of contrasting colours, her table a joy and her cellar filled with bottled treasure. It was a memorable weekend and conversation with her slightly sardonic sense of humour, which lit on every subject including herself, lingers in my mind.

Part of the Air Ministry was moved to Harrogate on the outbreak of war, and until permanent arrangements could be made officers were billeted around the town. For a while Doris had several under her roof and, since she was out a lot, said that in her absence they could help themselves to a bottle of wine for dinner. It was a little annoying when they would open at random a bottle of Latour '24 when plonk would have served them just as well, but that irreplaceable loss could be regarded as a contribution to the war effort. But she felt enough was enough when one of the young men made a pass at her. She complained to his commanding officer who was most upset and promised to do something about it. Next day he telephoned.

'Mrs Moore, I don't think that young man will trouble you any more; he has been posted to the Argentine.'

She was horrified. She would never have wished anything so drastic to befall him, and merely wanted him out of her house.

Denyse Clairouin came on a short visit to London. Although the admonitory question was 'Is your journey really necessary?', during the 'phoney war' travel was quite easy and she had a lot to do here. Lunching together we had no idea that it was the last time, and she asked me to keep £500 safely for her, which was eventually to cause me a certain amount of trouble. She was a beautiful woman – or rather, she had an utterly lovely head on a somewhat cumbersome body as if the two did not really belong together; but she was of such utter goodness that the whole of her seemed to glow.

Life proceeded comparatively calmly until June 1940, when everything suddenly fell apart. I watched from the bridge at Tubbs Hill Station as trains packed with dirty, bedraggled, exhausted men stopped while volunteers gave them soup, hot tea and sandwiches.

Stefan invited Margaret and me for a weekend to discuss the English publication of his *The Tide of Fortune*; Lotte was away. It was the first time we had seen his house in Bath, to which he had moved from Hallam Street. Almost any view of Bath is lovely, and the panorama spreading out below his study window on the first floor was shimmering in the hot sunshine.

He was deeply affected by the news which was getting worse and worse. As Prater writes of this period: 'The "aristocrat" had disappeared, his Jewishness was more prominent and the delicate hands transformed. It was the physical reflection of the deepest depression of his whole life.' He thought that England was totally lost; in his diary he wrote, 'I know what awaits us after the war – hatred because we speak German and are Jews.' He was unduly pessimistic; I knew a number who shared these attributes, yet afterwards never suffered from any such acrimony. However, the worst happened on Sunday morning when we heard on the wireless that the Germans had entered Paris. I have never seen anyone so completely shattered; he was speechless, shrunk into himself like a mummy – it was a heavy blow from which he never fully recovered.

Bob Low had left Twentieth Century-Fox and was the correspondent for *Collier's Magazine* in France. He told me long afterwards that when Paris fell he was in Tours. No one knew anything, except that sooner or later the enemy would come. At a hospital in the town a French captain, convalescing, gathered the walking wounded together, managed to arm them and set up a road-block on the Paris road. Bob went with him. It was a blazing hot day and silence reigned until, finally, they heard the unmistakable squeak and rattle of tank tracks. At last a big Renault tank hove in sight, covered with *poilus* like a swarm of bees.

The captain held up his hand and demanded, 'Who the hell are you?'

There was a plaintive reply, '*Nous sommes refugés militaires.*'

There were so many refugees driven before the German advance, and Denyse Clairouin was one of the vast mass. Somehow there were posts to and from Vichy, although they took a long time, and letters from

Denyse were directed through her great friend Winifred Nerney, the London representative of Doubledays, who distributed copies to interested parties. She wrote so vividly of her feelings and of what had happened:

Your note arrived here [Vichy] one week ago, together with one from Desmond F. and Laurence P. I simply burst into tears at their news, the first I had of my friends ... and at the feeling that they understood and were still fond of me ... I am settling into a kind of White Russian life, washing, ironing, mending, making tea and keeping a diary in this little hotel room which is all my universe for how long ... God knows ... Nights and days I am with you all, and so are all your friends here and in Paris, longing to see you all and be with you again ... It's difficult to give news. Not in my worst nightmares could I imagine what arrived. I left Paris on June 13 to get to Villers [her country house] where my aunt was – shut up with no means of communication – post, wire, trains or car. She was watching the Havre tanks burning, and with a load of refugee nephews there. As the road was already in German hands from Mantes to Lisieux, I had to drive for a steady fourteen hours to Le Mans, then up by byways. Once there, I managed to carry the cumbersome nephews to the nearest station working, at Argentan, 140 kilometres, and then we decided to wait and see. But the following night we were awakened by an order from the mairie to leave within two hours, as they were cutting water and electric supplies. So packing into the car my aunt, a lonely old lady, a forlorn couple – and five cats, we took the trail and for five days roamed about, mapless, breadless, roofless, petrolless, to Laval, Angers, Poitiers, Perigeux, up to Villeneuve-sur-Lot where some kind friends gave us a room at last – the whole trip with the usual accompaniments of bombs, shells, bridge-blowing-up, people dying on the roadside, disbanded and dying soldiers. But the worst of all was the lack of news then, and now the lack of reliable news. We remained two months living with our friends a kind of communistic life, digging, washing, cooking etc. Then I came to Vichy ... My aunt after a month there returned to Paris: I remained, hoping to get an exit visa to N.Y. which was finally refused to me twelve days ago, as they do not seem to like me. So I think I'll try to return to Paris – to help my aunt at least. Her smuggled notes are pretty distressing; she writes 'I'm hungry' begs me to find a way to smuggle even a few chestnuts to her – no heat at all. Twelve kilos of coal per household for cooking and heating. No butter, oil, potatoes, fruit, chocolate, coffee, tea, wool, woollen materials. Queues start at 5.30 a.m. for food. Of course at Fouquet's, Maxim's or the Ritz there is plenty for the Germans who go there. The misery and unemployment are tremendous, but the spirit is splendid; the harder times grow the better people are resisting. Our place in Normandy has been completely looted – everything stolen, mattresses, linen, pictures, souvenirs – up to my lingerie, which I had bought there! But I don't mind living as a tramp with one shirt, and darned stockings (another thing completely lacking in both zones) so long as in the end we can breathe again and be free to think and do whatever pleases us. Temperature is rising every day in the occupied zone, and in the other too, but it needs a good deal of energy to resist the daily hammering of propaganda by newspaper and radio, distorting everything. If only one could be active, work or fight, all would be well. The one thing left is gazing at the sky, listening to the engines and hoping ... and praying for all one's friends over there.'

She was not to be idle for long, with tragic results, as we shall see.

But long before these letters came in the autumn we were alone. Brendan told me that the cabinet's decision to fight on was carried by a single vote; it would not be difficult to imagine whose vote that was.

As it did for millions of others, Dunkirk changed my life. One of the first results was a drastic revision of the reserved occupations. The age at which it began for publishers was raised from thirty to thirty-five; as soon as this was announced I telephoned father and told him that I intended to go into the army. He decided that he would return to the office and look after things until I came back – if I did.

The next problem was that of Margaret and Nicholas. Not only was there a strong possibility – a certainty it seemed at the time – of invasion, but a probability of heavy air raids on London. I would be away anyhow and they could not safely remain at Gordon Place. We debated ceaselessly, for a decision was urgent, and at last made up our minds: they should go to the United States.

The Germans then guaranteed the safe passage of the *Manhattan*; filled with American citizens and their dependants, she would not be molested, but after her every ship leaving or approaching the shores of Britain would be at risk. All berths aboard were allocated by the American Consulate, in which we spent hours waiting. Understandably it was pandemonium. One vignette is clear in my mind: André Maurois in military uniform pleading for a passage – it was unworthy and undignified, and always makes me think of Edward Ardizzone's famous drawing, 'Priest begging for a lift in Louvain'. Anyway, in the end we were successful, the day came, and we went up to Liverpool. We had tea at the Adelphi, where the circular lounge was packed. As a present, and as a distraction, I had bought Nicholas the biggest box of toy aeroplanes that I could find. It contained every known type and in no time Nicholas had them all out on the floor and was busily playing with them under the feet of Polish generals, British brigadiers, naval captains and every other form of human life, all pushing and shoving and stepping over the maze of Dinky Toys.

Then it was time to go to the ship. At the dock gates we had to say goodbye as I was allowed no further, and it was short because we had already said all there was to say. We had agreed to put our marriage vows on ice for the duration, or until we were together again; three thousand miles apart, in what circumstances neither of us could imagine, it seemed better to have a frank understanding than wallow in possible guilt and subterfuge. It was numb because we did not know what kind of goodbye we were saying – for a year or perhaps for ever. I stood still watching them walk farther and farther away, Nicholas happily holding his mother's hand. Half-way along the dock he stopped for a long moment to look back, as though the penny had suddenly dropped and he was fixing in his mind an image of his father in case it was for the last time.

Feeling very much alone, I returned to the Adelphi for dinner, consoled myself with the best Burgundy on the list, went to a film and took the midnight train back to London.

I now had two tasks before me: closing up Gordon Place and getting into the army. Neither of them turned out to be simple. So many people had moved out of London that all the well-known furniture repositories were full, but I eventually found a firm which had room and would take everything away towards the end of July, when I wrote, 'The house is empty now, and very forlorn. All the furniture and most of our belongings went off in two pantechnicons.'

Immediately I began a detailed correspondence with Margaret, as I was soon also to do with father, and continued until my return to civilian life; both of them preserved all my letters and, since I had access to them, these have served me better than my memory or a diary which I never kept.

A few days at 'Idehurst', including mother's sixtieth birthday, were enlivened by the sight of a Dornier 'flying pencil', with two Hurricanes on its tail, just clearing the trees at the bottom of the garden and crashing, while Edward Hudson supervised the construction of innumerable tank traps which it was hoped would create a traffic block if ever the invasion came to Sevenoaks. Then I returned to London to attend to the office while I made my plans about the army. Meanwhile, several evenings a week were spent as an ambulance driver in a unit behind Barkers. The air raids had not started, so there was nothing to do except play stump cricket in the yard, but the *camaraderie* was welcome, wonderful, and warming. War is a great leveller and it engenders an atmosphere which is seldom found in civilian life; no one was interested in anything except that he found for himself by observation, in a way which is all too seldom achieved in a time of so-called normal life. It was a revival of the 'genius' which had inspired the Romans and expressed their unity, making their genius – 'a group of men insulated by blood but joined by common interests and purposes ... acquiring an entity of its own' – similar to the traditions of a regiment.

I could never forget or forgive one piece of petty larceny in those days. In such a time of crisis it was not surprising that all Germans and Italians were rounded up and packed into the Isle of Man until the sheep could be separated from the goats – if there were any. Among them was my doctor, Edward Elkan, who was a Jew from Hamburg. He was a wonderful doctor who had cured the ill health which had plagued me through the thirties. I once asked him what decided him finally to leave Germany, and he said that when the police had smashed down his front door, burnt his library and broken his collar bone he thought that it was time to go.

His wife rang me up in distress to tell me that he had been taken. I went to see her at once, offering what comfort I could, and assuring her that there was little danger of his being put permanently in a concentration camp – the understandable fear that constantly haunted all German Jews. Since I knew that he loved wine, I said that I would send him a case to give him a little solace. The case arrived at the concentration camp in Liverpool where he was incarcerated and, of course, was opened. It took him three months of haggling to get it; the guards had stolen two bottles and gave him ten – perhaps he was lucky that it was not the other way round. His release was delayed until December, and questions were raised on his behalf in the House.

Then I set about getting into the army, for I had no intention of waiting until my age group was called up. Being ten years older than the majority of those going into the services at that time, I dosed myself with a vast intake of glucose in order to make sure that I would appear even fitter than I was when I should be examined. Then I trotted off to the recruiting office in the Euston Road. The paperwork was done and the physical examination completed, only for me to be turned down for excess of sugar! By a stroke of good fortune one of the examining doctors was Eric Steeler, my E.N.T. specialist; I told him quietly what I had done, and he said not to worry, just eat no sweets and come back two days later. This I did and was passed fit. Then the question came: into what did I want to go? Conscious of my vow of 1930, I said that I wanted to be a machine-gunner. There was a pause.

'I wish you hadn't said that,' said the officer before whom I was standing, 'anything you like except that, which can't be done.'

'Very well,' I replied, 'I am ahead of my age group and I will be a machine-gunner or nothing.'

I left and went to another recruiting office in Whitehall, where the answer was the same.

I was not going to be defeated, so I asked for an appointment with Brendan Bracken at No 10 Downing Street. After I first met him in 1939 we had become good friends, but now I am ashamed at how much I badgered him for help when he had so much more important work to do.

He welcomed me and after a chat I told him what I wanted.

'I can offer you an immediate commission in the Royal Marines,' he said.

I thanked him very much but said that I did not want to be a marine, just a machine-gunner.

He sighed, 'All right, I'll see what I can do.'

Some days later he sent on to me a letter, which I have kept. It said that if I would present myself at the recruiting office in Euston Road I would get what I wanted, and it was signed by the Secretary of State for War!

All that to get one private soldier into the army! I had always thought it a myth that the armed services would almost deliberately make you do anything except the one thing you wanted, but now there seemed to have been some substance in the story. When Edwin Harper came back to Cassell's after the war, I knew that he had been in the navy. I said, 'With your artistic and design skills, you should have been in the hydrographical department of the Admiralty, but I'll bet you were a stoker on a minesweeper.'

Somewhat startled, he said, 'How did you guess?'

So here I was, back in the Euston Road where I started. I was told to report to the depot of the Middlesex Regiment at Mill Hill on 15 August, the date of the next intake. There was no need for my first expressed wish to have been frustrated, for the Middlesex, an entirely machine-gun regiment, was taking in more than a hundred men a month and there was plenty of room. Some of the intake were no more fitted to be machine-gunners than I was to be a fighter pilot or a sailor, yet they were forced into it – even if some of them were later forced out again.

I began to taper off my work at the office. A welcome discovery was that Nicholas Monsarrat, whose *This is the Schoolroom* I had published the previous year, lived opposite to me. He and his wife Eileen had a flat over Cullen's grocery store on the corner of Camden Grove and Church Street, the largest occupant of which next to themselves was one of those gramophones with an enormous horn that used to give the best possible tone. We became instant friends, but there was not much time left; he was going into the navy at the same time as I was going into the army. Nevertheless, the foundations were laid upon which after the war was built a friendship of deep and lasting importance to me, and I believe not without some interest to him.

The last three authors with whom I contracted were, as it happens, women. The most important book, to my mind, was *The Golden Reign* by Clare Sydney Smith, wife of the station commander when T.E. Lawrence was in the R.A.F.; she and her husband had friendly relations with him quite irrespective of rank, and hers is the only work written about this strange man from a woman's point of view. The second was a Canadian, Evelyn Eaton, and her first novel with us that year was *Quietly My Captain Waits*. She came from Fredericton, New Brunswick, the home town of Beaverbrook, of whom she had as low an opinion as I. She regaled me with stories from her own knowledge, of which the mildest concerned the tycoon's generosity in presenting a new hospital to the town and his obstinacy in insisting that it be built in the most inconvenient place, just where the local authorities did *not* want it, or not at all. The third was Margaret Trouncer whose *Go, Lovely Rose* was in the works but did not appear until the following year.

I also saw Walter Churchill from time to time. He had a squadron of Hurricanes, which he preferred to Spitfires because he considered the tighter turning worth more than a few extra miles per hour. He had been flying over General Corap's 9th French Army, which collapsed at Sedan where it bore the brunt of the unexpected German attack through the Ardennes; he said that they had shot down sixty-two planes for the loss of four of their own. He was one of the first pilots to be awarded both the D.S.O. and the D.F.C. With the collapse of the French front his squadron was ordered home, and they were flying sorties from Tangmere escorting convoys up the Channel. Since he needed glasses he never allowed the fact that he was short-sighted to become known because he would have been grounded, so when they took off for a sortie his eyes were his Number 1 on his right. Once contact was made he could see well enough for the ensuing dogfights.

The convoy work was tedious and tiring, and he liked to get up to London when he could to relax. I used to ask him sometimes to the *400* in Leicester Square, which was my favourite night-club. On one occasion, to entertain him, I unkindly routed out of bed a dear friend, Mechtild Nawiasky, who was picture editor of *The Observer*, and asked her to join us by taxi, which she was kind enough to do – but then she was a very kind person. It was the era of the bottle club, now long forgotten. You bought a bottle of spirits during licensing hours, drank as much as you wished during the night, and the remains were sealed with your name on it against your next visit. They were scrupulously honest.

Our furniture and my clothes were stored; our wines had gone to A.J.'s cellar at Finchingfield, my library to Walter's parents in Malvern. I waited for the day.

14 Trying to be a Soldier

At last the day came. I had been instructed where to report, but not
when; it seemed obvious that I must be there by midnight, so I took a
girlfriend out to dinner and finally arrived by taxi, rather drunk, at ten
minutes to twelve. I was not at all popular. The clerk who had sent me
my papers had omitted the one instructing me to report by four in the
afternoon to be kitted out. The next morning when all the others were
on their first drill parade, I was stuck in the quartermaster's store.

My platoon sergeant was named Jacques, and his Number 2 was
Corporal Budden. Both were very good instructors, though the latter
was much the nicer man; Jacques had a bullying streak in him which
came out if anyone was weak or incompetent. There was another
instructor, Sergeant Andrews, who had come back from Dunkirk; he
was an inspired teacher with a rugged personal charm. Instruction was
intense and conducted at a fierce pace because the invasion was
expected at any moment and there was a rush to cram as much as
possible into us so that we could be of some use, however small, if the
crisis came.

I was extremely happy and found the Vickers machine-gun every bit
as interesting as I had hoped. The only disadvantage I discovered was
that if one was given the order to mount gun, for which twenty-five
seconds were allowed, one inevitably sat down in a hurry on the back
leg of the tripod, with the result that one had a permanently bruised
coccyx. Equipment was short, so we had three guns to a platoon which
should have four. Two men had to go through the motions without a
gun, the loader lying down and the gunner sitting in the correct
position, the latter often to be assaulted, half in jest, with a roar of, 'How
many times have you been told to keep your thumbs on the bloody
triggers?'

Like every bunch of recruits, we were a mixture of all sorts. I enjoyed
the company of everyone in our two huge barrack rooms. There was
only one man whom I tried not to sit opposite in the dining-hall if I
could help it because his eating habits had to be seen to be believed; he
was harmless enough, but the way he shovelled his food into his mouth
and let half of it drip out again on to the table would have disgraced an
ill-bred pig.

I made two very good friends, and the fact that they were of my own

180

kind had nothing to do with class but simply bcause we had more interests in common, more things to do and talk about. Aubrey Jolly, a plump chap who had come back from the Argentine where he had been tutoring the children of a wealthy family, a man with a vast sense of humour, and Comte Raymond de Speville from Mauritius. Friendships then were precious; time might be short.

I had not been long at Mill Hill when to my surprise (after our acerbic exchanges of a few months before) I received a letter from Laura Riding. In it she asked for my advice: as a soldier I must know – were the Germans going to invade Britain? Obviously Private Flower, with about two weeks' service in the ranks, must be better informed than either the Prime Minister or the Chief of the Imperial General Staff. So I wrote back to her. Yes, in my opinion, it was certain that the Germans would invade this country; they would land on the coast of Kent or Sussex, overrunning the home counties; there would be fighting in the streets of London, but they would be held on the line of the River Thames; the eventual outcome was anybody's guess. I have no evidence that she received my letter, but the fact remains that she took the next boat to the United States and never came back. I learnt much later that she and Robert Graves had finally parted and she had acquired an American friend.

There were two recruit companies, and I got to know a Scot in the other one, Dickie Dickson, with whom I was to serve throughout the war and who remains a good friend to this day.

The beginning of the air raids on London introduced a new factor into life. The most used route was in over Sevenoaks and out over Mill Hill, so our part of the world became rather lively. The commanding officer laid it down that there was to be no retiring to the air-raid shelters because being killed by a bomb was no worse than being killed in action, and we needed as much rest as we could get in order to keep at our training to help withstand the still expected invasion. I can remember only one exception. I had been down to the Astoria in Charing Cross Road to see *The Mortal Storm* in which James Stewart plays a German teacher who is against Nazism. At the end one of the nasty little Nazis flees from his home horrified at the damage his beastly terrorism had caused; the last line is, '... and what now does the future hold for him?' As though in answer, there was a terrific explosion and the whole cinema rocked violently; a land mine had come down in the centre of Charing Cross Road, making a crater right down into the Underground. The film was over. I went out, skirting the crater, and walked through the wrecked buildings; there was no one about, and utter silence except for the drip of broken water pipes. I shouted in case there was anybody needing help, but there was no sound and I went back to Mill Hill. There I found everyone in the shelters, since the barracks seemed to be one of the evening's targets. I was glad we did not do it often; it was cramped, stuffy, dirty and unpleasant. The next morning a rather pale Sergeant Jacques said, 'Well, you nearly got rid of me.' He lived in married quarters at one end of the barracks; his wife had refused to go with their children to the shelter excavated in the side of a bank opposite, so he went by himself. A bomb landed in the entrance; fortunately there was a hole at the other end, or he would have been entombed.

I wrote about how these raids seemed: 'It's just like being in a permanent thunderstorm. Possible danger does not occur to one, until something comes down close. Then a bomb within, say, half a mile swishes with the same sound as a rocket makes going up, and for a second I get the feeling you get when you go over the top in a roller-coaster. Then there is the crash of the explosion – rather a sodden crash, like an enormous suet pudding being dropped on an echoing floor. If it is a good distance away things just rattle. If it is close, the building sways as if in a small earthquake.'

The raids were becoming more frequent and monotonous, but there were exciting moments – such as a sunny afternoon when nine Heinkels flew over our heads in perfect formation and were pounced upon by half a dozen Spitfires; the ensuing dogfight brought down two Heinkels, and one Spitfire made a forced landing.

The morning after one heavy raid we went on a route march, and during the last 'five minutes smoke' the sky was filled with the pages of books like a snowstorm. 'Hello,' I said to myself, 'some publisher's had it.' I picked up a few of the sheets, looked at them, and shouted, 'Christ, it's us!' I found out that our warehouse at Watford had been hit; it was the first of the three disasters we were to suffer.

Some lunatic decided to set up a bomb-disposal unit inside the barracks – hardly the most suitable place, in the middle of hundreds of men – and Sergeant Andrews used to go and watch the subaltern and his sergeant defusing bombs. With a five-hundred pounder on the table one morning the subaltern said, 'Hello, this is one I haven't seen before; Sergeant, give me a hammer.' Andrews said, 'Excuse me, Sir, would you mind if I go outside before you wield that?' and prudently withdrew. Of course the worst happened. Someone found the officer's head, but the only trace I saw was one forefinger with a few stringy tendons attached on the roof of a hut two blocks away.

Andrews was concerned in another incident which was psychologi-cally interesting. We were at bayonet practice, following the usual monotonous cry of 'In, out, on guard!' There was one chap in my platoon of Italian origin – I am surprised that he was conscripted – who was a gentle moron, a heaver of cement bags in civilian life. He refused to obey the order. Andrews said, 'Oh go on, it's only a straw dummy.' But the Italian said, 'Yes, but it might be a body and I couldn't stick a bayonet into human flesh.' The sergeant looked at him closely, saw the genuinely stricken look in his eyes, and said quietly, 'All right; skip it.' Shortly afterwards there was to be a boxing match between the two recruit companies and this same man – his name was something like Fazola – was asked if he had ever boxed and if not would he like to try. He said he would have a go. He was enormously strong with a wonderful physique, about a middleweight. The P.T. Instructor had one week in which to teach him the rudiments of self-defence. On the night he took a terrible shellacking, but was still on his feet at the end of three rounds. He stood there bleeding from the mouth, the nose, the eyes, the ears, but blazing with excitement. 'That was wonderful,' he said, 'can I do it again?' He was totally unsuited to be a machine-gunner, which, although hardly the Elusynian mysteries, did require a certain degree of intelligence.

A sadder case was a gentle soul named Davey, who had deserted from the merchant navy because he could not bear the sight of ships being torpedoed in the Atlantic, and joined the army. He brought out the worst in Jacques. One wet day we were practising clearing stoppages (of which the Vickers gun had eleven). It was Davey's turn and we all sat round watching. He failed to resolve the stoppage set up for him and got flustered; the more flustered he became the more incompetent he was, and Jacques started to make fun of him. Finally he was sitting behind the gun completely disintegrated with six belts of ammunition draped round his neck and Jacques jeering at him. He deserted the next day. With two strikes against him, what chance had that gentle soul in time of war? I suppose the police picked him up somewhere; I can only hope that he was hauled before a compassionate authority which would draft him into something simple but useful, where he could to some degree be happy.

It seems that I got on reasonably, because the P.T. sergeant asked me to give some fencing lessons, which did not work out very well because there were few pupils and we were constantly interrupted by air raids; and when we did a full shoot I was roped in as an extra instructor, which led to five hours non-stop on the guns, after which I could not hear a thing.

The Battle of Britain was now well under way, and the brilliant sky was criss-crossed from horizon to horizon by innumerable vapour trails. We watched, fascinated. The little silver stars at the heads of the vapour trails turned east. This display looked so harmless; even beautiful. Then, with a dull roar which made the ground across London shake, the first sticks of bombs hit the docks. Leisurely, enormous mushrooms of black and brown smoke shot with crimson climbed into the sunlit sky. There they hung and slowly expanded, for there was no wind, and the great fires below fed more smoke into them as the hours passed.

On Friday and Saturday morning the sky grew darker and darker as the oily smoke rose and spread in heavy, immobile columns, shutting out the sun.

At the same time Intelligence and Ultra intercepts of Hitler's orders indicated that Operation Sealion was off. With the danger of invasion removed it was decided at Mill Hill that two men per company could have weekend leave. A ballot was held and the first two names out of the hat were mine and a chap whose home was in Birmingham. We were free from midday Saturday but had to be back at all costs by midnight on Sunday. I went down to Charing Cross and sat on the top of the steps overlooking Villiers Street. There was still one bomber passing slowly over, not very high, gleaming silver in the sun. I decided to go to see the new Gary Cooper film, *The Westerner*, and then get to Sevenoaks in time for dinner. The film was very good but my decision was a disaster, for when I got back to Charing Cross the loudspeakers were announcing that the main line had been cut and there would be no more trains that day. I got as far as Camberwell and then stood on the main road south to thumb a lift, and a motor-cyclist stopped, saying that he was going to Sidcup (half-way home) and took me on his pillion. Down through Lewisham and Blackheath this gave me a prolonged broadside view of the docks. Columns of smoke merged and became a monstrous curtain which blocked the sky; only the billows within it and the sudden shafts of flame which shot up hundreds of feet made one realize that it was living, and not just the backdrop of some nightmare opera. There were fire-hoses along the side of the road, climbing over one another like a helping of macaroni, with those sad little fountains spraying out from the leaks, as they always seem to from all fire-hoses. Every two or three minutes we would pull into the gutter as a fire-bell broke out stridently behind us and an engine in unfamiliar livery tore past; chocolate or green or blue with gold lettering – City of Birmingham Fire Brigade, or Sheffield, or Bournemouth. It was something never experienced before – the excitement of fire-engines arriving to help from so far away, and the oily, evil smell of fire and destruction, with its lazy, insolent rhythm.

A friendly van driver helped me to finish my journey in comfort and good time for dinner. It was lovely to be at home, but the next morning I came down to breakfast a little grumpy. During the night a bomber had seen fit to drop a stick down Hitchen Hatch Lane. The first one destroyed the town hall and the last two bracketed our front gate. I remarked that I had enough of that sort of thing at Mill Hill without a bonus in Sevenoaks!

Some time after dinner on Sunday I said that I had better start back. The train was blacked out and the little blue bulbs gave a light so dim that one could barely see the people opposite. I found myself sitting next to an attractive girl – as far as I could see – and we talked as we started and stopped and started again on the lengthy journey to Holborn – for Charing Cross was still out of commission. There was a raid on when we came out of the station, and at that moment a big one dropped just opposite, by Saint Bartholomew's Hospital. I thought that was not good enough, so I shepherded her down into the shelters in the vaults beneath the station, which were packed. After about half an hour I said that, whatever the situation, I had to get back to barracks; the girl – I never knew her name – lived quite near and I advised her to stay put until the all clear. I went up and started west. I had only got as far as Holborn Circus when I was stopped by a warden who said that the rest of Holborn was closed because it was a shambles and there were several more buildings which might come down at any moment. I trudged through the deserted side streets which I knew so well; it was quite eerie – absolutely silent except for the drone of bombers overhead, the clang of fire-engine bells, and the regular 'crump, crump' of bombs falling and the blood-red clouds of smoke drifting across the sky. At Marble Arch I was lucky enough to find a taxi and the driver said that he was willing to take me to Mill Hill. I am sure that he bitterly regretted his decision. Another raid started and all the way up the Edgware Road we were pursued by bombs which burst behind us as though we were a fox which hounds could not quite kill. As I paid him the driver said, 'If I'd 'a known it was going to be like this, Guv, I'd never 'a taken the fare.' I felt desperately sorry for him as he drove away into the darkness; I hope he made it.

I got into barracks just after two, but my pal from Birmingham did not. Two days passed before he appeared; I do not know how hard he tried, but his story must have been a good one for it was accepted.

Soon after I arrived at Mill Hill there had been talk of selection for future officers, but, although I knew that my name had been put down, nothing happened until about six weeks later, during which I enjoyed myself and got extremely fit. Then one morning Sergeant Jacques stormed into the barrack room between parades and shouted at me, 'Why didn't you tell me that you had Certificate A?'

I said, 'Sergeant, if I have told you once, I have told you ten times that I have it.' (Certificate A was awarded for proficiency in the Corps at school; I do not know if it still exists.)

'Christ,' he said, 'you'll get me stripped. There's a Board on now. Put your belt on and get over there quick.'

I did as I was told, and eventually it was my turn to stand in front of three colonels sitting behind a table. The chairman asked various questions and then said, 'You know it says in Certificate A that on the outbreak of war you are supposed to report at once to the War Office? Did you do that?'

'No, Sir.'

'Why not?'

I said the first thing that came into my head. 'I didn't read the small print, Sir.'

My God, I thought, that's done it; there was no expression on the colonel's face, but he must have had a sense of humour for I was accepted.

A couple of days before we were due to leave, Aubrey and I invited Jacques and Budden out to supper. We took them to Odenino's, then a pleasant place next door to the Café Royal. Budden, who was good looking in a florid way, asked a rather pretty girl to dance; how he managed to perform in ammunition boots I do not know, and I cannot imagine that he did the floor much good. Jacques got very drunk. We took a taxi back to Mill Hill before midnight, and, as we did not think that he was in a fit state to go back to married quarters, we laid him out on a spare bunk in our barrack room. He fell asleep instantly, but half an hour later he woke up full of frenzied energy. He turned on all the lights in both the adjoining rooms and ran up and down with a rolled up newspaper bashing anyone who raised his head. An air raid had started and in the middle of this exhibition a bomb landed just outside, blowing in all the black-out shutters on the tall windows. The blaze of lights must have looked like the Crystal Palace. However we got him back to bed in the end, and darkness reigned.

The next morning Company Sergeant-Major Marshall, who produced a good W.O.'s voice despite having no roof to his mouth, tackled me and said, 'I've heard all about last night in detail. One more peep out of you and you won't go to O.C.T.U.'

Aubrey Jolly and I were good as gold and in the first week of November, saying goodbye to all our friends and specially Raymond Speville who went to a different O.C.T.U., we left for Droitwich. But before we went, I had a letter from Walter, who had been commanding 605 Squadron over London. He had been lucky; a Messerschmitt 109 put seven cannon shells into him, he baled out and the only damage was a splinter in his arm which needed four stitches. 605 added forty-two more kills to their score, for the loss of only four pilots. When he was well he was to take command of the first Eagle Squadron.

The machine-gun course was a long one – six months. There is not much to be said about it so far as the work is concerned, except that it was very intense; but there was a psychological aspect. On leaving Mill Hill I wrote, 'The one thing I really regret is that once more I shall be surrounded by people more or less of my own class, instead of a mixture of everyone which was so enjoyable a feature of the ranks. For two months I have been moving among men whose only interest in me has been whether I shaped up as an agreeable companion and likable fellow soldier: now I am climbing back over the fence again. I regret it.'

Droitwich I found a pleasant, rather sleepy spa; I loved the warm saline swimming-baths in which, like the Dead Sea, one cannot sink. Aubrey and I had acquired a reputation for being the two biggest scroungers around; if there was anything to be found, we found it. At tea-time on the first day Aubrey, with a triumphant gleam in his eye, whispered to me that he had discovered a shop which had unlimited chocolate off the ration. I said so had I. Both of us had discovered this tiny establishment tucked away in a side street, the owner of which made slab chocolate out of cocoa, vegetable oils and suchlike which was really palatable. I also came across 'Smelly Nelly's', a minute restaurant kept by an Italian woman who had an unlimited, and I am sure illicit, supply of eggs and bacon.

Another advantage of the town was that it was not very far from Malvern, so that I was able to go over quite frequently to see the Churchills for lunch, and they took me to a number of concerts; also Walter was able to come home from time to time on short leave.

Work proceeded quite happily. Our company commander was a quiet man like a benevolent schoolmaster. My platoon commander was a corpulent Geordie from the Northumberland Fusiliers who was a brilliant instructor. But the biggest character was the R.S.M., the youngest in the army, from the Coldstream. He was extremely good at his job, young, handsome and great fun off parade. One of his characteristics was that he knew the number of every regiment of foot and would never refer to them by name. For example, on his Saturday morning drill parade, if his wrath fell upon me from the Middlesex, he would scream, 'Wake up that dozy man in the rear rank from the 57th Foot!' Another of his mannerisms was that whenever he gave the command, 'Quick March!' he followed it with the cheerful admonition, 'Bend the knee and away you go!'

There were two regular sergeant instructors, supplemented by a territorial, Sergeant B.A. Brown, D.C.M., the son of a brigadier whose regiment had been the Black Watch. He was a cadet like the rest of us, but he had years of knowledge and also battle experience. As an instructor, he was a tartar, far fiercer than the two officially charged with the task. Little did I realize then that we were to serve so long together and remain friends for life.

One night a man named Gerry German and I were due to do sentry duty in the vehicle park. We said that it was ridiculous to get up twice during the night, thus having practically no sleep, and we bullied the sergeant of the guard into letting us do a double stint at one go, which was against regulations; it was also a mistake. The weather was bitter and the only place where we could keep warm was the boiler house of the factory in the car-park of which the vehicles were lined up. We had a good view of our charges and went the rounds constantly, but even so, the only thing which kept us awake was the endless roar of aircraft overhead. Good God, we thought, somebody's getting it; they were indeed – it was Coventry.

Later Walter told me that his engineering works, which made precision parts such as pistons for the Merlin engine, on the edge of the city had escaped. But he took seventy-two hours leave and in that time, studying the one-inch survey map, had found a disused tunnel and moved the whole thing underground.

I was given leave at Christmas and went to stay with my Aunt Blanche and mother at Dudsbury, near Wimborne. At twilight on Christmas Day I took one of my grandfather's 12-bores, a few cartridges, and went to look for pheasant, of which there were a lot in the area. At the bottom of the long orchard I saw a lovely bird playing hide-and-seek with me through the undergrowth. I realized that when he took off he would head over the river, into which, if I bagged him, he would fall and be lost. So I tried to outflank him, and as a result fell down the very steep wooded bank of the river, tearing all the tendons in my right ankle. I crawled back to the house and went to bed. But the pain got steadily worse, so finally during the evening an ambulance came and took me to Wimborne Hospital. After something over two weeks I could get about on crutches and went back to Droitwich. Major Dolly sent for me and said I had missed so much that I had better be put back a company – the last thing I wanted. I replied that for the benefit of the infantrymen we were still only being taught things which I, as a machine-gunner, knew already; this was true and so, to my relief, I was left alone – except of course that I could take no exercise. I spent the time re-reading the two books which I had taken with me in my knapsack, where the potential marshal's baton is supposed to lie. One was a book by Liddell Hart on armoured warfare, the other de Gaulle's *Vers l'armée de métier*. I wrote to Liddell Hart, whom I had not then met, asking his views about the mechanized use of the medium machine-gun in mobile warfare and daring to set out a few ideas; I was delighted to get a long letter back discussing the problem. Years later, when we were friends, I mentioned this to him, and there in his files was my letter and a copy of his reply; he kept everything. It is interesting, in a small way, that our views were similar – that twin machine-guns should be mounted on a bren carrier and roam about as required, which became the role of the Long Range Desert Group.

As the six months drew to an end, we had to think about what regiments we wished to apply for, and military tailors began hovering about to take orders for service dress. We also bought Sam Browne belts and the sergeant instructors polished them at night for a fee. Of course, I arrogantly had to go into Worcester and buy one from a saddler, which cost me dear because it was such superb leather that it had to be done twice – but what a belt when it was finished! I was determined to put in for a Scottish Regiment, and I would have been up the creek if I had not got my wish, for my lovely new uniform would have been useless. Of course, we could only choose machine-gun regiments or those having machine-gun battalions, but we were assured that anyone with a decent mark would get what he wanted. That left me with a choice of the Gordons or the Argyll and Sutherland Highlanders; I plumped for the latter.

There was a frightful outcry over the examinations. Our Geordie platoon commander did not believe in them; he contended that any instructor worth his salt knew his cadets' abilities, or lack of them, backwards after six months and could grade them much more accurately than any written examination could. So on the morning he came into our rooms before breakfast and told us what some of the questions were going to be; the other platoons were furious. But in fact it made little difference, if any, because there was really no time to bone up on anything one did not already know. So we did the papers and anxiously awaited the results. When they came, there was only one 'A' in the Company – a quiet man of Italian extraction called Lucarotti; there was a small handful of 'B+' which included Brian Brown and myself. So all was well; I was commissioned into the Argyll and Sutherland Highlanders and posted to the machine-gun depot at Gosport. I wrote the news to Margaret and got back five pages of well-deserved abuse from her – a Cameron by name and ancestry – for having the bad taste to go into a Campbell regiment.

Towards the end our company sergeant-major posted two rather splendid notices: 'All Cadets holding rank will hand in their brassieres [brassards] by tomorrow morning', and 'All those illegible for proficiency pay will hand in their pay-books.'

And the day came to depart. Aubrey Jolly and I left Droitwich together in his car, for he still had some petrol and was going east. During our time together we had become good friends, done much and enjoyed much together, and parted forever – just an exchange of letters was all. I had to get to Gosport, but thanks to Aubrey I was able to go to Suffolk first, to see Walter. Now a wing commander, he had just taken over the east-coast defences just north of the Thames. He had recovered from sinus trouble, which had caused him to relinquish command of 71 Squadron, the first Eagle Squadron of American volunteers – as I have said. He told me that when he first addressed them his opening words were, 'I have been appointed to make you into officers and gentlemen; at present you are neither.' It sounds like him, for he never pulled a punch in his life, and if it sounds arrogant, it contains within it a basic truth: that he, as a man of considerable experience, had the determination to bring his bunch of willing mavericks to that order which he knew was the only element which could help them to do their duty and stay alive.

Whatever he may have said, it worked. He was called 'Pappy' and one of his pilots has recorded that '(the) efficiency and aggressiveness (to me at least) was due entirely … to the intelligence, enthusiasm and outstanding personal leadership of Churchill.'

Now he had three airfields under his command, and his headquarters was at Debden, in Suffolk. I got there in time for lunch. With delight he showed me a map taken from a crashed JU88 on which the target marked in red was that airfield; it had been framed over the mantelpiece in the ante-room. And he said that his first act had been to halve the sugar ration of the ground staff and double that of the pilots who he considered needed it more, and the unpopularity of this in some quarters neither moved nor surprised him. After lunch we got into his car with his pennon fluttering from the wing to go round the station, men presented arms right and left, and as a very new officer I found it all very grand. Lots of the latest night fighters were drawn up with mechanics swarming all over them, and his own Hurricane stood ready for him to go wherever he wished at a moment's notice. When we got out of the car he said, 'Just a minute, I want to pop into the parachute store.'

We went into a hut where there was an elderly aircraftsman in charge.

'Where,' Walter asked, 'is Wing Commander Churchill's parachute?'

'Sir, Wing Commander Churchill keeps that himself.'

'Oh no, he doesn't,' came the kindly but firm reply, 'I am Wing Commander Churchill.'

Finally I had to go and we parted as close friends always part – until the next time; but there was no next time. I never saw him again.

At Gosport, 'we arrived yesterday afternoon – eleven in all, shining new officers just out of tissue paper, all shining brass and polished leather.' I was given a room with a charming young man, Donald MacLean from Tobermory on the island of Mull. The barracks were part of the huge naval complex around Portsmouth; they had somehow come into the hands of the army, but were shortly to be passed back to the Royal Marines. On the first evening we were given a talk by the senior subaltern on how to behave. The next day was a Sunday and there was a full church parade, and I cannot imagine what the platoon in front of which I was standing must have thought. During the first lesson I felt something uncomfortable sticking into my back; unobtrusive (I hope) investigations revealed that it was the buckle of my still unfamiliar Sam Browne – I had got the strap on the wrong way round. While we knelt for the collects I disappeared beneath the pew and put it right. That was a fine start.

There were frequent air raids. One night a single plane slipped through the barrage and dropped its load on the barracks; we had a busy time putting the fires out. But the next night was the big one. When the sirens went I was determined to stay in bed, but the darkness and the eerie silence punctuated by explosions got me down, so I dressed and went out – on to the flat roof of a neighbouring block and watched a remarkable display of pyrotechnics. On my left the end of our barracks was burning merrily again; on my right Haslar naval hospital was on fire. Across the water Portsmouth town hall was well away, and against the huge sheet of flame were silhouetted, unmoved and indomitable, the masts of *Victory*.

There was little to do. I played some golf at Lee-on-Solent; and if one was out on driving or convoy instruction it was important to pass down the High Street there at eleven o'clock in order to see Vivian Leigh out with her shopping-basket, since her husband in the Fleet Air Arm was stationed at the airfield. I also played a lot of badminton with an Argyll named Henderson, who was very good. There was an unusual hazard on one side of the net because an incendiary bomb had come through the roof and one therefore had to try to watch both the shuttlecock and the hole in the floor.

A senior Argyll, Major Percy Lothian, had a charming house near by with a lovely garden, where he and his wife entertained new officers in the regiment to tea. I was invited one day and treated to a vitriolic tirade; at all costs, he said, I must avoid 5 Battalion, it was worse than a slave hulk, and I must move heaven and earth to get myself posted to the 6th. He was so bitter that he annoyed me and, although I did nothing either way, I was happy when I was eventually posted to the 5th. It was not until many years later when I was asked by the colonel of the regiment to write the history of 5th Battalion, that I discovered the cause of his bitterness. When during the invasion scare of 1940 the battalion was part of the south-east defences, he was second in command. In an excess of zeal he had most of 'Bungalow Town' west of Shoreham razed to the ground because, he said, it interfered with his field of fire. Aesthetically the ramshackle buildings were an eyesore, but their demolition was unauthorized and incurred a vast sum in compensation to the owners. Major Lothian eventually departed under a very heavy cloud, which was never dispersed and which he never forgave.

At weekends the place was a morgue. So on 21 May I absented myself without leave and went to London where I stayed with a friend in

Chelsea. One of my obligatory visits whenever in London was to 100 Oxford Street, where George Shearing was the resident pianist and Carl Barriteau, one of the two survivors from Ken 'Snake Hips' Johnson's band when a bomb hit the Café de Paris, played clarinet. But that Saturday night was very bad. In the morning I walked over to see if Beatrice Warde, who lived nearby, was all right, which she was; and I contemplated the huge pall of black smoke over the City. I wondered if I ought to go down to Ludgate Hill to see if La Belle Sauvage was intact. I decided not to because I thought that it was either destroyed or it was not, so that in either case I could perform no useful service. I did not think of the third possibility, fire; nor, of course, could I be aware that the abnormally low tide in the Thames would render the firemen impotent. I have reproached myself ever since for not going. If I had seen the danger and if I could have persuaded those in charge to let me in, I could at least have brought out Wyndham Lewis' portrait of father, if nothing else. In fact fires were raging in the Old Bailey some distance from Cassell's; for the firemen there was no water and they had to stand helpless, watching the flames work their way from building to building. What the office fire-watchers or the business director, who I presume had some interest in the matter, were doing I do not know. On Tuesday La Belle Sauvage and everything in it, including all my personal belongings, was destroyed.

But my immediate task was to get back to barracks by Sunday evening. All the terminals facing south were knocked out, and I had to take a taxi to Clapham Junction to join the throng milling for a train to Portsmouth.

The destruction was of course a terrible blow to those running Cassell's. Although contingency plans had been made and worked very well, there was no knowing what effect the serious situation would have on the company's business.

Ever since I was four I had had attacks at intervals from a rumbling appendix which had always gone away, but now I had a bad one. While the pain was still tolerable I won the small-bore shooting championship of the barracks, for which I was given a very nice silver salver. But the appendix got worse and I went to the M.O. who gave me a chit to the surgeon at Netley Military Hospital, Southampton; but he said all that would happen would be that I would be given a letter stating that the operation had better be done at some convenient date in the future. Believing him, I got a Utility (the little 8-h.p. runabouts) and on 7 June was driven over to the hospital. I asked the driver to wait, to take me back with the expected letter.

I was examined, and the surgeon – an elderly man of great presence and charm – said laconically, 'I'll have that out.'

Frankly relieved I said, 'All right, I'll go back to Gosport and get my kit.'

To which the equally laconic reply was, 'You're going nowhere except to bed.'

Since I knew that we were soon to leave Gosport, I had to write a note to Jock Maclean asking him to pack up everything, and inform the adjutant. In due course the driver came back with my uniform trunk and bedroll – everything except my silver salver. Who stole it I never knew; but I was sad – it was a very fleeting trophy.

The surgeon said that my appendix was so inflamed that he could not operate until it had settled down, so I had a week of peace and comparative comfort. Mother came to see me, and after it was over the surgeon told her that it had been very bad, but I recovered quickly. The worst night was just after the operation. Southampton was the Luftwaffe's target for the night. As soon as the raiders' intention was established, all patients were evacuated from the ward – except me. I was told that I was too ill to be moved, but they put a mattress on top of me and departed. Alone in the huge room, I was in total darkness until a near-miss blew in all the black-out shutters on the tall windows. Sweating like a beast and unable to move, I realized that if there was another near-miss I would be showered with broken glass. My inability to do anything but lie there scared the life out of me. However, nothing further happened; the all clear sounded, everyone came back and I was released.

When I was on my feet again, I discovered that, as I had expected, Gosport was closed. I was ordered to report to Fenham Barracks in Newcastle, the headquarters of the most prestigious of machine-gun regiments, the Royal Northumberland Fusiliers.

On arrival I was posted to C Company, the only one in billets, about ten minutes' walk from the barracks. The company commander was a burly, sympathetic soul. Almost on sight he said, 'You're not fit, are you?'

Still feeling disagreeably weak, I said, 'No, I'm not.'

'I know how you feel,' he said. 'I was blown up on a mine at Dunkirk and I haven't got over it yet. I tell you what, you'll be messing officer, and instructor in convoy discipline.'

Not only was this kind of him, but it suited me down to the ground. It was impossible to spend too much time on trying to instil into drivers the absolute necessity of keeping the prescribed thirty yards between vehicles; they were so stupid or so idle that they either bunched up (a wonderful target in war) or straggled half-way across the county and the tail got lost. The importance is obvious, but an awful lot of petrol had to be used up trying to get the lesson across.

The messing was fun. I had an official allowance of about a shilling (five pence) per head per day, plus anything more we cared to put in, with which to supplement the basic rations. Every morning I walked down to market with my shopping-basket. I got to know all the shopkeepers and developed an affection for Geordies, and for Newcastle, which I have never lost. We had a good cook and I used to plan the meals with him, introducing a few dishes which I remembered from home. It worked rather well.

I used to look in at the headquarters mess every day and occasionally lunched there; it had an effete atmosphere about it which I had not encountered before. There was the Lord Mayor of Westminster who would never lower himself to eat in the mess, but he appeared in his blues around seven o'clock for a sherry or two while he was waiting for his car to take him into the city to dine. Then there was a regular officer who had the most terrible asthma and was quite useless. The bar in the mess opened at eleven and most days I had a drink before going shopping. At eleven fifteen sharp the door was pushed slowly open and this officer entered on all fours; he would crawl across to the bar where the corporal handed down to him two large pink gins, after which he was able to pull himself upright and stand on his feet.

Also there was an officer under close arrest when I arrived who still had not been court-martialled when I left. A subaltern had to be in the room with him round the clock, and the one on night duty had a terrible time. Every night the prisoner, with his escort, broke out of barracks and took a taxi to a gambling-joint in Whitley Bay. The prisoner, whom I only saw once, must have been a strong character to prevail upon officer after officer to accompany him on these expeditions. They were back before reveille; it was all right for the prisoner who had nothing to do, but the wretched escort had to face a day of parades without a wink of sleep.

One of the perennial problems, there as everywhere else, was security. No number of posters or lectures got the message over to a lot of the men. So one Oldershaw, Henderson from Gosport and I got permission to present a short play showing a plausible enemy agent talking his way past a sentry and then causing an explosion. It was a great success. The divisional commander attended and was so enthusiastic that he thought the show should be kept going. Oldershaw said that we were on to something and if we played our cards right we could probably go on touring round military units for the duration. I replied that I was sorry, but I had not joined the army to become a third-rate actor, and the matter was dropped.

The only work of unusual interest was an exercise one Sunday in which an army force attacked the Newcastle Home Guard, and I was appointed one of the umpires. Up at 2.45 a.m., we were ready for the exercise to begin at first light. I had the left flank of the Home Guard to look after, and it so happened that the army's breakthrough came here, so I had a wonderful time dashing about on a motor-bike watching tanks advancing and telling people that they were dead, which they were not inclined to believe. This reminds me that when Molotov died in 1986 all the obituaries referred to the home-made anti-tank bomb named after him as the 'Molotov cocktail', which was said to have been first used in 1956 when the Soviet army intervened in the Hungarian troubles. This is quite untrue, because in this exercise in 1941 the Home Guard had masses of them; I still remember the recipe for making them – a fairly useless piece of knowledge.

Before very long news was received that we were all going to be posted out and Fenham Barracks would be closed down or put to some other use. It was during August 1941 that the postings arrived. Three of us – oh joy – were to go to 5 Battalion in Stirling, Henderson, Donald Reekie, a Scot with an ungovernable temper who was devoured by a passionate hatred of all Sassenachs, and I. The battalion was not in the castle, the regimental depot, but in requisitioned houses huddled round the base of the hill.

With great good fortune I had found my home for the rest of the war. I have told the chequered story of this remarkable unit in the history of it which I was asked to write by the colonel of the regiment, General Sir Gordon MacMillan, which was published in 1950. I have repeated the bare bones, but there are also various matters for which there was no place in a formal history – some personal, some scurrilous, some I hope amusing which perhaps may go to show why I was so happy during the more than four years which were to follow.

We arrived at Stirling in the evening and were told where to sleep. The next day there was nothing to do because the commanding officer, Lieutenant-Colonel J.C. Cockburn, M.B.E., did not want to see us until the evening. So I wandered down to headquarters, and the first person I met was the intelligence officer, Harry Aitken, a tall, extremely good-looking Scot whose home was in Jamaica where his family had been for generations. He was a very special person and my affection for him remains undimmed.

Then at half-past six it was time to face the commanding officer. I was marched in by the adjutant and, standing to attention, looked down for the first time at the man, sitting behind his desk, who probably has had more influence on me than anyone else in my life except my parents. I saw a man about my own size, a precise, neat figure with black hair and shrewd appraising eyes which carried in them a twinkle of deep humanity – 'a terrifically handsome professional soldier, aged forty-one,' I wrote to Margaret.

I had already been warned that he was a tartar with a terrible temper. I was soon to discover that although he did have a temper, it was nicely balanced by an enormous sense of humour; and I became convinced that a number of his rages were simulated when he considered it necessary to put the fear of God into someone. I was to see, one day, a sergeant, a huge man, who had done something silly, stand before him visibly quivering. Colonel Cockburn was determined that the battalion, which he had not long taken over from Colonel Cunningham (whom he much admired) was going to be one of the finest units in the British Army. There was a great deal to be done; but to achieve his end he would spare nothing and nobody, least of all himself.

He succeeded, as time was to show. Known as the 'wee man' he was respected – and feared – because of the horrible consequences if one made a mistake. But now, when those who served under him come together, there is no one who does not feel and express his complete admiration and devotion. In fact the devotion always existed; there was not a man in the battalion who would not have done anything he asked or – to use the old cliché – died for him.

He taught me the meaning of discipline, which is a state of mind more subtle than blind obedience; of loyalty which if true can never be broken; of duty which banishes selfishness; and above all that there is only one standard, one target: the best.

On that first morning I stood motionless taking him in as he looked up at me, taking me in. He asked what I had been doing in civilian life and I briefly told him. Then I marched out. Afterwards the adjutant, David Simpson from Peebles, emerged and told me that I was to be assistant adjutant (one had just been dismissed for doing something silly). David and I hit it off and remained friends until his sudden death in the late fifties. He taught me what to do and I settled down quite happily. Whenever time permitted we played golf together on the municipal Stirling course, for we both had our clubs with us.

It was an interesting start. The hours were not so much long as irregular, because I was at the beck and call of the adjutant and the C.O., according to what was happening; on the other hand, I saw how a battalion was run and had access to all the secret files. In addition I was made battalion education officer, which meant keeping an eye on the men taking evening classes, arranging the films and lectures which came round, and trying to think up ways of keeping the men amused during the long winter evenings to come. But the duty which I enjoyed most was taking band parade. Sergeant Craig, at twenty-four the youngest pipe major in the army, was an excellent teacher and the standard was high. The band practised endlessly, but there was one formal parade on Tuesdays after tea. I stood on the steps at one end of the asphalt school playground which we used and listened as the band marched and counter-marched. When they had completed their programme Sergeant Craig saluted and asked if there was anything further I would like them to play. I always asked for *The Rowan Tree* and *The Black Bear*, the former for its beauty and the latter because it is the only tune for the pipes which has a syncopated rhythm. Week after week he always knew what I would ask for, but not a flicker ever crossed his face.

Another enjoyable duty was Highland dancing. Classes were taken by the regimental sergeant-major – for some reason always called the R.S.M., not Mr MacDougall as was the custom in many infantry battalions – and were obligatory for all officers, even such as the tall Lyle Barr who had been dancing since childhood. I suppose that was a good thing because it ensured that we all danced in the same style; and what fun it was.

The least pleasant chore which one had to perform at intervals was that of orderly officer throughout the night. We had one outlying company which lived on a new building estate called Raploch. It was reached by a narrow path through the woods round the hill on which the castle stands. Between twelve and one it had to be visited to make sure that the sentries were awake and all was well; it was a considerable walk which in the pitch dark was precarious, eerie and lonely. One night I found all the officers still awake. An argument had started. The 'Oxford

accent' of my predecessor as assistant adjutant had roused all Donald
Reekie's hatred of Sassenachs; in the ensuing row both had drawn their
skhian dhus. The only damage before they could be separated was a
deep gash in the Englishman's thigh; it had been bound up, had
stopped bleeding, and peace was restored. If word of this had got to
Colonel John he would obviously have been extremely angry. But the
sufferer neither missed a parade nor allowed himself to limp, whatever
the discomfort. Since the company commander knew all about it, and I
was a very new subaltern, I could see no reason for not maintaining a
discreet silence.

David Simpson was on leave in September when the message came
from the War Office that we were to be converted into an anti-tank
Regiment and leave Stirling. I took the 'Most Secret' letter into Colonel
John in a panic, but of course he knew all about it. I will not go into the
strange breach of security and the complicated hand-over to the I/9
Manchesters, whom the colonel always referred to as the 'Manchurian
Highlanders', for it is too long and I have already done so in the
'history'; but I cannot forget the pride and sadness of the last church
parade. I was in the rear and as we went down the hill I could see the
whole column of Jocks stretched in front of me. They were marching
well; they were marching with all the pride they could muster. And the
people of Stirling lined the streets and cheered and waved – and there
were a few tears, for this was a battalion of their own regiment that was
leaving them.

On conversion we were offered a selection of numbers from which to
choose, and it was decided that we should be the 91(A. & S.H.)
Anti-tank Regiment because the original Argyllshire Highlanders had
been the 91st Foot; the choice of so high a number was to do us great
harm in the future.

Our new home was not very far away. It was the small wool-spinning
town of Tillicoultry. I used to think that my handwriting was quite
clear, but I obviously flattered myself because we had not been there
long before I received a letter from mother addressed to 'Pilliconetry'
which was safely delivered. The town huddles beneath the Ochils, the
magnificent hills which roll north to south at one side of the
comparatively flat country in which Stirling lies; it was comfortable
enough but could be damp and cold.

I used to walk a great deal. At Stirling in high summer I had often
walked to the Buchanan Arms, on the Glasgow–Loch Lomond road, for
lunch on Sunday, spent a while by the loch, and walked back. Now,
before autumn broke into winter, I went up into the Ochil Hills. One
Sunday the regiment nearly lost my services. Far away and turning for
home, I decided to get down into a narrow glen and follow the burn
below to the road; it was not a good idea. The first twenty feet or so were
negotiable, but then I realized that it became a precipice. There was no
way down. I had to turn on to my stomach and go back up. I lost my ash
stick; I had no time to be frightened because, with no foothold, all my
thoughts and strength were concentrated in my finger tips which were

the only things keeping me from disaster on the rocks below. They held; my searching toes found some crevice and, a few inches at a time, I slowly reached the top. Lying exhausted on the grass, I realized that if I had fallen to the bottom there was little chance that I would have been found for a very long time, because I was miles from anywhere; I walked home severely chastened.

David Simpson soon went away on a course to familiarize himself with our new role, so I had three weeks acting as adjutant. The establishment of an anti-tank regiment being smaller than that of a machine-gun battalion, a number of men had to go, and there was a great deal to do. I wrote to my father on 16 November: 'To get sixty men away from the place takes a foolscap page of closely written instructions, + ½ page ditto when the railway goes and buggers the thing up – all worked out by your humble servant in the intervals of attending to all the battery commanders, regimental sergeant major and subalterns who all crowd into my office asking questions from when can they have leave to what time their men's diapers should be changed ... It is quite awe-inspiring to work under a C.O. who seems to have no thought in life except the regiment ... He is on the job longer than anyone else, and never forgets a thing. He expects every little detail carried out, and as he never forgets himself he expects no one else to. This morning at breakfast he remarked to me that he thought it would be a good idea to change the disposition of the sentries round barracks. The day passed in a flurry and it was not until I was walking down to the orderly room at half past six in the evening that I suddenly thought, 'Jesus – those bloody sentries!' so I toiled up to the guard room and had the alterations made instanter. I had only been back in my office long enough to write an order to the R.S.M. telling him to do the same every day in future, when the C.O. came in saying, 'Oh, there you are, Desmond; I see those sentries haven't been changed.' So with the smug smile of righteousness I said it had now been done.'

In consequence, being alone, I had to work in the office every night after dinner, and of that I have a fond memory. At ten o'clock I would hear the duty piper playing the Highland Cradle Song for lights out. In the dark silence the sound of the pipes echoed round the labyrinthine buildings now loud, now soft, until it died away, with a haunting beauty which for a few moments filled one's soul with wistful thoughts of some far distant land of peace.

Not all my memories were so happy however. There was a considerable turn-over of officers. One subaltern who had just joined us was a hard-bitten, not very attractive character who had fought in the Spanish Civil War. He and his wife were quite feckless and they had not been in Tillicoultry very long before the Edinburgh police turned up wanting to know why they had abandoned in their flat in the city a small armoury of grenades, pistols and other lethal weapons. There were constant heavy drinking parties in his lodgings. One day on the rifle range a colour sergeant, a crack shot, remarked that he would never hit the target because he was always drunk. The subject overheard him and out of the corner of his mouth said, 'I can shoot that man off the map drunk or sober,' and proceeded to do so. He was no good for anything except fighting, and I believe that he distinguished himself in North Africa. He did not stay with us long. But before his departure he crawled into my office early one morning wearing his steel helmet; his voice gone through drink, he whispered that he had lost his bonnet in an affray and could he borrow mine so that he could go to the mess for some breakfast.

Another morning David Reekie came in to see me. He said that he could not get on with anybody and wanted to go to the regimental depot, now merged with that of the Black Watch at Perth, to see if he could get a posting out. I knew he was unhappy, however much it may have been his own fault, and I felt sorry for him; so I said, 'I haven't seen you this morning, but if you are not back by dinner this evening I shall report you to the C.O. as absent without leave.' He was back, he did get his posting – whither I know not; but I was to see him again years later, still his old cantankerous self.

Here, too, I was faced with taking my first court martial. I believe that military law has now been changed, but at that time it was always the adjutant's duty to prosecute. But the first most interesting part, which also fell to the adjutant or his assistant, was taking the summary of evidence on which the commanding officer decides whether there is a case. This entails interviewing all potential witnesses and taking down their statements, which must be strictly factual; if one shred of 'hearsay' creeps in the whole statement is invalid. This is more difficult than it sounds, and I always found it an absorbing exercise in concentration.

The court martial was a case of theft, a gunner of impeccable reputation having been found with a stolen watch in his possession.

The prisoner's friend (defending officer) was Henderson. He came into my office and said, 'You're going to lose this case.'

'Why? What makes you so sure?'

'Because I know he didn't do it.'

'How do you know?'

'Well, I shouldn't tell you, but it will all come out in evidence.'

I was worried; if the accused was clearly innocent, which did not surprise me, no way was I going to prosecute him, yet the court martial had been ordered and it appeared an open-and-shut case.

Henderson came clean. It appeared that the prisoner, whom everyone liked and trusted, had gone into his barrack room and discovered a soldier, having rifled another's kit, with the watch in his hand. 'Don't be a fool,' he said, 'give it to me and I will give it back to its owner.' The thief gave up the watch and ran off; the prisoner was found with the watch before he could return it, and it was impossible to confront the culprit, a bad hat, because he had immediately deserted.

A fine kettle of fish, which I considered was quite beyond my capacity to cope with. So I went to the Judge Advocate's department at Division for advice. In the end a D.J.A.G. prosecuted, with me as his assistant. The president of the court was a lieutenant-colonel from the Royal

Signals; when he came to give his verdict he looked at the D.J.A.G. and said, 'Not guilty; that's what you wanted, isn't it?'

One evening that winter the proprietor of the Glen Devon Hotel not many miles away telephoned. He said that he had a V.I.P. coming who had never been in Scotland before, and to whom he wanted to show the best of Scottish hospitality. For this he needed a piper, and could we oblige. If we could, he would like me to come to dinner and bring a fellow officer with me. Colonel John said that he was quite willing for a piper to play if anyone was willing to, and the pipe major said that he would like to go himself. I asked Jack Wilson, a charming elderly soul who had been quartermaster, to join me, and the three of us set off in the evening.

It was a strange event. About four tables were occupied in the large room and all the diners seemed quite unknown to one another, though the face of one man seemed familiar to me. We had a remarkably good dinner, and when the haggis was brought in Sergeant Craig marched up and down in the hall playing beautifully.

After dinner we sat with the proprietor in the hall, while the man whose face seemed familiar stood in a telephone box across the room for ages and ages delivering a dramatic monologue.

I asked what was going on, and the proprietor said that now he could tell us. It appeared that the Glen Devon Hotel was from time to time used for secret meetings because the glen itself was so narrow that it could be closed at each end with complete security. The man who was paying his first visit to Scotland whose face seemed familiar was Beneš, the president of Czechoslovakia, and all the diners were members of his cabinet in exile, though they pretended not to know one another. Now, standing in the telephone box with voice rising and gestures ever more incisively dramatic, the president was making a speech by land line to London and thence relayed by the B.B.C. – urging the workers in the Skoda armament factories under German occupation to sabotage everything within their power.

On the subject of resistance, I heard from Margaret in December that Denyse Clairouin had been in New York, via Lisbon, gathering funds from her publishing friends for the French underground. They were generous, but begged her to stay in New York. She spoke on the telephone to Margaret who was in Philadelphia; she said she must go back because there was work to do. She had transferred her activities to Lyons, where she married an engineer, Jean Biche. He made aeroplane engines, and in 1942 the Germans asked him if he would make engines for them. In order not to have his works taken over by someone else more enthusiastic than himself, he agreed. What with labour troubles, shortage of supplies, breakdown of machinery, misunderstandings and other unavoidable obstacles, his total output up to the liberation in 1945 was one engine. It is a miracle that he got away with it.

Denyse was immersed in the Lyons underground. In the end she was caught by Barbie's fiends and put on a train to Ravensbrück. She never got there; the cattle trucks were packed so tight that she suffocated to death. In her memory is named the prize presented at the embassy in London each year for the best translation from French into English.

The general commanding Scottish Command was extremely keen on education and, unlike other areas, had inaugurated a compulsory scheme which included map-reading (always a British weakness) with mathematics, and English; teaching the Jocks how to express themselves, how to take down a message, synonyms, précis of prose passages – all to make them more articulate. For this I had just got all the stores in, blackboards, chalk, maps, protractors, 500 pencils, 20,000 sheets of paper – when another course came up.

All of us were sent, a batch at a time, to conversion courses which took place at Ilkley. We were in one big hotel which was very comfortable. Lectures were given in the ballroom, round the gallery of which were a number of bedrooms. During the first lecture on the opening morning there was a slight disturbance as Harry Aitken, never an early riser, emerged from his room in the gallery *sans* breakfast hastily buttoning up his battledress blouse. The hotel was not entirely requisitioned and there were quite a number of civilian guests. A much greater distraction was caused by the arrival of a rather good looking young tart who had booked a room. On her first day there was a queue of lustful officers on her side of the gallery, and the management was undecided whether to live and let live or ask her to leave. The matter was settled for them by the police who arrived the next morning to arrest the young lady for stealing a fur coat in Leeds. Notwithstanding such distractions, six of us got 'D' (distinguished), which shows that Colonel John's ruthless drive was having results, for there were some regiments which did not manage a single 'D'.

Early in the New Year we left Scotland for ever and moved south into Northumberland. Headquarters were in the small fishing port of Seahouses. The winter was severe, we were often cut off by deep snow, and I was amazed that the little early lambs, born into an unfriendly world, survived. And in the wild weather sheets of spray would shoot hundreds of feet into the air over the reefs of the Farne Islands.

We received a new war establishment, which always meant hard work and in this case a rather amusing result. After dinner Colonel John and I attacked it. By one o'clock in the morning we were exhausted, and baffled by one body who appeared to have nothing to do. Colonel John said that he would go to the War Office and find out what this man's duties were supposed to be. He took the morning train, and on his return late that evening told me of his visit. At the War Office he asked for the officer responsible for compiling war establishments, and at the end of a long corridor in a small office there sat a lonely captain. Colonel John explained his dilemma. Rising to his feet, the captain said, 'Sir, would you allow me to shake you by the hand? I have been sitting here since 1939 writing war establishments and nobody has ever asked me a question. You, Sir, are the first. This man has no duties; I put him in out of desperation to see if anyone would notice.'

At that time I got a letter from father asking if I could get down to

London as a farewell party was being given for Stefan Zweig, who was leaving for Brazil via New York. I did not know the colonel well enough to ask for exceptional or compassionate leave to attend the departure of an Austrian author who was leaving the country; two years later things might well have been different.

In any case it was too late. Stefan had made his decision and was on his way. Many years later I said to Donald Prater – from whose splendid biography all the quotations which follow are drawn – that I thought that I could have persuaded Stefan not to go. But to have had any chance of doing so, I would have needed to be in London all the time, not just when he had already booked his passage.

Such a presumptuous statement demands an explanation. For some time Stefan's feelings had alternated between deep pessimism and a sense almost of duty, expressed in letters to his many friends: '... An intellectual who leaves Europe now betrays her,' yet 'I know what awaits us after the war – hatred because we speak German and are Jews.' Although, 'Here we can fulfil a duty, merely by our presence,' but 'Those who still live according to the old ideas are lost.' And thinking of invasion, '... The Nazis shall not find me alive.'

He had been invited to lecture in Brazil and finally decided to go, 'Although,' he said, 'things look so frightful that a well-aimed torpedo would to my mind be the best solution.' It was his intention to return, but he decided that he would first go via the United States where he could use his considerable influence to help others who had to seek a refuge. It was just at this stage, I feel, that if I had been in London and able to see him daily I could have been of use. I have described earlier how close to him I had become in the years before the war. Of course, he had many friends, but all of them were of his own generation – eminent and respected figures who could commiserate but not inspire; and I am sure that many of them felt (and some more than likely said) that if he could get himself to South America, he would be a fool not to. What was lacking was someone from the next generation who could hammer at him, 'Forget the world of yesterday; we are going to win the war and we need you for the world of tomorrow.' I was twenty-seven years younger than he, another friend, Lord Carlow, more; but I was a soldier and Carlow was in the R.A.F.

So he went; and the intention to return soaked away like water in the desert sand. 'We can have no doubt,' says Prater, 'that the feeling had grown in him that his life was at its end, and that the thought of suicide – not for the first time – was now never far from the surface.' Before returning to Brazil from the United States he wrote to a friend: 'Back to South America on the old work and lecture business ... *Auf Wiedersehen unter oder oben*'; and to Jules Romains, 'It would be madness to return to England, where morally I am a foreigner and still a little the old "enemy alien".' To another friend, Feder, he said, 'The trouble is that when I used to write I was happy and full of enthusiasm. Now that's all gone.' On 22 February 1942, he and Lotte together committed suicide.

I did not hear of his death for a long time, and when I did, in a callous way, I suppose death had become a commonplace. But in the years since I have realized what a very dear friend I had lost.

Paul Frischauer left too – also for Brazil. But Paul, almost the same age as Stefan, was an extrovert and an optimist; so he made a success of his life there, moved later to New York and eventually returned to live out the rest of his days in his native Vienna.

When spring came I acquired a bicycle, and one sunny Sunday set off in an old tweed coat and trousers I had with me, armed with an Ordnance map, to visit a ruined castle on the cliffs about ten miles away. I had given no thought to the possibility of being taken for a spy, but on my way back I ran into the whole population of a small village, with the local constable, blocking the road. Of course I had my identity papers, but these could be forged; the constable cross-questioned me about my unit, the names of its officers and various other details until he was satisfied. I found it rather reassuring; far better a simple mistake than indifferent apathy.

At the end of that April two things happened. A man who was to become a dear friend arrived, and my job changed. The officer was a territorial from the Lanarkshire Yeomanry who became a great figure in the regiment, Tom Leys Geddes. He arrived when everyone was on an exercise and I was holding the fort. We lunched alone and I remember that I did most of the talking, telling him everything I could about the family of which he had that day become a part. He listened courteously – courtesy being one of his characteristics – and I hope that the picture I painted was a reasonably true one.

And I became M.T.O. (transport officer); another dear friend, Norman Reid (destined in time to be knighted as head of the Tate Gallery) took over as assistant adjutant and intelligence officer. I am not particularly expert mechanically, although machinery fascinates me, but in fact the duties of M.T.O. are really administrative, making sure that jobs are done in the right priority and co-ordinating the activities of the excellent mechanics and store clerks whom we now had. My warmest memory of this task was C.O.'s inspection of the transport. While Colonel John looked over the vehicles in general, I, in overalls, examined the engines and crawled underneath looking for oil leaks and the like. We had at the time a number of Quads, strange tortoise-like vehicles designed for towing the 25–pr field-gun, which had inside a mass of cupboards, the purpose of which was lost on us. They were of course supposed to be spotless. I do not know if we both were surprised or delighted to find in one a pound of butter and a collection of gramophone records.

Not long afterwards headquarters moved a short distance south to a rather pleasant house in a little place called Rock. There were always exercises, and since all the transport was out I would stay at home once more holding the fort. On one such occasion the mess sergeant, Maher, for whom I think the Spanish word *estupido* must have been invented, came to my office with a worried expression. When I asked him what was bothering him, he explained that the colonel had shot a brace of pheasant and had told him to hang them against the regiment's return, but would I come because he did not like the look of them. I went, to discover that he had hung them all right – over the kitchen stove. They were heaving like a man who has just finished a game of squash; they were two pullulating masses of maggots. I just said, 'Get a spade.' Surprisingly, he was not with us much longer, and was replaced by one of the great regimental characters, Sergeant Cushnagan.

It was about this time that, spending a leave in London, I thought that I would go and have a chat with Brendan. I rang him, and we spent some time talking in his office at Number 10. At three o'clock I was leaving, picking up my Glengarry and cane in the hall, when the front door opened and the Prime Minister came in.

'Ah, Desmond,' he said, 'what are you doing here?' I explained that I had been talking to Brendan.

'Come in for a few minutes,' he said, leading the way through into the cabinet room.

He sat down in his usual seat, in the middle of the long baize table with his back to the fireplace, and I sat beside him.

'Well, how do you think the war is going?'

It was in fact going very badly; but alone in that huge and famous room, what does a subaltern say to his prime minister? I waffled some platitudes, and, dearly as I loved him, that short interlude remains in my mind as one of the most embarrassing moments of my life.

On that same leave father told me that he had asked mother to divorce him; did I mind?

'Of course not,' I said, 'it's your life.'

As long as I could remember, they had never been really close; yet there was, and there remained, a bond between them, as I see from the later letters which have come into my hands since they died. I think they had not been divorced earlier because both were comfortable and there was no reason. Now they were separated geographically and father was in love with the beautiful Irish nurse who had looked after him in Weymouth Street half a dozen years before, so there was a cause; I was to have a stepmother.

It is interesting that when the case eventually came up father asked Lord Camrose please not to mention it in the *Telegraph*; the answer was firm and typical – 'I cannot promise that. If it is news I shall print it.' But it wasn't.

Rather more important, at this time Hitler was threatening to invade Spain in order to close the Straits of Gibraltar, and Churchill was contemplating an amphibious operation in retaliation if it became necessary. An ACI (Army Council Instruction) came out saying that anyone who knew any part of the coast of Spain well should report to the Admiralty. Knowing the coast north of Barcelona and being blessed with a photographic memory, I applied for a day pass and a railway warrant to London. When I told the pleasant Wren responsible what part I knew, she produced some photographs, including one of a British destroyer off Arenys – next door to Caldetas – obviously taken on that farcical non-intervention patrol during the Civil War. I talked for an hour and a half about the nature and gradients of the beaches, the nature of the terrain and the road system; finally I dried up.

'I'm sorry, I can't think of any more. I hope I haven't wasted your time.'

'Not at all,' the Wren beamed. 'Some people come here with all sorts of ideas and are out again in five minutes.'

It was an interesting exercise; thank God it came to nothing.

The regiment moved about a good deal in 1942, and improved in efficiency the whole time. The most beautiful place we were at was Keldy Castle, a shooting-box belonging to the Reckitts family, near Pickering in Yorkshire. The journey there was a nightmare. Little of the transport which was then in our charge was anything like new, and most was in no condition to last out a long day's drive under any circumstances, least of all with an extra heavy load on board. I brought up the rear, and, as the mechanics effected running repairs, more and more vehicles joined my party. This went on so long and so often that I finally lost count, and when we got to Keldy I was sublimely unaware of the fact that we had left one vehicle on the road. By a stroke of ill fortune that vehicle contained among other impedimenta Colonel John's servant, who arrived on foot some hours later.

It was not long before I was sent for. When he was very angry and trying not to explode, Colonel John used to go through the motions of chewing, though I cannot believe he ever had any chewing-gum. He was chewing that evening all right; he asked me if I would kindly explain why I had seen fit to abandon his servant in the wilds of Yorkshire. I cannot remember what I said, but it must have been, as near as dammit, nothing, because there was no sensible answer. Keldy was a lovely place. Surrounded by rhododendrons, it was miles from anywhere in the middle of vast moors of which the summer colouring was memorable.

From Keldy we moved to Thirsk racecourse for a short stay, much of our time there being taken up by a major exercise. This was always a busy time for the M.T.O., with almost no sleep, but extremely enjoyable; I recorded: 'I had plenty of unditching work to do, which I find fascinating. Since I have been M.T.O. I have become, of all things, an expert on recovering vehicles out of trouble; really, one never knows what one is going to do next in this war. I must say I find it most interesting, and few things are so satisfying as coming up to find the vehicle in some precarious position, sizing up the job, giving one's orders, getting ready, start up, then: the great moment – will she or won't she? Thank God, with a horrible sucking noise and a general slithering, she emerges from the mud on to firm ground. A most satisfactory sense of achievement results.'

Our brief stay at Thirsk was followed by a move of only four miles to Upsall, a house which belongs to 'Straffer' Gott, the general who should have taken over the 8th Army in the desert but was killed in an air crash, and replaced by Montgomery. It was a large house, with

Nissen huts snuggling round it like a sow with a litter of pigs; it stood at the top of a steep hill; the drive up to it was narrow, culminating in a right-angle bend and a small roundabout by the front door. The trucks carrying the men's kit and stores had to stop on the bend, unload, turn around and go down empty. It was obvious that there would be the most almighty traffic jam if it were left as a free for all, so Colonel John accepted my suggestion that I should have a wireless at the top of the hill, with a control set at the bottom, and that nothing should come up until given the all clear. This worked all right until one battery commander, a peppery little territorial, growing more and more impatient after about an hour of being told not to move, took matters into his own hands and led his transport up the hill. Of course the chaos at the top was total and no one could budge in either direction; it took the rest of the afternoon to sort that out and everyone lost their temper. I regarded this as a gross breach of discipline – selfishness, which is the cause of most indiscipline – and I complained bitterly to Colonel John. He listened with his usual quiet dignity and said nothing; I do not suppose that what I had said had anything to do with the fact that this officer left us shortly afterwards.

As the colonel set his standards ever higher, there were a number of casualties strewn along the way. Another senior T.A. officer left though I never knew exactly why. He was a most agreeable man, but he must have been irritating to serve under, or two dear friends of mine would not have put him under a cold shower in his service dress one evening after dinner. But one characteristic of his did get me down: he would always telephone headquarters about any order which was sent out; if there was anything about transport he would phone me.

'Desmond, how do you interpret para seven in this order?'

'Tommy, it's perfectly obvious; it means …'

'That's what I thought, but I just wanted to make sure.'

This used to infuriate me because I knew perfectly well why he did it: if he made a mistake, he would be able to say, 'Well, I did have some doubts about it at the time, and queried it …' and so the buck, he hoped, would be safely passed.

After years of virtual agnosticism, I found in myself during the war a completely fresh interest in religion. I am sure that this must have been quite common. There was no particular moment; it crept up on me. A great influence was the Church of Scotland, with which I had not previously been acquainted. Although the prose of the great English prayer book is magnificent, I had long become disillusioned by the monotonous and hasty gabble of many C. of E. priests who know it all by heart and sound as bored as their congregation is. In the Scottish church, where every prayer is extempore, each service is a new experience which can vary from the trivial to the sublime. This fascinated me, and after long and careful thought, at Upsall I offered myself to the elderly padre who looked after us as a candidate for reception into the Church of Scotland. He was a simple, sincere man who had been awarded the Military Cross in the first war for his ministrations to the wounded in no-man's-land.

He used to hold voluntary talks with the men, and I went to one of them to see how he was getting on. There were a handful there, and it was pretty heavy going. I asked him if he thought that Christ was a reincarnation of the Buddha. The object of my question was two-fold: I wanted to stir the meeting up a bit, and the matter is of the deepest interest to me. Mindful of Dryden's words, 'I have even thought that the wise men in all ages have not much differed in their opinions of religion; I meant that it is grounded on human reason. For reason, so far as it is right, must be the same in all men, and truth being but one, they must consequently think in the same train'. It seems to me that if God created the world, all its inhabitants are His children; and I can see no reason why He should choose a Jew at the eastern end of the Mediterranean as a manifestation of His presence and power, while apparently ignoring the needs and aspirations of the yellow, black and red peoples with which He had populated the greater part of the world. Frankly I do not believe that the Almighty would do such a thing, and the idea is merely a manifestation of the egocentricity of Europeans. There must be a wider answer, one much discussed at the present time. But our padre was silent.

Anyway he, a young signaller called Rennie and I stood under the trees and went through a simple ceremony which moved me deeply. I believe that when the day came when I had to preside over the burial of friend and foe alike in some wretched corner where no padre was available, I commended these poor remains to the mercy of God a little better than I thought I was capable of – or is that just sentimental imagination? I think that one thing, perhaps, which moved me towards religion occurred when I was on leave that September. I went to stay with mother. It was, as always, a happy time until the last day. I have a note which she wrote to father which says all there is to say better than I could: 'Poor Desmond had an awful blow on Saturday ... He saw in the *Telegraph* that Walter Churchill is missing and must now be presumed dead. I was sorry for him. I couldn't get a word out of him for some time.'

Later I came to know the details. Walter, with all his courage, drive and character, had risen to the rank of group captain when he was sent to Malta to command the Spitfire squadrons at Takali airfield. He must have told me before he went, because I remember he said that Keith Park had specifically asked for him. From there he led the sweeps over Sicily, and was hit by flak beating up the airfield at Catania. It was ironic that he should have lost his life in a Spitfire, which he never particularly liked. During my time I have been honoured by the friendship of some great and some good, some both; but I do not think that any other man has meant so much to me.

Socially Upsall, apart from the cold in winter, was fun. I shared a Nissen hut with Norman Reid, who bore with charm and resignation the constant blare of traditional jazz from my portable gramophone. My collection of records, which I carted around in cases, was always increasing because wherever we were I scoured the shops for out-of-print 78s, with gratifying results. Together we often went into Thirsk, and developed a catch-phrase. Entering the bar of the Golden Fleece Hotel, the centre of life in town, we would glance at one another: 'A drop of the old and bold?' Agreed; that was a large Irish whiskey (Scotch was scarce) and a pint of bitter.

The alternative to Thirsk was Northallerton, a charming sleepy little town to which recreational transport went on certain evenings. There I bought a silver lighter made by Clarkson, an aged silversmith who had been responsible for the dinner service of the Queen's doll's house. I gave it to father, and now have it back.

An undesirable officer newly posted to us whose name I fortunately forget was in charge of the fifteen-cwt truck going there one evening, and I asked if he minded my having a lift, as there was a film which I wanted to see.

The film was over and the pubs closed at eleven. At a quarter past I went into the inn which was the rendezvous, where I knew our chap was friendly with the landlord. He had his feet well under the table.

'The men are ready and waiting,' I said mildly.

'Let them wait,' was his reply.

I gave it a few minutes longer and then, returning, said rather coldly, 'I am taking the truck back in five minutes; if you are not on it, you can make your own way home.'

He was on it.

The colonel's eye soon fell upon him and he left us. His next posting ended rather suddenly when he was sent to prison for some appalling fiddle over 'grindery' (cut leather for repairing boots).

Such little things, perhaps unimportant in themselves, have stuck in my mind because they represent in different ways a trait, an inability or unwillingness to submit personal self to the demands of duty. There is nothing holier-than-thou about it – I made as many mistakes as anyone else, one of which will haunt me until the day I die because it cost life – but that is a different matter. To the great majority of my brother officers – and to a man all who went overseas with us – discipline implied being where one was supposed to be doing what one was supposed to be doing when one was supposed to be doing it, and nothing else. I got up to quite enough mischief at one time or another without placing myself at the risk of breaking this code. I was immensely proud to be in the 5th Battalion, the 91st, and any nonsense would have brought upon me Colonel John's displeasure and at its direst a posting out, which to me was unthinkable. Apropos, John Masefield wrote to his wife in 1915 from the field hospital in which he was an orderly, 'One thing comes over very clearly here, "the community of feeling". Just as at school, or in a monastery, one's likes become devotions, and dislikes loathings.'

Other ranks are in a different moral position. Barring accidents, no officer would return late from leave, one reason being that it means someone else has got to do his job for him. The private soldier has no such obligations and an extra couple of days may be well worth the fourteen days confined to barracks which will inevitably follow. But even so I only remember one man who made a practice of returning late, and he was such a character that we shall meet him again later. Furthermore the majority of the original Argylls possessed a long and fierce loyalty which reduced their misconduct to a minimum. Of course every unit has its regular delinquents, and I always think of the soldier who appeared with monotonous regularity on charges of idleness. His C.O. one day had had enough and sentenced him to ten days in the glasshouse, 'where,' he added, 'they won't give you much time to be idle.' With permission to speak, the prisoner expressed his feelings: 'Oh, thank you, Sir, I think you've done the right thing – because I'm a bugger when I'm idle, I'm a sod when I'm idle.'

There was fresh news from father at the office. He was talking of trying to get Margaret, who was teaching three days a week at the University of Bryn Mawr, back to run the educational department. I wrote, 'She will, I am sure, prove a help and a friend, if you need one, against the constant pin-pricks and petty irritations which I am sure Young and Gentry inflict upon you. They are a couple of woollen-headed reverse-wallahs.'

Apparently before my departure I had been promised the memoirs of Michael Fokine, though they did not materialize; but a letter was sent on to me from Albert Guérard – Pertinax, the most influential political commentator in France, whose book I had bought from Denyse Clairouin – to say that he had finished it. *The Gravediggers of France* came out in the autumn of 1944. Margaret acquired for father one very important book during these years – *One World* by Wendell Wilkie, whose early death was a tragedy for American politics – and he also got both of the two best American correspondents, Ed Murrow, and Quentin Reynolds whose first book had the famous title *The Wounded Don't Cry* (true; with very rare exceptions they don't). Quent was still in London when I came on leave and I remember his huge professional footballer-like figure and deep gravelly voice.

Sergeant Cushnagan was now firmly established in charge of RHQ messing. I liked him because of his dry humour, and I wish I could remember more of his remarks. One evening I asked him what was for supper; he said he could not remember, but would let me know. Shortly afterwards he brought me a drink and said, 'The menu, Sir,' handing me a slip of paper which read:

Green Turtle Soup

Sole Colbert

Chicken Maryland
fresh peas and sauté potatoes

Iced water melon

Coffee

and out of the corner of his mouth added, 'Beef as usual.' I think that it was this evening that the meat was the toughest it has ever been my misfortune to try to eat. As he was taking the plates away, I said, 'Cushnagan, that horse won the Derby in the year of Queen Victoria's Jubilee.'

Quickly and sympathetically he replied, 'Yes, Sir, I know; my father backed it.'

I think that the last word on Upsall was said by Sergeant Harvey, a grizzled territorial. It was decreed that there should be a night exercise in map-reading, for some reason always a weakness in the British army. At midnight the second in command, John Tweedie, asked me if I would like to go with him to the top of Sutton Bank to see how things were getting on. Long after everyone else had passed, a truck chugged up the winding hill with Harvey navigating; it came to a stop.

'Well, Sergeant,' said John Tweedie, 'how is it going?'

Somewhat testily the answer was, 'I'm all right, Sir, the trouble is half the roads aren't on this map,' and with a screech of tyres the truck set off in completely the wrong direction. I think they got back in time for breakfast.

15   Final Preparations

There was great relief in everyone's mind when the regiment was at last given a positive role: we were named as the anti-tank regiment of VIII Corps which was being formed for the eventual invasion of Europe.

Almost my last job as M.T.O. was a lugubrious farce. I attended a demonstration of wrapping the canopy of a three-ton truck round its metal stays to form a boat in which a 6-pr. gun could be ferried across a water obstacle. This worked perfectly and we paddled about in a big lake. Another method demonstrated was to haul the gun across a river with the aid of a thick hawser. I got very excited about this and persuaded the colonel to let me put on a show for the regiment.

We all went down to the Ouse north of York, where the river is about fifty yards wide. We got the top off the three-ton truck, made our boat, put the gun in and launched it. With a tearing sound like Smee's trousers in *Peter Pan* the canopy disintegrated and the gun went to the bottom. I had been conned; the canopy used at the demonstration had been good pre-war stock, while those available to us were wartime issue which tore like a handkerchief. Furious, I was determined to carry out the second part of the demonstration, which involved getting a heavy hawser across the river. Stripping off, I tied the rope round my waist and started swimming across the Ouse. A wet hawser, I discovered, can be very heavy, but I kept going and just made it to the other side. The gun was pulled across and honour was shakily preserved.

After that, or because of it, I was posted to 144 Battery; it was a pleasure to be under David Simpson again, first as L.O. and then commanding a troop.

In March the regiment drove out of Upsall for Exercise Spartan in great style and high spirits, in the knowledge that we were not returning, and that we had at last been appointed to a definite role with a rosy future. It took us two days to drive to the area in Buckinghamshire designated for the exercise, and on the way we spent the night in and around a large farm. Space was very cramped and Norman Reid and I did not like it at all, so we took our bed-rolls and retreated to the hay-loft of a large barn. It was a night to remember: I must have been asleep on my back because, waking up in the small hours, I found a mouse sitting quietly on my forehead.

As its name implies, the exercise was to some extent a large-scale test of the stamina of the troops involved who, it was apparent, would form a great part of the forces opening the second front. It was a pretty busy affair so far as we were concerned; we were moved backwards and forwards ceaselessly, and although most of us never saw the 'enemy' we had very little rest. But the weather was superb: warm sunshine by day and a sharp frost at night. To awaken at first light in the open with rime on one's hair and breathe the keen, sharp spring air was exhilarating. Although we learnt little about tactics, we discovered that by and large we were equal to the most strenuous physical demands that could be made on us.

After it was over we were sent to Norfolk; 144 Battery was in Sheringham and very comfortable. David and I played golf sometimes, though the excellent course was somewhat shortened because the holes along the cliff edge were mined. But the outstanding thing for me was being handed a telegram in the middle of one of David's conferences: it was a cable from Margaret saying that she had got her passage to the U.K. She had obtained a Canadian passport and sailed for England on a Fyffe's banana boat, in convoy: it was, of course, loaded with essential foodstuffs – there were no bananas. Indeed, when the fruit was reintroduced in 1946 some small children are said to have burst into tears on their first sight of such strange objects.

She arrived safely, and after a while our dear friend [Sir] Robin Brook gave us a lease on the two top floors of a house which he owned – 10 Devonshire Place, a few doors from the London Clinic – which was to be our home for a number of years.

I had by now discovered the particular traits of Colonel John. The first, of which everyone was in terror, was his ability, with an unerring eye, to appear at any weak spot where one least wanted him. The second was that, if one were called upon to speak, the only possible answer was complete honesty; any prevarication invited immediate disaster. I had a good example of both when we were doing a full charge shoot at this time at Foulness. The activities of one of my guns were abominable, so I was not surprised to hear the familiar quiet voice behind me:

'Desmond, your left hand gun is shooting very badly; who is the No. 1?'

'Bombardier Clarke, Sir; he only got back from leave in the small hours and I do not think he can even see the target, let alone hit it.'

I waited nervously, but at least I had told the truth; any prevarication would have produced a horrible explosion.

We were only two months in Norfolk, and then moved back to Yorkshire where VIII Corps was assembling so that its armour could exercise with the least possible damage to agriculture. We were under canvas on Strensall Common. Being next door to the depot of the K.R.R.C., many of us found the main attraction on the other side of the fence to be David Niven, and a very smart officer he was. At this point I was appointed adjutant; thus Norman Reid, as I.O., and I were finally working full time together. For a while Margaret and Norman's wife, Jean, lodged in the same house near the camp and a close friendship sprang up which has lasted ever since.

If anyone not familiar with such matters is interested, the position of adjutant is peculiar. One is promoted into a hard chore. It is not simply the executive office of trying to see that everything runs in accordance with the commander's wishes but there is, or should be, extraordinary trust. The officer commanding a unit has a very proud position but a very lonely one. There are only two people with whom he can be on any terms of familiarity: his second in command and his adjutant. If he is at odds with either of them his position becomes that much more restricted. It has been said that if a commanding officer and his adjutant are together for any length of time they finish up deadly enemies or friends for life. My complete devotion to John Cockburn and at the same time the knowledge of his idiosyncrasies which I had acquired made my long term of an office which can be full of pitfalls an enjoyable and a comparatively easy one, and a life-long friendship developed. Although so long as I served him I kept my place (I hope), to me he was always John, and so he shall be for the rest of these recollections.

While we were there our first seventeen-pounders arrived. This was a gun which equalled the power of the famous German 88. John insisted that on delivery every gun be stripped down. One was found to contain in its recuperator a twelve-inch file, an act of presumed sabotage which would have destroyed the gun and possibly its crew if it had been fired in that condition.

Our stay on the common was short, and at the end of July we moved to Filey, the seaside resort which contained among other things a large Butlin's camp. To my great sorrow Norman left us to do photographic interpretation in Italy. I am sure that it was a job after his own heart, but I missed him terribly. Life at Filey was fun. It included a ball for which various wives, including Margaret, came up to stay. The large Butlin's swimming pool had been emptied for the duration, but we cleaned out all the tins and dead cats and filled it with sea water which was very cold; there, the day after the ball, we had sports which were easily won by R.H.Q. largely because we had the very energetic and able P.T. Sergeant Mitchell.

In getting his team together, he asked me if I was a swimmer. I told him truthfully that I could swim a long way, but very slowly; so that if he wanted to put me in the longest race, I promised that I would finish – but it would have to be in my own time. So be it, he said, and I found myself committed to five lengths of the pool. It turned out exactly as I had threatened: I finished last, and the whole proceedings were held up while I doggedly fulfilled my task. Climbing out of the water, I was addressed by Couser, the second in command's driver, who said, 'The trouble with you, Sir, is you spend too much time on your arse.' I grinned; at least I had scored some points because I had finished while some had not.

One of the vagaries of war is the frequent changes of circumstances which cause the powers that be to have fresh thoughts. It was ironic that our neighbours were a battalion of Beds and Herts, which was being converted from infantry to the medium machine-gun – and our senior N.C.O.s spent all their spare time instructing the art, or science, which after such long experience they had been forced to abandon two years before! They thoroughly enjoyed themselves. Looking back, I suppose the renewed need for the Vickers gun was brought about by the terrain of Italy which had made the campaign there one long slogging match from mountain to mountain. The M.M.G., being water cooled, can go on firing for ever and a number of them together can deny ground to the enemy as effectively as and much more economically than artillery.

Things always seemed to happen while everyone was away: that September it was a full charge shoot. Alone in the office, I was rung up by Corps to say that our first six M10s were ready to be picked up at an ordnance depot some way away. (The M10 was an open-topped diesel – thank God – Sherman which when later fitted with the British 17-pr was to become the hammer of the German armour.) I rustled up enough mechanics who could drive and we went to fetch them. None of us had ever seen one before, but we made it back without hitting anything or anybody. Actually, driving a tank at a sober pace along a good road is very easy, but I got a thrill out of for the first time holding the tiller of a thirty-ton machine capable of 35 miles per hour.

While we were at Filey VIII Corps reached its final form and its purpose became known: somewhere in Europe there was to be a beach-head and it would be our task to break out of it. Since it was obvious that, wherever we landed, our advance would be impeded by large minefields, one of the first exercises which the new VIII Corps held was to practise the breaching and passage of troops with armour through such an obstacle at night. A sunken road on the Wolds represented the minefield, the sappers went through the motions of making the gaps and laid the tape up to them, placing the lanterns which marked them in the dark. John was gap controller; we had five gaps to look after, and in a conference at Corps H.Q. I suggested the simple identification signs for them, of which I can now remember only Hat (a top hat) and Diamond; as we shall see, they were used in the real thing, and I like to think that I made a tiny bit of history.

As R.H.Q. was not involved in any changes of equipment, the men were already fully trained and it was difficult to keep them occupied – particularly on wet days. I filled up a certain amount of time with setting quizzes to which they had to write down answers; it was quite fun. I remember two questions, which I put in one of them. First, who is President of the Soviet Union? They all put Stalin, except one driver, a card-carrying member of the Communist Party, who of course knew that it was Kalinin. Secondly, what are A.F.V., Char, and Panzer-kampfwagen? They are, of course, the same – a tank in English, French and German. Everyone knew Armoured Fighting Vehicle; most people understandably put 'tea' for 'Char'; but the answer which gave me the most pleasure was that 'Panzerkampfwagen' was a Turkish admiral.

We left Filey because it turned out that the accommodation had originally been requisitioned by the Air Ministry which wanted it back for the Free French air force. There was a certain amount of bad feeling, and we ended up rather scattered in the Driffield area, where we remained until the following March. Headquarters were in a little village called

North Dalton, which was comfortable enough but miles from anywhere.

It was here that I had what was probably the most ludicrous experience of my time in the army. Not long after our arrival there was a dance in the village hall and the villagers sent a formal invitation to the commanding officer; John said that he wasn't keen to go and asked me to represent him. So I appeared on the dot; all the women were seated in a ring round the room and the men were drinking at the bar. The band struck up and everyone looked at me to open the proceedings. I ran my eye round, walked over to the prettiest girl I could see and asked if I might have the first dance. We swung out across the floor, the admiration of all eyes until fate intervened. No one knew that in the very centre there was a patch of dry rot: this gave way and I descended to Mother Earth. The distance from the floor to the foundations was exactly the length of my calves, so, still holding my partner who looked down at me with mixed horror and amusement, the hem of my kilt just reaching the boards, I must have looked something like José Ferrer as MacLautrec.

My next experience of dancing was rather happier. For some time I had been suffering from a chronic sore throat, and I thought that there must be something wrong with my tonsils. The M.O. said that he could not see anything, but if I really wanted them out, I could. The operation at Scarborough Hospital was a success: my sore throat vanished, never to return. After two days I was turned out and sent to Harewood House, an officers' convalescent home, where I spent Christmas and Hogmanay.

For Christmas the Princess Royal gave every patient a book which she inscribed; for me it was a bitter-sweet present: *British Historians* in the 'Britain in Pictures' series which Paul Frischauer had suggested and we had turned down! At dinner the Earl stood everyone champagne. I have never refused a glass of champagne and I was not going to start now, but so soon after the operation the acid bubbles down my raw throat felt like red-hot coals. By Hogmanay I was much better in all ways, and could consume the champagne with relish. Soon after dinner the Princess demanded eightsomes; there was another Argyll officer, two Gordons and three Scottish nurses, and we started. She was a very good dancer. The Earl had gone away so she was alone, and after the dancing the Matron asked me to go and talk with her because I was rather older than the others. Once she had forgotten her shyness with someone she had never seen before and my natural respect had moderated, we talked about what the house was like normally – all the marble fireplaces were boarded over and the best furniture removed – and about eighteenth-century furniture and painting in general. Her charm and great knowledge bewitched me and we chattered on until the New Year came in.

During this time I had the leisure to think, and I let off a few of my ideas – some right, some wrong – to father in a long letter, part of which, over forty years later, is not without interest. My first point, about publishing, was mainly concerned with the impending prevalence of paperbacks (which had only started a few years before the war).

My second point starts from politics: do you agree with me that we shall have two things for certain – Beveridge in some form (when the present Long Parliament is dissolved there will be such a reaction that I do not think the Conservative Party will see power for ten years). What is that going to mean to us in our new Belle Sauvage? Education – masses of it; the Socialists will spend millions on education. New schools, longer years at school, new methods of teaching – and new books, millions of them ... I was excited to hear from Margaret in a letter today that you had had the offer of a Russian dictionary. Is it a good one? ... I look forward to hearing what has happened to it. Another of the small group of things which seem certain after the war is that the world will be dominated by Russia and the United States, with us clinging on by our fingernails if we play our cards right – and it seems to me a terrible gap in our line of dictionaries not to have a Russian one ... Don't forget to have masses of [German] dictionaries (including the little pocket one in millions – even if printed on lat paper) for the army of occupation – it's going to be there for years, I can assure you ... It is cold in this office in the evenings and I shall go to bed. But I feel better for giving you my views: I should feel much better if I were sitting with you.

We were still at North Dalton in the following March, when I very nearly came a nasty cropper. VIII Corps had already been inspected by the King and Queen; now it was Montgomery's turn. On the morning of the parade John burst into my office: 'You know it's take great-coats?' To my horror in all the reams of paper I had missed this small paragraph. Frantic telephoning followed: if only we could get through to the scattered batteries in time! I had visions of the 91st drawn up in impeccable order, soaked to the skin, and the great man asking 'Why are these men not wearing great-coats?'

We did get through; the men took coats and cleaned their brass on the way; and it didn't rain. The only thing Monty wanted to know was why the Corps A/Tk Regiment wore balmorals. After he had looked at us all, he went through his usual drill: standing on the bonnet of a jeep he summoned everyone to break ranks and gather round. It was, after all, dry and we sat on the ground. He made his usual speech: 'We'll hit 'em for six' etc. There can be no doubt that he was very impressive. I was sitting next to two of our N.C.O.s and they agreed; one said to the other, 'H'm, seems a reasonable sort of cunt.' There could be no higher praise.

The time arrived for us to move to a southern area in preparation for what was to come. Leaving Yorkshire on 26 April, it took us three days to motor down to Seaford. I found the drive through London very exciting, and rather moving. The main roads were closed for our passage and, preceded and followed by policemen on motor-cycles, we rattled down the Edgware Road, round Marble Arch, down Park Lane, Hyde Park Corner and so south. Although my home town, London seemed strangely remote; we knew that we were going to France – somewhere – and the people in the streets, some waving, were like the citizens of another world: which indeed they were, for we had for years now been living in a separate community, brothers of a lay order sworn in for the destruction of the King's enemies.

The regiment settled in comfortably in Seaford where there was a lot to do. First, equipment poured in; the M10s were replaced by new ones with 17-pr guns – secret, with the code name 'Fireflies' – and waterproofing had to begin all over again. Waterproofing was the covering of every join in the metal hull with black Bostic for going ashore through water. An enormous document like a bible arrived, which was 2 Army's orders for every possible contingency; my task was to extract from this only what a battery commander needed to know and reproduce it in a pamphlet of manageable size. It sounds simple, and indeed it was, but it took days of concentration.

I had one day off when I went up to London with a friend of mine, Rollo Spencer. We met Margaret for lunch at the Café Royal and were joined by Rollo's best friend, a fellow stoic, Noel Annan, now the distinguished peer. It was a very happy and civilized meal – the last I was to have until Harry Aitken and I lunched four months later in Brussels.

Meanwhile, there was one last court martial to deal with: a chap found loitering around some W.R.N.s quarters – whether just a Peeping Tom or trying to effect an entry I cannot remember. But any case involving service women had to be prosecuted by a J.A.G., so I only had to assist.

At last on 6 June we learned that the assault troops had landed in Normandy. On the following day John held a briefing in which he said, pointing to a large map, that the whole operation would hinge on Mont Pinçon. Of course it did, and the attack of the 4 Dorsets on this big feature became the subject of what I think is the best British novel about north-west Europe: Alexander Barron's *From the City, From the Plough*.

We were now ready and had nothing to do but wait. Peter Maxwell and I used to go at eleven o'clock each morning for a drink at the Cottage Club, a house run by an angular woman whose name I forget, but whom John always called 'Miss Screw-picket'. It was here that we encountered one of the less desirable elements of life: inter-service jealousy. Although the R.A.F. was always sensitive about being the junior of the three services, the vast majority of its pilots and air-crews, mostly very young men, were too concerned with their work to bother with trivialities: but there were a small number of those, as cocksure as they were arrogant, who liked to make trouble. Two such Peter and I met one morning. They had, they said, already made one sortie over France and would be making another later in the day; the tenor of their further remarks was that they were, as usual, doing the army's work for it, a job they had been at since 1940. The important thing was not to get into a fight, because that might lead to enquiries and being detained in England; so we said nothing, and let their sarcasm flow over the hatred in our hearts.

We held a last dance at regimental headquarters. My work was finished, the concentration had left me exhausted, and in consequence I let my hair down to such an extent that I danced a *Dashing White Sergeant* the wrong way round, the other dancers graciously making way for the adjutant's aberrations; after which, deciding that I had made enough of a fool of myself for one evening, I retired to bed.

16   Off to Work

We finally left Seaford in the small hours of 13 June, that is, R.H.Q. and
the two M10 Batteries. After a nightmare drive we finished up in a
concentration camp on Southampton Common, where we stayed for
four days – though the M10s remained in the streets where the drivers
were royally entertained by the local people.

On the evening of the 18th the order to move came, and at about half
past six the leading vehicles set off. The tanks were garlanded with
flowers by the inhabitants of the houses outside which they had stood;
there were roses in the muzzles of the guns, roses rambling up the aerial
masts, and a rose in each man's bonnet. As they drove through the
streets everyone was in exuberant form, shouting and blowing kisses at
every girl with any pretension to good looks. The crowds on the way
cheered and waved and threw more flowers, and older people in the
windows sadly raised their hands in blessing. Later there was a halt in
the middle of the city which lasted for several hours, and here Highland
dancing to the pipes of both batteries drew an enormous crowd.

Loading began at about three in the morning and was completed by
breakfast time. By daylight on the 20th the vast convoy finally
assembled in Southampton Water, and we were off. The voyage was
appalling; there was a full gale blowing – the worst June weather ever
recorded – and after the first day everyone was ordered to return home
except us: being, as the saying goes, 'operationally required'. We
plunged on with a destroyer escort. On one of the L.S.T.s (Landing Ship,
Tank) the M10s broke loose and threatened to burst through the frail
side of the vessel. In the party which prevented disaster one sergeant
was seriously injured and a very fine driver was killed.

On my craft I shared a cabin with Peter Maxwell. I had absolutely
nothing to do. Since I did not consider that feeling ill would do anything
to raise the morale of the miserably sea-sick soldiers in the main hold,
and as my duties would begin in earnest the moment we arrived, I
swallowed a powerful black pill kindly supplied by the Americans and
took to my bunk.

When we finally arrived off Courseulles it was smoother, though
there was still too much of a swell for landing. But one could peacefully
go up on deck and survey the remarkable sight of hundreds of ships of
every size and shape stretching as far as one could see. Finally, at low

tide the ship was run in and the flat bows were let down.

This was the great, long-awaited moment. I led the way in my Bren carrier which had been severely damaged in the storm. Steeling my heart, feeling like a cross between Balboa and Captain Cook and more romantic than either, with my piper Fraser beside me playing *The Campbells are Coming*, I gave the order to advance and plunged off the end into rather less than a foot of water; there was not even a splash, but at least we had arrived. The next day we were in a pleasant meadow a few miles inland where John had set up his H.Q. We dug holes, sat on the edge of them in the sun, and ate our horrible but sustaining compressed 24-hour rations.

Early the next morning I rode a motor cycle for the last time. In the small hours a message told us that a battery from the A.Tk. Regiment of the Guards Armoured Division, which was in the process of arriving, was to come under our command. Unfortunately no one knew where it was, except that it came under XII Corps, so at first light I set off to find them. The two possible map references I had been given drew a blank. Finally I came upon the Corps R.A.; there was no sentry to be seen and everyone was asleep. Stamping about, I finally found an elderly soldier with iron-grey hair standing on end, dressed in battle-dress trousers, a pullover and sandals, who had obviously got up for an early run off. I marched up to him and in a rather belligerent tone said, 'Are you anything to do with H.Q., R.A. here?'

He replied gently, 'Well, yes, I suppose I am in a way; I'm the C.C.R.A*.'

He was charming, and told me what I wanted to know, I found the battery and motored home to breakfast; stepping off the bike with relief, never to put my leg across one again.

After a few days we settled down in a farmhouse at Bretteville-l'Orgueieuse on the N 13 Caen–Bayeux road. The two S.P. batteries sunned themselves in a beautiful orchard across the road, waiting for the first move of the break-out. Here we stayed for some time. On 25 June *Operation Epsom* began, the attempt to bypass Caen on the south, the battle for which VIII Corps had initially been trained. Soon after it began our idyll at the farm was interrupted rather rudely by a salvo of shells which landed on the road just outside our front door. As there was no reason why the dose should not be repeated as often as the Germans had a mind to, John told me to prepare a headquarters below ground to which we could withdraw if the need arose; in fact it never did, but I set to with bucket and spade. It really was like that because the soil was pure sand; in no time we had dug a deep square room with shelves for the wireless sets and various other niceties. Then came the question of how to provide a roof for it. Looking around the farm buildings, I found a mass of long logs ideal for the purpose and soon we had laid the roof with two feet of sand on top of it.

That afternoon an elderly man with a beret pulled over one eye appeared and became extremely angry when he noticed that the logs had disappeared; he attacked me with some vituperation. Finally he

---

* Corps Commander, Royal Artillery.

came to the point:

'*Mais, alors, je suis ancien combattant, moi* ... I know the form. You can take our women, you can drink our wine, but you can't take our wood!'

I invited him to come and look at our lovely dug-out, where he saw that all his logs were intact beneath the sand. He was perfectly delighted and, after we had embraced, he went off down the road muttering happily to himself.

Later, when things were quiet, the farmer's wife returned with her children; there was room for us all. But she was horrified to discover that all her kitchen utensils had been 'borrowed', since we had nothing in which to cook save mess tins. She went about wringing her hands and crying, '*Où sont mes casseroles?*' A happy compromise was reached: the pots and pans were produced, and she very kindly gave us one or two so that our cook could continue to produce his culinary masterpieces.

In the days before we had to get down to serious work, Harry Aitken and I made a quick dash into Bayeux, which had been captured undamaged.

The shops were stacked with Camembert, Pont l'Eveque and Port Salut, for this had been the supermarket for the Germans in the west, and we could buy as much as we liked with the special money with which we had been issued – I still have a 100-franc note.

Epsom was a hard slog. It began with the breaching of a minefield, just as we had practised, outside a village called Le Mesnil Patry which John translated as Mess in the Pantry. The VIII Corps sappers used the signs which I had suggested in Yorkshire for the gaps – hat, diamond, etc. – and so on along the routes leading out from the gaps, snaking across the face of western Europe. Years after the war, motoring through France, I used still to see the little signposts, about a foot square, nailed to trees with 'my' signs on them; they gave a little tug at my heart – perhaps one or two may even survive today, old, faded and forgotten.

The battle went on until 1 July, struggling against nine Panzer divisions which comprised nearly all the German armour available in the west. It was a bloody business; in that one week fifteen Scottish divisions suffered 25 per cent of all the casualties it had during the whole year in Europe.

All battles go in fits and starts; as Graham Greene has said, 'So much of war is sitting around and doing nothing, waiting for somebody else', I wrote home, 'Like all wars since the beginning of time, so far as I can gather, this one is excruciatingly dull most of the time and highly interesting for short periods.' During one of the many pauses Harry Aitken and I were sitting in the sun on Epsom Downs – the long slope up to the hotly debated plateau – when a squadron of Messerschmitt 109s came back at tree-top height from beating up the beaches. They were beautiful planes, as graceful as Spitfires, and there was something uncanny in seeing for a fleeting moment the features and goggles of a German pilot looking down at us as we looked up at him. Hughes, David Simpson's batman who was on air defence, was not unnaturally taken by surprise since they came so fast from behind him, and, doing his best, he produced a sharp burst of Bren after they were out of sight.

Peter Maxwell and I also made a number of trips around for various reasons. On one occasion we heard that there was an M10 sitting in a field, apparently undamaged, and we wondered if we might be able to recover it. We drove down in a jeep and entered a small clump of trees. Sure enough, down the slope a hundred yards away on the other side of the field in front was the tank. It looked all right. Silence reigned. Then we saw a sergeant slipping quietly from tree to tree like a grey wolf in a forest.

Peter always had a very loud voice; 'Good morning, Sergeant,' he boomed, 'where are the forward defended localities?'

The sergeant whispered, 'You're in them, sir.'

As the fighting in Normandy was conducted from one field to the next and as the Germans presumably occupied the hedgerow against which the M10 was resting, the proposed salvage was not on and we drove home with regret.

Operation Epsom was followed by *Windsor* and *Jupiter* which ground to a halt, and, on our failure to reach the River Orne, the battle was called off. We held a salient sticking into the German front south of Caen; we had not broken out, but we had made Rommel's projected counter-attack to re-take Bayeux impossible.

Meanwhile on 7 July, one of the most heartbreaking incidents of the campaign took place. Montgomery having failed to get round Caen, it was decided at the planning level to bomb the city; there is much evidence that it was a purely political decision, for by this time Caen had lost its strategic value to Montgomery. Six hundred Lancasters and Halifaxes came in late in the day, dropping six thousand bombs. The earth was already in the shadows of night, and the sky itself was that electric blue which follows a day of cloudless heat. But the long line of bombers, stretching back towards England as far as the eye could see, was still in sunlight, and their metal twinkled like fairy lights against the darkening sky. The pathfinders dropped their markers like a shower of jewels reluctant to follow the force of gravity. Soon the sky was dotted with flak like a giant net through the meshes of which the aircraft flew on, apparently undisturbed. Next there was a mushroom of black smoke from the city, shot through with red and yellow flames, which mounted as slowly as the flares had seemed to fall.

It was an awe-inspiring sight, which I watched from the extreme forward position of the Canadians on our left, only a short way from the town. Militarily it was a completely useless operation; the Germans were not in Caen – they were three miles north of it and remained completely untouched, as we were soon to discover to our cost. I do not think that the raid even wounded one German, but it killed a large number of French families. Immediately afterwards Professor (Lord) Zuckerman and a senior staff officer presented an official report in which they stated that 'There was virtually no sign of enemy gun positions, tanks or German dead in the target area ... no targets of military value had been attacked.'

I must say that I am unequivocally opposed to the bombing of cities. At its best (from the bombers' point of view) not more than 10% of the casualties are likely to be military; the other 90% are civilian. In the case of Caen, the military casualties were 0% and the remaining 100% were our allies. As Peter Waymark (ex Bomber Command) has written in *The Times*: 'At the outbreak of the Second World War the bombing of civilians was widely regarded as a crime perpetrated only by fascist regimes. By the end of the war half a million German civilians had been killed in allied bombing attacks which destroyed more than 60 cities.' But the worst of all, of course, is Dresden, a city known at the time to be packed with refugees in addition to its normal population. The corpses were piled in the main square and burnt, for all cemeteries were full. When the air crews were briefed for this, they were given as the main point of attack the crowded city centre. 'Christ Almighty!' one navigator remembers thinking. 'It's women and kids. We've never done anything like that before.' After the raid a fresh false briefing was held, giving quite a different target, so that it could be filmed for the public. Even so, one ex-airman has written in rebuttal, pointing out that the war was not yet won, though how the death of something like a hundred thousand women and children was going to win it he did not make clear. 'I asked Sir Arthur Harris,' writes Sir John Colville, the Prime Minister's secretary, 'what the effect of the raid on Dresden had been. "Dresden" he said, "there is no such place as Dresden".' Charming.

When Harris took over Bomber Command in 1942 one of the first directives given to him read: 'It has been decided that the primary object of your operations should now be focused on the enemy civil population.' Harris himself seemed to come to the mistaken conclusion that he could win the war all by himself, a purpose to which he gave the lives of fifty-five thousand young men. Even the Prime Minister finally choked on the bone and on 28 March 1945 he wrote to the Chief of the Air Staff, 'I feel the need for more precise concentration upon military objectives ... rather than on mere acts of terror and wanton destruction, however impressive.' One recent verdict states clearly that 'With hindsight the rigid adherence for so long to the concept of area bombing had been shown to have been a mistake.' And the most senior living military critic has added, 'The disruption caused by the British air offensive to the German economy had been minimal and probably strengthened national morale.'* For years we had been boasting, 'Britain can take it'; what made anyone imagine in the first place that, if we could, the Germans – a redoubtable people – could not? The same military critic has written 'By then [July 1944] neither the morale of the German people nor their faith in the Nazi regime had been undermined by air attack.'

Like every unit, we had suffered casualties, and I motored down to the coast to Army (rear) to see the officer responsible about reinforcements. There was a tragically long queue of adjutants, sitting there patiently on the same mission. The door burst open and we were all overruled by a colonel commanding a unit of the Pioneer Corps. He

* Field Marshal Lord Carver, *Twentieth Century Warriors*, 1987

was tall, grey-haired, with a mulberry face that told a long story, and he walked with a stick. He came straight to the point in a firm bark: 'Lost a lot of men. Must have more. They may limp. They can walk with a stick. But I won't have crutches. Crutches won't do.'

The British salient was under constant shellfire, and on 12 July there was a tragedy. John had ordered that everyone during this static period must be below ground, but David Simpson found himself in a dilemma. The lead from his wireless set was not long enough to reach from his lightly armoured command vehicle to his fox-hole dug beside it. He could either go below ground and be totally out of touch, or remain in the vehicle ready to receive any orders that might be forthcoming. He chose the latter course, sitting with his liaison officer who had arrived from corps headquarters only half an hour before. A shell burst beside them which killed Lieutenant Price and gave David multiple wounds – from which happily he recovered at home. Tom Geddes then left his position as Captain G of 146 to take over command of 144, and I departed from R.H.Q. to occupy his place at 146 Battery under Geoffrey Lardner. (Corps A.Tk. Batteries had two captains because they were liable to be spread over large areas under different formations and might need two commanders, hence the Captain G. The other Captain (Q) was, as usual, responsible for supplies).

I joined them at the side of a field full of dead cows with their legs in the air, their bodies bloated by the heat, outside the hotly contested and ruined village of Cheux. Four days later I wrote to father: 'Life is either dirty, smelly and noisy, or cloisterally quiet, according to whether one is in the fighting or out of it.'

Infantry losses since landing had been so heavy that General Dempsey was warned that there were only sufficient reinforcements to keep him up to strength until the end of July. He therefore suggested a left hook by VIII Corps using three armoured divisions north-east of Caen, and Montgomery accepted the idea. For this purpose we made a horrible journey across country and finished up sitting on a forward slope facing the industrial suburb of Colombelles, north of Caen, occupied by the Germans, which should really have been the target of the big raid instead of the city itself. In the middle of Colombelles there was a tall factory chimney from the top of which a look-out had a very good view of us, and he used to amuse himself by calling down shellfire on us whenever he felt like it.

At night we slept in fox-holes, or rather lay in them, because there was little sleep to be had. Most of the night the Luftwaffe flew over us at a few hundred feet, dropping flares to see what was going on; their curiosity was rewarded, and on the 15th Ultra (now well known as having broken the enemy's codes) intercepted a German forecast of a large-scale attack to be expected on the night 17th/18th.

Operation Goodwood began at first light on the 18th with a flourish: six thousand bombers dropped eight thousand tons of bombs and the artillery fired a million and a quarter shells. The battle was a disaster. 'What VIII Corps was running into that morning was really top-class

German defence. The inadequacy of British Intelligence about German strength east of the Orne was unhappily demonstrated by the presence of perhaps the best defensive structure they had yet been able to prepare in Normandy.'*

In an interview Dempsey said afterwards to Basil Liddell Hart: 'Once it was evident that the armour was not going to break out ... I really lost interest ... in the operation by evening, and was ready to call it off.' Yet that very evening Montgomery sent a signal to Brooke, the C.I.G.S., saying, 'Operations this morning a complete success.' Who was kidding whom? It was this sort of tomfoolery which led his British colleagues at Allied Supreme Headquarters to take the lead in demanding Montgomery's dismissal.

Two hundred and seven tanks were lost, and, since the weather broke, the survivors could not have gone through the mud even if the very strong German opposition had melted away. So the corridor the flanks of which it was our job to protect was never established and we did nothing.

Everybody went off to the next job. We motored ten miles west and had five days with the weather fine again. We were spread over meadows next to some friendly and hospitable Canadians. There were five days of parties, a mobile cimema, baths for everyone, pipers piped and dancers danced. During this otherwise happy time there was one casualty: the battery cook. He had a fixation that death would creep up on him if he went to sleep, so he spent the nights roaming round in his greatcoat and tin hat. As a result he was in the last stages of exhaustion, quite useless, and had to be sent home. In his place for the time being we were lent by R.H.Q. Sergeant Cushnagan, for whom I always had a soft spot. One day not very long afterwards, he and I 'liberated' some eggs from a farmyard; as a treat I said that we would both have omelettes and I would make them. I fancied myself as an omelette maker, my sole culinary pride, and they turned out very well. As we were eating I said, 'By the way, Cushnagan, what did you do in Civvy Street?'

'I was head omelette chef at the Metropole Hotel in Brighton,' he replied.

What if my omelettes had been a failure and I had wasted the priceless eggs under the eye of a professional? My blood ran cold at the thought.

In Normandy the rations were liberally supplemened by the barrels of cider and countless bottles of Calvados found in the cellars of every captured farmhouse. Cider, unknown north of the border, had become familiar to the Jocks in England, but Calvados was something new. The fact that it is practically colourless disguised its potency, and I regret to say that there were instances of drunken driving and, less important, some very sore heads.

Another thing which may never be seen again was the escaper's kit supplied to officers and N.C.O.s with technical training, of whom there

* d'Este, *Decision in Normandy*, Collins 1983

was a shortage. It was supposed to help us in getting back through the enemy lines if we had a chance. It contained *inter alia* syrettes of morphia, benzedrine tablets, compressed food, a compass in the form of a fly-button and a map of north-west Europe printed on linen the size of a pocket handkerchief.

And then there was a sudden change: we were ordered to remove all corps signs from our clothing and vehicles. The final breakout, the great battle known as *Operation Bluecoat*, was about to begin.

The spoke of the wheel which was to turn south and then east was formed by XXX Corps and VIII Corps, while on our right General Patton's 7th Army had the longest but fastest way to go to get right out in the clear. The object of the secrecy was to try to hide from the enemy just how many and what British troops were taking over ground from the Americans in order to release them for what they called *Operation Cobra*.

On 28 July John was given command of 44 Brigade in 15 Scottish Division. It happened very quickly: everyone was naturally delighted at his promotion, but each of us, with varying degrees according to how close one had been to him, felt sad at not being able to say goodbye and wish him luck – for we were all on the move at the time. Fortunately it was not to be the end of the story, and, for myself, this remarkable man was later to become again an important thread in my life and remain a beloved friend.

Bluecoat began on 30 July. Montgomery signalled to the C.I.G.S.: 'I have ordered Dempsey to throw caution overboard and take any risk he likes and to accept any casualties and to step on the gas for Vire.' The movement forward was long and complicated, but by the 5th we had advanced over ten miles south and were facing a curve of which the end on our left was the high point of Mont Pinçon, on our right the town of Vire, and in the centre a small village called Estry – which was to be the object of the next day's attack. The weather was glorious; Geoffrey Lardner and I found a way up to the top of the ridge behind which we were stationed; our reconnaissance was a pleasant and uninterrupted stroll. The scented pine woods which fringed the summit crackled in the heat, and from the eminence we looked across a shallow valley of meadows to a long ridge a good deal lower and running almost north to south on which lay our objective. The slate-covered spire of the village church could be seen above the oak trees and orchards which surrounded it. On our left the one road, white with dust, emerged from the trees and descended straight as a ruler and bare of cover more than half a mile to a crossroads. Further to the left, screened from us by the friendly pines, were the thickly wooded Bois des Monts and the enemy's observers who had everything stretched out before them, just as we had. That lovely afternoon was the last walk and talk that Geoffrey and I had, and the penultimate time I was to see him during the war.

The battle for Estry began before dawn on 6 August, which turned out to be another glorious summer's day. For us it was far from glorious and the name of that humble little village is engraved as clearly on our hearts as Waterloo must have been on those who survived it.

In fact Estry was never taken, for, after defying the efforts of two brigades for a week, the enemy withdrew of his own accord. At the time none of us could see any particular reason for their enduring such unpleasantness and inflicting such slaughter, but with hindsight it is quite clear. On 2 August Hitler ordered Von Kluge to launch Hausser's 7th Army against the Americans at Mortain; there existed, he said, 'An unique, never recurring opportunity for a complete reversal of the situation.' Von Kluge signalled back, 'If, as I foresee, this plan does not succeed, catastrophe is inevitable.' If 15 Scottish had taken Estry, they would have poured down upon the supply route of the attacking Germans. Nevertheless, Von Kluge was right; the attack failed and led to the destruction at Falaise and Trun. The Germans quietly withdrew from Estry, which no longer served any purpose, and this small huddle of dusty houses and orchards, soaked with the blood of a thousand Scotsmen and littered with the remains of thirteen Churchills, became once more just a name on the map, a point on the road.

I have described this disastrous operation in considerable detail elsewhere, so there are only certain aspects which I feel I need mention here.

Brian Brown, with 1 Troop, moved first with a battalion of the Gordons, the commanding officer of which stated that 'there is nothing in the village, and we expect to walk in.' Information from the leader of the local Resistance that there were, in fact, five thousand German infantry and a number of tanks in Estry was ignored. The British advance was planned to follow a road which would take them not into the village but parallel with and in front of it, so that the further the infantry went the more they were exposed, without purpose, to the enemy's fire. The Gordons were followed by a battalion of the H.L.I.

In the late afternoon Geoffrey told me to take his tank and go to see what was going on. I found the Gordons and the H.L.I. with Brian's troop and a squadron of Churchills stuck; attempts to get up a ridge to the left to attack the village the proper way had, for a variety of reasons, failed. Up a side road short of the village 2 Argylls commanded by John Tweedie, with our K Troop, were equally stuck. I drove back with this depressing news up the long straight road Geoffrey and I had been looking at the afternoon before; as it was completely dominated by the Bois des Monts, anything which appeared on it was heavily shelled from one end to the other.

By nightfall the infantry had got along the road facing the village rather less than two hundred yards away; the Gordons and the H.L.I. had pooled their slender number of survivors in one force, and, by order of the C.O. of the former, the M10s were lined up along the road in completely ludicrous positions in full view of the enemy.

During the following morning the situation was not a happy one. The Gordon, senior of the two battalion commanders, refused to allow the M10s to be moved, so they remained as aiming marks for the Germans' constant attention. Various plans were formed and cancelled. Geoffrey went down in his tank to see for himself what was going on, while I remained at Battery H.Q.

I realized that something had happened when I was called to the wireless and told by Geoffrey to hurry down and not to drive right up to him as it was unhealthy. I took the half-track, that useful lightly armoured vehicle, stopped well short of the village and walked the rest of the way. I arrived at the ditch which ran beside the M10s just in time to get into it in a hurry.

The position formed a rectangle, of which we occupied one of the long sides and the Germans in the village the other. The long sides were joined on our right by another road which was dominated by a German Mark IV which sat beneath a calvary ninety yards away. A small party trying to make a plan for the dislodgement of this nuisance had been spotted by it and hit with a high-explosive shell at virtually point-blank range. An engineer officer was killed, Brian blinded by the flash (fortunately he recovered his sight in hospital), and Geoffrey wounded in the foot.

On our left there ran from us to them a narrow strip of wood which was to become my obsession.

Geoffrey and I sat in the ditch as he explained the situation to me. I unlaced his boot and found that the wound was minute, but his foot was swelling angrily. He then took me over to introduce me to the two infantry commanders. They were in a farmhouse about a hundred yards away, but even that we could only complete in three laps, diving for cover on the way.

Then we walked down the road together to the half-track, underneath which we sat talking for some time until there was a pause in the mortaring; then Geoffrey drove off and I went back to the ditch feeling very lonely. Three-quarters of an hour later he came on the air to tell me that the small splinter of steel in his foot had severed a nerve and he was being evacuated – to spend several months in hospital (afterwards he was posted to 1 Airborne Division and we only met again after the war).

The enemy had a variety of offensive weapons: medium artillery, mortars, the direct fire of his tanks, and a 'Moaning Minnie': a multi-barrelled mortar the only advantage of which was that, on discharge, it uttered an unearthly shriek which gave us a short warning of the impending arrival of its load of bombs. All these they used at regular intervals as the fancy took them.

In the pauses of quiet I got a huge hole dug with all the shovels available and ran the command tank over it so that its crew and I could live beneath it, able to withstand anything except a large direct hit.

During the afternoon, with a small party, I had another go to see what way there was of tackling the troublesome Mark IV, but he nearly got us with a burst of Spandau and three rounds of H.E.; we escaped but had to give it up. A little later a heavy concentration killed two very good sergeants. Corrigan, one of the dead, had been removed, but we arranged to bury the other, Hutchby, as well as some infantrymen at nine o'clock in the evening; the only padre left alive was the Roman

Catholic from the H.L.I., who said he would gladly officiate. As few as possible assembled around the graves we had dug, but we had been there less than a minute when the roar of approaching medium shells made us scatter with all speed. In the unearthly silence which follows a salvo of explosives, scarcely broken by the patter of leaves still falling from the trees, I crawled out of my hole and found the one who had not made it to cover. A wonderful man, Sergeant Orr Wilson, lay with a shell fragment in his forehead. The one doctor, who had so little time to get round the area before the next salvo, arrived at the double, said, 'I can't do anything for him,' and ran off on his way. I knew Wilson was going to die and I knelt beside him feeling useless. I took an ampoule of morphia from my escaper's pack and injected him: I thought that if he could feel anything it might be some small relief. I felt desperately unhappy. Looking up, I saw a ring of gunners who knew him well standing around.

'What the hell are you staring at?' I snarled. 'Get back under cover.'

And they went silently away. I was still kneeling there when the M.O. came round again, not in such a hurry, and Wilson was borne away.

I became more and more obsessed by the strip of wood on our left which connected us with the enemy. Eventually I went to see the Gordons' colonel; I pointed out that if the Germans attacked they would hardly come galloping across the open field to our front, but would more probably pounce on our defenceless left flank under cover of the wood. He agreed for once – an unusual occurrence, because the two colonels, condemned to sit and do nothing except watch more and more of their men depart to a happier world, were deeply depressed – and gave me permission to set up a strong-point on the far side of the trees made up of one M10 guarded by a section of machine-guns, so that we could at least watch our sensitive flank and supply route. Needless to say I did not get back in one lap; I had covered fifty of the hundred yards when I heard the roar – like that of a train entering a tunnel – of descending shells. With nowhere to go, I hurriedly lay flat. They burst all around me, and I was hit in the ankle, not by a piece of metal which would have penetrated, but by a flying stone. I hardly felt it at the time, but there were to be consequences.

I was back under my tank when Scottie, (Lt. G.R.D. Scott, later Captain), who had driven to within a discreet distance with the water truck, arrived; I was glad he decided to stay. Our next visitor was Sergeant Macdonald, whom I remember as the only Gaelic speaker we had, to say that one of the M10s was on fire. It was beside a cottage and, when this was hit, blazing thatch had gone down into every corner of the turret. Fire extinguishers had had no effect and soon, if nothing was done, the whole tank would go up. The only thing for it was to get inside the turret and remove the ammunition so that one could get at the burning straw. Fortunately this worked and in the end all was well.

Before the long, late twilight I walked over to the cow byre which was filled with the wounded, to see how our casualties were. No ambulances could get forward, so they just had to stay there, silent and waiting. In a sort of ante-room one man was sitting by himself because the sight of him would have unnerved the others; he had no face. There was no sound but the little regular plop as his breath blew bubbles through the blood. No eyes, no mouth, no jaw – if he lived, and I believe he did, all the wonders of plastic surgery would still leave him blind and dumb.

When darkness fell, things quietened down. It had been quite a day. I cat-napped under the tank, for I had one more job to do.

At about one in the morning I set off down the road to see if my strong-point, beyond the wood I hated, was all right; I trod delicately. When I arrived Hughes, he who was always late from leave but was proving a bonny fighter, was on watch. I climbed up and we chatted in whispers. All was well and after a while I gave him a friendly pat and started back.

As I passed the wood I knew instinctively that my enemy was there. It was so dark that he could not see me nor I him. Then like a fool, unseeing, I kicked a stone. In a flash I flung myself down and a stream of Schmeisser bullets screamed over me as he fired at the sound. He was evidently in the bushes not much more than ten yards away.

I lay there for a while then moved on soundlessly. I was very angry and wanted a cigarette.

There was no smoking at night, for in the dark a cigarette-end gleams like a beacon, so I ducked into a dug-out by the road where I was out of sight. By chance it was the home of the artillery liaison office. I lit a cigarette, told him of my adventure and added, 'I would like to beat the buggers up!'

'Why not?' he said and, after some quiet converse, the divisional artillery was got out of bed and shelled the village. It was a frightful waste of taxpayers' money, but relieved my feelings no end.

The next day it was decided that the whole brigade should withdraw and let John's 44 Brigade have a go from a different angle. Leaving Scottie, who brought J. Troop out beautifully with the infantry, I took the tank back to Battery H.Q. to see how everyone else was. We were shelled all the way up the long straight road as usual. There was a fork at the top and, tired and distracted, I said over the intercom to the driver, Big Mac as he was always called, 'Bear left.' Then as we got nearer I realized I was wrong and said, 'No, bear right.'

He also had had enough and his answer was laconic: 'For Christ's sake make up your mind.'

After a good night's sleep I walked down a track into a valley where the Gordons were resting to chat with the C.O. in happier circumstances than our previous conversations. On the way I looked across at Estry in the distance and saw the whole ridge erupting in one long sheet of earth and smoke; I found it difficult to believe that I had been in the middle of that on the previous day.

John's attack on the wretched village was no more successful than ours had been. But, approaching at a right angle to the road we had followed, Tom Geddes, commanding 144 Battery, was able to get a tank forward to a point from which it could bring its gun to bear on the Mark

IV, which as usual motored up to the calvary, but could not see it because of high hedges in the way. So Harry Aitken crawled forward until he was lying adjacent to it, on the other side of the hedge. From this precarious position he directed fire by hand signals; the fourth shot hit the turret ring and the crew baled out. Harry long after told me that he stood up then, and he and the tank commander faced one another over the hedge, but neither at the moment was feeling belligerent.

'The whole attack came to a standstill,' Tom wrote, 'and Brigadier Cockburn called on me at my H.Q. in a field half a mile back from Estry and seemed very disappointed.'

So ended the battle of Estry: the village untaken. Harry and I had the honour of receiving the Military Cross, but the place remained burned in our memory and we mourned the loss of so many good men and good friends to no purpose.

On 11 August *Operation Grouse* began, an endeavour by 3 British Division to push further on the right flank; it got a foothold over the next main road, the N812 from Vire to Vassy, and there stuck. 146 was lent for the operation. Confirmed in its command and told to put up a crown, I should have been happy, but I was not. As we all sat waiting for a German counter-attack which never came, I was in more and more pain. The bruise on the side of my foot had gone septic and, after the M.O.'s ministrations, there was a hole down to the bone which had to be packed every day with sulphonamide. I could not wear a boot, and was reduced to a bedroom slipper. Then it started to rain, but I found that the gas-proof wallet we were given in which to keep personal documents fitted perfectly over my slipper like a galosh. There was no penicillin yet and sulphonamide has a terribly depressing effect. Feeling suicidal, I sat day after day praying for the long-awaited counter-attack to come and finish me off. But as the drug did its stuff and the wound healed enough to discontinue using it, my spirits rose. I used to write home what news I could and I was furious some time later that father had been talking to a friend in Fleet Street and he sent me a cutting from the Londoner's Diary in *The Evening Standard* headed 'Carpet-slippered Major'.

The next move was a further attack by 185 Brigade of 3 Division south-east along the road from Vire to Tinchebray, in the direction of the Falaise pocket which was building up. They had the Coldstream Churchills of 6 Guards Tank Brigade under command, and Donald Hackston's troop of 146 was to go with them. No one knew where the Brigade was and finding them was an extremely difficult business; it included going down a cart-track preceded by a terrified cow which suddenly veered left to avoid our jeep and went up on a mine.

All was well in the end and the advance went on until it was brought to a halt by intense mortaring short of Tinchebray. The armour pulled off into the fields; everyone dug in and it was not wise to stay far from one's fox-hole. I went down again in the morning to see Donald and we sat chatting on the edge of his particular hole.

As he was quite happy, with no problems, I said that I would leave him after the next mortar attack. I duly got into my jeep and drove off, to be met by the R.S.M. of the Coldstream who politely asked if I would mind waiting for a few minues. I did mind very much, as I had no desire to be caught in the open. However, I then noticed a small group standing under a hedge not far away: the Churchill commander, Colonel Smith, was holding an Orderly Room and trying a delinquent. I could think of safer places to do it, but it was none of my business so I contained myself in patience until I could drive on, without any ill effects.

This was the end of the battles in France for VIII Corps in general and the 91st in particular. We settled down in comfortable fields at Fresnay, west of Flers, to get busy on very necessary reorganization. There was a certain amount of 'swanning' – a phrase which had come into use for driving about on non-military business. As neither of us had ever been there, Scottie and I decided to visit Mont Saint Michel. We started out through Flers in pouring rain, and were violently waved at by a French family; we stopped, and they asked us if we were going to Brittany. A remarkably sweet and very pretty girl had bicycled through the lovely sunny weather dressed only in a shirt and the briefest of shorts to see if her family in Flers was safe. Since they all were, she now wanted to get back to Portorson, the nearest place on the main road to her home. Nothing could give us greater pleasure. We strapped her bicycle on the back, she squeezed in between Scottie, who was driving, and me, and we set off. She spoke no English, and she and I chattered away in French; Scottie, a remarkably handsome man with an eye for the ladies, had but little French and he was good-naturedly seething. He worked on it and suddenly exclaimed, '*Mauvais temps pour bicyclette!*' As we splashed on our way, from time to time he would loudly and testily exclaim, '*Mauvais temps pour bicyclette!*' We parted from our beauty at Portorson, had a very good lunch, went over Mont Saint Michel and drove back.

Thereafter swanning was stopped because of the difficulty over petrol on the ever-lengthening supply lines to the forward troops. A day later our C.C.R.A. (Corps Commander Royal Artillery), Brigadier Matthew, a huge, very fat man who was a military martinet but at the same time a charming person, went up as passenger in an Air O.P., a light aeroplane, to see what was going on. Over Dreux, still in German hands, he was hit in the backside by a rifle shot from the ground and ended up in Flers Hospital. I went to see him and sat by his bed gossiping.

I could not resist it; I said quietly, 'I rather thought swanning had been stopped.'

He blushed.

By 1 September the advance northwards had gone far enough for the roads to be clear for further movement, and we set off to cross the Seine. In the night our route lay through the Falaise pocket. One figure is enough to illustrate the kind of destruction wrought on the German

Army in the west by steady attrition and the disastrous pocket: 'Kurt Meyer's elite 12SS Panzer Division at one time numbered ten thousand men, but by the final battles round Trun it was estimated that there may have been fewer than a hundred.'* It was horrible; the ditches were filled with the burnt-out wrecks of transport which had been bulldozed off the road, and in the moonlight the scene looked like the invention of a surrealist lunatic. Usually in the presence of death it is possible to hold one's breath and hurry by, but here for mile after mile we had to endure the sweet, penetrating smell of putrefaction. When daylight came we were given a tumultuous welcome by the people who were thereabouts more demonstrative than the rather dour Normans. We crossed the Seine at Les Andelys and settled down for three weeks on the edge of the Forêt de Lyon.

This huge forest had been the place which airmen had been told to make for if they baled out in that region because of the thick undergrowth and a well organized Maquis. We made friends with a gallant Frenchwoman, Madame Huguette Lambert, who had given refuge to many fliers: British, Canadian and American. Brian Brown met her first, and a number of us went to her small cottage of two rooms, with a step between them. Her worst evening, she said, was when she had a number of inmates and a German patrol knocked at the door, demanding to stay for the night. Bundling the airmen into one room, she shut the door and admitted the enemy to the other; she herself lay for the night on the step between the two rooms. If anyone had so much as sneezed, it would have been death for her, whatever happened to the escaping airmen; but it passed off all right and the Germans left in the morning.

During this stay 'Hammer' Matthew directed that battery commanders and captains G should go north to look at the new terrain. We decided to split the job, and Harry Aitken from 144 and I from 146 were the first pair to go. We found Corps H.Q. between Brussels and Louvain and then spent two agreeable days around Malines and Antwerp. Neither of us had been in Brussels before. I cannot remember if it was good advice or good luck which took us to an excellent lunch at the *Epaule de Mouton* in the glorious *Grande Place*, enlivened by a bottle of champagne which the only other occupant, a Belgian businessman, sent as a charming gesture across to us. We stayed that night in a comfortable hotel in Malines, and neither of us could sleep; we were so used to lying on the ground wrapped in a blanket that a soft bed was uncomfortable and we both just tossed and turned.

Then on to Antwerp which was eerie. The southern part of the city was in British hands, the northern half still occupied by the enemy; all jumbled up. Our first call was on the C.O. of an A.Tk. Regiment, who said that his 17-prs were having great fun shooting up barges of German stores coming down the river. In fact, he said, he was just going down to visit his guns and invited us to accompany him. For some reason we

* d'Este, *op.cit.*

declined and went off to look around. Near the contended area we found a sherry bar which was open. The ordinary German does not drink sherry, so the occupying troops had made virtually no inroads into the stocks. There were rows of bottles we had not seen since before the war: Tio Pepe, La Ina, Isabalita, the lot! It gave us a strange feeling, as we sat there making pigs of ourselves, to see a fighting patrol come past with fixed bayonets at the high port, so close were the two sides. Afterwards we went back to say goodbye to the A.Tk. Colonel, only to be told that he had been put in the bag. What an ignominious end to our military careers if we had accepted his invitation!

By the third day we were back in Brussels, were joined by Tom and Scottie, and then drove back through all the heavy traffic, including assault boats and motor launches on transporters, going north for *Market Garden* – the attack on Grave, Nijmegen and Arnhem – which began the next day.

When we reported back to John Tweedie, who had returned to us as our commanding officer just before we left France, we recommended that, since most of the roads in northern Belgium and – obviously – Holland were *pavé*, the M10s' tracks should be changed from steel to rubber. He accepted this and Peter Maxwell set off to get what stock was available. He got enough to equip all our tanks; in the fine weather no one else was interested. It paid off and in the horrible winter which followed we were about the only armour that could stay on the roads without skidding.

When Peter had got the tracks, we just had time to fit them in soaking rain before taking the road north to Holland. The regiment was divided into several columns. My task was to take the M10s of both batteries; they should not have been driven that long distance, but the army did not have enough transporters. My dear friend, Dickie Dickson, was O.C. my advance party and I told him that I would like to laager the first night on the Somme in High Wood, in memory of the West Kents which I so loved in my childhood, and the second on the field of Waterloo – preferably at the farm of Hougoumont.

We were leaving France, and I think that I should give this as our *envoi*: on one of our vehicles had been written in chalk:

> 'To the English we give our hearts
> To the Russians we give flowers
> To the Americans we give our regards
> To the Germans we give our undying
>   hatred.'

It never stopped raining the first day and we were late in; but we were even later out the next morning. One of the 3-ton trucks carrying our stores and kit went down into a First World War trench and it took hours to winch it out. We made an awful mess and I apologized to the farmer who said, 'That's all right. We are used to armies around here; but please God it is the last time.' The result of this contretemps was that we were outrageously late in arriving at Waterloo.

Dickie, who graduated from the University of Grenoble just before the

war and spoke perfect French, had done his stuff with the charming
lady who owned the farm of Hougoumont. She not only welcomed us
but put on a lovely supper for the officers (there were four of us), while
the men were bedded down comfortably in a huge hay loft. I had to
explain to the Jocks that, this being a national monument, there could be
no smoking in any of the buildings. They readily obeyed the rule and
many of them appreciated the honour of spending the night in a place
so hallowed in our history. I had not been there before and found it
fascinating; the huge wooden gates into the courtyard still pitted with
the bullet holes of 1815, and in the middle the little chapel which had
formed a first-aid post during the battle. The next morning there was
much taking of photographs and shaking of hands with *Madame la
Patronne* and her family before we went on our weary but fortunately
rather drier way.

The regiment finished up at Geldrop, a small town near Eindhoven,
with 146 a short way away in a village called Urkhoven. Our task was to
guard the right flank of 2 Army where there was a gap between that and
the left flank of 1 U.S. Army. There was no infantry and we were
apprehensive at first, but the Germans never appeared.

Life was extremely comfortable. The Dutch on the whole were
charming and all very dark, being of Spanish descent; and they had no
time for Queen Wilhelmina because in the whole of her reign, being a
fanatical Protestant, she had refused to visit her Catholic subjects in the
eastern half of the country.

On 9 October John Tweedie received a letter from Montgomery saying
that the regiment was to be disbanded. It was a horrible shock to
everyone.

The circumstances were as follows. 61 Division, not being in the order
of battle for Normandy, was disbanded as a formation. One of its units
was the 63 A.Tk. Regiment of which the commanding officer, Lieut.-
Colonel Thomson, could see imminent dissolution ahead. They were
territorials, the Oxford Hussars, in which Winston Churchill had served
as a young man and of which he was the Colonel-in-Chief. Thomson
appealed to him for help, and not in vain. Churchill wrote to
Montgomery suggesting that the Oxford Hussars might be used to
replace an A.Tk. regiment that had suffered badly or was otherwise not
up to scratch. The commander-in-chief had other things on his mind
than disagreeing with the Prime Minister on so trivial a matter and
decided (or his staff did) that the blow should fall on the regiment with
the highest number: us – which was pretty ironic, since we had chosen
91 because of our historic traditions. Everyone was angry, most of all the
C.C.R.A., who had not been informed of the impending change.
Interviews took place at 2 Army Headquarters, but Dempsey wanted
nothing to do with it. John Tweedie sent a letter at once to Lieut.-Colonel
C.P. Dawnay, MA/C in C, who replied sympathetically, but saying that
'He [the C in C] is however convinced that, whatever decision is finally
come to by the War Office, it will be in the best interests of the war effort
as a whole.' How wrong this proved to be can be seen from the events

which followed. The Corps Commander, Richard O'Connor, had not been consulted either, and when he heard he wrote to John Tweedie, 'I can only say there is no unit in the whole of the force under my command whose departure I regret more ... The whole tone of your unit is far above the average, the morale of your men is first-class and the fighting powers unsurpassed ...'

When John Tweedie informed me, I told him that I knew the Prime Minister personally (being his publisher) and asked if he thought there was anything in my going back to England to plead for the decision to be altered. He consulted 'Hammer' Matthew who thought it was worth trying and, as a cover, posted me on a one-week field gunnery course at Larkhill. On my way through London I rang up Mrs Hill, Churchill's private secretary for years whom I knew well, and asked for an appointment at the conclusion of the course – which I must say I enjoyed. Back in London, I went to Downing Street where I was received with the great man's usual warmth. He listened kindly and carefully and told me to come back the next day; it was now 17 November. He then told me gently that we were a second-line territorial unit; I said I knew nothing about that, but what I thought was more important was that we were a proven unit which knew its job, and I showed him General O'Connor's letter which he kept. He said that he would see what he could do. His action was to write a letter to the Secretary of State for War, dated 19 November, in which he said: 'We arranged with Montgomery that he was to disband some battered wartime-raised units, rather than drain white ancient regiments of modernized British yeomanry. The attached letter [that of General O'Connor] ... shows that the axe has fallen upon a very fine territorial unit. Surely some better arrangement than this one can be made to make a place for the Oxfordshire Hussars. I will, if necessary, telegraph Field-Marshal Montgomery on the subject ... With regard to the attached letter, it was brought to me by an officer, and I take full responsibility for his bringing it to me, and also for its having been written by General O'Connor. No kind of victimization is to be made in this case, as the communication must be regarded as privileged, and I am responsible for the use of it.*

The reaction of the Secretary of State for War was first to send a signal to 21 Army Group saying, 'Act quickly. Trouble coming,' and secondly to disobey the Prime Minister's final injunction.

I then put the whole situation to the Prime Minister in two letters, and stayed on in London for a further ten days, hoping for good news.

On the 27th I was told to wait upon the Prime Minister again on the following day at 5.45, as he had a cabinet meeting at six o'clock, at which our problem was on the agenda. I was taken to his bedroom where he had just woken up from his siesta. I helped him dress, holding his trousers for him and handing him his false teeth; then we went down in the lift together. On the ground floor the whole cabinet was drawn up waiting, and as we stepped out the Secretary of State for War glared at

* W.S. Churchill, *The Second World War*, vol. VI, p 613.

me as if he could kill me with his bare hands.

With the matter being discussed in cabinet, there was nothing more that I could do. After the completion of my course at Larkhill, I had had orders to report to a transit camp at Sunningdale, but I had telephoned the commanding officer and explained that the course was only a front and that I was on business of which I could tell him nothing. He was remarkably understanding, but by 29 November his patience was exhausted; he said that if I did not report to him forthwith he would post me as a deserter.

I went down to Sunningdale at once. The C.O. was very nice, but I did not like the news he had for me. Forty survivors of 1 Airborne Division who had refused to jump again after Arnhem were being sent back to Holland as infantry reinforcements under close arrest. As senior officer I was in command of the party, with a Captain Byass of the famous sherry family as my only help. I asked what I was to do with them when we got to Dunkirk, and was told to hand them over to the provost marshal. We went by train from Sunningdale to Dover, where I was extremely displeased that they were battened down below decks; I thought it quite unnecessary as no one was likely to jump overboard in mid-Channel. When we arrived, I was first down the gangplank and found a military policeman whom I asked where I could find the provost marshal.

'Oh, Sir,' he said, 'don't tell me you've fallen for that one! There is no provost marshal at Dunkirk.'

I was furious. I found a M.P. sergeant in a small office and told him that I had forty men under close arrest for him. By then there were thirty-six; between the ship and the office four of them had disappeared. I could not have cared less; I stamped off to find my way to the regiment.

When I eventually got back, I found that a lot had happened. On 18 November 'Hammer' Matthew, still very angry, having had a good look at the Oxfordshire Hussars, sent a signal to Army: 'Impracticable to relieve 91 A.Tk. Regt.R.A. by 63 A.Tk. Regt.R.A. for four months at least ... 63 A.Tk. Regt. ... unfit repeat unfit for war.' He followed this with a letter to the inspector of artillery at the War Office in which he wrote, 'It is clear from the official signal that the proposed change has no bearing whatsoever on our efforts to win this war ... So strongly do I feel about the way this project has been handled, that I have made it quite clear that if it proceeds as planned I shall be reluctantly compelled to consider my own position as C.C.R.A. 8 Corps ... I am shocked to think that such a raw deal can be handed out as a reward for such services, especially to a converted infantry regiment for whose future the DRA has shed so many crocodile tears.'

Discussions had already taken place over the desirability of keeping the best officers and men of both regiments and dispersing the rest into some anonymous limbo. The C.C.R.A.'s verdict that the 63rd was unfit for war seriously changed the situation. The final decision, which was put into operation early in December, was that the M10 Batteries of the 91st commanded by Tom Geddes and myself, were to be retained intact, while two towed batteries of the 63rd remained. The latter did not have a very happy experience in north-west Europe; they hardly fired a shot in anger, and their major task was to provide the guards at Belsen when that horror was exposed and occupied.

The matter was best summed up by Colonel Thomson who, on 1 December, wrote a detailed letter to the Prime Minister in which he concluded: 'I do feel it my duty to report to the colonel of the regiment my conviction that so far from the preservation of the Oxfordshire Hussars being achieved, the result will be the destruction of the two regiments concerned.'

Colonel Thomson disappeared, John Tweedie also went elsewhere and was promoted, and a new commanding officer was appointed: Dick Taylor, whose battery from the Guards Armoured A.Tk. Regiment I had set out on a motor cycle to find soon after our first arrival in Normandy.

For me the last word in the affair was a summons from 'Hammer' Matthew. I went to his headquarters and he said, 'I thought you might like to see this,' showing me an unpleasant signal from the Secretary of State for War, disloyally disobeying his master's instructions. It read: 'The officer who has been interfering in matters which do not concern him is to be severely disciplined.'

Hooting with laughter, 'Hammer' screwed it up and threw it in the waste-paper basket.

17   'The Phoenix 'midst her Fires'

Before the break-up could be effected, there was more work to be done. There was, for instance, a nasty battle around two small towns called Overloon and Venraij in which 146 was involved. It was a very bloody affair in all senses; nothing went right, infantry casualties were very heavy and progress was slow.

Yet there can often be a sinister beauty even in the most adverse situations. When one of my troop commands, 'Bing' Crosby, and I went forward at last light on the first day to see what we could, Overloon was ablaze and against the sheets of orange flame were silhouetted the diminutive figures of the infantry plodding steadily on with rifles at the high port, while on our right a Sherman and a Mark IV were engaged in a solitary duel, the tracer flying back and forth like beautifully coloured rockets.

There were far more mines here than anywhere else that we were called upon to fight in during the campaign. Bisecting the battle area from north to south was the main road from Overloon to Venraij; crossing the area at right angles to the road was a deep dyke called the Molenbeek, and at the point where the road crossed the dyke the bridge was blown. On the right flank thick woods, the Laag Heide, which 8 Rifle Brigade had entered on the previous day, ran out like a finger in the direction of Venraij, and formed an obvious springboard for forward movement (a fact of which the enemy showed himself by no means unaware). The whole area was overlooked by the church tower of Venraij, which was still standing in spite of the battering it had received.

The infantry, making a silent crossing in the early morning, was forced to advance straight across the open fields. The armour's efforts were completely abortive. The Churchills sent down to the Molenbeek to fill the dyke with rolls of faggots either bogged down before they reached their destination, were shot up, or found their task impossible when they got there. The tanks thereupon pushed round into the woods on to the right where they were shelled and mortared for hours on end, while a recce party went forward on foot in the hope of finding some way over the obstacle. Everywhere the fair green turf was a delusion, for as soon as anything heavier than a man attempted to traverse it, it gave way. Men were caught in the fiercest concentrations, directed from Venraij church tower, as they tried to get on. The 2nd Lincolns, for example, lost seventy killed in one small field when they were observed. To make the scene more horrible, the Churchills working down to the dyke to attempt bridging operations were forced by the narrowness of the track to drive over the bodies of their fallen comrades.

When the 1 Norfolks were decimated (and had soon to be withdrawn), they were particularly harassed by the high velocity gun of a tank so well hidden that it could not be identified. Finally we pin-pointed where it was, and Donald Hackston and I set off on foot to see if we could catch a glimpse of it and find a way of flushing it out. We walked a long way, so concentrated on what we were doing that neither of us saw the German signs, the red skull and crossbones and '*Achtung Minen*', until it was too late. I suddenly woke up and said rather uncomfortably, 'Hackie, we're in the middle of a minefield' and so we were. There was only one thing to do: walk out in single file, hoping for the best. Our hopes were not in vain, but as I walked, examining the ground and seeing nothing, I felt a foolish desire to walk on tiptoe – as if that might help. I don't think the enemy was fooling, but I heaved a deep sigh of relief when we were both safely back on the main road.

Then the whole regiment was sent north to guard the bank of the River Maas, the opposite side being held by the Germans. There were armoured cars of the Household Cavalry and ourselves, but no infantry – an extraordinary situation. Our role was purely a patrolling one, to make sure that the enemy did nothing and to do nothing ourselves. By day we went where we liked, but as darkness fell we holed up and the Germans took over. There was an eerie silence everywhere. We were not all that far from the border and the population was of mixed blood and largely pro-German. The enemy troops came across the river at night to visit their friends and mistresses; one of them picked up his clean clothes from the laundry in our village. My headquarters was a small railway station, and I made the mistake of electing to sleep alone in the station-master's cottage, he, being apparently a collaborator, having disappeared. I lay awake listening to the Germans walking round the house talking, holding my sten gun and expecting the door to burst open at any moment; I would not have stood a chance, and I did not enjoy it. One night they blew up the church towers in two of our villages, and the engineers said that it must have taken them several nights to ferry over enough explosives to create such havoc. But like every party, the joke wore off and what had at first been fun became a nerve-racking bore, as a prisoner captured by Tom Geddes confessed.

Later it was considered necessary to evacuate the entire civilian population, but I was not there by then.

On the morning of 29 October I was told to report at once to the headquarters of II Armoured Division at Deune, some sixteen miles south, as there was a crisis. What had happened was that 7 U.S. Armoured Division had been scattered; they had been put under British command because they were in rather poor shape, and since the Maas front was quiet they could set about pulling themselves together there. They were badly strung out, and this, of course, did not escape the

German Intelligence. Three divisions were flung at them, one armoured and reinforced with Tigers, and it is hardly surprising that they were blown away. It was a shambolic situation, in the middle of which I found myself alone in a jeep except for driver and wireless operator, waiting for my battery to arrive.

The front was propped up with infantry rushed from their successes on another part of the front. The American division withdrew, its morale not being improved by a string of Messerschmitts which machine-gunned them from tree-top height after dark when they were in a traffic jam just outside the house in which I was by then. It is an interesting example of how men can recover – as our own Highland Division did – that this same 7 Armoured Division, then fearful and inefficient, was to cover itself with glory in the Battle of the Bulge a few months later.

Operations went on in this area, often through heavy mud and rain, for the rest of the month, after I had gone home on 1 November to see the Prime Minister.

On 28 November General O'Connor was relieved of his command of VIII Corps and posted to India. Bitterly disappointed, we wanted to know why. Rumour said that he was tired; we thought that it was because he was a better tactician than Montgomery, who resented it; for, as Professor Howard has written: 'After Normandy Montgomery's arrogance became almost pathological, reinforced as it was by self-imposed isolation in which he communed only with a small group of young and adoring acolytes.' The real reason, the record now shows, was that O'Connor, scrupulously honest as always, refused to submit an adverse report on the commander of the 7 U.S. Armoured Division, General Sylvester, who had never stood a chance; which is another devastating example of Montgomery's hubris.

The fatal day marking the demise of the 91st finally arrived. Our men who had been cast off, after years together, marched to the station with tears streaming down their faces – literally. When I said goodbye to the RSM he could hardly speak, and even the hard-bitten old quartermaster, Charlie Ditcham, was crying. I have no doubt that those Hussars who were leaving for an unknown fate felt much the same, though they had not had the extra annealing element of fighting together.

Dick Taylor, a tall man with great personality, possessing one blue eye and one brown, and a great record in the desert, arrived to hold his first conference on 11 December – and did all he could to pour balm on very sore wounds. Everyone was frankly resentful, we Argylls because we regarded the Hussars as the cause of all the trouble, which they were; and the Hussars because by keeping the armoured batteries they considered that we had got the better of the bargain, which we had. He insisted that all regimental traditions were to be maintained and we all kept our own badges. The War Office did its best to spoil things by directing that the numbers of the armoured batteries be changed, but Dick decided that within the confines of 2 Army they should remain as they were; so we became 146 (A & S H) Battery.

Tempers gradually simmered down; I flourished an early olive branch by challenging one of the Hussar batteries to play us at football, and the atmosphere became very much better when we all moved into a big Dutch barracks and got to know one another. I suppose the wisest words on the subject were spoken by the 63rd quartermaster, Captain Bob Lewis – a splendid man – who said, 'Personally, I'm a bloody gunner and always have been, and I don't care a monkey's for all this Argylls and Hussars business.'

It was a bitter and miserable winter, the worst recorded since 1890, of which I have only one clear memory. Sitting in my tank one day with my top half out of the turret, I took off my gloves to light my pipe. Absent-mindedly I put one bare hand on the edge of the turret, to which it froze instantly and I had to tear it off, leaving behind the whole skin of fingers and palm. And the *pavé* roads, which were never intended for the weight of military traffic, disintegrated and the bricks stood on end, resembling a badly ploughed field.

At the end of January 146 was sent for a month to XXX Corps for the battle of the Reichswald Forest, and the operations eastwards which followed. Some months earlier Harry Aitken and I had been sent up to have a look at the forest from the Canadian forward positions, as Monty was thinking of attacking it with VIII Corps. We didn't like what we saw, and were very glad when we were recalled because it was decided that the position was too strong for the forces available. This time it was to be attacked in much greater strength. Everything was very wet, and with a large number of Churchills we made enough noise grinding up the hill to our positions to awake the dead, let alone the Germans about half a mile away.

The battle, called *Operation Veritable*, began at five o'clock on the morning of 8 February 1945, with a bombardment of the forest and its defences by 1,400 guns and a 'mattress' of rocket projectors; this went on for two hours, by which time the incessant noise had given me – and I am sure many others – a splitting headache. There was one disaster when a 25-pr lost elevation and put several rounds into the HQ of 154 Brigade just across a sandy track from me, killing a number of officers and men of the Black Watch. Then I shared a hole with Brian Brown, as we were all ordered below ground in anticipation of enemy counter-battery fire; but nothing happened. Then the attack went in. The weather was a greater deterrent than the Germans, who were in considerable disarray because the barrage had caught them in the open when various units were changing over. In addition we were facing for the first time ordinary troops instead of the perpetual Waffen SS, and the difference was most marked. A further hindrance was the enormous number of minefields, but we were lucky and lost some armour but no lives.

One of my troop commanders, Willie Williams, had sworn that he would urinate as soon as he was on German soil – the frontier ran through the forest; late in the afternoon he came up on the air with the simple message, 'Mission accomplished'. The same day, plodding about in the glutinous mud, I ran into General Wimberley, commanding 51 Highland Division; he did not know me from Adam, but he addressed me in agonized tones: 'An axis, I must have an axis.' There wasn't one through the sea of mud, but still the forest was taken.

Once the road south of the forest was cleared the advance continued eastwards towards Gennep. The floods around the town, caused by the Germans having opened the river dams, made it into an amphibious operation, and when, on the 10th, the assault began, there was only one road down which to advance, and it was shelled regularly. It was not a happy operation; and frankly I found Horrocks, the corps commander, rather off-putting – his 'gung-ho' attitude comparing unfavourably with O'Connor's quiet reserve.

When the next place, Heyen, was taken, VIII Corps, having lent us to XXX Corps, for the Forest battle only, wanted us back. We were furious as we had wanted to see the show through to the end, and disliked the idea of returning to whence we had come.

The next day we formed up on the road and started back. It was on this drive that a Canadian jeep in a hurry, cutting in and out of the traffic, swerved under the tracks of one of the M10s and the passenger in the back seat was beheaded; we were to hear more about that. When we had settled down in an orchard that night, it didn't seem such a bad thing to be out of battle after all.

In the morning we formed up again and moved on. As I was stationary at the head of the column waiting for the police to let me make a turn, an agitated D.R. drew up beside my tank.

'I've been looking for you everywhere,' he said, 'You are wanted at Div. H.Q.' We all pulled into a convenient empty field and I set off in a jeep. The B.M.R.A. was waiting for me with orders that we were to come under Command 52 (Lowland) Division immediately. Those of us who wanted more fighting were to get it sooner than we had expected.

In the end I found myself with 157 Brigade which had as its objective a big wood south of Heyen and then on to Afferden, the taking of which would open up a further stretch of the main road.

First light came the next morning in a thick blanket of fog. One troop set off with the infantry right-handed down a track and quickly disappeared from sight. When I went to see how things were getting on there was nothing but a white curtain; I was told that the leading troop was farther down the track and that Willie Williams, its commander, was away on a recce. I pushed on, and it was eerie driving through the fog, listening for sounds over the throb of the tank engine and straining one's eyes for any signs of movement. I found the troop deployed round some farm buildings. Willie had learnt from the infantry that the point at which the track joined the road was blocked with felled trees and mined, so he wanted to go on foot to find another way into the village. As getting his troop into action somehow was the most important item on the day's agenda, I decided to stay there myself until Willie got back. The first thing I did was to have the farm buildings searched. It was not necessary, I was told, because the infantry had done it. Never mind, I said, do it again. So we searched the farm and found plenty of evidence of recent occupation, but no Germans. Satisfied, I went back and stood on the back of my own tank. Ten minutes later I heard a movement behind me and turned round to see two young German paratroopers patiently trying to attract my attention in order to surrender! I was so surprised that all I could think of to say was '*Guten Tag*'. It appears that when they heard the tanks roar up to the farm, they had burrowed under a haystack and pulled the hay after them, so that they were completely concealed. I was grateful that they were not two young fanatics who desired to sell their lives dearly for their Führer.

Half an hour later Willie returned, perspiring and triumphant. He had found a way into the village, which was then taken. There was no counter-attack, but the Germans were determined by mortaring and shelling to make it as unhealthy a place as possible.

Eventually we went back to VIII Corps, and moved forward until one evening, 12 March, a few of us were playing poker with Colonel Dick when the telephone rang; it was 'Hammer' Matthew and the conversation was short:

'You want one S.P. battery commander to report to you tonight? Very good, Sir. His name? Flower, Sir.'

That was it. I packed some kit, got my jeep driver and set off for Corps headquarters, arriving at midnight. 'Hammer' had gone to bed, leaving a message that he wished to see me at seven in the morning.

His conversation was as short as his telephone call had been: 'The Rhine is going to be assaulted, and there will be a large air drop. Your battery will be the first armour to be ferried across the river on rafts, and you will go through to the airborne perimeter. Had your breakfast? Well, have it quickly. Your plane takes off at half past. You will report to the C.R.A. 6 Airborne Division at Bulford and make the necessary arrangements.'

A little artillery observation plane took me over the German lines to Eindhoven, where I caught the morning DC3 to Northolt. When I arrived I asked if any arrangements had been made for my return to Germany, but I was not surprised that no one knew anything about it. I took a taxi to the Ecu de France, where Lherian was pleased to see me, and rang the office. Margaret was out, so I left a message that if she would come to the restaurant she might find an old friend. She walked in at two, suitably surprised, in time for coffee and a glass of *marc de champagne*.

At Bulford I met Lieut.-Colonel Allday, C.O. of the 6 Airborne A.Tk. Regiment. He was charming and we had a great deal to talk about besides the business in hand, because he was a director of the big eponymous printing firm in Sheffield. The actual planning was a speedy and mildly hilarious affair, since I quickly found out that most people in 6 Airborne combined extreme efficiency with an inability to take anything seriously. On a table model we made a plan which, strangely enough, worked. The rest of my time was a round of social calls on the divisional commander, General Bols, and the brigadiers, so that if I appeared suddenly one day they would know who I was, and arrange for the right kind of ammunition and fuel to be flown in with the re-supply.

Getting back to Germany was a different matter altogether. There were four of us in a hurry, but on the morning of our intended departure Bulford airfield was fog-bound. So a staff car was produced to take us to White Waltham, in Berkshire, where conditions were said to be better. There an Air Force officer said that he had tried once without success, but was willing to have another go; so we piled into an Avro Anson and took off, seeing nothing until Box Hill loomed in front of our nose. With a screaming climb and right angle turn the pilot narrowly avoided it, and said that he had had enough. Back at White Waltham we got transport to Airborne headquarters, which were at Moor Park Golf Club at Rickmansworth. The club house is such a superb piece of Palladian architecture that I vowed there and then to join the club if I survived the war, and eventually did. In the end we flew to Brussels where we dropped off an airborne subaltern whose job was to lay secret markers on the banks of the Rhine. I ran into him some time later on the other side of the river and he told me that he had not done what he was supposed to do: the car to pick him up at Brussels did not exist, nobody knew anything about him, and his special equipment was never delivered.

While we were getting ready for the forthcoming battle, my tank *Zadig* which had carried me faithfully all the way from Normandy decided that it had had enough and would go no further. (When I was confirmed in the command of 146 Battery, I renamed all the H.Q. vehicles after the works of Voltaire. My tank was *Zadig* because it is my favourite of his tales: the half-track was *Henriade* and the slave-charger was called *La Pucelle* because of its well known unreliability.) Peter Maxwell moved with his usual speed and got me a replacement at once.

There was little sleep on the night of the operation. We were on high ground overlooking the Rhine, so we stayed up to watch two hundred Lancasters bomb Wesel, the ancient town which had been the starting point of the Gallic tribes' trade by water with Rome and had survived two thousand years without harm; now it was being virtually burnt to the ground.

At one we were having breakfast and afterwards moved down towards the river. A second breakfast, and at ten o'clock the air armada arrived. It is impossible to describe this tremendous sight adequately; it was even difficult to appreciate the magnitude of the huge fleet roaring so low over our heads. The Lancasters, Halifaxes, Sterlings, Fortresses and Dakotas flew in majestically, slowly, at eight hundred feet – a steady, solid phalanx like the pattern of a carpet in the sky for three hours. There was haze as well as smoke over the target area and the planes gradually disappeared into it before we could see the parachutes open or the mushroom puffs of the flak which met them. We watched anxiously as the planes materialized again, their task accomplished – some, happily only a few, with their engines smoking, losing height and seeking desperately somewhere to land. One Fortress I shall never forget. It came lower and lower over our heads, the flames streaming from it orange against the azure blue. As it passed us parachutes blossomed from it and we counted. One was a 'roman candle', the wretched man kicking desperately to get his 'chute open till the very last moment; it was just round the corner of the wood from me, and I was told that he went into the ground up to his armpits. Finally we knew that remaining in the blazing plane, alive or dead, was no one but the pilot.

I didn't get over the river, the greatest water obstacle in Europe, until eleven that night – twenty hours after we had lined up and set off. Leaving an officer (John Pothecary) to gather everybody together as they were ferried across, I set off in my new tank up the road which was supposed to lead to the airborne boys. The furthest sign of life I could find was the headquarters of a battalion of the K.O.S.B. The C.O. said that there was nothing ahead of him and he thought that the road was covered by one or two hostile anti-tank guns. The road gleamed white in the moonlight the few hundred yards to the woods where the paras should be. I told Big Mac to drive slowly, making as little noise as possible, and nothing happened. I found Brigadier Hill's headquarters just inside the big wood, the Diersfordt Forest; he said that his 6 Parachute Brigade was firm, but he could not let us go through the forest to join the rest of the division before daylight because the track was not in his hands. In fact, through the night there was small arms fire round us as the Germans and the paras played a sinister game of cops and robbers among the trees. I got on the air and in due course all the M10s bowled into the forest and parked. With everybody settled, I said that we would move at 7.15.

'And now,' I added, 'you can all get a good night's rest.'

They looked at me as if I were round the bend, which indeed I was; glancing at my watch I saw that it was already half past six.

We would not have got through in the dark; the Germans had heavily cratered the track, and it was quite a job even in daylight. But our reception when we got into the main divisional area was tremendous. Paratroopers stood up in their fox-holes and cheered, some threw their berets in the air; one even kissed my tank. By just appearing we had removed the haunting fear of another Arnhem.

We were a long time with the airborne troops and I found it most stimulating. I do not know whether it is that they are dropped into action comparatively seldom so they are not punch-drunk with continuous fighting, or that their training is so based on flexibility that they retain an open mind. At any rate they are very easy to talk to and get on with. One example comes to my mind. 6 Airlanding Brigade sent a battalion forward to take a small wooded hill before the advance could really get under way. This they did and I took a troop up to help them consolidate on the feature. The airborne 6-prs were dug in on the front edge of the wood, looking out over a vast rolling plain; behind us was some two hundred yards of meadow to thick woods in which we knew there was a German tank. I asked if I might make a suggestion; it seemed to me that the 6-prs could perfectly well look after our rear and cope with the Mark IV or Panther, whatever it was, while the M10s with three times the power and much greater range would be more useful facing forward at an unknown future. Agreement was instant; it was obvious, but I knew from past painful experience that from many infantry commanders there would have been endless objections, if not an outright refusal.

Like most soldiers, the paratroopers were not above a bit of looting, now that we were in the enemy's country. I shall never forget one of them slogging down the road in the long advance which now began. The weather was extremely hot; over his battledress and pack he was wearing a superb silver fox cape and as a result sweat was pouring down his face; I hope he got it home.

I suppose that taking what one fancies in the enemy's country is a practice general in wars since prehistoric times; the current phrase, starting way back with the eggs and wine in what was called allied territory – France – was 'liberating'. I certainly was guilty, if it was a matter of guilt. During this advance I came to a very large farmhouse near the Steinhuder Meer. The house was empty; the owner had fled. Searching the outbuildings I found one small room with shelves from floor to ceiling covered with wood shavings. Parting the shavings, I found underneath them the owner's huge collection of eighteenth-century porcelain. I thought that a reasonable small tithe was two little Meissen coffeepots. To the left was a door which I could not open. I shot the lock off, and the report of my revolver brought female screams of terror from the other side. Entering, I found a cellar full of nuns and schoolgirls. There were about four cases of hock, one in particular of magnificent Victorianaberg; and the walls were lined on both sides with bottled food like a grocer's shop. Wherever we went through Germany it was unbelievable to me how much food the householders had hoarded: hundreds of bottles of cooked meat, potatoes and vegetables of every sort. I suppose occupied Europe had been stripped to fill their store cupboards.

I said to the Mother Superior – as she seemed to be – 'I want the wine; all the food is at your disposal.'

As we loaded the cases, they were already hungrily falling upon and opening the bottles of food.

Not long after, 4 Tank Grenadier Guards came under the command of 6 Airborne Division, and 146 came under the Grenadiers. The time from that day until the end of hostilities formed for us the most happy and successful period of the campaign. With them there was not only friendship, but mutual respect. The tank brigades were equipped solely with Churchills, so that their make-up and tactics were different from those of an armoured division. The often maligned Churchill seems to me to have been the best tank designed by the British in the Second World War. Although the tank itself had originally been a British invention, the second time round we seemed to lack both the imagination and the skill to design anything comparable with the German Mk IVs, Panthers (the most beautiful tank designed by anybody) the Tiger or the Russian TR234. Even the excellent Churchill, however, possessed one serious flaw; whoever designed it did not foresee the possibility of a heavier weapon being needed to cope with the ever-thickening German armour. Therefore when the 17-pr became a necessity, it was discovered that the diameter of the turret ring was too small to accommodate the recoil of the larger gun. 'Fireflies', the 17-pr M10, were therefore needed to support them.

The Grenadiers understood both the necessity and the potential of the M10s and so kept them always close at hand for immediate use. There was a troop in support of each squadron, while I remained most of the time with their colonel, Lord Tryon. How I loved our days together; he was such a splendid man, always kind, always considerate and with an enormous sense of humour. Whenever he cracked a joke, which was frequently, he had an involuntary muscular twitch – a wink of the right eye, which made it appear almost lascivious. Later he commanded the brigade – the 6 Guards Tank Brigade which Montgomery had foolishly tried to have disbanded before 'Overlord'. And after the war he was Keeper of the Queen's Privy Purse.

After we had advanced about a hundred miles from the Rhine, the real gallop began. We carried the infantry on the Churchills and the M10s and the columns drove on at full speed until meeting opposition and dealing with it. The élan of the airborne men and surprising speed of the Churchills backed by the hitting power of the M10s gave very successful results. Our best advance in one day was forty miles. The German army was collapsing, and on 1 April I wrote home: 'This war has now become Fred Carno – you never know what you will meet next: five hundred German soldiers walking along by themselves, looking for someone to take them in charge, thousands of German soldiers changing hurriedly into civvy clothes and melting away, French soldiers – free after five years – wandering down the roads flying the tricolour and waving to us as we go by, Russian, Pole and Italian forced labour all free and all on the move – going anywhere, meeting on the roads, some going away from the front, some towards it, all walking just for the sensation of being free …'

But it was something of a false dawn; it was by no means yet the days of wine and roses.

On 14 April we arrived in Lüneberg, quite a large and pleasant town by the Elbe. The International Red Cross had declared it an open city since it contained a number of military hospitals, and so it was unmarked.

A strange experience: there were a large number of nursing orderlies at the hospitals, so that we were constantly mixing with field grey uniforms – a curious feeling to which we first became accustomed and then indifferent. In general, throughout the campaign, I do not think that any of us had any particular feelings about the Germans; the real enemy was an hypothesis – Nazism – which we were fighting to destroy, and the men with whom we were playing a macabre and often fatal game of cops and robbers were human beings just like ourselves. Both sides could be exceedingly nasty on occasion; yet sometimes when we came across a bunch of prisoners in a field or by the roadside, and they seemed as if they were waiting for Godot, or spectators after a football match which their team had lost, I had a feeling almost of compassion. It was only when some Germans – either SS or Hitler Youth – indulged in senseless cruelty that we got our dander up.

I set up my headquarters in a very nice house, the owner of which used to look in every day, slightly anxiously, to see how things were. He had a very good library, and I discovered that the books were two rows deep: in front were all the 'acceptable' authors, while behind them he had hidden all the great Jewish writers of the thirties: Stefan and Arnold Zweig, Leon Feuch-wanger, Robert Neumann and a lot more.

Opposite was a small hospital, made up of wooden huts in which lay men and women who were Russian labourers from a factory on the edge of town which the R.A.F. had recently attacked. There was no question of the slave labour being allowed into any shelters during the raid and as they fled from the falling bombs they were machine-gunned by the SS There were about two thousand bodies still littered about round the factory area. The wounded survivors were visited by a doctor once a day and there was one nurse. The Russians lay gaunt-eyed, too weak to move, in tumbled grey things which had once been bedclothes, bathed in their own sweat and the pus of their untended wounds. Our men took them food, sweets and cigarettes. They tried to show their thanks for the first kindness they had known for a long time. My servant, a delightful man from Bermuda named Mullins, came back across the road deeply moved; he went around murmuring, 'They kissed my hand, they kissed my hand.'

But far, far worse was a short distance away: Belsen. Riddled with typhus, the camp was abandoned by the Wehrmacht intact so that any surviving inmates strong enough to walk should not escape and infect the local population. The first British officer to be put in command of this horror was Dick Taylor, who took with him a battery of the Oxford Hussars as guards.

Photographs and films have since made everyone familiar with the appearance of this place, littered with dead to which were added every day those too far gone for any help. Mass graves were bulldozed and Dick ordered the SS to carry the corpses over to them: however putrid, one over each shoulder for a man, one over a shoulder for a woman guard. Films I saw on television in 1984 showed some bodies being dragged, but Dick told me that he had given the order for them to be carried. Some guards vomited, some refused to obey the order and were shot out of hand by the horrified and infuriated Hussars.

Most of the local population denied all knowledge of the camp's existence, but they were lying. Again I wrote home: 'The SS guards at that camp, who lived in great luxury, pillaged the whole neighbour-hood. For instance, one of them turned King's evidence and told our

C.O. where the swag was buried: on investigation suitcase after suitcase of brand-new watches from the local jewellers were unearthed – so many that after helping themselves quite liberally our chaps handed over to their successors a 3-ton lorry-load.' Only one man was honest, ironically the town butcher; he said he knew perfectly well from the stench what was going on.

One of Dick Taylor's problems was what to do with the camp commandant, Kramer. Finally in the basement below the mess he found a huge food refrigerator, and, since there was no electricity supply, decided to put him in there with a sentry outside. Someone in town repaired the bomb damage and the current came on: a furious banging from inside the refrigerator made the sentry open the door, and Kramer indicated that he demanded to see the British commander. He was marched up to Dick and complained that he was freezing.

Dick said he was sorry about that, it was a beautiful sunny day and Kramer was perfectly at liberty to go out and walk about the camp.

'Oh, I couldn't do that; they'd tear me to pieces,' was the reply.

'Well, it's up to you; you go outside or you go back in.'

Kramer went back in; he may have been very cold but he survived, to be tried at Nuremberg and hanged.

There were still a lot of Germans in front of us. Again I wrote home, 'The day before yesterday a beastly little Hitler youth shot a Grenadiers' medical orderly in the back and killed him while he was bending over a casualty dressing his wounds in the middle of the road; he had red crosses all over him and the range was only twenty yards, so there was no excuse.'

Operation Enterprise, the crossing of the Elbe, which began on 29 April, was less pleasant than that of the Rhine. Armour had to wait until a bridge was built, on the far side of which the route went through wooded country up a steep track difficult to negotiate, so that an enormous traffic jam developed. For a long time I sat in my tank, stationary in the middle of the bridge. During this pause the R.A.F. umbrella made a slip; one lot went home to tea before its relief had arrived. Almost at once a squadron of Messerschmitt 262s dive-bombed the bridge. Obviously they missed: I do not think that even the *élite* pilots who flew them were accustomed yet to the speed of the jets, so much greater than anything they had known before. I was told afterwards that I should feel honoured because I had received the personal attention of the commander in chief of the Luftwaffe, the great Adolf Galland. He was cruising high over the river in a light plane, ordering his scarce jets in whenever he could see an opportunity. It was an unpleasant experience watching the twelve planes screaming down towards me one after the other in line ahead, and their sound was new to the ears. Today every child is as familiar with the sound of a jet engine as the clang of a letter-box, but then they were brand new, in action for the first time, and for the first time one heard it, like some giant tearing a bale of calico.

In this operation I discovered one of my limitations: seventy-two hours without any sleep whatever was my maximum; I could not keep my eyes open.

There were not all that many days to go, and I have a few last memories. A night drive through a blazing forest, the tinder-dry pines set on fire by the tracer of the leading tanks. The many shades of red and orange of the wall of flames crackling upwards on both sides of us were awe-inspiringly beautiful, even though destructive. It was like something out of *The Ring* and, with my head out of *Zadig*, I found myself singing the Fire Music from *Walküre* as we drove onward through the heat.

Even so near the end, no one was safe. On the 27th I wrote to father, 'I am not feeling particularly well disposed towards the Germans. One of my men was quite lightly wounded recently – two bullets in the flesh of his thigh – and was evacuated in an ambulance. This, red crosses notwithstanding, the Germans saw fit to ambush, so now instead of being at home recovering this young man is a charred and unrecognisable corpse.'

And I stood on the top of a hill in the sunshine with a Grenadier officer looking out over the last plain. A sniper's bullet whistled past my ear and I thought, 'What a silly way to go', being careful not to stand on the skyline again. The same afternoon I was jeeping round, having a look at the side roads, when I came face to face with a whole squadron of Panthers, brand-new, never in action, with the factory red paint still on the bolts of their track bogies. They were coming in to surrender. I was alone, and a chill went down my spine when I thought that a zealous young Nazi could have bagged me as a last blow in memory of his now defunct Führer. They would have driven on, and when my body was found no one would have known. Yet in fact I had little to be afraid of – an observer said, 'The terrifying scourge of Europe were now remarkably docile and well disciplined.'

We entered the historic Hanseatic town of Lübeck on 8 May. I requisitioned extremely comfortable rooms in a fairly new block of flats and all the men were found good quarters. My feelings of cheerful indifference towards the Wehrmacht did not extend to the civilian population, which was quite a different matter. I wrote home: 'The part we are in is inhabited by people about as well off as ourselves, who have not suffered at all from the war, and like so many well-to-do people are horribly selfish ... If only I could find one German who would face up to the fact that he had voted for Hitler, I should feel better ... The apparent unpopularity of Hitler in a country which for twelve years yelled and screamed with delight whenever he appeared is a twentieth-century miracle.'

It was V.E. Day, and for us the war was over. 'Now,' said the King, 'we can take up our work again, resolved as a people to do nothing unworthy of those who died for us and make the world such as they would have desired.' *The Guardian* was a little more qualificatory: 'We have solved nothing. We are no nearer the Golden Age. But at least we have stopped the onrush of evil. We have won the right to hope.' In

Lübeck we had no such lofty hopes; we celebrated – some more than others. After dinner Brian Brown, Scottie and I went on to the roof. Parked in the street below was a row of Churchills with a sentry in charge of them. Brownie light-heartedly fired a signal flare and as I watched it floating down I realized that it was going to land uncomfortably close to the sentry, and I yelled, 'Get down quick.' Sure enough the sentry's reaction was a whole magazine of sten which whistled past. The last shots had been fired at us.

18   Uneasy Peace

Lübeck was lovely, busy and prosperous. Contrary to what had been claimed, the only building the R.A.F. had managed to damage was the cathedral; the rest of the city had not got a mark on it. Near the station was a warehouse containing a vast amount of hock and moselle which the N.A.A.F.I. took over and rationed out a dozen bottles at a time on request. I canoe'd on the lake, and strolled through the medieval streets eastwards to gaze curiously at the Soviet army; the junction with our great allies was a couple of hundred yards beyond the edge of town.

Four days later we moved north to our final destination, Kiel. At first the battery was just outside the city at Labo, where as headquarters we had two houses, one as an office and one as a mess. The owner of the latter was a retired officer of the Hamburg–Amerika Line who spoke perfect English. When he was dispossessed he said, 'I expected this; it's nothing to what our people would have done in England. Here are the keys, and I'll look in every day to see if there is anything I can do.'

We had a cook and two servants who were naval personnel. Somewhere along the way someone – I think Donald Hackston – had 'liberated' a record of the Horst Wessel song, and every evening it was played before dinner while we stood to attention around the table with our right arms raised in salute. What the Germans thought of this charade I do not know, but the cook did not poison us and the servant waited upon us politely.

In these early days there was complete chaos, in the midst of which the man for whom I felt sorriest was our M.O. He was the Hussars' doctor and quite elderly. It somehow fell to him to examine physically the exalted Nazis who would in due course be brought to trial at Nuremberg. Among them was Goering; he ran over him, looking in all the usual places – mouth, nose, ears, rectum, but it never occurred to him that the field marshal was so gross that folds of fat covered his navel, and it was therein that the fatal cyanide pill nestled until the time came for its owner to use it.

Regimental headquarters was in a large Luftwaffe barracks which, being outside the city at Holtenau, was intact. I mention this for one reason: it is the only time in my life that I have seen a vomitorium. There was a skittles alley in the basement, and in the lavatories opposite the porcelain equipment was built at chest height into the wall, with handles to hang on to while in action. Since obviously a standard make, it was probably a feature of every officers' mess, but it was the only one I ever saw. It is typical of German thoroughness to recognize that since young officers were obviously going to drink far more beer than they could possibly hold, they should have somewhere suitable to dispose of it and, like the ancient Romans, return refreshed for more.

Every day we were pestered by German soldiers asking where they could sign on. To the question 'Sign on for what?' they replied, 'The new army; you're going to fight the Russians of course, aren't you?'

When told that we had no intention of doing any such thing they went away disconsolate and bewildered.

Throughout the war the R.A.F. had been pounding Kiel harbour with enormous effect so that everything was destroyed except the submarine pens, the huge concrete roofs of which were barely dented by the bombs which fell on them. Snugly inside lay several two-man submarines; I got into one and thought that it would need a very dedicated sailor to take it into action.

The city of Kiel, although not the main target, was considerably damaged by the constant raids. But the real shambles was brought about by the American air force in the last days of the war, when it could not have made an iota of difference except to bring misery to everyone who had to live there. Somehow the Germans made do; at intervals along the streets there were stove-pipes sticking out of piles of rubble with a thin wisp of smoke coming from them as the people lived under the ruins of what had been their homes.

The next move proposed to us made me very angry; we were told to take over a block of flats in the city, but I was not having it. The mains had burst (hastily repaired) so that the basement was three feet deep in water. Our predecessors had methodically broken up every stick of furniture in the entire building and dumped the lot downstairs in the water; as a result they had to sleep on the floor, had nowhere to sit and no tables at which to eat. I was not prepared to have my men submitted to such conditions. I went to Corps and I got my way; and we were moved to a large barracks which contained the office of 'Hammer' Matthew, now military governor of Kiel. It had water and light, but no sanitation, no windows and little roof. The last was simple; we had several builders in the battery and in no time they had scrounged enough tiles and got to work. About the sewers we could do nothing, and the latrines we had to dig were quickly alive with rats which swarmed over every open space and all the nearby ruins.

One morning Scottie, who drove round with his eyes open, was in a state of high glee; he had found a warehouse containing a large amount of plate glass. I asked him to take a 3-ton truck – and a tank to show that we meant business – and bring back the lot. Of course, we had glaziers among us also, and in no time, using up every sheet, our windows were replaced. Then the C.R.E. (Commander Royal Engineers) drove into the barracks and reprimanded me for seizing the glass, which he said he knew about and had intended to ration out to those in need around Kiel.

I muttered about striking while the iron is hot, first come first served, and similar *clichés*; his reproof was so gentle that I think he had a sneaking sympathy with us for having got on and done something.

That was Scottie's last fling with the battery. The splendid headquarters of the Kiel Yacht Club had been the German officers' club and it was quickly reopened in the same capacity for us. Scottie was appointed manager and ran the establishment with enormous success. He lived in, with one austere sergeant to protect the virtue of the twelve waitresses who slept upstairs – one very beautiful. They possibly had not the slightest wish to have their virtue protected, but it had to be because otherwise, sleepless, they would have become exhausted. Scottie got hold of some wonderful clarets, and Château Margeaux 1924 (Château bottled) was on the list at 70p. However, not all the drinks were up to that high standard. There was a small jazz band, and one night I put my glass of German gin down on the top of the piano while I talked to the pianist; when I picked it up again, the wet rim had burnt a circle through the varnish, and I thought 'My God, that's what we are pouring down our gullets!'

At first we were very busy. Just outside Kiel there was an oil jetty at a place called Mönkeberg, backed by a natural grassy amphitheatre. To this came ships of every size and description loaded with the garrisons of all the Baltic islands, coming in to surrender. We took over guard duties from the Oxford Hussars. The weather was hot and dry, and the Germans remained in the grassy bowl until about five thousand had accumulated. Then we marched them off.

The SS were separated, put in or lolled about outside a large concrete bunker. Some of the Germans had strong views about us; one sergeant grinned and said, 'We know you Argylls, you are the British SS.' Nor was his view unique. When one ship was coming in, those on board shouted, 'To whom are we surrendering?' When they received the answer 'To the Argylls,' they cried, 'No, put off again quickly, go somewhere else – anywhere else.'

Apart from the bad SS record for atrocities against civilians, the Waffen SS were great fighters, so I suppose that these German remarks were a form of compliment.

The problem of what to do with all these men coming in from the islands had been solved by closing off the Heiligenstadt Peninsula which protrudes into the Baltic; this was entirely administered by a German corps H.Q. organization, rations being supplied by the British. At the check-point there was a reception committee of three colonels. From Mönkeberg it was a two-day march and we broke the journey overnight at a disused brickworks.

We marched them off in large batches; one morning we left the amphitheatre 15,000 strong. We had all sorts, from children of twelve in uniform who wept bitterly, to one old man of over eighty who, when asked what he had done in the previous war, explained that he had been too old to be called up; it had taken a Hitler to get him into uniform. Most of them had huge kitbags, far too heavy to carry in the summer heat, but they would not give them up – some, no doubt, because they had signed for the contents and were still afraid that they might be charged if they lost them, some because the crammed bundles of clothing represented their sole possessions. And they all stank, a distinctive smell which was peculiar to them. We had two 3-ton trucks at the rear of the column to pick up those who were really ill – about a hundred on average. Those heavy kitbags could be lethal, and one day we had six deaths from heart failure by the roadside; as soon as the last breath had sighed from the worn-out bodies a swarm of German civilians seized the kitbags and looted the miserable possessions of their own countrymen. But many of the local populace in the villages we marched them through turned out with wine, milk and water for them as they passed. One woman, standing with her legs apart and a mug of wine in her hand, laughed at one of my men as he marched the prisoners by, which was rather unfortunate for her. He fired his rifle at a range of ten yards between her legs, narrowly missing her chances of motherhood, whereupon she fell flat on her back in a dead faint.

I offered a seat in the front of one of the trucks to two colonels, both over sixty. The first was very frail and obviously was not going to complete the march. He said that this was the second time he had been a prisoner of the British – the first had been in Palestine in 1918; he found this second experience more agreeable.

The other was a bull of a man, as straight as a ramrod, whom I liked very much. When I offered him a lift, his reply was polite but abrupt:

'My men march – I march.'

And when we got to the brickworks I asked him if he would tell his men that there were plenty of latrines and I wanted the place left clean in the morning. Shouting for silence, he began his address with the ringing words:

'*Ich will hier keine Schweinerei haben.*'

We had dealt with about thirty thousand by the time we were relieved by the other battery under Tom Geddes.

In our barracks there were twelve soldiers under a sergeant-major to do the cleaning. They were all tank men, quite young, and the sergeant-major was excellent. As my German was rusty, I did not speak it, but used as interpreter a genial sailor who had lived for years in New York and had the vilest Bronx accent I have ever heard (a friend had persuaded him to return to the Fatherland just in time to be called up). After a while the Panzer boys got lazy. They had it too good – not much work, plenty of food; evening passes – so I told my seaman that I wanted them on parade in their quarters at nine the next morning. On the dot I walked in; the sergeant-major called them to attention, fingers extended flat down the seams of their trousers in the German manner. I told them that their work had gone to pieces, they were idle and useless and a lot more, and, further, if they did not get down to the job, they would be confined to barracks until they did.

I listened carefully as my sailor told them gently that the major was not quite happy. When he had finished, I snapped, 'That is not what I said and you know it; now start again and tick them off properly.'

He looked at me, his mouth open; the secret was out – I understood German.

I was soon forced to use my German. As military governor 'Hammer' Matthew had sent for the mayor of the city to discuss discipline, and he wanted me to interpret. I protested that I was very rusty, but he said it did not matter because he would rather put up with that than bring into confidential matters someone whom he neither knew nor trusted. Sweating, I was deeply relieved that it went off all right.

On another occasion he said that he was going to visit a factory and wanted me to go with him. As we drove alone into the woods north of Kiel he said that a commission on armaments was coming round the next day – three officers, one British, one American and one Russian – and he wanted to see the hidden plant first. We arrived. From the ground the place was quite invisible, and I doubt if anything could be seen from the air either. We were met by the boss – it was Helmut Walter, who designed the V.1. He had one of its engines on the test bed and he started it up for us; at close quarters the comet's tail of fire which everyone at home knew so well was extremely impressive and the noise hideous. We saw his other invention, the snorkel, which enabled U-boats to remain submerged for long periods. And, taking up most of the factory space, was his – fortunately uncompleted – peroxide-driven submarine which would have been able to remain submerged indefinitely, as nuclear submarines can today.

'Hammer' asked if he would like to work in Britain; yes, he said, he would like that very much. Then we both recoiled when he added, 'But let me make myself clear; I will work only on weapons of destruction.'

Many years later I heard the end of the story. He was eventually brought to Britain with seven of his colleagues and assigned to Vickers at Barrow-in-Furness, where his presence was resented and a fiasco resulted.

We left him with his nasty thoughts. I do not think that the inspecting commissioners ever found his factory, but there was a banquet for them the next night in the huge mess of the barracks where I had seen the vomitorium. It had a gallery in which a military band was to play. Panic set in at 4 p.m. – the bandmaster discovered that he had not got the music of the *Red Flag*. A flurry of jeeps was sent in all directions; at 7 o'clock one officer returned triumphant. Dinner was at 7.30, and the musicians had half an hour in which to rehearse the unfamiliar Soviet anthem. It was a good dinner. In due course 'Hammer' rose and proposed the King, and we drank as the band played the national anthem. Then 'Hammer' proposed the health of Generalissimo Stalin and the glorious Red Army and the *Red Flag* was played. What no one knew was that it is the custom in the Soviet Union for toasts to be replied to, so the moment we sat down the Russian colonel (I think he was) rose to his feet and made a gracious speech in his own language, which is one of the most beautiful in the world. Whereupon the bandmaster, who had his back to the speaker anyway and probably would not have known a Soviet officer from an Eskimo, enthusiastically struck up *The Star-spangled Banner*. It was a disaster and the Russian hit the roof. He said it was a filthy plot to make fun of him and he was leaving right now; it took a considerable time, through the interpreter, to persuade him to remain at the table.

'Hammer's' great pride and joy was Goering's motor yacht *Karen II*. She was found some way inland at Mölln, where she had been taken for safety and was in the charge of an elderly married couple. A German crew was put on board and she was sailed back to Kiel. 'Hammer' was a generous host and gave parties, to one of which I was invited. There were about four of us, including Peter Maxwell. We embarked in the late afternoon and sailed down the Kiel Canal. A German steward served drinks on deck in the sunshine; all the girls cycling along the towpath waved. It was warm, peaceful and idyllic. We tied up to the bank for the night. After dinner we went ashore duck-shooting at last light, and eventually to bed. 'Hammer' and I shared the main cabin – he had the field marshal's bunk and I had Emmy's. At first light we had another go at the duck, a swim in the canal, breakfast on the voyage back and on first parade at eight-thirty.

The main difficulty after a year's fighting was trying to get back to spit and polish. We had been frequently filthy and often looked like a gang of scarecrows in any old clothes; now badges had to be polished, trousers had to have knife-edge creases, buttons had to be done up. We had not only won, but we had to be seen to have won. Buttons undone were a great trial and I developed a mania on the subject. Inspection on parade at eight-thirty was the first order of the day, and I finally became so exasperated that I announced the next man found with a button undone would be on a charge.

The very next morning a man unfamiliar to me – for changes of personnel were already taking place – was improperly dressed. I screamed, 'Sergeant-Major, take his name!' I held an orderly room at ten; I was fed up with this nonsense, and when the wretched man was marched in I put on a simulated rage and shouted at him. When I had finally run out of breath, I was startled by a refined and gentle voice which said:

'Oh, Sir, I am so sorry. I wouldn't upset you for the world. I was only posted in at two o'clock this morning and had no idea that my mistake would so distress you.'

Totally deflated, I could only say, 'Well, I hope you will enjoy your stay with us. March out!'

It was not only the men who had to be smartened up; the tanks too needed cleaning and completely repainting. When they were done, I inspected them with my sergeant-major, a charming Irish-Glaswegian named Byrne. It was a thoroughly sloppy job and I ordered the whole thing to be done again. The struggle to get the required smartness was depressing, and I realized how John must have felt when he was trying to make soldiers out of us four years before. In an effort to cheer me up,

Byrne produced a pearl of wisdom: 'Sir, the trouble with this battery is that everything that's in our favour is against us.'

All the depressing nonsense was driven away by my delight when Brian Brown walked into the office one morning and, standing in front of my desk, said, 'Satisfied?'

There on his chest was the brand new crimson and blue ribbon of the D.C.M.* which he had sworn never to wear until he knew that his brother, put in the bag in 1940, was alive and well. He had just had the good news. In the highest spirits, we had a particularly strenuous bout of cricket that afternoon. This he and I played together in the long narrow concrete passage upstairs in the barracks. One of us bowled fast while the other hit hard, and the ball shot like a bullet from one end of the seventy-five-yard corridor to the other. It was highly dangerous but great fun.

The most frequent visitors to my orderly room were those returning from hospital after treatment for venereal disease. With the arrival of penicillin the cure was quite quick, but the doctors used to keep all their old blunt needles so that the injections would be as painful as possible. The girls in Kiel were riddled with pox, which was hardly surprising. In the first place, prostitution was illegal in the Third Reich, so that the clandestine brothels lacked any kind of medical supervision; in the second place the shortage of rubber in Germany made condoms so scarce that the rate of VD rose alarmingly; and in the third place after VE Day four and a half million German soldiers remained in captivity in the Soviet Union which increased pressure on the sex-starved female population at home. Although Eisenhower had issued an order 'No social intercourse of any kind with Germans will take place', there was no way of keeping men off the girls, and by the summer the situation was so serious that in their sector the Americans jokingly compared it with the farce of Prohibition in the twenties.

In the army of Julius Caesar any soldier who got a dose was flogged, and, worse, Richard III had his delinquents hanged. We could not go that far, but Montgomery, the son of a bishop, was not interested in obtaining proper supplies of prophylactics, and consequently, although medical officers issued free on request what condoms they could get hold of, the incidence of disease was high. I reckon that by the time I left in November, over 40 per cent of 146 Battery had been infected.

As they returned from hospital to duty I had each man marched in. The first, inevitably, was Hughes, the irrepressible ex-pug who never

* His was a remarkable feat. A sergeant in the Kensingtons, the machine-gun regiment of the 51st Highland Division, he was like all of them cornered at St Valery in 1940. Gathering his men, he laagered on the clifftop in a tight bunch and surrounded the position with barbed wire. During the night the Germans rattled on the wire to get a reaction if there was anybody there. Next morning, making a rope of rifle slings, they descended the cliff to the sea and swam out to a British destroyer lying two miles off the shore. The last man said miserably, 'I can't swim,' so Brownie took him out on his back. It was not an experience that one forgets easily, as I know from once sharing lodgings with him; he used to mutter in his sleep, 'The wire; don't touch the wire.'

came back from leave on time and never fired at a German tank without hitting it. When he was marched in our conversation was brief and to the point.

'Well, Hughes, are you quite cured?'

'Yes, Sir.'

'What are you going to do now?'

'Go out and get it again, Sir.'

So summer went on. There were sports, football, entertainments and no duties except keeping smart and reading about the fighting in the Far East. Then suddenly the end came.

Victory Day was celebrated on 15 August, and it was the proudest day of my years in the army. 'Hammer' Matthew nominated 146 Battery to fire a royal salute of 101 guns in front of the town hall of Kiel.

We did not have much time in which to get ready. Everything had to be spotless and gleam where it should gleam. We had to have 101 rounds of blank, plus a percentage for misfires; Corps had not got enough, so Brian had to tear off to an army dump which made up some more in a hurry. I had a clipboard marked up to 101 so that I could tick off each discharge, and a stop-watch so that I could give the order to fire at ten-second intervals over the wireless from my tank. A large crowd of citizens watched.

It was as well that I had the chart in front of me. We had one misfire and I had immediately to give an order to the next gun; I certainly would have lost count if I had not been ticking them off one by one. It was rather difficult to keep a straight face when one of the rounds made up so quickly only just went off and with a sound little more than a deep belch there dribbled from the muzzle a torn brassière, shredded panties and a collection of old newspapers.

It was chaos that evening. At the officers' club someone had got hold of a quantity of illuminating rockets and used as a target *Karen II* lying off shore. As she sat there brilliantly lit by the descending golden rain 'Hammer' went berserk. He was running up and down the verandah shouting 'Stop it! Stop it! Leave my boat alone, you'll have her on fire!' She survived and is still around, having recently passed through the hands of the man who tried unsuccessfully to forge Hitler's diaries.

Soldiering was over. All the territorial Argylls departed. Dick Taylor had gone home to Northumberland and our colonel was now O'Grady, a regular officer. My own time was drawing near, and I gave a party for the whole battery. On the eve of my departure I received a letter from a gunner, written on behalf of the battery, wishing me luck; I had always hoped that they had for me a little of the very great respect which I had for them, but it is difficult to know, and to read what was sent to me moved me to the bottom of whatever heart I have.

One evening in November I set off on a packed train. The Channel was smooth, and happily I had managed to get a cabin to myself. Over the address system a last appeal was made for men to surrender any arms they had; I was bringing a Luger with me, and – thinking what do I really want this for? – I opened the porthole and threw it out. Even so, at

Dover the first kitbag opened had a weapon in it, and after that every single thing had to be turned out and we were there for hours. I declared a not very distinguished fur coat which I had bought for Margaret on short leave in Copenhagen, and the Customs officer was charming. Turning it over and over, he kept up a muttered commentary: 'That's not a very good skin; and look here, this bit's not so hot either; oh, I don't think I can charge you anything on this, Sir.' By late afternoon I was home.

Perhaps my last thoughts about the army are best summed up in a letter which I had a few weeks later from Scottie, who was still in Kiel.

There had recently, he wrote, been a spot of trouble. One of our sergeants, it appeared, had encountered a German officer, a sergeant and eight other ranks late one night. They came to blows and the Germans were routed. The officer rather unwisely decided to sue for assault. The civil court, deciding that the matter lay outside its jurisdiction, referred it to the military authorities; before a Judge Advocate General evidence was given by both sides, the officer appearing in the witness box with a glorious black eye. When he had heard all that there was to be said, the J.A.G. gave his verdict: 'I am pleased to learn that one Argyll is still equal to ten Germans. Case dismissed.'

19 Another Kind of War

It was winter and people were coming back from all over the world. Life was like a journey through country once familiar, picking out old landmarks and finding others changed or gone for ever. There was no Walter any more, or A.J. who had died in 1941 from the illness which had begun before my disappearance, some friendships were casualties of passing time and diverging ways, patterns had changed, people had moved; but others were renewed as the news of one's return got around. André Simon rang up to ask if I could lunch with him on a given date at the Ecu de France, and I arrived to find that he had invited six of my close friends to welcome me home; I nearly wept – only that dear warm-hearted Frenchman would think of such a kindness.

Life returned as far as possible to its pre-war form. Very soon after my return I joined Moor Park Golf Club, as I had promised myself two years before because I so admired the superb eighteenth-century clubhouse. There I got to know a member who had been in a Japanese P.O.W. camp where he was senior British officer. Neither his health nor his nerves were yet back to normal and, as I saw in the dressing-room, his body was a mass of scars because, despite his position, the guards had been in the habit of bayoneting him from time to time as a form of sport. Nevertheless he told me of a conversation which it would be difficult to forget.

Every prison camp everywhere contained electricians who from scrap metal and chance thefts somehow managed to construct a wireless set; this camp was no exception. One day my friend passed two sergeants sitting in the shade of a tree with the set hidden between them, listening to the BBC overseas news. It was not good; the Germans were driving deeper and deeper into the heart of the Soviet Union, and one of the sergeants was very pessimistic: 'I reckon the Russkies have had it; they'll be beaten and then it's all over.'

'Don't you believe it!' said his companion, 'Russia's a big place, they won't give in, they can go on retreating and retreating. If they have to, they can retreat behind the Urinals.'

On 1 January 1946 I went back to Cassell's. We were still in the temporary offices in Holborn which had been lent to us by Crittals, the well-known metal window firm, when La Belle Sauvage was destroyed. They had space because their normal work was at a standstill and a lot of their people were away. With the war over their staff and their functions were returning to normal and, although they were very understanding, they wanted us out. We knew this and the hunt was on, but we stayed where we were for a few more months.

Space had been kept for me; it was an alcove with a desk in it and an elephant track passing from the staircase to the medical and publicity departments. I have seldom felt so spare as I did on that first day, sitting at a desk crowded with a blotter, a few sheets of blank paper and a pencil. Where was I to start? How was I to start?

Five years had passed during which, of course, father had added a number of new authors to the list – some made famous by the war, such as Ed Murrow and Quentin Reynolds. Also there were others with their eye on the shape of things to come, such as the Fabian economist, G.D.H. Cole. Yet it was in a way comforting how many familiar names remained, which made it seem almost as if one had not been away at all. There were still Warwick Deeping and Ernest Raymond, R.C. Hutchinson, Louis Bromfield, Alec Waugh, G.B. Stern, Mary Roberts Rinehart, Sheila Kaye-Smith, I.A.R. Wylie, H.A. Vachell, Robert Hitchens, Evelyn Eaton, all the popular novelists, and a favourite of mine John Gloag, who in his daytime activity as an advertising agent was to coin one of the best-remembered slogans: 'If you want to get ahead, get a hat.' And Erle Stanley Gardner was as prolific as ever.

Father must have been fully aware by 1945 that at the war's end there would be an army of occupation, long before he got my letter from Kiel on the subject, because that summer appeared *Cassell's War and Post-war German Dictionary*, containing terms that servicemen would need and such Nazi terms as they were likely to come across. It was edited by Dr Carl Brinitzer who was in the BBC German Service.

That spring the sixth volume of Winston Churchill's speeches appeared, not surprisingly entitled *Victory*; so ended the memorable series which I had set in train during my last days as a civilian. But they had a notable appendix: in the summer the speeches which the Prime Minister had made in Secret Session appeared in a fascinating small volume.

Once things were rolling I would need a secretary. Along the elephant track I noticed passing back and forth a beautiful dark-haired girl who looked a likely prospect and I found out that her name was Elizabeth Smith. One day I stopped her in her passage either to or fro and asked her if she would care to be my secretary.

Rather grumpily she replied, 'I suppose so.'

I told Bill Angell, the Company Secretary, that I had asked her and received what I took to be an affirmative answer; he smiled and said, 'That is what she was hired for.' It appeared that she was the youngest daughter of Reginald Smith who had at one time been a considerable power in the British film industry; hence he knew Laurence Pollinger. The time came for Elizabeth to get a job and her father asked Laurence if he had any ideas, and he, knowing that I was alive and would be returning, suggested Cassell's. She was fitted into the publicity department for the time being.

In February father retired for the second and last time; he withdrew to his native Dorset, buying Tarrant Keynston House in the village of that name, not far from Blandford. Meanwhile Aubrey Gentry and I looked all over London and the only premises that we could find were on either side of St Andrew's Hill, a little street south of St Paul's Cathedral which had only two claims to fame: Shakespeare once owned a house there, and at the bottom were the offices of *The Observer*. They were cramped quarters, but they would have to do. Business was on one side and I was on the other with the Editorial Department on the fourth floor below me. Shortly after the move we had a tea lady who at the end of her first week asked for an interview with the Business Director. Ushered in to Aubrey Gentry, she said, 'Sir, I wish to report a serious dereliction of duty. For five days now I have taken tea to the fourth floor and I have not seen anyone do a hand's turn of work; they are all just sitting there reading.'

My chief editor was dear Arthur Hayward who had been in the firm since his demobilization from the Royal Artillery after World War One. Edwin Boyce was still sales manager. The task before us was formidable. Our back list was a pale shadow, since during the war years pretty well anything had sold, even if it was printed upside down in Cyrillic. Our dictionaries, of which we were so proud, were a mess and little could be done as paper rationing was still in force. Another valuable work badly in need of attention was *Brewer's Dictionary of Phrase and Fable*; it was not only out of print, but out of date. A complete revision was begun by Arthur Hayward, Margaret and myself. My particular provinces were Australiana and war-time phrases; I had a protracted hunt for a suitable explanation of 'Kilroy was here' – I hope I got it right in the end.

Father had always been interested in the history of warfare, so it was not surprising that he asked me if I would take him round some of the places where I had been in Normandy. I suggested that we should go in the Whitsun holiday, and we set off in my car from Boulogne.

In the few days we had, we saw a lot. When we were at Cheux, where one of our drivers picked up and so named a terrified little puppy which went all the way to the Baltic, waxed and grew fat, I asked father if he would mind if I nipped across a field to a spot where I joined 146 Battery, living for some days in a dry ditch partly covered over with a solid roof by a German before me. I wanted to see if my burrow was still there; it was, and what is more in it lay a pair of socks with my laundry mark!

Estry was a 'must'. It had not changed, and Brian Brown, who made a pilgrimage to it in 1985, said that it is still the same now and that any Briton who fought there is remembered and made welcome. At the crossroads short of it still lay the Mark IV, the commander of which had got out to read the signpost, and no one had bothered about the crew who had died when our 17-pr knocked it out – their skeletons remained inside. In the village I met the schoolmaster, the member of the Resistance who when he had tried to tell our commanders the German layout found that no one would listen to him; we talked at great length and father took a photograph of us together – I still have a long letter from him.

Then to Caen. Poor Caen; I knew that the university had been destroyed, so I got in touch with the librarian, Mlle Dupasquier, who still flourishes and was then an enchanting young blonde, and she invited us to tea. I asked her how many volumes had survived from the ruins of the university library, and she said 'One.' I thereupon offered to send her all the duplicates I had in my Voltaire collection, and this was the start of the rare book collection in the new library. That was the extent of my original intention, but, like Topsy, 'it growed' and I found myself searching antiquarian booksellers for rare French books which were then still not appreciated – things are different now – and sending over parcels. This was to produce a result of which I never dreamed.

The next important matter seemed to be the re-establishment of relations with our close friends across the Atlantic. Aubrey Gentry was in favour, and added, 'Your father, in an excess of enthusiasm, bought the British rights of an anthology of world poetry edited by Louis Untermeyer. It is a very good book, but we can't publish it because it is huge and would take up almost a whole year's paper ration. Will you talk to Simon and Schuster and see what you can do about it?'

So I set off by air, and took the best part of four days on a B.O.A.C. DC-8. Heathrow did not exist and all flights west started from Hurn, near Bournemouth. On day one we all arrived at Bournemouth West Station and piled into a coach on which a representative of B.O.A.C. said that it was a mistake, we should not have been sent down from London as the plane was not ready; so we were deposited in a comfortable hotel at Sandbanks. After dinner we were told that we must be dressed and ready for departure at 1 a.m.; I thought this sounded extremely unlikely and went to bed, determined that if this hare-brained scheme turned out to be true they could go without me. On day two I came down to breakfast at a normal hour and found all the other disgruntled passengers, who had dutifully got up in the small hours, eating. After sitting around all morning there were no signs of movement, so after lunch I went for a walk. Soon my conscience pricked me and I went back, to find a scene of great activity – we were off! Or were we? By no means; we settled down to a long wait at the airport. In the dark we finally took off, and as we did so the next plane was already on the runway – it was one of the very new Constellations, determined to prove that it was *the* great step forward in passenger aircraft. By the night of day three we had stopped to refuel in Ireland and Iceland and were running into a blizzard as we approached Newfoundland. The pilot announced that the weather was too bad for him to get into Gander and he would cross the island and try Stevensville on the west coast. As we made our approach through blinding snow, only two passengers were awake; the man across the aisle from me and myself.

He said to me, 'Did you see what I saw?'

'I did indeed,' I replied.

Out of the window uncomfortably close to the tip of our wing had been the navigation lights of the Constellation which had hunted us the whole way, determined to reach New York first. We hit the runway; the Constellation disappeared into the wall of snow and had not been located by the time we continued on our way. On day four we refuelled for the last time at Boston, and finally hit New York, tired but relieved.

After checking in at the Elysée, a charming hotel next door to the beautiful Lever building, my first thought was to get some money. Margaret's cousin Bill, who was in command of the American police at London's Marlborough Street, knew that I was going to be a bit pushed on what we were then allowed and suggested that if I would give him a cheque for £100, he would give me his for $450 (that makes ancient history!). Taking this to my favourite bank on Madison Avenue I sat down at a table, as one does, with one of the managers and presented the cheque.

'You know,' he said, 'we've been asked by the British government not to do this sort of thing, but we know how short of currency you are, and we like to help. Do you know anyone in New York?'

Yes, I did, and I rattled off the names of some well-known publishers like Alfred Knopf, Harold Ginzburg, Bennett Cerf, Stanley Rinehart ...

'Oh, Mr Rinehart; he banks here. I'll give him a ring.'

He disappeared and returned a few minutes later with a broad smile on his face.

'Mr Rinehart says we're to give you whatever we have in the vaults.'

It was a worthwhile trip and, although I did not come back with any masterpieces, all my friends in the profession were as kind and hospitable as ever. I have generally found that the heads of American publishing houses are extraordinarily kind and extremely efficient, and the same goes for their right-hand men, but below that level personnel can be deplorable. It is typical of the country – the stars shine bright; while here, with some outstanding exceptions, the good are seldom so good and the bad are certainly never so bad. On the other hand, I am writing of an age which is now past; most of the American giants are dead, and it is beyond my competence to express an opinion about the present calibre on either side of the Atlantic.

Then Alfred Knopf – whom Alistair Cooke described on his death as the greatest American publisher of the century – was always Alfred, and I regarded him almost as a relation; Ben Huebsch was as gentle as ever; Stanley Rinehart as kind as he was over the bank; Cass Canfield at Harper's sounding vague while being nothing of the sort, and so on.

A new friend was Roger Straus; just out of the navy, he had started a firm called Farrar, Straus. Johnny Farrar was a strange man credited with impeccable literary judgement who had previously been with Rinehart, and the new combination made a considerable impact on the American publishing scene. Later they were joined by another partner, Robert Giroux, and the name of the firm was accordingly enlarged. As well as his good taste, Roger was a man of means and used his consequent freedom of movement to good purpose. In the thirties the two best international lists had been Viking because of Ben Huebsch's European background, and Knopf because of Blanche's avocation. In the next generation Roger's penchant towards international literature quickly made his list outstanding. In the following year I was able to buy from him the British rights of Carlo Levi's *Christ Stopped at Eboli*.

This remarkable book is about Levi's native Calabria, the toe of Italy where the poverty was so great that Christ was said not to have penetrated beyond Eboli on its northern boundary.

The book made a considerable impact and I was proud to have it on our list. Everyone was talking about it, even two women in New York who always made their hair appointments at the same time so that they could gossip. Under the dryer one said, 'Read any good books lately?' and her friend replied, 'Yes, actually I've just read a wonderful book – had a funny sort of title: Somebody stopped at Eboli.'

Then I went to Simon and Schuster. They were then – I do not know if they still are – the only firm in which every member of the staff had to be Jewish; today this may seem discriminatory, but anyway they were a singularly happy firm. Dick Simon I knew best in those days so that it was upon him that I called first, then Max Schuster came in, and I brought up the subject of Louis Untermeyer's *Anthology of World Poetry* and our paper problem.

'That,' said Dick, 'is a matter for the company treasurer; let's get him in,' and he phoned for Leon Shimkin to join us.

When Leon had sat down, I said my piece again. He thought for a moment, then said:

'As I understand it, you have signed a contract which you are unable to honour owing to circumstances beyond your control.'

'That is so.'

'Tear it up.'

The only thing he added was that he would like me to write him a letter explaining the circumstances so that he could send it to Untermeyer.

I have never forgotten that, perfectly representing the complete straightforwardness which was so characteristic of them, and, after Dick and Max were no more, of Peter Schwed whose dry staccato humour I enjoyed as long as I was in business.

Leon Shimkin, a small dark man who crackled with electric vitality moved on afterwards to become a considerable tycoon in publishing, and I lost touch with him. But years later he was brought back to mind when I was playing golf with Alfred and Bennett Cerf. On the second hole Alfred topped his drive which just trickled on to the fairway, and he exploded, 'Oh, Shimkin!' Bennett reproved him, 'Alfred, Alfred, do not take the name of the deity in vain!'

But one of the important results of my visit was to get to know much better Thayer Hobson who ran the William Morrow Company after the death of its founder. Throughout my story I refer to people who become 'friends'. There are friends and friends; all are more than acquaintances, but a few are people who become part of one's life, of whom one may ask anything, and for whom one will do anything that they may need; among these, in addition to Walter and Charles Hasse, John Marks and John Cockburn and Charles Ede, I counted Thayer Hobson.

The first annual general meeting after the war was memorable. Living in the country, father was still chairman, and firmly of the opinion that shareholders would flock to this meeting – the first in the still fresh days of peace – so it was decided to hire a hall off Fleet Street to accommodate the mob. We directors sat at a table across the top of the room; rows of chairs stretched almost as far as the eye could see. On the stroke of eleven father got to his feet and began the chairman's address: 'Ladies and gentlemen ... ' The entire audience hung on his words: sitting on a chair in the centre of the front row and watching him with unwavering golden eyes, it consisted of one large black cat.

At much the same time I was asked to be dinner secretary of the Double Crown Club, in succession to Holbrook Jackson who had held the office for twenty-one years and thought that was enough; he was not well, and in fact had not long to live. The secretary (as opposed to him who arranged the dinners) was my old friend Ellic Howe, who added, 'There is going to be a presentation to Holbrook Jackson at the anniversary dinner in September – and when you have done twenty-one years, you too will get a presentation.'

I did not think that was very funny, but the years rolled by, the members put up with me, I lost count of time, and suddenly in 1968 when we were dining at Waddesdon Manor I was presented with a glorious Regency decanter with round its neck a silver label designed by Hans Schmoller. It is customary to say that one is taken aback, but on this occasion I really was because, being barely conscious that it was the twenty-first year, I had long forgotten Ellic's jocular prophecy.

It was a job which I enjoyed, but one which I could not have done without Herta Ryder, later my secretary, who comes in shortly. It was she whose patience was tried by delinquent members (always the same ones) ringing up long after the closing date to ask if they could come. My main task then was the table plan, watching out for personal quirks and duplication.

We settled down at Kettner's in Romilly Street where we always dined except on special occasions out of London. On the whole the food was good and the price was reasonable but there was one disadvantage: on a well attended guest night the room was packed and got very stuffy. Various members protested and I tried hard to make a change, but I could not find anywhere larger which could match the price. From my years of office two incidents stick in my mind.

The eleventh and last rule of the club states that 'Any member failing to attend one dinner in the club's year shall be considered to have resigned, except in view of reasons accepted by the committee.' At the beginning of a new year it is normal for the president to write to any delinquent during the previous twelve months. This led to the affair of John Betjeman, who had been elected a member in 1940, why I do not know: whatever interest he ever had in the club soon waned and he never came to any dinners. Eventually, in 1947, his name was tabled at a committee lunch, held normally at the Etoile, which in the thirties was used almost exclusively by people connected with books and graphic arts. It was pointed out that he was not only a delinquent during the season immediately past, but had not been to a dinner for years; Rule 11 should apply. Even James Shand, who was president and could be very firm, was reluctant and thought that we should give him another chance; he would write to him. Another year passed; no Betjeman. The new president, Christian Barman, was rather equivocal; he said, 'I know that Betjeman should be asked to resign or be expelled, but I don't want it to happen in my year.'

Twelve months later the situation was unchanged, and under Noel Rooke, a much respected founder member, no one seemed to know what should be done. Since as a permanent member of the committee I had to sit through the same charade annually, I finally exploded: 'This is the third year and is simply making a mockery of the rules. Either you expel him or you get a new dinner secretary, I don't mind which, but it must be one or the other.' Reynolds Stone said, quietly, 'I suppose you know that you will be expelling a future Poet Laureate.' I thought he was joking, but he was of course proved right. Finally Reynolds added, 'If you will let it go, I will myself bring him to the next dinner.'

In due course the table plan was done and these two were naturally placed together. During dinner it was part of my duty to look round and see that everyone was present – or not. There was one empty chair; I caught Reynolds' eye, but he looked down. Afterwards he was bewildered: 'We were together all day,' he said, 'and then about six o'clock he gave me the slip.'

Dear Reynolds! After that even he acquiesced – but for about a year afterwards Betjeman signed his letters as 'ex-member Double Crown Club'.

During the war Nicholas Monsarrat had produced three small books on the corvettes in which he served and then commanded. Now he produced his first work since demobilization: *Depends what you Mean by Love*. Many people will have read this, but I want to mention it especially because I think that it contains some of the finest prose he wrote. It is made up of three stories. The first, the love of a man for a woman, is explained by its title *Leave Cancelled*. The second, *Heavy Rescue*, the love of a man for his job and his country, describes the death of an old navvy beneath the wreckage of a bombed house as he tries to rescue a child, and is the most poignant. The last, the love of a man for his ship, is called *H.M.S. Marlborough will enter Harbour*, the proud signal that the captain hoists when he has resolutely nursed his stricken wreck with its few survivors back to safety. I admired this one so much that five years later I commissioned James Holland, one of the leading marine artists of the time, to do an illustrated edition. It is a handsome book and my enthusiasm for it was shared by others – when I went to Malta a little later I found a small bookseller who thought so well of it that he had bought enough copies to give one to almost every citizen in Valletta.

Nicholas was now British information officer in Johannesburg, and on leave from South Africa he said to me, 'In three years I will deliver a novel about the Western Approaches.'

In the same year Margaret and I received a visit at 10 Devonshire Place from a man somewhat younger than I, tall, with a large nose, like a blond version of the great Duke of Wellington in his prime, named Charles Ede; why he came to our home rather than to the office neither of us can now remember. Earlier in the year, with Alan Bott and Christopher Sandford, he had started the Folio Society. Bott, as founder of the Book Society, the Reprint Society and Pan Books, had the business experience; Sandford had printed fine books all his life, acquired the Golden Cockerel Press from Robert Gibbings in 1933, commissioned work from many of the new illustrators, and was trying to reduce the cost of good printing to a level which people could afford. This was to be the primary object of the Folio, using all mechanical means to produce handsome illustrated classics at prices which compared favourably with those of a straight text. They decided that they needed a reputable trade publisher to handle their books. This was of the greatest interest to me, and, with Bryen Gentry's assent, an agreement was entered into.

It was not a good time to be launching a new venture. The retail trade was still unaccustomed to the fact that the boom times of the war were over; booksellers were over-cautious and suspicious. The books had a mixed reception, of which there was a typical example when the second list was being taken round by our representatives. Our sales manager, on being rung up by an excited bookseller who said, 'These Folio books are wonderful; why haven't I heard about them before?' replied, 'You'd better take a look round your shelves; you had half a dozen of the last title.' After two years of hard grafting it became apparent that the formula was not right, and Folio was converted into a subscribing members' society, became immensely successful and remains so to this day. Nevertheless, twelve months later there was a financial crisis. Alan Bott was nearing the end of his life and wanted out, so Cassell's became shareholders. Bott's place on the board was taken by Ralph Vernon-Hunt, while Christopher Sandford became less and less inclined to come up to London from his lovely home in Leominster. I remained on the board for more than twenty years, for much of the time as chairman, but more important was the fact that Charles and his lovely wife Liz became friends who remained always kind, and at one period were of the greatest help in a time of crisis.

Father seldom left Dorset except for the occasional board meeting, and, with Aubrey retired, I was in charge of operations. Bryen, although short on experience, was doing wonderfully well; Arthur Hayward, nearly old enough to be my father, was my *eminence grise*. The first thing I tackled was pensions, which had never existed in Cassell's. Today, when Social Security is a matter of law, this may seem extraordinary, but forty years ago, without having gone into the statistics, I would say that firms which had schemes in existence were very much in the minority.

I discussed it with Arthur and found myself faced by a dilemma: should the scheme be contributory or non-contributory? I was in favour of the latter because I considered it was something the company owed its employees in an industry which is never particularly well paid at the best of times. I was told that opposition to this was raised by a packer, Len Aylott, who had been in our cricket team before the war. I asked why and was told that he considered it an unfair weapon in the hands of the directors who, in the event of an industrial dispute, could threaten to suspend the scheme. Frankly, I was hurt that he should imagine that I would allow the board to take such an attitude, so I said, 'Sod him,' and put the non-contributory scheme through; two weeks later he died of a heart attack and his widow was the first to benefit.

I must admit that I did not get around to the workers' committee about which I had written enthusiastically to father during the war; it is difficult to say whether I forgot because I was so busy or whether it was a case of the mind putting aside the difficult and inconvenient. But we did give shares to some members of the staff so that they could represent their colleagues at the annual general meeting.

Allen Lane was in New York at the same time as I was in 1948 and asked me if I would like to go with him to see Martita Hunt who was enjoying a great success in Giraudoux's *The Mad Woman of Chaillot*, and he added that his American attorney would be coming. The attorney turned out to be Mrs Harriet Pilpel, an enchanting woman of great beauty who enjoyed the reputation of being about the toughest lawyer in New York City. From then on I never went there without calling upon her and if there was any legal business to be done for the company I always asked her to take care of it. There soon was.

From the mists of time our language dictionaries had always been handled in the United States by Funk and Wagnell, an old-established house then not in the best of health. In the previous year I had been approached by two publisher friends either of whose firms would have been ideal – Cass Canfield at Harper's and Bennett Cerf of Random House. Searching through our records, I was alarmed to discover that there was no contract between Funks and ourselves – in the nineteenth century the arrangement was probably made by an exchange of letters now long lost, or simply by a handshake. I could see no way by which I could terminate a contract which did not exist, so I consulted Harriet Pilpel. In the end she negotiated a proper contract and Funks pulled their socks up. Meanwhile I called upon Bennett Cerf, and when he again asked about the dictionaries I explained the difficulty and added that I had put Harriet Pilpel on to them. He exploded: 'Desmond, you bastard! It shouldn't happen to a dog!'

Bennett was a character whose enormous vitality took him far beyond the bounds of publishing, a major television personality and collector of wit and wisdom. He was explosive and one never saw him without something happening. At this same meeting he tore an enormous strip off me because in the wretched last days of the British mandate in

Palestine ships of unhappy refugees were being turned away; yet, vitriolic as he was, when he ran out of breath we remained friends. Some years later, in 1955, he said, 'I always knew you British were crazy, but sometimes you go too far. The other night I was taken to the cinema to see a damn fool British picture about a ridiculous bomb that bounced along the water!'

'But Bennett,' I said mildly, '_The Dam Busters_ was an act of war,' and, shaken, he exclaimed, 'Jesus, you mean it's true?'

That trip I came back with two good books, the authors of which both became my friends. One was _The Crusaders_ by Stefan Heym, a story of the Second World War. Stefan is Jewish and left Germany for obvious reasons in the thirties, becoming an American citizen and marrying an American wife. During the war in Europe he was sent forward in a tank to address the German front-line troops through a loudspeaker, and from his experiences came _The Crusaders_, a splendid novel. When the contract was signed he and his wife took me to lunch, and over that lunch Stefan and I became friends and have remained so to this day, through many vicissitudes.

He was horrified when the United States started the Korean War – so much so that he posted his decorations to the President, renounced his American citizenship and went back to Germany. He lives in comfort in – what used to be East – Berlin, a man concerned with humanity and not with 'isms', who speaks his mind with a sincerity which can be uncomfortable.

Then I went to see Adelaide Shearer at Rinehart's, in those days one of the best editors in the business – a beautiful woman with a limp, rather like Viola Garvin.

'I don't think I've got anything for you,' she said, 'but there's a manuscript here which came in this morning; I haven't even looked at it yet but you're welcome to take it away and see what it's like if you wish.'

I read it overnight and excitedly phoned her the next morning recommending that we both buy the rights at once; it was _The Arabian Bird_, Constantine FitzGibbon's first novel. Constantine had had an interesting war in the American army. Not long after _The Arabian Bird_ he moved to London and I got to know him well. His third novel, _My Cousin Emily_, made his name, though I remain attached to his first, a later edition of which he dedicated to me. He drank too much, and was brave enough to write a book about the problem with the same honesty that Richard Burton showed on the small screen – a problem I was later to know all too well.

It was at this time that Basil Liddell Hart came to Cassell's, and was to remain with us for the rest of his life. His first book on our list was _The Other Side of the Hill_, which resulted from his long interviews with the German generals, and it was hailed with excitement. It was an impressive work but in the end not alone; for instance, a similar book, which has recently been reprinted, was written by Milton Shulman who as a Canadian journalist also saw all the German relics.

Soon after that we published _Pattern of War_ by Sir Francis Tuker who had commanded 4th Indian Division with conspicuous success in the western desert. He was a fine, handsome man, tragically crippled by arthritis at the end of his life, a good writer with a clear, incisive mind. He must have been a delight to serve with, and I can imagine the sharpness of his tone when on the field-telephone he retorted, he told me, to Ritchie, the 8th Army Commander, who wanted him to pull back from Sollum to Sidi Barrani after the failure of 'Crusader': 'No one can retreat half-way; Alexander couldn't, Napoleon couldn't and I'm sure you can't either; I shall withdraw to Mersa Matruh.'

During this time I came to realize that my secretary, Elizabeth Smith, had considerable literary gifts, and as we were in need of an extra editor to cope with the expanding programme, I shifted her to that department under Arthur Hayward, where she proved to be very good at dealing with authors and smoothing any feathers which might become ruffled.

She was followed by a cheerful beauty who looked after me for nearly two years and then left to get married. Her successor in 1950 was to remain my keeper for longer than anyone else and to become far more than a secretary – much more a personal assistant, an ally as well as a friend – throughout the busiest years of my life: Herta Ryder.

Originally arriving as a refugee from Germany, Herta was already married to John Ryder, a fine typographer and typographical historian, late a director of The Bodley Head. When she came to St Andrew's Hill and I first saw her – a small, almost frail figure with a face of placid beauty and a low-pitched gentle voice – it took me little time to engage her, and I mark the day white. Her extraordinary gifts soon became apparent; the actual work of publishing she took in her stride, and my extra-mural interests which were to grow with time never seemed to bother her. An exquisite woman with exquisite taste, a pillar of the edifice and later perhaps more of a crutch, she did everything without a murmur, though there was to be much of which she deeply disapproved. She combined all the virtues which I would have looked for in a much-loved sister, if I had had one, with the abilities of the Business Woman of the Year.

During 1948 David Ascoli came to see me at St Andrew's Hill. He was looking for a position, but added that if nothing was immediately available there was something else that he could do for a year. I liked him very much, and he went away while I set about thinking how I could fit him into the organization. I came up with the idea of a subsidiary list, to be called after our old home – the Idehurst Press – which would consist of specialized books of a nature as yet unspecified. When he came back a year later I offered him this vague brief which he accepted. So he joined Cassell's and became one of its most important figures in the ensuing decades. Born in India, he was the younger son of the head of Dunlop's rubber plantations in Malaysia and his mother, whom I was to meet often, lived to a great age in this country. He had had a hard war, early in which he suffered a personal tragedy which I feel left a deep scar.

He was a man of considerable charm, enormous enthusiasm and

great ability; his faults, for we all have them, were that he could be short-tempered and sometimes dictatorial. Circumstances were to make his period of running the Idehurst Press a short one.

In February the following year a notice appeared in *The Bookseller* which said that the British Command in Germany wanted six publishing directors to go over in pairs and advise them as to what should be done about the industry in the territory under their control. I sent my name in and was drawn first out of the hat with Mervyn Horder of Duckworth's, whom I had not met before. We had to go to Berlin.

Various problems there needed solution; among them was the future allocation of paper, of which, as in all European countries, there was a great shortage. An elderly and highly esteemed publisher, Rowohlt, had just pulled a fast one; he had applied for and been granted a large quantity of newsprint with which to start a paper, but instead used it to print novels in newspaper format which were familiarly known as 'Ro-ro-ro's'; while the British governor admired Rowohlt's ingenuity, he did not want anything similar to happen again. Consideration had to be given to the provision of a completely new issue of school books as those in use were riddled with National Socialism and warlike similes; in elementary arithmetic, for example, there were questions like: 'A Tiger Mark VI tank leaves Frankfurt at the same time as a Panther Mark V leaves Stuttgart; the former travels at 18 kph, the latter at 32 kph and the distance between the two cities is 110 kilometres – where do they meet?'

Mervyn and I got on very well together, and when we came back submitted a report which is now ancient history. It was a bitterly cold February; Big Ben froze, a feat which it repeated four decades later, people in London went to the theatre with rugs, while Bryen and I at St Andrew's Hill moved into one office for body-warmth and received a surprised Elliot Macrae of Dutton's (why he chose to come at such a time I do not know) both wearing woollen scarves, overcoats and flying boots – the last Bryen of course had, and I had bought a pair because they kept one's feet warm in a tank.

We travelled through the night by train; apart from the darkness we could see nothing as the blinds had to be drawn while we passed through the Soviet zone. When we arrived at Charlottenberg station we were met by a very smart Hussar officer who introduced himself as our Cicerone and drove us to our hotel. He said that we would of course want a bath and he would return at ten o'clock to see what we wished to do, since our first morning was free for sightseeing before we started work.

I was down first, talking to our guide, when I saw him look towards the stairs and wince. One of Mervyn's great assets is his wry, penetrating sense of humour, but I do not think that he would claim any great physical beauty. Coming down the stairs, he was sensibly dressed in a heavy overcoat with a vast muffler round his neck; his drawn hawk-like features with their sharp black eyes were encased in a Balaclava helmet on top of which perched a trilby hat. It was a remarkable sight.

What we wanted to see first was, of course, the Chancellery. I shall never forget Hitler's study, it was the most terrifying room I have ever been in: enormous, like the concourse of a railway station, and the walls, the floor and the ceiling were all of blood-red marble. Through a french window we walked a short way across the garden, a bare patch of churned earth, to the bunker. There several floors below ground were the rooms of the Führer and Eva Braun, plain grey concrete, as claustrophobic as a rat-trap. Then flight after flight of stairs, on each landing of which guards must have stood, until in daylight we could breathe fresh air again. It is all long gone now, demolished by the Soviets – in a way historically a pity, yet perhaps just as well so that no misguided neo-Nazi might be tempted to make a shrine of it.

Berlin was just one great pile of rubble then; there was no Wall yet and one could go where one pleased. The Tiergarten looked rather like the Somme in 1919, shell-holes almost overlapping and the remains of a few twisted tree trunks. Just 'our' side of the Brandenburgertor was – and is – a large memorial to the Soviet dead on which two soldiers stood motionless day and night. Beyond the Gate the other way stretched Unter den Linden which had already been rebuilt as a showpiece by Stalin in the heavy, unattractive style associated with him, now fortunately long frowned upon by Soviet architects. The Adlon Hotel was gone. The devastation appalled me – but years later I was to see worse.

Just after I got back from Germany Aubrey Gentry went to Australia and New Zealand. There was reorganization to be done to the company's premises, but to me his most important action was the appointment of a literary adviser from Melbourne University, and thus the first of the hopes which I had expressed to father during the war came true. But it was a hectic three months and took a terrible toll of Aubrey; not long after his return his health broke down and he suffered a severe stroke which paralysed his left side, and took a great deal out of him mentally. I have written some harsh things about him and I cannot retract them; I retain bitter memories of the frustration I had often felt – a blank wall too hard and high for me to climb. But I always respected his business ability, and I must say that for much of the time he was a kindly man and a good friend. He stayed on for the best part of a year on a part-time basis, but the fire had gone out of him. He retired in favour of his son, Bryen, who had come into the firm on his release from the Fleet Air Arm in February 1946. Bryen was just as able, and in addition possessed one gift which his father seldom displayed: the willingness, having weighed up the odds, to have a go. We became close friends and worked together in perfect amity at all times. But he too possessed the Gentry temper, rigidly controlled until once, years later, in difficult circumstances it slipped its leash.

Out of office – to his own surprise and that of many other people – Winston Churchill had decided to embark upon his *History of the Second World War*. The book rights he placed in the hands of Lord Camrose, while the foreign rights went to Emery Reeves, an interesting man. Reeves, born Imre Revész in Hungary, had during the thirties run an international news service, and Churchill had been one of his contributors. When war was approaching, Churchill urged him to settle in London and sponsored his naturalization papers. Reeves handled the world-wide rights admirably, and also frequently entertained their author at his house, La Pausa, outside Menton, to which I was also asked and witnessed Winston enjoying himself having his leg pulled by Reeves' beautiful Texan wife, Wendy.

Through father's close relations with them, I had come to know well the remarkable brothers, Lords Camrose and Kemsley. Although the latter was always extremely kind to me, I had a personal preference for the former. He was a large man, a cross between an elder statesman and Buddha, but there was a twinkle in his eyes and when he spoke, for he was a man of few words, a smile could wander across his rather stern features and be gone so quickly that one wondered if its existence had been a trick of light. From time to time he would summon me to his office at *The Daily Telegraph* to ask me questions about the state of the publishing industry in general. He sat behind a huge desk on which I never once saw a piece of paper; and I remember his personal assistant, a tall lean man, whose efficiency, I am sure, assisted admirably in keeping the desk in its immaculate condition. Sitting alone with this dynamo which worked so silently, I developed a love and respect which after many years remain an affectionate memory.

But on this occasion there was the specific matter of the War history which, following the author's promise, was to be offered first to us. There had been some informal talk about an advance of £20,000; Camrose came to the point quickly: 'Desmond, you will have to pay more; the advance is £25,000.'

Agreeing without demur, I went back to St Andrew's Hill to tell Aubrey Gentry, and it was then that I realized what an effect his stroke had had upon him. When he was in possession of his full powers there would have been a spirited discussion, possibly a bitter argument; but now he hugged his poor left arm with his other hand and said rather plaintively, 'Do you think it's worth it?' I said that of course it was, and the tremendous success of this great work was not only a triumph in itself, but a major factor in increasing our freedom: it joined our dictionaries as part of our sheet-anchor.

Later in the year Churchill delivered the first volume, *The Gathering Storm*. There can be little doubt that this is the best of the six volumes which make up that great work, and the reason is not far to seek: dealing largely with the events leading up to the outbreak of war, it is Churchill's views in his own inimitable prose. The subsequent volumes are to some extent the great man's fusion of the facts laid before him by his researchers, among them General Pownall, Commander Allan and Bill Deakin, although all are liberally laced with flashes of original felicity. The manner of his presentation of it to us was interesting. He had each volume set up at his own expense by the Chiswick Press in 14-point type leaded for easy reading, and galleys were pulled on extra wide paper to allow for his corrections and emendations in the margins.

I am told that he had upward of twenty revises before he was sufficiently satisfied to issue the text to all those with whom he was contracted. Seventy sets of galleys of normal width were then pulled and sent to all concerned – we, for instance, received two sets – and these were known as 'The Seventies'.

From my own experience of bibliography, the preparation, correction and issue of so many sets constitutes publication – the definition of 'to publish' which I have found in every dictionary I can lay my hands on says 'to issue'. I know that my view is not widely shared by bibliographers, but, what I consider all-important, it is upheld by Frederick Woods in his bibliography of Churchill. How many sets of The Seventies have survived no one knows; many were thrown away in the offices setting the type afresh in periodical and book form. I treasured one complete set for many years and finally gave it to the British Library. The author asked me several times if we could not use his type on which he had spent so much, but unfortunately it was too big for commercial use and I had to decline.

I took as much trouble as I could over the format. I asked Percy Smith, the then eminent elderly calligrapher, to design the lettering on the binding and the chapter initials, and Lynton Lamb, one of the best British lithographers, to do the end-papers. The text was to be 12-point Bembo, leaded; and the author approved the specimen page.

We set aside every shred of paper we could and in addition received a liberal allowance from the Moberly Pool (a reserve held during paper rationing to be released for worthy causes, presided over by a committee of six publishers). In addition stereo moulds of the type were taken and sent to Australia and New Zealand so that editions could be produced in those two countries. But the interest building up was enormous and I could see that we were going to be in trouble. If we went ahead as we were, we would not have enough copies to meet the advance orders on publication day and the trade would abuse us for our inefficiency; if we reduced the type size we would be departing from the format which the author had approved. After agonizing thought, I decided to reduce the type to 10-point, 2-point leaded – quite legible, if not ideal. This gave us 15,000 more copies and enabled us just to meet our subscription orders of 90,000. I did not think that I had heard the last of it, nor had I.

Not long after publication I was telephoned by Lord Camrose: would I be at *The Daily Telegraph* office at 6 p.m. on a certain day; our author would be there. I dreaded the meeting but my bacon was saved by the abolition of paper rationing forty-eight hours before the appointed date.

We met in a small office, not Camrose's usual one; he at the head of the table while Winston and I faced one another. The meeting was short and sweet. After a few introductory words from Camrose, Winston gently chided me for departing from the agreed specimen, adding that many of his friends to whom he had given the book had written to say that they would be happy to read it as soon as they could find a magnifying glass. I explained the reasons for my action, and the explosion which I had feared did not take place. After a few more well merited grumbles from across the table, I said, 'A second edition is required immediately. I will be happy to have the whole book reset in the originally agreed size.' Honour was satisfied and we all went home in good humour.

The only hiccup with the 'Seventies' was over the third volume which was due to be delivered at a time when there was a printing strike, and it brought about the sole occasion on which I had the effrontery to be rude to the great man. I was at my wits' end trying to make some sense out of the chaotic situation when my phone rang and the inimitable voice rumbled:

'Desmond, there are no printers.'

Harassed, I snapped, 'What do you expect me to do? I didn't start the strike.'

I was not reproved for my rudeness as I deserved to be; he just put the phone down. In fact, he had the proofs cyclostyled.

There was a good deal of ill-feeling in Britain, both among booksellers and members of the public, over the fact that each volume of our national hero's History appeared in the United States a considerable time before we could get our edition out; some did not hesitate to suggest that it was sheer inefficiency on the part of Cassell's. Actually there were several unavoidable factors, but however much and however often we pointed them out, no one believed us. In the first place the first print of the British edition was three times as large as that in the United States, and therefore took three times as long to machine; furthermore, the American maps were only in black and white while many of ours were in colour which took up a further length of machining time. But the most retarding factor was the correspondence which Churchill received from the work's serialization in *The Daily Telegraph* and *Life*. Every point raised in every letter which came in, however trivial, had to be checked and, if discovered to have any foundation, taken into account. We received as many as twenty-five lists of corrections and emendations to some volumes before the author would release them – for he considered the British text the one by which he wished his work to be remembered.

Whether it had anything to do with my narrow escape over the size of the type or not, I do not know, but previously I had always agreed with Ian Fleming's view that only God and the King should be called Sir (out of the services), until I found that admirals and generals were so addressing the great man and thought that I had better do likewise. As a result of the work involved, one of the joys of publishing the War History, and the long-contracted-for *History of the English-speaking Peoples* which was to follow, was having to go to see the author frequently – sometimes at Chartwell, but more often at Hyde Park Gate. Appointments at the latter were always in the morning, when he stayed in bed conducting his private affairs before getting up for the day's public business. He had a large bedtable across the bed in front of him on which were two bricks covered in green baize so that he could rest his elbows. Whatever the time, one was always offered a whisky and soda and a large cigar. I had a friendly bet with his lawyer as to which of us would be the earlier recipient of this customary hospitality. I rang him up one day in triumph: 'I'm back to 8 a.m.!' 'That's nothing,' he replied, 'I'm on 7.30.' 'Then all bets are off,' I said 'I can't go on.'

Unkind things have been said about Winston's alcoholic intake. He was one of those people who need a great deal of fluid, and I must say that I never saw him without a glass on his bedtable; I must also say that they were the weakest-looking drinks imaginable – water or soda, with a minute splash of whisky so that they should not taste of absolutely nothing.

In the late forties everyone in this country, those who had been in industry as much as those who had come out of the forces, was painfully aware of our condition: tired from the effort of six years – years which had been claustrophobic for those at home, nostalgic to those away. The camaraderie of wartime was wearing thin, food was even shorter and tempers frayed. Only a further effort to export everything exportable could save us; it was almost as bad as the situation in which we find ourselves today. Swim or sink: and looking over our arrangements to achieve the former rather than degenerate into the latter, I saw one great country in which I thought that we were doing lamentably badly – Canada. There was only one way of finding out what was or was not going on, and that was to see for myself.

But before I could set out on my exploration there was another crisis. Edwin Boyce was a very senior and experienced sales manager, a position which he already occupied when I entered the firm in 1930, and during the war there had been talk of inviting him to join the board. I liked him personally, and I think he liked me, for we remained friends until his death, in spite of what was about to happen. Swim or sink; a very disturbing rumour was reported to me, so disturbing that I asked him to come to my office immediately. Our conversation was short.

'In spite of the conditions in which this country finds itself, it has been reported to me that you have categorically stated that you will not fill any export order until all home orders have been completely met. Is that correct?'

'That is correct.'

'Then you are dismissed.'

There was no time to argue; there was too much to do to afford the luxury of constantly checking a senior executive's activities. Matters were not improved by my blunder in appointing someone who turned out not to be up to the job; having done which, I departed to Canada. But I must anticipate the end of the story. When I came back it became apparent that my unfortunate choice would have to go; father insisted on coming up from the country to carry out this unpleasant task himself. But we had the replacement to hand: all thoughts of the Idehurst Press were abandoned and David Ascoli was offered the job, which he accepted – provided it carried with it a seat on the board. This was agreed, and he immediately entered upon his highly successful career of sales director.

It is not central to my story to describe the theatre – although I have mentioned Robeson's *Othello* – but I feel I must record our seeing Arthur Miller's plays because their appearance was such a milestone in theatrical history. The first was *All My Sons* in 1947, a revival of which in 1988 was described by *The Times* critic as 'an epic explosion'. The manufacturer of aircraft parts who, during the war, supplies faulty goods for profit which results in the death of twenty-one pilots – one of whom is his own son – was played by George Colouris. Since I had seen him in so many films, I had always thought of Colouris as American, but I later discovered that, although he had been in Hollywood for twenty years, he was English; his performance was magnificent.

Miller's second and greatest play, *Death of a Salesman*, appeared in 1949. The part of Willie Loman, who 'fights to the last against unsympathetic employers, an unhelpful wife, self-centred sons and his own weakness in order to salvage something worth while from his life', was played by Paul Muni. We had seats in the centre of the front row without knowing that Muni would deliver his soliloquies on a little apron stage jutting out just above us; if I had leant forward, I could have touched his feet. Never before or since have I been so close to a great actor, so that the briefest almost imperceptible movement brings home the full tragedy of his words; a remarkable experience, a remarkable actor and a remarkable play.

Three years later, on the dot, Nicholas Monsarrat delivered the novel which he had promised; it was called *The Cruel Sea*. Reading it at once, I was so impressed that I ordered a first print of 60,000; but this was nothing compared with the avalanche which followed when it came out. I never permitted a cheap edition (except for a limited licence to Allan Lane for 500,000 Penguins) and the last time I looked at the figures some years later we alone had sold in hard cover at the original price 1,330,000 copies – which I believe is a record for English fiction.

20   Triumph and Trouble

The best way of finding out what I wanted to know in Canada seemed to be to fly out to the west coast and work my way back, getting off wherever the plane came down. I was told that I should take a train in order to appreciate the splendour of the Rockies, but I do not believe that anything could exceed their beauty from the air: the endless chain of snowy peaks, stretching from one horizon to the other; and there was a small addition: high on one mountain was a farmer ploughing a lonely furrow, breaking soil previously untouched by man; after all these years later I suppose that barren slope must now be verdant fields. Perhaps as we flew over, that was a cause for sadness because man was encroaching further on one more piece of the original environment, as he has set about destroying the world everywhere.

In Vancouver and British Columbia I ferreted out every bookshop and talked to the managers.

Calgary was my favourite town – a crisp, alive place with the best evening paper I have ever seen anywhere. At Lethbridge, where the golden wheat bending before the elements shimmers as far as the eye can see, I commented on the wind to an airport official who was most contemptuous; pointing to a large iron ball hanging inertly by a chain from a tall pole, he said, 'When that thing's out horizontal, that's a wind.' The excellence of the bookshops in Winnipeg surprised me, but after all it is an important university town.

In eastern Canada I discovered one feature which surprised me considerably: the flat refusal of anyone – be he bookseller, policeman or official of any kind – to speak French. If I asked a question in French it would be answered in English; a conversation begun in French would quickly be switched to English. I do not believe, though the thought must arise, that my French is so bad as to cause *Canadiens* to recoil from it in horror: after all, their own form of French is a stock joke on the variety stage of *La Belle France*. They seemed, on the contrary, deliberately to shun it, as though it were a forbidden tongue, as Catalan used to be in Spain. Today, I understand – for, alas, I have not been in French Canada for some time – the case is very much reversed and anyone not speaking French is shunned like some rather undesirable deaf mute.

I did what I should: in Quebec I stayed at the Frontenac, trod the

Heights of Abraham, and ate delicious food at bistros in the old town; I loved it all, but the hub of the wheel lay in Toronto.

What had I learnt? The outlets across the country were much more extensive than I had anticipated, for in addition to the many proprietary shops, there were excellent book departments in every branch of Eaton's and the Hudson Bay. The most disconcerting factor was the dreadful warping of the covers of British books. The reason was not far to seek: this country has a very damp climate, the boards are hydroscopic and, when exposed to the high temperature of Canadian central heating, dry out and warp. The only solution then was to use expensive millboard, but by now new materials may have solved that problem.

Some booksellers praised the service of British publishers and said that they got a book quicker from London than they did from New York, which was gratifying, though puzzling. If these booksellers had to get their books all the way from London, what were our Canadian representatives doing with their time?

Then, of course, I saw McClelland & Stewart. I did not particularly like George Stewart, but I must confess that I did not know him very well; whereas John McClelland I had known since 1930 and I both liked him and respected him. But when I asked them why they did not sell more British books, their answer was that they found it easier to sell American books, which was hardly music to my ears. I reached the conclusion that the only solution to our problem was to be handled by an organization in which the furtherance of British books was paramount; and it so happened that just such a body was about to open up – British Book Service, to be run by an experienced and formidable battleaxe, Ann Orford, with whom I was to get on extremely well.

I returned home and, after putting all my findings to the board, wrote to McClelland giving his firm notice. Soon afterwards he came to London, not just to see me, I am sure, but to visit all his other agencies. He asked me why I had not told him of my views while I was in Toronto. On the one hand, there is little point in telling someone that he is doing a lousy job if you feel convinced that there is no chance of improvement; and on the other, which is what I said to him, I was not a dictator and such a decision had to be made – and was made – by the whole board. I felt sorry for McClelland personally, but never regretted the move to British Book Service.

Going away for a summer holiday is hardly worthy of record unless something special happens, and perhaps 1949 deserves a few words. We went to Talloires, on the Lake of Annecy. Talloires is tiny, mainly composed of two memorable monuments: the famous restaurant, Père Bize, and the Hôtel de l'Abbaye in which we stayed – more recently notorious through the arrival there of Baby Doc and his entourage after their flight from Haiti. It was an ancient monastery, with thick walls, cloisters and great comfort. At one point the Meynells appeared; and Francis' son, Benedict, and I swam across the lake from Talloires, where Cézanne sat when he painted his famous picture (in the Courtauld) of our target on the other side: the Château de Doing. Our families accompanied us in a boat; Benedict waded ashore at the château, while I got cramp about twenty yards from shore and was towed – I could have made it in a crisis, but I thought honour had been satisfied.

Other guests in the hotel were Florence Eldridge and her daughter Penny; her husband, Frederick March, looked in but could not stay long as he was filming somewhere near by. Down in what were once, no doubt, the monks' wine cellars, there was what is now called a discothèque. Jiving was all the rage, and some of the locals, in their teens like Penny, would come in the evening and furiously exhaust themselves in their idea of the new dance. Mrs March exclaimed, 'Penny, what *are* they doing?' and Penny, baffled, replied, 'I don't know, Mommy, but it's awful cute.'

Of course when the time came to pay, I was short; but the proprietor, a charming man with whom we had become very friendly, said not to worry since he and his wife were coming to London for a holiday at the end of the season.

From my initial concern with Voltaire my interest in French literature had now broadened in all directions like the delta of the Danube, and from John Hayward's magnificent exhibition of English poetry at the National Book League in 1947 I had an idea: how about an exhibition of French books?

The period in Albemarle Street under the directorship of John Hadfield was the most exciting in the history of the N.B.L. John believed that the league should be one of the cultural centres of London and that its consequent prestige would bring it great power in the world of books, and he further believed that the exhibitions during those years were the league's greatest achievement – 'They were well attended, attracted much publicity and had significance from a literary standpoint.' But all aspects of the trade did not produce sufficient funds to support that way of life; they took the league too much for granted, until eventually it shrank from malnutrition. Of course it continues today and does much valuable work, but its targets are different from those of forty years ago, and in that bygone atmosphere I asked John Hadfield if he would like me to mount an exhibition to be entitled *A Thousand Years of French Books*, and he said, 'Yes' but banteringly bet me that I wouldn't make the thousand years; I swore I would and went to work (in the event the earliest exhibition was pages from a manuscript of the eighth century).

A few days after the decision to go ahead I ran into Gerry Hopkins, great nephew of Gerard Manley Hopkins, who was in the Oxford University Press and was one of the finest translators from French at that time. We knew one another well but met less often than I would have wished. He wanted to know what I was doing and when I told him, he asked me if I knew the French cultural counsellor, René Varin; as I did not, he said that this was essential and asked the two of us to lunch at the Garrick. So I met a man who became a most dear friend, a companion with whom I worked closely for many years to our mutual advantage.

René was a very big man with remarkable pale grey eyes, a heart of gold, a deep love for and encyclopaedic knowledge of our two countries. He came from Versailles, which remained his home throughout his life. He knew well the keeper and all the custodians of the great château, which he always referred to as his 'country cottage'. He was in England at the time of the fall of France and Winston Churchill entrusted him with a delicate mission: Britain having supplied the French with two units of the latest radar, these were now in the Vichy half and it was imperative that they should be destroyed. The mission was accomplished and René was appointed C.B.E. But, as I had discovered in connection with the crossing of the Rhine five years earlier, the authorities can make the most elaborate arrangements for getting someone to his destination, but nothing more: after that he is on his own. There was no way that René, an undisguisable figure, could get out again; and, since he had been a pilot in the first war, he found himself air adviser to Marshal Pétain. He had a high old time feeding the aged marshal with depressing information which stressed the increasing superiority of the R.A.F. over the Luftwaffe.

Varin was by far the most active of the cultural counsellors whom I have known since I had the honour of becoming on friendly terms with the French embassy through the exhibition which I was about to organize. From now on we met constantly: at our homes, at his office and in restaurants; he was never idle, always seeking, probing.

But I do not think that there can be any question about our most successful coup. On the telephone one day René said, 'Barbara Hutton has the great carpet from Marie Antoinette's drawing-room; what should I do about it?'

I said, 'Leave it to me.'

By one of those chances almost as rare as winning the pools, I knew Barbara Hutton's favourite aunt, an acquaintance of Margaret's parents, who lived just down the road from them in Ventnor, New Jersey. In the past I had spent some time with her, making myself as agreeable as I could, because she was a dear old lady and seemed lonely. Now I wrote to her, asking if she could mention this to her niece. The enormous carpet was lying rolled up in the vaults of Coutts' Bank in Paris; if it were given to the château, there would be some suitable recognition. Seven months and various letters passed until finally I was able to ring up René: 'You remember that carpet you wanted.'

'What carpet? Oh, yes, I remember.'

'It's yours.'

How many millions of visitors must have filed by it now, filling to perfection the large room for which it was designed – one of the most beautiful French carpets ever made.

As long as he was here (and after) we were very close, and I think I once aptly described him. Two years after this I put together and translated most of Voltaire's dicta about this country. Published by The Folio Society, it was called *Voltaire's England* and I dedicated it to René, 'whose love of England and sardonic appreciation of her crochets and foibles has much in common with these pages by his illustrious compatriot'.

We quickly reached agreement on the exhibition. I would make up my mind what I wanted to show and would raise all the exhibits I could from British sources; where I was stuck René would see that help was forthcoming from France. As a first step he introduced me to Julien Cain, who was not only head of the Bibliothèque Nationale but inspector general of the libraries of France. This was a success and very important, since the fact that he took to me was, I am sure, responsible for the support and harmony which marked my relations with the heads of departments in Paris.

Everyone was extraordinarily kind and two of the people whom I badgered invited me to their homes so that I could choose what I wanted: the Earls of Crawford and Leicester. At Balcarres I was given the run of the library and certain loans were agreed. They were small books and Lord Crawford said that he would deliver them to Devonshire Place next time he came to London.

I went to Holkham alone and it was a memorable weekend. The other guests were Lord Leicester's brother-in-law and W.O. Hassall, his part-time librarian who worked at the Bodleian. With permission all Saturday and Sunday I went through the thousands and thousands of books, quite apart from the famous treasures assembled in what might be called the 'official' library; for example, a very rare edition of Perrault's fairy tales I found in one of the loos. After supper on Sunday we settled down in a comfortable warm room, again once the staff quarters, and Lord Leicester said, 'You and Hassall sit the other end and make up a list of what you want. We'll sit by the fire.'

Hassall and I got down to work, and suddenly looked at one another, slightly startled by a fragment of conversation which wafted across to us.

The brother-in-law said, 'I see you've brought down the fishing book,' to which the musically-devoted Earl replied, 'Yes, I thought I'd keep it handy. Trouble is there's nothing to read in this house.'

Like a detective story, one clue led to another; how, for instance, did I discover that M. Georges Weibel in France possessed the only manuscript pages of the Goncourts' Journals not under lock and key in the Bibliothèque Nationale?

My most exciting discovery was pure chance. I knew that there were French illuminated manuscripts in the library of Dulwich College, so I went to have a look; there was a handful but, as the librarian agreed, they were not particularly important, nor in good condition. Knowing the broad nature of my search, the librarian helpfully suggested that I should see Eric Parsley, the French master, who had some interesting things. I went to see Mr Parsley, who turned out to be a gentle soul, not unlike the actor Bob Hoskins to look at. Yes, he said, he had one book which he felt would interest me for my purpose.

There used to be in Stockwell, south of the Thames, a dealer in waste paper named Salkeld, who was also an antiquarian bookseller; strange things would turn up in the masses of paper which passed through his hands, and I had profitably called upon him several times. He was in the habit of sending notes to the school, which was not very far away, when he had anything which he thought might interest Parsley.

When during the war Holland House caught fire – not through enemy action – and the famous library was damaged, Lord Ilchester was so disgusted that he ordered all books even slightly affected by fire or water to be disposed of. Sacks full appeared at Hodgson's in Chancery Lane and a number of them were bought by Salkeld, who sent a note to Parsley one day to say that he had something. The note was brought to the master in class and he consulted his pupils: should he go in the mid-morning break or would it keep till afternoon? 'Oh, sir, do go in the break,' they all cried, and he did, returning in triumph with his prize – slightly water-stained at the edges – for which he paid 7s 6d. (36p).

Anyone interested knows that Madame de Maintenon, the morganatic second wife of Louis XIV, founded her school for girls at Saint-Cyr in 1694, and persuaded Jean Racine, who was so disgusted by the reception of his magnificent *Phèdre* that he had given up work for twelve years, to write two plays on sacred subjects for her girls to perform; the first was *Esther* and the second *Athalie*. Eric Parsley's loot was a first edition of *Athalie*, 1696, with the bookplate of Saint-Cyr and inscribed on the title page by Racine to Madame de Maintenon. Of course I arranged to borrow it.

I shall complete the story. After the exhibition was over and I returned the book to its owner, I asked him what was going to happen to this extraordinary treasure, and he said that he really didn't know because none of his family was in the least interested in anything French. He would, I think, have sold it to me, but for once my acquisitive cupidity was subdued, for my conscience told me where the book really belonged.

I said to René, 'What would you do if Eric Parsley were to give his copy of *Athalie* to Versailles?'

'He would be invited to France, shown privately over the whole of the château and Versailles, and royally entertained' was the reply.

Eric Parsley liked the idea, so he was king of Versailles for a day; and his *Athalie* lies in a glass case in Madame de Maintenon's drawing-room, the same room in which the girls rehearsed the play in the king's presence three centuries ago.

During the organizing of the exhibition I had to visit Paris frequently, and was able to stay at the hotel which before the war Stefan Zweig had urged me to try: the Hôtel Beaujolais, which had the added advantage of being five minutes walk from the Bibliothèque Nationale. The hotel, which, alas, no longer exists, was in the Palais Royal; it was very small and had no restaurant, though, if one could afford it, there was the Grand Vefour downstairs on the corner. I used to telephone the charming couple who ran it well ahead of time to ask for a room on the first floor, since all these retained their painted ceilings and *boiserie* from the *Régence*. Jean Cocteau, Jean Marais and Colette all lived just to the left, and the last of these once said, 'Am I not lucky to have this exquisite view of the gardens of the Palais Royal ... to watch and to hear the children and the birds ... to see the day appear each morning.' I was lucky too.

Another wonderful surprise came from François Porché, Keeper of Manuscripts at the Bibliothèque Nationale. I had been able to bring together an exciting collection of illuminated manuscripts from British sources, but Porché – a delightful, puckish man – said that he wanted to add to it. When I asked him what he would send, he put his finger beside his nose and replied, 'I won't tell you.' I said that I would have to know soon because I had to write the catalogue entries and send copy to the printers; seeing my point, he stated that he proposed to send the *Psalter* of Saint Louis and *The Small Hours* of the Duc de Berry, two of the finest manuscripts in the history of French illumination. I was staggered, and indeed later the French press made a fuss that these two treasures, which had never before been allowed outside the library, should go abroad.

There was no Rabelais or Villon in this country, or Louise de Labé, the greatest of France's three great women poets; the Bibliothèque Nationale filled all the gaps and I lacked for nothing. Eventually the cases of treasure were loaded on to a security van and escorted by a posse of motor-cycle policemen to the Dunkirk train, where they were put into a compartment with Jacques Guignard, the Keeper of Printed Books, and the door locked. The point about the Dunkirk train was, of course, that the same rolling stock crosses the Channel, so that the compartment was not unlocked until it reached Victoria Station, where the contents were escorted once again by the police, to Albemarle Street.

The exhibition was opened on 30 September by Duff Cooper, the British Ambassador in Paris. It had a good press of which I remember best a long article in the still lamented *News Chronicle*, by Edward Penning-Rowsell, now a well known wine expert. I took him round and at the end he asked me for some reason what I had done in the war, so I told him. His laudatory article the next morning stated, 'I was shown round by ex-Commando Major ... ' No sooner was I in my office than my telephone started ringing, and I remember the unmistakable voice of Scottie remarking, 'You've been busy since I saw you last.' I rang up Penning-Rowsell in a fury and he apologized, explaining that his copy had been altered by the night editor who did not think that the Argylls were glamorous enough. Today, of course, the regiment is fashionable; but what an example of how much faith one can put in press reports!

Also the exhibition was the occasion of the first visit by the royal family to the Book League. The Queen expressed a wish to see it and brought with her Princess Margaret, then an enchanting eighteen. René Varin showed the Queen round and I followed with the Princess. On the following day Queen Mary decided to come. While I was waiting for her arrival, John Hadfield said, 'You know her reputation for minutiae; you'd better have a catalogue with you.' I thought I knew all about every exhibit, but I took his advice. I felt sure that the Queen Mother would ask me a question, and it came when we were looking at an enchanting little eighteenth-century binding which was a late entry, not in the catalogue: 'Whose arms are those?' My answer was positive but unsatisfactory: 'Ma'am, no one knows – neither I nor the owners of the book, the Bibliothèque Nationale.'

As we neared the end of the exhibition, John Hadfield remarked to me, 'I suppose you have got an export licence for sending the exhibits back to France?' I was flabbergasted; it had not occurred to me that a licence would be required for returning French national property, but I immediately slapped an application in to the Board of Trade and it was refused; since the compartment in which they came had been locked at the Gare du Nord and unlocked at Victoria, the books had not passed through Customs and it was claimed that there was no evidence of entry. The impasse was brought to an end by Duff Cooper who sent a message to the Board of Trade, saying that unless they stopped being silly there was a strong possibility of diplomatic relations being broken off between France and Great Britain. The treasures went home safely.

Eighteen months later Julian Cain sent me a wonderful present; he had had a copy of the catalogue bound in red morocco by the bindery of the Bibliothèque Nationale, using on the spine the brasses of Louis XV; it is a superb binding – and in his covering letter he said that he was pleased to learn that my work had been noticed: I was to be made *Chevalier de la Légion d'Honneur*. When the day for the investiture came, Margaret and mother came to see me make a fool of myself at the embassy. In a high state of nerves, when I walked forward to have the lovely decoration pinned on me, I of course forgot that one is kissed on both cheeks, and as I started to walk backwards I had to be brusquely seized by René Massigli before I retreated beyond his reach.

Another of the lenders to the exhibition had been Paul Hirsch, who lived with his dynamo of a wife, Olga, in Cambridge. They were very hospitable and always welcomed their host of friends – together until Paul's death in 1951 and Olga for years thereafter until her own death. Both of them were great collectors: his subject was mainly the history and bibliography of music, while she had the most remarkable assemblage of pattern papers ever seen. At his home in Frankfurt Paul had opened his library to students as early as 1909, and it remained available until their departure from Germany. As a partner in the large company of iron merchants which bore his name, as well as being on the board of many other concerns, he had to travel a great deal, and since, being Jewish, after 1933 they were constantly at risk, he kept to a strict timetable while he was abroad, so that Olga at home would always know where he was. It was agreed between them that if the situation became critical Olga would send him a cable in simple code – such as 'Mary had a little lamb' – which meant that he was under no circumstances to return to Germany but proceed to England.

The cable was sent in 1936, and Olga began clearing up. At that time, however brutal they might be to those too lowly to defend themselves, the Nazis were positively respectful to the rich and powerful, allowing them to remove with them all their personal possessions – in their eyes good riddance to bad rubbish. A Nazi official lived in the Hirschs' house to supervise Olga's packing and put his official seal on every case as it was filled and closed. He was kept liberally supplied with liquid refreshment as with a benevolent eye he watched everything, including the kitchen stove, done up. But even he balked at a narrow painting about a foot high and three feet long, and Olga was outraged, insisting that she must have the picture – the portraits were those of her ancestors. Dubiously the official agreed, and the painting eventually hung in the Hirschs' dining-room at Cambridge. It was, in fact, Goya's studies from life of all the Spanish royal family in preparation for his great painting of them which is in the Prado.

After the French exhibition I paid the first of several visits to the Indian sub-continent – with all its magic and pathos. Independence and partition had come and gone, and although we were represented in India most ably by Allied Publishers, an Indian firm, Pakistan was a blank. Two things happened within a few months of one another. An extremely pleasant Englishman named Davies called upon me and said that he had set up an import business in Karachi and, if we had not made other arrangements, would like to represent us; this we quickly fixed up. And soon thereafter I found myself in touch with the Pakistan Cultural Attaché, Tony Latif, a Kingsman, though somewhat younger than I. We liked one another and he urged me to visit his country, which I decided I should do.

I flew to Karachi, which was then the capital, where Latif had arranged for me to be put up in a government compound, somewhat sparse but perfectly comfortable, where a kind elderly bearer looked after me. Davies was doing all right. Outside business his passion was racing, and he took me round his stables; he had about a dozen horses in training, all immaculate and each with its syce who looked after it with pride and joy. There is little to say of Karachi, a large and sprawling port, but I fell completely in love with my next stop: Lahore, a superb and graceful town which remains my favourite in the sub-continent. As Latif had advised, I had written ahead to Faletti's Hotel booking a room, keeping a copy of my letter, because, he said, they were quite likely bluntly to say that they had never received it. But they had (not so the next time – lightning never strikes twice) and I was given a room with a log fire blazing, for Lahore can be chilly.

I love the palace of Jahangir, as indeed I love all Mogul architecture, but there is about that particular place a lightness which in some ways brings to my mind the two hundred years later Zwinger at Dresden. I like the thought of the emperor, on the many sunny days, in his bath in one corner of the huge precinct in which he received petitioners, the hot tap brass, the cold of lead, so far in advance of his Elizabethan contemporaries in far-away England. What more beautiful than the domed ceilings of the harem – black honeycombs, symbolizing to the Muslims the void between the atoms, inlaid with small gold stars which, when a taper is lit, shimmer and gleam like the floor of heaven.

After a short stop in Rawalpindi I arrived in Peshawar, my first call being upon the British DHC: he was away but his young stand-in was pleasant and chatty. 'I don't know what you are doing here,' he said, 'but please don't try and drive up into Waziristan; the natives are not friendly. Several times the army has sent up loudspeakers telling them it's all right, the British have gone and they are now free and independent, but each broadcast is greeted by a volley of rifle fire, and now patrols can only go up into the hills in Bren carriers.'

I had no desire to go into Waziristan, but I did want to go up the Khyber Pass to the north-west frontier; I hired a car and driver and set off. No one who has any respect for the British army can fail to be moved by the huge carvings on the limestone cliffs of the badges of every regiment which had served on the frontier. At the sight of a white man in a car an old turbaned stone-breaker beside the road sprang to his feet and saluted. The little villages a maze of houses all enclosed by forbidding mud brick walls; every man going about his business in the fields had slung over his shoulder a Lee-Enfield rifle 'acquired' from the British army; and every woman 'beautiful with the assurance of princesses' walking slowly along the road with a water pot on her head had perfect Greek features – for they are the descendants of Alexander's generals who ended their days here. At the frontier I was gazing past the two Afghan guards at the road winding through the mountains towards Kabul, when a very smart Pakistani sergeant turned out the guard and saluted; I felt rather embarrassed – I had no hat, so I could not salute back, a slight bow and 'Thank you' was all I could manage. It was only when we started again downhill that a horrible truth was revealed: the taxi had virtually no brakes. Thank God there was nothing coming the other way as we rocketed down to Peshawar and I stepped out, safe but shaken.

And so south and across the border to Bombay to meet P.C. Manektala, the eldest of the three brothers who then ran Allied Publishers so ably, the other two having their offices in Delhi and Calcutta. Manektala was an enchanting man, as charming as he was able. The day on which I called for the first time was a shocker – the temperature was in the high nineties, which was fine, but the humidity made it like the steam room of a Turkish bath. I like heat, but this dampness was a bit much and I said that I was suffering; 'You're suffering,' he retorted, 'How about me? I come from Kashmir.'

In Old Delhi the Cecil has gone now; it was a comfortable, solid hotel with a wonderful garden, but I could not see it surviving after the two elderly English ladies who owned it died. Now I am sure that it has been replaced by a glass and concrete box similar to all the other glass and concrete boxes from Spitzbergen to Tierra del Fuego. Few people would go to Delhi for the first time without driving south through the swirls of red dust to Agra for the Taj Mahal – 'accepted by some as the aesthetic epitome of civilization, by others as a simple story of a Mogul's love for his wife who, in 1630, died in childbirth.' Either way, it is a wonder of the world which commands silence. Perhaps the most moving view, though not the most majestic, is from the window in the Jasmine Tower the other side of the Jumna whence Shah Jehan, imprisoned by Aurengzeb his son, gazed at the shimmering tomb in which he would one day join his wife.

Calcutta struck me as a place with little to recommend it; I know that the cows which roam the streets are sacred, but they are also dirty, insanitary and a nuisance. But I cherish the memory of a schools inspector who had come in to Allied Publishers especially because he heard that I was going to be there. A tall man, speaking with a voice of quiet dignity, he said that our elementary readers were very good and much used by the schools in his area, but he did wonder if, perhaps, when we were reprinting we could reconsider some of the text. For example, he recently inspected a school where the Cassell readers were in use: 'Now, children,' he had asked, 'What is your favourite bird?' 'The robin,' they all piped with one voice.

There are no robins in India.

But Calcutta was paradise compared with my next destination: East Bengal, now Bangladesh. Davies in Karachi did not extend his operations to the eastern part of Pakistan, and, since we were not represented there at all, I thought I ought to look into it. Unable to find out anything about accommodation in Dacca, I had written to the British Council library there for advice and they had replied that as there was no hotel in the city in which they would like to see me dead, they had arranged for me to be the guest of the Deputy High Commissioner. (Today I am sure there are ample hotels, including a Sheraton or a Hilton or both.) My host and hostess were most interesting and hospitable. Previously he had been a financial or political adviser to one of the Maharajas, and his wife never ceased to lament what she regarded as a considerable worsening of their fortunes; she did not like Dacca, and neither did I. When I remarked upon the large number of elderly men on the plane from Calcutta, rather seedy with not too clean turbans and looking as if they could hardly afford the fare, the DHC said, 'Don't you believe it; they are all smugglers and very well off indeed.'

Living in great comfort, I seem to remember a warning from my host to keep my eye open for snakes crawling up the bathroom waste-pipe. It reminded me of a story about the great Durbar of 1911 which I was told by Wynford Vaughan Thomas, whom I used to bump into at irregular intervals during the war and always found hilarious. It appears that in their Imperial Majesties' progress round the vast country, there was no way to avoid their staying at one Residence which had no sanitation. The bathroom to be used by the royal visitors was hastily fitted up with all the necessary mechanical arrangements, including a cistern with its conjoint chain. How it worked was that when the plug was pulled a small flag sprang up on the roof above, whereupon a patient bearer sitting beside it poured a bucket of water down the pipe.

After a long discussion at the British Council library I was not sufficiently excited to start an agency in East Bengal, and flew back to

Karachi. On my last night there, Tony Latif and his German wife took me to their favourite restaurant for dinner, a little upstairs room on a narrow street where the food was superb. I have never been able to find anywhere else the sweet we had to end that lovely meal; it was called 'The Shah's Delight' and consisted of a wafer of beaten silver wrapped round a special nougat, so that the flat taste of the metal offset the sweetness it enclosed. Never to see him again, I remember what he said that night: 'We have too few capable civil servants in this country; those of us who do a decent job are working ourselves to death. I shall not live long.' He died, worn out, at forty.

My own contribution that year was the only long book that I had written to date, although I had done a good deal of translation. When General MacMillan became colonel of the Argylls he decided that he would have a volume published about every battalion active during the second war, and asked me if I would undertake the 5th (91st). I jumped at the chance, which I regarded as much an honour as an order. It took a long time and involved much delving through reports filed in the War Office, as well as choosing photographs from among the twenty-seven thousand of north-west Europe in the Imperial War Museum. Great help came from two of my friends; it turned out that Tom Geddes had kept a diary and Brian Brown had carried a camera – both activities contrary to orders, but both extremely welcome when they generously put their material at my disposal. Thomas Nelson published the whole series extremely well, and I am happy to say that my volume soon went out of print.

We also published Margaret's book on *Victorian Jewellery*, which was the first major work on the subject and remains a standard source book. Years before the war she had become interested in what was then an almost totally neglected subject, and with her usual thoroughness had gone into it deeply as well as acquiring a considerable quantity of exquisite jewellery herself. She said that I drove her into it; if I did, I knew that I was on to a good thing. She made a superb book, both in text and illustrations, which sold edition after edition for many years as the subject came into fashion. Now prices for good pieces have risen sky high, and fresh experts have applied their talents to the same subject; but she was the first – and in my not unprejudiced opinion, still the best.

Meanwhile I had decided to combine business with pleasure by producing a *History of Golf in Britain*, which was finally to appear in the autumn of 1951; I chose the contributors myself. I asked Sir Guy Campbell to write the essay on the early history of the game and the development of equipment. Henry Cotton wrote on the style and principles of the swing – and one of the stupider omissions of my life is that in the years when we used to meet I never asked if he had time to give me a game. The story of golf in our lifetime was covered in three chapters by the three best writers in the business. Bernard Darwin produced the first, on the period before the First World War; I had met him earlier because in the thirties we published a book by him on John Gully, the prize-fighter. The next, the period between the wars, was written by Leonard Crawley, whose work I liked as straightforward without any pretensions – although as a golf correspondent it was slanderously said of him that he never stirred out of the club house bar and got all his information from others who had walked round. I thought that his article was good, though I took issue with him over the description of his matches in the Walker Cup, and persuaded him that it was less pretensiously assuming to write of himself in the first person than to refer to 'Crawley' doing this or that – there seems to me to be a great difference between an essay under one's one name and an anonymous article such as that in *The Times* in which their most famous golf correspondent, describing an incident in the Worplesdon foursomes, wrote 'Mr Darwin then retired behind a bush to kick himself.'

The third, the modern scene, was entrusted to Henry Longhurst, the felicity of whose style made him the only writer on golf who can be thought of as in the same class as Darwin. I got to know him well and admired him, for, though he had certain peculiarities, he had above all a God-given gift of humanity. We were later to publish his *Spice of Life* and *My Life and Soft Times*.

While the book was in preparation I went to St Andrews to see Guy Campbell, and we played the Eden course; he had a lovely swing and had been runner-up in the Amateur Championship the year I was born. Sitting in the Big Room afterwards I was about to suffer one of the most embarrassing moments of my life.

'You know,' he said, 'you ought to be a member of this club.'

Passionately fond of golf as I was, I hardly aspired to membership of the Royal and Ancient; I had never given it a thought and would not have known how to go about it if I had.

Guy went on, 'There's the late colonel of your regiment over there; he will propose you and I will second you.'

With that he went across to General Gervase Thorpe who was writing a letter, and there ensued a quiet conversation which I gathered was going well because there was a certain amount of nodding.

Major General Thorpe was old and he was deaf, but he was kind. He started to fill out the form and suddenly bellowed 'Desmond, which battalion did you command?'

'I didn't, General,' I bellowed back. Every newspaper from *The Times* to the *Daily Worker*, every periodical from *Country Life* to *Punch* was lowered to see who was creating such an unseemly disturbance. My heart sank, but it need not have done. Owing to the gap created by the war years there was hardly any waiting list and to my pride and joy I was elected comparatively quickly.

In the same year *The Little Princesses* by Marion Crawford was offered to me. There was a terrible hullabaloo over the book; it was said that the author had broken her undertaking not to write or say anything when she had entered royal service to look after the two children. It was pretty mild stuff when we consider the appalling invasion of privacy and harassment with which every member of the royal family is persecuted

292   *Fellows in Foolscap*

today, but twenty years ago its production gave great offence to some people, and was remembered still with distaste on the author's death in 1988. My view, right or wrong, was that since it had been written someone was certain to publish the book anyway, and not care how much offence it gave. That being the case, I could not see why we should not do it, *provided* that it was submitted first to the Palace, rather than let it fall into the hands of certain publishers I could think of who would have no such scruples. In fact, however great the official disapproval, only two small cuts were made – one of which I was sorry to see made because it was extremely funny; but I do not think that my publishing the book endeared me in some quarters which take note of such things.

I think that I endeared myself even less by publishing in the following year the memoirs of the Duke of Windsor: *A King's Story*. I have recorded earlier that at the time of the abdication I was very much a 'King's man', deeply distrusting Stanley Baldwin, so that it was of more than usual interest to me to have the opportunity of meeting my idol of fifteen years before. Arrangements were made with Sir George Allen, the Duke's solicitor, who, I think, approached me in the first instance; the rights were not bandied about. The text was written by an American journalist called Murphy, with of course the Duke's fullest co-operation, and on the whole he made a pretty good job of it, except in minor details. There was a woman concerned with the serialization rights with whom I used to go over each chapter as we received it; occasionally we shook our heads over some things which the American did not know and the Duke did not notice. There was a moving description of the train bearing the coffin of the late King arriving at Charing Cross Station, and our minds boggled at the thought of the complicated traffic arrangements which would have had to be made to get a train from Sandringham to approach London from the south. The train came in, of course, to King's Cross.

Much, too much, has been written about some aspects of the character of Edward VIII and whether he would have been a good king if what happened had not happened, but no one has cast a shadow upon his personal charm as a man. Thirteen years his junior and an ardent admirer, I was captivated when he received me in London and at his house in Paris near the Arc de Triomphe. He took great interest in every detail of the book and I was careful to show it to him at every stage. Knowing that he loved golf, when I rang up his secretary to say that I was flying to Paris with the binding case, I asked if I should bring my clubs with me; the answer was yes, because it was not easy for the Duke to find people to play with. I flew over in the morning, the Duke liked the binding case and said that he thought the Duchess would wish to see it. A footman took it upstairs and brought it back with her approval; but I never saw her – I do not think that I was an important enough visitor for her to leave her room.

We motored out to Saint Cloud for lunch; having flown from London, I was hungry, nevertheless I felt embarrassed tucking into a steak, cheese and wine, while my host touched only raspberries, yoghurt and Perrier water. And so to the first tee; we played level, having the same handicap at that time, 8, and the Duke was a tough nut off his handicap. But there is one thing no one can teach – putting; he was not at his best on the green, and I knew it. After some holes he had a six-foot putt for a half; he looked at me, and I looked at the sky. He measured it with his putter and looked at me again, but I still looked at the sky. Golf is a great leveller, and I did not see why I should concede to my illustrious host a putt which I would not concede to anyone else in a tight game. He missed it.

At the annual dinner of the Book Trade Representatives' Association it is customary for the president to have as his guest of honour a distinguished author from the list of the firm for which he works. In the following year the president was our West End representative, Ken Smith, who asked me if I thought that the Duke of Windsor would come; I said that I had no idea, but that I would ask him. The Duke accepted, but fate intervened; King George VI died, the Court went into mourning, during which there was no question of a member of the family appearing in public. The speech which the Duke had intended to make was read for him by Max Aitken. But later, as some recompense, he came to a private luncheon which Ken Smith gave. He seemed to enjoy the atmosphere of respectful affection which filled the room; and at the end, when he left, he paused at the door and looked back at us with a gentle, almost sad smile; it was adieu.

I have mentioned how pleased Julien Cain had been with *A Thousand Years of French Books* and its success, so much so that he proposed that there should be a return match in the Galerie Mazarine at the Bibliothèque Nationale. I was all right on French books, but I did not consider myself competent to organize a similar exhibition of English literature; I said that I would like to be organizing secretary, and a powerful committee was formed. It included Frank Francis, Keeper of Printed Books and later Director of the British Museum, as chairman; A.J. Collins, Keeper of Manuscripts; Howard Nixon, Assistant Keeper in charge of bindings; Percy Muir, President of the International Antiquarian Booksellers; and John Hayward. All except Collins were people whom I knew well. In addition there was Harvey Wood, head of the British Council in Paris with altogether six other representatives, including Enid McLeod, a remarkable and distinguished figure who was to become the first woman to hold a senior British Council post overseas. Also there was a picture committee headed by C.K. Adams, Director of the National Portrait Gallery.

The exhibition was to open in 1951, so that we had two years in which to prepare it. It was quickly agreed that T.S. Eliot should be asked to open it, and he accepted. That was about the only thing that was settled quickly; the committee met often and spent the whole of the first year wrangling over what authors should be represented; the second year passed choosing the exhibits and writing the catalogue, which was my job.

The chief wrangle was over Charles Morgan, whose reputation has always stood higher in France than in his own country. In 1940 he had written an 'Ode to France' and given the manuscript to the Bibliothèque Nationale which, not unreasonably, they wanted to show. The consensus of the committee's opinion was that Morgan did not merit a place, though Frank Francis from the chair said that if the French were so keen his inclusion could really do no harm. But Frank had reckoned without John Hayward, with whom at that time T.S. Eliot lived in Chelsea. John had innumerable connections and his help was invaluable, but – partly because he was by nature acerbic and partly because of his physical handicap – there were times when he could be plain bloody-minded. His rejoinder to Frank's reasonable attitude was categorical: 'If Charles Morgan is included, my lodger will not open the exhibition.'

Morgan was not included; the French were quite mystified and not a little hurt.

It turned out to be a remarkable exhibition, partly because being under the auspices of the British Council, which was highly regarded, we were granted loans from sources which might not otherwise have been available – such as the Bodleian. It got off to a flying start with the superb *Benedictional of Saint Aethelwold*, then at Chatsworth, now in the British Library, and gleaming in the centre case at the Anglo-Saxon Exhibition there in 1983 – a jewel of the school of scribes and illuminators at Winchester where Saint Aethelwold was Bishop. It was supported by a galaxy of beautiful illuminated manuscripts. There were first editions of every work of prime importance, but autograph manuscripts have always been of particular interest to me, and here I think that we were most fortunate. The earliest was a fragment of Hakluyt's *Principall Navigations*, but the procession really got under way with Jonson and Bacon; there were no poetical manuscripts of Donne or Herrick because at that time none was known, though some have come to light since. The greatest riches were from the Romantic period onward.

Quite different, and more moving than all the morocco and gilt, was the first exhibit in the section devoted to bindings: a seventh-century gospel bound at the time and, according to a thirteenth-century inscription, found in the tomb of Saint Cuthbert when it was opened in 1104.

While the Paris exhibition was taking shape Francis Meynell and I were asked to select the hundred finest books in print, to be shown at the great festival later in the year. As a pre-run they were exhibited at the National Book League in Albemarle Street, and the display was to be declared open by Princess Marina, Duchess of Kent. On the day I took the chair, with the Princess on my right and Francis on my left. The Duchess of Kent, as everyone will remember, was perfection: lovely to look at and always dressed impeccably. Francis made a speech about the exhibition and then, thanking her for coming to open it, added, 'Never have I seen anyone look so beautiful while doing so.' Her head snapped round as he said that, but when she looked at him and realized that he was in deadly earnest, she gave an adorable, almost shy smile.

At the same time my private life fell into grievous disarray. It is easy to blame everything on the war, but the fact is that the separation inflicted upon so many families throughout the country played havoc with many marriages. First while Margaret was in the United States and then after her return we had great expectations; perhaps we expected too much. Perhaps the bond between us which for a long time had been so strong had through circumstances become weaker, and vulnerable to the unforeseen.

Although I had switched Elizabeth from being my secretary to editorial, I still saw a great deal of her, for she was still on the same floor because our quarters at St Andrew's Hill were so cramped that there was nowhere else for her to go. As I had expected, she was a very good editor.

From our daily contact I realized that she was nursing a secret unhappiness and set about finding out what it was; eventually I discovered the answer, but in the course of exorcizing it we fell in love.

Robert Graves once wrote, 'Being in love with two women used to be the most troublesome of my inconsistencies.' It is a dilemma and the more one thinks about it the more insoluble it becomes. I told Margaret who said gently, 'You poor thing.' In a whirlpool of indecision I said to Elizabeth that I could not leave my wife and son, whereupon she made up her mind that she had no desire to stay in England. I rang Larry Audrain, a friendly Canadian who ran the British Book Centre which Brian Batsford had started in New York, and asked him if he had a vacancy; he had.

But my feelings for Elizabeth were deeper than perhaps I realized and were not so easily put aside. A detailed description of ensuing events would be as tedious as it would be impertinent: it is sufficient to say that an impasse developed in the face of which I ran away. Leaving notes for father and Bryen Gentry, I packed a trunk and left for New York – it seemed for good.

Elizabeth had found Larry Audrain a kind and amusing employer, but she moved on to a better job at the British Information Office. She lived in an apartment on the West Side which belonged to some Canadians who, when I appeared, would soon be returning, so we were likely before long to have no home and little money.

To solve the first of our problems I turned to Thayer Hobson who since the war had rapidly become such a close friend; he was a much-married man and sympathetic to such problems. In no time we were installed in the town apartment of some friends of his who were not coming back until the autumn.

It was a sweltering hot summer. I was given the courtesy of the splendid Grolier Club library where I spent the mornings writing catalogue entries for the exhibition, which in the afternoon, sweating in bathing trunks in the apartment, I typed out and airmailed to Herta; she would collate them and send batches on to Jacques Guignard who was translating the material at the Bibliothèque Nationale. Not unnaturally this roundabout procedure elicited a sour comment from John Hayward: 'A fine exhibition this is going to be, with the secretary sitting on his backside in New York.'

Both being busy, we did not go out much; but on one occasion I took

Elizabeth down Broadway to Jack Dempsey's restaurant, one whole wall
of which was a mural of him taking the world title from Jess Willard in
1919, and postcards of it were on every table. The great man himself was
sitting across the room and I asked the waiter if Mr Dempsey would sign
cards for us; he replied, 'That's what he's here for.' A short time later the
huge figure came over and shook hands, completely crushing my
fingers in the process. He asked my name and I told him; he said, 'No,
your first name' and signed the card 'to Desmond'. Next Elizabeth gave
her name and he said, 'No, your last name'; I realized that in the United
States no public figure could address a card with her first name to a
young woman for fear of blackmail.

As a result of this absence I missed the Festival of Britain. I had
commissioned two books for the occasion, one of which was Bill
Brandt's *Literary Britain*, of which all the lovely photographs (plus a few
extra) were shown at the Victoria and Albert Museum in the autumn of
1984. I also missed the publication of *The Cruel Sea* which was celebrated
by the release of a mass of coloured balloons from St Andrews Hill, and
father, who had come up for the occasion, had kittens every time one
exploded as they were filled with helium, fearing that so many would be
lost that the show might be spoiled; after which the nautical author was
at the helm of a steamer which took the company's guests down the
river. Had she sunk with all hands, there would have been vacancies for
a large number of aspiring literary critics in London.

Eventually the situation changed and Elizabeth and I returned to
London. I was still in time for *Le Livre Anglais* and in November I went to
Paris to arrange it with Howard Nixon and Ruth Atkinson, a New
Zealander from the British Council. We spent two nights there and went
around together. On the first evening we saw *The Damnation of Faust* at
the opera; devoted to Berlioz, I knew the work well, but after that
wonderful performance I failed to understand why it is not always
produced as an opera instead of in the concert hall. On the second
evening we saw that Grock was appearing at the Cirque Medrano and
hastened there expectantly. The great man was in his seventies then and
I suppose that through films, photographs and descriptions everyone
knew every detail of his act. But it did not make the slightest difference;
we were reduced to helpless laughter by the perfection of his delicate
timing, the absurd violin, the drawing of the grand piano towards him
rather than shift the seat, and his musicianship when he finally got
around to playing. People, particularly when they go to Sadler's Wells,
think of Grimaldi whose memory is ever green, and I remember with
pride that I can say 'I saw Grock.'

The day of the opening arrived. Jacques Guignard, soon to assume
charge of the Arsenal Library, had been working till all hours at night to
finish the catalogue, and I must certainly take a large part of the blame
for this; the printers promised five hundred copies for the ceremony and
they arrived in the nick of time. Very few people heard much of Eliot's
speech as the microphones broke down and he had a very quiet voice.
While *les invités* were milling round the cases I slipped out for a breath of

fresh air and found him sitting alone in the back of a car in the library courtyard, so we sat and talked until it was time for us to drive off to the Ministry of Culture. When we arrived the first act of the Minister, Joxe, was to invest Eliot with the *Légion d'honneur*, which seems to have come as a complete surprise to the recipient and to have given him considerable pleasure. Then lunch, it was a pity in a way that it was a *jour maigre*, but nevertheless the fish was delightful. I was put next to François Mauriac and was so involved in talking to that distinguished writer, soon to be given the Nobel Prize, that I remember little of the rest of the company.

At the end of the exhibition, unlike the previous show in London, we did not have any difficulty repatriating the exhibits.

21   Country and Western

The time came to look for a home; both Londoners, Elizabeth and I decided that it would be a good idea to start a new life in the country. After a long search we found an early sixteenth-century cottage called 'Tignals' in Headley just over the Hampshire border.

'Tignals' belonged to an elderly widow, Mrs Deane, who lived there with one of her daughters. She started to show us round and, having done the house, we went on to the outbuildings. I peered in through the half-open door of a potting-shed in which was a chemical thunder-box; over her shoulder Mrs Deane said, 'Don't bother with that, it's the gardener's place with one of those ENSA things.'

After we had seen everything, we were invited to stay to tea. As we chatted, the daughter, Biddy, asked what I did and I said that I was a publisher. 'Oh,' she said, 'we have one in the next house just up the road: Tony Barrett.' Tony, my friendship with whom had been cut short in 1939 by his disappearance into the H.A.C. and with whom I had lost touch! What sort of thing did I publish? I mentioned W.S.C., of course, and, since everyone was talking about *The Cruel Sea*, Nicholas Monsarrat. 'Oh him!' said Biddy, 'He knows this place well; he had an affair with my sister when she was here.' It seemed that fate had decided that we should live there.

As well as the massive beams and the huge fireplace in the hall, the house had its pleasant surprises. Taking a pickaxe to some odd-looking bricks in the kitchen revealed the original Tudor bread oven, its curved bricks so beautifully fitted together that no mortar was required between them; and a man hired to remove brown paint from the dining-room floor with a machine had not been at work long before he ran across the hall crying 'Madam, madam, come and look.' Stripped of paint glowed the dark honey of the sixteenth-century elm floor. The grounds were interesting: rambling outhouses which must have stabled half a dozen horses, greenhouses growing melons and grapes, and an acre field beyond. In a slight dip and largely surrounded by woods, it was a small world of its own, a world in which our three children began their lives.

Before the war I had known Tony Barrett extremely well and to find him now, with an enchanting wife, Bunty, and children, near by got life in the country off to a flying start. The monarch of the area was Commander Sir Stephen King-Hall (made a peer just a few months before his death), who lived about half a mile away. Tony introduced us to him, explaining that we would be moving into 'Tignals' in due course, and we soon met all his extensive family. He had made a great success of his 'News Letter', which had a circulation of 100,000, and founded the Hansard Society (for the study of parliamentary history), the publications of which he eventually asked Cassell's to distribute. He was what is generally known as 'a character', a leprechaun preserved in salt from years at sea, and in his deep voice he would speak in conspiratorial tones as if some secret, either ominous or obscene, lurked near by. For all his knowledge of the ways of the world, there was about him still an air of artless innocence – the whole rounded off with warm-hearted generosity and kindness. He farmed quite a bit of land. At one point, before we had moved in, he said that he presumed we would need a man for our own land, and if that was so, he knew of someone whom he could recommend. An appointment was arranged and a tall, fine-looking man appeared in the yard; it was a cold day and he was muffled up in an old RAF overcoat, and even before he opened his mouth to speak in deep measured tones, I realized that he was right. So life began with Arthur Small, as fine and good a man as I have ever met; he started work at once.

We also decided to keep a pig for breeding. We intended that there should be a succession of them and, rather unkindly, decided to name them after Queens of England. The first was Alexandra and the day she was delivered we were on our honeymoon, so we sent a cable, 'Welcome. Hope the rations are all right.' Arthur Small, who did not know us very well yet, was most concerned and walked up the road to Bayfields Farm to consult Bunty Barrett: did it mean that someone he didn't know about was coming to stay? Should he lay in some food? Bunty giggled and said, 'No, you fool, it's the pig.'

Alexandra had a long and apparently happy life. Later we put her to a boar and she produced a wonderful litter over the arrival of which Arthur watched lovingly until all hours of a very cold night. Then there came the great Landrace fashion and I thought of going into breeding seriously. We had published *Watching the Certain Things* by Ralph Wightman who, in addition to writing so well about the country, was a popular broadcaster with a wonderful Dorset accent. He lived in Puddletown opposite two of my great-aunts, so, knowing him, I wrote to ask his advice. His reply was typical:

'Why you publishers can't stick to your own bloody business I don't know, but if you must have a Landrace boar I suggest you try ...'

Allen Lane once described to me a programme of 'Any Questions' at which he was present and I have never forgotten it. Freddy Grisewood was the question-master and Ralph Wightman was one of the panel. The latter was a great beer-drinker and had done very well by the time he arrived at the studio, where he did even better, so that by the time they were on the air he was somewhat comatose and took little part in the proceedings. In despair Grisewood, thoroughly disgruntled, said, 'The next question comes from Mrs So-and-so of Such-and-such who would like to ask the panel: do novelists make good book reviewers? Now, Mr Wightman, I think this is one for you.'

Ever since I have had anything to do with publishing this has been a vexed question which ebbs and flows like the tide on a desert island beach; at one time it is thought to be a task best left to professionals – for example Ralph Straus in the *Sunday Times* – at another it suddenly becomes fashionable to employ novelists without any regard for their ability as critics (it is their names that are wanted, usually to little purpose).

Wightman opened one eye: 'Huh?'

'The question, Mr Wightman, is "Do novelists make good book critics"?'

There was a long pause, then: 'Of course not, bloody lot of back-scratchers.'

On the whole, apart from Arnold Bennett and one I can think of today, I rather agree with him.

We were married in May 1952, and set off by road for Spain. Rowland Winn (not yet Lord St Oswald), whom I had originally met in 1948 through publishing his novel *Lord Highport Dropped at Dawn*, based on his own experiences in Yugoslavia, and with whom I got on very well, was being married at the same time; he said that since obviously he was not going to spend his honeymoon in his own home, we were welcome to stay at 'Las Columnas' outside Algeciras.

He had been at 'Las Columnas' when he received a cable from the commanding officer of his old regiment, the 8th Hussars, saying in so many words, 'Going to Korea an officer short. Why not get up off your backside in Spain and join us,' which he did. Since he had broken his thigh when he parachuted into Yugoslavia he limped and above all wanted a job where he could sit down, i.e. in a tank; but when they got there he was told that he was to be liaison officer with the Turks which entailed walking up and down every mountain in the peninsula.

The Hussars were mounted in Centurions, then the newest and most advanced tank, and in the retreat from the Imjin river they had to go first in order to make certain that no disaster could cause one to fall into the hands of the enemy. In a back area they pulled off the road to rest, and while they were there a convoy of huge American trucks pulled up for a five-minute smoke on the opposite side of the road. All of them were driven by coloured GIs, like those on the Red Ball route which had thundered endlessly across north-west Europe.

Rowland asked one of the drivers what was going on up the road and the answer in a Southern drawl was:

'Ah dunno, Sah.'

Rowland pursued the matter: What had the man seen? Was there any gunfire? Was there anything?

'Ah dunno, Sah; Ah's second-class soldier.'

What in heaven's name, Rowland exploded, was a second-class soldier? This demanded deep thought before an answer could be given; finally:

'Second-class soldier? Ah guess when you'se advancin' Ah'm behind you; when you'se retreatin' Ah's in front of you.'

This being several years before Franco closed the frontier, we drove from 'Las Columnas' into Gibraltar and put our names in the book at the Convent, the lovely white building which is the Governor's residence, because the Governor was none other than General MacMillan, Colonel of the Argylls; as a consequence we were asked to lunch.

I asked him how he got on with his opposite number, the governor of Gibraltar Province, and he said that relations were fine. It was customary for the Spanish governor to make an official call on the governor of the Rock, and for this occasion General MacMillan had had a military band flown out from the U.K. which impressed his Spanish guest, none of whose predecessors had been accorded a similar honour.

And Gibraltar Day?

Little posters were put up in all public places, cafés, lamp-posts, telegraph poles, bearing a succinct statement:

'Tomorrow is Gibraltar Day. Anyone creating a disturbance in this province will go straight inside. Signed: Bajamonde, Governor.'

It was the quietest day of the year.

St Andrew's Hill became increasingly cramped, and in any case I did not think it was a good headquarters for a major publishing firm. I thought the time had come for us to set about our own building. Bryen and I looked all over the place, and eventually found the ideal site at the corner of Red Lion Square and Theobald's Road in Holborn. The contract was signed on 13 December 1951 and our architect got started, but it was years before we moved in.

Three personalities graced the list in 1952. We published *The Golden Hand*, the first novel of Edith Simon, a woman of quite remarkable gifts. German and Jewish by origin, she is one of those outstanding writers from Conrad to Stoppard who have added grace to a language not originally their own. She was also always expert in the visual arts, and with the passage of time her writing has disappeared into the shadows behind her painting and sculpture so that every year at the time of the festival in Edinburgh, where she lives, a new show opens: always an enchanting surprise – for she has as many gifts as the facets of a trap-cut diamond.

Also in the list was *The Moving Finger*, the first novel of John Ross Macdonald who under various combinations of his three names has become one of the great writers of detective fiction.

Recently we had published Adolf Zukor's *The Public is Always Right*, and at this time the great movie mogul was in London with his wife, during his eightieth year. We had tea with them and he said that if we were ever in Hollywood we should contact his son at Paramount. We said that we well might do that because we were planning to go to Australia and we might just as well travel westwards, and he said that he would warn his son to expect us.

The chief event of 1953 was the publication of the sixth and final volume of *The History of the Second World War*, which had sold in enormous quantities. In celebration of this I was invited to lunch at Chartwell, and took the precaution of going down to Westerham by train. Author and publisher lunched alone; it was a wonderful meal, and was the only occasion on which I ever saw Winston the slightest bit high – a condition in which I spontaneously joined him. After a bottle of champagne as an aperitif, we sat down and he soon remarked:

'You must admit, Desmond, that I have made a prodigious effort.'

'Yes, Sir, you have made a prodigious effort.'

Another course, another bottle later, he exclaimed, 'You must admit, Desmond ... ' and I again concurred. It became rather like Scottie's reiterated *'mauvais temps pour bicyclette'* in Normandy. After the port decanter had passed back and forth so often it can't have known which way it was facing, and the brandy had swilled round its balloon, we were still agreeing solemnly on the prodigiousness of the effort. I left my wonderful host in happy mood as I, enraptured and a little sleepy, took the train back to London.

Now there would be a return to the *History of the English-speaking Peoples*, the long-postponed work for which father had originally contracted. I realized that the £20,000 paid for the coypright must long since have disappeared and that some gesture would be fitting not only to whet the author's appetite but also in recognition of his considerably changed position from that of twenty years before. I suggested that the sum paid should be regarded as an advance on account of royalties for the book rights alone. This was accepted, and the author turned contentedly to work.

Through René Varin I had come to know Versailles well; he had taken me over most of his 'Country Cottage', including Madame du Barry's suite (open to the public now, but not then), Louis XV's lovely bathroom, Louis XVI's study and the *salle d'atours* of Marie Antoinette. The last is an enchanting small circular room in which the Queen used to see her lady-in-waiting every morning to decide what she should wear that day. It had recently been done up in its original blue watered silk as a changing-room for our Queen on her first visit to the château, when she attended a performance in the refurbished opera house. I do not think that anyone could match René's devotion, but I too had fallen in love with the place and suggested to him that we should together mount in London an exhibition which would represent something of the glories of Versailles. Jack Morpurgo, now head of the National Book League, was in favour and we set to work. It took most of the year.

To coincide with the exhibition I translated a selection of the memoirs of Saint Simon called *Louis XIV at Versailles*, which the Folio Society published. It must have been this book and the exhibition which prompted George Macy a little later to ask me to make a much larger selection from Saint Simon; this made two handsome volumes which the Limited Editions Club published in New York in 1959.

As with the exhibition of French books five years before, everyone was supremely helpful and it was a gorgeous display. The authorities in France once more surprised and delighted me with their generosity, and there was one exhibit which I never dreamed we would have a chance of showing in London: the *Gazette des Atours de La Reine*, lent by the Archives Nationales. I have mentioned the *salle d'atours* to which Marie Antoinette descended from her bedroom, where her lady in waiting handed her the *Gazette*. This was a leather-bound blank book in which was mounted a cutting of the material of every dress in the royal wardrobe, with the name of the dressmaker, and the Queen marked in pencil what she desired to wear at the day's various functions. To turn these pages, as I did before I locked the volume under glass, was to see the last glories of the *ancien régime* in a shimmer of multi-coloured silks.

At the end, as René had said that he would see to the return of everything to France and Jack Morpurgo was happy to look after all the exhibits which had British homes, I had arranged to leave for my first visit to Australia.

We flew first to Toronto to see British Book Services, and to our surprise were met at the airport by Igor Gouzenko, whose *The Fall of a Titan* we had recently published. Gouzenko had defected from the Soviet embassy at Ottawa in 1945 and had given a great deal of information. He was kept under wraps by the authorities and always had a bodyguard of Mounties – I did not see them at the airport, but then I do not imagine that I was supposed to. He was a dark, quiet, not very attractive little man, with a beautiful wife, Svetlana, who also wrote a book which we published.

Earlier I have described Anne Orford, head of the British Book Services, as a battleaxe, and I do not think that is unfair; she was as hard as nails in business, honest and straightforward, and I liked her. On our last night there was a trade party in full swing in our suite when I heard the bell ring in our bedroom which had its own door on to the corridor. I went to answer it and found Gouzenko standing outside. I invited him in but he declined; holding out a package, he said, 'This is for you,' turned round, and disappeared. 'Was he alone? Oh, my God!' Anne said when I told her who it was. I do not care if one defects from A to B or from B to A, nor what hardships one thinks one is escaping or what amplitudes – mental or physical – one hopes to gain; I still cannot believe that anyone can say farewell to his country without leaving behind the remnants of some roots so harshly torn up. Gouzenko's hobby was painting; the package was a landscape in oils of birch trees along the banks of the River Don that still flowed deeply within him and emerged through the brush that he held in his hand.

Then to Los Angeles, where I had booked a chalet at the Beverly Hills Hotel, which Commander Whitehead considered the best hotel in the world. I had known Teddy Whitehead before he was sent to the United States by Schweppes to find out why their tonic water was not selling. Tall, with an enormous blond beard, he was an advertising agent's dream, and soon full-page ads were appearing of him in every kind of gear with the line 'Commander Whitehead says ...' It must be among the most successful campaigns ever launched, and we later published his story with one of the best punning titles, 'Schwepped off my feet' –

and the tonic sold. I rang Zukor Junior who was expecting us; he invited us to lunch the following day in the studio canteen and then took us to have a look at the film then in production. Alfred Hitchcock was making *Rear Window*. It was a bad time because the set was being changed while Grace Kelly, James Stewart and all the actors were resting in their caravans, but a good time because the director was not too busy. Zukor spoke to him and he came across; his first words were, 'How's your father?' When I got home I took it up with father who said almost off-hand, 'Oh yes, known him for years.' Since he was not a great movie-goer, I do not think that he either knew or cared that his old friend of the twenties had become a figure before whom one practically genuflected.

Since the date of our visit to Australia did not particularly matter, I had timed it to coincide with the final of the Davis Cup, and had written to Cyril Denny asking him if he could get tickets for the match.

We settled into the old Wentworth Hotel. Thirty years ago the Davis Cup was an entirely amateur affair and the departure of Sedgeman to the professional ranks gave Harry Hopman, the great Australian captain and coach who became a Cassell author, the opportunity of using as his defending team for the first time two teenagers, Lew Hoad and Ken Rosewall. Both of them became so famous, but already as youngsters they were as different as they could be; Hoad a tow-headed muscular power player, Rosewall a dark-haired waif who, one thought, could never beat anybody until, having with perfect touch manoeuvred his opponent where he wanted him, unleashed his unbeatable backhand. The Americans were experienced: Tony Trabert and Vic Seixas, with William Talbot as non-playing captain. Honours were even at the end of the first day. Hoad beat Seixas and Rosewall lost to Trabert. But on the morrow the United States went into the lead, taking the doubles with a great match in which Seixas was the best player on court. Talbot was staying in the Wentworth and that evening, as he was dining alone, we sent a note over asking if he would care to join a couple of Limeys for coffee, adding that we had nothing to do with the press. He came across, sat down, thanked us for the rider, and was charming. In the course of conversation we asked him how he accounted for Seixas, who had not played all that well against Hoad, producing such a startling performance in the doubles. 'Psychology,' he said, 'Tony Trabert and I spent two hours this morning standing over him in his room repeating "you are a great player; you are going to play well this afternoon".'

On the last day the stadium was packed for the reverse singles. We got back to town in the evening not only exhausted by the excitement but deafened as well. Hoad beat Trabert to even the score and the cup depended on the final match: Rosewall v Seixas. The Australian L.T.A. had telephoned Rosewall's parents, who kept a grocery store somewhere up-country, and told them that the winning or losing of the cup might well depend upon their son – how about coming in to watch? Mr Rosewall said he had to mind the shop, but his wife would like it. She was about three seats away from us and got so excited that she stood up most of the time and screamed at the top of her voice. I do not know what effect she had, if any (apart from deafening us), but her ewe-lamb ran out the winner and Australia kept the cup.

After that work began, and the more I saw of Australia and the more Australians I met, the more I loved them and their country. Though I deserved to get my head bitten off in Adelaide; it wasn't. With the Dennys there was the usual party for the book trade in the South Australia Hotel. It was very hot – so hot indeed that the manager sent word that gentlemen might remove their coats, the first time such a thing had happened in that excellent establishment within living memory. I was due to make a broadcast to go out at nine o'clock that night and in the middle of the party the recording man arrived. I took him to my bedroom as the only place where we could be quiet. I said my piece and when I had finished he said, 'We still have a few seconds left. Have you any other message you would like to give to the Australian people?'

I was hot and I was tired from meeting so many people, and I snapped, 'Yes; if you can't send us any better wines than you are sending at present, for God's sake don't send us any.' Although it was said in the heat – literally – of the moment, it was not unjustified. The stuff arriving in Britain at this time was hogwash; none of the lovely wines of the Barossa Valley or the Hunter River were obtainable. Happily that deplorable situation is now completely changed.

The next day, which was equally hot, we were taken by Harry Muir, then the king of Adelaide booksellers, up the Barossa Valley to the home and vineyards of the Hill-Smiths. The younger brother and his superbly beautiful wife had been at the party, but I then met the elder brother and found that we shared an interest in illustrated books, of which he had a fine collection. He asked me if I would like a glass of sherry and I gratefully said yes. It was like a fine very dry Manzanilla and ice cold; asked if I would like a refill, I accepted and complimented him on the wine. Casually he remarked, 'Now you see why we don't send you any; we drink it all ourselves.' This was the only reference which told me that my ill-tempered remark the night before had gone out on the air. But it did not spoil a happy day with charming people whom I remember with affection.

Then on to Sydney. The weather was very hot, so we spent some time on Bondi Beach which is only a taxi ride from the centre of town. I wonder if anyone reading this has ever been 'dumped'; I was, and I found it a terrifying experience. We have all seen photographs of the huge breakers on which the indomitable surfers ride in. Going out when they are big is easy because one can always dive through them, but coming in is another matter because of having to avoid being caught by a big one which is just breaking. I was caught – the local word is 'dumped'. The force of the water took me down to the bottom of the sea where it was dark and I was so disoriented that I did not know which way was up. My lungs bursting, I finally surfaced, very frightened, and I thought of raising my arm, which is the signal to the lifeguards that one is in trouble. But no, dammit, I would have one more try, and I got in. Half an hour later the red flag went up; the seas were too big and the beach was closed.

New Zealand was our next target, and we were lucky to make the journey before the end of the flying boats. In Sydney a taxi took us to the gloomy concrete pen where the Sunderland sat in the water like a vast albatross with its wings oustretched. Flying through the night, we came down at Auckland in sparkling sunshine, but I do not think that either of us was prepared for the vast billows which overwhelm the whole machine when the hull re-enters the water.

It was a quick visit, confined to Auckland, because I had to do something about our representation in that fair country.

Eric Westbrook, who had been one of the British Council members assembling the *Livre Anglais* exhibition in Paris with me, was now keeper of the Auckland City Art Gallery, remarkable for having the best collection in the world of Frances Hodgkins. He gave a party for us at which I met a woman to whom I took an instant dislike which I realized was mutual. I asked Eric who she was, and he said that she was the woman who was going to interview me on the radio the next morning; she was very well known in the business. I was to be at the studio at half past nine; I groaned, but turned up as instructed. With extreme distaste she asked me random questions which bore no relation to one another, and inwardly I thought, 'This is going to be the disaster of all time'.

Just before the hour the red light flashed and she remarked coldly that we would be on the air in thirty seconds. From half an hour of depressing and inconsequential conversation she had constructed a scheme of questions which led me from one period to the next, from one author to another in logical and stimulating succession; she was quite brilliantly expert. When it was over she walked out without a word; we still hated one another's guts, but my dislike was at least tempered with admiration.

At that time we were represented in New Zealand by an Australian called Avon Davies. He was a well known 'character' who lived near Wellington at Lower Hutt; he was old and he wanted to retire. Taking advantage of the last fact, the most important decision that I made was to separate our business in New Zealand from Australia; to me branches in these two wonderful countries, fifteen hundred miles apart and with little in common except the language, would be much better on their own. Some years before I had taken on for PR duties at St Andrew's Hill a young man of whom I thought highly, Michael Felgate-Catt, and when I got home I asked him if he would like the challenge of opening an autonomous branch with its lines of communication direct to London. He accepted, opened an office and a warehouse in Auckland, and made an outstanding success of the job.

We started back, staying on the way with friends in Kuala Lumpur. I managed to squeeze in a round of golf which was so bizarre that it is worth a mention apart from the pages devoted elsewhere to the game. I played with the professional, a Yorkshireman named Verity, and the temperature was well over 100 degrees. Golf is not a particularly easy game at any time, but that morning it was made more difficult by the fact that every time I got to the top of my swing there was a burst of machine-gun fire. I asked Verity what the hell was going on and he said that terrorists had cut the road from Kuala Lumpur to Jahore and the army, under the newly arrived General Templar, was dealing with the matter.

'Whereabouts?' I asked. 'A few miles away?'

'No,' he said, 'the other side of that wood,' pointing to some trees just beyond the clubhouse.

The battle was not going to stop for my convenience, and the distraction resulted in a distinctly mediocre performance.

22 Exhibitions and Exhibitionists

There are many sides to publishing. The obvious one, the side which would occur to most people, in choosing from the books offered by literary agents or the authors themselves, and purchased in forays overseas to the United States or France. Even this is no simple matter. A successful publisher is one with whose taste a sufficiently large number of people agree: there can be publishers whose discrimination is shared only by a small body of the like-minded, and they will find it difficult not to end up in Carey Street. And there are different strata of the reading public for which different publishers can successfully cater; I would not, for example, have enjoyed publishing the novels produced by Mills & Boon, but it cannot be denied that the directors of that firm are masters of their *métier*. It is a venal sin to publish books outside one's own bailiwick, a sin of which I was sometimes guilty; I should not, for example, have published the novels of Godfrey Winn which were without merit, and, furthermore, I found him a rather tiresome individual.

Another facet is the making of books: either seeing to it that someone who has a story to tell tells it with that persuasion and help may be required: or seeing to it that a book is created for which one feels there is a need. This latter is satisfying fun.

Finding myself constantly referring to a French *Dictionnaire Historique*, published at the end of the last century, which covers literary figures as well as purely historical ones, I realized that there was no reference work in the English language covering the whole of world literature. Through bibliography I knew Dr S.H. Steinberg and asked him if he would assemble a team to prepare the work which I had in mind. He consented; offices were found for him and his assistants in our warehouse which was then in Tooley Street, near London Bridge, and they laboured for four years. The result appeared in 1953: *Cassell's Encyclopaedia of World Literature* (a completely revised edition edited by John Buchanan Brown appeared twenty years later). Proud as I am of the famous authors and great books which appeared on the Cassell list during my time, my colleagues and I were but the *entrepreneurs* – 'half grocers, half pimps' Céline called us – who gave the words of others to the world; so if my career had any merit, I would like to think that much of it lies within the covers of the encyclopaedia.

To return to Voltaire, one edition of his works which every collector wishes to have on his shelves is the seventy volumes known as the Kehl Edition, published 1785–89; it is remarkably handsome, printed in Baskerville's type under the aegis of Caron de Beaumarchais, the famous author of *The Barber of Seville*. Baskerville, who had once been printer to the University of Cambridge and enjoyed a great reputation in Europe, died in 1775, and for a while his widow continued the business as a type-founder. The complicated story of what ensued has been admirably told by John Dreyfus in *The Survival of Baskerville's Punches*, privately printed at the Cambridge University Press in 1949. Briefly, Beaumarchais, a man of parts with a finger in many dubious enterprises which included gun-running, bought all the author's manuscripts after Voltaire's death, and set up a company to acquire punches from Mrs Baskerville from which to make the type to print them, and then three mills to produce the paper for the edition. Censorship would not permit the work to be done in France, so Beaumarchais obtained the lease of an old fort at Kehl, just across the border in the principality of Baden-Dourlach. But with the changed circumstances of the revolution, he moved back to Paris and took the punches with him. They remained in France, changing hands several times until in 1936 they were bought by the type-founding firm of Deberny & Peignot, the eminent head of which became an honorary member of the Double Crown Club in 1947. I got to know him quite well while I was in Paris preparing for the *Livre Anglais* exhibition.

It occurred to me that these punches were of decreasing practical use and would no doubt be welcome in Cambridge not only because Baskerville had been University Printer, but because the Press was building up its collection of historic types. Stanley Morison's remark when I mentioned my idea – 'You haven't got a hope!' – was sufficient to spur me into action; I approached Peignot myself and also invoked René Varin's support. When it appeared that Peignot was favourably inclined, the University printer, Brooke Crutchley, sent his No 2, John Dreyfus, to Paris to make sure that these punches were the right ones, for the vicissitudes of the Baskerville types over the last 150 years formed a complex story which Dreyfus himself had unravelled in his book. He found the material to be genuine; Peignot was willing, and I felt very happy to be present at a ceremony on 12 March 1953, when he gave to the University Press the best part of 3,000 punches, the majority of them Baskerville's own and some used in the production of his great folio Bible at Cambridge in 1763. They had come home.

Nicholas Monsarrat published that year his first novel after *The Cruel Sea: The Story of Esther Costello*. This led to an unfortunate contretemps with Alfred Knopf, and it says a great deal for the strength of my personal relations with him that they survived it unimpaired. Esther Costello, a young blind woman, is raped and the trauma restores her sight. This is a not impossible phenomenon, but unfortunately Alfred and Blanche Knopf considered the book in bad taste and an insult to their friend Helen Keller, the blind celebrity. Whether its taste is good,

bad or indifferent, I think that it is a good novel. Any correlation with
Helen Keller was absolute rubbish, and I wrote saying so to Alfred. But
nothing could make him like the book; he published it as silently as
possible and let it die.

Nicholas, not unnaturally, was furious at the extinction of his novel
and vowed that he would never write another book for the Knopf
imprint, and they in return pointed out that he had signed a three-book
contract and would fail to complete it at his peril. Stalemate. Nicholas
had a perfectly good agent, but because of my connections with the
American publishing scene I had a finger in the ensuing pie. A book,
Castle Garac, was cobbled together with which Knopf had every reason
to be satisfied since it was a Literary Guild choice. The way was now
clear for Nicholas to move over, as I suggested, to Thayer Hobson and
the Morrow list on which he remained for the rest of his life.

Since 1946 Nicholas had served in the United Kingdom Information
Office in Johannesburg, and it was to him that journalists had to go for
information about the situation during the Mau Mau period in Kenya,
and these years were important ones in his life. It was there that he met
a high-powered and beautiful South African journalist named Philippa
Crosby, to whom *The Cruel Sea* was dedicated – so high-powered that
she rather enjoyed her nickname, 'The Cruel She'.

What the relations had been like between Nicholas and his wife,
Eileen, during the war years and immediately thereafter I do not know,
for I had not seen her since our short acquaintance in 1940, when I had
found her charming; but whatever they may have been – and they
inevitably involved a great deal of separation – they did not survive the
new comet in the southern sky. Nicholas was divorced and married
Philippa.

Philippa was certainly beautiful and possessed great charm; unfortunately she had one shortcoming with which I am all too familiar: she
was an alcoholic. A long battle ensued, but in the end the bottle won;
there was deep sadness in his voice when he finally said to me, 'I am
sick of stomach pumps.'

His next novel, *The Tribe that Lost Its Head,* which appeared in 1957 was
based on his acquaintance with the Mau Mau and their atrocities. He
said to me that if he had put all that he knew into the book it would have
been so revolting that no one would have believed it and few would
have read it. It is from this period that his bad relations with the press
date. He was disgusted by the blood-lust of journalists and their probing
for filthy details which he refused to give; they in return found him
stand-offish and unhelpful. There was no love lost and, although his
writings were treated on their merits, I do not think that the press even
to the end of his life went out of its way to be kind to him.

By now Nicholas, Margaret's and my son, was finishing at school. I
wanted him to go to King's, but the Dean (an old friend of mine) said
that at that time to be the son of a King's man was a distinct handicap.
Nicholas was pleased; he said, 'I have just wasted five years at school; I
am about to waste two more in National Service, and I want to get on

with a job of work.' When those two years were finished he had various possibilities before him. There was a long silence while he thought about them, and then one day he said to me, 'Would you give me a job at Cassell's?' Releasing a pent-up sigh of relief, I said, 'Of course.'

Although I was naturally flattered at the time, I always thought that my appointment to the board after only one year's service had been premature; so I think that I erred in the other direction before suggesting to my colleagues that Nicholas should join us. But the day came and the board was stronger for his presence; it was where he belonged. And his command of the typographical design of our books was outstanding.

It was at this time that I came to know Count Alfred de Curzon, I do not remember how or why, but I found him an appealing old gentleman; he was the French Consul in Portsmouth. I invited him to run over our French dictionary and make the necessary corrections for a new edition, and also asked him to revise our French Phrase Book for Travellers. Although I was never enamoured of this series, they did have their uses and were quite steady sellers. I was horrified to discover that neither the Count nor the Editorial Department nor myself had done our stuff when I received a letter from a disgruntled customer who questioned the value of such a phrase as, 'I would like to order a partridge pie for twenty-four.' This was so obviously ludicrous that the only reply I could make was:

'Dear Sir, If you have never ordered a partridge pie for twenty-four, you have not lived ...' (although I spoiled it by going on in more serious vein.)

Old Curtis Brown had died and the head of the firm which he had founded was now his son, Spencer, whom I cordially disliked – while on the best of terms with all his colleagues, I presume that my feelings were reciprocated, for he only once sold me a book and did me one serious disservice. He loved meddling and moving people around like pieces on a chessboard; he had a zany laugh and whenever I heard it I was filled with forebodings.

Among his clients was R.C. Hutchinson. I did not rate Ray Hutchinson as great a genius as father considered him; to me he was a fine writer whom I was proud to publish and whom I respected for his craftsmanship and as a man. For decades he had been father's client, but after father's retirement he and I became friends. Quite suddenly he left, and there has never been any question in my mind but that it was a put-up job and who put it up. Knowing what Ray meant to father, who was still titular head of the firm, I would have expected after a quarter of a century a visit – or at least a telephone call – from a good agent to explain that Ray was not happy and why or, at worst, simply to say 'Sorry, after all these years he feels like a change.' But no, Machiavelli remained in the wings. I would be delighted if someone could prove to me that Spencer did not say to Ray something like 'I can do better for you; think of an excuse and get quit of Cassell's.' The outcome, anyway, was a letter from Ray announcing his departure: the reason he gave was that I had put the wrong sort of jacket on his first book with us twenty-two years before, and to make this long-forgotten and irrelevant point took him no less than eleven handwritten pages of beating about the bush. I was too sad and angry to argue; but I felt a certain sardonic glee when the jacket which his next publisher, Collins, put on his first novel to appear on their list was a picture (anathema to Ray) which would have sent shudders even down the collective spine of Mr Mills and Mr Boon.

The one book Curtis Brown did sell me, which came out in the spring of 1954, had an interesting history. He telephoned me to ask if I would be interested in *The Scourge of the Swastika* by Lord Russell of Liverpool. Concerned, as its title implies, with the evil deeds of the Nazis, I found the book valuable but probably with a limited market and I estimated a print of 5,000 copies. That would probably have been the end of the story had not the Lord Chancellor taken it upon himself to disapprove of Lord Russell having written the book as a Judge Advocate General and one of the prosecuting counsel at the Nuremberg trials – this in spite of the author having taken all the steps officially required of him before starting to write. When Lord Russell, naturally incensed, resigned from the Judge Advocate's department, it became front page news and in consequence the book sold edition after edition like wildfire. Of course I was delighted, but it is perhaps a warning that inter-departmental quarrels are sometimes better conducted in private – and kept from the press: a foretaste of the fun and games which enlivened the year of grace 1987 over *Spycatcher*.

As the eightieth birthday of Sir Winston Churchill fell in 1954, we thought that it would be pleasant and proper to produce a book in honour of the occasion, and as editor Sir James Marchant brought together 'a tribute by various hands' entitled *Winston Spencer Churchill: Servant of Crown and Commonwealth*. In addition to the trade edition there was a small issue bound in full morocco with an unusual *justification du tirage*: 'Six copies of this book have been printed on hand-made paper. None is for sale.' No 1 was graciously accepted by Her Majesty the Queen, No 2 was for the subject, the third went to the British Museum, the fourth to the National Library of Australia, the fifth to father and the last remained in the company archives. We wanted to present his copy to Sir Winston personally as a surprise, and with this in mind I went to see Lady Churchill to ask what arrangements she felt inclined to make. We sat in the small drawing-room of No 10 at the end overlooking the park. Although she was always charming, for obvious reasons I did not know her as well as I knew her husband. He had, I think, a sixth sense – in fact Sir John Colville in his memoirs has said the same thing; So the door opened and he came in, feeling that something was going on and wanting to know what. He was greeted with great firmness: 'Mr Flower and I are discussing business. Go away.'

He went.

In the end, on a convenient date as near the actual day as possible, she asked the whole board to tea in the big drawing-room, and the Prime Minister seemed pleased with the book.

The autumn of 1955 saw another exhibition with which I was concerned. The Fourth International Congress of Bibliophiles was to be held in London and a powerful committee was in charge of the arrangements. Howard Nixon and I found ourselves organizing an exhibition at the National Book League, the object of which was to delight our visitors from abroad with the richness of some of the private libraries in Britain.

Howard was then Assistant Keeper of Printed Books at the British Museum in charge of bindings. He gave thirty-eight years of distinguished service to the museum, and after his retirement became librarian of Westminster Abbey, which his father had been before him, living in the Little Cloister near by where he had been born. I had known him for more than a decade. Long before we had been together in Paris at the time of the *Livre Anglais,* and we had got on extremely well. He had succeeded the great Geoffrey Hobson of Sotheby's as the country's leading authority on bookbindings, whose son Anthony was close behind him. We settled upon the collectors whom we would pursue and divided the chase between us.

Her Majesty the Queen graciously lent from Windsor a superb copy of the psalter which Fust and Schoeffer published at Mainz on 14 August 1457. Several of the dozen lenders had been most generous to me before, the Duke of Devonshire, the Earl of Leicester, Sir John Murray, Major Abbey, Henry Davies, Albert Ehrman and his wife. Lord Eccles contributed from his magnificent South American collection, and the Duke of Wellington invited me to Stratfield Saye where I could look at the library begun by the Iron Duke. Each selection was prefaced by a description of the library and its origins written by the owner, or his librarian. A change from manuscripts, printings and bindings from the past was a group of books from Cyril Connolly's collection which he called 'Homage to the twenties, a decade of light and hope, the last perhaps and when I first awoke to the magic of the contemporary.' And he began his introductory note with a sentence which is as interesting as it is provocative: 'Collecting is a means of extracting order from chaos, or providing sanctuary for genius or survival for the unfittest, depending on the collector.'

At this time books about the war were still pouring out – we were to have some distinguished ones ourselves in the next few years – and *Vain Glory* which I had commissioned in the thirties came back to my mind. I decided to do it again, but this time there would be no attempt at wagging a warning finger, which had been such a frost before. This had been a war about which I felt passionately and wanted to see all of its nastiness encapsulated in one book. I teamed up with James Reeves, the critic and poet who was a friend of Robert Graves. He, having the worst eyesight short of blindness I have ever met had been confined to the home front, which therefore was his province; I dealt with all activities on land, at sea and in the air. I took masses of books home from the London Library and pored over them after dinner; I quickly developed a nose for 'the right stuff' and could detect a phoney more quickly than I

could dry rot. Passages which seemed to me suitable were typed by Herta
Ryder, many of which were subsequently edited out; the poor woman
must have typed in all about three million words, and it is impossible for
me to repay my enormous debt to her. It took a long time to select and edit
it down to 1,100 pages, though I was well aware that it had one serious
weakness: the prodigious efforts of the Soviet forces were not well
represented. The reasons were simple: I would not include something
which I could not read myself, the Russians were much slower rushing
into print than other peoples and English publishers were even slower in
undertaking translations when the books did appear; furthermore of
what sources were available one eminent critic wrote that they were 'so
choked with official patriotism that individual emotion is obliterated'. I
received a pained and perfectly justified protest from the Soviet authorities, but at that time there was absolutely nothing that I could do to put
the record straight.

After three years' work and a year for production, the book finally came
out in 1960 under the simple title *The War, 1939–1945*. It was, I am happy
to say, well received and sold well; Cass Canfield took the American
rights for Harper's, gave it a fresh title – *The Taste of Courage* and sold even
more than we did. It is a little invidious to quote a review of one of one's
own books, but Orville Prescott in *The New York Times* put our desire and
purpose so well that perhaps I may be permitted one: 'World War II is
only history to millions of people who rarely read history. If they could be
persuaded to read *The Taste of Courage* it would never be history again.
They would understand the nature of modern war and, perhaps be better
prepared to prevent or endure another.'

During 1955 Alec Waugh delivered his new novel, *Island in the Sun*, a
large, very good book from which was to be made a very bad film (apart
from the beautiful start, tracking on to the little Caribbean island, and its
haunting song by Harry Belafonte). It appeared in the following March.
The grapevine in publishing operates with remarkable speed, and if one
has a good book the trade seems to know about it almost as soon as one
knows oneself. Sure enough, Nancy Spain, the *Daily Express* literary critic
whose straightforward honesty I had always liked, came to see me and
said, 'I hear you have a good book from Alec Waugh;' we had a chat and
then she asked how many we had printed and I told her: 19,000. Alec was
not a particularly good seller, and the largest first edition we had
previously printed was 12,000 of a fat novel he had given us before the
war, called *The Balliols*.

I was not aware at the time that Evelyn Waugh had written in *The
Spectator* that literary criticism at Beaverbrook Newspapers had suffered a
serious decline since the days of Arnold Bennett in *The Evening Standard*
and D. H. Lawrence in the *Express;* this was, of course, perfectly true, but
it earned the personal enmity of the proprietor.

Nancy Spain's review of *Island in the Sun* appeared on publication day
and I read it with horror. In it she stated that the book had subscribed
more than the first editions of all Evelyn's novels put together. I rang her
up at once and said, 'Nancy, what have you done? You know that what

you have written is completely untrue.'

'I got the yellow paper,' was her answer.

When I asked her what she meant, she explained, 'In the yellow paper Beaverbrook sets down exactly what one is to write, and if one doesn't write it, don't bother to come back next week.'

The subsequent developments have been admirably set out in Mr David Hooper's book on libel cases. Evelyn wrote to his agent, A. D. Peters, who represented both brothers, 'I have wanted for a long time to catch the *Express* in libel ... there should be no difficulty in proving malice,' and also told Alec that he was proceeding. The case was heard nearly a year later and I had to be there to state in evidence how many copies of Alec's book we had printed. Evelyn, of course, won and was awarded £5,000 damages, the same amount that Beaverbrook had to pay for another spiteful libel the following week.

The middle fifties produced a succession of strong lists; of the authors which were included in them, some I never met, several I saw but once – such as King Peter of Yugoslavia and Marshal of the Air Force Sir John Slessor; but one I came to know well. Most people think that *Defeat into Victory* was a great book, and with Sir William Slim (as he then was) I formed a relationship which went far beyond even the best of terms which a publisher can expect with an author; it would have been (to me) a valued friendship if circumstances had permitted us to meet more often. Complete devotion, enormous ability and abundant humanity were combined in the make-up of a great man. Obviously I never served under him, but no one who did, I am sure, got anything other than his deserts – good or bad; but that jutting chin boded ill for the idle or inefficient.

One day he asked me to lunch at the Athenaeum and, over a glass of sherry, said that the food (at that time) was so bad that he had ordered lunch and hoped I didn't mind. We went in to find smoked salmon already on the table, and when we had consumed it a little waitress, not a day over eighteen, appeared and simpered, 'Did you want anything else?' The firmest of military voices replied, 'I have ordered two steaks; GO AND GET THEM.' The poor child scuttled away like a frightened spider.

He had a great admiration for Ernest Bevin and explained the reason. Soon after the war the Attlee government was considering army pay and Slim, as Chief of the Imperial General Staff, was called upon to attend at No 10. When the meeting began the Prime Minister made it clear that rises were being considered only in the pay of other ranks; commissioned officers were not to be included. Slim was furious at such blatant injustice and his rage shook Attlee who was so disconcerted that in a worried tone he asked Bevin what he thought about it. After a pause the Foreign Secretary rumbled in his deepest tone, 'Every man deserves the rate for the job.' That killed any further thought of discrimination.

In the autumn of 1955 we published *In the Thick of the Fight* by Paul Reynaud. I, in common with many others – despite the stature of de Gaulle – still regarded him with the greatest respect because of his wish in 1940 to move his government from Bordeaux to North Africa, an aspiration in which he was outvoted by his cabinet colleagues who preferred an armistice – he spent the next five years in jail. Some years before, when the contract had just been signed, Margaret and I had been invited to lunch at his apartment in Paris. There were about ten of us altogether, and, apart from the small, neat, rather bird-like figure of our host the *Président du Conseil* (a title which in France is kept for life after a term of office), the man I remember is the butler. In morning coat and white cotton gloves, he admitted us with enormous dignity on our arrival. After general conversation over an aperitif we nearly jumped out of our skins when he opened the door and bellowed in the voice of a sergeant-major (which he may well have been), 'MONSIEUR LE PRÉSIDENT EST SERVI.' But he endeared himself to both of us by the conspiratorial tones in which he whispered the name of the château and the year of the delectable wines with which he filled our glasses.

Major-General Von Mellenthin brought us *Panzer Battles, 1939-45*. He was to Rommel what Freddie de Guingand was to Montgomery, and if by some transmogrification they could have changed places I do not think that the result would have been much different; he was a good man and a fine soldier.

And Eartha Kitt's *Thursday's Child*. She was young, at the height of her fame, an exciting *enfant terrible*. Since she was in London I asked her agent where she was staying so that I could take her to lunch; he said that she was at the Mayfair and warned that she was so temperamental that when she was displeased she could just get up and walk out. I asked her to the Jardin des Gourmets and she could not have been sweeter. After a happy lunch we walked together down Greek Street and I asked her to come with me into the grocery shop there while I bought a *fromage de monsieur*. Now choosing a *fromage de monsieur* exactly *au point* is not a matter to be taken lightly – it demands complete concentration, and when I had made my choice and looked round, she was gone. I paid and went out, standing on the pavement in a dilemma. Had I offended her by dragging her into the shop? Should I go to the Mayfair or go back to my office and phone the hotel from there? I was still debating with myself when I felt a little hand on my arm. 'You thought you'd lost me; I've only been to the loo,' she said with an impish expression.

I saw her once more on that visit, though I cannot remember what I wanted to ask her – does one need a reason for calling upon so attractive a woman? She asked me to come up and I found her in a white négligé, stretched out on the sofa like a dusky Madame Récamier. It was a great strain.

David Ascoli, while still sales director, was beginning to play an increasingly large part in the literary side, and to him were due many of the important sporting books which came to us around this time: Ferenc Puskas, the great Hungarian footballer; Harry Hopman, the genius behind Australian tennis; Ian Johnstone, captain of the Aussies' test side; and Pat Smythe.

Pat Smythe was very young when she and Prince Hal made their meteoric rise together in show-jumping; a girl of great charm who, with no one to give her a leg up into the saddle, had by sheer hard work made it to the very top – the kind of success story that no one can resist. So we expected great things for her first book, *Jump For Joy*, Nor were we disappointed. David was a wizard at promotions for books in which he believed, and he laid one on for this. He booked a whole block of seats at Olympia, where the jumping was that year, and invited a number of leading booksellers.

I had not met Pat before that evening; when the programme was over and David was busy despatching the booksellers, I went down to see if Elizabeth and I could be of any help and asked where she was staying; I was told that she would share the horsebox with Prince Hal. It sounded rather uncomfortable but obviously she was used to it. I asked then where she was going to eat and was told that she would not be having anything. That was too much; 'Nonsense,' I said, 'You have just won and you cannot go to bed without supper. We will all go out.'

But, she said, she had no clothes to change into. 'Leave it to me,' I answered with a confidence which I did not entirely feel.

I rang up Hatchett's in Piccadilly which I had always liked and where Chappie D'Amato's band played very well and asked the *maître d'hôtel* for a table for our total of eight – but, I said, there was a snag: one of our guests was Pat Smythe and she had only her riding-clothes. 'We will be happy to see Miss Smythe whatever she is wearing,' he replied at once.

We set off in our various cars; David, who had become very fond of Pat, brought her in his and they arrived at the side entrance in Dover Street. The ladies of the town were as thick on the ground as pigeons in Trafalgar Square, and one of them, when she saw Pat get out of the car, remarked in a loud voice: 'Things have come to a pretty pass when one has to wear boots and spurs to drum up a bit of business.'

Pat was not amused.

Thereafter we published all her books. Prince Hal – there is a photograph somewhere of us all grinning like zanies when, in an alcove at Martinez', we presented her with a bronze of that lovely sensitive horse. She began a successful series of stories for younger horse-lovers, and the years rolled by. The last time I saw her ride was at Hickstead where we took mother in the middle sixties. Pat came round for a few words with mother, who was sitting in the sun enjoying life. Then Pat met Sam Koechlin who was in the Swiss team at the 1963 Olympics, married him and had two daughters. After Hickstead I did not see her for many years; but when I did, I found her little changed and just as charming.

Living in the country, we did not go often to the opera, but there was one great occasion. In June 1955 the director of Covent Garden discovered that Tito Gobbi and Renata Tebaldi were both on holiday in London, contacted them, found them willing, and as a result there was a sudden announcement that there would be three special performances of *Tosca*. Like a great number of other people, I rushed to the box-office and, lucky to get any seats at all, bought two in a box right over the orchestra. I do not expect to see another Scarpia as good as Gobbi (whom I was to hear in this role a number of times) and Tebaldi was at the height of her great career. Both were in holiday mood.

Before the war I remember Maurice Rena telling me that his friends in Italy were asking him if he could not persuade the B.B.C. to get someone to run their news programmes in Italian who knew the language intimately, because they were becoming a joke to which everyone listened for the wrong reasons. For instance, it was announced that Count Ciano, the Italian Foreign Minister, had gone to Berlin and called upon Ribbentrop, his opposite number, to exchange *'gesti amicavoli'*; this would appear straightforward, but at that time there was a common use of the phrase meaning 'obscene gestures'. From our box at *Tosca* we could see into the wings, and there whichever of the two stars was not on stage was going through *'gesti amicavoli.'* trying to make the one who was singing laugh. But what a wonderful performance!

In 1955 was Basil Liddell Hart's sixtieth birthday. He sent me – for my interest and amusement, he said – an article from the *Frankfurter Allgemeine Zeitung* entitled 'The Clausewitz of our Age'. The author, Adelbert Weinstein, had the same impression as I had of 'the greatest military thinker alive today', describing how 'During the course of the afternoon which I spent as his guest at Wolverton Park, Captain Liddell Hart may well have used fifty matches to keep his pipe alight. Each time he got it going he would take a puff, bend his knees, lean his tall, spare frame against a corner of the chimney-piece beneath which the fire blazed, begin to talk – and let his pipe go out.' In sending it to me, Basil added, 'I don't feel sixty, and hope I am not yet an "extinct volcano". Nevertheless, I can now appreciate the irony of the fact that I was partly responsible for reducing the retiring age of generals in the British army from 65 to 60.'

Soon after the war Basil was commissioned by the Royal Tank Regiment to write a history of the Tank Corps which turned out to be a lengthy, complicated and expensive project. As early as 1948 I was already in correspondence with the Representative Colonel Comman- dant of the Royal Tank Regiment, General Hobart, that 'erratic genius' who commanded the 'funnies'* in Normandy and subsequently became Lieutenant-Governor of the Royal Hospital at Chelsea, which was why I was invited there for Oak Apple Day when all the pensioners parade in honour of their founder, King Charles II.

The stumbling-block was a matter of procedure: the R.T.R. committee, understandably, wanted to have a number of copies which they could make available at a reduced price to indigent ex-members of the regiment, and the question was whether they should pay for the production of the book (with our technical assistance) which we would market, receiving a royalty of 22½ per cent for our pains, or whether we

---

* 'Funnies': a division of Churchill tanks for special purposes such as mine clearance, flame-throwing and bridge-laying.

should produce and publish the work in the normal way and supply their requirements at an agreed price; over this block they stumbled for years.

By 1955 we were no nearer a solution. Basil wrote to me that the original R.T.R. subvention had already run out in 1948, since when he had put in £5,000 of his own capital and £7,000 which he had received from his edition of *The Rommel Papers* to continue the work. At long last agreement was reached (we produced the book and made them a price) and *The Tanks* finally appeared in two volumes in January 1959; it was extremely well received. Basil had by then returned to his *History of the Second World War* which was already much delayed and which we finally published in the summer of 1970.

I was now visiting New York regularly once a year, and in 1955 I thought that it would be a good idea to tack a holiday on to the end of business so that, although I would be away from the office twice as long, I would only have one interruption in my routine instead of two. I asked Elizabeth if she would fly into New York and help me finish the reading and return such books as I had decided against before we set off. After the usual enjoyable chasing from publisher to publisher, I went to spend the last weekend before Elizabeth's arrival with Thayer Hobson in Tucson, Arizona. It was nearly a disaster.

The plane left New York in the morning and was due to arrive at Tucson in time for dinner at eight. The first hiccup came in Washington when the pilot announced that we had a dud engine which would have to be replaced. This took a considerable time; when we finally left plus the additional passengers I found myself sitting next to a young man who was going to Phoenix, the next stop after Tucson, and we got talking. We next came down at Nashville, where the pilot on the intercom told us that the new engine was no better than its predecessor and would have to be changed again. Neither my young friend nor I felt like sitting in the airport lounge for hours, so, making sure what time we had to be back, we asked a taxi to take us to the nearest decent hotel in town; and here, for the first time, we encountered the liquor laws of Tennessee which were then, to put it mildly, idiotic.

We walked into the bar and asked for two Scotch and soda. The bartender said he was sorry, he could give us the set-ups, but we would have to get the Scotch at a liquor store. We asked where was the nearest liquor store and he replied, 'In the hotel lobby.' So we walked to the store in the lobby, all of twenty yards, and bought half a bottle of Scotch with which we returned to the bar. Since we were not going to leave any behind, the result of this pantomime was that we both drank more Scotch than we had intended which, unless the state laws are drawn up by the liquor barons, was not the object of the exercise.

We took a cab back to the airport and were soon once more airborne; but our adventures were not yet over. After some time we ran into an intimidating electric storm; lightning danced along the wings like St Elmo's fire and the plane bucked like a steer. The pilot came down at Oklahoma City and said that he was not prepared to go any further unless the weather improved. It was now the middle of the night and my young friend, deciding that he had had enough, departed into town to find an hotel. I was left alone in the airport lounge with, since Oklahoma is a dry state, nothing to sustain me but root beer through an indefinite wait.

The weather did improve and the pilot decided to move on. As we approached Tucson, I wondered what I was going to do at four o'clock in the morning and could only presume that I would have to cat-nap at the airport until daylight when I could telephone Thayer. Judge of my surprise when I got into the building to see Thayer there with one of his colleagues, Sam Lawrence, who was taking the same plane on its next westward leg. Thayer said, 'We knew all about the delays because of Sam. And I have some news for you: that is the last plane into or out of Tucson. The engineers have gone on strike.'

Thayer and Isobel had an enchanting house out of town on the edge of the desert. I sat by the pool and looked out across the pale sand dunes dotted with tall cacti reaching into the deep blue cloudless sky – this is Apache country, and at night coyotes wandered round the house and occasionally howled.

I explained that I had to be in New York early on Monday morning to meet Elizabeth and he, being the wonderful man that he was, spent the whole of Saturday on the telephone trying to find a way round the affected area, for the strike was not nationwide; in the end he succeeded. I had to start west first, to Phoenix, then far north; in the end I got to Kennedy Airport half an hour before the London plane was due.

We cleared up and started south; our first holiday objective was New Orleans. At that time there was no hotel in the Vieux Carré, but a Cassell author recommended the Montcalm which was right on the edge and, further, sent an introduction to a charming lady who called upon us and was extremely kind. Knowing of my interest in jazz, she took us to call on a very old lady with a two-fold object: to hear her talk and play the piano (see Appendix on jazz) and to see her home in St Charles Avenue. It was the most magnificent house, built at the end of the eighteenth century, like Tara with which millions have become acquainted through the film of *Gone With The Wind*. The grand piano at which she sat looked dwarfed in one corner of the drawing-room from the ceiling of which hung the original crystal chandeliers sparkling in the sunshine which poured through the tall windows. Then she took us to one of the cemeteries where the water table is so near the surface that the dead have to be 'buried' above ground.

By ourselves we wandered through the Vieux Carré, an ambiance which for me has only one rival: the Marais in Paris. At one point on Main Street, Elizabeth remarked laughingly, 'I don't suppose we shall see a streetcar named Desire.' 'What's that?' I said, pointing, as a tram trundled towards us with the famous name of its destination (a suburb) on the front.

We ate at Anthoine's; like all rubberneckers, we went up the Mississippi in a paddle-wheel show-boat with a jazz band on board. Then we were off to Mexico City.

I had had a visit not long before from one John Grepe who had opened a British bookshop in the city, and made up my mind to put on a bit of publicity in the hope, probably quite vain, of impressing the Mexicans with the fact that we produced English language books as good as and cheaper than their mighty neighbour to the north. I had also written to the Cultural Counsellor at the British embassy saying that I spoke Spanish and would he be interested in my making a broadcast about British books, to which he had replied in the affirmative.

I went to see him with the English text of the clarion call which I wished to sound. He was a really delightful man with one artificial hand covered with a black glove. He said he would have it put into Spanish and we made a date for the following morning, when I returned to the embassy, a short walk from our hotel. The text was ready and I was put in the charge of two young locals whose task was to convert my Castillian into Mexican Spanish. We had a small room to ourselves and worked away until they were satisfied, then I taped my oration.

There followed one of the most embarrassing moments of my life. It was nearly lunchtime and as I was leaving I ran into the Cultural Counsellor, who said that he wanted to hear the recording. Unfortunately there was a tape player right there in the hall and I had the shaming experience of listening to my own voice with my host and all the servants standing round. I know that my voice is much deeper than I think because I had heard it played back some years before when I had made a recording for the B.B.C. German Service, so I was not dismayed but merely abashed to hear my sepulchral tones groaning out in a Spanish with which I had hitherto been unfamiliar.

Our next stop was Cuba. Havana, where Sergeant Batista still had four years to run, was like any American city except down by the harbour where the architecture is charming. At our hotel, the Ambos Mundos, I had asked for the room in which Hemingway wrote *For Whom the Bell Tolls*, but the manager apologetically said that he had felt obliged to give it to a young American couple because they were on their honeymoon. Hemingway's *Pilar* lay off-shore, gleaming in new paint. We looked in for a drink at the Florodita bar for a very good reason. It was Hemingway's favourite haunt in town, and it was here that Hotchner was bidden to meet him for the first time in 1948. Hotchner in *Papa Hemingway* says, 'At that time the Florodita was a well lighted old-fashioned bar restaurant with ceiling fans ... the bar was of massive burnished mahogany: the barstools high and comfortable, and the bartenders cheerful, skilled veterans who produced a variety of frozen daiquiris of rare quality.' Air-conditioning had replaced the fans by now, but the daiquiris were still of rare quality; they should be, they were the attraction, for it was behind that massive mahogany bar that the mixture was invented.

It is a short hop from Cuba to Jamaica, where Harry Aitken and his newly married wife Anne had invited us to stay. I was longing for the moment when we would see him at the airport, for fate had separated us since he had broken his legs in a jeep accident towards the end of the war in Germany.

Harry and Anne took us over a large part of the island of which my memories are very vivid. The beauty of the Blue Mountains. The vulgar horror of Montego Bay. Harry getting lost and stopping in a tiny village to ask the way, adopting the sing-song patois to which today the Caribbeans in London revert when they don't want the whites to understand. Coming at night upon a Revivalist meeting and sitting in the car out of sight so as not to intrude upon the soul-baring cries of those who felt the spirit within them.

And finally Port Antonio, the charming harbour town in which our ship was waiting and where we said goodbye. It was fourteen years since Harry had first shown me, the new boy, round battalion headquarters in Stirling, and I left him with regret, fortunately not for ever, and bid farewell to a beautiful island which I am not likely to see again.

Our ship was a banana boat, the last coal-burner making her final voyage before going to the breakers' yard, and our captain was admiral of Fyffe's fleet. We leant over the rail watching the fruit being loaded. The labourers, mostly women, carried the bananas on their heads and received a tally every time they loaded a stem into the hold; at first their movements were leisurely, but as the hours passed they speeded up and by sailing-time they were running, to collect as many tallies as they could.

We made friends with the Third Officer, a Trinidadian named Carlton Goddard who came to see us at home several times afterwards when he was in port. He took me down to see the engine-room and the stokehold. The latter was as near hell as anything I have ever seen: the huge banks of coal ranging up to the deck above, the infernal heat, the fire-doors open casting a lurid orange light over the filthy figure standing before each one with his wide-panned shovel, and the monotonous movement: dig, swivel, heave with a practised flick on to the hungry flames.

Twelve days at sea without sight of land, it was a lovely voyage and, though the old tub rolled, she did it slowly and with dignity. When we got to Avonmouth Arthur Small was there to meet us with the car, and we stood briefly watching the ship, passengers and baggage ashore, being moved upriver to unload. A group of stevedores threw the lines which the crew catch to pull up the heavy hawsers attached; everyone missed and the ropes fell back on to the dock. The ship moved on slowly, majestically, while on the bridge the captain's mouth was opening and closing like Mr Punch in a fury, too far away for us to hear. I sent him a postcard to thank him for a happy voyage and added that I had seen the trouble with the lines and imagined what he was saying. He sent back a postcard, 'You couldn't. I was using words you never dreamed of.'

23   New Horizons

After Bryen Gentry and I had settled on the Red Lion Square site five years before and our architects (the actual designer was John Osborne) had been busy ever since, a space was levelled and there came the question of laying the foundation stone. The day on which this was to take place would be a great day in the history of Cassell's, a proud day for father who had brought the firm to its present eminence and an exciting time for me: some way towards my ambition of seeing us once more decently housed.

The first question was the stone itself. René Varin and I were still as close as ever, and he made a suggestion which surprised and delighted me: would I like a piece of the Château de Versailles? The answer was obvious. It appeared that some work was being done on the balustrades of the opera House, and René had sent over to London with the compliments of the French Government a block quarried in 1779. It was shipped to England from the Port à l'Anglais at Marly where on the river the Sun King had had his private palace. One portion was smoothed, to be carved with the name of the layer and the date; this I asked Reynolds Stone to do, while engraving a plaque about the stone itself. A silver trowel was obtained for the ceremony.

Who should lay it but our most distinguished author, if he was willing? Sir Winston Churchill said that he *was* willing and the date was fixed: Saint George's Day, 1956.

We decided to invite to the ceremony a selection of Cassell authors, literary agents, booksellers, printers, the press with, of course, members of the firm, and entertain them to a lunch afterwards with father in the chair. The total came to just over eighty and the problem was to find a building suitable and not too far away; happily the new headquarters of the Royal College of Surgeons in Lincoln's Inn Fields was the right size and available. A blue-and-white striped marquee was set up over the area, the company assembled, and Winston arrived at noon to perform the ceremony which the trade periodical, *The Bookseller*, reported so well that I cannot do better than quote it: 'When celebrated persons engage themselves in this ritual it generally proves to be a somewhat formalistic business – a hand on the stone, a perfunctory scrape with a trowel and a timid tap or two with a gavel, and that is that. But when the job is entrusted to a veteran member of the Amalgamated Union of Building

Trade Workers it is an entirely different thing. Sir Winston smoothed the cement with an expert hand and, when the stone did not come down absolutely to his satisfaction the first time, he had it raised and lowered again. Not until he had tested the result with a spirit level did he pronounce the stone well and truly laid.'

Sir Winston and Lady Churchill with father and my stepmother were borne away by car to Lincoln's Inn Fields where they were put in the President's office with a liberal supply of champagne. I had done the table-plan and dashed to the hall quickly to help the guests find their places as they straggled in from Red Lion Square; I was busier than the doorman of the Ritz on Derby Day. Inevitably it took a long time – some had cars to be re-parked, some stopped to talk to friends, some lost their way – and at one point father dashed out in a frenzy saying, 'For God's sake hurry up; Winston says that if he doesn't get his lunch soon, he's going home.'

Such extreme action fortunately was not necessary; at last everyone was seated and lunch began. It was a good meal as city catering goes. Father spoke, I presented the author with a leather-bound copy of the first volume of *The History of the English-speaking Peoples* which was published that day, and then there was a superb gesture from René Varin. He made this the occasion to present to Winston from the French government a silver medal with on its obverse the effigy of Napoleon cast from the original die approved by the Emperor and on the reverse simply:

A
WINSTON CHURCHILL
Vainqueur de la Guerre
MCMXXXIX – MCMXLV
Le 23 Avril 1956

When Winston got up to speak, we all rose and cheered him. He spoke of the long association he had had with the company and wished us happiness and good fortune in our new home.

During lunch a note was passed up and Lady Churchill, sitting next to me, asked what it was. It came from Eartha Kitt saying that she wanted to meet Sir Winston, and Lady Churchill remarked, 'I wouldn't do much about that if I were you; Winston is not mad about coloured people.' I had no way of knowing whether he held the slightest racist feelings or not, and in any case there was nothing I could do about it one way or the other.

At the end I dashed out to see that the cars were ready and the drivers alerted; as I returned Winston was just emerging from the hall smiling and chatting happily – with Eartha Kitt.

That July the 28th International Congress of PEN was held in London. After being in the book business for so many years without any particular interest in PEN, I had recently begun to take a more active part and had become very friendly with the secretary, David Carver.

He was a tall, handsome man who had been a singer; it was he who had recorded all the English folk music which Paul Frischauer had produced as cultural propaganda early in the war, and then he had been ADC to the Duke of Windsor in the Bahamas.

At his request I had taken the Chair of a House Committee to consider the pressure which existed at the headquarters, which were in Glebe Place, Chelsea, and try to find ways of raising money to buy the house next door. In spite of the presence on the committee of such figures as Roy Jenkins and Sir d'Avigdor-Goldsmid, we did not achieve anything.

Money problems seem endemic in cultural organizations like PEN and the National Book League; people who admire them and use them are lavish with their praise and little else.

This congress is now thirty years back, but even then I was aware that David Carver was not happy about PEN's position and its finances.

As an adjunct to the congress I felt that there should be some exhibition to give the many members from abroad something to look to as a diversion from their conferences, and I thought of a show to be entitled 'England – her friends and visitors.' David Carver liked the idea and Jack Morpurgo said that he wished to have it at Albemarle Street.

I was capable of doing the book side, but I thought that the artists, who were just as important, were beyond me; so I asked Anthony Blunt at the Courtauld Institute if he could recommend anyone who would collaborate with me. He suggested Dr Anita Brookner, who came to see me at St Andrew's Hill. I found myself discussing my little project with not only one of the leading art historians of the age, later the first woman Slade Professor at Cambridge, but also an extremely beautiful and devastatingly attractive woman. I had obviously no idea, nor I am sure at that time had she, that within less than twenty years she would be one of the best living English novelists.

We came to terms and started work. It was great fun. On my side, one of the books which was written in London and had to be shown at all costs was *Das Kapital* by Karl Marx. It is a rare book, but I knew who would have a copy: Ian Fleming, in the remarkable library which Percy Muir formed for him containing the first appearance in print of everything, fact and theory, that you could think of. He had generously lent to me before. The exhibition, which showed first editions and autograph manuscripts from Alfireri to Axel Munthe with paintings and drawings from Hans Eworth to Kokoshka, was well received.

It has been said that everybody has one novel in him, and I now had a good example of this: a manuscript – why do publishers who will only consider books which are typed always refer to them by this misnomer? – came in with the striking title *The Dead, the Dying and the Damned*, a novel by D. J. Hollands, who had served in the Korean War. The reader to whom it was sent for a report was James Turner, who had been junior to me in Field's House at Lancing and now wrote poetry, and novels about a detective called Rampion Savage which we published with moderate success, and was an extremely good critic whose judgement I trusted; I also liked his rather odd, dry wit. He sent me his views which were so vitriolically abusive that I was startled; but then, on second thoughts, I remembered that James was a pacifist, so, inversely, the book must have character to have got under his skin to such an extent. I decided to read it myself and found that my suspicions were not groundless. It was an extremely well written bitter denunciation of the horrors to which this young man doing his National Service had been subjected, a cry against the bestiality and the burning – does anyone now remember the napalm dropped by mistake on our own men (no more horrible than dropping it on anyone else), and the heroism of the Gloucesters? I bought it and we sold 20,000 copies. I never heard anything further; Hollands had got his one novel out of his system.

In June the University at Caen, to replace that totally destroyed in the war, had risen sufficiently from the ground of its new site to be declared open; the occasion was to be marked by great festivities and the bestowal of honorary doctorates on representatives of various countries. To my astonishment I was informed that there were to be two British representatives, Anthony Eden and myself; nothing could have surprised me more and few things could have given me greater pleasure.

This was the vice-chancellor's great day; he had badgered the Government for money and now the result of his labours was to be declared open. A huge audience sat in the sunshine watching the ceremony, at which Gladwin Jebb, the British Ambassador, stood in for Eden. As the beautiful stole of white fur, red and blue silk, with the city's arms embroidered in black and gold was pinned on me, I was touched that laid out in glass cases were the best of the books which I had had the pleasure of giving to the library.

This honour cast a long shadow. Seven years later Lord Thomson of Fleet gave a dinner for Beaverbrook's eighty-fifth birthday, to which I was invited. I once had the uncharitable thought that Roy Thomson laid it all on to dispose of the guest of honour, who was brought to the top table in a wheelchair by his valet, wheeled out again in due course, took to his bed and died. But I am sure no such idea flitted through our host's mind. Beaverbrook, for whose dictatorial villainies I felt the utmost contempt, spoke brilliantly – his last speech and I doubt if he ever made a better one.

I was sitting next to Ifor Evans (later Lord Evans of Hungershall) with whom I had a strange relationship; we had known one another for years, we met seldom, yet we were both delighted when we did. At the time I was bothered by a tiresome situation at Red Lion Square. Nicholas was in charge of all design and jackets and his activities often took him away from the office. During such times if someone rang up for 'Mr Flower,' unaware that there were two, the switchboard had the habit of putting the callers through to me, and some of them were irritated when I had not the slightest idea what they were talking about. I thought that this problem could be solved if I were to assume the title of Doctor, so I explained the circumstances to Ifor Evans and asked his advice. He said, 'Of course you can use it, until you get something better.' I know that it is considered cocky to use an honorary title, but in this case it served a practical purpose; and once done, such things are not easily undone.

A more frivolous aspect appeared some years later in Brisbane. The best bookseller in the city. Watty Thompson, was always very kind to me and I held him in great affection. I believe that I was the only Pom member of his Thursday Club, a group of his friends which met each week after hours, in the basement of his shop, for a few jars. After a round of golf there came into the changing-room another friend of his. Watty introduced us and added acidly, 'Both Doctors, one science, one literature, and neither of you could cure a dose of clap.'

Publishing was exciting all through the fifties. To go through the books in detail would be a lengthy bore, but I may mention that our lists contained Vivian Fuchs, Neville Duke the test pilot, Stirling Moss on Le Mans, at long last the memoirs of Gigli, and an interesting study of sea warfare 1939–1945. And *Heads and Tails* by Aarge Thaarup, a fashionable milliner; for this David arranged a party the surprise of which was to be when the author would suddenly produce a specially designed hat and throw it to Leslie Caron. Thaarup was outrageously late and I could see that the beautiful actress was getting restless, so I went over and tried to pacify her by saying that there was a reason for her staying; the surprise was no surprise to her since she said, 'Yes, I know, but if he doesn't buck up I'm going.'

Allen Lane comes back to my mind at this point because my relations with him were a little peculiar; we met at irregular intervals, yet there was a bridge between us which when crossed seemed always familiar. Should we come together after months, it always seemed as though we had just parted and one of us might re-start, 'As I was saying ...'

He had flamboyance, flair, a selfish will yet great idealism. I asked him once what he was doing for his holiday and he replied that he would as usual be going on an archaeological dig, preferably in the Middle East – 'It cleanses the mind and exercises the body.'

'And how,' I asked, 'do you get there?'

'I drive. I have a Bentley which I keep in Calais for the purpose.'

In those few words appear to me the characteristics which I have attributed to him. A slightly lengthier *rencontre* had more notable repercussions.

At this time, and for many years, the circulation of all Penguin publications, in wrappers or rebound, through public libraries was prohibited. I felt that there was a considerable market for the Pelican originals – which had been described as pioneering a social revolution in Britain when their publication began in 1937 (in this materialistic age they have been declared redundant from the spring of 1990) – in more permanent form. So at one of our occasional meetings over lunch I asked Allen if I might have the hard-back rights. He said that he could not agree to that because it would be showing favour to one publisher at the expense of the rest. I quite appreciated his point, but added that I would like him to lunch with me at the same place in exactly twelve months' time, when I would put the same proposition to him.

1958 came and we sat down to enjoy one another's company as we always did.

'Now, Allen, how many publishers have asked you for the hard-cover rights of any of your publications in the last twelve months?'

'None,' he replied, 'you can go ahead and do what you like.'

So we did, choosing what we considered the cream of the Pelican titles. We called our selection the Belle Sauvage Library, and they were printed mainly in Czechoslovakia. This was not taking bread out of the mouths of British printers, because in this country there was a big log-jam, which the fairly long runs of a batch of fresh titles would only have made worse. The Czechs have always been good printers, but censorship was a nuisance; one book containing something which they considered politically questionable they would not touch, and it had to be moved to Holland.

That year, at last, we moved into Red Lion Square, and to celebrate the event we published *The House of Cassell* which I had originally commissioned Simon Nowell-Smith to write in commemoration of our centenary in 1948. I had known him for many years and always had the deepest respect for him; he is in the truest sense 'a man of letters', who can turn his hand to anything – such as running the London Library for some years – yet will not turn it to anything which he thinks is not right. In this instance when I asked him he said that he would do it provided that he did not have to write about anybody living – which meant that he would stop at 1907 when father entered the firm. I have heard it described as the best history of a publishing firm yet written – up to his stopping, that is. It took the best part of a decade longer than anticipated; and it was to be brought up to date from 1907 to the laying of the foundation stone in Red Lion Square by a fairly pedestrian, but I hope accurate, account written by Arthur Hayward and myself.

Father after so many years of wonderful work felt less and less like coming up to London from his beloved Dorset, so he was happy to be named President while I took the chair.

A year later the quadri-annual International Publishers' Conference was taking place in Vienna and, since in nearly thirty years I had had little time off except normal holidays, I decided that Elizabeth and I should make a 'sabbatical' trip, taking in the conference and meeting our Czech printers. We took the car to Ostende and headed for our first stop, Brussels. Our car was a Jensen 641 in British racing green; it was the most beautifully designed model of that splendid marque and was much admired wherever we stopped throughout the journey. On to Cologne, a visit to which I regarded with mixed feelings. I have expressed before my extreme distaste for the bombing of civilian targets and I was not looking forward to seeing scars on the face of the city I had loved, yet a macabre curiosity made me want to find out what had actually happened.

Most reports of aerial bombardment are inaccurate and over-optimistic – if that is the right word – as I had found out during the war when I entered Lübeck which was claimed to be destroyed and in fact had not got a scratch on it. But in the case of Cologne the R.A.F. had done a fantastic job of precision bombing, in fact so accurate that there must have been a good deal of luck as well as good judgement. The cathedral survived, yet they had destroyed the Hohenzollern Bridge just by one side of it and the railway station which lies immediately on the other. Not unnaturally, the overs had destroyed the Dom Hotel in the square and my favourite Romanesque church a hundred yards away. Of course, from the recently printed remarks of an ex-pilot, it may be – less flatteringly – that the bombs were aimed at the cathedral and as usual missed. Anyway the Excelsior Hotel on the other side of the square survived, and there we stayed.

When it was time to go I loaded the bags and headed the car on the road out of town. Elizabeth came out fuming.

'Don't you ever bring me to this bloody country again,' she said as she got in. I made no reply; my mind was still in a state of ambivalence, sad to go, yet equally sad to see holes in the ground where buildings which I had known so well had stood – and also because I realized from past experience that she must have just been subjected to a typical piece of Prussian impertinence.

We were heading for East Berlin. At that time there were no diplomatic relations between Britain and the German Democratic Republic, to which one could only go if one had an invitation. Through the good offices of Stefan Heym I was invited by the Writers' Union (I forget its official title) and when I had to make this known in London, I was reminded in writing by the Foreign Office that we went entirely at our own risk and that in the event of trouble there was no one to whom we could appeal for help. On that condition we drove eastwards, through Hanover where I saw the worst destruction next to Berlin – with very little done about it – and on to the frontier post at Helmstadt. Here the delay was interminable; there wasn't much traffic, but we sat there for a very long time without anything happening. By the time we entered the G.D.R. we were by my reckoning some two hours behind schedule.

We finally reached the checkpoint at Marienborn, south of Berlin; here our passports were stamped, since Helmstadt, for all its delays, had only been interested in who we were and where we were going. Patiently waiting for us was our cicerone or watch-dog, whichever way one cares to look at it: he was a charming man in his forties; in the first capacity he was invaluable and in the second, if it existed, he was tactful and accommodating. He got in the back of the car and directed us to our hotel near the main railway station, where he said *au revoir* and that he would see us in the morning.

Things had changed in the thirteen years since I had been in the city; the Iron Curtain had come down, although the Wall was not yet built. From the eastern side of the Brandenburg Gate, through which we could not pass (though the two Russian soldiers still stood motionless on their memorial inside the British sector) we peered at the Tiergarten growing up again. There was no longer any trace of the Führer's

Chancellery; but Unter den Linden was a fine street, even if the Stalin style which I had seen when new was beginning to show its age.

Our happiest day was the Sunday with Stefan Heym and his American wife, whom I had met years before in New York. We drove out to the tranquil house where he lived, and still does, in a tree-lined street in the suburb of Grünau. It was a hot day and we spent it on his boat, picnicking and bathing. The vast lake was a mass of yachts, their coloured sails like a scene that Tissot might have painted; everyone in East Berlin seemed to have at least a sailing dinghy.

The next day we drove with our cicerone to Potsdam to visit Sans Souci which survived, although Frederick's Neues Palais had gone. Voltaire meant more to me then than he had when I was last there thirty years before, and I stood in his room at the far end saying a little prayer. The gravel terrace below the wide shallow steps was thronged and the largest proportion of the crowds were Soviet and Chinese officers. The Chinese wore utilitarian uniforms like dull blue denims, with peaked caps to match, but the Soviets had one of their crack Guards Divisions in Berlin at the time, and looking at its representatives with a critical eye I have seen no smarter soldiers anywhere in my life.

We went on to Dresden later that afternoon and arrived after dark. Since 1945 everyone has known about the wanton destruction of Dresden, but nothing had prepared me for what I saw when we emerged from our newly built hotel the next morning.

I had walked through the crumbled streets of London in the eerie silence which follows the bombers' departure; I had heard over my head the menacing roar of the armada on its way to Coventry; I had driven among the needlessly ravaged beauties of Caen; I had stood with incredulous detachment in the desert which had once been Berlin. But Dresden saddened me beyond measure, partly from aesthetic sentimentality, and partly because the shambles which I saw spread all around me seemed the fruit of no more than last-minute vicious spite, almost like a foretoken of *Annie Get Your Gun* – 'Anything you can do, I can do better.'

The large hotel in which Goethe and I both once stayed was a gravel promenade beside the river. With loving care and as a matter of pride the exquisite Zwinger had been built again in all its sparkling beauty; after that the Dresdeners had disconsolately moved down the road and started a new city; life had to go on while they mustered their strength to do something about the rest of the ruins.

Surprisingly one of the few survivors was the art gallery, and an unexpected pleasure was to see the wonderful collection newly rehung. At the end of the war the Soviet authorities had taken the paintings away and cleaned them; and when they returned them, they all looked dazzling – except Giorgione's *Sleeping Venus* which they said was too fragile to touch.

In the late afternoon we bade farewell to our companion; as he said that he must get back to Berlin, and we were on our way south to Prague. I asked him if we had all the papers that we needed and he assured me that we had; he was a good man and we parted affectionately, but all too soon I was to find that he was mistaken.

We arrived shortly before seven at the German frontier post which was occupied by a man and a girl both in their twenties, both good looking and both very friendly. I bustled in with my papers and passports and all was well until they asked, 'Where is your exit visa?'

I explained that I had been assured that I had all the papers required; but no, I needed an exit visa. Where could I get an exit visa? In Dresden. But I had just come from bloody Dresden and had no desire to drive all the way back there. Then they had an idea; the head of Police in the chief town of the *Kreis* (I think it was Pirna) could issue the permit, if he was available. They telephoned. Yes, he would be happy to oblige and would remain in his office until eight o'clock. Seldom has the Jensen moved as fast as it did back up the road down which we had just come.

Arriving at Police headquarters, I asked Elizabeth to stay in the car while I went inside to find the boss. Then I was very thoughtless; the Police chief was such an interesting man that we sat talking politics, I quite oblivious of my poor wife who, by the time I came out, was lonely and apprehensive.

We sailed through the German border the second time, parted with smiles and waves, and drove half a mile to the border of Czechoslovakia. The post was manned by two officials, one of whom spoke only Czech while the other also spoke German. The latter looked at our passports and then struck a thunder blow:

'These visas are out of date.'

I had applied to the Czech embassy in London well in advance because I expected that it would be a slow business. At that time the visas stipulated precisely the day and the month on which you intended to enter the country. The embassy clerk had not turned his rubber stamp far enough and instead of stamping '20 May' he had entered '20 April', and not understanding a word of Czech I was blissfully unaware of his mistake. A month out made the visas automatically invalid.

When I asked what we did now, the official said that he would have to ring Prague, and, when I asked how long that might take, he said that the last case they had had took five hours. I went out to the car with the joyful news, and Elizabeth, who had had a few qualms about this journey from the start, announced (hardly surprisingly) that she had a sick headache. The two officials were most concerned and in no time they whipped up a large cup of black coffee which the Czech-speaker took out with a smile of commiseration.

Actually, the sanction came fairly quickly and with handshakes all round we set off.

I had been told that everyone in Prague spoke German – although there were some who preferred not to use the language of their erstwhile occupiers. So when I got into the city and the main road began to splinter into turnings in all directions I decided to ask before I got even more lost than I was already; but at one o'clock in the morning German-speakers were conspicuously absent. Finally I accosted a

friendly pedestrian who had no German but offered by signs to take me
to our hotel, the Alkron. I by signs indicated that I had a wife and a car
just round the corner, and he by signs indicated the way to a taxi-rank
where one of the drivers was sure to speak German. I did as I was 'told'
and, as usually happens in this sort of situation, it turned out that we
were quite near the hotel.

Our few days in what is one of the most beautiful cities in Europe
were as happy as they were fully occupied. We met four representatives
of the printing office; the two of whom we saw most were George
Theiner and Milós Porkorny, in addition to whom there was a tall
handsome man who, not surprisingly, displayed a marked liking for
Elizabeth, and a fourth who had never been out of Czechoslovakia but
whose hobby was London of which he had an astonishing and
encyclopaedic knowledge. There was not a great deal of actual work to
be done, it was more a matter of getting to know one another and going
over problems, which were few. We of course saw all the proper sights;
apart from these we were asked what we would like to do, and then
some of the restraint appeared like a little iceberg bobbing in the open
sea. I said that we would like to meet Method Kaláb, not only to pay our
respects to one of the world's greatest typographers but also to bring
him greetings from the Double Crown Club of which he had been made
one of the first honorary members in 1925. Milós and George expressed
themselves delighted because they had never seen him, which surprised
me; again I felt that there was some reason why it would have been a
little unwise for them to have known the greatest living Czech printer.
But they would get in touch with him on our behalf. After a delay we
were invited to tea by Kaláb and his wife. The great typographer was a
short, reserved, gentle old man, and though it was no more than a
gesture I think that he was pleased that a member of the club had called
to pay his respects. It gave me the germ of an idea which did not bear
fruit until over a year later.

Eventually the day came to leave for Vienna.

The Alkron was at that time the best hotel in the city, large and
comfortable. Beyond reception is a dance floor, surrounded by a salon
with little tables, at the far end of which, by the dining-room door, is a
stand from which a waiter dispenses coffee – Italian espresso, or Turkish
which is not to everyone's taste, but very much to mine. Staying in the
hotel was an American, short, fat, red-faced, pompous, the kind of
person – every country has them – who should never be allowed a
passport because he does nothing but harm to the image of his
homeland. Elizabeth and I had nicknamed him the 'turkey cock' and
disliked the sight of him intensely.

At eleven our friends came to wish us *bon voyage* and we all sat at one
of the little tables. I thought that I had better go up to the room to make
sure that the bags had been brought down and when I returned,
satisfied, Elizabeth said, 'It's a good thing you weren't here just now, or
you would have had a row.'

'What happened?'

'The turkey cock came in and right across the room bellowed at the top of his voice, "gimme a cup of coffee, and don't give me any of that shit you gave me yesterday".'

She was right; he was such a disgrace to a country which has meant so much to both of us that I do not think I would have been able to keep my seat.

By the evening we were settled in Sacher's, one of my favourite hotels in the world. We stayed in for dinner, and, since I have always found German and Austrian wines too sweet for my taste, I asked the *maître d'hôtel* if he would bring us a bottle of the driest wine he had in the cellar. It was pure Austrian nectar, very light in colour with a wonderful nose, and as dry as a good wine from the Loire. He came back a little later and asked with some anxiety. 'You did mean the driest?' And when I told him that we thought it perfection, he sighed, 'Thank goodness for that; I can't give it away.'

We had arranged to meet Tony and Bunty Barrett in Vienna and afterwards drive them to Venice. The conference was like any other conference; but I got some fun out of listening to speeches in German and then switching over to the interpreter to see what he was making of the prolixities of German syntax. On one occasion there was a never-ending sentence and he wearily remarked, 'I'm waiting for the verb,' and then, what seemed hours later, 'I'm still waiting for the verb.' But everything was dwarfed by a performance at the opera put on for the occasion by the Austrian paper-makers. When I got home and showed the programme to David Ascoli, he remarked that it was the finest cast of singers which could have been assembled in the world at that time. But I can only recall the glorious voice of Elisabeth Schwarzkopf, then at her finest. The opera was *The Marriage of Figaro*, conducted by Von Karajan. I had never seen him before, so it was a surprise to watch him enter the orchestra pit at the double, pick up his baton without so much as a glance at the audience, and away at a fast gallop. Not for nothing did someone say that what most people record on four discs he will get into three. He took the overture at a sizzling pace with the sparkle of diamonds and it was electrically exciting. The whole performance was magic; but much as I love the opera, I still think it is an act too long.

It was with considerable regret that I left Vienna with a full car for Venice. For a long time I have tried to analyse why I retain an affection for some towns and take a dislike to others. Perhaps it is brought about by my reaction against general opinion; for instance, I am very fond of Bilbao for which most people cannot find a good word, and I do not particularly care for San Francisco because, although charming, it is over-praised. Yet this cannot be the whole explanation because I love Grenada and Florence, two places which are described only with a monotonous stream of superlatives. Order and tidiness appeal to me, which is a good reason for admiring Dubrovnik, and I dislike anything which is complacently content to live on its reputation. Never in my life had I had any desire to go to Venice, but on this occasion there were two good reasons for doing so: first, I was in a minority of one to three, and secondly it is the height of arrogance to hold an opinion of any sort about a place which one has never visited.

Alas, my worst forebodings proved to be not without foundation. I found the place dirty, smelly, down-at-heel, neglected, like a woman once proud and beautiful now akin to the piteous state of Blanche Dubois in *Streetcar*. Once the stronghold of a mercantile and conscienceless aristocracy which lived on selling slaves to the Levant and the raw material of armaments to its own enemies and which patronized a school of painting which, with the ever-blessed exception of Giorgione and the early work of his illustrious pupil, is not to my taste. Of the palaces on the Grand Canal, Will Durant concedes that 'We must picture these not in their present deterioration but in their fifteenth- and sixteenth-century heyday' – a feat of the imagination which I found beyond me.

Yet to dismiss such a jewel in the crown of civilization as spurious would be short-sighted and childish. The panorama coming back from the Lido I felt as exciting as a glimpse of some promised land. The Piazza di San Marco is as familiar as the Taj Mahal and, like that marble miracle, exceeds all expectation. From our bedroom window I drew a silent breath at the beauty of Santa Maria della Salute and thought of Sargent's lovely painting of it which I had known since I was young.

Saying *au revoir* to the Barretts, we went on our way. One of my targets was to call upon Professor Pietro Rebora and congratulate him on our Italian dictionary which he had recently completed and which was going through the press. I had written from London of my impending visit and asking for two recommendations: an hotel in Florence, and a place to have a few days rest from driving; in both he turned up trumps. Still dazzled by the mosaics at Ravenna and the drive over the Apennines we arrived in Florence at his hotel. He had written 'Do not be put off by the exterior, but be grateful that it is quiet'; for all its great beauty, Florence is an excruciatingly noisy city and in the main square a café orchestra playing the latest hit *Arrivederci Roma* was barely audible above the traffic.

There was no point in staying at another city, Milan, and I thought that we could afford two nights on Como at the Villa d'Este, an hotel which I had always wanted to see, and indeed very luxurious it is. Having drinks before dinner on the terrace we were fascinated by a party of Americans at the next table who were having a violent row; we expected fisticuffs at any moment. By unashamedly listening we discovered the cause of the fracas: they had travelled so far and so fast that they could not agree among themselves in which country a certain church was located, let alone in what town.

The next morning, suggesting that Elizabeth should take a boat on the lake, I set off on the fifty-mile drive into Milan to see Professor Rebora, and a very hairy journey it was. The moment a long, low car in British racing green swept up the drive from the hotel on to the autostrada, the Italian drivers went berserk. Hounded by Alfas, Maseratis, Ferraris and other lesser breeds, my foot flat on the floorboards, I averaged 120 mph, which was not bad in those days, and entered town undefeated but a little nerve-racked. The next day I took Elizabeth in rather more sedately so that we could worship before Leonardo's *Last Supper* which, although I understand that the present restoration work is revealing great things, even then was in much better condition than I had expected.

In answer to my second question – where to rest – Professor Rebora had recommended the Isola dei Pescatori on Lake Maggiore; as before, he was right. Having garaged the car in Stresa, we were rowed out to the tiny island and a charming small hotel. The peace, the quiet only broken by an occasional bicycle bell down the island's one street, sitting on the rocks in the warm sun gazing at the beauty of the lake disappearing into the distant haze, strolling round the nearby Isola Bella where the white peacocks strut proudly through the terraced gardens was perfection.

We left with regret, for we had a date at Le Mans. There we had a rendezvous with Bryen Gentry who flew in from London; we all arrived on time and it was a happy reunion. Everyone who is interested knows from television what the Vingt-quatre Heures is like, if he has not indeed been there himself. It is enough to say that there is the peculiarly rare atmosphere which is enjoyed by the few sporting events which are *hors classe* – like the Derby, the Grand National or the Indianapolis 500. And Jaguar won.

We brought Bryen back with us. The 'sabbatical', the longest drive of my life, was over; the car had purred the whole way and there had been never so much as a puncture, never a mishap and never a dull moment.

24 Excursions and Alarms

Paperbacks: Their Past, Their Present and Their Future was the title of a paper which I read to the Double Crown Club in the spring of 1959, and it seems to me to have been the most worth while of my various offerings to them. My guest that evening was Allen Lane. The past and present spoke for themselves, and my views about the future were not so far out – except that I did not foresee the full extent of the vast avalanche which was to overwhelm the market. Ellic Howe liked it well enough to print it as a small book, to which Allen wrote a Foreword. In reviewing it, *The Times Literary Supplement* said, 'Others beside publishers could well ponder his prophecy that the paperback publishers in America will soon be bossing the whole business.' I had another go on this subject at the annual Booksellers' Conference that year when I quoted the latest American paperback figures which were 3,000,000 and it is obvious what an enormous investment by printers and papermakers that represents. William Jovanovich, the respected head of one of the big American firms – Harcourt Brace – had recently said that 'Millionaires have of late discovered that book publishing ... can be most stimulating ... and publishing stock prospectuses are found on the tables of stockbrokers everywhere.'

I said then that there was a tendency to buy the hardcover rights of a book because of confidence in making a fat deal, and cited the case of a publisher who rejected a book because he had not been able to arrange already a paperback sale; to me that was the absolute negation of the ethics of publishing and there was serious danger of its becoming the norm.

That was thirty years ago, and I think that it did become the norm; it was a phase through which publishing had to pass. Today there are enormous prices being paid for titles which have quick paperback potential, and books which have no such attraction are handled by a number of smaller publishers, some of them very good, which have mushroomed since the time of which I was speaking.

On the other hand, of recent years there has been a surge of amalgamations – every well known publishing house seems to belong to someone else or is itself the centre of a conglomerate, so that on examination it can be seen that the industry is largely in the hands of a few – the millionaires of whom Bill Jovanovich was speaking years ago, and by one of whom he was for some time being pursued. For example, in 1986 Allen Lane's brainchild, Penguin, acquired from Thomson Michael Joseph, Hamish Hamilton, Sphere Books and Rainbird ('a major extension of its hardback publishing arm') and is itself a sub-division of Pearson. Another millionaire, B.T.R., is involved in a publishing empire with Paul Hamlyn's Octopus which together acquired Heinemann at about the same time, and this is a classic example of the progress of publishing.

William Heinemann founded his imprint in 1890; it became a public company in 1932 and belonged to the American house of Doubleday who put in charge A.S. Frere, a well known director who was there when they bought it. Then it was acquired in 1961 by Thomas Tilling whose money came from the sale of their bus company when London Transport was formed. In 1986 the new move was described in *The Times* as 'the biggest merger in the history of British publishing', and when it was announced, B.T.R.'s shares rose within two hours by £6,500,000, and its chief, Sir Owen Green, declaimed that 'We take a bullish view of publishing for the coming ten to twenty years.' In itself, there does not seem to be anything wrong with being a millionaire, though I am sometimes reminded of the song in *High Society:* yet the point which I am trying to make was emphasized recently in *The Observer* which said, 'Nowadays publishing – no longer an occupation for gentlemen – is jammed with marketing wizards, and vulgar money-spinners are accepted in the best literary society.'

In other words, there are now two breeds of dog: one very large, with many tails which have grown to such an extent that they wag the body, the other, a smaller breed like a terrier which has no tail at all. This is not necessarily a bad thing so long as it conforms to the old tag, *mens sana in corpore sano:* on the other hand, whether the *corpus* is actually *sanum* remains to be seen. Sales of paperbacks overall are no longer increasing, and in the United States alone during 1985 fell by 50,000,000. 'The paperback industry is desperately worried ... Now horns are being drawn in ... Most alarming of all is the high percentage-level of returns to paperback houses ... The paperback certainly has a past. But what of its future?' one critic of publishing wrote in the spring of 1986. All appeared not to be well, however bullish Sir Owen Green might feel; 'Publishing appears to be going through the San Francisco earthquake,' one director of a famous house said a little later in the same year, and this critical situation, it has been noted, is 'despite all the nationalization and reorganization which has taken place'; another director at the same time added, 'What publishers need is a good kick up the pants.'

Perhaps in the spring of 1987 they got it, with the biggest burst of wheeling and dealing seen to date. The publishing industry became headline news, and too complicated to detail here; anyway, those sufficiently interested will have read in the press about the two-way transatlantic traffic.

In May 1987 *The Times* carried an article headed 'Publishers re-write the profits handbook with acquisitions,' with photographs of two of the 'hungry' (sic) millionaires. They sound good, but there are certain drawbacks inherent in these transatlantic conglomerations, with their concentration on money (which their heads would deny). A member of a prominent English publishing house referred to one on the air late in 1989: 'If you have people in New York or Los Angeles saying to editors in London what kind of books they should be doing and what kind of margins they should be making, what direction the editorial policies should be taking, I think there's a problem. You have the accountant in New York who is saying 'We must grow the company' [a new Wall Street phrase]. Well, you can't grow a publishing house at 15 per cent per annum unless you win the Booker Prize every year.' Those who see roses all the way point to the enormous sums of money which the conglomerates have available now for certain authors – though unfortunately those authors are almost without exception concocters of sludge. This has led to 'fears of a devaluation of literature into a supermarket, as Edna O'Brien has lamented'.

The publisher whose broadcast was quoted above added; 'We talk about publishing *houses* and it is, traditionally, a house, a small group of people living in a house working with writers. It is not a company. It is not a big business.' In the present altered conditions, it is as well to remember that in the past all the firms so busily amalgamated were founded by individuals who followed their own fancy; their successes and mistakes were of their own making. As that great publisher Ben Huebsch wrote: 'The important thing is that an imprint be purposeful; at its best it should be representative of a personality.' Peter Owen, an independent publisher for nearly forty years, has said: 'If good books – as distinct from pieces of mediocre merchandise – are to be published in the future, it will be necessary to have strong independent publishers.' I defy anyone, however able, to run an imprint which is part of a conglomerate entirely to his own satisfaction – despite the assurances of the big boys that the heads of their multiple divisions have complete autonomy. Of necessity he has the ultimate group balance sheet hovering in the background like Banquo's ghost; he is driving a car with the handbrake on. And in all the almost frantic wheeler-dealing nothing has been said about the authors who are not TV meat, who are trying to get started, or about literature. As Peter Owen, again, says: 'Our strong literary heritage is under threat from the values of the conglomerates.'

'Now thesis has provoked anti-thesis, and small publishers are back in fashion,' Melvyn Bragg wrote at the end of 1989. One movement in this direction was the foundation of Bloomsbury Books by Miss Calder, in order, she said, 'To give the author what he wants.' This move back towards sense and good order has been continued by various individuals, all once leading figures in firms which have been sucked into conglomerates, who have departed disgruntled and set up their own imprints. But still the plague of the conglomerates – unlikely to work in the long term – continues.

The last years of the fifties produced for us the memoirs of Lord Avon, who invited me down to Wiltshire for a most enjoyable lunch; he was charming and friendly. Nevertheless I had heard some alarming accounts – R.A. Butler recorded Eden's acute sensitivity to all forms of criticism and the raggedness of his nerves; there was something which made me instinctively wary (and I am not being wise after the event). Fortunately there quickly appeared an affinity between Lord Avon and Kenneth Parker, our chief editor in whose capable hands I was happy to leave all dealings over the volumes.

And at the same time we took *Beloved Infidel* by Sheila Graham, the East End London girl who became a reporter in Hollywood. As an admirer of Scott Fitzgerald, I was deeply interested in her first account of her life with him; by the time they came together his wife was in the lunatic asylum and he was cracking up. She came to London for the publication and I was half attracted and half frightened by the blonde beauty who had become one of the 'unholy trinity' – with Hedda Hopper and Louella Parsons – the sarcasm of which was the bane of the film industry. She and Fitzgerald, she told me, had two flats in Hollywood, one above the other. In 1940 he died in her flat; that being a more moral age, and inert bodies weighing a ton, she had to enlist the porter's help so that the great writer could be discovered upstairs in his own premises. Nearly twenty years later she was to write a more explicit account of the affair.

One should have no favourites, but I look back with special pleasure to *Speech is of Time* because I had the highest admiration for its author, Sir Robert Menzies, personally, as a statesman and as a writer. We gave a launching party at the Savoy and I can see the smile on his face as he left and I said to myself, 'That is a man I would like to see again'; I did.

We also produced *Venetian Blind* by William Savage. Although we had published many of his books, this is the one which I remember particularly because I think that it had the best jacket we ever gave him. As an espionage novelist he was a forerunner of Deighton and Le Carré, who may be the vogue now but neither writes better English than Savage. His agent was Innes Rose, the senior partner in the firm of John Farquharson, whose offices were opposite us in Red Lion Square.

In sending me the first William Savage manuscript Innes said, 'It is a *nom de plume,* and if you like it I will tell you who it is.' It turned out to be R.H.M. Clayton who had been one of my house captains in Field's House at Lancing. We had not seen one another since; he was now a high-ranking civil servant and a golfer. We resumed our interrupted friendship and enjoyed a successful business partnership for more than a decade.

The most spectacular event was the publication of *A Silver Plated Spoon* by the Duke of Bedford, which was the highest light of David Ascoli's promotional flair. Ian Bedford agreed to the event taking place at Woburn and was enthusiastically co-operative. The whole of the near-by hotel was booked to accommodate booksellers and ourselves. Dinner was served in the banqueting hall using the gold plate – apparently the first time this had happened since Queen Victoria and the Prince Consort had visited Woburn. The main speakers were Lord Mancroft, renowned for his eloquence, and the delightful Canadian television star, Bernard Braden. I had to speak last and to follow two such experienced orators was not easy; at least I had to try to be light-hearted. It used to be characteristic of the Beaverbrook Press to make snide remarks whenever the fancy took them, and in an account of this dinner I was looked down upon from a great height for telling what the reporter haughtily considered a *risqué* joke about Sir Thomas Beecham. Years later I was delighted to find this harmless anecdote printed in a book of the great conductor's aphorisms; times change, occasionally for the better.

As the XVII Olympiad was to take place at Rome in 1960 I thought it would be a good idea to do a book of essays by the winner of a gold medal at each of the games since their revival. I suggested to Harold Abrahams, with whom I was still in touch, that he should edit it and we worked out the contributors together. Everyone who was asked accepted, wherever he or she lived in the world; they were an impressive collection, including Douglas Lowe. Fanny Blankers-Koen of Holland, Zatopek of Czechoslovakia and Kuts of the Soviet Union. I discovered somewhat to my surprise that Avery Brundage, the autocratic American secretary of the games, had won gold for the pole-vault in 1912. I was so pleased that another Chicagoan accepted: the immortal Jesse Owens, who to Hitler's fury dominated the Berlin games in 1936.

I love Chicago and never miss an opportunity of going there, so I arranged to pick up these two manuscripts on my next trip. Brundage, an hotel tycoon, was out of town, but he had left his essay with his secretary for me. Then I went to call on Jesse Owens.

Apart from my own particular interest in running, it is difficult when one meets a famous athlete to analyse how much of one's impression of a man who won four gold medals and held the world record of every sprint distance and the long jump is straight hero-worship, and how much is unbiased. I can only say that he welcomed me as warmly as I have ever been welcomed in my life, and in five minutes we were talking as if we had known one another for years. Of course in a black face a broad smile is particularly gleaming, but I can see the sweetness of his expression now. I asked him what he was doing and he replied: 'The Mayor of Chicago sent for me and said, "Get the kids off the streets. Never mind about the money, just get them off the streets and keep them occupied," and that's what I'm doing.'

We could certainly use a man like him in the country now.

I could have stayed all day, but after an hour, I reluctantly thought that I had taken enough of his time and got up to go, gratefully pocketing his manuscript. From his office, he insisted on walking with me to the elevator, a neat, slim figure, not very tall. The trouble with athletes who keep fit is that they have no conception of their own strength. As the elevator arrived he put his hand affectionately round the back of my neck and shook it; my spine felt like that of a rodent severely mauled by a terrier. And he said, 'Goodbye and good luck.'

I didn't deserve any more good luck than I had just had.

Thayer Hobson retired from William Morrow at the end of 1959 by which time Isobel, his wife, who had been my hostess in New England, New York and Arizona, was dead. It was a sad loss to me in the publishing world, but fortunately not the end of our friendship. In the following year H.L. Davis, who had been famous for his *Honey in the Horn* which had achieved a huge success which he had never been able to equal, died in Mexico and Thayer found himself literary executor. Going down to Mexico to sort through the vast mass of papers, Thayer fell in love with Bette, the author's widow, and married her. It was the last of his several marriages and a very happy one. They tried living at her home in Oaxaca, which is fairly far south, but it was too high for Thayer's lungs which had been badly damaged by gas in the first war, so they moved to Texas – to Comfort, which is some twenty miles outside San Antonio.

Here he and Bette started to breed apaloosas, the beautiful piebald horses seen comparatively seldom in England. In 1964 he wrote to me: 'I have been brooding about combining the apaloosa operation with a quarter horse* racing programme. Last Saturday, on the theory that one might as well be hanged for a sheep as a lamb, to my own surprise as well as everyone else's – at a dispersal sale near Forth Worth – I bought a 12-year-old race mare who has produced some of the best and finest running horses in the last few years … It looks as though I will have to pull myself together and live at least one more year! (I have even *considered* giving up smoking).'

He lived more than the year he wanted, but he never did give up smoking. When I went to stay with them at Deer Ledge Ranch outside Comfort and saw him for the last time, dying from emphysema, he was forced at intervals to put a mask over his face and inhale pure oxygen; but it did not stop him smoking. Nothing would change him, the dry wit remained unimpaired and everything was still as ludicrous as it had always seemed to him. He could not go out of the house, but Bette took me into San Antonio, an enchanting small town with one quarter of the old white Spanish streets gay with the sound of running streams and ablaze with flowers. Modern San Antonio has grown round the erstwhile loneliness of the old mission, opposite the entrance of which now stands the general post office; but inside the walls it is cool and quiet and visitors have to be reminded to take their hats off, for the central building, in one room of which James Bowie died, is still a chapel. Although I felt sure that it was the last time, there was no sadness when I left: we knew one another far too well for that. He died on 19 October 1967.

As the market for books on jazz increased and my own interest was as strong as ever, I noticed in the American *Literary Market Place* that a small firm with alleged communist leanings, Twayne, was going to publish the memoirs of my idol, Sidney Bechet; I applied for the British rights at once, and found myself owning the whole thing. A young woman

* A type of horse bred in the United States with a remarkable turn of speed which, as the name implies, races over a quarter of a mile.

named Joan Williams had persuaded Bechet to talk on tape, but she had no plan and the result of all this recording was a mess. There was wonderful material in it, but no order, so I had to take the whole thing to pieces and reassemble it; the last chapter, as published, I found somewhere in the middle of the jumble. It was far from complete; one of the things about which I particularly wanted Bechet's views was the ballet, *The Night is a Witch*, for which he had composed the music. He was now living in Paris, so I arranged to go over and talk to him. I was very excited to arrive at Le Bourget and see waiting for me the jazz musician – or 'musicianer' as he would say – whom I admired above all others; he drove me to his home where his cook-housekeeper gave us a good lunch. He had an office in town and we spent the best part of two days making tapes, which I later gave to Tulane University in New Orleans for their historic jazz collection. There was no time for more, and we agreed to meet again when I had prepared a questionnaire so that we could complete his life to date. But it was not to be; shortly afterwards he went into hospital and never came out again. He died in May 1959. Left with an incomplete book, I was now so soaked in his idiosyncratic style that I was able to write the remaining chapters (except, as I have said, the very last one) from the existing printed records. It must have come off all right because when we published *Treat it Gentle* in 1960, a letter arrived from a lady in Boston who was born in New Orleans, thanking us for doing the book which had the authentic tang of Louisiana, particularly the last chapters!

In the spring of 1961, together as usual for the last part of my New York stay, we had an example of something which seems, alas, to have been all too common. I knew well Frank Taylor, a tall, extremely young-looking man who was mentally ambidextrous; he spent six months of the year as a publisher in New York and six months on the west coast as a film producer. On this occasion he was in New York in the act of changing hats because he had been appointed producer of *The Misfits*, the script which Arthur Miller had written to be made into a film by Clark Gable and Marilyn Monroe that summer. Frank said that it had already been decided that the musical accompaniment was to be provided by a solo guitar and he had been looking round for the right player. Now he thought that he had found him, playing in a nightclub, and Marilyn Monroe was coming that evening to hear him; would we care to join in? Of course we would.

It is extraordinary how quickly rumours get around; when we arrived, near ten o'clock, there was already a small crowd waiting at the entrance. We sat with Frank listening to the young man play, and he was very good. Midnight came, but no Marilyn Monroe; the crowd drifted away; we went home to bed; the musician packed up his instrument and departed, the most disappointed man in New York that night. Why did she promise? Did she forget, or did something else turn up, or perhaps she never had any intention of coming.

After our return from the long drive round Europe I had a phone call from Method Kaláb's daughter, who lived in England, asking how her father was; she had heard of my visit by letter, but had not seen him for many years. In Prague there had been the germ of an idea in my mind and it now grew; I wanted to see assembled at the National Book League an exhibition of books from Czechoslovakia where the standards of production are so high, and invite Kaláb to open it in celebration of his 75th birthday. The Czech authorities agreed, a splendid display of books was assembled, and Kaláb arrived early in October 1961, with Milós Porkorny who was to read his paper for him since he had little English. The exhibition opened in Albemarle Street on the 13th, and after that Kaláb visited Manchester, Leicester and other schools of typography at which he could answer the questions of advanced students. What he did in between his official appointments was no concern of mine; my duty was solely to see that he returned at the proper time to his homeland, which he did. Afterwards he wrote me a charming letter and sent me a beautiful specimen of his typography. I cannot believe that the Czech authorities then, in view of his prompt return, can have taken exception to his having seen his daughter; they certainly would not today. It was for the last time; he died in 1963.

Needing more room, we moved to another sixteenth-century house: Wray Farm, Reigate. It was beautiful, but haunted by sadness. Houses have characters and, although Wray Farm cannot be held responsible for the conduct of its occupants, eventually the sadness, whether pre-ordained or fortuitous, had not been exorcized by the departure of the previous owners.

We had not been there long before there was a considerable flurry in the publishing world, in which I became involved in a peculiar way. Stanley Rinehart, who was in London, asked a number of friends in for drinks. During the party I noticed Graham Watson of Curtis Brown and Peter Watt (A.P. Watt's son, soon, alas, to die young) with their heads together, so I went over and jokingly asked what two such eminent literary agents could be talking about. Graham looked at his watch and said, 'I suppose *The Times* has gone to bed by now; we might as well tell him.'

The news concerned the excellent publishing house originally founded under his own name by Michael Joseph when he left Curtis Brown. Now his widow, Anthea, was deputy chairman, the firm belonged to *The Ilustrated News* which in turn belonged to Roy (later Lord) Thomson who then owned *The Times*. It appeared that three directors of Michael Joseph – Charles Pick, Roland Gant and Peter Hebdon – had resigned and the news would break the following morning. The story from the Thomson side, and for all I know it may be no more than half the truth, was that these three gentlemen had asked for more money or they would walk out and, when Roy Thomson said that he would not negotiate under duress, walk out they did. The *Daily Telegraph* some days later, on 17 January, reported that the three were joining a syndicate to take over Jonathan Cape, but nothing came of this. In the end Pick and Gant went to Heinemann, of which the former eventually became managing director and now recently retired; Hebdon reneged and asked for his job back.

That evening I felt very angry. I had always liked Michael Joseph who had built up a good list, and now his widow, whom I had never met, was to be left short-handed for what appeared to be purely mercenary reasons; somehow the possible disintegration of a fine list upset me in the way one might feel seeing a beautiful ship blown on to a reef. I happened to have the home telephone number of Denis Hamilton, the managing director of the Thomson Group, so I rang him to ask if my services could be of any help in keeping things tied down in the high winds which were sure to blow. He said he would be pleased, and so my association with Michael Joseph's began.

Anthea accepted me, fortunately, and we worked well together. She eventually married as her second husband Macdonald Hastings, whom I had known for years in the Saintsbury Club, and they lived in Hampshire with great happiness and contentment. My first task was to write, as a quasi-independent body in a less personal way than Anthea could, to all the authors, assuring them that the departure of three executives whom they knew well would make no difference to the efficiency of the firm. In the end they all decided to stay except two: Monica Dickens, who left for personal reasons, and Richard Gordon, author of the 'Doctor' books, for reasons which were never clear to me. Spencer Curtis Brown was Gordon's agent and he gave us both lunch at the Reform Club, but he was of no help in explaining why his client wished to go to another house; I was not heartbroken.

No sooner had I made this move than David Ascoli offered to come in on the sales side: it was a kindly, spontaneous and welcome gesture. He eased off after Peter Hebdon had returned with his tail suitably between his legs, but I remained on the board for eight years, although once the ship had sailed into calmer waters I took no further part in daily business and only attended formal meetings. As the company was doing well I could not contribute anything further, as the Thomson chairman, Gordon Brunton, gently pointed out, and I was happy to withdraw.

Getting to know this remarkable man, now knighted, was one of the bonuses of the adventure. He wielded great power in the Thomson organization; a man of iron, whose hand was gloved not in velvet but in vair; a man who, if he wished to tell someone to take a running jump, would do so with such courtesy that, I am sure, he would be thanked by the victim; a man who saw things with such clarity that disagreement was impossible.

The other bonus, smaller because less frequent, was to see something of Roy Thomson. How different he was from that other newspaper proprietor, unlike whom he had a marked disinclination for interfering in the policies of his various enterprises; he hired men whom he trusted and left them to their devices. He did not send commands on yellow paper, vengeful notes issued regardless of the consequences. He was a careful man who liked order. He peered from behind his pebble-lensed glasses with such lack of ostentation that a stranger might be forgiven for not recognizing the needle-sharp perception which lay behind. Though prepared to lose millions on *The Times*, which he may have regarded as an expensive hobby or a pious duty, he hated waste. None of his executives was allowed to fly anywhere first class; he always flew economy himself and insisted that what was adequate for him was sufficient for his staff – though they were welcome to drink themselves silly on champagne if they so desired. To sit next to him at lunch was as restful as having a drink with an acquaintance at one's golf club. He was an habitual reader of who-dunits; I always sent him every one we published, and he never failed to say that he found them welcome. I was once told of his method of going home at the end of the day (I presume that he came by the same method); I hope that it is not apocryphal, because it is so typical of his practicality. At the appointed hour a chauffeur was waiting at Gray's Inn Road with a Rolls-Royce to drive him to Holborn Underground station where he took the train; at the end of the line another chauffeur was waiting with another Rolls-Royce. Practicality without parsimony!

It was in the following year that René Varin, to my very great regret, went back to France, after being Cultural Counsellor in London for nearly twenty years, an unusually long time in any diplomatic post. He was so good that the Quai d'Orsay was reluctant to move him, but finally, because of age, the time had come for him to retire. Although I was to see him again in France, there would be no more lunches at the Stafford – a favourite of his – and no more plots together for the benefit of France. But before he left he was to do me one more good turn: he asked me if I would become *Président des Comités de l'Alliance Française en Grande Bretagne* in succession to John Lehmann, who in turn had followed T.S. Eliot. This was a serious matter: to be titular head of the British branch of the organization responsible for the furtherance of French thought and culture throughout the world. I was perfectly well aware of how much my spoken French left to be desired, but, feeling that this shortcoming was outweighed by my admiration for French culture, I accepted.

My first duty was to call upon the French ambassador at the Embassy in Knightsbridge, where I went in a state of some trepidation – which I need not have felt, for a kinder reception would have been impossible. Geoffroy de Courcel must rank among the most distinguished figures in the last fifty years of French diplomacy and has enjoyed a scintillating career. He had arrived as ambassador to the Court of Saint James in 1962, but was no stranger to London, for in 1940 he had been *Chef de Cabinet* in General de Gaulle's Free French government. After a spell in the field as a captain of Spahis Marocains, the Baron came back to the government again *director adjoint* for the rest of the war. He returned as ambassador from a series of high appointments in occupied Germany; it is some indication of his success that he remained here for a whole decade and in 1965 was given the prestigious title of *Ambassadeur de France*. The embassy residence, always beautiful, became a wonderful place to visit, and the Courcels were not only very hospitable, but together were the most magnificent couple I have ever seen: he tall, blond and handsome, while Martine was small, dark and exquisite – an innocent enchantress with whom everyone (within the bounds of propriety) was in love.

My tenure of office, which was to last just over eight years, would have been quite impossible if the secretary had not been the character he was. Pierre le Dilicocq, already OBE for his services in this country, was a man of great stature and immense charm. His diplomacy was infinite; his private opinion of some of the members of the committee over which, with his help, I was called upon to preside was unprintable, but, ever unruffled, he was at all times polite to everyone. We got to know one another very well and I relied on him totally. On my next visit to Australia I expressed fraternal greetings to my opposite numbers over a memorable meal in Melbourne.

Before that visit there was a decision to be made at Red Lion Square: for some time we had been faced by a growing dilemma over the Medical Department. Although we had some titles which were highly regarded in the profession, our list was not big enough to command sufficient attention in the trade; either we had to get out or find some means of enlarging it. By chance we discovered that the highly respected firm of Ballière, Tindall & Cox would not look unkindly on an offer for dynastic reasons. Dennis Tindall had one daughter, Gillian, who was a writer on the Cassell list – I had published her first novel, *No Name in the Street*, in 1959 and had a very high opinion of her talents – but he had no son. Terms were agreeably arranged during 1964, and our two lists together were sufficiently substantial.

The alliance produced one strange repercussion: Gillian Tindall came to see me and said that in the new situation she could no longer be published by Cassell's because it would smack of nepotism. With anyone else I would have argued and pointed out that my fiction list had no connection with nor was it affected by the Medical Department; but she is so upright and of such austere probity that I could see that her conscience would not let her go on. It reminded me of a similar incident in the thirties. Whatever the merits of Eliot's *Murder in the Cathedral* as a play, I was completely bowled over by Robert Speaight's performance as Becket, and when he offered me a most readable novel, *Angel in the Mist*, I was delighted. We got to know one another and remained on very friendly terms until his death. Nevertheless, after one more novel he formed up and said that his conscience would not allow him to be published by any other than a Roman Catholic house. Similarly I could not see what difference it made, but he departed to Douglas Jerrold at Eyre & Spottiswoode with my blessing.

Also before my next visit to Australia I managed to achieve an ambition I had tentatively suggested to father in a letter, which I have quoted earlier, written from Kiel nearly twenty years before. I asked Bryen Gentry, as vice-chairman, to go to Australia and change the status of our organization there from that of a branch into an independent company. So Cassell Australia was born: a close cousin rather than a respected servant. I was appointed President while the power lay in the hands of Cyril Denny as Managing Director, and his second in command, Jim Moad. I was extremely happy and, although there was to be some stormy weather, it became a fine business. At the same time I asked Cyril Denny to set about building an educational list that was in the tradition of John Cassell and because I wanted the new company to play an integral part in Australian life. Cyril pointed out, defensively, that each state had its own school system, to which I replied that we should start with Victoria, since our headquarters was in Melbourne, and if the authorities in any other state liked our books and adopted any of them, that would be a bonus.

I was now reaching the age which can too often be filled with sadness because those dear to one are reaching the end of their time. In 1964, one of my most respected friends in publishing died: Ben Huebsch of the Viking Press. He was described by Alfred Knopf – and no one could know better – as 'regarded with more genuine affection by a wider circle of colleagues, in England and the countries of Western Europe as well as back home, than anyone in our industry.' Ben always stayed at Athenaeum Court in Piccadilly. We had lunch one day at the Ecu de France and, since I knew his tastes, I asked him to walk with me to Fribourg Treyer, then still in their old shop at the top of the Haymarket, and run by my prep school friend, Roy Bridgeman-Evans. I asked Roy to sell me a box of fifty of the best cigars he had, which I gave to Ben. At his age I thought that Ben should take a taxi back to Athenaeum Court, but no, he said, he would go by bus and we waved goodbye. That night the time came, and, as his old colleague Marshall Best wrote, 'He met it with characteristic grace, sitting at his desk in his London hotel, a cigar in one hand and writing a letter to his son at midnight.'

For some years father's health had been declining. His legs would no longer take him into the garden which he loved so much: the straw hat, now tobacco-brown with age, which he had worn while planting his beloved dahlias hung unheeded on its peg. The Wimborne works had been sold. Still having to inject himself twice a day, drinking a good deal of whisky which his doctor permitted, he no longer wasted time and energy on dressing, but sat in his favourite armchair with his bath-robe clutched round him, thinking thoughts that no one will ever know. My stepmother, in her moments of clarity, could not have looked after him more lovingly, and gradually he became too weak for her times of aberration to bother him any more. So, as summer came with a blaze of flowers that he would never see, he sank into a coma.

I was now forced to make a painful decision. The city of Liverpool decided to honour its most distinguished living man of letters, Nicholas Monsarrat, with an exhibition in the public library, the first time that the City Fathers had taken such a step. There was to be an opening ceremony on 11 March, and I should be there for two reasons: Nicholas was my friend, and I had been his publisher for twenty-five years. In my dilemma I rang up father's doctor, whose verdict was unequivocal: 'I cannot tell you when the end will come, but I can tell you that your father will not recover consciousness; even if I were proved wrong, he would not recognize you. You can be of no help; if you have anything to do, do it.' So I went to Liverpool; the exhibition was a grand affair and I met Nicholas' father, the city's most distinguished surgeon, properly pleased as Punch. The next morning I returned to London and immediately rang Tarrant Keynston; the telephone was answered by my son Nicholas' sister-in-law who had kindly been helping; her message was short: 'Your father died half an hour ago.'

The shock on arrival at an end already expected is not traumatic only a dumb sense of deprivation that a loved one has gone for ever. He had always wanted to be buried where he could see High Stoy and in spite of his having been so long a Quaker, the rector of Fontmell Magna allocated a plot just inside the churchyard, fifty yards from the house where he was born, with a clear view of the rounded hill that had meant so much to him.

After the funeral which was private, there was a memorial service in the crypt of St Paul's Cathedral; Ernest Raymond, the oldest living Cassell author and a life-long friend, gave the address in which he said, 'I owe my whole career to him.'

The news on the radio of his death and the obituary in *The Times* brought me the heavy task of replying to over a hundred and fifty letters, cables and messages from all over the world. Having watched him slowly losing his hold on life, having sat beside him during the final coma when he was alive but could not hear me speak, having walked beside him since I was a child, it was harrowing to read the words of those who thought of him still as he had been; the motionless head on the pillow was turned back to the man of both incision and gentleness. From Deyá Robert Graves was as succinct as always: 'I have heard so much in his praise and nothing ever to the contrary.'

Into my own life it brought the last letter I ever had from Michael Fletcher, then Military Attaché at the British Embassy in Bonn. He wrote of our canoeing, of my 'instructing him in old architecture' and said 'His death has brought back many memories of your mother of whom I was particularly fond.'

There were so many little things that I found in my mind from the long years like sea shells scattered on a long, long beach; mostly trivia, but all endearing. I smiled when I remembered saying to him once, 'You know there *are* other composers besides Handel: let me take you to hear one of *my* favourites: Berlioz' *Messe des Morts*, and when I asked him tentatively in the interval what he thought of it, his grave reply: 'It's superb, magnificent ... Handel might have written it.'

After death there is always the mournful clearing up. I found that father had made me his literary executor. My chief concern was the Handel collection; I think father realized that it would have to go to meet estate duties, because towards the end of his life he had suddenly said to me, 'I want it kept together and I want it to stay in England'; of course I felt the same. But even if circumstances had been such that I could have kept the collection, I do not think that I should have – nor could, because it was very large.

I asked Percy Muir, with his assistant, Laurie Duval, to make a valuation; and while they were doing so I thought about its possible destination. London and Cambridge, the two places with which I felt most closely connected, were already well served – the British Library (as I have said) and the Fitzwilliam are full of Handel; but what about the northern half of the country? What about the Hallé Orchestra which has for so long given music-lovers such great pleasure? So I gave the first offer to the Manchester Public Library, which has a splendid music collection, and I had to look no further. It was accepted and sits there all together, beautifully catalogued a decade ago, well used and the subject of research which has already produced a quantity of unknown Vivaldi from one of the Aylesford volumes.

Among the letters which I had received was one from Sir Winston Churchill. It was a decade since he had written to me, and after all those years the phrases were similar but the *panache* had gone out of the signature. He was now ninety, no longer holding office, no longer writing so far as I knew, with so many of his life-long friends gone before him; I thought that the appearance of a face the only recommendation for which was that he had known it for a quarter of a century might be of fleeting interest. So I telephoned and was asked to go to Hyde Park Gate one afternoon. We sat by the fire in the small sitting-room to the right of the entrance hall. It was not particularly easy, for I had not come with anything special to say and I did not wish to bore him with trivialities. He sat still like a big retriever tired from a long day's shoot, drawing slowly on a cigar and mangling it as he had always mangled them. And he was very deaf; he had long had a hearing-aid but it gave him no pleasure. After a while I heard the front door open and voices in the hall, not loud; through the heavy door I could not hear what was said and barely knew who it was. But sounds beloved have a strange affinity to the ears, as I had known so long before with Seton Gordon and the pipes, and the distant voice was a familiar melody; his head rose. 'Ah,' he said 'Clemmie's back.'

It was in January 1965, that the end was reached, a day few living then will not remember. Of all the innumerable tributes the one which I liked best was that of Sir Robert Menzies, broadcast from the crypt of the cathedral, and I admired it so much that I asked him if we could make a little book of it. He was agreeable, and we had an edition of 500 printed in Australia of which Nos 1-250 were in the gift of the author, and with his permission the remainder were reserved for the friends of Cassell London and Cassell Australia. It had a noble peroration which ended, 'His body will be carried on the Thames, a river full of history. With one heart we all feel, with one mind we all acknowledge, that it will never have borne a more precious burden, or been enriched by more splendid memories.'

It was not long after that John Hayward departed. Considering the nature of his illness which had forced him to take to a wheelchair in the early thirties, it is remarkable that he lived into his sixty-first year. I had become accustomed to his bitter wit, his sarcasm, his denigration of everything, because there was kindness hidden there like a thin vein of gold in hard rock; and his standards of scholarship were of the highest. Until late in his life he used to get about a good deal, and there were always helpers willing to get him to the door and into a taxi after a lunch or dinner; and as the wheelchair was lifted in through the door, he would reassure the driver with a lordly 'Do not be alarmed; it has all been done before.' I felt touched by the confidence which he had in me, and I do not know how or why it began. If I was present he would always prefer me to get him downstairs, saying to others 'Don't bother, Desmond will do it.'

No one who really knew him disliked him; as Kathleen Raine has written: 'His malicious, delicious wit was an aspect of the dignity which never allowed us to pity him.' And to Graham Greene it was an extraordinary misapprehension that he might find John's physical appearance ugly: 'That powerful head ugly? That twist of the half-paralysed arm, as the agile hand seized a cup or procured a cigarette? A cripple, yes, but there are few men I can remember with greater vitality ... he was certainly not a saint, but he was the bravest man I have ever known.'

At this time there began one of the great disappointments of my publishing life. Laurence Pollinger came to see me, and the fact that he expressed a wish to do so indicated that he had a matter of importance in his mind, for at his age and with his standing he did not need to go out to publishers. He sat down, lit his pipe, and asked if I would like to publish William Saroyan. Would I indeed! Saroyan was one of my literary heroes. I had read his first volume, *The Daring Young Man on the Flying Trapeze,* when it came out in 1934, and *The Human Comedy* is a novel which I place in the highest rank of the astonishing age of American fiction which began in the twenties; I liked his natural, almost conversational style, and his concern with the basic goodness in people. He was not as well known or appreciated in this country as I thought he ought to be and I welcomed the opportunity of trying to do something about it. In this we failed; four books later he was no better appreciated and selling no more than when we started. I was bitterly disappointed and had to confess to Laurence that there was no point in our going on. Perhaps the title of the last book we published, at the beginning of 1970, was sadly ironic: *Don't Go But If you Must Say Hello to Everyone.*

Next it seemed time to go to Australia once more, to see how the new company was getting on, and we decided to go eastwards round the world this time. It was a journey full of incident. A quarter of a century ago the *étapes* on a long flight were still comparatively short, which added interest and variety, though it was no longer obligatory to leave the plane during refuelling if one had no wish to do so.

There were only two other passengers besides ourselves in the forward compartment of the aircraft; immediately in front of us a large woman of uncertain age with peroxide hair whom we called 'the brassy blonde,' and opposite her a tea-planter of enormous proportions who was to us 'the man mountain'.

The first stop was Rome, where we were offered the choice of a repast at the airport or an excellent box lunch on a coach into the city, which we took; a chance of visiting St Peter's, the Coliseum and the Baths of Caracalla was not to be missed. It was quite a long stop; after we had taken off, darkness fell, and the cabin lights were turned out for the six-hour flight to Teheran.

In the deep gloom the man mountain moved over to the brassy blonde and got to work. The whole plane shook with the violence of their 'copulation immense' – to use the famous BBC spoonerism – and if there had been any cups around they would have rattled. Eventually the man mountain returned to his own seat and fell asleep; so exhausted that when we came down at Teheran he did not stir. But the brassy blonde got off and her place in front of us was taken by a young mother with a tiny baby in a bassinet which she placed in the aisle between herself and the slumbering giant. Off again eastwards towards Pakistan, and after some time the man mountain awoke; looking at the tiny child beside him with surprise, he turned over, and before going back to sleep made just one comment: 'Christ, things happen fast around here.'

We got off at Darwin, where one of our most respected Australian authors came out to the airport for a chat: Douglas Lockwood, a 'skin brother' of the Pintubi tribe in the outback, with the name of Tjampitjimpa. Then we had been invited to stay for a few days by Tom Ronan for whom I had a considerable affection; I liked his novels and I liked him. He was a hard-bitten, hard-drinking man from the outback who seemed uneasy in town; gritty, yet within him a lambent imagination – a blend which I feel has given so much to the Australian character. The first novel of his which we published in 1954 was *Vision Splendid,* about cattle-herding in the northern part of Western Australia; it was a lovely book and had in it one of those memorable lines like the opening of Nick Monsarrat's *This is the Schoolroom:* taking a phrase from Banjo Patterson, Ronan wrote, 'And he saw the vision splendid, and that's all he bloody well did see.'

Tom was waiting for us outside the airport at Katharine, which is some two hundred miles south of Darwin in the Northern Territory, and drove us in his jeep to the interesting house and national monument in which he and his wife lived. In 1840 a Dutchman had said, 'I see a great future in this land' and as an expression of his faith built this house of stone; nearly a century and a half later the full potential of the Northern Territory has been little more than scratched, but the Dutchman was right – it is there.

Arnhem Land, the name of that part of the Northern Territory which forms the big bulge at the top of the country, is a strange mixture. Round the stone house lay rich grassland, and wallabies peeped shyly from every bush; but if we wanted to see the big red 'roos, Tom said that we would have to get up at four in the morning when they came in to drink at a small lake beyond the trees. We did, and found a couple of them beside the water. They let us get within a hundred yards of them, then rose to their full seven feet, ears twitching; Soon they were off in their huge, leaping gallop.

But much of the land is flat and barren, the earth the same red as that of India; trees stand apart with bare trunks and foliage only at the top; ants build their extraordinary nests like minarets as much as eight feet high; and the climate can vary with extreme rapidity. Tom drove us about fifteen miles across country to visit a citrus-fruit farmer who came from Gloucestersire. Behind our host's house was a canyon some sixty feet deep at the bottom of which a tiny stream meandered. He pointed to a corrugated-iron building in the distance beyond the chasm and said, 'You would not believe than when my wife's labour began I took her to that hospital by canoe.' Later, sitting in the garden which loving green fingers had created, Tom, uneasy because it was autumn, noticed a cloud the size of a man's hand in the otherwise brilliant sky. 'Come on,' he said, 'we're off; if that comes this way, we'll be here a week.'

Bumping along a dirt-track which wound for miles between the bare trees and towering ant hills, we went to call upon the warden of an Aborigines' reserve. He was a kindly man and, I am sure, looked after the people in his charge well. No one would call the Aborigines a beautiful people – as for instance the Bedouin Arabs can be – but they are gentle, quiet and introspective. As this is the only large gathering of Aborigines that I have ever seen, I must presume that their wistfulness is brought about by their being basically nomads who are tied by well-meaning officialdom to one place with nothing to do; if they are wandering, they are occupied in the search for food, but when their rations are provided daily without effort, time must hang heavy. But they still have their wonderful gift for the decorative arts, and have produced a school of painters every one of which is a faithful, if less gifted, imitator of the superb Albert Namajira, one of the great landscape painters of this century.

Tom said goodbye to us as we took the early morning flight some nine hundred miles to Cairns in northern Queensland. From Cairns we sailed the twelve miles out to Green Island, which I had chosen because at that time it had the only underwater observatory.

It is indeed a green island, a pear-shaped domain only a few feet above sea level, small enough for a leisurely walk round its sandy perimeter, while the observatory down in the coral is remarkable, with fish of all brilliant colours swimming by and peering in curiously as the occupants gaze out spell-bound.

The hotel had a central block and chalets scattered round it through the woods; it was there that after lights-out disaster struck. Mosquitoes are one of the forms of life which do not like me (I am sure there are many others), but in the morning Elizabeth was horribly bitten: her whole face puffed up and both eyes nearly closed. She asked me to see the manager and ask if there was any magic cure for the swelling because if not, she could take no more and would have to go back to the mainland. I walked straight into him outside our door, a nice bloke padding round in shorts and sandals. I told him about Elizabeth's troubles.

'What about the nits?' he asked.

Somewhat testily I groaned, 'No, no, not nits; I'm talking about mosquitoes.'

Then the penny dropped; 'nits' in a Queensland accent is 'nets,' and the lad who had shown us to our chalet had forgotten to point out the mosquito netting, stowed in a box above the bed. The remainder of our stay was idyllic.

Before he left to take up office as Governor-General, Slim had said to me, 'If you visit Australia, be sure to come and stay with me.' As soon as I knew that we were going, I wrote to him and in reply he invited us for the weekend, adding that at that time he would not be in Canberra but at Admiralty House, the Governor's residence in Sydney.

Admiralty House is handsome and comfortable, situated at one end of Sydney Bridge on the edge of a bluff past which flows the deep-water channel of the harbour. Consequently ships practically brush the trees at the bottom of the garden. Slim loved ships and there was a lot of traffic during the Friday evening after we arrived. It was clear and warm by then and with the french windows open we could hear the throb of the propellers as a ship approached, and we would go to the end of the garden and lean over the fence to watch her go by. Then there was a particularly deep rumble; Slim exclaimed, 'Ah, there's a big one!' and set off excitedly towards the windows, brushing past Elizabeth with a boyish, 'Sorry to go first; protocol, you know!' And it was a big one with glittering lights, nearly as tall as the cliff. How he loved those ships and how he relished every facet of life.

The next morning his secretary told us that there was to be a big dinner that night for all the Ministers gathered for the Commonwealth Finance Conference due to begin on Monday. I suggested that perhaps it would be better if we went out for the evening, but she said that, on the contrary, as house guests we were to be included. It was a very large gathering. Sitting between the New Zealand representative and his wife, I found it difficult to think of anything to say to them, since they were dull but worthy as some people from that most beautiful country can be. Elizabeth was put on the right of the South African Minister, for it was still eight years before that republic would leave the Commonwealth. Havenga was a crusty old Boer and I suppose Lady Slim thought that putting a beautiful young woman by his side would be good for him. He was the last of those who had fought against us at the turn of the century, and looked something like Ernie Bevin. This placing was not a tremendous success, for when he spoke, which was seldom, Elizabeth had great difficulty in understanding his thick Afrikaans accent and could, in turn, think of little to say to him.

Half-way through dinner Slim called from the head of the table:

'Havenga, how many British bullets have you got in you?'

'Seven,' the old man growled, 'but I bear no malice.'

Our stay ended on Sunday night and we took a taxi across the bridge back to the Wentworth Hotel, which, like so much else, has, I gather, now been pulled down and rebuilt.

After doing everything that needed to be done, seeing all the trade and drumming into Cyril Denny once more the need for an educational list, we departed for New Zealand. There are fifteen hundred miles of water between the two countries, but there is a much wider gap between the characters of the two peoples. I have met with so much kindness in both countries that any criticism of either seems rather like biting a friendly hand. One of the grounds of difference is that Australia is very conscious of its size and geographical importance, and in consequence is more international; while New Zealand remains devoted to its Scottish heritage. Not that New Zealand is going to be pushed around by anybody, as her firm attitude over the Greenpeace fracas with France shows clearly. New Zealanders are unlikely to be as abrasive as some Australians can be; they are more gentle, though equally they are unlikely to be as exciting – the number of great artists in different *métiers* produced by Australia in relation to its small population represents easily the highest percentage in the world. There is a streak in the Australians similar to one in so many Americans: they always expect to win. The New Zealanders do not expect always to win, but are delighted when they do. Basically, it makes little difference; in both countries there is a wonderful hail-fellow-well-met atmosphere which takes you as it finds you.

Michael Felgate-Catt was making a first-class job of the branch, and with his wife, Elizabeth, we set off by car to visit as many of his clients as we could. The first stop was Hamilton. We had found on our last visit that it was the custom of the country to eat disastrously (to us) early in the evening, but here the hotel was kind enough to give us dinner at eight. We were the last to leave the dining-room and an attractive waitress was already laying tables for breakfast. As the building was new and only just opened, I was surprised to see a mouse waddling along the skirting and said to the waitress, 'Do you see what I see?' glancing over her shoulder at the tiny visitor, she returned to her work with but few words: 'Hungry, I suppose, like the rest of us.'

Crossing to South Island we were soon in Christchurch to see Bertie Whitcombe, the venerable head of the famous book wholesalers, Whitcombe & Toombs. On the first day Michael and I paid a business visit to his office, and the following morning he gave up his time to drive us through the beautiful countryside for lunch in the hills. I do not know how old he actually was, but he seemed like one of those big tortoises which live forever – and a very nice one.

As we drove to the first appointment, Michael said, 'I'm sure that he's going to ask you for an extra 2½ per cent and I replied that what discount Michael gave in his own territory was his own business, and I did not propose to interfere. Sure enough, the spiel began; life was hard, trade was bad, overheads were rising – all the usual difficulties which would be magically solved by an extra 2½ per cent. I listened sympathetically and made no reply to the reiterated suggestion.

Before we left Michael went back to the office to book orders, and Bertie said his last words: 'Mr Catt Felgate,' (he always got Michael's name the wrong way round) 'your chairman is a hard man.' I didn't feel it; I gave him a bottle of whisky of a good brand he had not come across and I liked him. May he rest in peace.

From New Zealand we started home across the Pacific, first to the ochre-coloured earth of New Caledonia and thence to Tahiti, where the plane refuelled. We had already decided to break our journey and had made a hotel booking in advance. Twenty years ago the island was paradise on earth, and I made up my mind that I would like to end my days there; but on my last visit a rather nasty building was going up, and I became fearful that if I were to go back now I might find that the gentle beauty with which I had fallen in love had grown brittle.

The hotel in which we stayed outside Papeete was in the usual form of a central administrative and restaurant block surrounded by bungalows; it was charming, everything built in the local style of wood and thatch. In front of our bungalow was a row of palms, a sandy beach and the lagoon – for it is a mile off shore to the coral reef on which the ocean waves break in an endless roar that lulls one to sleep and is the first welcome on awakening. From our veranda we looked across at Moorea, twelve miles away, easily recognized by its twin peaks which appear in so many of Gauguin's paintings. Papeete is the only town on this lovely island that is no more than a circle of vegetation and sandy beaches round the base of an extinct volcano covered with such thick jungle that its summit was reached for the first time only in 1929. Cruise liners come through a gap in the reef to the busy port.

When Bourgainville took possession of the island for France in 1768, he commented on the happy health, good nature and easy morals of the natives, but the scientists who followed managed to damage seriously the first of these qualities. They insisted on changing the diet of the islanders whose teeth as a result are subject to a form of decay for which modern science to date has found neither prevention nor cure. When the second film of *Mutiny on the Bounty* had been made there four years previously a number of beautiful young girls were needed; all applicants were interviewed and a choice was made. Before shooting could begin the dentist had a big job on his hands: he had to remove all the blackened fangs from the lucky candidates and replace them with gleaming full dentures. Since M.G.M. was paying them *per diem* as much as they would normally earn in about six months, the girls had to check in their dentures after each day's work to prevent absenteeism; at the end of filming they were allowed to keep them.

The making of the film had two effects on island life. Up to then no one in Tahiti had ever worn anything above the waist, but, at a time when even the topless beach at St Tropez was in its infancy, there was no way that the Hayes Office was going to tolerate so much flesh, however beautiful. So the girls appearing before the cameras had to wear brassières of the same patterned material as their skirts; this quickly became all the rage, and by the time we arrived there was not a bare breast to be seen. The other effect was merely an inconvenience. Since all the technicians were in the customary hurry to get from A to B, everyone was given a Lambretta; and the little machines became so fashionable that in the morning and evening the congested streets of the town were like a hive of angry bees.

A total disaster of which I have been told is the closure of Quinn's Bar on the waterfront. There used to be a saying that if you stayed long enough in three places in the world, sooner or later everyone you knew would come by: Piccadilly Circus, Raffle's Hotel in Singapore and Quinn's Bar in Papeete. Now it seems there are only two.

In Quinn's there were small tables scattered about the room, and an oval bar at which sat a selection of the most comely tarts in town, waiting for custom over a neglected warm beer. One beauty caught my eye: she could not have been much over seventeen but already her teeth were black; when I went again a year later she was still at the receipt of custom, but without a tooth in her head. One morning a Matson cruise liner docked at eight; two hours later the passengers were ashore and the crew could follow them. One drawback of American ships being dry is that every man's first requirement on coming ashore is drink, and only when he has got a skinful will he begin to think about women. Idling in Quinn's around noon, like everyone present we jumped when there was a loud crash: the First Officer had fallen off his bar stool and was too drunk to get up again.

For a change of scene and a quick one before lunch we strolled to another pleasant bar about a quarter of a mile along the water-front. The only patrons were two American sailors having a long conversation in English with a couple of tarts. One of the sailors looked about eighteen and this was probably his first time away from home; his companion was older and had obviously been told to look after his young friend, who was toying with the idea of a bit of action. His mentor was against it. The pendulum swung back and forth; finally the favoured tart began to lose patience and said, 'Well, do you want it or don't you?' Senior said disapprovingly, 'Time we got back to the ship,' and Junior made his last plea: 'Oh, c'mon, it'll only take a New York minute!'

But prudence prevailed; they left; and we too went home soon after, fortunately unaware that we had indeed left paradise behind.

As the months passed the intended educational list in Australia was never far from my mind, because I was certain that this would secure the position and the future of the new company. Writing to Cyril Denny from time to time, asking how he was getting on, I became restless as I got from him either no answer or a non-committal reply. 1965 became 1966 with still no evidence of any activity, so in the spring I wrote asking him precisely how many titles he had in hand, and the answer came back, 'None.' I am like my father in many ways, I am sure, and one of them is having a breaking-point beyond which fury overcomes reason. For example, in the old days at La Belle Sauvage he would not allow any whistling outside his office, and on one occasion rushed out and sacked an offender on the spot – whether the culprit was actually employed by

Cassell's was to him irrelevant. I had that feeling now a whole year frittered away – I could not and would not bear it. I cabled Denny to reserve me a room at the Windsor, an hotel in Melbourne which I liked, and flew out at once.

The next morning I asked him to come and see me, putting the same question to him face to face and receiving the same answer: in the last twelve months he had done nothing. So I fired him on the spot, and then appointed his No 2, Jim Moad, to take his place. After the dust had settled, I realized that Cyril Denny had been quite incapable of founding an educational list; he was loyal and hard-working, but totally lacking the imagination to know even where to begin. If I had been reasonable I should have invited him to retire, and if necessary insisted that he do so. Subsequently I discovered that Jim Moad was given a rough ride by some people in the trade who thought that he had had some hand in the affair, but they were wrong – Jim would never stoop to any such action. Ruthless and hasty I may have been, and I do not think that my action helped Cyril Denny, for, having lost his wife, he did not live very much longer. But for Cassell Australia it was another story; Jim Moad was a wonderful head of the firm and rapidly built a list of impressive proportions which put it in the position for which I had always hoped.

My duty done, I went slowly homewards. First to Canberra, having by telephone made an appointment to see Sir Robert Menzies. The city was still under construction – the lake which Sir Robert had decreed should be its centre-piece was dug, though the water was still to come – but it was on the way to its appearance as one of the fine capital cities of the world. I was somewhat apprehensive because a political crisis had arisen resulting in a snap election and it was obvious that the Prime Minister would be extremely busy.

Just before eleven I reported to the government building in which he had his office and, hardly to my surprise, the man on the door said, 'I doubt if he will see you; he's holding a cabinet meeting; but I'll try.' To my delight I was whisked straight upstairs into the presence, and when I expressed surprise because of the meeting, he said, 'I've sent them out to have a jar because I wanted to talk to you.'

I repeat this not because of any compliment to myself, but because it is typical of the big-heartedness which perceived that, twelve thousand miles from home, I had made the additional journey (albeit not a very long one) down from Sydney specifically to call upon him. A smaller man would have sent a message saying that owing to unforeseen circumstances he was too busy. Years ago I had heard that some Australians resented his position as a world figure when he had, in their view, been elected solely as their Prime Minister – the same criticism as had been levelled at Billy Hughes during the first war. And I was saddened more recently to learn that his reputation lies under something of a cloud because of his internationalism. All right, he was by immediate ancestry a Scot and very pro-British; but was he any less an Australian than an immigrant Japanese pearl-fisher or an Italian tomato-grower?

Undoubtedly he had charisma, which Donald Horne first noted being used in a political sense at this time, adding, 'It is to the charismatic social sense, not to charismatic *individuals*, that we can attach our faith in the magic of change.' It is to that change which Australia is looking forward and in which it is now involved – not back to individuals all too strongly connected with a fading past.

I could not possibly cross the Pacific without a stop in Tahiti for a stay of several days. I noticed a sinister portent from the previous year: the presence of the French army and concrete buildings springing up on the edge of town. Perhaps the earthly paradise was already becoming a little sophisticated. I thought about it as I took off for Canada, where I had a little business.

It was fortunate for me that the international publishers' conference, which, as I have said, takes place every four years, was about to start in Washington, so I flew down from Toronto. The headquarters was the Hilton Hotel, just opened; the architect had had a good idea, but one which did have certain drawbacks. The building is in the shape of a starfish; the centre is a solid bank of elevators from which bedroom wings extend like tentacles. Fortunately my room was near to the elevators; when I had settled in I went downstairs and ran into Alfred Knopf who was not happy; in fact he was fuming. 'I've paced it out,' he said, 'and do you know how far it is from our suite to the elevators? Just over two hundred yards; it's ridiculous, and I've told the manager so. He was very contrite and said that he would have us moved at once. And I said, "For God's sake don't do that – Mrs Knopf has already unpacked!"

These two remarkable people – who were my oldest American friends, since I had known them from childhood – were too different to live together and too fond of one another to be entirely apart. Their interests diverged widely and the gap was too great to bridge even if either had felt inclined to make the effort. Both of them expected the highest standards and were intolerant of shortcomings. Alfred was tall, majestic, incredibly funny and passionately devoted to music. Blanche was tiny, neurotic and slightly arrogant – frankly some people, including father, did not like her – with a very real and very deep interest in French literature. She seemed to lack Alfred's lust for life, as though somewhere she had taken the wrong turning and could not find the way back. I could not imagine what she did when she was alone; she was so desperately short-sighted that I could not see her reading a book, though of course she must have. I always wanted to pick her up and cosset her; had one summoned up the courage to commit such an act of *lèse-majesté* she would certainly have been surprised but possibly delighted.

Blanche was a city cat and Alfred a country dog, a circumstance over which they agreed to differ. She lived in a New York apartment and he had a house at Purchase, each enjoying the hospitality of the other whenever it suited. And when they went to the international conference they always enjoyed a suite together. At Barcelona in 1957 Elizabeth and

I took them out to a really Spanish restaurant, and it was the happiest event of the conference. That was the conference which was enlivened by a passionate speech from Robert Maxwell demanding that a vote of censure be passed condemning the censorship in Portugal, to which one of the Portuguese publishers replied, 'I agree with everything you say, but I beg the conference not to pass such a motion; we have to live there.'

Two invitations to Blanche's apartment were disasters, for neither of which was she responsible. The first occasion was a dinner to which she invited Elizabeth and me to meet Carl Van Vechten and his wife – adding that he was now off the bottle. When we appeared the Van Vechtens were already there, and he was stoned; without a word he sat stuffing peanuts into his mouth with the concentration of a starving monkey. At dinner he ate what was put before him and his contributions to the conversation were an occasional grunt, and after dinner he was removed. It was sad to see a man so big physically and mentally reduced to the level of a harmless moron; and when we left later Blanche said ruefully, 'No one told me he had a relapse.'

The second incident was nothing more than pure frustration. Blanche invited me for drinks one evening and it was a large gathering which completely filled her long living-room. There is nothing more calculated to enhance a thirst than to see drinks in the offing and not be able to get at them. I stood at one end of the room with an empty glass while in the distance, like a mirage in the desert, was a table of bottles which I was unable to reach. The reason for my frustration was that sitting on the floor, cutting the room impenetrably in half, was a large circle of devotees, among them Thornton Wilder, to whom Jean-Paul Sartre was outlining the plot of his new play.

Long ago Margaret once said that through some similarity of vocal cords Americans speak French with much better accents than the English – a remark which she has forgotten and a theory which she no longer accepts. Thornton Wilder could add nothing to her thesis if it was ever true; he spoke French with a vile Middle Western accent. Although I admire his writings and he was a charming man, on this occasion I could willingly have throttled him. Every time Sartre ran out of steam and there was a promising pause, the sonorous voice of Wilder would exclaim, 'Mais, maître, say marevay-yer, continuay,' and the master, nothing loth, would go on for another half-hour.

Blanche died in 1966. Not long before Alfred had merged his firm – which had published sixteen Nobel and six Pulitzer prize winners and was famous as much for its standards of craftsmanship as its quality of writing – with Random House, although his identity remained unimpaired. In the following year he married again, a lady whom I never met because during my decreasing visits to New York he was always away in Arizona for his health. Finally in 1984 he died at the age of ninety-one – a man whose high ideals and personal kindness remain to me ever green; a man whom H. L. Menken described as 'By my standards the perfect publisher.'

A contemporary of Alfred was Cass Canfield, head of one of the oldest publishing houses in the United States: Harper Bros. Cass took my war anthology which he re-titled *The Taste of Courage* and did even better with it than we did. A number of times he invited me to his house in the country for the weekend, which generally included a round of golf. On one occasion he rang to say that he would send a car to my hotel to pick me up, and added, 'By the way, the Priestleys are coming. Do you mind?' Jacquetta Hawkes, then Mrs Priestley, I had run into at various parties over the years, but J.B. I had never met, though I knew he had a reputation for plain speaking which did not please some people, and I suppose prompted Cass's question. But far from minding, I was delighted at the chance of meeting Jack Priestley, whose *Johnson Over Jordan* I particularly admired, and in fact it was a very happy weekend. They were already in the car when it came to pick me up. After some opening chat, he kindly congratulated me on our *Encyclopaedia of World Literature*, adding that the modern section could do with a bit of looking at; that sounded ominous, but he went no further. My reply was non-committal but I made a note to look up the entry on him at the first opportunity. It was all right, but I presume not as fulsome as he would have wished.

Everyone had been at the Washington conference, and, although it produced no results, it was not so boring a scramble as the Frankfurt Book Fair. It was the end of a journey of melancholy duty and personal pleasure.

25   Cracks in the Fabric

Since several of us now had our fingers in the pie, our lists, which had always covered a pretty wide field, were assuming an even more variegated look. Besides myself, there was Nicholas (now in his late twenties), and Kenneth Parker (chief editor, who had been elected to the board); David Ascoli also was taking an increasingly important interest in the literary side. No two of us had quite the same taste.

Nicholas in 1962 had gone to the United States to see his grandfather, and while he was there had a run round the publishers, returning with one book of particular interest: *Guerilla Warfare* by Mao Tso-t'ung and Che Guevara – a book which would be unlikely to feature on the list of any American publisher today.

In more orthodox warfare the one eminent figure who characteristically had not leapt immediately into print was Field Marshal Lord Alexander. He had captured people's imagination in 1940 when, after Gort's recall, he had commanded the beach at Dunkirk clad in immaculate service dress; since when throughout his campaigns he had always appeared spick and span, with no touch of flamboyance. After the war, since his retirement, there had been nothing but silence. I was approached by John North, a writer on military history, who had had a number of long interviews with him and believed that these talks would make a book. Having read them, I agreed, the Field Marshal agreed, and the result was *The Alexander Memoirs* which came out that year. North and I were invited to lunch at his home in Windsor Forest, and I found him exactly as I had expected: handsome, quiet, diffident and rather dubious about the whole operation as though it were against his will that his silence should be broken; perhaps it was.

In the same period appeared *The Game of Kings*, the first novel of Dorothy Dunnett who continues to reign today among the queens of historical novelists. There are some who do not like history in fiction, but for the multitude who do her tales, described by critics as 'immaculately researched and deftly plotted,' are a must. An Englishwoman who was married to a Scot, then the editor of *The Scotsman*, I found her, as well as a fine writer, a delightful addition to the charms of Edinburgh.

Believing that nothing in this world is totally black or totally white, I considered that there might be a place for an unbiased and unfettered life of General Franco, a man who to some was a saviour and to others anti-Christ. In every human being, even a dictator, there must be some good I thought. Stalin, on whose conscience lay the murder of Trotsky, his equivocal attitude to the Warsaw Poles in 1945, the dilution of the revolution into a bourgeois twilight, still made the backward Soviet Union completely literate – by force where necessary. And Veronica Wedgwood has pointed out that Oliver Cromwell, my least favourite figure in English history, introduced opera to London.

As we know, power corrupts and absolute power corrupts absolutely, and I deplored the continuation of the Caudillo in office. I had presumed that having restored stability to Spain after the Civil War and having performed an admirable balancing act during the Second World War when the Peninsula was in a position of great peril, he would make way for some form of representative government; but my hope was premature and my illusions shattered, partly through the obduracy of the army which has so often acted as a brake in Spanish history. But the land was dear to me as to so very many others, and its ruler, whatever his qualities, was a figure of importance, so I wanted a true balance sheet on the aged tyrant in Madrid.

I wrote to John Marks asking if he would be interested in writing the book, provided we got the necessary assurances. He said that he was willing, so it was arranged for Bryen Gentry and I to meet him in Madrid for a conference with the Foreign Minister, Señor de Castiella. It was a long and interesting discussion. The Minister said that he could not give us the exclusive rights to the Caudillo's biography, to which we replied that we did not want this – what was essential to us was an assurance that John could write the truth as he found it without danger of interference or censorship. The result of it all was that John was given official assurance that nothing would be withheld from him and there would be no interference; so we signed a contract, and shortly afterwards sold the American rights to Elliot Macrae of Dutton's.

Time passed and Elliot became understandably restive and I too felt worried, although I had long become used to John's tardiness; now I was forced to badger him. As a result he somewhat testily sent me a pathetic small notebook; now thoroughly alarmed, I found out that he had had a stroke. Gone was any thought of the book or of Duttons' money; John was ill. His second wife, whom I did not know well, brought him back to England to end his life in the Middlesex Hospital. He died in July 1967. On the day of his funeral Robert Graves and I were having lunch and then took a taxi; Robert, on his way somewhere else, dropped me at the church door at three o'clock. As he got out and for a moment towered over me, I did not realize that this too was a long farewell.

Somewhere around this time I began to drink too much; one never knows exactly – it creeps up on one, but I was at about the same age as father when the problem got at him. I do not know whether it was hereditary, coincidental or from the same cause. I was at the height of my career and working extremely hard; like father I had always done a considerable amount of writing, and that, together with reading manuscripts at home, adds up to a work-load which can in the end take its toll. Perhaps this work-load idea is just an excuse – thousands work just as hard without suffering any ill effects – or perhaps it was just an inherent weakness which brought about a collapse, for there is now a strongly held theory linking alcoholism with genes. Whatever the cause, the time came when I found that my love of wine was being indulged too often, other than with meals; a gentle slope turns into a steep decline and reaches a precipice; firm ground degenerates into a bog. Ghosts can be exorcized, but their disappearance may only be effected after years of anguish which cause heartache to others and shame to oneself. Although I can, happily, write in the past tense, I may never forget that the French word for a ghost is 'un revenant'; and, to change the metaphor back, anyone who has had this problem, though he may walk once more with confident tread on solid ground, must watch every step forward to ensure that no unsuspected trap lies in his path.

I am writing this because I believe that those who have been submerged but have struggled back to the surface to swim successfully should say so, as witness that it can be done; help may be needed, but if the will is there, a renewal of life is perfectly possible.

Going to a health farm one summer, to relieve the tedium I worked on a translation of *1940: The Fall of France* by General André Beaufre, which we brought out late in the following year. Although I think I made a good job of that, I was surprised while I was there to receive a visit from Bryen Gentry who, sitting in the hot sun by the swimming-pool, suggested that I might like to retire – a suggestion which I brushed aside. Perhaps, like father before me in similar circumstances, it would have been a good thing if I had. But whatever my capacity or incapacity at the office, there can be little doubt that I must have been nearly impossible to live with at home.

In spite of damage to the track, the train did not leave the rails immediately. Some good ideas still came to me in my eyrie at the top of Red Lion Square. One which had been suggested by Margaret in a letter during the war came back to me: a Hammett Omnibus. We had all his novels except one – *The Thin Man*, which had been published by Heinemann; if they would lease their famous title to us, we could put together the complete works. When they consented, I thought that it would make an agreeable kind of Neapolitan ice cream if we sandwiched between the novels some short stories previously unpublished in England. This so stirred the interest of Lillian Hellman that she wrote an introduction for the volume, and came to Red Lion Square when she was passing through London. She was getting on – two years older than I – but her dynamism was still there, and I hung on every word from a woman who had written a play as bitter and brilliant as *The Little Foxes* and had stood up to McCarthy with the immortal words: 'I cannot and will not cut my conscience to fit this year's fashions.' Now the fashion is to aver that her dynamism covered a shallowness and inaccuracy which amounts to virtual untruth; but I still pay her some respect for that remark alone, which must be on the record.

My mind also went back to literary autographs, of a perennial interest to me, and I thought again of Tim Munby who was now librarian at King's in Cambridge. Unfortunately too busy, Tim suggested his successor in the old job he had occupied at Sotheby's: Peter Croft.

I followed up his suggestion, quickly came to terms, and Peter Croft and I began on a 50-50 basis. Since I went regularly to the United States, my main task was to procure material of the American poets which particularly interested me – especially the negro poets such as James Weldon Johnson and Langston Hughes. Both of us were very busy and the years slipped by almost unnoticed but, as Peter said, this turned out to be an advantage since, during this lengthy period, among his exciting discoveries were the only known autograph poems of Donne and Herrick. Our selection was not completed until the late sixties, and editing began. Frankly, as I have made clear, this was not a very good time for me; and when I had to admit that I could not decipher and transcribe a poem by Steven Vincent Benet which he asked me to do, it was obvious that the 50-50 partnership had gone out of the window. He has been described as lacking in social graces and an uncomfortable colleague, but at the same time there could be no question of his passion for truth and accuracy. So *Autograph Poetry in the English Language* finally appeared as his book in 1973. That I felt a little hard done by was of no importance compared with the excellence of the two splendid volumes, and we remained friends – in fact, I spent an afternoon with him in King's, where he had become librarian on Tim's death, only two days before his sudden and fatal illness.

Although life at Reigate was generally happy, there were storm clouds in the distance of which neither Elizabeth nor I took cognizance. At one of the frequent parties I was introduced to a handsome woman with whom I spent the whole evening talking, not only because she was a very good conversationalist but also because she was a bookseller. She was running the bookshop at Westminster Abbey, and from little more than a postcard and souvenir stall, in the words of the Dean, 'under her management the bookshop was transformed, and became one of the best shops of its kind in central London.' I was interested enough to find out that the trade had a very high opinion of her, and then put the matter out of my mind.

Some years later I drove up to Stockport for the Publishers' and Booksellers' annual conference. Having got my room, I walked over to the conference hall just as a talk was ending, and the speaker descending from the platform seemed familiar. I asked who she was and the answer was 'Rosemary Augdahl'; and we came face to face, said hello, and there was an explosion.

After the first few days of these conferences the publishers withdraw and leave the retail trade to its deliberations; I drove home, of which the explosion had severely undermined the foundations. In the end I departed from Wray Farm with an abruptness which was inconsiderate, cruel and ill-mannered.

What did I want that I had not got? What could I wish that I would leave a wife to bring up three delightful children on her own? I am very lucky that I have been forgiven. Then I was muddled, my self-confidence was evaporating and I felt close to despair without knowing what I despaired of. Josephine (I did not think 'Rosemary' suited her and used her second name, which stuck) and I should have known better, but the fact that we did not may indicate some need, some void into which we fell.

She was now running the University of Warwick's bookshop, which she had started. Despite her beauty and brains she did not seem to have had a particularly happy life. She had been married twice. By her first husband she had a son Anthony, who was reaching manhood; the second was the Norwegian ambassador to the United Nations. She was a woman of extremes: brief bursts of violent temper could suddenly interrupt her otherwise tranquil and loving kindness. There was a degree of uncertainty engendered possibly by wondering – with Ant, whom she adored, grown up – whither her life was going, but more definitely about her unstable health which was to become of vital concern.

When the heart interferes with the head, the result seems like an eclipse of the sun – all around is a kind of twilight in which nothing is certain; what should be a simple selection of right from wrong is confused by blurred outlines. There was no animosity; but a state of ambivalence, for which I must accept responsibility, abrogated clear-cut resolution for a year, twelve months of sand sifting through the hourglass which, all unknown, held so little more.

Meawhile I had no home. But Charles and Elizabeth Ede came to my rescue and invited me to live with them, which I did for a considerable time. We had been friends for twenty years, but for all our closeness to one another their great kindness shone like a beacon across a stormy sea.

But I could not impose upon the Edes for ever; several furnished flats followed. Finally Josephine gave up her bookshop at Warwick University, took my name, and we settled down – first in a tiny flat in Hampstead, and then near Baker Street where I was to live for the next twenty years.

To add to the other disasters, in 1967 after seventeen years my dear, long-suffering, much-loved Herta Ryder decided to leave. I was too depressed even to ask her why and I knew well that any attempt to dissuade her would be quite useless once she had made up her mind. Nearly twenty years later at a Cassell party I did pluck up the courage to ask her and her reply was a complete surprise; it was a matter of conscience, an expression of her deep disapproval of three dismissals of personel, none of which (even one in editorial) did I make myself, but, like at a more exalted level Truman's 'the buck stops here', as chairman I had to accept responsibility.

The only good thing which happened in that disastrous year was the appearance at last of *The Letters of Ernest Dowson* on which Henry Maas and I had been working for twenty years. *The Times Literary Supplement* gave the book a whole page, and since the reviews were then still anonymous I do not know who it was who wrote this most perceptive study of the poet to whom I had devoted so much of my time since the early thirties. In it the reviewer wrote, 'The Letters leave an impression of courageous industry in unfavourable conditions, but only modify the prevailing image of Dowson.' Exactly! Later editors and critics go on repeating the same old slanders like so many gramophone needles stuck in a groove.

Once the die was cast, Voltaire, alas, was as homeless as I; offered at Sotheby's, the collection was bought as a whole by the University of Texas where it still lives complete.

During the same year mother died. After the war she had bought a small house with a charming garden, not far from our old home 'Idehurst'. She would have no one living in the house with her, but had daily help and an Irish gardener called Paddy Kane.

A regular date for a number of years was in early summer when I stayed with her to play in an open golf competition called the Americas Cup at Wildernesse; Paddy Kane always caddied for me. The two golf clubs at Sevenoaks each had a competition open to players with handicaps of 4 and under: that at Wildernesse was called the Bishops' Bowl (after a renowned local golfing family) and the one at Knole was called the Kent Cob. They were always arranged for Saturday and Sunday of the same weekend, so that visitors from a distance could stay over and have two days of good golf. Paddy, who played off 4, usually entered, and mother, who never lost her love of the game even though she could no longer play, had the same conversation with him every year resembling that which Queen Mary had had many years before at Sevenoaks Hospital.

Paddy would raise the subject when they were in the garden.

'I think I'll enter for the Bishops' Bowel this year, m'lady.'

'Bowl, Paddy.'

'Yes, I usually do quite well in the Bowel.'

'Bowl' ... and so it went on, never with any change.

About three years before her death she had a severe stroke. Elizabeth and I had taken her out for the last two occasions before that – to Hickstead to see Pat Smythe, as I have mentioned, and to the Albert Hall to hear Rubinstein, for she loved piano music. For some reason he had had a poor reception in the provinces that year, so when he walked on to the platform that Saturday to the enormous applause of a full house, his heart was touched and he played more beautifully than I had ever heard him before. Nor was it lost on mother, a golden memory for her last concert, and she was very quiet as we drove her home.

Although turned eighty, she still rejected every effort to get her to have someone sleeping in, so that when during the night the stroke came she was alone. She managed to crawl down the stairs to reach the telephone, but it was too high; with enormous effort she managed to unlatch the front door and then spent the rest of the night on the floor. The first person to arrive in the morning was the paper boy. Finding the door ajar, he pushed it open and offered his wares to the prostrate figure: 'Your paper, m'lady.' However, he then had second thoughts and went next door to raise the alarm.

In time her final illness got its grip on her; she had cancer of the oesophagus. Unlike father, whose life ebbed away in unconscious innocence, she was fully awake and deeply humiliated by the unpleasant symptoms as she grew steadily weaker. She was lovingly cared for until the end by the very nice woman who had come in daily for years and now at last slept in the house.

In the November of 1966 Kenneth Parker had come into my office with a typescript which he said he found intensely interesting and would like me to read; I did so and also found it good, but I thought that we could not take it unless we were given the all-clear by our libel lawyer; the book was *The Story of P.Q.17* by David Irving. What was to follow was a notorious case which is described in great detail by David Hooper in his book on libel, *Public Scandal, Odium and Contempt,* published in 1984, which is so detailed that what I have to say about the matter cannot be written without reference to this circumstantial account.

For those who have not read the book or have forgotten the case, I may explain that *P.Q.17.* was a British convoy bound for Murmansk, the destroyer escort of which was commanded by one Captain Broome. The Admiralty, in the mistaken belief that the giant *Tirpitz* had put to sea from her Norwegian hideout, sent a signal for the convoy to scatter and in the consequential absence of armed escort it was tragically decimated.

Talks began at Red Lion Square, examining the book paragraph by paragraph, at which the parties involved were Bryen Gentry as vice-chairman and business manager whom it would most concern, and Kenneth Parker, the director who had first read the book, on the one hand, and our libel lawyer on the other, plus the author. I took no part in the talks myself but Bryen kept me up to date because the final decision would eventually be mine. The discussions took place almost daily and were of great length, going on sometimes until eight o'clock in the evening.

David Hooper's book rather gives the impression that we seemed to have been negligent or carefree about the whole thing, though I do not suppose that it was the author's intention to give that appearance; certainly in fact no one could have taken more care than we did. There is one passage lending colour to such an impression to which I must really take exception: 'Broome's previous involvement with Cassell had been when he acted as naval adviser for the filming of a book by Nicholas Monsarrat, a Cassell author.' Whatever the situation may be today, Mr Hooper should know that nearly twenty years ago a publisher had nothing whatever to do with the film rights of the books which he published, and was neither concerned with nor even aware that a film was being made from a work on his list. I had never heard of Captain Broome and only knew that he had been connected with a film when Monsarrat, during the subsequent case, mentioned him to me disparagingly.

That we did not take the matter lightly is indicated, I think, by the time factor. The author submitted the book to us on 9 November 1966, and it was not until the following March that our lawyer gave us the green light and assured us that the book was safe, and we signed a contract.

It would appear that a minimum of one sentence and a maximum of one paragraph passed unnoticed and were subsequently considered to impugn Captain Broome's honour and that of the Royal Navy. Of course, if you throw a stone into a pond the ripples spread and if you wear the right spectacles the whole world looks different; I am sure that the book contained further passages which, while not in themselves defamatory, added fuel to the fire once it was lit.

A great deal of coming and going followed and the book was not published until June 1968.

Captain Broome sued us for libel, having, I was told, been guaranteed his costs if he lost by certain interested parties; but he did not lose – he was awarded very large damages indeed.

Would matters have been any different if, as chairman, I had taken part personally in the discussions before the contract was signed? I do not think so; one hires a first-class lawyer, a well known specialist on libel, and if he says that it is in order to publish the book I cannot see what reason one has for not doing so. If that expert's view turns out to be diametrically different from the law's view, that is just too bad for the publisher.

Twenty years later the book has been safely republished, because the release of the Admiralty's secret papers has disclosed that Irving's allegations were well founded. However, so far as Cassell's is concerned it is far too late; and anyway Captain Broome is now dead.

The damages given against us, heavy as they were, would have made little difference to the firm in the long run, but a more serious, indeed fatal, shadow was soon to fall upon us.

Better news at this time came from Jim Moad who wrote to say that Cassell Australia was now so successful and the staff had increased to such an extent that their offices were quite inadequate, and he suggested that we should build our own premises; as this fulfilled all my hopes, I agreed with alacrity. A site was bought in north Melbourne and the new building was ready in the following year. After the opening ceremony, which I attended, the staff moved in: the editorial, production and advertising departments, and the educational manager. It was all Jim Moad's doing, but I could not help feeling extremely happy after more than twenty years of scheming, planning and progress. Looking back, it is interesting that the educational department, over the foundation of which I had made such a fuss not all that many years before, was now large enough to need its own manager under Jim.

I could not be in Melbourne without calling on Sir Robert Menzies, whose autobiography *Afternoon Light* we had published in the previous year. He had retired from politics in January 1966 and had a small private office in town. It was an affectionate meeting because I think that both of us realized that it was likely to be the last; I left with regret because I regard him with Churchill and Slim as the three greatest men I have had the privilege of knowing.

As I said at the beginning of this chapter, David Ascoli's was one of the fingers in the pie which helped to broaden the lists of which I was officially in charge.

He now felt that he had spent enough time as sales director and would be better suited if he became literary director. I have always liked David, and until his death last year I still thought of him with affection; I admired his drive and his cornucopia of good ideas, so I readily agreed. I did not appreciate that I was putting myself out of work; I was chairman and I had my own authors, Kenneth Parker had his, but the advent of David officially as literary director placed the future of the firm's programmes in his hands. He naturally saw all the literary agents and, with the exception of A.D. Peters, Gerald Pollinger and Innes Rose who were personal friends, I had too much respect for them to take up more time in their busy lives talking about books for the same list. Perhaps I was over-diffident in this, but that was the way I felt; I was in the chair but I was no longer of much consequence in the publishing field. With my eyes open I had made myself a cipher.

During the second half of 1966 we published three books about various forms of violence, none of which bore any relation to the others.

Marshal of the Royal Air Force Lord Tedder's memoirs were appropriately entitled *With Prejudice*, for it is quite alarming although, I suppose, not surprising, to learn how bitter were the wrangles which never ceased in the high command during the Second World War; but the author had no interest in his publisher, nor frankly had I in him, so we never met – a pity, because there were questions which I would have liked to have asked him, particularly about Caen.

Alexandr Kerensky, the last premier of the Russian Duma in July 1917, swept away by the Bolsheviks five months later, was much more concerned when his memoirs were coming out, and visited Red Lion Square. It was a cheerful meeting; possibly the fact that I had known his younger son so well in the latter days of the war may have had something to do with his interest. Gleb Kerensky is an engineer; when the Argyll-Oxford Hussar amalgamation took place, he commanded our R.E.M.E. and saw that our tanks were looked after well.

The third was *Spain, the Vital Years* by Luis Bolín. Luis I got to know well and after his death saw his American wife regularly in Madrid or London. The story of his getting Franco, who was Governor of the Canaries, to Morocco was as good as any fiction. Although, as I have made clear earlier, a military rising in 1936 was widely expected, even by members of the Republican cabinet, those concerned in it had to proceed with great caution. Bolín therefore came to England and at Croydon hired a commercial pilot to fly him in a de Havilland to Ceuta, where he told him to fill up and await further instructions. The pilot was surprised to be asked next to fly to the Canaries, but he did as he was told, picked up the general and brought him to the mainland to take command of the Moroccan troops. During the war Bolín was the nationalist press officer, and his reward at the end of the struggle was to be appointed Minister of Tourism, in which office he made his one great contribution to his country: the Paradors. The first of these delightful havens, the hunting-lodge in the Gredos near Avila, was given to the nation by the Marqués de la Vega Inclán in the reign of Alfonso XIII. But the development of the magnificent range which we know and admire today was set in motion by Luis Bolín.

We had two of the American block-busters – Irving Wallace and Irving Stone – both of whom I liked very much personally. And three authors who were friends as well as clients whose work I enjoyed: Vincent Brome, Allan Prior and Oswald Wynd. Notably, the first brought to light Father Pat O'Leary whose exploits in the Belgian underground have made him well remembered. The second a good companion, especially watching cricket. And the third, with his charming wife, gave me much hospitality at their home in Crail, above the harbour, looking straight out to the rocky island offshore.

Although we did not know it, the beginning of the new decade would be our last great year.

Anne, Portrait of a Princess by Judith Campbell was interesting because photography was one of Nicholas's main interests at the time, and he went up to Balmoral to take all the pictures for the book. Looking at them again recently I was once more impressed by how good they are. Of course, they had to be submitted to the Palace, and again – as had happened years before – I was sorry that one was vetoed which I thought charming: the Royal Family standing on a terrace in the garden and one of the young princes rooting about in his father's sporran to see what treasures he can find. But the most beautiful by far is one of Princess Anne affectionately snuggling her horse.

A 'first' of importance was *A World of My Own* by Robin Knox-Johnson, the first man to sail round the world single-handed and non-stop, a deeply interesting book by a charming man.

In planning the lists David would come to me and say, 'I want ten titles from you for the autumn,' and in view of the attitude which I had taken towards the literary agents, I was often hard put to meet his requirements. I did suggest Rex Bellamy who was then the best writer on lawn tennis in this country, and *Bryant on Bowls* when that great player had reached the height of his career.

It occurred to me that Ian Fleming was so precise in the details of the hardware carried both by 007 and his enemies that he must either know a great deal himself or have a very good adviser, so I wrote to him and his reply was the last communication that I had from him before his death. He got all he needed, he said, from an expert named Geoffrey

Boothroyd, who, when I approached him, agreed to write for us a comprehensive work: *The Handgun.*

The last book of genuine importance for which I was myself responsible, *Printing and the Mind of Man: a Descriptive Catalogue Illustrating the Impact of Print on the Evolution of Western Civilization during Five Centuries,* appeared in 1967. It was a noble large quarto designed by John Dreyfus and superbly printed by Brooke Crutchley at the Cambridge University Press, with a double-spread title page cut by Reynolds Stone. In 1940 Stanley Morison had organized at the FitzWilliam Museum in Cambridge an exhibition to celebrate the fifth centenary of Gutenberg's invention in the west of movable type. The catalogue was printed, but the exhibition never opened because of the fear of air raids. Nonetheless he never abandoned the hope of seeing an exhibition or a book on the subject, and thought the 11th International Printers' Exhibition of Machinery and Allied Trades (acronym IPEX) to be held in London, at Earl's Court and Olympia, in 1963 to be a golden opportunity. He suggested the idea to Percy Muir and the exhibition, which was a great success, was organized by Percy and John Carter, assisted by Nicholas Barker, H.A. Feisenberger, Howard Nixon and S.H. Steinberg. Since I knew all of them, I was not entirely surprised when I was offered the resulting book, though I was honoured and delighted.

Morison lived just long enough to see the publication of what is now a standard book on the subject; it sold well and there should have been a second edition, but by the time one was required such matters were beyond my control.

We worked on, we worked hard, but we did not know that the demon sharper had a card up his sleeve to trump the next trick.

26   The Fall

Not long after the *P.Q.17* case a well known publisher of central European origin bought all the Cassell shares he could obtain on the market and offered them to the New York firm of Crowell, Collier, MacMillan, saying he thought that Cassell was ripe for a take-over bid. The Americans bought the shares and, if one of their directors was right about the price they paid him, he did very nicely. In due course they made their offer; it was a good one, but none of us was interested. However, our attention was rather painfully fixed upon the matter when the legal position became clear.

Years before I had said to my father that, while I had no idea what his intentions were as regards his will, nor did I expect or wish to know, I begged him not to leave a lot of Cassell shares to me, since I might not long survive him and two doses of estate duty in quick succession would be crippling. I suggested rather that he should leave whatever he thought fit to my children; he agreed with this and created a trust for them of which Bill Angell was the main trustee.

Bill and I had always got on extremely well, although I did not have a great deal to do with him since his dealings as secretary, were with the business director. His translation from Cassell's to a similar position in a friendly firm had nothing to do with me, although as chairman I had to acquiesce. Now he came to see me and in a perfectly friendly way pointed out that the offer was a good one, and if the trustees did not accept it they were guilty in law of betraying their trust. I was staggered; we were trapped and there was no way out. So the firm was sold against our will and we became part of a group of publishers under the control of Crowell, Collier, MacMillan.

As chairman of the group the Americans appointed an English retired diplomat who was a charming man, but could not be expected to have any great knowledge of publishing, and what useful purpose he served or was supposed to serve I never discovered. The chief executive was a hard-nosed American with little feeling or goodwill, and I cannot pretend that I was sorry when later I heard a rumour that, very much to his own surprise, he found himself abruptly fired in New York City.

The actual responsibility for Cassell's was in the hands of an American of what I might call the higher second echelon, although I was still nominally chairman. I have said earlier that although throughout my

372

working-life I had always admired, indeed almost revered the great American publishers, I had a poor opinion of the second echelon – though I can recall three notable exceptions. There was a rapid turnover of these types occupying the London position and they did so with varying success: the good, the bad and the indifferent – sometimes feeling their corn, sometimes making a real effort to get beneath the skin and be part of the set-up in which they found themselves. For it was not an easy job to rule an English staff whose ways were different from their own – not better or worse, but different – and be answerable to an American boss who would bite their heads off as soon as look at them. Perhaps it was for this reason that another English director was appointed to the headquarters of the group – to oil the wheels, so to speak. If this was the intention he must have been a sad disappointment because he turned out to be no more than a rather indifferent postman who had only one answer to a question: asked, for instance, if one might blow one's nose, his reply would invariably be, 'I'll have to phone New York on that.'

The first Cassellite to rebel was Bryen Gentry. Over lunch at the Royal Thames Yacht Club, of which he was a member, the Gentry temper for once overcame him and he had a noisy altercation with second-echelon Mark 1 which, I gather, thoroughly upset the dining-room; he then told us at Red Lion Square that he was resigning. One and all we begged him to do no such thing; even Bill Angell, who had no particular reason to love him at that time, tried to make him change his mind. But he was adamant – he left and founded his own firm, Gentry Books; and then a few years later, all too soon, he died. He was a friend who had meant a great deal more to me than even our respective fathers had to one another.

The next departure was that of Nicholas. Not having wished to go to university when he was eighteen, he had now in his thirties begun work at Bedford College, then a part of London University for evening students. Since the sale of the firm meant that on the one hand he would never succeed me as chairman and on the other he had received a considerable sum for his shares, he walked out and went full time to the university. The result was a first-class degree and he followed this by devoting himself to ecology and writing a thesis on the history and development of the New Forest which earned him his Ph.D.

I had taken the first step back up the hill when in October 1969 I placed myself in the hands of Dr Silvio Benaim, one of the two people to whom I owe the fact that (so far) I am still alive. But while my health took a turn for the better, I became more and more worried about that of Josephine. Her brilliance and business ability were countered by a streak of unsureness and instability – I don't know what it was – which caused her to make two attempts to take her own life. But more alarming were the attacks, increasingly frequent, of some disorder of the nervous system which would bring about an almost trance-like state accompanied by physical instability. I never discovered the name of the disorder and she did not want to discuss it, nor did her very reputable doctor seem able to find a cure. Whatever the cause, the attacks became more baneful and more frequent, until the night came in July 1970 when I put her to bed virtually unconscious and she was soon asleep, never to wake up again.

How the terrible news spread I never knew and was too dazed to ask. Nevertheless that evening I was taken to dinner by Michael Goodman-Smith, still technically my brother-in-law, who had come up from Watford for the purpose, and given a bed by my old friend Edward Hudson, so that I would not be alone; two acts of charity and kindness for which I will be for ever grateful.

Another thread was cut in the same year when Pierre Le Dilicocq's long term as secretary of the Alliance Française in Great Britain came to an end and he was returning to France. He had the O.B.E., but was most properly created C.B.E. for his great work in Anglo-French relations. I could not face starting afresh with a new secretary and, since I had been president for over eight years, I thought that I should offer my resignation. At the same time the Baron de Courcel was leaving the London embassy for a high position at the Quai d'Orsay. A chapter came to an end at the *dîner de clôture* at the annual *Assemblée Générale* of the Alliance. The ambassador elevated me from Chevalier to Officier of the Légion d'Honneur, and at the end of dinner Pierre asked for the decoration back; mine was delayed in the post so the ambassador had pinned his own on me, and I felt doubly honoured. I stood on the steps as he and his wife were driven away, leaving London and taking with them the particular magic which they had bestowed upon the embassy. Pierre and Madeleine Le Dilicocq went too, but they left a little of themselves behind: their beautiful daughter Nanou married an Englishman.

The year was rounded off by my being invited somewhat brusquely to retire. I cannot blame Crowell, Collier; I was sixty-five, my office had become a sinecure and I have no doubt that my continued presence was a nuisance. It was done surgically and the arrangements were all that I could expect.

David Ascoli remained, increasingly frustrated in his endeavours to carry on a list worthy of the House of Cassell, with the big names which had customarily distinguished it. I cannot, nor would I if I could, detail the story through the several years that it lasted. Just at the end a system was introduced whereby if he wished to contract for a book, he should submit a request for agreement to the man sitting in the chair which I once had occupied. Accordingly one day he sent a chit upstairs which came back cryptically annotated:

'Who is Fischer-Dieskau and what authority has he to write about Schubert?'

This was too much; he resigned, and the fall was complete.

27   The Empty Quarter

Not many years had passed before the affairs of Cassell's took a most disturbing turn. After the sixties when 'we never had it so good' a cold wind blew and only the sturdy could endure against it. In 1981 the general book division of Cassell's was closed with losses unofficially estimated at £500,000 a year, and Jeremy Greenwood, the director in charge, said that 'the division's long record of losses had made it less able to cope with the recession than other publishers'. Notwithstanding the setback of the *P.Q.17* case, the then directors of Cassell's had handed over a thriving business, and to have destroyed it so quickly was a remarkable achievement. Further, those in charge undid all the work that I had done in the Antipodes by putting Australia and New Zealand together again, and for some reason moving headquarters from Melbourne to Sydney – though Jim Moad himself refused to budge. Truly Locke said, 'Error is not a fault of knowledge but a mistake of our judgement.'

Crowell, Collier sold Cassell's to CBS, under whom it went on publishing medical and educational books, while retaining the most famous authors. Now it is once more in the hands of a British proprietor, and all those still around who knew and loved the old firm have already seen a heart-warming renaissance – a new life.

But all publishing is hard work in a changing world; as Sam Lawrence, the present head of William Morrow, recently wrote to me, 'When Thayer moved to the hill country around Texas and raised horses he told me that he thought horse-racing was a saner business than book-publishing. I didn't agree with him then, but I do now.'

Meanwhile, there is a Spanish saying, 'Take what you want from life – and pay for it.' Had I taken what I wanted and was the bill now lying in the saucer on the table?

No longer a publisher, I neither knew what to do next nor how much time I had in which to do it. Two sayings kept rattling round in my mind: Graham Greene's, 'We are served or damned by our thoughts, not by our actions,' and the wise words of that well upholstered girl from Nashville, Dolly Parton: 'The way I see it, if you want the rainbow you've got to put up with the rain.' It was awfully wet, so I wrapped myself in history which had commanded part of me from my early life.

My interest was quickened from an unexpected quarter. At Walton

Heath, which I had joined a number of years before, I played a round
with a new member, got to know him and discovered him to be one of
the most remarkable men I have ever met – Patrick Gilbert, who had not
long before been appointed as the first lay head of the S.P.C.K. One day,
after we played our round, he said that he had decided to broaden the
front of the society, whose sole purpose as its name implies is the
promotion of Christian knowledge, by founding a new imprint
publishing social studies, psychology, any serious subject. He asked me
if I would like the position of editorial consultant and I instantly
accepted; so on 27 September 1972 the Sheldon Press was born, and I
worked happily with its director, Darley Anderson. At the start, with my
knowledge of the American scene, I think that I was of help, and for a
number of years I read and advised on manuscripts. But eventually
Darley found a successful niche in the publishing field, specialized
rather than general, in which I could be of no help to him; so, after more
than a decade, I asked to be relieved from duty.

There was also a certain amount of writing to be done. Since he had
first opened a wine and cheese bar near the British Museum in the
thirties I had known Tommy Layton, and published several of his books;
ow he was editor of the quarterly produced by the Anglo-Spanish
Society. I began to write articles which he accepted, and he
commissioned a long series on the bulls. Also I made a new friend in
Alan Ross, who asked me to write for his excellent *London Magazine*.
This, together with various commissions and working on this book,
occupied much of my time; and there was travel.

Visiting my elder daughter, Susan, who was at Stanford University,
we decided to drive down the lovely Pacific highway to Saint Simeon,
Hurst's famous palace. So big is the house that it takes three tours to go
over it all; the one we selected finished up in the cinema to watch films
taken by Hurst of some of his celebrated guests, and their names were
given out. As we got on the bus to go back down the hill I thanked our
young guide and remarked that he had not mentioned the most famous
of the guests in the films playing tennis.

'Oh, I'm sorry,' he said, 'who was that?'

'Big Bill Tilden.'

He went the colour of beetroot. Considering that California is
notorious as Gayland with San Francisco as its capital, I was surprised
that the peccadilloes of the greatest of all tennis players have even now
been neither forgotten nor forgiven.

Although homosexuality is another way of life of which I want no
part, I think that the American treatment of Tilden was abominable.
They put him in prison; Nabokov made fun of him in *Lolita* as a tennis
coach, Ned Litam, which, spelt backwards, reads 'Ma Tilden.' And in
1953, the last year of his life, he was invited to play in the National
Hard-courts Championship, then forced to withdraw because of public
protest. 'He just turned away,' said the tennis pro who offered the
invitation. 'Jesus, it was awful. The poor old son of a bitch.'

There was a renaissance at this time, when Margaret and I became again good companions, travelling far and wide together every summer between 1976 and 1983. Since today so many people go everywhere, all that seems worth recording are the things which remain in my mind as jewels.

In Kenya how many visitors have seen a lioness which has just killed a zebra waiting for her man to arrive after she has summoned him from his idleness two miles away, and her hungry cubs waiting patiently in the stalls, with equal patience the hyenas in the dress circle knowing that their turn will come while, behind, in the upper circle, the vultures, their scraggy necks sunk between their shoulders, stand motionless, resigned to a long delay before they can pick the bones – all that will remain.

It is said to be very unusual to see pairs of lovers in the lion family close together, as we did; they prefer to perform in solitude: and what a performance it is! The lion mounts the lioness, who remains prone, every twenty minutes for forty-eight hours like clockwork, after which he has had enough and goes away, probably never to see her again.

It was the translation which I had made in the early thirties of Paul Morand's *Air Indien* which, Margaret said, gave her the idea that we should go to Peru, a country in which there is so much to see besides the incredible Inca architecture. Magnificent as the ruins of Macchu Pichu and Sachsachuan are, the thing which remains most clearly in my mind is the last surviving Indian co-operative which, tending then the soil which it still tends now, had the right of direct appeal on all matters to the Inca himself.

On the winding train journey up from Cuzco, the ancient capital, to Juliaca, the end of the line, I saw high above the hills a condor which I am told is a rare sight today.

One year a tour round Sicily. Surely Syracuse must be the most interesting place on this beautiful island. Where else is there a church built round a temple so that the nave is flanked by rows of Doric columns? The desecration of the mosque at Córdoba by the imposition in its middle of a Christian cathedral is terrible, so why is it different to enclose an ancient temple? It seems to me that it is the arrogance and lack of taste which is so offensive at Córdoba, whereas Sicily still simmers in the past, inland are still the vales of Theocritus, there has been no change, merely a gentle progression as though the newer stones enveloping the sturdy columns merely added one more tribute to the gods. The wide theatre on the stage of which were first performed the plays of Euripides. And down the road the only Greek bath I have ever seen. Roman baths, from the splendours of Caracalla down to the steam-room of a villa in Gloucestershire; but what did the Greeks do? They were such great talkers, great philosophers, that it should be no surprise that round the heating is a semi-circle of terracotta armchairs, so that sweating should not interfere with their conversation.

In Israel I do not believe that many of the sacred places one is shown present anything more than agreeable legends; but in Nazareth one is face to face with the fact in the small synagogue in which He took His barmitzvah and the only well in town from which His mother drew water, while the modern cathedral is a horror.

The Dead Sea was no surprise because it is just like the brine baths at Droitwich; but the scriptorium where the scrolls were written seemed almost as if the scribes had just gone on holiday, leaving an ink-well ready in each desk. The huge rock pile of Masada where the Jewish garrison died rather than surrender is very familiar, but what are still there which interested me are the huge earthen ramps constructed by the Romans so that they could get their battering-rams up to the gates of the citadel high above them.

A visit to the Soviet Union was our last journey together; both of us wanted to see the tomb of Tamerlane.

As one drives in from the western airport (Moscow has five) the first thing that pulls one up sharp is the huge, severe and dignified memorial which marks the point at which the German troops were halted in their advance on the capital: it is frighteningly near – there just down the road are the tall buildings of the city. Unlike Alexander and Kutuzov, Stalin decided to go back no farther, and seeing that monument so close brings to mind the desperation with which the Soviet soldiers fought and died to hold the enemy back from the very heart of Mother Russia.

The National Hotel is in the centre of the city, and as I stood on the doorstep in the morning watching the crowds pouring out of the Underground, I thought how remarkably they resembled a similar crowd at the same hour in London, Paris or New York. It was nippy and there was still ice on the Neva; just before we moved on came May Day on which winter officially ends, and it is the duty of every citizen to go on to the streets with a shovel and clear away the remaining snow. When I thought of London where one might imagine that it is the duty of every citizen to throw away his cigarette packet, his hamburger container or his bag of crisps and his beer can to add to the general filth, I shuddered.

Our journey towards our target began with a flight south to Bokhara, which gave us an immediate sense of the vastness of the Soviet Union. On a map Bokhara is very near Moscow, but in fact it is a longer flight than that from London. There a day at the races was a pleasant change from more serious activities; as in a number of countries, trotting races are preferred to ordinary flat racing. The last number on the card was a camel race, and the afternoon ended with *Buz Kashi*. This is a game from Afghanistan in which two mounted teams struggle for possession of the carcass of a goat; it is a tough business and in wilder climes often results in the death of at least one of the contestants. Genghis Khan is said to have invented it, using the heads of prisoners instead of a goat's carcass.

From here on south everyone speaks Uzbek, and the children have to learn two new languages: first Russian, and then either English or French. I discovered that virtually everyone of what we call the middle classes or bourgeoisie – both terms of opprobrium in a Communist state – spoke one or the other. Whether the same applies to the Asian republics, I do not know, but in the European republics I was constantly surprised by a state of education quite different from that in our island. As an example, in Samarkand I walked to see the tomb of Tamerlane by moonlight when it is particularly beautiful, and on the way there was a young man sitting on the pavement; seeing, by my clothes I presume, that I was a foreigner, he addressed me in French so I stopped and chatted for a while.

The building itself is magnificent, and it is typical that within it Tamerlane, who could not read but took delight in the company of wise men and poets, should have given a larger tomb to his teacher than the one designed to receive his own remains when the time came. How strange an animal is man: here was one who could have so much feeling for beauty, yet destroy his fellow beings in such numbers that to read the story of his life is sickening. Perhaps Sir Walter Raleigh was right: 'All men are evil and will declare themselves to be so when occasion is offered.'

There is so much to see. But the thing which will stay for ever in my mind is the Yurt – the tent of felt stretched over bamboo poles, warm in winter and cool in summer – used by the nomadic tribesmen and easily transported to wherever the pasture is best. These tents seem symbolic of a life which goes on unchanged as it has gone on for thousands of years and will go on years without end – far removed in space, time and inclination from a Kremlin beset by technical problems, economic troubles and the machinations of its enemies.

Louise, my second daughter, married a Korean whose parents live in Japan, just outside Osaka. When she bore a daughter it was their first grandchild, which of course had to be shown to them as soon as possible; I decided to go with her. Since my host and hostess were Korean, I did not meet many Japanese people, but I shall never forget the party to which they invited a number of their friends; it was hilarious, for Koreans have a boisterous sense of humour. As to Japan itself, there is no country to which I have ever been that has made me feel so much a stranger in a strange land; I might have landed on another planet. Accepting all their technological and mechanical efficiency as read, two overwhelming impressions remain – the beauty and the cleanliness. I like everything being spick and span with no litter in the streets, buying stamps in a post office where they are handed across the counter in a cellophane envelope, the custom of taking one's shoes off before entering a house; I like the Japanese bath for which one first cleans oneself under a shower and then sinks into the family tank of hot water up to one's neck to stay as long as one likes, which is remarkably soothing.

The sense of beauty is spellbinding. Knowing that they are great show-pieces cannot possibly prepare one for the magic of the two ancient capitals, Nara and Kyoto. The buildings are as lovely within as they are without, and around them lie age-old gardens assembled with the careless precision for which they are justly famous. And everywhere, particularly in the great wooden arches, is that distinctive red which is seen nowhere else in the world.

The studied politeness, the scribes who paint complex and beautiful kanjies as you watch, the Kabuki theatre are but symbols of a tradition so deeply ingrained which make more understandable the harsh reactions which in unhappier times, can meet those who offend against it. At the top of a long flight of steps in Izumi, outside Osaka, is a simple cenotaph erected in memory of the conscientious objectors who were executed in prison during the Second World War. A coloured paper fish flies over the near by house when a child is born. A remarkable people, a mystical mixture of beauty and brutality.

About then I had one more month in a nursing home. My son David, deciding that it was not a good idea for me to look after myself entirely alone, went to a well known employment agency to find someone who could take care of lunch; they thought they had a suitable candidate on their books. He brought her to see me; very tall, he came in with a small figure who scarcely reached his shoulders. A deal was quickly arranged.

Sophia Margaretta, née Komorska, is the only child of a father descended from one of the oldest families in Poland and a distinguished Russian mother. She has intense pride, and a never-fading love of the deep forests in which she was a child, the vast estates of her parents and her Bochwic relations in what was eastern Poland. While the pride makes her impatient of stupidity and incompetence, she is filled with loving kindness and generosity to people of goodwill and those in need. In 1939 she left her homeland with her mother when their country was invaded from both sides and their estates overrun. Educated thereafter in Paris and Scotland, she married a Lithuanian doctor in the British colonial service. After he had been for a number of years medical officer in St Helena, to which distant island she remains devoted, he served in Sierra Leone. And there, deeply loved by the army of patients whom he looked after with such selfless devotion, he died. That her heart was broken is hardly surprising, that her health collapsed little less so. She left West Africa with her memories, a detailed knowledge of and liking for the various tribes which inhabit that variegated area. After a slow recovery, circumstances were such that she had to work for her living – in Spain Ibiza and Madrid, and in Prague, eventually returning to this country.

During my life I have known many people exiled from their homelands and, whatever the reason for their departure, there are few exceptions who have not wounds of differing degrees of pain caused by violent separation from the roots left behind. The exceptions are the very rich for whom the making of money has stultified every other feeling. But of them all, those in whom the nostalgia is most insoluble and never forgotten are those who come from the proudest and most tragic of countries: Poland.

This was the woman who came at midday; and, as we sat over lunch, there were the most violent political arguments, for not only our views differed, but our approach to them. She sees everything as black or white, while, as I have said earlier, to me everything is grey. But that in itself was less important than the fact that she saw to it that I mended my ways. Gradually the professional engagement changed and grew into a personal one. As it deepened, she became the second person, following Silvio Benaim, who saved my life and saw to it that I lived to write this book, for what it is worth.

Now we are happily married. Apart from the sense of security, an added benefit has been our visits to Poland to see the remains of her family, and some of the wonderful treasures – one of which I never thought I would live to see, Chopin's birthplace.

It lies twenty-five miles west of Warsaw – beautiful, peaceful, revered – and unscathed because a Soviet divisional commander in 1945 issued an order which said, 'We are now approaching Zelazowa Wola; anyone firing anywhere in that direction will be court-martialled.' But it is people who make places; and I have been charmed by the courtesy of the Poles in general and the kindness of my Polish cousins in particular. I say 'my cousins' because it is a typical custom there that the cousins of a spouse on marriage regard themselves formally as kinsmen of the new arrival.

Long ago, Hemingway wrote, 'Part of you died each year when the leaves fell from the trees and their branches were bare against the wind and the cold, wintry light.' It is late autumn now, and as Sophie and I walk together through the woods the shafts of the setting sun slant lowly through the trees. Perhaps she is thinking of her beloved forests at Paulinovo, perhaps I am walking back after the duck have flighted in for the last stand. It has been a long time.

Appendix 1

Cricket

I do not think that I have ever met anyone who is indifferent to cricket; people either think that it is needlessly complicated and lasts too long, or they regard it almost as a religion. Never much good as a player, I have long been devoted to watching the game.

Playing

I was always a butter-fingers. A lot of my trouble, I believe, was psychological: if I saw a catch coming my way, my reaction was that I was sure to drop it.

During my university days and my time at home, four years in all, I played for the Sevenoaks 2nd XI. Sevenoaks was always a centre of cricket, and there in the eighteenth century Roger Pett made the best bats. On one unforgettable occasion I was summoned to the 1st XI, a good club side, unforgettable because the match was at home – on the Vine, the oldest cricket ground in regular use in the world (Hambledon only enjoys a memorial game once a year). The first fully recorded match was in June 1744, and in the pavilion are the score cards of 'The Duke of Dorset's XI v The Rest of England'; the Duke was a great figure in the history of cricket and he lived at Knole which is still the home of his family, the Sackvilles.

I came to no harm in the field and was sent in fairly low down – about No 8; 'Don't try anything fancy, just stay there,' I was told. In spite of my orders, a half-volley outside the leg stump was more than I could bear and I despatched it for six in the direction of Knole Park. We won, I was not out, and got back to the pavilion to face a withering rebuke: 'I told you *not* to do anything fancy.' Nearly forty years later I thought of that when I was talking to my friend Allan Prior, such a good novelist and television writer, who used to play in the Yorkshire League. He, too, received a ball which deserved what it got, whereupon the old pro at the other end walked slowly down the pitch and in sombre tones said, 'Tha' doosn't 'it fowers afore loonch.'

Not long after I went into Cassell's I thought that it would be a good idea to have a cricket team and started enquiries round the house to see what talent was available. I found that we could just about manage, with a friend or two of mine topping up the numbers and the skill. The Packing Department produced a really first-class wicket-keeper, trained by the great Strudwick of Surrey and England, and our two best bowlers; Accounts contained an enthusiastic but not brilliant all-rounder and a bowler of donkey-drops of such sublime simplicity that batsmen treated them with deep suspicion; and from the Art Department came our assault weapon, a left-hand fast bowler who produced a bewildering mixture of full tosses, bumpers and wides, with some very good balls in between. For a short time we had a beautiful opening bat, a young chap who, alas, soon went to a better job elsewhere.

I cannot now think why, but I never bowled myself; and I got over my catching jinx by fielding usually at silly mid-wicket. This had several advantages: I could see what was going on; if a hot catch came it would either stick or if it went down nobody would be surprised; and in the kind of village-level cricket that we played it shut up quite a wide arc which the batsmen had not the skill to avoid.

The next thing was fixtures. We were wanderers with no ground of our own, but it was not too difficult to get enough games, mainly in the trade: Hazell, Watson & Viney at Aylesbury, Butler & Tanner at Frome (an all-day game in Somerset), the B.B.C. 2nd XI, Dickinsons the paper makers, the Sun Engraving and a few villages where we had an 'in'.

Our umpire was Packe, who in the office looked after incoming manuscripts; and Margaret, one of the comparatively small number of Americans who, like J. Paul Getty, really uderstand the game, was a remarkably efficient scorer.

Lord Camrose very kindly gave us the use of the nets on the *Daily Telegraph* ground at Sidcup for practice on Thursday evenings. In addition, Oliver Simon and I used to have a lunchtime net once a week at Jack Fingleton's school in the basement of Dolphin Square. One day the next net to us was occupied by Learie Constantine bowling to H.M. Garland-Wells; it was astonishing how the great West Indian, off a short run, made the ball fizz and accelerate off the matting on to the bat.

We called ourselves the Savages and had a rather nice claret-coloured cap with Pocahontas in gold on the front. The best of the friends who joined us when we were in need was Edward Hudson, whom I had known from childhood in Sevenoaks and who in addition was my solicitor; he was a lovely bat, his style characteristic of the purity which is found in Kent, the best examples being the Cowdreys and David Gower.

Francis Meynell, Oliver and Bobby Simon ran teams for which I played from time to time. Francis had a fixture every Whit Monday against Great Yeldham, the village in which he then lived. One year, being short, he asked if I could bring someone and I asked Edward Hudson. Edward was always diffident and self-critical; he was going in first wicket, and throughout the opening partnership sat padded up muttering. 'This will be a disaster ... I wish I hadn't come ... Francis will never forgive me ...'; when the time came he rattled up 71 with consummate ease. Centuries were rare at this level, and the only one that I can remember was scored by Michael Fordham, the child psychiatrist, playing for Bobby Simon at Bourne End; he was so excited that he took a wild swipe at the next delivery, got a top edge and hit the ball into his own face.

I have described how we happened to have a fixture with the Motor Union Insurance on the day when Nicholas, my son was born in 1935. The two friends whom I asked to strengthen the side were Francis Meynell and a doctor, Tom Garland, who had narrowly missed a Blue at Cambridge; I had to take a risk and be there to captain the side. This is what happened, on a lovely sunny day.

The ground was beautiful, smallish and like a billiards table – you could have pitched a wicket anywhere in the outfield. Beyond one end was the main railway line to the west. Some of our opponents met us, and my bag was carried in by their wicket-keeper, a charming man. Conversationally he remarked that this was a very high-scoring ground, and on the previous Saturday Owen-Smith (an England amateur) had scored a century before lunch.

They won the toss and batted. I opened with Tom Garland bowling very fast downhill and down wind; they were soon in trouble and were all out for 120. I walked in with the wicket-keeper who was not out and he was most despondent; 'That score's no good on this ground,' he said, 'we've had it.' Our batting went well, the high point being a huge six hit by Tom Garland into a passing train, and the ball was carried off to Paddington. By the standards of those days, I suppose we behaved badly; knowing how condescendingly I had been treated, the Savages riotously cheered every single. I went in No 4 to be with Francis for the kill, and we beat them by seven wickets. Rather pettily they refused to play us the following year.

Not long before the second war Alec (a devoted cricketer) and Joan Waugh bought a house on the edge of Silchester, and for certainly two years we had a wonderful fixture which he generously arranged. Margaret and I drove down for the weekend; the boys came down by train. Alec sent a bus to pick them up at Reading station and gave them lunch. He was a medium-pace bowler, and when I came in he got the Silchester captain to put him on; a friendly duel always ensued and honours were pretty even. Afterwards Alec gave the boys supper and the bus took them to their train.

After the war Edrington, the wicket-keeper, did not come back and I had no heart for starting the Savages again. In fact, I only played twice myself: once for the fathers against Nicholas's prep school and once for Edward Hudson in Sussex.

Watching

The pleasure of a lifetime as a spectator has been and still is endless; and from it there are some things which I cannot forget.

I got off to a flying start; my prep-school friend, Bunny Jacques, and I became schoolboy members of the Oval just in time to see the last Test against the Australians in August 1921. In a series of three, the Aussies had been all over us in the first two, but this almost endless game made cricket history and ended in a draw. Bunny and I saw every ball of the match which Wisden says 'declined from serious contest to a farce'. The Australian captain, W.W. Armstrong, over-fat and over-age, fielded in the deep, put his cap on backwards and read a newspaper ('to find out whom we're playing,' he said). This is history, but R.W.V. Robins told me that I was the only person he had met who actually saw it. Macdonald and Gregory, both very fast, bowled an average of five bumpers an over; they were best dealt with by Ernest Tyldesley of Lancashire who put his bat up beside his face and, as the ball reared, turned through ninety degrees, scoring four past square leg. Of course eventually he mistimed one and was hit in the face.

Different people get pleasure from different things, and I am one of the many to whom grace is more important than sheer skill. For example, I got more enjoyment from watching McCartney make sixty at Canterbury than I ever did from a Bradman double-century; indeed, although there is no question that Bradman is the greatest run-making machine there has ever been, Margaret once put it very well: 'He either plays back or hits a boundary – it's a bore.'

As to skill, I respected the sterling qualities of men like Bill Edrich and Ken Barrington without being at all moved; yet even these honest workmen cannot be redeemed by their personality, as with the likes of Maurice Leyland and Patsy Hendren.

My all-time favourites among batsmen have been Hobbs, Hammond, Compton, Worrell, Border and Gower. They all have the same characteristic: having twice as long in which to play their shots as anyone else – rather like Alex James playing football for Arsenal in the thirties who had such an instinctive sense of position that he never ran – he walked.

Australian Test players regard Hobbs as the best batsman ever produced by England, perhaps not surprising as he made twelve more centuries against them than any other player. He too not only had all the time in the world, but played his shots with superlative grace. There was one in particular which I shall never forget. Mother and I went to the Oval in 1926 to see the Gentlemen v. Players match, which was such an enjoyable fixture until all became one, though not all the other. Hobbs, captain of the Players, made 82. To one ball he took two leisurely strides down the pitch and swung his bat in a slow, full, graceful arc. No one knew where the ball had gone until there was a crash of breaking tiles at the top of the pavilion roof; another six inches and the ball would have cleared it into the Kennington Road.

Later I used to allow myself two bats a season and always bought them from Hobbs' shop in Fleet Street. The great man would be sitting behind his desk; having selected a couple for weight and lift, I would lay them before him for his approval, and he would nod with grave courtesy.

Wally Hammond was not as tall as Hobbs, and stockier; 'Someone once wrote that Hammond coming in to bat was one of the sights of the cricketing world – like a galleon moving in full sail.' His off-drive, in which he sort of leaned over the ball, was for years seen by millions, whether they were interested or not, on the posters for Players' cigarettes. In a test match I once saw him slightly mistime one and Stan McCabe, the bowler, bravely tried to catch it just above the ground; it split through the Australian's hand and still went for four. In August 1938, Margaret and I went to Lord's for the Test against Australia, and when play began England were in rather poor health at 29 for 3; Hammond, who had yet to score, came in with Charlie Barnett; by the time stumps were drawn he had made 240.

Although he did not make a big score, I shall always associate Worrell with the match at Lord's in 1950 in which the West Indies beat England for the first time; their most loyal supporter, always in a morning coat with bowler hat and badly furled umbrella, was ecstatic, as were the rest of the coloured spectators – on that day Henry Newbolt's 'deathly hush' departed from the cricket scene for ever, and within forty-eight hours the Lord Beginner's lovely calypso, 'Cricket, lovely cricket/At Lord's did I see it', was on everyone's lips.

As an aside, there is a little piece of social history which has impinged in a small way on cricket. Many years ago, in the days of the Raj, it was not only condoned but positively encouraged that single civil servants or businessmen working in India should acquire Indian mistresses; it kept them happy and out of trouble. At the end of their tour of duty they would return to Britain, sometimes callously leaving their lady pregnant. When the baby arrived the mother, registering it, would be asked the name of the father which she either did not know or had forgotten, so she would be asked what his occupation had been, and this would be the child's name, and, in time, the name of the child's family. These names have persisted for generations, and those who have watched the players who have helped India to her present eminence will remember Merchant, Engineer and Contractor.

Among bowlers I had two favourites in the fast department; Larwood for his incredible accuracy – he was just as hard to cope with going away outside the off stump as he was when ordered to bowl at the body, a tactic, Robins told me, suggested to Jardine by H.D. Nourse, the captain of South Africa; and Keith Miller, a master of the unexpected. But spin bowling always fascinated me: Rhodes, Mailey, Grimmett, O'Reilly, Ramadin, Valentine, Gibbs, Wardle, Laker and Lock – I saw them all, but my favourite was Hedley Verity, who on a drying pitch once took fourteen Australian wickets in one day. He was a wonderful figure with such a beautiful action, and I feel a twinge of sadness still when I remember that he died of wounds in Italy as a captain in the K.O.Y.L.I. But Margaret's favourite was always Doug Wright, quick for a spinner and alleged to be the most difficult to play on a quick wicket. He could turn the ball prodigiously and startle the batsman, the wicket-keeper and often, I think, himself.

All great men, and there were so many more – Woolley, Hutton, May, Sobers, 'perhaps cricket's greatest all-rounder', Hadlee, Imran – for instance, but perhaps when stumps are drawn, though we were never paid, I join with Mary Mitford who in 1820 wrote, 'The cricket I mean is a real solid, old-fashioned match between neighbouring parishes where each man attacks the other for honour and supper, glory and half a crown a man.'

Appendix 2

Golf

The first golf lessons I ever had were given to me when I was twelve by Hills, the greenkeeper and pro at the Wildernesse; we lived in Sevenoaks and this was the nearest course. At that time father and mother both played; he was about to give it up, but she continued until the Second World War.

In those days the Wildernesse clubhouse was a group of nissen huts at the tiny village of Godden Green; what is now the 7th hole was the 18th, and the present 8th (a much more difficult hole than it looks) was then the first. On the death of Lord Hillingdon, who owned the land, there was panic that the course might cease to exist, and arrangements were quickly made with Lord Sackville for a new course to be constructed at Knole Park. In the event, not only did the Wildernesse survive, but Lord Hillingdon's mansion became the clubhouse; this necessitated making a new 1st and 18th hole, so that players could get away from and finish at the new headquarters – this enabled two rather bad holes across the Seal road to be done away with. Knole Park flourished, and with its growth as a dormitory town Sevenoaks needed at least two clubs anyway. Mother belonged to both and in due course was Lady Captain of each. After I no longer had any connection with the Wildernesse a completely new clubhouse was built in its present location and further rearrangements of the course became necessary; but still sixteen of the eighteen holes remain as I knew them as a child – and one's first course always retains a special place in one's memory.

Among my acquaintances in King's, at Cambridge, was one Bond, a golf Blue who was son of the Master of Trinity Hall and in 1928 we decided to drive down to Moor Park to watch the match between Walter Hagen and Archie Compston. Although Compston won 18 up and 17 to play, there was only one interesting character on the course, Hagen; he had probably not been to bed the night before, and zig-zagged from rough to rough, but he could not have cared less and it did not in any way interfere with his winning the Open two weeks later. The stories about Hagen are, of course, endless. He was not very good about money, and this may have been the occasion on which, when he arrived back in New York, he had to borrow the cab fare from the ship to his

389

hotel; although, to be fair, the purses then were minuscule compared with today.

Sir Guy Campbell told me that he was stewarding on the 8th at Muirfield when Hagen won again. The 8th is a dog-leg to the right, then a par 5. On the fourth day Hagen noticed that the crowds had trampled flat the rough which filled the elbow of the dog-leg, and, asking Guy to move the spectators right back, he deliberately drove into what had once been thick grass, leaving himself an easy 5 iron to the green for a birdie. This so enraged the committee of the Honourable Company, of which the magnificent course is the home, that they planted thick trees to ensure that no such indignity could ever be perpetrated again.

Jimmy van Allen – now, I gather, the uncrowned king of Newport, Rhode Island – is a wealthy man who was at one time interested in publishing and had a share in William Morrow in Thayer Hobson's time. Very kindly he asked me to have a round at Piping Rock, on Long Island; where Hagen had once been pro. One day, he told me, there was an eighteen-hole professional tournament and a member, going into the shop, was surprised to see Hagen showing no signs of taking part. The great man said he could make more money minding the shop, and, when the member expostulated, replied, 'All right, go back to the clubhouse and if you can raise a bet of $5,000 that I don't equal the course record, I'll play.' In a short time the member returned and the bet was on. The record was then 66. The 18th is a drive and a medium iron; his sixty-fifth stroke was a little strong to the back of the green with about a twenty-foot downhill putt. He was a wonderful putter, with the same reputation as Bobby Locke has had more recently, and no sooner had he struck his sixty-sixth stroke, long before the ball had entered the hole, than he threw his head back and shouted, 'Pay up, suckers!'

In 1937, when Margaret and I intended to holiday in Saint Jean de Luz, I took my clubs and had a round at Hossegors on the way. I played alone, with a caddy to guide me. In those days I had very sharp eyesight; when I hit a full 2 wood, the caddy said, 'I didn't see where that went,' and I replied, 'It went down a rabbit hole' – when we got there, he put his arm down the hole and said, 'By God, you're right.' At Saint Jean de Luz the pleasant course, Chantaco, belonged to the father of France's greatest golfer at that time, Simonne de la Chaume. They had an open day, and for the medal in the morning I was paired with an enchantress, Mile Vilmorin (of the seed firm, the French equivalent of Ryders), who had a long handicap and went round in a net 59. When I remarked that her handicap hardly flattered her, she blushed and admitted that she had recently had quite a lot of lessons from her friend, Simonne. In the afternoon there was a long driving competition, which I was leading easily when René Lacoste, Simonne de la Chaume's husband, appeared; she asked him why he wasn't in the competition and he said because he didn't feel like it. Retired from tennis, he was a hypochondriac, and on that blazing hot day, at her insistence, he reluctantly removed a racoon coat, peeled off several sweaters, removed various scarves and finally outdrove me by about ten metres.

My last round before the second war was the Lancing Old Boys' meeting at Liphook, a course which was to become important to me later, and I played with Bunny Millard, the father of Lancing golf and one of the moving spirits of the Halford-Hewitt. The clubhouse was in the Links Hotel, and the course began and ended with two blind holes, which are its only flaw. Bernard Darwin said that the best inland course in the south of England was either Woking or Liphook and he could never decide which; knowing both backwards, neither can I. After the war the brewery which owned the hotel decided that they did not want the golfers back, and since there was fortunately enough spare ground a new clubhouse was put up – which meant bending the 11th into a dog-leg 18th and using the old 11th green for a new short 1st. Immediately after the war builders were busy building homes, and the only accommodation permitted was some ex-army huts – and thereby hangs a tale.

In the army I carted my clubs round with me wherever we went, before departure overseas, and the best courses I encountered were the Old at St Andrews (as I have said earlier), Ganton and Gleneagles. The most exciting match in which I took part was at the last of these, not long after I had been posted to 5 Argylls. The battalion played against 52 Scottish Divisional HQ, foursomes all day. In the morning I played with David Simpson (both of us handicap 7), but the real fun was in the afternoon. Lyle Barr (2) and I played against one off 4 and his partner who had just been posted in, whose name I did not catch and who complained the whole way round that his clubs had been lost with his luggage. It was exciting and Lyle – a great man in all senses – and I lost on the last green. As we were walking in I asked who the man was who had complained all the time, and Lyle said, 'That's Gordon Peters, the Walker Cup player'; thank God I didn't know, or I would have blown up.

Immediately after the war I joined Moor Park, as I had promised myself, and there the pro was Arthur Havers, who won the Open in 1923, in spite of having the reputation of being a very bad putter. I had some evidence of this while playing with him in the Hertfordshire Alliance at Berkhamsted (a lovely course on which all hazards are natural and no bunkers are allowed); at the first hole he drove, I put the second about twelve feet past the pin and his putt back was neither short nor long but went straight to cover point at an angle of 45 degrees. But he was a charming man.

Another less agreeable memory of Moor Park was finding an acquaintance of mine fuming in the dressing-room; he had just contested the final of one of the club competitions with a man who was known to have had to leave another club for cheating. These two, playing on the shorter course, were all square after eighteen, and went back to the 1st to continue the battle. This first hole is traversed by a road to Rickmansworth. My acquaintance (let us call him 'A') drove down the middle, his opponent ('X') cut his into the rough behind a clump of trees. Their activity was watched with interest by an old man and his small granddaughter. After searching for a while X said to A, 'Are you sure that ball on the fairway is yours?' A ill-advisedly replied, 'Of course it's mine, but if it will give you any pleasure, I will go and identify it.' No sooner had his back turned than X shouted, 'All right, I've got it!' The penny did not drop until A heard the old man say to his grandchild, 'We can go home to tea now, dear; this gentleman is in the middle and that one over there has just dropped another.' A was so furious at being suckered that he promptly lost the match.

When I went to live at Headley, in Hampshire, in 1952, I immediately applied for membership at Liphook, was accepted and granted the same handicap as that which I had had at Moor Park: 6.

In 1950 I was delighted and flattered to be asked by Bunny Millard to play in the Halford-Hewitt. I played eight times for Lancing, four years with the same partner who then inexplicably gave up the game, and twice as an older hand I partnered young golfers far better than I who were appearing for the first time. I was involved in one really exhausting match, never forgotten. Playing with Eric Pamberton (alas now dead), we were two down with two to play and I was studying a rather curly uphill eight-foot putt when I noticed that a lot of people had appeared round the green; I soon learned the reason: we were two matches all with King's, Canterbury, and the result depended on us. I holed that one, and gave Eric a decent drive down the 18th; he asked me whether he should take a 4 or a 3 iron, and, knowing that at all costs we had to be up, I suggested the larger club – whereupon he hit a beauty through the green into elephant country. I hacked it out to ten feet and he holed, which was good enough and we went on to the 19th. From a good drive I lifted my head and very nearly put us in the ditch; he scuttled it on, and with a half we went to the 20th. This and the match we won, and from the nervous tension and concentration I think I have never felt so tired in my life.

Foursomes I have always found more interesting than singles, and I think that I have been better at them; there is more psychology and a great deal of art in when to speak to one's partner and when to keep one's mouth shut.

I never discovered why there was a period – despite the presence of Gerald Micklem, a member of Wildernesse and one of the nicest men one could wish to meet – when the Old Wykehnmists were so unpopular; perhaps they brought it upon themselves. At one time they had in their side a young man who played in white cotton gloves, of which he seemed to have an unlimited supply. If any match goes to the 19th at Deal, there is always a large crowd on the balcony of the clubhouse in front of which it runs. He of the white gloves was involved in such a match and it was his turn to putt; donning a fresh pair, he stood over the ball and waggled and waggled until he hit it ten yards backwards – to ironic cheers from the mass of spectators. On the other hand, I think that the great success of Scottish schools in recent years can be traced back to my old wartime friend, Lyle Barr, when he was captain of Fettes. For years the descent of the Scots on the Kent coast was such a thrash that they were incapable of good golf; but Lyle insisted on iron discipline with such effect that other Scottish schools were similarly inspired, as the records show.

In 1957 I got to the age when I was eligible for the Mellin Trophy at West Hill, for those, now fifty and up, who had played for the second thirty schools in the Halford-Hewitt; the first thirty compete in the Bernard Darwin Trophy at Woking. In 1960 I appeared for the first time with John Godfray whom I originally remember as a fast bowler. The last couple of times I partnered a man of the cloth, and on the very last occasion was summoned when Bunny Millard was obviously scraping the barrel. In the dressing-room after the first game I said to him, 'You didn't expect me to win that match, did you?' and he replied, 'Frankly, no, I didn't.' All Lancing golfers owe an enormous debt to Bunny, and when I presented a trophy to the society I asked that it should be named after him.

Besides Lancing, I belonged for many years to two golfing societies: N.A.G.S. to which I was introduced by Bunny Millard who was at the time a printer and the P.B.G.S.

N.A.G.S. which stands for Newspaper and Advertisers' Golfing Society, was the first trade golfing society, founded in 1925. Elected in 1948, I was captain in 1968. It was a rather hazardous term of office because in the first weeks the secretary had a severe stroke. Fortunately he had a part-time assistant who stepped into the breach, and between us we struggled through; I say 'struggled' because we discovered that the invalid had kept no notes and there was not even a list of the holders of the society's various valuable trophies – in fact it was not until a year later that the last one was tracked down. I never won any singles event, but had quite a good record in the foursomes.

P.B.G.S., as might be guessed, is the Publishers' and Booksellers' Golfing Society, which was also founded later in the same year; I did not join until after the war, but seem to have made quite good progress, because I was captain in 1950 and 1951 – why two years when the normal term of office is one, I have no idea. That I was no use at anything but foursomes was belied when I was playing with Peter Locke in the spring meeting at New Zealand about ten years later. New Zealand, near Woking, where every fairway is lined with rhododendrons, is at that time of year a picture. My handicap at Liphook had gone up to 8, but I managed a gross 73, dropping two shots in the last two holes out of sheer excitement. 'Peter says I have probably won the scratch prize,' I said as I handed my car to Paull Harrap, our secretary who gave me the kind of pitying look usually bestowed upon a child that thinks it has found gold, saying, 'I doubt it,' then, on looking at the card, added, 'My God, you have.'

I also played several times for the Stationers' Company in the Prince Arthur of Connaught Cup at Wentworth, which is for teams from the City livery companies. We were runners up in 1960 (one of five times) for which the Master gave us a lunch, and won in 1964 – one of the four occasions on which the company has been victorious.

My election to the Royal and Ancient came through in 1951, and I have
remained a member ever since. The first autumn meeting I attended was
the following year, and, playing as usual in threes (of whom one was
Ronnie Alexander, since captain) we went off behind Roger Wethered.
He drove far to the left on to the 18th fairway, and in my ignorance I
thought what a terrible shot; but with more knowledge I learned that it is
the easiest way to play the hole. As Henry Longhurst said of the Old
Course: 'Like any other work of art, in music, painting, sculpture, writing
and the rest, why expect to appreciate it fully at first acquaintance?' And
Peter Thompson, the Australian who won the Open five times, has
written: 'You either love it or hate it, at least at first acquaintance. Bobby
Jones tore up his card at his first attempt at a score, and then later fell to its
charms, ending up a confirmed *aficionado* ... The course, almost entirely
nature-made, has a subtlety no man can ever completely fathom. There is
a razor-edge between success and failure at every turn;' and again,
'Considering the ever-present wind, it means a constant battle either to
make distance with the shots or apply the brakes to keep from going too
far.' This is very true: take, for example, the 10th, a short hole which has
on the left of the green a huge bunker in which a professional once took
ten during the Open. I got into the habit of going every year for the
autumn medal, and at that hole used every club in the bag from a driver to
7 iron, according to the wind.

My greatest pleasure was in the foursomes match against the Town, in
which with various partners I never lost a match.

The ten years during which I was a member of Liphook were the most
interesting of my golfing life. The members received me most kindly
when I was elected in 1952, within a few years I found myself on the
committee and in September, 1958, was elected captain at a tragic
meeting. Alan Macbeth, the husband of Doddie who nearly won the
Ladies Championship in 1924, was in the chair at the annual general
meeting and was proposed and elected president. But the hut which
served as a lounge was filled with smoke and was so hot that it soon
became apparent that Macbeth was in distress. Dr Sam Pope, a senior
member, ran out to his car to fetch his little black bag but there was
nothing he could do; within half an hour the newly elected president was
dead.

The subsequent atmosphere of gloom gradually wore off and by the
time I came into office as captain on 1 January 1959, life was back to
normal. A pal of mine, Charles Bannister from Petersfield, and I were two
of the most vocal members in urging that such a fine course deserved a
better, permanent clubhouse – in addition to the fact that the army huts
would not last much longer anyway. Eventually plans were drawn up, it
was found that the new building, furnished, would cost £24,000, and in
August a successful appeal was made to the members to take up
debentures. W.K. ('Granny') Clarke, a solicitor in Dorking, as chairman of
the committee sent out the appeal, and said to me, 'You are as much
responsible for all this as anyone, so you will jolly well stay in office till it's
finished' – as a result of which I had the unusual experience of remaining

captain for three years.

During the spring we had the Great Tree Scandal. The course was laid out in 1922 by Croome, with Tom Simpson giving advice – two of the greatest designers of their period. The 15th hole is a dog-leg to the right, up a hill on the crest of which, 190 yards from the tee, Croome placed a bunker which one might attempt to carry, thereby leaving an easy second to the green – or there was a safe way to the left of the bunker for those who could not or would not make it; to the right of the bunker was thick heather. In the course of time a group of very tall, very beautiful ash trees grew up on the tee-ward side of the bunker which thereby became out of play, a lovers' trysting place and repository for cigarette packets, beer bottles and other garbage. The only remaining way to play the hole was the 'safe' route; when Peter Arliss had a round with me he said that he would go to the right of the trees and see what happened; he lost his ball. This was to me a ridiculous situation; I consulted Dick Kenyon, a most senior and experienced member, who agreed with me, and Tom Simpson himself who also took my view. Therefore I asked the secretary, Bill Williams – a crotchety old sailor with arthritis who was about to retire – to have the trees cut down, the bunker resanded, and when he said 'Is that an order?' in the old services style, I replied, 'Yes.' Sam Pope, another senior member whom I have mentioned, wrote to me on 22 March: 'Congratulations on your energetic powers in restoring the drive to No 15 to its full and original value. There is bound to be sorrow at the loss of that attractive clump of trees: but in a very worthy cause.'

Sorrow there was, and the complaints book was filled with angry protests by outraged members for years to come.

When I moved home from Headley to Reigate, I had perforce to leave Liphook and was accepted as a member at Walton Heath, where my days were pleasant and undistinguished, ending when I could get round no more.

Random Recollections

Bryen Gentry once raised a side to play the local T.A. regiment across country from Ditchling Beacon to Brighton racecourse, holing out in a Benares brass bowl beside the winning-post. A lost ball was abandoned without penalty. Playing with Dwye Evans of Heinemann, I think I lost every old ball I had, but turned in the best score: 101. The next C.O. of the regiment did not think it funny and the match was not repeated.

At one of the courses round Atlantic City I was playing with the English professional, sharing as usual a coloured caddy. In that country all approach shots are played high and pull up short on the lush greens, so at one hole the pro said to me, 'Now play a Scottish run up.' So I did and the ball, never rising more than a foot, finished (thank God) by the hole; the caddy's eyes popped out of his head and he exclaimed, 'Bah Jeesus, Ah never saw such a thing in all ma life.'

Dennis Passmore, a printer by profession whom I knew in N.A.G.S., played off 8 at Denham when he moved and joined Walton Heath. Time passed and he asked Miss Paul, almost the only lady secretary in the business at that time, when he might expect to be given a handicap; she told him not to worry. In due course he received a *printed* postcard: 'Mr Braid has decided that your handicap will be: 8'; the great man had watched Dennis on the first tee and made up his own mind.

Playing in the Seniors at Woking was always fun. Anyone who has been there will remember the pond beside the 18th green, into which a hot-headed acquaintance of mine flung his club on fluffing an approach shot. Repenting, he returned the next day with his fishing waders to retrieve it; seeing him, the caddy-master said, 'While you are at it, Sir, would you see if you can find His Honour Judge So-and-so's 3 iron which he deposited there last week.'

Friends in Australia were always extremely generous hosts and I enjoyed many rounds, particularly in Sydney and Brisbane. After a round with Albert Alexander, of Dymock's Book Arcade in Sydney, at the Concord Club, the A.G.M. was taking place, and I was under a shower when the chairman said, 'I hear that we have here today a member of the Royal and Ancient.' Shocked into urgent action I dried, dressed and went into the meeting and expressed fraternal greetings; whereupon I was made an honorary member and presented with the Club tie.

In Sri Lanka I went up, as most people do, to Newara Eliya, a lovely course with a climate similar to that of St Andrews whence all the gorse which lines the fairways was brought. I played with the pro, Urquhart, who was very upset because all his stock had been destroyed by the wine steward, whose supplies were in the same building which he, having fiddled the books, had had burnt down; the price of a fire-raiser at that time was four rupees. On one tee, with its back to the jungle, I had the honour and was addressing the ball when he remarked, 'This is where the tigers live'; a neat piece of gamesmanship.

Altogether I played in fourteen countries, from Canada to New Zealand, and according to the list which I kept something over a hundred and twenty courses, and met 'a host of people who conceived and nourished some strange glamour in the hitting of a little ball round an agony of green acres' – always with infinite pleasure. I have hit so many bad shots which I prefer to forget, and a few good ones that are more likely to stick in one's mind. I suppose a hole in one is a good shot, since it is achieving what one is trying to do, and I have only succeeded once, on the 13th at West Hill in 1970. It was my first year in the Mellin Trophy with John Godfray; we were two down, but this unexpected blow so shook the opposition that we won the match. Once at St Andrews everyone was practising for the autumn medal, the year that Doug Saunders had played out of the bunker on the left of the 17th to within six inches of the hole. I found myself in the same dreaded pit and an acquaintance by the flag, a nimble version of Sydney Greenstreet, said, 'I bet you can't do what Doug Saunders did.' I put it within a foot of the hole. This is not so difficult in a friendly game when there is not a fortune on it, and if you keep your head down and your eye on the ball – but we don't; and if we did, golf would neither be such a devilish game nor half so much fun.

Appendix 3

Jazz

Virgil Thomson, the classical composer, some years ago affirmed that 'Jazz is the most astounding spontaneous musical event to take place anywhere since the Reformation'. My interest in 'Trad' or 'Mainstream' grew, almost uninvited, at the same time as my concern over the colour problem; when I was at Cambridge I already had an extensive library of books by and about the American Negro.

After coming down from the university in 1929 I went to Paris to see Margaret Coss, and took her (as recorded) to Zelli's, a plush night-spot in Montmartre. There was a good band – Zelli would come on to the floor and invite us to dance to 'the music of ten thousand musicians' – but between sets a Negro played piano which really rocked. It was a landmark for me. The sparkling cascade of notes, the masculine, almost brutal left hand really sent me; I could not take my eyes off the dark face which looked round at the audience with placid indifference, an inch of dead cigar rooted firmly in one corner of the cynical mouth – an indifference deserved, for by and large we were a corny audience. It was James P. Johnson, now such a legend, but then only in his middle thirties.

In 1930 in New York when father and I went to see the film of *All Quiet on the Western Front*, between that and the second feature Paul Whiteman's band played, and a male trio – the Rhythm Boys, of whom Bing Crosby was one – sang. Whiteman was not great on solos, but during one number he pointed and a small dark-haired man got up at the back and took four choruses of inimitable beauty. The silver trumpet (for it was made of silver) produced a tone of a brilliance the like of which I have never heard since, and there was total command, yet at the same time a sadness which was unforgettable. It was Bix Beiderbecke, just returned to the band after a breakdown and with only a year to live. I claim to be the only person left in this country who actually saw and heard him – a claim which no one has so far disputed.

Two years later when Margaret and I were in Berlin we went to Haus Vaterland, one of the two large establishments which catered for every taste, and, drawn by the sound, we went into the Wild West bar which was made up like a log cabin; the rafters rang with the driving soprano saxophone of my first, my greatest and my lasting idol – Sidney Bechet.

Bechet was one of the musicians who look exactly like their pictures, and he photographed well. I saw him again twenty years later at Jimmy Ryan's on 52nd Street; the lines were deeper and the hair greyer, but apart from that he did not seem to have changed a bit. He looked so solid, he stood so square, and walked slowly. He seemed completely removed from the audience, and the only sign he gave that he was at all interested in the music those around him were making was that he might close his eyes and concentrate the harder.

A further hearing was in 1954 when Elizabeth and I drove into Paris from the south and noticed from posters that he was playing at Olympia that evening. We had dinner as quickly as we could, but even so when we got there those wonderful high, bounding phrases were already echoing through the theatre – it was a hot night and all the doors were open. The house was full, the standing room was sold and they were sitting in the gangways; when I expressed my deep disappointment the manager did a charming thing: he turned his back and went on counting the evening's takings. Not until Bechet's last glorious phrase had died away, the whole place reverberating with the whistles and stamping of a full throated French applause, and two flics came in, did he turn round and say 'Monsieur, I told you that the theatre is full, you will have to leave.' We had heard what we had come to hear – free of charge.

My last memory of Bechet was more personal and much later, as I have described.

When Margaret and I were in the United States in 1936, I have mentioned that we went to hear and dance to Benny Goodman's band, then at its superb best. An interesting feature was Lionel Hampton on vibes, almost the first time a coloured man played in a white band; Goodman's clarinet, Harry James on trumpet and Gene Krupa drums were, of course, splendid but best of all for me was Jess Stacy's piano. Stacy became another of my idols; he could follow an ensemble, retaining the tension of what had gone before, with a solo of four or five choruses of underlying strength and exact construction, yet marked with his own overtone of nostalgia, and hand on to what came next with no lessening of drive.

The other big band we heard that time, as I have described, was that of Cab Calloway, which had recently taken over from Duke Ellington at the Cotton Club South; he was at the height of his Minnie-the-Moocher white-tail-coat era, and was the greatest personality there until Bill Robinson came on. I was interested to learn from Big Bill Broonzy years later that Cab Calloway was considered by musicians as about the best band leader to play for – understanding and generous.

The centre of Mid-Town jazz in New York 52nd Street was a mass of small joints of which the Onyx was typical. It was a rather gloomy place, all black – hence its name. Stuff Smith had his trio there, the other two being Jonah Jones on trumpet and Cozy Cole drums. (John Chilton's *Who's Who* mentions a sextet, but I can only recall those two players.) Many people say that the violin has no place in jazz, although its home-made cigar box variety seems always to have been used in the Deep South. I never heard Joe Venuti, but Stuff Smith and Stefan Grapelly (who enjoyed such a revival in his old age) were masters. In those days Stuff Smith was a lean, trim, rather light-skinned figure of inexhaustible vitality. From time to time he would cock his battered top hat over one eye, but generally he just played, bending forward, his mouth open, humming and crooning to himself and never still for an instant – in contrast to the impassive Jones who sat sideways to the audience just blowing his fine trumpet as if in a trance.

In the early years of the war I was a member at 100 Oxford Street, and went there whenever I was on leave. Blind George Shearing played good barrel-house piano, and Carl Barriteau, the clarinet who was one of the two survivors of 'Snake Hips' Johnson's band when the Café de Paris was hit, always brought the house down with 'I can't dance/I've ants in my pants'. Jiving started earlier than has usually been accepted, because it was going strong by 1942; I wrote to Margaret about 100 Oxford Street then: 'The room falls into two parts, the floor on which very young things dance wildly and throw one another through the air like trapeze artists; the other part includes the serious critics (among which I number myself) who sit or stand round the band the whole evening.' The band that night in November was Kenny Baker trumpet, Jimmy Skidmore tenor sax, Shearing piano, Tom Bromley bass and Bob Midgley on drums. Sometimes George Chisholm joined in on trombone.

On one leave I went to a night-club which Adelaide Hall had in Soho; she did not sing, but a pianist called Sowande played, and I spent the whole evening sitting talking with her – and very charming she was. When one table got rather animated and glass was crashing, the worried waiter came to her for advice; she just said quietly, 'They're young, they're enjoying themselves; let them be.'

Naturally when I paid my first visit to New York after the war, in 1946, I wanted to hear all I could; it was a fruitful period and fresh haunts were beginning to open away from 52nd Street, although that was still going strong. The best music I heard that time was played by Red Allen, J.C. Higginbotham, Jimmy Shirley and a bass. Although he had faults, I liked Allen and I think that my admiration began with that first acquaintance. It was a small joint, and empty, so that they did not need to blow their heads off. Higginbotham, small and precise, attended to his trombone and only from his darting eyes could one tell that he was not a mechanical machine. Jimmy Shirley was just making his name as a guitar player and was anxious to impress, though shy. As there were only two of us and the barman there, Red Allen wasn't going to get a hernia, but blew softly, firmly, imaginatively for his own pleasure. But he was an extrovert who leaned forward as he played, as though wanting to draw his audience to him (unlike Armstrong who always leaned backwards), and pounded a final chorus until the last note, when he would tear his horn from his lips with his right hand and swing his considerable backside the other way.

I was to hear him many times in the future, often at the Metropole on

Broadway, with Buster Bailey, who was very good looking and had a wonderful technique, and Herb Flemming on trombone. I always asked him to play *Rosetta,* his opening cadenza of which I found exhilarating, and it got so that if he saw me come in he would make it his next number without being asked. Two of his own favourite numbers which he always played during the evening were Jelly Roll Morton's *I thought I heard Buddy Bolden say* and *Who stole the lock on the Henhouse Door?* Many years later, the last time I saw him, he was playing at Crawley, and as Wray Farm was more than half-way I asked him to supper, and afterwards we drove him to the concert. Before we left home I asked him if he would play for the children; he willingly took out his horn and played *Happy Birthday* pianissimo, which was not a great success – I had been hoping for a chorus of *The Saints* – and my daughter Louise, who was very small then, whispered, 'Daddy, I don't think he's very good.' But he was; my favourite trumpet player and a very nice man.

I went to Eddie Condon's, where Condon seldom was, but Joe Sullivan was playing – the next best white pianist to Jess Stacy in my book; a burly figure made even bigger by his rough tweeds, with tousled hair, thick-lensed glasses, a red face and strong, stubby fingers. I asked him if he would play for me *Gin Mill Blues,* which I had always admired on record, and he obliged with power and abandon.

Mary Lou Williams was in town; she had composed many well known numbers during the thirties, was a great name and always ahead of her time. Just then she was playing piano on her own; I hurried along and, although she played beautifully, I remember the *décor* more than the music: the place was all red and white, and she sat at a white grand piano in a red dress; she was also beautiful and it was a vision not to be forgotten.

George Shearing had moved in New York and had got his trio together at a cool cellar down town. I did not realize that he had suffered a sea change; expecting the same barrelhouse that I had heard less than a decade before, I listened rather sadly to the new Shearing for a while and crept away. Ed Hall was playing at the Café Society Uptown which involved him in wearing a natty blue tuxedo with light blue facings which did not seem to be doing him much good. The Stuyvesant Casino had jazz every evening at that time – later it was confined to Fridays – and I took Katharine Brush to hear a very good band headed by Art Hodes, which included Harry Goodwin, Albert Nicholas, Baby Dodds and Pops Foster.

In the following year Margaret and I spent our holiday with her parents at Ventnor, outside Atlantic City, and were only fleetingly in New York. Nevertheless there was time to hear Billie Holiday at the Onyx, which seemed a suitable setting for her. She was extremely tall, wearing a straight black dress, the usual camellia in her hair, and in the gloom her face seemed almost luminously pale. She looked over the heads of the audience with an expression of utter contempt as though she were in a world of her own; poor Billie, with all her troubles perhaps she was. Anyway the macabre black setting and her frightening presence made *Strange Fruit* almost unbearably sinister.

Atlantic City during the summer attracts good bands, and this time Count Basie was playing. I am no lover of big bands, but to me his was much the best. He was himself going through a phase then of playing very little, just single notes put into pauses which sustained and enhanced the rhythm; much later, towards the end of his life, he played more freely. Their best number, to me, is *Harvard Blues*, with its slow, descending chords, and Jimmy Rushing sang the sad refrain so well: 'Rinehart, Rinehart, I'm a most indifferent guy'. Between sets I went over to him – all of him, he was immensely fat – and asked him who Rinehart was. Rinehart, he explained, was a very wet student at Harvard where they have the same pernicious system as most other American universities of electing freshmen to fraternities. Rinehart was so wet that no fraternity would have him and he felt very lonely so he got into the habit of going beneath the windows of his own rooms and calling up to himself to make it seem as though he enjoyed a popularity which he could never achieve.

In 1949 we published Rudi Blesh's *Shining Trumpets*, and when I looked him up in New York he invited me to come to a studio where they were recording for his programme 'This is Jazz'. The thing that I remember best is Rudi explaining what he wanted in a retake, and during his long disquisition Babe Dodds and Albert Nicholas were enjoying a private joke, not listening to a word he said; they knew it all.

At the Village Vanguard, way down town, Leadbelly was beginning to make a name again after release from his prison sentence – a great singer. And at the same joint Chippie Hill was still good. After she had finished I went to the men's room and passed the open door of the kitchen; she had put her spectacles on and was tucking into an enormous steak, with her skirt pulled up over her knees – a homely, unintended view.

In 1950 I had taken on Big Bill Broonzy's book and, as I had to go to Chicago, arranged to meet him. It was the first time that I had been to the black quarter of Cicero and in those days before desegregation I felt, and was, a stranger; but his apartment was most civilly pointed out to me. He was not at home; a nice young white girl who was waiting told me that he had gone to meet two boys just up from Kentucky who needed help. Eventually we spent some time together, but the following evening was the most interesting. We passed the hours together, sitting with a bottle of whisky between us, while he played guitar in all the different styles to be found throughout the States, explaining each as he played.

The only other musician I could find in town was Doc Evans, a competent cornet without great character.

A year later I heard Armstrong, Ellington, Bechet, Conrad Janis, Dizzy Gillespie and Art Tatum – the last two at Birdland. Gillespie was still young using that curious angled horn to play some lovely music. Tatum I could not get on with at all; he was practically blind and I have a theory that he developed his style – more notes to the minute than anyone else – to show that he could do it. No feeling, no soul – the same as his descendants such as Oscar Peterson, who is saved by his personality: a smiling humanity which Tatum lacked.

I have recorded that in 1953, on our way to Los Angeles, we stopped in Chicago and the effect that the martinis at the Ambassador West had upon us: Elizabeth went to bed, and I struggled out because Muggsy Spanier was playing at Bill Rinehart's. I had been wanting to hear Spanier for years, as his constant use of the mute was so interesting; there was only one other like him, Charlie Shavers, whose tone was much lighter. Spanier was magnificent and I went happy to bed.

Coming in from the airport at Los Angeles Elizabeth, who knew my taste well, exclaimed, 'Do you see what I see?' It was a poster; Jess Stacy was playing in town. We went at once after dinner. Stacy had a small band, and at the end of a set came over to sit with us. I told him I thought that his solo of *The World is waiting for the Sunrise* was one of the most interesting in jazz, but the recording was so bad that one could not hear half of it, so he said that he would play it for us – and did, superbly. Then the band came back, and he decided to play one of his own compositions, which was interesting; he said to them, 'This is one you've never heard. I'll play two choruses, and then you take it away' – and take it away they did, extremely well. Jack Teagarden also was in town, but was said to have just come out of hospital, and played abominably; on the other hand, Kid Ory had a small place where he was in superb form and, in his seventies, seemed as fit as Teagarden, a much younger man, did not.

Next year was the one in which we decided to take our holiday on the end of work in New York, and among the places we visited, as I have said, was New Orleans. The old lady to whose lovely house we were taken was Mrs Burt Kierns and, like Broonzy before, she sat and played every style of jazz piano that she had ever heard in her life – and there were plenty. Years before she had known Nick La Rocca when young, standing on street corners whistling through his fingers begging for money for a trumpet, and when he had bought it he never had any lessons. One day she found him sitting on the sidewalk, and he said, 'Lady, you can write music, can't you? I've got some tunes running in my head; would you write them down if I hum them to you?' She got paper and pencil, drew some staves, sat down beside him and wrote while he hummed two tunes. One was *Tiger Rag* and the other was *The Original Dixieland One-step*, and she had to sign an affidavit that he had dictated them to her.

In town we heard Santo Pecora's band, with himself on trombone, George Giraud trumpet, Harry Shields (brother of Larry) clarinet, Ronnie Du Pont piano and Monk Hazel on drums; I have a note of it, but I do not remember them very well. Much more clearly I recall Paul Barbarin's band, because they played very well and I recognized the banjo player whom I had seen often in New York, so I asked him his name: it was Danny Barker, Barbarin's nephew.

By now in New York 52nd Street was practically finished, with only Jimmy Ryan's still flourishing and Wilbur de Paris an almost permanent fixture. I thought him an awful show-off, and the standard poodle which he brought in on a lead for the evening's work was rather like him. But his brother, Sidney, was another matter; he was a beautiful trumpet player, and when he took a solo he turned away and leaned down into a world of his own. The inimitable Pops Foster was on bass, and I promised him a bottle of brandy one night which I forgot, now it is too late.

A player whom I used to pick up whenever I could was Wild Bill Davison. Purists derided him for his coarseness, but I liked his tremendous enthusiastic attack. Once I asked him what he did after the place closed, and he said he high-tailed it out of town to Long Island where he ran an antique business. Some years later I bumped into him in a doorway and asked, 'How is the antique business:' He did a double take and just answered, 'Packed it up long ago.'

Everyone will remember that Armstrong came to London in 1956 and played at Earl's Court, which he filled. But he was really doing little more than going through the motions, good as those motions were, and the most interesting player was the trombone, Trummy Young, whose solos *The Times*, when he died in 1984, described as 'technically brilliant and breathless'.

And nor must London be forgotten, for in the thirties we had Nat Gonella and after the war Humphrey Lyttelton, when he played Trad, and still have John Chilton whose pure tone and lovely pianissimo are to be heard with George Melly's singing. And a great clarinet, Wally Fawkes, known to readers of *The Observer* as 'Trog'. Through Albert McCarthy, whom I knew for a while and then lost, I went to a recording studio in north London when *Fishmouth Blues* was cut, and the Fawkes clarinet was superb.

A great musician whom I never really appreciated was Ellington – except for the two inspired numbers *Mood Indigo* and *Take the A-Train*. In the same way as I have my dislikes in classical music, it is simply that I got no pleasure from listening to him.

Today the Americans have become very up-stage about Jazz. As James Lincoln Collier has said in his biography of Louis Armstrong, 'They [the coloured musicians] did not think of art – they had to entertain to live,' which is true; but even he can write that 'one of the most enduring myths about jazz is that, scorned in its native land, it was first appreciated by Europeans,' but is it a myth? Now there are historians galore who seem to resent any outside interest in the marvellous entertainment that men like Armstrong, Bechet, Buster Bailey and their followers provided. Eddie Condon said, 'We don't go over there and tell them how to jump on grapes, do we?' and judging by his own occasional and not very inspiring performance on the guitar, no one would have been very much the wiser if he had. Otis Ferguson in the *New Republic* calls Panassie's *Hot Jazz* 'a standard source of extremely valuable misinformation,' yet, when I published that book in 1936 it had no rival, no equal, and what did the Americans produce to correct such misinformation? Nothing. They were conspicuous by their silence, although since it was their music and the wonderful men who made it were all around them for the hearing, perhaps they thought they did not need to write about it. But the men have gone, so they missed their chance; now they are frantically digging in the graveyards.

There is something very human about the words of Eubie Blake, in New Orleans on his hundredth birthday: which run through my mind as I grow old, 'If I had known I was going to live this long, I would have taken more care of myself.'

Index